see page 96!
All my love
Mary

Treasured Poems

of America

Summer 1990

Sparrowgrass Poetry Forum
Inc.
Sistersville, West Virginia

Copyright 1990
By Sparrowgrass Poetry Forum, Inc.

Published by
Sparrowgrass Poetry Forum, Inc.
203 Diamond St., P.O. Box 193
Sistersville, WV 26175

Library of Congress
Catalog Card Number 89-063046

ISBN 0-923242-05-8

Introduction

THIS, the Summer 1990 edition of **Treasured Poems of America**, contains a wide selection of work by poets from across the United States and Canada. Also included are the new winners of the Distinguished Poet Awards, sponsored by Sparrowgrass Poetry Forum, Inc.

Some of the authors are new to the field of poetry, while others have a long history of writing and publishing. You will find, as you read their work, that every poem offers a new and unique vision. I've enjoyed my correspondence with each of the poets, brief though it must be. I'm sure you will enjoy their work.

Welcome to the vibrant and exciting world that awaits you as you turn the page.

William H. Trent
Editor

The **ABOUT THE AUTHORS** section begins on page **285.**

The **INDEX OF AUTHORS** begins on page **317.**

IN GRATITUDE

That you have held these blossoms in your hand,
Even hurried their withering by picking them
or by prodding your fingers among the cabbaging petals.

That you have stayed to watch these red and violet tissues
shrivel and blacken at the edges.
That you have stood in the quiet dusk, waiting,
and then come back in the thick wet morning
for the next blossom.

That I have been known so well by you —
known as a thing that blooms and fades and blooms.
That you have been so patient and are patient still
to see which it will be at last.

      —Carolyn England Ritchie
      First Place Award Winner

WHAT GRANDPA GAVE TO ME . . . .

On a crisp fall day,
I took the bus.
From Water Street — my 5th grade school —
down Western, up Main, down Walnut, and up Fifth,
then up Paint — to the middle school.
Grandpa waited as Tom pulled to the curb.
I ran to meet him,
enjoying thoughts of the walk to come.
We turned the corner,
heading down Fourth.
I just had to cross the street.
There — the buckeye tree.
Grandpa kept each and every one.
They were from me.
The first two ever lifted from the cool ground
stayed close to him, warm,
where I too loved to be.
Grandpa held my buckeyes near
just because I gave them.
I sometimes wish grandpa's pocket
still held my buckeyes.
Grandma gave me grandpa's buckeyes,
    my buckeyes?
              Both.
What grandpa gave —
A part of him,
now a part of me.

      —Amy Cox

KEEPER OF SAKES

Sweet Marie, keeper of sakes
Curator of the family treasures
Filing diplomas with expired coupons
Baby curls in tea boxes
Photographs loose and at large
Forgotten gifts for grandchildren
Letters, cards, newspapers and magazines
Stockpiled memories
Insurance against the years
Sentimental mementos

        Alzheimers took you prisoner
        Sentencing your last years
        There's no time for reading
        Only garbled conversations
            Nonsense
            Confusion
          And tears.

Sweet Marie, what do we do with the collection?

      —Mary Sjaaheim
      Second Place Award Winner

MY FIELDS

These are my fields,
These fields of growing wheat
That lean toward harvest
So a hungered world may have
           its bread to eat.
These fields are mine that change
Dusk through to dawn
From deepest green to lighter tinge
With golden, swaying tips upon.
With heads so swollen,
Dough-filled, yet a gloried dream
Of augured grain, to fill, to glut
Stout granaries beam to solid beam.
These are my fields
That, hasting to their yields
Wave gently in the summer breeze,
With promise of a wealth of fragrant loaves.
These are my fields.

      —Irene Taylor Day
      Fifth Place Award Winner

JUICING THE LEMONS

We carried them across the Florida border
curves of lemon rind peeking
through loosely spaced boards of a crate.
In evening when the lemon sun
looked dipped in pools of orange-magenta paint
we opened a few with your pocket knife,
hand-squeezed drops in oil
to eat with dandelion greens.

Halved, they're piled, a pyramid
waiting to be juiced,
crushed in the machine like light
liquified.
A woman in ancient Egypt
blocked her lover's sperm
with a lemon half.
Another hearing lemons
prevented conception
kept a half beside her as a talisman
and let her lover kiss her
in the overgrown grass.

      —Amy Sherman
      Fifth Place Award Winner

ANGELS HAVE NO FEET

I made a snow angel on your grave
yesterday. In the space of body and
wings I lay, hair clotted with snow,
wetness seeping into blue-jeaned
legs, breath white on steel.
Remember when we lived on South Pearl?
Some winters were without snow and
sometimes it fell so deep we would sink
to our knees. That was the best time for
angels, you said, chasing me out to the
yard, and we laughed and threw our arms
and legs wildly until the backyard was
covered. Angels have no feet, you said,
they only need wings.

I tried to chip the ice from your
stone, my tears were not enough
to melt it; I'm hoping the sun
will warm it away and Susan,
do you have feet?

      —Kathleen A. Worbois
      Fourth Place Award Winner

A LITTLE GIRL I LOVE

I saw a little girl I love
    on crutches
        today.
She reminded me
    of another little girl
        long passed,
Trying to explain
    to her playmates
        the braces on her legs
And wondering if they thank
    Heavenly Father
        when they run.
I think I know
    how that little girl I love
        feels
Because the little girl
    long passed
        was me.

        —Sue A. Osbourn

ALONE

The little boy
    sits in the park
alone
still
on splintered swing
staring
into the cold
like a seagull
perched
at the edge
of a deserted jetty
in December surf
listening
to silent laughter
of other children playing
knowing they can not hear
their smiles

and he is happy

        —Dennis J. Zegan

A SONGBIRD'S DEATH

Yesterday I watched
    as your feline captor
    carried you
    like a newborn kitten
    across the yard.

You singing your heart
    to the sky.
It was only natural.
A song of absolute trust
    coming through the bushes.

Then Silence.
The song of existence
    lifting you
    on wings of light.

Today I watch
    as your feline captor
    tosses your lifeless body
    around in the grass

    awaiting the resurrection
    of a once-alive playmate.

        —Sarisa Love
        Fifth Place Award Winner

FLAGS

These iris are free-range, not wild like their Siberian sisters
    Startled wide-eyed in a ditch or rising with a clamor
Of wings from the brake, beating out a rhapsody
Whose wildest chords cannot be heard lest you go mad.

How do they grow them one at a time in the hot house?
Bloodless, beardless, and pale, born to bring mnemonic grace
To Italianate entryways. No, these sisters will bloom today
And tomorrow, furling the exploded parachute of yesterday's bloom
Beneath today's glory and beside tomorrow's taut bud.
Yes, they are tame but not diminished. Their music is our music:
The piccolos of Memorial Day, playing cards clacking
On bicycle wheels, the rocker's squeak, lilacs close thicketing.

They still bear the name of the goddess, Iris of rainbows.
Does she point to a time when men and women will ride together
On fierce ponies through thunder claps and rolling skies
And laugh with the ecstacy of being earth-born and nursed on spirit?

        —Destiny Kinal
        Fifth Place Award Winner

CRACKING WALNUTS

We're cracking walnuts on the back step of the apartment,
    Kneeling on the ice and cold cement,
The nuts between us in a towel.
We're taking turns and Ben swings two-handed
With the flat of the hammer into the pile
While I hold the towel closed.
We're bunched and bulky in our coats
And the hammer twangs against the cement,
Walnuts roll away, and quick thin patches
Of white breath come and go between us.
My forearm, wrist, and fingers tire quickly,
The muscles tighten, and my shoulder aches
As I press the pile to show him
Where to hit the single nuts remaining.
We open the torn towel
And bend, heads down, on cold knees
Over the light brown chambers of the inner shells.
The odor of the broken meats swells up like a storm
And we are leaves riding on the wind.

        —Peter Trumbull
        Third Place Award Winner

THE HARVEST

The summer's past and will not come again,
    the seed pods fallen and the weeds grown tall.
My turn has come to tend the orchard now,
take tenderly the speckled fruit in hand,
and turn the soil along the tangled paths.
My spade is lighter but will have to do.

Through many seasons your deft hands would prune these trees,
trim the once-perfect rows where wild unruly grass begins.
You were the giant of these well-kept fields,
and I the princess, running barefoot down the enormous leafy aisles—

Now with weathered hands grasping a useless hoe,
you gaze bewildered, while the last blaze of sun
filters through veined leaves, at the ripe hazy globes
you cannot gather.

I'll bring the laded baskets home to rest,
and when the chill of autumn settles in,
clasp hands, and lead you gently from the gate.
And we will sit together by the hearthstone one more time,
when that cold wind begins,
when the harvest is done.

        —Doris Henderson
        Fifth Place Award Winner

ALPHA

As I walk back through the past
Glancing at the paintings hanging on the walls
Better I leave
The memories there are shadows of things that never
were
Passed so quickly
As the little girl so full of anger
Tossing her hair
The young woman playing a role
Missing what was real
It seems as if life started so late and flew
And now I'm here
Past the noon of life
Not so different from the little girl
In hopes, dreams, the possibility of tomorrow
How wonderful
How strange

   —Merra-Lee Block

PORCHES

The window is up and the wind a drowsy breath
When you push away from sopped supper-plates
Just in time to find the sun hovering
Beneath strips of violet clouds like pages
And above a violet strip of trees the field
Lies against in the distance where the heat
Caresses the naked rows like the sheer fingers
Of dusty spirits. Cicadas are raking their wings
About the time you ease into the swing
And offer a gust of sated breath. The chains
Creak with the slow sway while the rocking chairs
Sit idle but expectant, their seats and backs
Washed in dusty orange. Across the seat
Of one, the yellow cat lies still, his fur
Rising and falling in careful measured breaths.

This is how you watch the story of the day
End: An ancient weathered book comes
To a dust-settling close, and the sun becomes
A marigold slowly pressed between the frayed
Violet binding of the trees and the night.

   —Joseph Holmes
   Fifth Place Award Winner

A 20 LINE POEM

Singular is the heart that beats within one's chest.
Two are the souls that twine together at
Three a.m. when outside is dark and quiet and inside
Forgotten dreams are remembered.
Five p.m. eyes meet over tea.
Six candles burn and reflect off
Seven faceted crystal from which wine toasts to
Life and Love are consumed at dinner at eight.

Nine lives has a cat but we only one.
Ten or more pictures taken at holiday,
"See us eating dinner in Spain at 11 . . ."
One dozen images of lives spent together

Warm mornings consisting of sweet smells
  Rumpled blankets
Soft skin
Hands entwined as windows watched
Smiles exchanged when presents bought

Universal images of
People loving life in a
Twenty line poem, too long and too short.

   —Sarah Bittleman
   Fourth Place Award Winner

DISTANT MEMORIES —
ASYLUM FOR MY DREAM

There were three boys
In that building,
Apartment in the back.
Whatever happened to them
I do not know.
The middle one was cute:
Why was I
In such a hurry,
Where was I running to.
Ah, yes, I had a dream
Tucked under my arm —
Running to keep it
Unblemished —
Dragging that tired dream
Wherever I went —
Running — oh, running
Till the sun
   disappeared.

   —Ellen Malis

SUMMER LONG GONE

Sweet Judy, can you recall
The days of summer heat
When waves of burning air swirled
And rose above the street?
Our backs to the fence, breathing in
The sorrowful thick evening air
Waiting for mornings, later on,
When all the colors you used to wear
Would make you sad as you were on that
Crazy beach when you swore with eyes like
Circus rings that you could not teach
Me a thing I hadn't already taught you.
And now as I turn away from the light
That keeps burning all night in your
Quiet room, I feel the familiar bite
Of adolescent pain as it digs its
Teeth of innocence into my desire.
Sweet womanly child, I yearn to find
Where our beginnings have led us
And why you ultimately left me behind.

   —Andrew Epstein

FOR EVERY MONKEY CHILD

For every caged-up monkey child
We must produce a living wild
Limb-laddered tree where he can flee
When danger signs alert—escape from
massive human hurt . . .

A tree to monkey up and find respite
From lemming urge, freeway kills
And all our over crowding ills—
A friendly tree where he can astronaut
Alone, or with a friend—spend the night
Or afternoon, exploring skies,
The stars and moon—as guest of birds
Beyond the sound of "NO, NO!" words . . . . .

A tree for every mother's child—
Escape from ghetto walls, urban sprawls
People blight, where he can find his own
Birthright . . . vision fuzzy-free
Set on Infinity.

We must produce a living wild
For every caged-up monkey child.

   —Lola B. Graham

MOM

Have Faith,
Believe,
That's what I'm told.
It's hard you see,
She was my Soul.

—Wilma C. Vuolo

KIDS

Warm icicles
melt
only to form
new puddles
on the ground.

—Robert Ballo

THE EMERGING GOD

God moves
from the ooze
of the sea-bed
through three billion years
to the lover's nest
where man and his mate
in fusion wed,

and the living fire
gives birth
to the higher
and higher —
the growing God,
both Son and Sire.

—Harold R. Hodgson

RAIN COATING

Woman waving her fan
roasting corn
move not but stay
rain-coated body
slick . . . cool
all over

rush not but enjoy
time in the rain
luxury in wetness
sensing the feel
every curve of the body
nothing else
can be so close.

—Jean Polisoto

APPLES

Look at them
Sly — happy
A lapful
Of apples
All cousins
With similar
Smiles
Oh Adam
Green Adam
You hadn't a prayer
Did it have to be
Waiting round
Like a Monday
Ripe as a Kiss
So many sunny
Red apples
There

—Mary Esther Frederick

PILOT

In the privacy of a pink dawn . . . after spinning a safe cocoon,
witness the birth of an airborne gypsy.
At high noon, observe the private navigation of fearless flying,
        like a tiny carefree kite.
Sunset . . . sailing on purple clouds of individual freedoms,
        like a spaceship without the mysterious masks of dusk.
By the midnight moon, guide your tired body to a secret landing,
        after an impulsive night flight . . .
Daily you are envied as you soar, joyful butterfly,
        who packs no parachute.

1988 Dedication: To my mother, Lathelle, who taught me to grow roots and wings.
        —Sharon L. Strandberg

THE RUGBY MATCH AT FIREBASE JULIE

History books are solemn and speak in whispered reverence of wars:
        Nearly 10 million were butchered
In the barbed wire wasteland of mud, craters, corpses and ruins of
The Great War that promised to end all wars.

Young men hugged their lost limbs like teddy bears
While being hauled to field hospitals in ambulances.

Some kicked footballs "over the top" as they emerged from
Grave-like ditches for a coin-toss with The Destroyer of Worlds.

Small wonder the ground between trenches was called No Man's Land.
Their dreamselves saw it as a rugby field for boys at play.

A half century later on Asia's Dragon Tail:

Shortly after midnight, five NVA battalions charged over the barbed wire
And poured into the middle of Firebase Julie,
Just a couple of "kliks" down the Dragon's Tail from Cambodia's border.

Snake-tongued tracers streaked red across the jungle skies over Julie's
Game of Blind Man's Bluff, "You G.I.? You G.I.?"

A nightmare scream rose solitary above the din of battle,
"Mommy! Mom, where are you?"

Too bad the boys' mothers weren't there to watch and put a stop to it.
They'd have said, "The hell with History. Get home right now!"
        —Michael Kluznik

SWANS AND LILIES ARE USUALLY WHITE

—This is a sacrifice to the gods of the written word, so turn back now
        if your sensibilities are easily shocked.

At the risk of martyring this brute to the cause of Art—
Thus keeping alive a bloodless, gibbering beast—
A hatred of all things passionless and bland
Compels me to slaughter this whimpering creature
Before its capacity to diminish worthier efforts realizes its potential.

Verily, despite the manifold vagaries and transgressions
Of generations of wayward wordsmiths,
I beseech the mighty, illustrious muses
To accept this awkward, pedantic satire
On behalf of all incompetent scribblers the world over:

May the ink shed here today assure the safe passage
Of vessels of every description—or lack thereof—
From one fell bank of the Styx
To the One True Savings Bank of Anthologized Everafter;
And may the rock-hard heads and concrete hearts

Of overburdened editors wax penitent and gladsome
Upon receipt of all manuscripts hereafter dispatched.
. . .
And now, in deference to centuries of theatricality (and so-called fair play),
I hereby preserve for posterity my victim's weary legacy:
"Head for mirth. While everyone comes to grief, some die laughing."
        —D. S. Biggs

THE DARKNESS AND THE LIGHT

There are two kinds of darkness — that which comes over the night and that which comes over the soul.

In both there is hope.

In the darkness of night, there are millions of tiny stars — reflections of a sun, not far away, waiting to dawn.

In the soul is also a light, a dawn, a new day. For in each soul GOD planted a seed. You need only believe in him to make it grow. Serve him and not only will it blossom, it will fertilize the seeds of other souls.

In each of us there lies the power to cultivate the seeds of faith, to give hope to a lost soul.

Go forth, and give light to darkness "In him was life and the life was the light of men. The light shines in the darkness, and the darkness has not overcome it." John 1:4-5

—Dora Martindale

THE FENCES

I walk the twisted avenue of fate,
Following wherever it leads,
Helpless in my own to break from my path.

When I was younger, I used to envision fences,
Enclosing my walkway and protecting me from failure.
I think I know those fences aren't really there, but for me

They Are

The fences stretch high around my path,
Offering tiny glimpses of the world outside fate's road.
I think, maybe once, a long time ago I wanted to leave this path

The Fences Stopped Me

I tried to climb them and they pushed me down —
Laughing and pointing.

I sat huddled on my narrow avenue, surrounded by my fences.
They whispered to me and called to me, "Try, try. Leave your path . . ."

Then They'd Laugh

Now I've stayed on my path,
Resigned to follow it to the end and not to climb

The Fences

—T.L. Sheptak

INTERLUDE OF LAUGHTER

At this time of her life she found herself always ready to laugh and when it wasn't a deep belly laugh or a melodious dignified laugh, it was a silent secret smile, a spontaneous turning up of the corners of her mouth. She seemed to have no control. This laugh or rire (French-to laugh is a nice word. To say it one is almost obliged to smile) came without warning. It needed no great purpose.

It was as if the past three years of grief and then silent sorrow, the eventual slow coming back to life had unexpectedly released a string that had been strung too taut for too long.

All of a sudden she felt different, freer, almost giddy. She was extravagantly happy and couldn't quite fathom it, but she didn't care. This delirious aliveness was too precious to analyze. She hugged it to her each night and in the morning discovered that she still embraced it.

Change had evolved in her. She was no longer the same woman. Often she was unrecognizable to herself. Perhaps it was her acceptance of this "new" person that accounted for her present joy.

Whatever the reasons this interlude of laughter would hopefully return again and again and again.

—Gloria M. Schulte

LANDING IN NEW YORK

Heads and tails
Ribbons of light
Red and white
Knotting the night.

Over the slab
The bird circles round
Touches down
Welcome to town.

—Katie Sherrill

BLIZZARD

All night
The wind blew fiercely
A continuous crescendo
Of howling treble
And roaring bass
Rattling the shutters;
Interrupting our sleep
With its violence;
Sending sheets
Of the new fallen snow
Whirling in every direction.

Next morning
The wind
Is almost quiet,
Its night-long tantrum
Spent.

Marble sculptures
Cover the fence rows,
Towering ocean waves
With gentle gusts
Of powdery sea spray rolling
Off their overhanging crests;
Ribs of desert sand
And miniature
Himalayan mountain peaks
In Nature's outdoor gallery,
White marble
Like Michael Angilo's Pieta.

—Mildred Hansel

I WEEP FOR THE HEROES

I weep for the heroes,
All Hallowed and dead.
Asleep in their chambers,
of Uellum and thread.

I weep for the leaders,
All twisted and rent.
With quick changing faces
And backs firmly bent.

I weep for the athletes
That prodigious class.
With bodies of Iron
And conscience of Glass.

I weep for the parents
That Janus-ized lot!
Who spin minds like tumblers
And feed on the rot.

I weep for the children
For them most of all,
Their minds full of visions
Their stomachs, of gall.

—Sean McCarthy

THE POET'S OTHER HALF

We are different
That one and I
That one is content to be content
I thrive on that which does not content me
That one finds purpose in obscurity
I am nothing if I am not heard
What an odd combination we are
But I do not question
That we belong together
Sometimes that one squelches my pride
Sometimes that one needles the air out of me
    so I do not float away with my ego
That one holds the line that keeps my head
    above the clouds
That one loves me
Even though we are so different
And that one reminds me that loving the other
    is where it's at
When all my lofty ideas
Drift away

—E. A. Townsend

I'D LIKE TO BE A LIGHTHOUSE

Standing alone on a pillar of stone
Buffeted by howling winds and crashing waves
I'd rise like an enormous erection
In the middle of the malestrom
Hurling a defiant, "Fuck you!"
At the night and the storm
and at all the forces that darken life

Unwavering, my light would warn the world away
From rocks and shoals that surround me
Alone and aloof I'd stand
Guiding storm-tossed travelers
To smoother waters
And gentler breezes

In calms between I'd bask in bits of sunlight
Ever alone, yet never lonely
Reflecting on storms past and weathered well
Confident and sure that nothing now
Save the gentle erosion of time
Can ever bring me down

—Horst Uttech

OH! TO SHORTER DAYS

Shuck the sun split hay,
worn down old by days;
itch and burn my knees
which grazed the rusted ground
under too many yellow-white skies,
my neck blistered with beat and ache.

Is good, the shadow of the great, god oak;
my eyes closed to the buzz of sound,
drifting off to cooler falls,
and airy, fanned rooms where loose curtains fly.
Give me just one brisk breeze
and an hour of silent rest,
how grateful I would be.

Oh! To shorter days when at night
few crickets call, and covers do not wait alone
in the hope chest at the foot of the naked bed;
when children can play at noon and
windows stay shut without a thought.
I'll soon be there, dancing
under the fiery, fickle trees.

—Christine Fulmer
Fifth Place Award Winner

AUTUMN NOSTALGIA

I would like to go gather up the turkeys again,
Run skinny and free through winter-brown fields,
Scratch my legs on withered weeds,
And yell childish curses at the stupid beasts,
"You can't go home again," they say,
"You can't go home again,"
But if I could:
I would stand beneath the cottonwood tree,
Feel the soft moss in the watering tank,
And when the first bright stars of evening appeared,
I would walk back to my Mother's yellow kitchen,
Watch Dad pour a glowing glass of bourbon,
And cut off a chunk of cheese,
And if he said, "Here, taste this,"
I would reach out my hand.

—Sharon Ready

PLIABLE YOUTH

I once touched the softness
of your cool and fragranced form —
then I moved abruptly
and you bounced top to bottom
bumping your way — billowing back
bouncing . .
I touched your sides
and held you gently between my palms.
I walked you to the corner
taking a moment to shake you again
and watched the sun play with your image.
Oh,
to drink in your sweetness when you are warm . .
and see you tense when I set you aside.
I love your tempting ripples and folds —
the fruitful contents within your form.
I shook you again and walked you from the corner
to Mrs. Smith's door
where she set you down
with the rest of the jello.

—T. R. Frisby

RHAPSODY IN BLACK

Yo . . . they told me I was Black,
and when that wasn't bad enough,
They let me find out I was
A woman. Damn.
Weell, fuck it . . . .
'cause by the time I found out,
I was poetry in motion — I was a rhapsody in
        Black,
free as a raven,
blacker than night, and just as cool.

But they couldn't have me be nobody, not even me
And they tried to stomp me out,
like roaches.
But I'm a rhapsody in Black,
so I flew like that raven,
And sang MY song — I stayed cool . . . .
and my rhapsody got hotter.
And I'm still a rhapsody in Black, with a streak
        of lightnin' in my hair,
and they still try to stomp me out . . . .
but all they can see is the lightnin',
and IF they manage to stomp that out,
there's still my song.

—Victoria Sharice Campbell

DESIRE'S ONLY OPTION

The moth chases the flame,
   It feels no heat,
There is no pain.
The light is so sweet.

Blindly it flutters toward the glow.
Drawn by nature's passion,
There's but little else to know.
The light is so sweet.

Wings singed it falls to die.
There is no regret,
Ne'er a question why.
The light was so sweet.

Another moth watches the first expire.
It hesitates a moment,
But then feels the desire.
The light is so sweet.

—Donald Carte

LILIES IN THE RIVER

Songs of sorrow dance in my head,
   Like lilies in the river.
   So beautiful and so lonely,
   Around and around they go.
   Never dancing with another,
Choosing themselves as partners.
Sometimes I am sorry for them,
Because they look so awkward.
They never seem to notice though,
   Maybe they really don't care.
After all I made them like that,
I could have made them different
But then they wouldn't be unique.
   I wouldn't want that for them.
   I wanted them to be special,
   So all could admire them
   I didn't want a symphony,
   I just wanted to be heard.

—Linda Ann Thorburn
Fifth Place Award Winner

MY COMFORT

Come, walk with me through
   This community in which I live
And see,

A city within a city
A garden of beauty where,
Roses, dandelions, poppies,
All adorn each other
A cultural, artistic center
Of talent, that touches the heart
And mind
A complex of many backgrounds
That complement each other with
Style and grace
Colorful Chevrons, Brownstones,
Tall all-embracing Towers,
And petite Townhouses that delight
The heart, as you walk the
Spacious pathways
Young and old all growing and working
Together

Yes, it's CO-OP City of which
I speak
The metropolis of unending pleasures

—Patricia Gladen

FRANCIS

Fatty always made the biggest splash.
   Says I, "A dime says no one makes a bigger!"
From then on, me and Fatty went halfs—
'R almost.
We'd divvy up their dimes; but Fatty kept their sniggers.

He was especially good at the cannonball.
Jesus! The water seemed grateful to jump outta his way!
So, how it was, I couldn't figger at all
That Toothpick beat Fatty one tar-hot day.

Toothpick did win fair-an-square though.
Why, he splashed clear up to where God is!
And poor Fatty, wearin' a smile for a halo,
Was shiverin' with the rest of us losers—I says,

"Fatty, you're a sport . . . What's your name anyway?"
"Francis," he says, kinda happy and big-eyed.
Then, he ran off and hugged Toothpick that tar-hot day,
And everybody but me and God were surprised.

—Sara Gill Berg
Fifth Place Award Winner

SOMEWHERE REVISITED

Sometimes when we're least aware
   A strange thing comes to be:
We hear a distant echo from buried memory.

Anything can strike the chord—
Both commonplace and rare—
The sight of southbound swallow;
The scent of snow-tinged air;
Seeing hearthfire red ablaze or azure summer sky;
Hearing rousing tavern song or lieder lullaby.

And then, within a heartbeat,
We sight familiar shore,
With half-remembered feeling
That we've been here before.

It's over in an instant
(If reckoned in our time;
Such moments must be measured
By far and diff'rent clime).
We pause, still filled with wonder
At this elusive toll evoking in our being
Nostalgia of the soul.

—Emily McCormack

TIME

She walked passed flower filled booths
   where people might have been
and saw a man scrubbing a white carpet
as though it were fit for the foot of heaven;
The purple cry of a deaf man fell upon his own stone ears
and the empty bread box of the mother of eight
edged in on her most morbid fears;
The sky grew increasingly bleached and spare
the ozone layer worn thin
as across the dunes of time
man's solemn smile grew dim;
But on she spent her secret breath
in search of whence she came
and saw a marred and reckless form
There begged to know its name;
Lo, in tears she scurried on perplexed but not in vain
for the ravaged hand familiar and crude
came forth to sign its name.
                    TIME
Time, it said. It has always been the same.

—Stephanie Bryan-Reed

12

CONJECTURES

Polarized forces,
  Two countries are dichotomized by political principles:
Subjugation_____Liberation
Exigencies effect reformations:
    Concessions_____Regulations

This natural rhythm of growth
Propels them towards conjointment.

Ultimately, the remaining contention will be
The empowerment of authority.

      —Laura D. Quigley

LOVE'S HABITATIONS

Liebestraum, liebestrode, liebesleben and liebeslode,
  Each dream of love has its abode

Above the lintel, newly laid,
Paolo and Francesca swayed,
Resting from eternal flight
Through the dark and endless flight

Before the doorway, carved in wood,
Dante and Beatrice stood
All their soul within their eyes,
Dreaming still of Paradise.

While before the hearth, in slippered ease,
Sat Abelard and Heloise.

      —Lilian P. Brinton

NIGHTSONG

Orion's back is arched across the sky;
  The shy moon simpers in a gown of cloud.
Sounds of the screech-owl's nightly hunting cry
In this vast silence, echo wild and loud.
Together, Love, we gaze into the dark
That stretches to the very lap of God.
Officious shooting stars attempt to mark
The stately paths which agéd planets plod.
Infinity of never-ending space
Raptures our mind; our awed eyes veer away.
We are so small, huddled in this huge place,
Fearing the dark, and desperate for day.
  We know, though dazed by endless night above:
  The greatest mystery of all is love.

      —Mary Gaynor Bryan

JOY

I feel your walk beside me this cold, clear night.
 Companion to the sky of lights so bright and
shimmery that trees stand winter-silhouetted
against it. More vivid this luminescence than
from the moon, curiously missing from sight.
And night's chill kiss, like your fervent whisper,
brings a tingling pink to my cheeks.

They all but fill the sky, this night's good stars.
Logarithmically far from here, but sage guards
to the heavens while our humble world spins
seasons below. I lift my face to them as to
your love, awed by the immense brilliance.
So calm and bright they must be like those
lights that guided wise men long ago.

Legends. Legacies.
Our romance with the eternal,
an uplifting thing.
Like your good warm smile,
sweet beyond imagining.

      —Marie Caldwell

INVERSION

I must have wept as the sun set.
 Dark water under an orange-striped sky
Sighed each time I stared by—
Toward receding rays,
Preceding lights of previous days.
Watching heavens and water reverse!
An expanding universe horizon
Beckoned me to feast my eyes
On twinkling beasts and magic myths—
Whose existence twists with mine.

      —Samuel T. Rimmer

INVITATION

Through fields of glorious goldenrod
  Who tilt and whirl, and bob, and nod,
Tossing out their saucy greeting —
'Tho well they know the summer's fleeting
Off with the breezes, frolicking, flirting,
Up through the maples' silver skirting
Ruff'ling their bonnets' lacy edge
Of orange and yellow, gold and red,
Where winds have whistled winter's warning
Leaving diamonds of dew to dazzle the morning
Come walk with me, come share the splendor
Of the summer's sweet surrender.

      —J. DuBois
      Fifth Place Award Winner

HOLLYHOCKS

The Hollyhock a poor man's flower,
  Not delicate — like a rose.
And no matter how hard you tried
Through the alleys they all rose.
Protecting our view from garbage cans
And the men who sold their wares,
On horse drawn wagons,
Chanting loudly "Rags, buy your rags,"
To ears with other cares.
The Hollyhocks paid no attention,
They grew up straight and tall,
And with their tough and rugged beauty,
Was one with one and all.

      —Vilma Yacos Michalski
      Fifth Place Award Winner

SUMMER'S SHADOW

The heat: palpable
  half-formed sweat a second skin
    gray-dark room
    chatting
sunlight outside in golden pools
the season of heat is coming
    dreams of cool, clear water
    in the back of the mind
next to thoughts of the upcoming graduation
    battered shoes
    abandoned
    like sand-scoured desert rocks
black-socked feet next to them
part of a whole, but disconnected
    summer's weight
    and summer's wind
    are coming
you can scent them in the air
see them on the horizon
    they glitter in people's eyes

      —Melissa Caruso

FALL COMES TO THE FOOTHILLS

A spider webs
from the boxwood
to the water spigot.
A flock of blackbirds fly low;
leaves drift to the ground,
acorns fall on acorns.
His garden gone to seed,
an old grasshopper sleeps
on the pimento.
As the sun sinks
the last cow entering the barn
bellows one more time.
    One year now . . .
    on wood he stacked
    lichens still grow.
And beyond my window
this starry night
I turn in my hand
one sycamore ball.

       —Nina A. Wicker
       Fifth Place Award Winner

FOR KYLE

B efore you,
I never thought of wrinkles and
    age and the
    elderly men on the benches.
    The ones that chuckle at
    your energy and life as
    you run in the grass.
I hold you and think of
    mothers in long dresses and
    aprons holding their
    baby boys
    singing the same lullabies
    running fingers through
    downy soft hair.
And as time returns to the present
    my heart softens at the thought
    that someday
You will be the one on the bench
    watching life run
Before you.

       —Jocelyn Moran

FROM MY BACK PORCH
DURING A BRIEF RAIN
12/9/87

Like tiny spheres of rolling light,
They course — the bright terrenes,

Beneath the brooding latticework
Outside my window pane.

In time, a shimmering tear-drop-thing
Bleeds off the beaded strand,

And plummets downward eagerly,
To greet my outstretched hand.

But the miracle is not, I think,
To catch a glimmering world in flight,

For in my palm it splashes:
Wet! And teases me,

To bow my head
To lifted palm,

To taste a pool of fallen light . . .

       —Mike McLaughlin

SUMMER DAZE

T he grass beneath my bare legs is warm
a warm that seems to radiate from the Earth's core
The sun beams down
Heat meets heat
But it's a good heat—growing weather
Skin tightens and tingles in the glow
The Earth cradles me
The breeze is a warm cool, enough to dry my brow
I hear
Cynical chuckling of swallows
The distant metalic saw buzz of a Heat Bug
I see
Puffed sparrows perched on windmill
A moth drunkenly dances from marigold to grass blade
The air is laden with the dry smell of green
Crickets sing of Fall
Swallows swoop, regroup and dive again—peppering the lofty
    swirling lake of blue and opal
Invisible currents tousle a thousand leaves—stirring the sound
    of a thousand flames

       —Melanee Colleen Buckentin

THE HAUNTING DOROTHY G.

P ine cones and fresh cut watermelon smelling
    grass;
Button-eyed, curly-haired scotties and night
    blooming jasmine's saccharine aroma remind me of
    Dorothy.
Fast convertible white Buicks and smoky, smelly,
    happy hour bars;
Tight legged slacks, and stacked scandalous paperbacks
    remind me of Dorothy.
All night talks and late night snacks with opinions
    too severe;
Aligned lacy couches; evened out rugs; and squared
    picture frames;
Crossword puzzles; burning cigarette ashes, and
    coffee stained cups;
All knowing of people; vodka and tonic; meat filled
    with wine; oysters on the half shell and snails
    remind me of Dorothy.
But Dorothy isn't here anymore. And that reminds me
    more of her than anything else.

       —Joseph Posner

DECEMBER COFFEE

S at across my early morning coffee
From a lady wrapped in
Wool and thought all quiet
Looking out the window
Waiting for . . . I wonder what
Drew her out in the December
To lean upon a counter and
Breathe the stain of age that's coming from the walls.
And listening but I didn't hear her order
"Only coffee" over twice
To warm her swollen fingers
Around the cup —
Then, gently, she eyed around
To see she was alone
And waiting just for that, it seemed,
So weary when she stood, then draped,
In a long but warmish coat and
Turned to step into December —
And as she left I kind of hoped
That somewhere she was loved . . .

       —Ann Griffiths
       Fifth Place Award Winner

THE OFFERINGS

Friends come, they bring the best they have
of food, loving embraces and words.
To them, more than to me,
their words sound hollow,
like a ping-pong ball bouncing in an empty, rugless room.
It is the best they have — all they have —
and they know it is nothing.

Some of them have been here and stand with me
but stand beside the memory of their own beloved
taken with little or no warning
just as life was handing over some control.
They say little as we hold each other long
While we go beyond the room.

But in the silence that answers every offering of love
the song of Rachel rings,
"For he is not."

—Jessie Holden Buttram Line 16: See Matt. 2:16-18

MARIA — marie antoinette

I want to sell my hair to you
old woman.
Use it to hide beneath;
It was of no use to me.

Look in the mirror.   Me.
Ready to hear you.
Given the chance,
would you steal my diamond earrings?

        Wait for the begonias.
        Pick them so you don't
        prick
        your fingers.

                Scrape the web's residue
                off
                your limbs.

                A carriage is outside
                waiting.
                The driver beckons mumbling —
                happy are the little cakes.

        —Mitra V. Komeily

HEDGE LIFE

From my perch on the deck chair
I look across the yard
and see the cat staring intently at the hedge
separating our house from the woods.
It is her post. Day after day she sits or paces
along its length, hoping for what?
I have seen the occasional wren peek through,
squirrels hot-footing over the tops of the branches.
Still she peers through the microscope of a cat's eyes
the same as I gaze into this morning sky wondering:
among those leaves are there contingencies
for boredom? Are there weevils and aphids dancing
a mating dance for the sheer joy of it?
Fungus relentlessly breeding with a mind to it?
Bag worms and blister beetles munching on leaves
and enjoying it? Is there a celebration?
If I close my eyes, I can almost hear
music floating over the lawn
the hallelujahs of the holy leaf rollers
and lace bugs like new brides humming.

        —J.D. Lords
        Fifth Place Award Winner

CICADA

The harsh undulation
        of your rasping voice
in the hidden silence
        where you hunch and mourn
in the evening
tells me . . .what
                the end
of summer means
                and yet, somehow,
inside (me) a new year music
emerges to drown the dirge
                from your dark thicket—
freshly-singing
        joy
                beyond all seasons.
        —Charles M. Campbell
        Fifth Place Award Winner

AN ALMOST PERFECT FREEDOM

In fact, perfect freedom lies
only in perpetual repose
past daily bread, banking dreams
freedom from want and wish

Closest in essence
freedom's next best
knowing what you want
then wanting it enough
to be, despite the rest who
rush to crush your choice,
through eyes that see not
who it is you are, not
who it is you want to be,
but who they want
and who they see

Only yours and yours alone
privilege, vision, obligation,
quest, despite the rest
to pursue the who and what of you
to your own expectation, your own best.

        —Pat Freeman
        Fifth Place Award Winner

FOR ALL OF MUSIC

Let it play on, to
caress perplexed minds;
it's a spiritual gift.
A saxophone reflects
traditions of folklore.
Pass it on
        this tale of survival.
                separation
                push & pull
                assimilation
                isolation
                adaptability
It encompasses all
with a loose tender touch.
There are drums,
harmonized heartbeats, of
a people rising
above political ambiguity
and social strife.
Play on for all of us.
PLAY ON.

        —J. Wardell Brown

As I watch and see how the city swells
I wonder where it is leading
For under the crush of progress
Nature is fast receding

I long for the dirt beneath my feet
And the sight of endless trees
But all I find are traffic signs
And the cracking of unused knees.

—Joseph G. Bell

HOMESICKNESS
Hour follows day and week, spinning
Out across the plains, the shadows
Meet where trees rise up
Eager and few in the western
Sky.
Into rivers of light
Clouds fall slowly, one by one.
Kneel here for a moment,
Near to all you thought you'd left behind,
Enter this expanse of wind and
Solitude, then turn with gold and dusty day to
Shining edge of night.

—Meghan Merker

ON SEEING JOANNE AFTER HER DEATH
You
were in the bank
in part of a face, today

I wanted to capture you;
I wanted to steal your ghost
out of the solidity

what was it
you wanted;
what caused you
to have paused inside a smile?

a woman
touched me, from across
the age-worn room;

I withdrew, to another year;
I withdrew, turning away
and breathing-in.

—Katherine Lockwood
Fifth Place Award Winner

FAREWELL
She sighed and shook her head softly.
   "I wonder where all the years have gone.
   Is it possible, I, too, was young once?
   So many years, so very many years."

She moves little now since —
But, no need to mention ravages of age;
The results are obvious and manifold.
Only the heart achieves immortality.

   "I do so hate to have them call me old.
   What do they know of so many years
   That they may cut and measure life
   And say when one should be done?"

Her years were many and her memory dim
Of the near-distant past,
But, oh, the dreams of years gone by
Were hers to final breath.

—Bernadine Robertson
Fifth Place Award Winner

UNANSWERED QUESTIONS
When winter comes and flowers die
We ask the question, why, oh why;
Do things so beautiful fade away,
To make room for another day?

Our lives are much the same you see;
To us they're precious as can be.
We question why must this one go;
We needed, cherished and loved them so;
But Christ knows best, he knows why;
We'll understand better by and by.

—Joyce Seay Mask

ODE TO PAIN
O miraculous pain, I shall not survive,
Unless I cure myself of your desire
And all the waking aches you are and claim to be.
Stand me not in awe of your terrible majesty
But give me heart to learn and the seer's eye to see
What pain is and all that maddening pain can be.

Though saddled with this distress, I will to healthiness
   aspire,
Lest I be cursed to grim nudity and to burn
Like elemental fire in a goldsmith's changeless urn.
Do give me cause to remain steadfast in my dream
   (made free) alive
And never to what I was and feared to be return.

—Kenneth Viabert Jones

WHAT IS MY ILLNESS . . . ?
What is my illness that I sicken so?
What reason for my symptoms of duress?
The surest remedy I quite forego:
I languish near the source of my distress.
My agonies stem not from a disease,
Nor from some dire infectious malady.
No hideous defect which, by degrees,
Directs my might and will toward tragedy.
Just as some slight recovery seems sure,
I fail before full vigour can regain —
For that which brings about my only cure,
Is that which also leaves me wracked with pain.
   Your influence is cure and bane in one;
   I drink you in, am strenthened, and undone.

—Stephen W. Speaker

THE BED
Through mists of darkness a bed stands,
Swaying to and fro abundantly filled,
With wails of pot bellied babies,
With tremors of dying old men,
With voices abruptly stilled.
Within its folds come cries of "Freedom"
By young men with faces old
With blind men with faces painted
With black faces, stiff, cold
From the freezing "Wind of Hate"
that chills the bones,
that clutches the heart,
as lips of many silently scream
"Too late! Too late!"
As the bed with its load of humanity,
Slowly sinks to the floor
with great groans and creaks
All is quiet within as it becomes
just another part of this world's insanity.

—LaNay Roshawn

Cold crow caw
Dagger scream of jay
Under fortified bounderies of mocking birds
The cyclic seasons exploit the humble bee
While leaves reign no more
As Autumn's scythe lays castles bare
Exposing secrets of mourning doves
As monarchs flee
Escaping flowers destiny

—Daniel Pickham

BAGGAGE

He takes his igloo with him everywhere
as if it were his shield or amulet
and flirts with silences. Why should he share
even his emptiness? Who ever met
a paragon of Eskimo like this?
Grateful that pride has slammed his door on pain
and helped him build his citadel of bliss,
why should he play caring's charades again?
He pets his dog and cat. They're all the liv-
ing things he needs. What does he have to prove?
Why should he playact willingness to give
warmth never his, temperate zones of love?
His igloo is the only home he needs.
He carries it wherever winter leads.

—Louise Jaffe
Fifth Place Award Winner

FROM A HIGH PLACE

The site where summit meetings should take place
Is at a summit; standing on the brink,
We have respect for life. Just once to face
Endangered beauty makes us stop and think
Of what is in the balance. Here we see
It all boils down to basics: chunks of stone
That shelter tiny life forms (you and me,
Wild flowers, every dear thing we have known
Or hope may be). From this frail rock collection
We draw our whole existence, or we fail.
Oh pray all sides may make the same connection:
The world, and no one nation, must prevail.
    If such a view as this could be revealed
    To all her people, earth might still be healed.

—J. Holan
Fifth Place Award Winner

Dedicated to:
    Erica and Justin (My little "Bulls")

Two children
Sleeping Soundly,
Among an array
Of pink bunnies
And brown teddy bears.
Oblivious to the T.V.,
the cars outside, the scratch of my pen on the paper.
I envy them.
How I wish to be surrounded
by pink bunnies
And brown teddy bears,
So warm and soft.
To be comforted in knowing
My security is in the
Hands of a babysitter.
A babysitter who loves me enough
To write a poem about me.

—Jeni Zeh
Fifth Place Award Winner

REVERIE

Young Petal swims with Playmate Breeze
—in Ocean Air—

    hands clasp
    spirits meet

Brother Song rides the waves—
            is breathed in—
            is passed along—

    cloth sways
    minds rest

    Central Park, 10 a.m.

—Tressy Pawlik

MY FEATHERED FRIENDS

I hear your mournful sound
Each morning as I awake,
I see you there on the ground,
Searching for food with your mate.

The wren is chattering from its perch,
As robins feed their young
Nestled in the weeping birch,
Until they can leave the nest.

Oriole, finch and meadow lark
Join in the chorus,
As sunbeams pierce the dark,
Proclaiming a new day.

—Lila Tonn Schmidtke

EGRETS AND I

Egrets fly in the evening
between Recovery Hill and Mount Royale
white as pure souls
in the golden sun of almost-dusk
flying serenely, surely
in a certain course
daily

they know their course
feeding ground to rookery
and in the soft dawn
reverse

those lovely, unsouled birds
so sure of their course
so sure
and I am not

—Betty Brown Hicks
Fifth Place Award Winner

ON BOSTON COMMON
OCTOBER 18, 1988

How long to stay, this place to rest
With poems heard and books to read
Of places known, indeed the best
This quiet place to fill my need

As churchbells toll the time of day
My reverie they do not break
To passers by I seldom say
But from their smile some pleasure take

Yet in my heart your beauty lies
As autumn winds through turned leaves blow
Some sadness still, behind these eyes
In knowing soon that I must go

—Creimetion

SEASONS

On a soft spring night
I drank the wine of moonlight,
heard the music of the stars,
touched the good green earth
And was made whole.

On a crisp fall day
I looked up at the
tangled skeins of wild birds
against a clear blue sky,
and cried aloud at the iron bonds
that held me fast bound to earth.

—Carolyn S. West

PAUVRE TANTE

Her hands quake constantly.
Her right eye blinks incessantly.
Her mouth twitches . . . always.
She laughs off-cue,
She spurts a sentence fragment with
    no one's ear in range.
She is a child in a woman's guise.
She is running circles around herself,
    wondering why she is dizzy.
    She is tarnished silver;
    cracked glass;
    tattered linen.

—Theresa Deal

WINTERIZED

Bedtime calls me
to cocoon myself
    beneath covers of warmth.
I find my bed — my sleeping nook —
    with wild-flowered sheets and cases
    mother's log-cabin quilt
    and the turned-on blanket

At a set morning time
    I'm alarmed awake
    to split my cocoon
    peel it away
    layer after layer.
Finally, hatched out,
    like a sleepy moth
    I get hours of freedom
    to fly around.

—Mabel D. Gilmore
Fifth Place Award Winner

THUNDERSTORMS

Ink black majesty on
Soundless wings approaches;
As if in pain roars from
A wasp's sting striking out.
In a sheltered dove
Noah's deluge remembered;
Perched, observing soaked leaves
Like so many slaves beaten
Hang unconscious from
Dripping whipping post stems.
While Gaea's children scramble
To evade her wrath, her justice,
Amidst a crescendo of light and sound
Highlighting aristocratic,
Tar stained clouds;
Pronouncing their judgements
Then moving on . . .

—David Ace Condor

FLIGHT PATHS

Craven images of flight are spectral in appearance
We, the flightless, see by chance
They in their full fury
In that fury, fury in beauty
Beauty is revealed in the soaring
Long, lonely, flight paths
And yet, they need not fly alone
To reveal themselves
Cast aside the spectral cloak
And look
Our flight paths cross.

—Jon Kennedy

POSSUMS AND PERSIMMONS

As the winter starts to approaching
and the leaves on the Persimmon trees
    starts turning brown
and the beautiful sweet Persimmons
    starts falling on the ground
and the Possums starts to feeding
    on the Persimmons from the tree
    it brings back childhood memories of me.
    but when I'm dead and buried
    and planted beneath the ground
underneath the Old Persimmon trees
    the Possums will still be
        walking around.

—C.L. Butler
Fifth Place Award Winner

THE DESPAIR OF RETICENCE

If only to be capable of voice, telling secrets
of the sweet liquid of babbling,
the solid repugnance of seething
Or of the dreaded ache of pouring rain.
And only, only, again to express in the way
that used to move the clouds to utter pictured words,
to move the sun to flame dark painted skies again.
If merely for the sputtering instant while candles die,
If solely for the stretch it lacks to blink another's eye;
Enough it would be just to warm the skin again,
to taste the coursing heat in a curving mouth again,
to once more feel soft solace in the now bleak and bitter eyes,
Or only to touch; to hold, the once-delicately intricate hands,
now twisted, gnarled, and aged with mourning and cold.

—Jennifer Kozlowski

THE VOICE OF MASS AVE

The voice of Mass Ave was like a whisper
    That day you turned away
Washing over me the rhapsody of our nights in Harvard Square
When Love was young and unspoilt by agendas
But the Charles River flowed through my heart with the
                brandy of industrial waste
And I drank deep and well of its forgetfulness
That night when the Moon was pregnant with my words
And the dilated drone of the city traffic sang
in acappella echoes against the wet street
Sheets of driven rain through the calling pain
And your answering machine gleams the same caustic refrain:
If you leave your name and number at the sound of the beep,
I will get back to you when I cannot sleep
And tears are deep in the throat of the night
I slip and sight the eyes of the morn
Upon the perfect concave awn of the library at M.I.T.
And I ride the writhing rain
Into the unremitting urban Sea

—Simon Schattner

18

Mother dear we love you so
    We hope you never have to go
But, if you go and leave us all
God will catch us in our fall
Then when you hold us oh, so tight

It's then and there we see the light
And when that light goes through and
Through
Then and there our love's anew
                —Melissa Renee Thomas, age 13

STRANGERS

I cannot reach you, though I have tried.
You seem much like the clouds . . .
Tempting, yet forever out of reach.
Like this unknown distance between us . . .
Guarding you faithfully from my passion.

Your image stays in my mind as if painted
By some famous artist.
Impressions of my heart resting in your hand,
While raindrops dance upon your shoulders.
The skies are gray and beautiful.
I kiss the wind and we remain as strangers.
                —India R. Stanley

RONDEAU

How long ago they seem, the tender years
That sang with joy, or throbbed with quick-hot tears
So tense with life that their atonal stream
But enriched the song, then made its joy supreme
When love resolved the undertones of fears.

Ideals were lyric summits to revere,
And every discord made the heights more dear.
All seasons bent their music to this theme;
How long ago they seem.

The rhythmic seasons now seem more severe;
Or is that failing cadence in my ear?
Somewhere there must be new strains to redeem
The melody of days I used to dream —
            How long ago they seem!
                —Ruth Greenlee Brown

PRISONERS OF WAR

The night approached, drew fire, immobilized,
                    and we clashed.
Continuous waves of darkness broke down my defenses,
                    and so she emerged victorious.
Through many battles I had wept
                    and so I closed my eyes and slept;
            I closed my eyes
                in unconditional surrender.
For the light that never broke
                I freed the trace of hope
As my soul's candle tumbled over
                    with the fresh blood on the floor.

So all you lonely, weary travelers
                who journey through the night
And come looking for a candle
                to assist your weary sight,
Don't bother clasping on the knocker—
                smell the blood inside my door.
Here you'll only find a sleeper
                and a prisoner of war.
                —Laura Fitzpatrick

OUR FRANNIE

Black Monday thundered into our
lives and stole her fast away.
    Those snappy dark eyes taking in
all life
    That quick smile and that sudden
laughter from within
    Those busy hands their myriad
tasks performing
    Those seemingly untiring feet ever
on errand's way.
    As a butterfly she flitted among
us assisting here, consoling there
    Sharing herself everywhere.
    Perchance in some sublimer time
we'll feel a brush upon our shoulder
and our startled gaze will reveal her
standing there with
    "Surprised you, didn't I?"
                —Maxine McCannon

TAP

It's a risky evolution
this spinal tap
of precious fluid
leaking from the grandeur
of your column

Ganglia, like grapes, hang
from branches of your vertebrae
tied in tenuous strings
of muscle and nerve

Wind through the armor
of my navel, like a spiral phallus,
that spews forth essence
to entangle our womb
with the mystery of form

Reach my trunk of knotted wood
as illumined brains of spine unite
We drip and spatter waves of fluid
and plunder abruptly

into the gradual wake of dawn . . .
                —Donna M. O'Donovan

RIVER OF SATIN

I found my grandmother
Lying in a river of white
Face up, made up,
She was not long of this world

Do you want to say goodbye to Grandma?
No, I already said it
She can't hear me
The roar of satin rapids
Drowns out my voice

I carried part of this river in my hands
And moved her to a horrible place
We followed her to a delta
Hollows cut by satin into the ground
The river holding everyone underground
Where satin conceals its darkness
Where satin reveals the loom
Where death weaves satin

If I could wade this river
I would bring her back
            —Gary Baird
            Fifth Place Award Winner

DESERT

Sand dust lifts in a gentle breeze
skims along the dunecrest,
a soft, delicate hiss,
and settles in my footprints.
The dawn will say I was never here.

—S. Bryeans von Schmacht

GOING TO A PARTY

Put on your nicest mask
      with all
the happy jingling sweetish smiles!
Arm yourself
with phrases of politeness and clichés!
Then walk in
to all the womyn (!)
who greedily wait
for their share of you.

Bite back
when attacked!

Don't give them
a single damn share of yourself!
Even if your mask
might crack apart.

—Birgitta Fryksén

A candle softly glowing
incense fills my air
gentle rain drops outside
cat at my feet purring
like monks chanting hymns

my heater comes on
chanting its song of warmth
curling the dust motes
about my toes and the cat's . . .
we snuggle into ourselves

a pull at my pipe of visions
and excursions into the spirit
a caressing sip
at my coffee cup
my toes tingle . . .
and i feel the claws of my cat.

—wm peter stravinsky

COULD I

Could I watch you in the morning
      brush your teeth and take a piss.
And when you would leave for work
I'd give you a great big kiss.

Could I go with you after work
to the baseball games at night.
And when I would fall asleep
you could hold me very tight.

Could I go with you on Sundays
for a very long long walk.
I could hold onto your hand
while we had a long long talk.

Could I sit on your lap someday
I'd pretend you are my dad.
And wrap my arms around you
I would feel so very glad.

—Alice M. Kary

A PAISLEY WOMAN

Rosanne on the outside
  Lola Falana on the inside
Equally delighted with diamonds or daisies
A paisley woman, aware too soon, awake too young
She knows too much of the world
Not enough of herself
A misshapen pearl encrusting a volcano
She struggles to pour herself upon the icy shoals
Burdened by her opulent shell
She dreams of dancing in the streets
A paisley shadow of potential lava.

—Judy Kendrick

BEAUTY

In dimlit shop on narrow winding lane
  Where dust lay thick but beauty still shone through,
I saw a glist'ning crystal bowl of blue;
And seeing, I was oh so young again,
Beholding weeds in crystal robes of rain
Where Queen Anne's Lace and Primrose stand askew;
I gently part tall stems with timid shoe
And find the gleaming crystal bowl again.

Oh happy questing heart of childhood years
That seeking beauty, finds her in the weeds;
Today I found you in this clear blue glass;
You shine through ashes, dust, desire and tears;
I clutch my tiny pack of flower seeds
And weep for those who all unseeing, pass.

—Martha Bigelow

SOLUS

I drift and wake, await your late-night call
  from Oakland, Utica, Bangor, New York,
and watch the winter lightning's pale flames fork
frail absences in air. Your letters all
find me where I fall still, unseal desire
and spill fresh news of rosemary and rue,
laughter and longing hair, false starts and true
confessions. Were you come before this fire
kindled against bleak night, I'd sooner light
our son to sleep, hang up your Christmas cape,
put off this poem and let my lips undrape
the dawn behind your eyes. Torn skies requite
such fancies; and alone, love's fragile art
transcends the random weather of my heart.

—David V. Rowland
Fifth Place Award Winner

MARATHON WOMAN

She reeks willpower. Don't stop her!

   Her legs have forgotten how not to run.
Her body is a marionette that
      sadistic gods are bounding about.
Her skeleton has melted inside her
      jelloed tendons.

Florence Joyner, Jesse Owens, feel
      shame at your ease in winning.

Her soupy brain boils inside
      pressure cooker skull.
Her sweat gleams, waxing tanned skin.
Her oil slick of hair is plastered to forehead.
Her eyes dull, like a dying vulture's.

Put your mothering instinct aside.

—S. M. Finn

AUTUMN'S EMIGRE

Wayfarer — the autumn's emigre
Keeps a finespun journal, painstakingly.
This soul possession of inquietude bequeathed
Ripens unto folio, befitting the breeze.

Thus, claiming roadsides in a filigree . . .
Whence golden hushes . . . the frivolities;
To lavish prose in a fluent finesse
Comes this quaint little peddler of leaves.

— Amanda L. Crow

CLEANING OUT THE CLOSET

You opened my soul
forcing me to make a conviction
stating fact based on reality

gently dusting off each porcelain vase and
chinese teacup as I make this transition from
one life to the next

life begun with treasures stored in boxes
wrapped in tissues or papers
wads and wads of them assuring that nothing will break

cobwebs hide but lights reveal
as they reach the corner cracked by time.

— Louise Eleanor Lynch

WHERE HAVE WE GONE

Where is everybody
I'm here
Where are you
Where is everybody
Where are the birds
Where are the squirrels
They said it wouldn't happen
I thought the weapons were only for defense
Someone lied
They said it wouldn't happen
it did
A nuclear war has come
We left Yasgurs' farm
We got away from the garden
And now the raven is all
that is left

— William Morrison

GIGGLING CIGARETTES

I saw my mother's cigarettes
smiling and giggling as she consumed
their deathly vapor.
The fingers of its smoke held tight
to her clothing refusing
to let free,
spreading its carcinogen scent
throughout the house.
I know you won't believe me,
but I heard them bickering at each other,
fighting their way to the top of the pack
wanting to be next in line
to disperse their harmful seeds.
I have to praise them
for shaping my mother,
into a helpless slave of habit.
Upon their destruction,
they will return,
for their great strength is
fortified in my mother's infinite addiction.

— James Illetschko

I SPEAK, BUT GENTLY
FIND THE TIME TO LISTEN . . .

The worms. they eat away at us all.
creating in us all a form
that first i lead, then follow.
i am pressed into service by a word only.
one that speaks many lines. a voice
that is barely heard above the wind,
but is heard by those who
profess a worthier knowledge.
they are the scholars, and we —
their students — we are almost nothing.
our flesh is all we have. our minds
have been taken from us and
given into more subtle hands.
hands that know how to shape a soul —
and yet somehow cater to an urge
that as timid mortals we find
in our fear of one another.

— Eugene A. Sylvester

MIDDLE AGE IN MIDDLE AMERICA

Nearing four o'clock in the afternoon
Friday, July, very hot and
Two kids — about ten — next door
Are cranking out a variety of words
And grunts that indicate unimpeded
Energy and unimaginative play.

Their presence scours my life
Like a Brillo pad — but my surface
Is Teflon and I scratch
irrepairably.

When I'm sixty, I'll not even "abide"
These creatures. But now,
In middle-age, in middle-America
And trapped by limited housing
Selection
I suffer and abide in equal
Amounts.

The senses dull — it is no surprise
The landlord's name is Brown.

— James A. Pearse

RIVERDALE REVERIE

I sit on the aluminum folding chair
Gently held by its interweaving colored bands.

Six or seven empty chairs line the rails
Of the Wolmanized wood deck —
(Guarenteed not to rot for thirty years)
— Empty. Like silent hosts — waiting.

From the center of the redwood table
Sprouts a giant, collapsed umbrella
That, in the fading light, appears
As a great sleeping flower.

The paling rose sky beyond the graying trees
Fades upward to a milky blue wash,
And the now green-blacked wooded rock shelf below
Gives up drifting, shadowy shapes
Like silent guardians of the woods.

Aware now of the comforting chorus
Of night crickets — insistent and eternal,
I surrender willingly to my senses
And breathe a silent "Thank You."

— Len Weingarten

BUTTERFLY'S WINGS

Butterflies are free to be
All that they are called to be
Just as they easily spread their wings
So are we free to do the same thing.

But others choose a different road
Bogged down by life's heavy load
But in Jesus we have the choice to be
Light in flight as the butterfly's wings.

—Mary F. Moore

TO RICHARD

I can feel you inside me —
all warm and glowing.
Sighing, I close my eyes
    and my heart begins to sing.
You hold me close, tight;
    the contentment is intoxicating.
I taste your lips on mine,
    the sweetest of kisses.
I reach out to touch your cheek;
    then you are gone — a dream.
Tears fill my eyes, I whisper your name;
    awake now, I smile — knowing.
You are always inside me —
    in my heart, my blood, my soul.

—Lisa A. Sherrod

REBUTTAL

High in the Andes
    Deep in Some Nation
Where my grandfather ruled
There by the golden forest
        He fought for his honor

        Towering in the Andes
        Deep in No Where
Where my father toiled
There by the vanishing river
        He obeyed for a potato

        Triumphant in the Andes
        Deep in No One's Land
Where I grow someone's coca
Here in my hovel
        The gods slay our foes . . .

—Matthew Dean Martin

That night when with the dusk
Your sudden smile, leaden-sweet
like cherries on the bough,
entered the sacred stillness of my soul,
offering what life had not intended —
dimly I first apprehended the mild mystery.
Oh, how it crept up on my cognizance!
restoring visions long since lost
to the exhausted bones of perception,
ending at last the singular, anguished dance.

Vanguard of kisses they stood,
your talc-white teeth,
arrayed as the marbles of Sounion,
lustrous in the lemonglow of moonlight.
In slenderest sleep
I dreamt of my pale death,
safe in the circle
of your man's embrace.

—David Marsh

A FATHER'S LEGACY

A convert disease
within me lies;
crave to appease
in liquid guise.

The need succumb strongly urges,
yet neither want nor desire.
Emotion, feeling, beauty, purge
for the horror of these just require.

When you die, victim claimed,
what stays but the poison, reap.
I am afraid, afraid
of the bitter thoughts I'll keep

        all within a bottle.
—Catherine Stoddert

BOUND

Wisteria climbs
grey boards,
collapsing the house.
It hangs out its lavender
from the eave.

Wearing the same blue dress
she flops on the door step
worry lines worn deep.
Two children sift sand
at her feet,
another feeds at her breast.

He bends over the fender
of a yawning truck
to fix a dead heartbeat.
No shirt.
Grease and sweat blend
strange ointment
of hope.
Determined to make
it work.

—Carolyn Smith

DIRECTIONS

If I were as sure of my direction
        as you are of yours
    I'm not so sure you would
            want me
        as you do now.

For my uncertainty makes you
            strong
    just as your persistence
        makes me weak
    and perhaps, just perhaps,
        we function best
            together
        in that way.

    We pass the hours
            talking
    as if nothing else matters
        but the words
    that pass from our lips.

    You seem content with that
        I have yet to learn
            that
        and so,
    maybe you'll teach me.
—terri

Too afraid to cross the others border,
for fear of having to identify ourselves,
we march around the boundaries of each others lives,
and trample the flowers that once grew there.

—Hal Adkins
Fifth Place Award Winner

FOR MAYA ANGELOU
You weave your words with
angelic caresses and effervescent
vivaciousness,

you encourage my soul
and
boost my spirits
and
make me laugh and cry — sometimes
simultaneously

you are a diamond with a sparkling
ubiquitous light. THANK YOU!

—Ramona Cooper-Beverly

THE BEAUTY OF
THE MORNING
The beauty of the early
morning is easy to see;
All the butterflies, sparrows, and
morning glories.
I see busy bumble bees buzzing all
around,
I also see the mist and fog coming
from the ground;
I see spider webs covered with dew,
I see so many beautiful things, do
you?

—Hollie LeAnne Carney, age 10

WINTER
In the frozen barren ground
wooden giants stand all around.

The friendly trees are sleeping now
with snowy frost upon their brow.

When spring returns then we shall see
once more the birds and green of tree.

And in the silence of the wood
we walk and talk as humans should.

And in our quiet gentle way
we thank The Lord for every day.

—Edna M. Hardy

RAINBOW
A very pretty rainbow
What a lovely sight
You'll never see a rainbow
When your eyes are shut tight
If you walk into a rainbow
You'll see some pretty towers
And in those pretty towers
You'll see some pretty flowers
And in those pretty flowers
You'll see some little girls
Who come from little flower cups
With little creamy swirls

—Aliya Rahman

DAISIES
Daisies dozing during the day
Wind blowing their white skirts at night
Daffodils chatting away
Bees buzzing, making honey,
dreaming all day.

—Debra Lee Dowling

Have you
Have you ever looked out the
window on a windy day at the
wheat field and see!

See how
See how the tops the whole
field look like the waves on
a sea

I have seen the sea

and

I have seen the field.

—Martin Gatto

THE SNAKE MAN
I saw him
Through the dilapidated grey fence.
He came out
Of his snake harbor shed
In his W.W. II (or was it W.W. I) coat
With two of them wrapped around him.
He saw me,
Disgust and horror showed on my face.
That crazy old man,
The frightener of little children
A local legend —
"THE SNAKE MAN,"
Looked at me and said,
"I've seen you with your pen."

—Diane McDonald

CHOPPING DOWN BEANSTALKS
Giants once walked this path
idols forged of
gold in a
cold fusion of self-importance and greed,

but their feet were made of clay
and when fate rolled a bomb
their way they crumbled
into artifacts
fairy-tales
and déjà vú

—David O. Bowles, Jr.

MARION'S MUSHROOMS
Funny umbrella.
Standing off the porch,
Four heads within it,
We hide from the rain
And the stormy skies.

We chat, but mostly
We laugh at our spot,
Apart from the house,
With raindrops bouncing
Off the umbrella.

—Catherine Gergesha

AUTUMN

Relentless wind
Drives red yellow leaves
Tumbling through browning grass.
Cold cutting wind
Rustles through barren trees
Blowing summer away.

—Josann Rutsch

LOVE IS A STEP HIGHER

Love is a step higher
Than fire and flood.
Love is a step higher
Than the spilling of blood.
Love is a step higher
Than death in the field.
Love is a step higher
Than the swords that we wield.
Love is a step higher
Than man's foolish pride.
Love is a step higher
Than all that we hide.
And who are we
I say
To stand and keep Love
From having Her way.

—Scott Brumfield

LOVE ALWAYS SHINES

Illuminated by your smile
Fascinated by your charm
Inspired by your touch
Words will never be
Enough to describe a
Radiance as pure as gold
Each and every new day
Your love always shines true
Only to magnify two-fold
Unleashing sensual desires
Rapture divine — only two share
Wakening the very senses
Of each other's existence
Making life in general
Advance with a definite purpose
Never eluding its own destiny.

—Katherine M. Happle

COMRADES

Winds of a distant place
Blow memories in my mind
A time long ago
Of comrades left behind
My brothers
In a horrid place
A land of ancient time
A tear of pain
A smile of brotherhood
The thoughts still live on

But yet the question?
Ever present in my life
What purpose do I exist
With brothers on my mind
No day goes by
I do not cry
For comrades left behind.

—Harvey L. Wasserman

HISTORY REPEATS ITSELF

You have to cancel tonight and
I'm supposed to be happy that you're verrrry sorry.
Goddamn phone machine.
Is it the truth or
is it memoreX?

—Susan Simpson

SPRING

The howling cold of winter passes; Sounds of spring arrive:
Chirping of birds as they prepare their nests,
Bees encircling their hives.
Cool mild breezes aroma the air with heavenly scents of flowers,
Surrendering your subconscious mind for hours, upon hours, upon hours.
Barefoot walks on moist sandy shores,
Permeating your body as the warming sun allures.
Young mothers with strollers sit in the park,
Watching their children frolic till just before dark.
Colorful kites of paper, cloth, or wood,
Engulfing the wind as it positively should.
School will be dismissed and children will cheer,
Till the school bell tolls at the next school year.
Soon spring will pass and summer will near,
But fear not: Spring will arrive again next year.

—Susan Silva

SOUND OF THE CYMBALS

The successional value of a day without light,
Is uncharming.
The reality of wit is lying to the mass of poverty,
That seems to the the Baudclaire limit,
Lying in avenues that comb the street.

The true intention of native values, that move through life,
On stiletto heels more quickly than,
A concave instrument,
That begs of the seduction, of a power house of logic, is convincing.

To name the rebel factor, that jumps from leaves,
In candid motion,
Meets the mind of comfort, like the Latin beat,
Of aforesaid rock,
On a decanter of wine,
Is its sister prism of philosophy of rhythm.

—Lisa Miller

TREBLINKA

Empty eyes stare out of sunken sockets at a world gone mad.
Concertina wire surrounds her pain and suffering, holding
it close with a million razor sharp points, shredding not
only her body, but her dignity as well.
Nothing shows through her eyes, if her dreams were to do so,
they too would be taken from her, and used to benefit the others.
Emaciated limbs quiver with the effort to make them function,
make them hold the small still bundle she cradles in her arms.
As she is roughly shoved into line for the "showers" —
the bundle falls — she is led screaming into the low building,
where the hiss of gas slowly silences both her hysteria and her life.
Inside the fallen bundle, a tiny body no longer breathes.
The golden crown of curls, no longer visible through the filth and lice.
The dancing blue eyes, now covered with an opaque film.
The once smiling mouth, now curved into a rictus of horror,
through which one by one the maggots crawl out to
taste the flavor of the "THIRD REICH."
God weeps quietly for the fate of man.

—Charlene Wood Villella

MY BIRTHDAY

All day smiles that glow, as the wind does gently blow.

Another day but something new, another year that I've been through.

All the bridges that I crossed, all the feelings that I tossed.

Through another year we'll go and on that special day again, I'll find my Birthday is my friend.

—Battise

PREJUDICE

If you don't look like them
Then you're not at best
They won't settle for anything less

When you do nice things, you'll be likely to regret it
They don't care as long as you get it

If you do something wrong
They don't forgive you
Then you'll be named Chink, Spic, Jew, Polack, Guinea, Honky or Nigger

Why do they say this
Does it make them proud
It only brings your ego down to the ground

When they say they're sorry
Can you forgive them
Or turn your back, and hope to never see them

It doesn't matter what you do
Try never to show them they got the best of you

It is embarrassing, rude and offending
What can you do
Prejudice is never-ending

—Jennifer Trodden

FRIENDS

Whom do you confide in and tell your most intimate secrets to, your friends, of course!
Who knows your heartaches and woes, your friends, of course!
Who stands beside you through thick and thin and picks you up when you are tired and worn, your friends, of course!
When you are lonely and all alone, who calls you on the phone and says "Come over to my home," your friends, of course!
Who, when a loved one passes away, stands by your side and lets you know, sorrow will pass one day and good memories will replace the loneliness you feel today, your friends, of course!
Who, when you were born, held you close in her arms your precious friend from the day of birth, your most beloved friend on earth, your Mother, of course!
But, who is the best friend of all?
Who took our sins to the cross and paid for them with His Life,
Who saved us from the terrors of Hell and gave us that hope and love we know so well.
Our most precious Friend Jesus, of course!

—Frances Boose

GRANDVIEW
A Time to Remember

High on a hilltop
Surrounded by tall comfortable trees
There is a grand view.
Laughter, joy, running, jumping
Let's go for a ride
Along a crooked path. Past a worn shed
To a green pasture of rolling hills and deep ravines.
A few cattle grazing by a small pond about to burst its seams.

Rain, Rain, Rain
Will it ever end?
All things must come to a close.
Tears, Sighs, Disbelief
No this cannot be.
Are we in a dream?
Back along the path
We must go home.

Below rich land with tall corn and red crimson milo.
Fertile from hard work and toil.
Not an easy life. But the only one.
Home at last.
Grandview, peaceful and serene valley.
A world with much love and laughter,
Yet fears and tears.
Faith will keep us all together.
Time to go. At last restful sleep.
We are in a dream.

—Amber Linn

FIFTH YEAR

With an old baggy pair of overalls and a brightly painted face,
this clown of a man with a lump in his throat began to present his case.

I have come to offer a proposition and if you so agree,
the riches of this world I'll give to you or at least those which are free.

Upon your soul I will bestow my love, as much as you can stand,
and in return all I ask of you is in marriage you offer your hand.

A lack of words and tears in her eyes had signalled more or less,
but the tremble he felt in her soft embrace provided a welcomed YES.

So the clown would marry the princess and forever change his life,
the girl that stood before him would soon become his wife.

Married they were amongst their friends, their vows exchanged outloud,
tears in their eyes overshadowed by those which flowed within crowd.

Five long years have come and gone since their wedding day,
both have taken the test of time, both received an A.

Oh heads of hair have begun to thin and the waistlines are up not down,
but the clown still loves the princess and the princess still loves the clown.

—Randy C. Holbrook

THE PROCESS

Caterpillar
slow, furry
crawling, inching, resting
takes time to grow
de-furring, developing, beautiful
unraveled, free
Butterfly

—Kimberly Louks

TRINITY

This church stands tall,
a Beacon white
to fill the needs
of those who live.
We work, we play,
we see this site;
Our needs fulfilled,
we'll sleep this night.

—Ron E. Mangel

BIRDS

Birds, birds, fly up so high
They can fly, they can fly
up to the sky.
They can stand on trees
They can almost touch the cloud,
When they sing their song,
They say it out loud.
They tweet while they fly
They stand with their leg
We hope people don't kill animals
When we beg.

—Hemant A. Mehta, age 6

OLD TREE

I am an old tree.
I wonder when I will die.
I see my friends dying.
I hear their moans and groans.

I am an old tree.
I think of living forever.
I like my thought.
I wish I could live forever.
I know I can't.

I am an old tree.

—Jeremy Coston, age 13

Roses are red
Violets are blue
It's hard to believe
That you're twenty-two.
You're getting older by the year
And grayer by the day,
I'm five years younger,
But I'll get there someday.
You're a great older sister
And my best friend, too.
You're caring and nice
And a pretty cool dude.
It's the end of my poem,
I'm sorry to say.
But I just wanted to wish you
A Happy Birthday.

—P. D. Kurth

MY MOTHER

In a treasured book of memories, she holds a special place,
With her pleasing personality and ever smiling face.
To me she was a priceless gem of which there was no other
Filled with true unselfish love — my Mother.

I loved to hold her toil-worn hands and kiss her wrinkled brow,
And hear her tell of yesteryears as only she knew how.
She taught me how to make a home to share with one another,
As only one like she could do — my Mother.

Through toil or strife or sorrow, she took it on the chin,
Yet no one knew just how she felt, way down deep within.
She only thought of doing good from one place to another,
That's why I'm proud to tell the world — She's my Mother.

As she walked down the path of life, years added one by one,
Yet the light that shone within her eyes was like the rising sun.
I'll shout with joy from coast to coast, till my voice they'd like to
smother,
If someday folks can say — I am like my Mother.

—Lilly Erickson

THE ABSENCE OF MOTHER

I wish that I could call my mother and talk with her a while.
and surprise her with a sudden visit that always made her smile.
How often I do think of her, memories from way back when
the things I wish I should've done, the way things could've been.

The thing most often that comes to mind from all the memories that
I store
is the surprised, pleasing smile she'd have as I walked through
her front door.
I can sometimes hear her laughter as it echos through my mind
and would laugh at her as she laughed at me and we'd laugh
until we cried.

How I wish I could just reach out and hug her oh so tight
and make sure all was well with her as the day turned to night.
Hands that knew the pains of labor, a heart as good as gold
her share of grief and loneliness, her dread of growing old.

So many things I took for granted as a child so often does
but mothers seem to know these things, it's all a part of love.
The void I have within my soul, the pain within my heart
the days I spend missing her, since her eternal part.

—Patricia E. Trero

THE LEAF'S SPIRIT

One day near the end of April — while sitting in the sun,
A crackling sound caught my ear — t'was a last-year leaf on the
run.
The breeze set it down beside me — for it seemed to have
something to say
"I can stay for only a moment — and then must be on my way.
There's nothing left here to cling to — and no place really to go
With all this beauty around me — I look out of place I know.
But since you're good to take notice — even tho' this beauty
surrounds,
Have no feeling of sorrow for me — for this too, is one of life's
rounds.
This time last year I was blooming — and was part of this beautiful
view
I can say I've lived a full lifetime — and I'm happy in this life,
too."
Just then the breeze came back dancing — and lifted the little
brown leaf
Dancing away with it sprightly — it showed no sign of grief.
I thought to myself at that moment — "My outlook on life should be
As wise as that little brown leaf's — who left its spirit with me."

—Cae U. DiFerdinando

THE POTTER IS STILL AT THE WHEEL

It started in the Garden of Eden, the Potter was at the wheel
As he scooped a lump of clay from the earth, to form man in His own appeal
A potter must have patience as he shapes and molds the clay
Just as Jesus is with us, when we sometime go astray
We are exhibits of the potter, not quite ready for the kiln
Let's not forget the Potter is still at the wheel
Shaping and molding our lives as we live from day to day
So that we can be a light to someone along life's narrow way

—Donald Woods

RIVER PASSING GENTLY

Walking through a timeless blizzard, an honored rain storm,
The sweltering charm of a sunny day,
It becomes a vault of futuristic haplessness,
Seeming to race through each second steadily.
Passing backwards, through the abbreviation of faltering takes,
It plows sceneless, like rigid straps that still exit together.
It rests like tables, and whims of silver.
Could this florid love, of seasons yet unknown,
Become an Appotomax, in the history, of a small planet?

A comet passed over the still water gems, of a cut stone horizon.
Do you think that this passage of endeavors,
Could dance, away, into the Tiffany pose of sunset,
Leaving for a beach of bliss?

I still count the country clover, and doves, remissing about a legend
incognito.
Its very pale forgiveness, suggest that I could walk,
Hand in hand, out of the climate of a given situation,
And still fly blithely into the taste of its realm,
Over Dionysis like consternation of livid, vital suggestion.

—Lisa Miller

MY GOODBYE TO GRANDMOTHER

I am walking down a long dry road covered in dust.
There are many holes in the road and many paths leading from it,
But I know to stay on the road.
    I look into the sky and see an eagle soaring above me
And I feel that I am with him.
When he plunges toward the earth my heart is seized with pain and
            unshed tears,
But when he climbs back into the sky I burst
With the joy of living and loving.

    Grandmother,
This is how I saw your life.
We will miss you with every passing day.
You will not be there to hold onto our dreams
When we think we are lost,
To wash away the tears,
Caused by our fears.
You will not be there to hold our hands
When life makes its strenuous demands.
When we wish to stop living, who will make us feel that we must?
You were special to every person you met.
You touched a part of us that was secret,
Yet shared.
I know that you can't hear my words of praise.
I just wish we could have had a moment for us to say:
Thank You for giving us all of your days.

    I wanted to run when they came to say . . .
    But it isn't true.
    You shall live in our hearts for the rest of our days.

—Marlene Bawcum

PEACE IS SONG

Like the rose you sang to me.
gentle petals; sweet melody
        sing to grow
        listen to me
        tell me please
    I need to know
The drifting release
    for which I long.
    My inner peace;
That PEACE is SONG.

—Kathy Crabill

I'LL FIND YOU THERE

Sleep, honey, sleep
I'm sorry we must part
But memories I'll still keep
Of you owning my heart

Goodbye, sweetheart, goodbye
I will miss you so much
But I will really try
To always keep in touch

Fly, my dear, fly
To the heavens up above
'Cause when it's my turn to die
I'll find you there, my love

—Sharon Lee Hasselman

AFRICAN VIOLETS

The table by the window
    is cluttered with little pots,
profuse dull green leaves
with many colored spots.
Flowers so perfect in form
almost hide the bed of green.
Petals of bright purple hues
centered by golden beads are seen.
Old caring hands pick leaves
of those fallen dead and dry
knowing full well someday
God will, when they too die,
pick them from life's garland
with dry flowers from the ground
alive again and bright in hue
and place them in His crown.

—Eleanor Whitekettle

ADULTHOOD TRANSCENDS
ADOLESCENCE

Unbridled tenacity,
    Self-centered desires,
Deliberate words:
    Biting, cutting, caustic.

Where is the softness,
    The concern for others,
The humility and the empathy
    Of one that abhors impertinence?

Concealed, like the tulip bulbs
            in winter.
Obstructed by impetuous whims,
Waiting to emerge from a
    metamorphosis
Into a delightfully compassionate
    individual . . .

—Jane L. Smith

PRELUDE OF DECEMBER

Autumn leaves of crimson
cascade, e'er so gently.
to a sun-glistened stream —
dancing, with beauty and furvor;
to a prelude of December.

—Ryan David Bassett, age 15

HERE AND THERE

I thought about you today
And I had to turn away
To see if maybe, just maybe
You'd be standing there.

But it was only a breeze
With a strong scent of the seas
And for a moment, the moment
Your heart beating here.

—Barry Setser

MOTHERS

Soft yet Strong
Deep rooted feelings showing
Veins bound by strong rope
Severed at times
But never cut through
Fiercely protective tenderly
caring
Pain and heartache unquest-
ionably
A life time of love

—Rebecca Anderson

You can't see it, touch it
When felt, you don't realize
You feel it.

It's guised in the forms of
Pleasure, pain, anger, and shame
And when in limbo, it even
Takes the blame.

A simple, yet dominant state
Created to demise or elate.

An affair of the heart,
One that befuddles and mires
In effect, the glory of a
Pair of desires.

—Michael E. Dunlap, Jr.

FALL

The cool breeze of the wind,
the smooth draft in which
it spins. The colorful leaves,
bare trees the pretty sight of
Autumn
Piles in which the children
play on a shiny day.
Laughter and joy in
everyway is surely a great
sign of:
Autumn Day
Sneezes and watery eyes, Fall
brings a surprise. Fall here,
Fall there, Fall brings allergies
everywhere.

—Katisha Nishaun Stipe, age 11

NOVA

Grandma left us today
"For heaven," Mom said.
I saw her twinkle goodbye to me.
"So long," I called.
I know she heard me
Because she twinkled again.

—Lory Bertsch

SALVATION'S SONG

I

The Gospel Message is the Truth, that teaches man what's right
and wrong.
It showeth mankind how to live and brings with it a song.
A song that thrills the heart and soul, a song we all may sing,
If we accept this vital truth, and let Him live within.

II

Salvation's Song, Salvation's Song, Oh! what a joy this song to sing,
To know the joy and peace it brings, forgiveness of my sins,
As Jesus said come unto me, and I will give you rest,
I went to Him and found it so, and how my soul is blessed.

III

When time for us shall be no more,
And we have crossed o'er Heaven's shore,
Forever there to enter in, "Salvation's Song" to sing,
To meet our Saviour face to face, and sing of saving Grace,
What joy 'twill be for you and me in all Eternity.

—Rev. David Blaskowsky

A REAL DREAM

There's walnut bark clinging to the climbing bending limbs.
The leaves turn touching colors as the summer season readily ends.
Well, fall has grown nearer now and the dew is nearly gone.
It's forming into crystal frost for the cold, but early rising dawn.
The birds are steadily searching for some scarce and hardened feed.
Down on the ground where to be found, is delicious, discarded, seed.
Then winter comes and the snow that's fell, begins to glisten all so
bright.
As the sun shines down so gleamingly a beautiful rainbow light.
It's a feeling of peace and thankful love to assuredly see all of
these.
Even the sight of the given bark that's clinging to the walnut trees.
But most of all what deeply touches, this real affectionate heart of
mine,
Is knowing the Lord will bring back always that splendid beauty of
the spring-time.

—Wendell Darren Rigg III

MOTHER'S BIBLE

I picked up Mother's Bible, all around me felt like Holy Ground.
I felt the brush of a breeze from an angel's wing.
And a warm glow did abound.
My heart was stirred within me, I felt the touch of quick'ning calm.
I picked up my Mother's Bible and I heard an angel's Psalm.

I heard the angels sing the song of Vict'ry until Death.
I felt the way she felt then, it took away my breath.
The time, it was so long ago when she would hold me close and say,
"Sister,
Don't you know that I love and pray for you each day?"

But, the Bible's all I have now for Mom has drifted away.
Into places I can't go just now but age brings me closer each day.
But,
I felt the same as she did when I hold my loved ones close.
I picked up Mother's Bible and heard the singing of the Heavenly
Host.

—Sue Hunt Carter

The water sparkles less —
The birds fly low.
I go!

—June R. Swetman

MY PRECIOUS GROWING GARDEN
My precious growing garden
Is made up of four special little ones
For whom I must have loads of patience, love, and pardon.

Jessica tall and slender as a willow,
Bending over to give the little ones a helping hand or hug
Until at night her head she lay upon her pillow.

Luke, wildly growing as a milkweed with its fuzzy head,
Lives day by day and each day to its fullest
Until at last the day is done and he snuggles down into his bed.

Stephanie sunny bright and such a clown, our little daffodil,
All day teasing and tormenting, an impish smile upon her face
Until at last her day is done and she is laying still.

Candice still a little clinging sweet pea vine
Crawling, crying, sleeping little, always wanting held,
Until finally far into the night she gives up the fight, this
    little baby of mine

God has entrusted this precious growing garden to my care,
To teach and help and pull the weeds that will sneak in
Until at last they each are grown and out of Mama's hair.

—Heather Boyer

PREY
Many times, I ran this trail; with winged heels, I prevailed.
Though dangers came, from every side; I ran like wind, lest I died.

Of this day, I do fear; raging dogs, everywhere.
I ran, I jump, I broke the air; praying that, they'll disappear.

I look, I saw no victory; only a dried up maple tree.
If I could get, to what I see; before these hunters, capture me.

With all my might, I run to thee; the feel of heat, close to me.
If I could get, to yonder tree; I just might claim, this victory.

The darkness of fear, came over me; I felt their paws, about my knee.
If I could get, to that tree; I could change, what just might be.

I deadly screamed, my destiny; as sharpen teeth, entered me.
It was not far, from distant tree; when all my hope, seem to flee.

Blood and Pain, they covered me; as raging wolves, claimed victory.
I close mine eyes, to Death I see; that came beneath, that Maple Tree...

—LaVerne

A SERVANT'S HEART
Give to me, Lord, a servant's heart that bends its will to Thine,
That quickly hears Thy least command and makes Thy wishes mine.
Let me obey the still, small voice that speaks within my soul
Of all Thy bidding unto me — my will in Thy control.
Might Thou mine effort undergird as I strive Thee to serve.
Make all my effort, Lord, to please; that I'll Thy smile deserve.
Let all my labor give Thee joy and rise unto Thy throne —
A savor sweet of sacrifice unto Thee, God, alone.
Let not mine eye search temporal things, earth's token favors seek —
Expecting wealth or praise of men because to me You speak.
But let mine only recompense for all my servitude
Be, "Well done, faithful child of Mine" — all earth's allures eschewed
In favor of Thy presence sweet, as I Thy face, Lord seek.
Let me, dear Master, look to Thee in full, n'er just oblique.
And when my labor here's complete, naught more for me to do,
May I rest, Jesus, at Thy feet — eternally with You.

—Sandra L. DiNello

A SPIDER'S WEB
Diamond threads spun
From leaf to leaf,
In shiny splinters
Of an odd motif.

—Christina L. Vaughn

FAITH CHALLENGES DOUBT
Doubt sees the obstacles
Faith sees the way
Doubt sees the darkest night
Faith sees the day
Doubt dreads to take a step
Faith soars on high
Doubt questions who believes
Faith answers "I"

—Inella Hoggan

FRIEND
You used to walk with me
Now I walk alone
You used to talk with me
Now there are no words
You used to laugh with me
Now the laughter is all gone
You used to comfort me
When things were down
You used to be my friend
Where did we go wrong?

—Doriana Mercedes

GARIBALDI
Garibaldi, Garibaldi the
king of the sea.

We all watch him swim
freely on this cold fall day.

We watch him swim in his
bay.

Garibaldi, Garibaldi the king
of the sea.

We all watch him swim freely.

—Lindsey Williams, age 9

LOVE
Love, it is like a long
river's path
It is allowed to flow freely
and swiftly until it comes to
a dam, where it is stopped.

The dam, may stay shut,
forever locking the river in,
or open up and let the water
go once more on its path.

There are many dams that
the water must overcome
to get to its final destiny,
an ocean.

It reaches the ocean and
is allowed to forever flow
freely.

—Karen Youngberg, age 13

ODE TO AN OUTDOOR DAD
(Written for Father's Day, 1989)
Hey there, Dad, with greying hair; you've slowed down some but we're still a pair
It seems that now our places have changed, and life itself is re-arranged
How I recall days long since past, when I was slow, and you were fast
You'd say "Hurry up!" then sit and wait, while I tried my best to match your gait.

But there were things a boy had to know, like "How does moss know where to grow?"
And "why do geese fly in a vee? If I can see a fish, can it see me?"
"Why are thistles sharp and spiny? Why is frost so white and shiny?"
"Why does a deer drop his horns each fall? Why does an owl make such a scary call?"

Life's mysteries, some unknown yet. Sometimes we'd talk, sometimes we'd set
Each listening as the world passed, and time sped by so very fast
The hours, the days, the weeks, the years I shared with you my youthful fears
And in your own wise, thoughtful way, you made me what I am today.

One does not overnight become, a man; I know he is the sum
Of all the parts life sends his way, and a Dad who guides him day by day.
        —Paul R. Jukes

LIFE IN A NURSING HOME
As you know, your days on this ole earth are numbered—
So, live your life fully, even, with cares encumbered.
You may move from place to place with a troubled mind,
Leaving familiar things and many a friend behind.
But we, as thinking people, meet the daily trials,
With a strong will, a brave heart and determined smiles.

So, hey! Just look at me! I'm living here in a "Nursing Home" — "I am alive!"
I have a roof over my head and there are many things from my past I can revive . . .
Making friends, singing, playing and listening to music and going out to a store,
Watching T.V., socializing and sharing experiences with others that can open
That door . . . . . .
To relationships with my fellowman that gives meaning to my life.
I am, "not," yet, ready to vegetate in a corner to wither and die.

Many times I hear you say, "You are in a Nursing Home, you can't have a life there."
I say unto you, "Yes, I live in a Nursing Home and I live life to the fullest, here."
I find that as each day comes, it brings with it a feeling that I am still "me,"
That I can do many things even if my mind and body are not as they used to be.
But when that last door opens and I know that my time has come to go —
I'll think back and say, "Yes, I lived a good life in a Nursing Home, that I know.
Yes, a darn good life." . . . .
        —Wilma Pierce

A TURNING POINT
There is a dullness in the air unlike anything I've experienced before.
        Yet, also a haughtiness — cold, though somehow alluring.
            What is it about this place that draws me in?
                I find myself returning often.
        The view here is astounding, not unlike that of a dream.
    All around it seems I am surrounded by circles and circles of land,
            Each circle having a uniqueness all its own.
                One can find hope in these circles somehow.
                    And again I return.
        I never quite understand the importance of my being here;
                Here in this dark, spell-binding place.
            Yet, I feel compelled, almost required to be present.
        It is as if my life, my entire well-being depend on it.
                The dullness grows heavier.
            I find myself weary and my thoughts wander.
    I begin to concentrate on the circle to my right — almost instinctively.
        Each breath draws me closer to its center and I find myself falling,
            Spinning toward and finally into its luminous core.
                    It is done.
I'm left with a sense of complete, never-ending peace — one I can call my own.
        —Amy Jo Anderson

THE KNOT

I was tired when I got down off that tractor late the other night.
All the stuff inside my body felt so bruised and weary from the fight
with this hard and rocky, worthless land. I thought as though it seemed
that the very earth beneath my feet absorbed my strength and self-esteem.

Twenty-three steps to the back porch, yes, I counted all of them inside
my head as I approached the door and saw, with half a wondering eye,
that the setting sun had splashed its red light on the sky so brilliantly.
Soon the stillness of a summer's eve would bring a restful sleep to me.

And then out through doorways in my house, I heard my woman gently say:
"Would you like something cool to drink? You have had such a tiring day."
I smiled, momentarily, her voice was soothing in my ears,
and then replied to her in kind: "Yes, my darling; yes, my dear."

The kitchen smelled of dinner as I washed the dust from off myself
and noticed that the work clothes had been folded neatly on the shelf.
And, later, as I ate the food so carefully prepared for me,
we talked of all the day's events and laughed at life quite carelessly!

That evening, as I lay in bed, my wife had cuddled close to me,
I thought of how my life had been completed through her destiny.
As sleep rolled down upon us both my heartfelt love for her became
a whisper in the dark of night that spoke the sound of her sweet name.

—Marc C. Di Giuseppe

THE BRAIN

It flings the fire of genius found in creative thought —
It rings the cerebral spirit of wisdom's prudence —
It stings the subconscious core of the mind's reflective heart —
It slings the divine sparks of pragmatic and philosophical sagacity —
It brings the calculating and cunning scintillations of brilliance —
It wings the circumspection and discriminating criticism of perception —
It swings the powerful mental faculties of comprehension, reason and
talent —
It pings the sharp witted dexterity of profound aptitude —
It zings the thought provoking psyche of mood and memory —
It sings the sensorium of enlightenment, foresight and intellect —
Only the Brain can both praise and please the glory of God, —
Only the human brain can understand the inevitable unity between force
and nature —
Only the human brain can fulfill all righteousness.

In an unfriendly world there is more wasted brain potential than
can be endured by anything but love. Again, there is a great need to
raise the human collective brain capacity from the depths of darkness to
the light of love.

—Barzillai

THE QUEST

One hundred years ago Earth time, we left this starry void,
to search for other forms of life and share ecstatic joy.
We know that other life exists, we cannot be alone,
    our physic soul demands we find that deep rimmed ageless home.
One hundred years is but a day in time warped outer reaches,
    the aging process slows to nil in suspended animation.

With laser beam we travel on, beyond where light rays bend,
    the probing sensors on our craft reveal that space must end.
Beyond this field of awesome force, there is no space or time,
    in utter darkness a shield so black that light rays fail to shine.
This is the end of cosmic space, a nothingness prevails beyond,
    a point where space and time stand still and both become as one.

To other stars, we head our ship, our frenzied search goes on,
    we have to find a living soul before we head for home.
Then from the endless depth of space, a murmured voice comes through,
    "Get out of bed you lazy boy or you'll be late for school."

—Russell Knox

Father help us
    to remember.
What you would like
to have us do.
Help us to be
Strong and Loving.
Help us to be
True.

—Mary H. Njos

A KISS

A kiss is
the lips' embrace
A brief enclosure
of a tiny place
And leaves
no visible trace
But a smile
On my love's face.

—Karen Palicki

BICYCLE ROW

See the bicycles
All in a row
See the students
Riding low
See the tanks
In Tiannamen Square
See the people
Just not fair
Gonna ride my bicycle
Away from here

—Lawrence Murren

For one brief moment
    I felt someone
        dancing with me.

Shadows cast by light
    upon the wall
        moved gracefully

In familiar patterns
    across the floor,
        and then I saw

A darkened window
    reflecting me —
        dancing alone.

—Andrea Moody

WALLS OF STEEL

I'm clenched in
But never show fear
When I'm surrounded by —
These Walls of Steel

They push and prod . . .
Thinking it's a joke
I've got feelings too
And they are broke

They'll never know
Just how I feel
Surrounded by —
These Walls of Steel

—Muzz Glover

TO AN ORIOLE

Oh bird of bright and golden hue, with mellow notes so old, yet new.
Your voice is heard before the dawn has pierced the early hours of morn.
Before the robin opens his eyes and sends his song upward toward the sky.
Swinging high upon your nest, thou has called me from my rest.

Would my home were built so high, away from vandal's wicked eye.
Swinging there among the leaves, a house of wise and cunning weave,
Thy priceless treasures hidden deep, while torrents fall, and whirl winds sweep.
Carefree and happy, swinging still, obeying the laws of thy Master's will.

Would that my life might ever be, faithful, true, like a bird carefree.
Trusting our Father's hand to guide from all the storms my soul to hide.
Father give me a trusting heart, what ever happens, will never depart.
Whether it be on land or sea that God in His heaven take care of me.

> **—Jean W. Williams**

WARMTH

Think about it . . . Warmth . . .
Isn't that a really strange word? Think about it for a minute. Warmth . . .
It seems that the more you say it the more obtuse it becomes.

Is that because it should be rendered and received more often than
talked about?

I have some warmth . . . but I have no one to give this warmth to. I
think I have warmth. I did once. I don't believe I'm cold. At any
rate I try not to be cold. Some people have been cold to me. Is it
because I have no warmth?

How do I find out?
How would you find out?
Could you?
Can I?
Will I?
Are you warm?
Do you have warmth?

Warmth . . . Isn't that a real strange word? Think about it for a minute.
Warmth . . . It seems that the more you say it the more obtuse it becomes.

Warmth . . .

> **—DaNett Asher**

A Conversation between The Song and THE SONGBIRD

I can move your world on a mere note, such is the power I have

ON THE CONTRARY MY FRIEND,
MY WORLD IS MUCH MORE POWERFUL, THAN THE STRENGTH YOU POSSESS

I am mighty, you are small
To use my power on you,
is as to use a cannon to disperse fleas

MY POWER IS A STRENGTH OF MIND
I CAN OVERCOME YOU, BY THINKING YOU AWAY

I don't believe in wishful thinking

SAY WHAT YOU WISH,
WISDOM AND KNOWLEDGE ALWAYS PREVAIL

Perhaps, but I can control your dreams!

YOU HAVE NEVER BEEN IN THE SOUNDS OF MY DREAMS

If I were, you would be powerless to stop me.
To me, you are but an image

AH, BUT AN IMAGE IS MORE THAN A WHISPER

Is it? A whisper holds the power of persuasion

NOT UPON THE WISE
AN IMAGE IS BELIEF,
AND BELIEVING IS LIFE

> **—Heather Johnson**

THE MANGER IN THE STABLE

In the little town of Bethlehem, by the Sea of Galilee,
A little child was born one night, he was sent for you and me.
His mother was a virgin, and she was blessed by God; to bring his
Son down to the Earth, to walk upon this sod.

Joseph, the husband of Mary, mother of the sweet Christ Child, was
visited by an angel who said, "In your wife there is no guile."
Many times to this place Joseph had surely been, but it was different
this night, there was no room at the inn.
So they went into a stable, for shelter through the night, and Mary was
delivered, of the One who is our light.

They named this little boy Jesus, it was the Lord's command.
He came to be our Saviour, so hold onto his hand.
They laid him in a manger, that was filled with hay.
The Christ Child slept on through the night, until the coming day.

Now friends, what I have written is certainly not a fable.
So let us thank our God for Jesus, and the manger in the stable.

—**William G. Perryman**

THE PAIN OF A TREE

In the middle of a field there stood a tree, twisted and dead.
I approached it one summer's day, and to it I said,
"How does it feel old tree, how does it feel to be dead?"
He looked up at me and he shook his head.
"It's a terrible feeling of remorse and numbness, it hurts to be dead."

As I started to leave I looked back over my shoulder,
And I saw a great limb fall and land beside a boulder.
The temperature now became colder and colder,
As I sat and watched the tree grow older.

I returned that night with sorrow in my eyes,
For I could see the tree in pain and could hear his silent cries.
I lit a match and burned the wood,
While staring intently there I stood.
The licking flames danced around,
As they burned the tree to the ground.
As the fire was extinguished by the downpour of rain,
My conscious was relieved that the tree would feel no more pain.

—**Shane Lemons**

A LETTER TO STUART

The world has tumbled upside down and turned sideways too this year
The dreams I thought most sure to be seem to have disappeared.
Seem to have disappeared, my love, but are they forever gone
Or temporarily without a place while more immediate things go on?

Let's not be hasty nor demand too much as we struggle to adjust
Our lives, careers, all future plans make retention of the past a must.
"This too shall pass" the prophet says though a painful present reigns
The joy and laughter of yesteryear will eventually surface again.

But time moves slowly, decisions now must deal with needs today
A short term solution, a long term loss, what gain and in what way?
The future seems more clouded now and though the view is bleak
Hope lives eternal deep inside, 'tis God's gift to man when weak.

The world would have us all believe escape is the best way forward
Or does it really leave us here to fight the same wars over?
Separation, divorce, American life confirmed by magazine and TV
But if God's will, then why the hope, the pilot light within?

My love goes with where e'er you go across the whole wide earth
And a part of you remains with me tucked safe within the hearth.
A part of you, unique to you, made of the love you gave to me
Which fills a space within my heart and will never empty be.

—**Shirley Anderson**

WINTER FUN

Angels, snowmen, fun
and games.
That's what Winter's for.
Snowballs flying in the sky,
Winter's in the air!

—**Ellen L. Hoopfer, age 10**

Football
hitting tackling
strong heavy muscular
pads hard catching punting
weather cold hot
injuries running
Baseball

—**Rob Seelman, age 12**

And through the air
there met our spirits
Gently did they touch
and then depart.
How is it that with his
eyes he can touch my heart?
And as I feel . . .
How can I bear to have
this soul depart?

—**Janice Manzolillo**

GOD'S GIFTS

God's gifts are to us human
beings and all things on earth.
Without his gifts, we
wouldn't be on earth.

God's gifts are beautiful.
His love means a lot to us,
his caring and knowing
that we are alive.

And to learn his knowledge
and government, and to
thank him for each day,
and for his many blessings.

Amen.

—**Mary Spinks
Charles Jr.
Charla O'Neal**

EMPTY?

How do I feel so Empty
when I am with you?
Why did I ever get this
way?
Maybe it was the things
you would never do or say.
All the times I said
"I love you"
were so hard to say. 'Cause
the few times that you did
say those words, it was like
child's play.
I can't explain the way
I feel when you do hold me
and say these words.

I've never felt that kind
of Empty before.

—**"Babet"**

33

MIRRORS

The azure sky radiates
over the glimmering,
crystal-clear water
forming mirror-like reflections.

—Maria Valeri-Gold

Heavy hands of liquid granite
Molding the iridescent music
Of a flute of glass
The wind plays,
Whistling by the countenance
Of uncounted eternities
In an eyeblink:
The wind and the clouds.

—Bruno Glos

MEMORIAL

I never knew a single vet,
yet as I read, my eyes are wet

It must be the human ties that
make me weep because they died.

It doesn't have to be her own.

Every mother of a son
feels the loss of even one.

—Virginia Carlson-Foat

WELD

Dedicated to John Wesley Jones, B.E. (Boilermaker Extraordinare)

Always clean the pass before, and pray for penetration,
For solid welds that picture true, no pins or slag inclusion.

In and out and weave about, consistency's the key.
Travel speed is puddle width for perfect uniformity.

No cheaters here, my eye is clear, whip hand is calm and steady on.
Penetrate and pour it in, weave and whip, or walk along.

Arc flare and crackle-hum, the metal melts and flows.
Forty-five and drag along, hold and build, and so it goes.

The rod's a stub, the pass is done, by now you know the drill.
Electrode steady, 'till you're ready, now lift and crater fill.

A special dread is overhead, got to hold the metal flat.
Icicles and falling fire, down your neck and off your hat.

Arc-flash and eyeburn, tears stream and spots dance.
Slag burn and flesh peel, holes in shirt and shoes and pants.

Lung sear and ravager, poison gas and choke.
Jobs play out before their time, the coupon didn't bend, it broke.

Now check the job, examine weld, paycheck time is drawing near.
Chip the slag and use wire brush, are undercuts or pinholes
here?

Hum-crackle sweet ozone, acrid fumes and scorch leather.
Finish the job and roll it up, now's the time to take a breather.

—Dock Jones

Many times I worry you in my times of
despair, but I know you'll listen and always be there.
To lessen my misery and lend me a hand
To help me and guide me any way you can.
When life's troubled waters try to drag me down
under, and my mountainous problems try to tear me asunder.
I know where to go, when there is no other, for
comfort and love to Dear Sweet Mother.
Today is your Birthday, May God grant you lots,
more, cause you're needed on Earth as much as before.
When God, calls you on that beautiful day and life's
prisons of darkness have floated away.
Heaven shall celebrate and the Angels be glad, for they've
gained a great Pilgrim from this world so bad.
Our loss on Earth shall be Heaven's gain. You deserve an
Eternity with no more heartache and pain.
Somehow Happy Birthday doesn't seem to say, what
I'm trying to express in my own kind of way.
But it'll have to suffice for there is no other? Happy
Birthday, I Love You, My dear sweet Mother.

—Boyce Edens

THE LOVE THAT WAS

The house was filled with laughter and joy
Because of you husband you and your boy
In the winter you would chop down a Christmas tree that was tall
In the summer you would catch the leaves that would fall
In the fall you would sit by the riverside
In the spring your son would slide down the slide
But the future past day by day
Your husband got sick and past away
Your son's only five he does not know
He said on vacation his father did go
But now it has been over six years
In the little boy's eyes you only see tears
He left when he was five and know he's eleven
For now he knows his father's in heaven

—Shari Neidig

DISTANCE MAKES A DIFFERENCE

Off in the distance I saw a blurred figure,
I grabbed for my gun and held on to the trigger.

As it kept moving forward and was quickly approaching,
I prayed God was beside me, giving me coaching.

I felt His presence but not too close by,
As the figure moved closer His presence grew high.

As the figure had reached me, I lost all my fright,
Suddenly God's presence was gone, the figure vanished from sight.

—Kelli A. Murphy

TRUE LOVE WILL CONQUER ALL

The many miles that keep you apart.
The lonely, lonely nights.
The striking of the midnight hour —
When you lie awake yearning for each other's touch.
When things are blackest and you are at the end of your rope.
A thought, a picture, a little note — some faint memory —
Helps to make things seem a little brighter.
Being willing to sacrifice or hurt yourself to help another.
When you cannot get each other out of your Minds, Hearts, or Souls.
No matter how bad things seem, with all your troubles and woes.
When you are in each other's arms and you hear those precious words —
You know: No one will ever separate you again.
Even your largest problems seem trivial.
Then you will understand —
That "TRUE LOVE WILL CONQUER ALL!"

—Bridget Talbot

JUST LET ME GET MY CHAIR

"Oh, Mommy, let me help you 'cause I know it would be fun
To help you stir up cookies and then watch them bake 'til done."
"But, Honey, are you big enough to stand a way up there?"
"Oh, yes, I know I can, Mom. Just let me get my chair."

"Now, Dear, you need to wash your hands; you've played outside
     all day.
Just wait a minute and I'll help — oh, what did you say?"
"Can I do it by myself, Mom? I won't get soap in my hair."
"But can you reach . . ." "I know I can — just let me get my
     chair."

"Mom, why are parents always big and children always small?
That's something I just never, ever figured out at all.
But I suppose if kids were big that folks would always stare.
But you know what, Mom? I'm big as you — when I'm on my chair."

—Connie Clapp Collins

NATURE'S SYMPHONY

Let the earth break forth with praiseful song and in utter joy sing,
Accompanied by nature's symphony, "He's King, He's King, He's King!"
Let the sea in all its vastness roar up with waves that clap
Their hands in glee,
"He died, He rose, He lives, He has set me free!"
And the hills sing their songs as gently the wildflowers blow,
Joy to the Lord! He's coming back, do you see His glow?
For He is robed with honor, with majesty, with light,
The heavens, a starry curtain; the angels, messengers of the night.
The clouds are His chariots He rides upon the wind,
And as far as east is from west He removed what we have sinned.
You bind the world together so that it shall never fall apart,
For You ride upon the wings of wind filling every heart.
You assign the moon to mark the months and the sun to mark the days,
Hallelujah! My life is full with nature's symphony,
And I shall sing You praise.

—Lois R. Batchelor

THANK YOU

The Lord is good,
  so good to me
For he forgives
  continuously!
Thank you Lord,
  always and ever,
For loving me and
  giving up on me — never!

—Nora P. Jennings

Rippled waves among trees.
A short breath,
A sigh.
He turns over
Naked.
The sun dances
In his hair.
Touching him,
I smile.
Secretly we laugh
At each other.
Two children
Playing a game
Of discover.

—Cheri Budzynski

DESOLATE

I sit in my room
Do nothing but sit.
Sit quiet in gloom
Deep in my pit.

I sit through the night,
Sit all through the day.
None know of my plight,
None care anyway.

While I stare at the wall,
Entrenched in my sorrow,
The dog trots down the hall,
My pain felt in her marrow.

My mood took its toll,
But the dog I embrace.
Pain leaves my soul,
And a smile takes its place.

—T. J. Weldy

A dew drop
oh so crystal pure
if I look at you
if I really see,
see the very wetness of you,
an elementary need
of life.
I see through you,
the leaf
upon which you rest,
magnified in size,
like a teardrop
intensifies the reality
of those who cry.
I see into you
and I wonder,
Oh dew drop
are you but one of many
when God cries?

—Brenda Kay Mudd

A pot-bellied stove
Squatting on stout bulldog legs
Growls its contentment.

—Rex Holt

THE FOG
The swirling fog
Is a gallant wraith.
O'er all the town,
He spreads his misty cloak.

—Nancy Parson Dennis

AT THE END OF A RAINBOW
At the end of a rainbow is
my favorite place.
At the end of a rainbow
everyone has a happy face.
And at that place I'm one
of those people with a happy
face.

—Donna Dickson, age 9 3/4

A YOUNG BOY . . .
A young boy
        reached down and
        picked a dandelion.

He shook the flower,
        scattering its seeds
        among the grass.

Then with one quick breath,
        he blew
        the rest away.

—Wanda Kinzie

LIFE
Life is so great!
But somedays you wonder?
        How you are going to make
it through the day?
Then something happens;
things fall in place; with
help of God!
        Don't rush have
patience with yourself
and others.

—Sam Holman

CAN IT BE LOVE
Always thinking of you
Only if you knew
Oh I need you so much
I can just feel your touch
Can it be love

Every time you're near
My heart beat so fast
It just keep pounding
Only when you're around me
Tell me can it be love

You turn me on
I'm your clock
This feeling just won't stop
I've never felt like this before
Can it be love

—Brenda Shoots

How many are the gifts of God for which we've never thanked?
The use of eyes, of hands, of feet, of money we have
        banked?
Whence came our health, the peace, the joy — all given
        to us free —
Our very lives and our free choice to serve or takers be?

How many hurts and ills now healed were never once
        thanked for;
New chances given to start anew — impossible before —
Protection given, the hope to strive, to never again give up!
Have we once thought of gratitude as we empty
        our filled cup?

"In everything give thanks" you see, the good Book clearly
        states.
Do we obey or grumble over lack or empty plates?
There were ten healed; and one gave thanks rejoicing to
        be fine.
God does meet needs! He never fails! Are we like
        the one or the nine?

—Bathbetah

OH, LORD
OH, Lord I see You in the mountains;
        Your beauty comes shining through.
Why is it always that way in everything You do?

OH, Lord I see You in the oceans;
        Broad, deep, and blue.
Just as I picture Your eyes smiling down in love.

OH, Lord I see You in the grassy meadows;
        Waving constantly in perfect rhythm.
Are all people, who get to heaven, going to sing like larks and dance
        like David?

OH, Lord I see You in the clouds;
        All different and wonderfully made.
But on the day You return, Oh, Lord, the clouds will fade in
        comparison to you.

OH, Lord I see You in so many things,
        Every day is a new look at You.
Lord, when I see you face to face I'll see all heaven through you!

—Rebecca S. Murphy

OUR LIVES ARE JUST BEGINNING
We've shared so many things
        For so long we wanted to be on our own
You are finally spreading your wings.
Now that we're here, we often wish we weren't grown.
I know we had a rough childhood
People say that's no excuse
To change things we wish we could.
When we get down, all we can do is shake it loose.
It's much harder to make it than most
But you are showing everyone that you are a man
To your succeeding, here's a toast.
To your striving 100%, I give you a hand.
We are closer than any brother and sister could ever be
We've experienced things most people never will
The one that understands you completely is me.
I'm watching you climb over that mountain, it's real.
Don't get discouraged, hold your head up high
Our hearts are slowly mending
You aren't just spreading your wings now, you are getting
        ready to fly.
Our lives are just beginning.

—Emily Dawn Doyle

I KNOW A PLACE

I know a place, somewhere, where the grass is soft and green.
Where tiny life is everywhere, whispering and chattering unseen.
Where lovely shade trees everywhere bid welcome with open arms,
Sweet flowers bloom, the river slips by and there's thousands of
        untold charms.
And maybe in the leafy green the fairies romp and play,
With just a shadow now and then but, I really couldn't say.

I know a place where in winter, it's a winter wonderland.
The soft snow covers everything, sent down by an unseen hand.
When night falls there, in its own special way,
It's a place of enchantment, as well as the day.
For the tall pines whisper and nod and sigh,
And off in the distance there's a lone wolf's cry.
An old owl hoots and the rabbits skip by,
While a big hunter's moon gives its light from the sky.

Now I've been told by someone I know,
That they've seen fairy shadows on the new, soft blown snow.
And if you should ever go there, you'll find it's really so,
It's a wonderland, a fairyland, in the winter, this place that
        I know.

        —June K. Taylor

TRYING TO SURVIVE

Today was Tuesday, 27, it was a beautiful summer day.
    All the birds in the sky, seemed to just fly away.
Everyone and everything, seemed so alive, all except me, I was trying
to survive.
The heat from the sun, as each ray touched my bare skin, as I
looked toward the sky, far up in the trees, sat a little brown wren.
When each little drop of perspiration, fell from my face, my thoughts
were of mountain streams, such a lovely place.
My small grandson asked for advice, asked a question or two, if I
didn't give him an answer, he'd feel real blue.
I'd try real hard, to do all my chores, when my mind was so far
away, near beautiful ocean shores.
To survive today, I'd think pleasant things, of a lovely dove, lifting
off its nest with graceful wings.
The branches from the trees, I had just snipped, Oh, what a thought, a
tasty banana split.
Yes, dreaming is so easy, when you're trying to survive.
But the reality hits you, when true friends arrive.

        —Jeanette M. Nettles

MORE THAN A BABE

The wise still seek Jesus — He's more than a Babe,
    For He grew in God's favor, perfection portrayed.
He ministered daily, confounding them all,
For even in childhood He acknowledged His call.

He spoke with great wisdom, to scholars' alarm,
And yet blessed the children with mercy and charm.
He walked among sinners, the poorest on earth,
Shunning honor and riches for Heavenly worth.

He healed many, fed thousands, raised others to life,
Bringing joy and contentment where once there was strife.
While He prayed in the garden, His own men asleep,
He hid not from soldiers, His mission to keep.

He endured a mock trial with scourging and shame,
While He said not a word in defense of His Name.
Then He bore His own cross to the place of the skull,
Where in death He declared sin's account "Paid in full!"

In a new tomb they laid Him to await the third day,
When in triumph He rose, as the stone rolled away.
So don't bow at His manger; don't worship His cross,
For the grave could not hold him — mankind's gain, Satan's loss.

        —David L. Adams

NISE

My nymph.
My beautiful maiden.
Oh how wondrous life is
    With you.

The exuberance you so
Easily bring out of me
Can be extracted by no other.

In the act of libation,
I raise my chalice and say,
"I love you."

—M. L. Eckert

EPITAPH

All at once I fled from thee,
    for life within my death.
Bringing 'bout an end to me,
    while grasping final breath.

Now I've found a place to rest,
    which will a harbour give.
Peace I find in earthly nest,
    now I no longer live.

Final come the days of life,
    enjoy as honey sweet.
Bringing end to days of strife,
    enjoying life's defeat.

—Edward Alexander Sosnowski

A LITTLE LIE

A little lie that I have told,
    To cover up what's there,
Knowing that to play the game,
You must take all the dares.

A little lie — that's all it is,
But I know to keep it small,
I must tell another one,
And hope that will be all.

But now I'm in too deep,
Another lie I hold,
To cover up the first one,
I wish I hadn't told.

—Annette June McMichen

SAILING TOGETHER

The years move by so quickly,
    and then very slow,
like an ocean of surprises
tide high, then low.

But partners in marriage
travel along the same trail,
sometimes stormy, then calm,
but together they sail.

And that's what's so wonderful
about love between two,
it's not just some feeling
that's always exciting and new,

But rather, a commitment
to travel this life
together, forever,
Husband and Wife.

—Linda Michener

SPRING

I have heard Spring: when birds sing their sweet songs, when the wind blows through trees, making a soft whistling sound, and when bees buzz while collecting honey.

Can you hear Spring?

I have seen Spring: on the green grass growing in a field, when on dead branches there are traces of new life, when the snow melts and the daffodils jump up from the ground in joy.

Have you seen Spring?

I have smelt Spring: in yellow sunflowers and red roses, at barbecues and in that fragrance after it has rained.

Have you done it yet?

I have tasted Spring: when I tear a blade of grass, tilt it, and let the dew drip into my mouth, when I eat blackberries which I have picked off a bush, and when I squeeze honey from honeysuckle onto my dry lips.

Won't you please join me?

I have felt Spring: when the little drops of rain dribble down my shirt, on a warm day in April a cool breeze blows by me, when I catch a softball at a game.

Will you not join me?

—Sam Mukherjee

That muggy night, just crawling with recycled unwanted heat,
I flipped on my outdated set.
Tonight so humid; heavy, almost opaque,
Caused me to be too lazy to even switch the channel.
So I watched a comedian, suited in suit,
Talking to the camera, talking to me.
His chatter-like style was plain, yet I did find him amusing.
He rattled on and on displaying satire at its best.
I laughed about freedom fighters burning our flag,
And snickered as he joked of men killing men over money.
I chuckled at his talk of accidental infants denied a chance to live,
And I giggled when that silly man said countries argued over which had more toys.
This show was such an ironic parody, I ought to watch it more often.
Then, a second later, I reached for the power knob.
And as the ghostly glow faded from the screen,
I bawled; a screaming-type crying.
An uncontrollable fury raging a lump in my throat.
For the item I'd last seen flashing brightly before my eyes,
A neon invitation mocking a tombstone fit for all.
A frightening sorrow to discover I had watched the 11 o'clock news.

—Lisa Marie Rovito

COUNTRY CALLIN

A cabin in the valley, fully built, hand hewn.
Blood, sweat, and heart sounds, molded with a melody to croon.
Dreams tugging, seeking fulfillment, with her to live here, a longing is imortune.
The front porch, two rocking chairs, hand in hand, memories of another full moon.
A still voice on high, gently caressing the heart, dreams soon opportune.

Fields plowed, stock fed, chores done, close of another day.
Troubles, life's cares just outside our door, stay at bay.
Close times, family ties, we make memories to inlay.
We sit to biscuits, ham and blueberry cobbler on display.
All take hands, she says "Love, thank Him as we pray."

We linger there, Love, kids, and me.
Frightful cold outside, cuts to the bone with pure agony.
Staring into them, her flickering fingers breaks the ebony.
They warm us to our soul, tis their destiny.
Family clock tickin, lightered knot popin, in perfect harmony.

Way back of yesterday is the origin.
Past Great Grand Mamm, deep within my kin.
Echoes, loud in my soul, sends the need wild, a-throbbin.
This dream must be fulfilled, "Country Callin."

—M. Stephenson Wilhite

THROUGH MY WINDOW

The shabbiness of a home-made barn
Against the green and yellow of wild weeds
Choking young trees
Under the crystal-blue sky
Invaded by electric wires.

—Sarah Stansell

A SADDEN LIFE

Once I once lived a sadden life,
filled with horror, grief and strife.
Sometimes I would like to disappear,
run and run til no one's near.
I'm filled with guilt and despair,
for I am a murderer can't anyone
       hear?

—Jordana Jarjura, Age 10

POETRY UNMASKED

Poetry to me is like water over rocks
Like winter's snowy blizzard
Like children's building blocks.

Some of it comes easy
Some freezes 'long the way
Some builds and builds upon itself
And never goes away.

The poet dips into his soul
And pens the words sublime
Reaching into rocks and ice
And building blocks of rhyme.

—Joy Crawford

A POEM ABOUT PHILOSOPHY CLASS

Once upon a time
I knew where I was going
Round and round
I'm spinning
Seeing it all fly by
I'm a part of it
But where does my existence
    fit in?
I'm here, there and everywhere
But what does that mean?
I want to know the answers
But the questions
      don't even come.

—Colleen Stein

TV DAY AND NIGHT

Daytime TV is not for me,
I dislike soaps and game shows;
Sadness I can do without
Nor am I the one to shout
My praises for those zealous
    game show contestants.

Nighttime TV is my cup of tea
With shows like Nightline and 20/20;
Cartoon specials like Garfield the Cat,
    Peanuts Gang, things like that.
Mind boggling to some but enjoyable
    to me.
They're a temporary escape from reality.

—Marjorie Persing

WHAT I SEE

Silence is everywhere
Silence, silence everywhere
Ashes are falling
Ashes falling to the ground
Look at the land, look at the trees
Death is what I see

—Cindy Elleman

ALONE

When I'm alone if I sit quiet
I can hear the birds chirp,
or the trees sway in the wind
But there isn't nothing better
Than being alone with you
Me looking into your big blue eyes
And them looking back
Touching your soft face
Feeling the love between us
But now I'm alone to think about
The quiet, peaceful moments we once had.

—Kelly Porter

Time now is quickly running out
From the mountain top I should shout,
Have you confirmed your reservation?
Are you ready for your salvation?
We can love and honor and obey
But falling to our knees we need to pray.
God, give us the faith so we can see
Your plan is always what's best for me
Give me courage and let me stand tall
Heaven is for the asking after all
I do believe, I really do
So, St. Peter will you let me through?

—Betty J. Pellman

THE BELL JAR

I can feel it, this bell jar,
Hovering overhead so threateningly.
I reach out to grab a star,
Instead I touch glass; the jar drops slowly
And as it drops, I feel so alone,
Cut off from the rest of civilization
But the jar doesn't care; cold as stone.
Very soon, I come to the realization
No one can now save me.
Thoughts of safety come much too late.
So, I sit 'neath the glass dying slowly
As under the bell jar I suffocate.

—Chris Robillard

HINDSIGHT

An oriole sang above my head
But I was busy in the strawberry bed.

A hawk was soaring through the skies
And I didn't think to raise my eyes.

The flowers were fragrant — like the rose
But I was involved in hanging up clothes.

The little ones spoke in poetic rhyme
But I didn't really listen at the time.

Now that I'm old, I wonder and ask,
"Why did those years go by so fast?"

—Janette W. Plassmann

FOR DAVID:

Sleep's transition to awaken
Meanders in and out, above, below.
A nightly journey that must be taken
Through dream liquid we drift and flow.

Some enter sleep without a warning
Placed by accident in an unknown scene
That has no night and has no morning.
Death's transition to a being.

Drift on through the quiet shadows
Toward the light that freedom shines.
Enter the world of no tomorrows.
You've just unlocked life's lonely binds.

—Greg L. Avery

MY CHILD

The years go by so quickly
It seems like yesterday
I saw your tiny smile
It stole my heart away.

The years go by so quickly
A teenage boy appears
We shared so many treasures
Your dreams, your hopes, your fears.

The years go by so quickly
A man now here I see
But to your gray-haired mother
MY CHILD you'll always be.

—Phyllis J. Russell

ANOTHER DAWN

The beginning of the end
I believe is finally here.
From the ground beasts descend,
bringing horror, fright, and fear.

The children are hungry and crying.
Satan's number will not be shown.
Soldiers and civilians are dying,
But the reason is yet unknown.

Smoke and fallout fill the air
As destruction and death goes on.
The land is becoming dry and bare.
Will there be "another Dawn?"

—Brandalin Rachelle Dampf

CLOUDS

A horrific face scowls upon
Mine as my eyes are
To the heavens.

A dancing horse prances
By another ugly face.
My neck begins to ache.

Swirls of imagination
Halt as my mind goes blank.
Nothing is there anymore.

Turquoise and clean white
Are the colors I want to see
But gray is reality.

Millions of eyes look down
Upon my own.
I want to smile but can only frown.

—Karen L. Graves

GLADIATOR

He marches on through the foreign land,
Fighting battles hand-to-hand,
Many a soldier has he slain,
With his sword, axe, and chain,
Underneath his opponents armor and gear,
There's a frightened man who wants to shed a tear,
And yet he kills more and more,
As if it's his destiny or his chore,
But, the time will arrive,
When he has not another opponent alive,
And the rest of his life will be lived in shame,
Whatever soul is left will look down upon his name.

—Chris Nelson

I'd like to be treated more fairly
But instead I'm treated like a child
I'd like to be praised for good
But instead I am condemned
I'd like to think someone cares
But underneath I know
I'd like to be myself
But instead I'm pushed into the shadow of someone else
I'd like to think I'll change someone's life
But what if it never comes true
I'd like to be seen as I really am
But no one has ever looked inside
I'd like to be treated more fairly
But this will probably never be

—Trisha Jensen

FREE

I think that I shall never see
A world where everyone is free

Free from triggers firmly pressed
By those who would enslave the rest

Free from envy, hate, and greed
And naught for those who really need

Free from gossip's ugly face
With loneliness to take its place

This evil we can not condone
Nor seek to change it on our own

How sad for all humanity
That only death will set us free.

—Gaye Fletcher Bloom

Here in the quiet all alone
I lend my thoughts to you
Turning the pages of yesterday
When skies were always blue.
Here in a room of memories
I ponder on moments we've spent
Recalling all the good times
And all the places we went.
How good it feels to view your face
From a faded photograph
And reminisce the good ol' days
When we would always laugh.
As time goes on, it heals the scar
of losing someone dear
Yet in my book of memories
I'll always hold you near.

—Linda Lallier Campbell

GOLLY GEE — JOLLY ME!

Things would sure go amiss
If I didn't keep my lists
Of the things I simply must do.

Gifts to make —
Gifts to bake —
And the time that it takes
To do all the gift shopping too.

It's hectic — it's frantic
It's hurry up — rush!!
If I'm going to be ready, you see.

But change any part
Of my holiday spree —?
You can bet your sweet life
I would not — not me!!!

—Shirley B. Johnson

BALLOONS, BALLOONS, BALLOONS

Balloons, balloons, balloons,
Way up in the sky,
Where do they go,
How high do they fly?

Yellow, green and red,
Like dots against the blue,
They soar so far away
They're almost out of view.

Where do they finally land,
Or do they stay up high,
Up among the clouds,
Forever sailing by.

—Eunice Julin Wegge

AN OLD FRIEND AND LOVED ONE
GRANDMOTHER

But I do pray for heaven's sake that if you
Die before I wake, that they are blessed with
One such as you.

The only one that can see us through the
Good times, the bad times, for me and you!

You're the one that's always there, to give,
Take, and always share!

Willing to do anything, for anyone, you see,
Your life has just begun, and you will
Live with me for eternity!

—Stephanie Ivy, age 13

LOVE'S GLOVE

Lost in a world of hate and confusion
I've come to the conclusion
that nothing ever is as it should be.
Looking through the haze trying to see
where to find some love
that will fit like a glove.
As the clock for love goes on
I am strangely drawn,
like a magnet, to you.
I never before knew
who you were,
but I know you're the cure.
Now the haze is gone
and you have drawn
around me a glove
of your endless love.

—Katrina Crocker

PIANIST'S HANDS

The wet sweaty hands,
So big, skipping and jumping
all around the keys.
Hitting key after key, after key —
Left hand first, right — second,
Vibrating fingers after pouncing
on the keys . . .
High jump, BAM!

—Kent Pugliese

SUN

Bright, Warm
Shining, Lighting, Coloring
Eastern, Apollo, Artemis, Southern
Sparkling, Glowing, Darkening
Dim, Cold
Moon

—Jim Preston

PASSIONATE REGARD

Blinded affection,
Torrid rejection
to what society permits us to have.

The passion within us,
The constant chagrin must
never cease the love that we share.

Violins strumming,
Lovers keep humming to
sounds of their everlasting dream.

While sincereness provides,
Sorrow subsides
to the love that I'm feeling for you.

—Raven O. Tyler

BALLOONS

Balloons, Balloons, they fly so high,
Balloons, Balloons, they roam the sky;
Balloons, Balloons, some green and some blue,
Balloons, Balloons, the colors so true;
Balloons, Balloons, a round one I see;
Balloons, Balloons, heading for the tree,
Look at that green one over there!
It's about to get a twig tear!
Balloon, Balloon, here I now stare,
Oh, Balloon, Balloon, I would not dare . . .

POP!

—Emily McLaughlin

EPHEMERA

Where does a thought go when it's lost?
Where does a dream go when it's through?
Where does a song go when it's ended?
Where, pray tell, where on earth are you?

Is there a stage where songs keep singing?
Is there a pillow where dreams must rest?
Is there a place where thoughts keep thinking?
Is it not true it was all for the best?

I hope a whisper is still remaining
I hate to think this ephemera has been wasted.
But the thought, the song and the dream are gone
Like mellow old wine that was only once tasted.

—Mary Louise Dua

IN A SOUTHERN SKY

I have been many places
And have seen strange things
    But the strangest thing
I've ever seen was high
    in a southern sky.
Out of the blue in a
    flash and a zip, from the
    west to the east it went.

Round as a saucer
    a bright green
The strangest thing I've ever seen.

—Rossenell Duncan

OUR PRECIOUS MOMENTS

The raindrops fell softly upon
    our heads.
The puddles splashed beneath
    our feet.
I remember those days we walked
    in the rain.
I can still feel your kisses
    so sweet.
The years have been long
    since you left me,
But with God's help I keep
    pushing on.
I remember so many quiet
    moments, we shared,
And I keep on enjoying our home.

—Mary Francis Leamon Long

DESERT FIRE

Lo! Good earth don't ever
    let us go
    For we may not be able
to show
    The warmth from the desert
fire so.

    It claims we have nothing
to share
    Only the spirit, which we've
taken from all.

    The desert fire will never
be at shame,
    But once recognized,
        Will never be the same.

—Eva Fitzgerald

MY FRIEND

You came
    in my darkest
hour to give me courage.
You gave a tender touch, desire
to live.

You gave
a smile, burning
the dead leaves of my mind,
enabling me to grow new dreams,
to clip

and trim
debris of life.
The me I am today
is new. My heart was born again
and sings!

—Louise Wilkerson Conn

LETTERS

I send you letters in my mind.
    In thoughts I talk with you.
Memories sprinkle through my days
Of friendship that stays true.
When empty paper isn't filled
I do not mean to be unkind.
When things I feel I long to share,
I send you letters, in my mind.

—S. H. Bosworth

LITTLE GIRL

Ashley Marie Bernardi
    Little girl with a beautiful name
Which goes with your smile and big
    eyes of blue
Such pretty blonde hair, that you have too
With your sweet little ways and the
    things that you do
Dull days are bright because of you.
This old world's never been the same
From the day that you first came.
Ashley Marie Bernardi
Little girl with a beautiful name.

—Pamela A. Bernardi

BLACK CINDERELLA

Six weeks passed,
    Got to hurry. Lord knows — I don't want to worry.
Lest my true hair begin to show —
KINKY, COARSE, and LACKING GLOW.
All my friends say, "Girl, you got problems. Get a
touch-up; Go and solve them."
But, will the chemical I douse on my hair straighten the
MIXED UP MIND beneath the KNAPPY HAIR?

In this world where "LIGHT IS RIGHT" and "DARK HIDES FROM
SIGHT," wide nostrils have ceased flaring. Full lips have
ceased blaring. (Lips which used to sing in an EBONY SOUL,
now a soul BLEACHED.)
Where did OUR soul go?

We're beauties born of our own despair, and yet we don't
even know. When, my BEAUTIFUL BROTHERS and SISTERS, will WE
let OUR TRUE BEAUTY show?

—Danita Gibson

FROM A WOMAN TO A GENTLEMAN

The concept of my image, is not one
    that demands to be superior nor inferior
to the role of man; Because, I don't
mind being a woman to a man that's
a man. Being at his side to hold him
or loving in his arms to console him
with the meaning of honest equality
none lesser nor greater than he.
    Because Gentle Gentleman of unique
Qualities you impress me with your
Expressions especially when your emotions
Influence a repetitious ecstacy that releases love continuously.
Your effecting affections send after effects
That does me just. I tend to grow
tender under your touch, controlling
my excitement is out of my control
as you arouse every part of my
soul. So by Popular Demand
I annouce you
        My Man.

—Kheynda

IT'S FAIR TIME

The hustle and bustle of the fair
  The smiles and laughter of people everywhere
The sound of the carousel
The screams from the joy rides
The barkers trying to get your attention
There's something exciting about fair time.
The foot-long hot dogs, carmel corn and
              cotton candy
Rainbow-colored balloons, big teddy bears
    and all things dandy.
It's fair time, come one, come all!!

—Mary Edwards

A COWHAND'S LIFE

A cowhand gets up early in the morn,
  He puts on his shirt and jeans that are torn.
He eats his breakfast which isn't very filling,
He still does his work even if he is not willing.
He saddles his horse and readies his rope,
When it comes to roping he is no dope.
He gathers the cattle in a herd or a bunch,
He has a small break to eat his hot lunch.
He comes back from work with a smile or a frown,
He is very tired so he lays down.
Then he sleeps till the next morn,
Gets up puts on his shirt and jeans that are torn.

—Tucker Henson, age 10

LIKE FATHER, LIKE SON

Seconds seem like hours
  upon all the dead flowers.
Shots ring through the ears
covering all your fears.
Mothers letting their sons go
with nothing coming back to show,
but yellow tinged letters
and little boy sweaters.
She brings flowers every Sunday,
remembering how he used to play.
How he'd say "I love you,"
and promising he'll come back too.
But not like daddy did.
MOM I'm not a kid.
Like father, Like son.
On his account the war was won.

—Heather Gates, age 16

FLAG OPTION

Still it flies . . . . . unfurls:
  The "Rocket's Red Glare"
Was trivia
Compared to this.

This . . . . . besmirchment
Of its stripes:
The dimming/damning of its stars.

An unjust devaluation
Tragically climaxed in burning.

Still it flies . . . . . unfurls:
And there will always be

Those who stand
Proudly
And salute it.

—Mary Guinn

KIDS SPORTS

Sports are made for competing
  And kids are made for fun

Parents can't stand the defeating
  And kids ask — who won?

Look parents before you gripe
  It doesn't matter to win

And it is not coaches trite
To teach that to lose is no sin!

—John James Garrett

FEARS

Unicorn tails and golden
  snails and rabbits feet at night.
All these things you think,
my dear, will keep you away
from fright.

But let me tell you
now, my dear, for it might
keep you away from trouble.
For when you worry about
your fears, you only make
them double.

—Sarah E. Butkus

LITTLE BITTY BOY

Little bitty boy with big brown eyes,
    sat on my knee.
He sat so quiet, looked so wise, though
    he's only three.
He's found a place in my heart,
and from him I would not part.
Little bitty boy with big brown eyes
    smiled up at me!

Little bitty boy, deep in my heart,
    here you belong.
When time goes by and you're a man,
    walk tall and strong.
You have an extra special way,
That makes me love you every day.
With a lasting love, sent from up above,
    you can't go wrong.

—Elise M. Scates

THE LITTLE PICKLE

Pickle, pickle, in a jar,
  did you come from very far?
Were you plucked from off your vine
    just as you were doing fine?
Did they break your tender stem,
    cutting off your life just when
    all of us began to wonder
    if you'd become a big cucumber?
But now you'll not go very far;
    just wind up in a pickle jar;
    covered with vinegar and other stuff.
Life for a pickle's mighty rough!
Soon you'll be poked and cut and chewed,
    along with many kinds of food.
Peristalsis comes into play
    to start you, pickle, on your merry way.
Into the stomach you will go
    with other juices, to make you flow
    on through the body to every cell
    to make us strong and feeling well.

—Everett Odoms

CHURCH CENSUS

Oh, I can count them one by one
  Within this sacred place;
Each bare, each smartly hatted head,
  With Sunday morning face.

And marvel that so many came,
  There is no empty pew,
For I am not unlike the rest.
  I think in numbers too.

But only God can view the hearts,
  That He alone can search,
And tally those who worship Him,
  And those who're playing church.

      —Vance B. King

OBSESSION

What demon lies upon my soul?
  Preventing me from being whole.
Incessant need to run away,
I can't, I won't, kneel to pray.

There is no God!, the fool expounds,
In self-delusion, as he drowns.
This head in crazy torment lies,
Spirit ebbing, slowly dies.

Dying not but living hell,
Swing not in this God-less spell.
Never-ending journey low,
What power in me makes this so?

      —Bob Culliton

DAWN'S PREMIERE

All's quiet on the ship deck.
  The waves are wishing well . . .
With God's coins in the sky.
Islands dressed in night clothes
Lie still sleeping in the deep
Dreaming . . .
Dawn's Premiere!

Lights launched,
Laughter lies
Waiting for the sun season.
All aboard the morning deck!
The ship is shining,
Smiling,
Simply, with the sails of the sea.

      —Caroline

HOLY ONE OR . . .

A shadow of darkness
  upon the light.

A drop of hell from
  an eye of heaven.

The war, God versus Devil.

Who is this?

Who is chasing me in my dreams?

Who is chasing me in the night?

Who is chasing me in the day?

Who is taking over my life?

Is it the Holy One, Unholy One, OR
  is it me?

      —Brandy Cummings, age 13

AFFIRMATION

Each year the hillside orchard
  Is a sentient, vibrant thing,
Full of joyous gaiety
And redolence of spring.
Each tree bears proof of kinship
To wind and rain and sod.
Each bud's an acclamation
Of the gloriousness of God.

      —Elinor Cheney Mogford

GOD FORGIVE THIS THANKLESS SOUL

I wake in pain,
  Somehow my legs unfold.
I hate the aches and pains
of growing old.

I moan and groan
How life it is not fair,
I hate each day,
spent mostly in a chair.

Yesterday, I went to town,
There was this little child.
His arms and legs hung useless;
I looked at him, He smiled.

      —Virginia Anne Cordill

SUNRISE

I saw a glorious sunset,
  It ended a perfect day.
So colorful, it saddened me
  To see it fade away.
And as the shadows deepened
  And darkness filled the sky,
I thought that, like the sunset,
  We, too, are doomed to die.

I saw a brilliant sunrise
  Upon the following morn.
My heart was filled with gladness
  To see the world reborn.
And as the dark was vanquished,
  By the dawn, so death shall be
Because Christ died to save us
  On the cross on Calvary.

      —Grace R. Crow

ODE TO STEPHANIE

O!, sweet and sparkling grandbabe,
  Your antics are a joy.
You oft reverse from glee to fret
Much as a wind-up toy.

Your darting ventures to the wilds
Cause worries for your elders,
But your return with smiling face
Brings forth true heart melders.

We would you did retain your shoes
When promming on the outside,
But like most other little girls
You dote on shedding rawhide.

Small Steph, you came to us
To have a lengthy stay.
The warmth you lend defies compare
So please don't leave, we pray.

      —Lee S. Trimble, Jr.

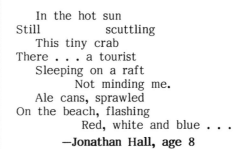

MY LIFE IN A TIPI

May we join as one.
May we follow one path.
May we journey that path together.
May our "Lonesome Dove" join us.
May she follow that same path.
May she learn and branch off.
May she remember that path is forever open.
May we join together for many suns.
May she find the return to the tipi her home.
May she build her foundation with love of her own.
May the journey of "Bald Eagle" fly over
   the "Bright Waters" each day for always.

> —Kathleen Gove Frantz

LIFE'S FUTURE A DREAM

Life's future is a dream.
A dream . . . Focused by the will of
the mind.

   Yes, the mind. A thing we do
not fully comprehend.

   Yet we comprehend the dream.
The dream, becomes the will of
the mind.

   The will makes the dream reality,
reality is in the future.

   Therefore the future is a
dream.

> —Joe Hillje

CALIFORNIA NIGHTS

Two people hand in hand
   Silently walking in the Pacific sand
As the last of the soft and quiet
   waves come in sight
And in the last of the maroon
   sunset night
They move close together without
   a sound
Still they don't know what they
   have found
It must be love
Yet they ask why
For if it wasn't love
It would just be a dream in
   your eye.

> —Mercedes Marie Valadez

AFTER ALL

After all the many years
   After all the joy and tears
After all the loving and giving
After all the every day living
I still smile when I see your face
I still want your sweet embrace
I still thrill at your touch
I still respect you very much
After all our ups and downs
After all the smiles and frowns
After all our times of strife
After all the thorns of life
I still love the way you smile
I still love your special style
I still come running when you call
I still love you after all

> —Delores A. Dixon

In the hot sun
Still   scuttling
   This tiny crab
There . . . a tourist
   Sleeping on a raft
            Not minding me.
   Ale cans, sprawled
On the beach, flashing
            Red, white and blue . . .

> —Jonathan Hall, age 8

HOPEFUL

Soaked in the rain,
   the spirit drenched.
Oh, feel such pain!
Your soul commence
to inch through a layer in your mind
and leave a thought of love behind.

The pain, still there
and have no shame.
Yet, your spirit, now bright
took a turn, just the same
As the love in your mind —
getting warm as a flame.

and such love in your soul
. . . . reflecting your goal . . . .

> —Erlinda R. Reyes

RAIN

The raindrops fall in my eyes
   And resemble the tears I once cried
When I was all alone, without you
Well, I guess it's over between us
Still, I'll always love you
And treasure all our memories
We even had fun, when the sun
was behind a cloud
but now the rain melts my heart
Though it used to rinse
the evil from my soul
I'm crawling back into the shell,
You once brought me out of
But my heart bleeds for you, near me
And the rain, is my only friend
And is as lonely as I.

> —Nicole Misialek

RAIN

Outside the rain falls,
   I cry for the millionth time.
It seems only right somehow,
That now the rain and I cry together.

I can't believe you're gone.
What will I do?
You were my sunshine, my life.
Now I have nothing left, nothing,
but the rain and my tears.

You said this was a mistake,
that I'd be better off this way.
How do you know? Are you
crying tonight?
No. Because you're the one who
said Good-Bye.

> —Cathy R. Bush

BANKED FIRES

From Zimbabwe the stars crash down
to nestle on the shores of Mozambique
In the dark they make party lanterns
The jellyfish glow opalescently
it's a good time and the crabs dance
The waves try to join in, grasping
for leverage, withdrawing
with a sputter time
and again. Mexican hats
swagger along the twinkling
trail of the periwinkle.
In the morning the sand is all shuffled
people say what happened here
and underneath the bright umbrellas
the stars are gleaming secretly

      —Erika Mailman
      Fifth Place Award Winner

Poem Written In Response to Dylan Thomas' "Prologue", Collected Poems

Aye, I found you Dylan Thomas
Though led astray by the "dogdayed
Night." Yea, led into the Welsh mist
Of curlews and owls. Led and lost,
Looking for some pattern and rhyme
I waded through, time after time,
Through hooting and "coo-rooing,"
Yea, the whole "hullaballoing
Clan" of dove, and of deer and rook
Gathered here to prologue your book.
Aye, I found your center
And proceeded there to enter
From the middle, your devious
Scheme. Not found here your obvious
Rhyme. Working outward line by line
As of mornings first subtle shine
Softly flowing from liquid quill,
Wrought precisely with crafty skill,
Gentle rhyme. I was led astray
But, I found you Dylan Thomas.

      —Elaine Deja Williams
      Fifth Place Award Winner

THE FUSING OF MINDS
OR
THE BLENDING OF NATURE

Children walk
amongst unfamiliar ground separately;
divorced from one another
enjoying alone, the coolness of spring's
grand debut.

Before their eyes, life flowers slowly . . .
dew meets grass,
sky falls to sea,
lightning bears thunder
and an audience cries with pleasure
with hands that sing in unison.

The world is one
with sun and rain.
The children are one
with minds that blend.

And,
the earth swells
to cushion the trail
of one lone traveler.

      —Lisa A. Mazzeo

NIGHTS'

Nights' stillness
Nights' quiet
Nights' dangers
Observe the stillness
Break the quiet and
Caution the dangers or
The nights' terrors will own you

      —Susan Wright

CONFUSION

Confusion comes as such surprise
It appears upon our staring eyes
Our brain tries to cue us in
Only to be confused again.
The question is how long does it last
When will this eerie feeling pass.
If one could tell such things as we ask
The world wouldn't be such an awful task.
As time goes by we realize
Confusion is brought by our own demise.
Just take the world one day at a time,
For there is never a mountain you can't climb.

      —"Breezeway"

THE REUNION

Through salt drenched eyes he peered
To focus baby brother long endeared,
But, when those eyes their lids did clear
Saw one near aged as he; draw near.

The younger grinned, though arms gently around embraced,
Hid internal rage at what this damaged brother faced.
His seventh mobile decade split by nature's sudden whims.
Enchained by shaking tongue and deadened limbs.

Baby brother's eyes did plead of him if he'd reveal.
"Why did he not die, so I'll not feel?"
Irate iris shot without gleam,
"Life is not what it does seem."

"Therefore, to you this fettered life has this to give."
"Why don't you feel, that you might live?"

      —Mathias F. Kolding

THE COST

We are seeds of ancient races
From Time long past, from forgotten places
We have come to Now.

Walking here — treading what has been
We stumble, falter tentative
Abstractly instinct finds paths, paths, paths . . .
We walk, we walk, we walk.

Our words are echoes lost in silence
Sunlit days fade into night
    Stars unblinking witness battles eternal:
    Good against Evil/Dark versus Light.

Drawn out lives in daily struggle wasted
On labors never known, for fruits seldom tasted;
    Bread and gold and glass and meat
    Smoke and silk and whiskey neat
Things — bought and used, broken, then lost.

Happiness sought and paid for
Life unregarded, left unlived . . .
The cost.

      —Leeland Morgan

A DOVE

A dove,
Whiter than a fresh, untouched snow
Softer and more gentle than a furry baby kitten.
Flying higher than the sky
Untouched by the filthy air that would
    pierce his virgin lungs and send him
    Eternally downward to the sea,
    To be washed away forever
And remembered,
by none.

—Arlene Lewis

THE HAWK

As the morning comes to light
The red-tailed hawk takes to flight
He soars off high into the air
And all small prey must then beware

For ages past and years to come
The hawk has ruled the sky
With strength and power he has become
The king of all that fly

From mountains high and the valleys low
In summer's heat and winter's snow
As men observe these birds so great
Man must help to seal their fate

—Anders Klemmer, age 11

SUCCESS

What if time is mere illusion,
we have always loved each other
and always will.

What if all of us are part of one,
all hungry when one is hungry,
all related.

What if all our limits, we impose.
The stars are ours for the reaching
and we don't.

What if life is our eternal souls
choosing to play awhile on earth,
and then depart.

What if our reason for being
is to be joyous and to love.
Have we succeeded?

—Ross P. Buckley

TELL ME

Little sparrow
Have you no fear?
Tell me why
You venture so near.
Rippling wind
Where is your start?
Tell me how
You create dune art.
Busy honeybee
Do you ever slow?
Tell me where
Yesterdays go.
Christ, my Lord,
Can you hear me?
Tell me why
I can't be as free
As the bird, the wind, and the bee.

—Susan Hurl

THE WIND

The wind whispers the secret
of the night, it howls and howls as if
in fright.

The trees do sway and topple a
bit and then they stop and quietly sit.

The wind seeps through the darkness
rustling the leaves. They flutter down as
if in ease.

The moon doth show and then is
gone, but the wind still stays to sing
its song.

—Hilary Dunham, age 12

MY DOG

A delightful pet, in sable coat
such loving joy, you do emote.
Little black paws, and black-tipped tail
with favorite toys, you do assail.

A prancing dog, a dancing beggar
cajoling me, for treats to give her
Guarding, protecting, alerting me
when things aren't right, where eyes can't see.

I treasure highly, each glowing day
when the two of us, can once again play
God's plans for creatures, however small
brought love, contentment, and peace to us all.

—Charles J. Myers

COLORADO MORN

Masses of cold and shimmery gray,
give way to amethyst, pink and green.
and on the far horizon,
shards of silver are seen.

In that morning burst of radiance.
in the clear and crystalline light,
silently, they melt away,
the shadows of the night.

Mingled scents pervade the air,
in the cool and lucent morn,
and high above the mountain tops,
a glorious day is born.

—Lillian Peacock

FAIRIES

Fairies walk along my pillow,
And dance upon my bed,
And whisper sweet enchanted thoughts
To roam about my head.

Daisies in the sunlight,
Drifting with the wind
Fairies strew them everywhere
To make my troubles end.

The rain is softly falling,
On petals of a rose,
Fairies sprinkle dew on me,
And strike a happy pose.

Fairies slowly calling—
Singing out my name.
My dreams are so much sweeter,
Since the fairies came.

—Ladonna Fulgham

WHEN I SIT AND PRAY

When I sit and pray everyday
I grow closer to the Lord,
He helps me through the day
He helps me through the night,
He guides me with His light
Now I have better sight,
Because He shed His blood
I have His love.

—Diane L. Watt

WHEN EVE REACHED UP

She plucked forbidden fruit,
Then shared with Adam
Her feast of revelation.
He chose freely, and
Eagerly he partook of all
She set before him.
Then, Adam cleansed his palette;
Gobbled grace guiltlessly;
Withholding from Eve a portion of
His forgiveness.
Rather than ask to savor his sorbet,
Eve merely watched him,
Tasting instead a bitter residue
That tainted her tongue forever.

—Lois Anne Edelman

THE ROSE

It's only a tiny rosebud,
A flower of God's design,
But I cannot unfold the petals,
With these clumsy hands of mine.
The secret to unfolding flowers,
Is not known to such as I.
The flower God unfolds so sweetly,
In my hands would fade and die.

So I will look to Him for guidance
Each step of every day,
And I will trust in Him to lead me
In each and every way.
For the path that lies before me,
My Heavenly Father knows.
I will trust Him to unfold the moments,
Just as He unfolds the Rose.

—Annette Christine Jerfita

OVER THE GARDEN WALL

Walking in the early morning,
Answering the bird's first call.
Returning footsteps find me looking,
Over the garden wall.

There it sits, our cozy house,
Roses climbing 'round the door,
Painted daisys, hollyhocks,
Pansies grace the garden floor.

A slip of this, a start of that,
Reminders all, of friendships dear.
Stepping stones pass the garden seat.
I'll have my morning coffee here.

Through the meadow the sun shines red,
Over the garden wall,
Up the path and through the gate
A neighbor is coming to call!

—Louise Johnson

HOLDING HANDS WITH JESUS

I'm holding hands with Jesus
the winds begin to blow
No matter where they take me
He'll never let me go
Even when the day is calm
And all seems it's best
Jesus Christ is holding on
His love will never rest
Knowing that we all must die
The time will come around
Knowing that His holding hand
will raise me from the ground.

—Scott Dennis Upchurch

YOU'RE NOT ALONE

The Heartiest of men will weep,
When all alone and trouble's near,
He'll toss and turn, and try to sleep,
His heart is overcome with fear.

Flowing tears run down his cheek,
He thinks no one will ever guess,
This hardy man, now so meek,
Like a little child in his loneliness.

But God sees this sad and tearful sight,
For a constant vigil he has kept,
It isn't weakness to cry at night,
For the Bible says even "Jesus Wept."

—C.J. White

A WORLD OF PEACE

If we could live in a world of peace
And not a world of war
This world would be so wonderful
The way God meant it for

With man's greed for power
And to take control
He has lost contact with Jesus
And cast away his soul

With atomic power
Some one with foul play
Will destroy all God's creations
In some future day

—Richard Hall

GRANT THAT I SHOULD ANSWER

Like the lyrical ascension
Of a note upon a scale,
Without pause, without retention
With momentum nought can quell

Grant that I should answer, Father,
Every nuance of Your wishes,
With the negative not bother,
Nor give ear to the suspicious.

To allow not scorn nor scoffing
Doubt, mistrust, nor unbelief
Cast a shadow on the offing
And bring to Your Spirit grief.

Grant attainment of the measure
To my being, Lord, allotted;
Change to wine this melting glacier
To be with Thy Spirit besotted.

—grace g. glaros

LOST TIME

Time is a lost treasure,
    more valuable than gold.
It can never be bought back,
    once it has been sold.
So before it's lost forever,
    in a place called Memory,
Look beyond what could have been,
    and make it what could be.
Because the future is the present,
    and soon will be the past.
The painful lesson I have learned,
    is that life goes by too fast.

—Laura L. Fogarty

SALVATION

The wellspring bubbles, bursts forth,
    Soaking the ground around it,
Permeating the air with its fresh scent of purity.
It leaves me with feelings of absolute cleanliness,
humbleness, holiness.
The water itself is free from any impurities;
Blue crystal.
One is almost afraid to enter it,
Lest one defile it.
Yet we cannot resist it.
It draws us near and then suddenly washes over us.
With the gentleness of a lazy stream it takes hold of us.
With the force of a torrential flood it swallows our soul.

—Perrin Nelson Smith, Jr.

THE WHIPPOORWILL

O, why did you ever learn to whistle
    That lonely call of the whippoorwill?
Didn't you know, for the rest of my life
    At twilight time when thoughts are still,
The plaintive cry of that desolate bird
    Would wing its way through the evening blue?
With a start, I would think it was you that I heard.
    Your call was so perfect. Your whistle so true.
You never could know with what sorrow and pain
    A longing would grip me, that nothing can fill,
For your smile; for your laughter; the gleam of your eyes;
    That cute, jaunty tilt of your work-cap bill.
O, Daddy! Why did you learn to whistle
    That lonely call of the whippoorwill?

—Betty Fortune McGuire

CHEPSTOW ROAD BEDSITTER

Often I have wondered how many
    Lives
Sit in furnished rooms protected
By ghostly dreams and ancient
Desires.
Often I have wondered
What these dead walls would
Say
If gags were removed.
Would love rise up and haunt
This chamber, soft with lilac
And trimmed with satin?
Or would Death seek out
Its dark domain
Charging us with silence
Within these skeletal walls.

—Janis Wital

FORBIDDEN

Love is as sweet as a bird's song
    as tender as a careful caress
To be loved is to breathe life's spirit
    it is to live to the fullest
But to have love snatched away
    to be forbidden of its warmth
One finds emptiness
    and therefore death

—Vera Medina-Norton

BOO RADLEY
(From "To Kill a Mockingbird")

Is it true, the things they say
    About the sad and lonely one?
At night does he sneak out to play,
In the dark, seen by none?

If we could see inside his mind,
Cast aside his hiding veil,
Who knows what secrets we might find?
Answers only time will tell.

Will he stay locked up inside,
Hidden in that scary place?
From what menace does he hide?
Will he show his hidden face?

—Ken Godwin

LIFE IS LIKE A FERRIS WHEEL

Life is a ferris wheel
    At a country fair . . .
Each ticket holder knows the feel
    If he likes to dare.

The roustabout will set him down
    And activate the ride,
Soon the movement takes him 'round
    On the upward side.

Higher, on the wheel, the rise,
    Stretching out the view . . . .
At topping out; blue the skies,
    then downward turn is due.

Sinking down the thrill retreats
    As one backward goes,
Then new faces claim the seats,
    the ride is done, he knows.

—Jim Sweet

WE CAN STAND

The war you say is drugs;
    I solely disagree.
What is the war then you ask;
Just think a moment with me.

Let's get to the root of the source;
Remember how it used to be?
When the Bible guided your course;
Not your peers or commercial T.V.

Charity begins at home;
This works if God is there.
No matter where you may roam;
He keeps you in his care.

Now you know what the war is about;
Which weapon do you choose?
For me I'll take the one with clout;
Without GOD —— We lose!

—Helen Louise

Where have the years gone?
Like sirens in the night
they pass so swiftly,
Leaving in the stillness only dim thoughts
and fading memories.
Oh, but the times were good —
Bad ones, to be sure,
not easily forgotten.
Life goes on. We live.
Thank God for life!

—Susan Robertson

ILLUSION

One dark and foggy night,
A shadowed face appeared.
Attached to it was a figure,
Whose transparency I feared.

I saw but not two eyes,
That glowed a fiery red.
A blood-curdling scream I heard,
That filled my heart with dread.

At last when I'd stopped running,
What I'd seen began to dawn.
I turned for one last look,
But the shadowy form was gone.

—Renee Hewitt

SHADOW IN THE MIST

I see her huddled in a doorway,
Seeking refuge from the cold.
A door is opened, she's pushed away.
Poverty has her in its hold.

As I walk by she grabs my hand.
I bring myself to look at her.
She rises but she cannot stand.
Life has done her more dishonor.

There is no sparkle in her eye
Besides the tear that's always there.
She lifts her palms up to the sky
In hopelessness and sad despair.

I give her a dollar without a sound.
She takes it and clenches it in her fist.
I walk on quietly, not turning around
'Til she's just a shadow in the mist.

—Dawn S. deGraffenried

ACCEPTANCE

I feel so weak and helpless
From all life's hurts and pains.
I feel defeated often
More losses than are gains.

Sometimes I want to dig a hole
To crawl inside and hide.
From all the woes and problems
That build up deep inside.

I don't like to pass my worries
Onto others that I know.
In front of friends and lovers
A strong spirit I like to show.

But now and then I do break down
And sympathetic my friends will be.
They understand and show they care
By accepting me as me.

—Deborah Ann Allsop-Ahern

ALMOST BELIEVED

You came to me upon false notions,
Stayed with me until I was deceived.
Loved me only with intimate contact,
Backed away when I almost believed.

Talked to me only when questioned,
Answered me without concern.
Neglected my only desire,
To be loved and not burned.

I reached for you when you were falling,
But my grip was not that strong.
To hold you up while I was learning,
That you would be gone before too long.

—Nancy Lyon

ABSENCE

Someone, leaving is a sad thing, I know,
Just say all you have to.
Before they must go.
Be happy you had, the time you two shared,
For it's priceless you know,
Those friendships are rare,
Someday, be sure,
That your paths will meet again,
Cause there is, no end,
To any true friend,
For time and space,
Can only keep you apart,
So for always, remember,
You'll have each other, at heart . . .

—Teresa A. Preis

UNTITLED

I can feel the loneliness in the air.
The paintings that once adorned the walls
Are no longer there.
The knickknacks that reminded me
Of happiness are gone.
In fact, this has become only an
Architectural structure.
Empty, except of dust and lint.
Things that say no one lives here.
A place to sit by yourself,
And remember,
What happened in days past
And what will never happen again.
Since you are no longer here.

—Cameron J. Rountree

RIVER'S RUN

Beneath the river's run I see,
a beauty far surpassing me.
Who with a side-long glance from thee,
does take the one true love from me.
With hopeless heart does beg and plead,
his heart she steals away from me.
To water's edge he flies in deed,
to die in vain for loving her, the sea.
And now her siren song both wails and mourns,
for death now takes his due.
In loving her his heart was torn,
for me who waits on troubled shore.
And now beneath the river's run I see,
his heart now undone, for me.

—Lisa Shawn Byerley

PEACE

Peace, Peace, At last it's come —
The glorious mist of loveliness,
The world abloom with blossoms fair,
The sunshine warmth enduring.

Peace, Peace, At last it's here —
The chains of fear are broken;
The freedom to drift, just filled with joy,
Taking comfort in the Spirit.

Peace, Peace, At last it's come —
It belongs to you and me.
Happiness and love are all about.
With the security of the truth —

—Mary Evelyn Lotterhos

THE HUMAN TRAGEDY

To live and breathe the air of earth;
To know the times of day and night;
To feel the breezes that gently blow,
And never know the true "Light;"

To feel the shade of a spreading oak,
Or the pleasure of tasting what we eat;
To drink the waters of earth's springs
And maintain an attitude of self-conceit;

To see the grass, the flowers, the trees
That grow forth from this earth's sod;
To see, to feel, to enjoy all these
And never know the source is GOD!

—Frances Taylor Smith

HOLD UP THE LIGHT

We were taken from Africa unlikely to return,
The ways of the Americans we were to learn,
Beaten, tortured and forced to obey,
Our lives as slaves lasted many a day,
But now my friends those days are gone,
To slavery, I say, "so long."
Come one, come all,
Come go with me,
Let's visit the land of the noble free,
America's opportunity has opened the door,
So that we can allow our ambitions to soar,
We African-Americans have been given the chance,
To make our lives abundant,
We African-Americans have been given the right,
But it is up to us to HOLD UP THE LIGHT!!

—Suzet M. Montgomery

LIFE'S ROAD

Life's road is quite unending . . .
  with curves and ruts, embankments steep;
And one may wonder where it leads
  or what the journey may impart.
But if one stays upon the path
  and keeps one's sight from turning not,
The bumps and jolts that life does bring
  produces treasures, quite unseen.
'Cause if the road were smooth as silk
  and wide and broad, without a hill;
One hardly would appreciate
  that life was worth the living.
For life is filled with ups and downs
  quite like a road so near, yet far . . .
It's travelled both by young and old
  which leads but onward, homeward bound.

—Jolene Bearden

PRAISING OUR LORD

Praising our Lord singing a new song
  Praising Him above for His glorious love
Praising seeking Him to strengthen us
Praising praying keeping His sayings
Praising playing stringed instruments
Praising sounding trumpets and timbrels
Praising dancing playing harps and organs
Praising our Lord for His amazing grace
Praising singing in joyful glory to our Lord
Praising clapping hands glorifying rejoicing

—Maria Lizzie Darby

OUR FOSTER SON

This little one came into our life,
  He knew not trouble, he knew not strife.
Surely life for Him will not be bright,
Until there is no line between black and white.

Like other babes he does all normal things,
For us he's Love, He's king of Kings.
But one big thing, just isn't the same,
God made him half black, and without a name.

His soul is his to save someday,
In spite of what others do or say,
He'll serve his God as best he can,
And prove that color hurts no man.

—Dorothy Frahm

AWAKENING COMPASSION

Silver clouds and shades of gray was all
  that I could see, as a room full of faces
swam before me. They all looked the same,
They all sounded the same. The only diff-
erence was the name. First impressions
are taken too seriously, you have to stop and
hear all the wisdom waiting there. Observe
closely this sea of gray, as all the personalities
come into play. Words of sorrow, gladness and
pain all falling as a gentle rain. Lifeless faces
begin to glow, as my compassion starts to grow.
The spirit of death always so near, taking the
ones I've held so dear. Still I went to this house
of death, I had to see my angels go to their
final rest. The body was old, the spirit was
young, in God's heaven they shall be as one.

—Doris J. Oakley

THOU SHALT NOT CRY

Look at it suspended there,
  touching nothing but the wet and rotting ropes
by which it hangs
over a sea of pain.
Like a foggy mist
liquid, but dense,
a frozen lake of boiling blood
with levels rising steadily, steadily,
from the dripping of tears
which tear through my broken spirit
slicing a deeper incision
soon to scab over and heal
as at long last
the ropes rip,
drowning my loneliness
in a spring of new hope.

—Dixie Lynn Anderson

MY BROTHER

Everyone has to grow-up—
 Either it will be sooner,
Or it will be later,
Someone will be sad and miss him:
    Mother, Brother, Father, Sister . . .
    or Best Friend.
I know when my brother leaves,
    my fighter, arguer, and my best
    friend will leave.
When I see him next he will still
be my best friend, BUT
    He will be changed.
No more fighting me, but fighting
    to be free.
That's going to be the way;
    "We'll see,"
But I hope he still will love me!

—Jenn J.

MY PAL "DADDY"

You come and go,
    in and out of sight;
I'm always happy to see you,
    morning or night.

My eyes light up,
    and a smile always appears;
Especially for you,
    even between my tears.

In your big strong hands,
    I always feel secure;
Whether you are changing my diaper,
    or gently tossing me in the air.

Your glasses intrigue me,
    they are so fun to grab;
And your whiskers tickle,
    as I give a big hug.

I'm a rugged little rascal,
    Grandma says you were too;
So I'll give you a warning,
    I want to be just like you.

—Melanie D. Abel

GOING BACK

The hills were all ablaze
    With red, gold, orange and green;
Bright blue skies with clouds of white—
A truly breath-taking scene.

I drove down a narrow lane
As far as I could see;
The hint of fall was everywhere,
Great works of art to me.

Passing by a quaint old house
That was once my Great Aunt's home
Brings back treasured memories;
But now stands all alone.

I thought of days gone by;
Time spent there as a kid
Stays forever in my mind;
The fun things that I did.

The poor old roof is sagging,
Porches have fallen in.
It made me sad to see it;
I shan't go there again.

—Geraldine Wolfanger

ANSWERS AND QUESTIONS

The moon rises, oh so fast,
    As I hurry to make it last.
My life passes just as quickly,
As I stop to ponder glibly,
The sun sets rather slowly it seems,
As I wait to dream my dreams.
Why is life so hurry up and wait?
You're either early or you're late.
These problems to some would be droll.
To ponder about on one's evening stroll,
Isn't it interesting to search one's mind?
The answers to questions one might never find,
To of failed to succeed, but to have never tried.
To lose out on life, because of one's pride.
To get excited and shout about.
To feel sad and cry, and really pout.
To know you're alive and not made of stone;
But to never ask and feel like a clone,
Would be sad to exist and feel dead.
Not knowing the answers to questions that lay in your head.

—Shirley Aniol

BELIEVE

My dearest one — I know things seem tough
You feel like a failure — You've had enough
But just remember there's always a light leading the way
You just have to find it with each awaking day
Reach into your heart and you will find
The faith and strength — It's one of a kind
Open your heart and it is there
A God that loves you and really does care
Just accept Him and you will see
Just how easy it can be
To ask and to receive
All you have to do is believe
I know this to be very true
Because of so many times I have prayed for you
I give you this poem with love and hope
That you will find the answers of how to cope
As long as we are together and have our love
We can conquer all — Far and above
Just remember all these things are true
Mostly — My Darling — I love you . . .

—Melinda C. Harrell

FROZEN IN TIME

Sometimes time is like ice frozen in time
There's a place in your heart where dreams are inside
There's a time, a place where words were spoken
There's a place where your heart can never be broken

If I could freeze this moment in time
my heart would know for sure if you were mine
I would place your memory deep inside
I couldn't leave it there long because true love won't hide

Sometimes memories are too hard to find
I was in a different place in another time
When your memories knock on your door
then maybe you'll find what your heart's looking for

Sometimes a heart is frozen like ice
where it's cold and it's dark
with memories that are torn apart
When your heart is like steam when the snow melts
it can turn to sand like sea shells

I know what we're feeling deep inside
we'll be together forever frozen in time

—Melanie Adcock

OUR BABY BOY

A baby came to live with us
What a happy time this was!

A baby needing so much care and love
A special little gift from God above.

This baby boy, though very small
in a short time became our all

Our whole world revolves around this little boy
Whose little smiles and coos bring us joy.

Why should we be so richly blessed
for all this happiness, though we'd done our best.

A little boy with a dirty face
Has come to fill the hearts empty space.

A little boy with torn blue jeans and a broken toy
Has won our hearts, he's our pride and joy.

—Naomi Peugh

THE SWEET GOODNIGHT

Watch as the evening sky starts losing its
lights.
   See how darkness spreads her cool dark
fingers out to bring the night,
   Her hand stretches out across the way,
   Showing us the close of another day.
   Her fingers are wide as they inch across
the blue,
   Watch close as other colors are cascading
through.
   Her magic finger does things unknown,
   Now the light is slowly going see all
the beauty she has shown.
   How gently darkness caresses the sky,
   And the little clouds as they pass by.
   But now her journey is nearly done,
   She kisses the valley and tree tops
goodnight on her run.
   All the daylight has faded and gone,
   Nightfall has come like a blanket on earth
so warm and strong,
   Like a mother who knows what is best,
   Darkness puts her child earth down for another
night's rest.

—Karen T. Davis

LISTEN TO THE LONELY

A child on the steps of an orphanage crying.
The tears streaking his little face.
Is there any use in trying?
I only want a home to call my place.

The pretty teenage girl with a face so sad,
A mother that doesn't care, an alcoholic dad.
Is there anywhere to turn?
Yes, the drugs, living in the streets somehow.
Do you think they will notice me now?

A soldier in a foxhole in this terrible war
He screams "Why are we here when life could be so
much more?" As his buddy next to him is hit with
a grenade and his life is gone, in this needless war.

The father is buried, mother is left
Who will take her? Who will it be?
In such a large family there surely must be one—
But then again is there none?

Listen To The Lonely

—Sharon Lee Crump

OUR ANNIVERSARY

Fifty years ago this year
   Which is drawing very near
To this man I gave my heart
For until death do us part
We have had our ups and downs
But still much happiness we have found
With one darling girl and two sweet boys
There has been a lot of pride and joy
Then come the grand-children smart and bright
And a great-grand child that is our delight
Now that we are growing old and grey
I would not change things in any way
And when the time comes on that great day
A home in Heaven with God I pray
And to walk the streets of silver and gold
There we will never grow old.

—Florence Cravens

MY STRENGTH

The God who made this great round earth
   Has been beside me since my birth
He's held me up when times were rough
And helped me be sometimes tough

He's been my strength, He's nurtured me
With faith in Him, I somehow see
That though my life is not the best
It will be better, before I rest

Through all the bad times given me
His love has been there endlessly
Helping me to find my way
Learning to live from day to day

I bless the God who made this earth
And been beside me since my birth
Without His love I would be lost
Like those who never count the cost

So day by day I kneel and pray
He'll ever guide me on my way
Until the time I am no more
He'll lead me straight to Heaven's door

—Nancy Cartwright

Dedicated To A Dear Friend In Our Senior Park Who Passed Away Recently.

We said goodbye to you today,
   Our eyes were filled with tears
But our minds and memories will never cry
Over our friendship through the years.

We still remember your smiling face
No matter what your sorrow.
You always looked ahead, it seems
To a fun filled glad tomorrow.

You knew your heart was on a balance scale
      To be — or not to be.
But the sincere trust in the God you loved
Caused you to thank him on bended knee.

If only us, who are left behind,
Could follow your beautiful faith
There'd be a much loved and happier world
And in God's hands always be safe.

As you laid there in your last long sleep,
So relaxed, so comforted, so free,
We could only hope we'd meet again
In the heaven that's meant to be.

—Mabel M. Amsden

GENTLE LAMB OF CALVARY

Oh gentle lamb of Calvary
You gave your life so willingly.
Only the father's will would you do
To show to all that your love is true.

Jesus is the name of this lamb of which I speak,
Sent to this earth his father's will to keep.
His love is the same yesterday, today, and forever
On him should we trust and doubt him not ever.

He will come back to this earth once again
But not as a babe, a boy or a man.
He will be king and lord of Lords
To reign forever with his crown and his sword.

—Diana L. Westbrook

JUST A FRIEND

Who will help you, day by day,
    with all the things you wish to say;
And be there on the day you pray
    to help you drive the blues away.
Or, take your hand so you won't sway
    as you go down that path of gray.
If only for one hour you play,
    who hears the call? Who says, "OK?"

Then, when you're coming 'round the bend
    and you feel driven to wits' end,
Your need for love, your need to depend
    on someone to help your spirit ascend
Will call out for a person to end this trend.
    Who can it be with a heart to lend?
Who gives you pleasure with no problems to tend?
    You know who it is! . . . . . . It is . . .
            . . . just a friend.

—Caren L. Eyre

WINTER MONDAY

The heat of the house feels warm and cozy,
    The cheeks of my children are so pudgy
and rosy.

The sweet smell of cookies baking
makes my little girl smile,
She asks "Mommy can I have one now,"
I say "dear in a little while."

The weather is cold and Christmas
is near,
I can't wait to play Santa Claus
again, this year!

We have a new son and a daughter
from before,
My husband groans and says "Instead
of one there are two to buy for."

The plans to buy a new home are under
way,
I hope to be out of this tiny place by
May.

New plans and dreams are what we
all live for,
My husband says "You are never
satisfied you always want more."

My baby boy is napping now
and I'm brushing my daughter's hair,
Cartoons are on T.V. and I'm
going to rest in my big rocking chair.

—Dawn Reneé

UNSPOKEN WORDS

I hear love's voice sailing through hollow air,
    Being transported by feelings I bear.
It penetrates boundaries I prepared
To prohibit the entrance of love's dare.

Now I must compete with the incomplete,
Fraudulent, world view——that I should not treat
My new love with kindness, only deceit
And carnal desire——like sensored male meat.

If I must bear love's stinging blow alone
Unknown to his benevolent mind's throne.
I shall purely be a modern martyr.
Jest will sight, "Did God forget his daughter?"

And still, soft, unspoken words sail through springs
of fain, moist air——love's voice hath hailed wings.

—Jeannine Spurlock

FANTASY

These tears that trickle down my face
    Slowly stain my fine knit lace
For life just hasn't been at all
A bowl of laughs or merry ball.
It took me for the longest ride,
Laughed at me as I danced with pride
Convinced me to this very day
That everything would go my way
And so these tears that I do cry
And tears to cry 'till the day I die
For I've been fooled by life the "game"
My heart will never be the same.
With my token wasted a ride well ridden
All who watched have run and hidden
Life played me for a simple fool
While I thought I was being cool.
And so I've lost, with yet to find
Life will never be too kind
To people who dream, just like me,
Living off of fantasy.

—Terri D. Fimbres

LOVER'S BLUES

God why does it always happen to me?
    Why did she have to leave?
Where did she go?
How is she?
What can I do?
Why do I have the lover's blues?

I want to hear her voice over the phone,
I want to see her face one more time.
I want to kiss her lips once again.
I want to be with her every hour of the day.
I want to tell her I love her so.
Why do I have the lover's blues?

What I have no doctor can cure.
There is no stopping the pain in my heart.
My stomach aches from all the suffering.
My dream of us has all but vanished.
Can't we start over again?
Why do I have the lover's blues?

Will I ever see her again?
When and where will the suffering stop?
How come I am all alone?
Can my life go on without her?
Will I lose her and, she doesn't know how I feel?
Why do I have the lover's blues?

—Gary Elton Brown

CLOUDS

Clouds are, in some sense,
Mediators between the heavens and the earth,
Material in substance rising from the deep,
Carrying heavy burdens on the winds of mighty worth.

They are ethereal in lightness,
Without visible support,
Moving in serene and gentle majesty —
Loveliness in shapes of every sort.

They shine in the flush of dawn,
Like islands of flame in a sea of fire,
And they blacken the night with darkness
Or shake the mountains with thunders of desire.

They can rush through the howling heavens
Or move serenely along the azure deep,
Often charged with angry lightnings
Which provoke nature to shudder and weep.

But that same nature sings with joy
When clouds that are pregnant with rain
Pour their blessings upon a dry parched earth
To relieve it of sorrow and pain,

—Marjorie N. Wessel

FRIENDSHIP

A friendship is like a pattern of lace
each stitch, a time—an experience—a face

Birth, death, joy, tears
    all life shared, that made up the years

Stitch by stitch, an intricate design
    some stitches dropped, then left behind

No patience to mend them, then finally one day
    we fold up our handwork and put it away

Stored in the past, lives take a turn
    years melt away, but memories return

One day we dare to retrieve at last
    that delicate handwork we shared from the past

Gently unfolded
    precision no measure

Once seen as imperfect
    now viewed as a treasure

We've picked up our needles
    no stitches to mend

I'm so glad you're back
    I missed you — My friend

—Joan M. Perna

DARK STORM

If you hear the wind scream softly
    In the night of sudden darkness —
Please don't be alarmed,
    It's only memories passing through me.

And if you feel a silent warmth
    Caress you close — caress you softly —
It's just my breath,
    Whispering "I Love you" in an ocean of compassion.

And if a gentle flow of rain
    Reaches out and drifts you slowly —
It's just my tears
    Saying "I want you" —
And I'll storm until I have you next to me . . .

—Dee Douglas

MY GARDEN OF FLOWERS

I planted my garden of flowers
With oh, such love and care.
I spaded and dug and labored so hard.
I wanted my garden to be so fair.

The miracle of life in my garden grew
And the blossoms gave great joy;
But as the sun grew hot and days grew long
My garden became a forgotten toy.

One day in need of beauty
I went to my garden so fair
And found only weeds and thistles instead
And I wept as I lingered there.

When the days were hot and dreary
Why did I not water with care
The garden I started so eagerly
Instead of giving up in despair?

Oh, don't neglect your line of duty,
Knowing God sees when we cower;
Keep out the weeds and the thistles;
Have a life of beautiful flowers!

—Hilda M. Clingan

ODE TO A MYSTICAL GEM (jim)

We share . .
    the sun rise
    the sun set
    the same blue sky
    the moon at night
    the stars . . .
Even the four winds.

We share . .
    the music of a raindrop
    the texture of a universal tear
    whose origin is the same.

We share waiting for the next time around.

To connect to the Divine Sparkle . .
    through your guidance is all . . . .
    I never expected to share.

I AM . .

Now a GLOW united.

—Joy Wind

DYING LOVE

Would you love me more with freedom,
If I just up and passed away?

If I lived among the angels,
Would you then know what to say?

Would I be easier to love,
If I were not here?

If my loving eyes,
Were never again so near?

Could you whisper in my ear,
And love me in your heart?

Could you feel the same,
If we forever were apart?

Could you love me now,
While we are both still here?

Or will you learn too late,
When all that's left are tears?

—D.R. George

OURS: BUT NOT REALLY

A long time ago a miracle happened
Poseidon fell in love
And to prove his love he made a bold
    but delicate creature
A wild creature with eyes that could
    hold a sea of concern and sympathy
A beautiful, magical creature
He called it the horse
He gave it to Demeter
Tonight I follow the prints of the new
    moon that burn hot in the sand
I follow them with tears in my eyes
They lead me to the sea
Demeter is there
And together we wave good-bye
    to a creature
        that was ours . . . but not really.

—Aime

FOR EDWARD: AGE 3

I have a special little friend
He is my nephew, too
He's why my days are sunny
And why my skies are blue.

No one else has such a smile
No one could take his place;
He, only, laughs the way he does
With sunbeams on his face!

Our love has kept me going
Through cloudy days and fair;
Whenever I have needed him
He's always been right there.

Wherever he may wander
Wherever he may go
The memories of our happy times
Will set my heart aglow!

He's happy and he's beautiful
He's my pride and joy,
He's found a place within my heart—
My Special Little Boy!!

—Linda M. Leib

A LONELY ROAD

Restlessly I strove
Through the corridors of time
Searching for a glimpse of you
Everyone walks a lonely road

One day you rescued me along the way
Nurturing my heart sheltering my soul
You let your eyes dwell on me
You cast a spell upon me

You said open your arms to love's illusion
Blend our hearts in wild confusion
Soon I depended on you
For love and everything

You happily spun my life
On the dial of time
Soon I depended on you
For love and everything

My senses leapt in joy
I was smiling in the rain
Laughing in the sun
For I was your chosen one

—Marianne Lazur

MORE

Do I love you as much as you love me? I answer more
Needless to say, that you are not sure
I guess the fault must lie in the past
When the same words were spoken but nay did they last
So we give just a little and the rest we hold out
Leaving ourselves room for that possible doubt
It is really our loss that we won't give it all
Like a tree we should nurture it, and let it grow tall
Our love is like the birth of a child,
Like the first sign of spring,
Like the bloom of a rose a most beautiful thing
With each breaking day life means so much more
Now that I have you to love and adore
So with all of the love that I have to give,
I want you to have it as long as I live
Darling let's not hold back as we're just passing through
Not knowing at all when the end is due
Do I love you as much as you love me? I love you more

—Barbara Gibbons

QUESTIONS

The young boy gazed into the universe
And turning to the old man asked haltingly,
Where do the heavens end?
If I knew that, the old man answered,
I would know all there is to know
About life and death and human destiny.
"But I want to know!" The child's voice
Became a plaintive cry.
The old man thought for a long time.
Life, he said, is not what you have been
Nor where you have gone, not laurels you have
Earned or battles you have fought.
It is not whether you are rich or poor or
Judgment by whom you know or who you think you are;
It is simply this!
On this day, regardless of what is right or wrong,
At this very instant in time, it is not what was,
Nor what will be but what you are
At this moment out of all eternity.
And this knowledge, you will discover,
Will reveal to you where the heavens end.

—Artis M. Cain

MY ANSWER

Once I went alone to a quiet place, and
There I prayed to God.
I knew my prayer he would answer.
But when I had prayed, my answer seemed not to come—
Only a silent reply.

So again I prayed—more fervently than before
Yet again no answer could I hear.
Only the same silent reply.

Now the third time I prayed
And again for an answer did wait
"Surely," I thought, "this time my answer will come."
Yet I heard—only the same silent reply.

As I knelt upon my knees, I cried—
"Lord! Why has my prayer not been answered?"
And the Lord said,
Three times you have prayed; Three times I have heard;
Three times I have answered.

The first was with the morning sun—
The second, when you read my word—
The third was in the voice of a friend.

—Terry Evans

IT'S SUMMER NOW

It's summer now
As I pass along the way
I see greenfields that I did not see yesterday.
I see the sky that harbor above, I see the black birds that
   fly like doves.
I see small streams that flow beyond their birth
I see cotton fields that have yet to be unearth
I see the gins that have closed their doors from work that
   will never be no more.
I see these things as I pass along the way,
   things that were that are not here today.

—Shayla

THE AWAKENING TIME

Cold, crisp Winter removes his coat to become
   The splash and slush of Spring.
Gray, colorless dawns ripen into the
Rose glow of the Awakening Time.

Sleepy squirrels hurriedly turn into the
Jesters of the leaf world,
Their antics overshadowed by the sudden appearance of
A flock of exclamation marks, blackbirds by another name.

Rain . . . to sun . . . to rain . . . to sun;
The life giving cycle reinstated.
Bud, new shoot, leaves, color,
All join in the shouting, living, breathing circle!

Faint flutterings and chirpings
Explode into the great courting chorus,
Forerunner to the new voices that cry out in hunger
From twig-strong, mud held, feather-lined homes.

The death of Winter meeting new life.
The old turned to new.
New? The old reborn?
Re-creation building on Creation, in the Awakening Time.

—Lorelei Pittack Halstead

FORWARD OBSERVATION

I

Serpentine mountain stream trailed by hidden paths
   Dew covered foliage conceals a stealthy soldier
Water buffalo stand in a shroud of misting breath
Along a ragged ridge; muted dawn.

II

Nouc mam lazily wafts from early cooking fires
Behind him, at waters' edge; a straw metal shanty village
Each day begins thus . . . for centuries
For centuries, war and peace have bartered here.

III

On the mountains' far side; daylight splinters
A rock quarry gapes and grows into a living scar
Spewing black exhaust, bulldozers discard foothills
Foreign soldiers patrol a defensive perimeter.

IV

Futility enfolds the aging warrior
Beneath this soil lie a millennium of ancestors . . .
Screaming over machinery, a rocket slams into the quarry
Whispering into a small transmitter, he corrects trajectory.

V

Ignored by paved roads, meandering cart paths expire
Scanty rice paddies await peasants who await rice
Folk lore enshrines the ancient work; the noble toil
Below the mountain, sleeping children inherit dreams.

—James M. Williams

DAWN ON THE BAYOU

The boat sits motionless in the water
   Still . . .
Not a ripple is seen.
The mist rises like a ghost
Across the water deep.
No sound is heard.
The cypress trees
Keep watch like sentinels.
The world of the swamp.
Then, like a burst of fire,
The sun peaks through.
The world of the swamp is alive again.
The birds sing
The alligator grunts, and
The snakes slap the water
As they make their way for
The start of a new day.

—Sarah DeCuir

SUMMER DAYS

The sweet smells of summer
   drifts through the air
   beckoning the children
   with wonders to be shared

Adults have that smile
   that promise of fun
   that twinkle in the eye
   that Summer has just begun

A time when we sleep
   out under the stars
   to the crackling of the campfire
   and the whispers that whisper far

Into the cool clear night
   sleepy little ones wonder
   at stars that are so close
   and seem to be without number

The secrets that were told and kept
fears that were calmed and laid to rest
Tired and weary we soon fall sleep
joy and contentment, happiness and peace

—Elizabeth G. Snow

THE CAREGIVER

Forty-three short years ago
   We vowed to share our wealth,
We vowed to love and honor
In sickness and in health.

If I knew then what I know now
I'm sure I'd do the same,
Despite the fact that life has turned
From years of joy to pain.

While fate had been quite kind to us
I'm often now in tears,
It's not the way that I would choose
To spend our "Golden Years".

Rather then give up on life
I'll do the best I can,
Tho it gets harder day by day
I'll take care of my man.

From big and strong to weak and frail
It hurts to see him fade,
But I will do my best to keep
The promises I made.

—Louise C. Thomas

ADOLESCENCE

Amidst the scattered springtime torrent rains,
a brooding bluebird rests atop a bough,
And feeble lightning to a point remains
Some muted throbbing vestige for right now.

Responding to the gently pulsing wind,
Unraveled wet and darkly verdant vines
Induce the flagging nature to rescind
The harsh and heavy nature it refines.

Persistent storms rebuff the springtime plea
for quiet inactivity, and time
and time and time again reality
Asserts upon itself a storm sublime.

> Without the scattered showertimes of spring,
> No bluebird's brooding happiness will bring.

—Bennett Zon

LOVER'S PLEA

I wish there was some one out there
Who would love me too . . . the way I care

But it never seems to be that way
No matter how I hope and pray

I give so much — I guess it must be me
I don't possess what needs to be

I always seem to hurt my heart
I've really known this from the start

I just don't learn — I'm such a fool
I just can't follow this simple rule

To keep away from what is naught
This bitter lesson I've been taught

I need someone who cares for me
who's loving, warm, tender and free

Who calls on me to spend my time
Making him happy, making him mine

I've suffered enough over the years
Many a nights were filled with tears

If someone out there hears my plea
Maybe you're someone just like me

—Karen Maziasz

MEMORIES

When at eve there's no more light
and my eyes I try to rest,
shrouded memories of past
come along the night to last,
you at their center like a light
all dressed up in gold and white.

I can feel I start to weep
when the efforts of my quest,
to forget you as I must,
make me lose my cool and rest;
those that come during the sleep
those that last while it is deep.

Why your presence every night
making my pain oh! so deep?
why should you come to destroy
the bright memories I keep?
Those I saved from yesternight,
those that we truly enjoy'd?
Didn't you say to be loved
will never match loving might?

—Carlos Freymann

RAIN

Up in the sky the clouds are grey,
Rain is coming, they mean to say.
Rain to help the farmers' crops.
And when the rain ceases and stops,
The world is so fresh and yet so new,
Like a layer of newly spread dew.
The earth is so peaceful and so still —
The plants are contented — they've had their fill.
The birds are rejoicing it seems!
And, out comes new sunlight beams.

Now the clouds have nothing to say,
And, people watch every day —

For when again the clouds are grey . . . .

—Rebekah Bowser

PRECIOUS MOMENTS

The most precious moments that I know
Are when I'm alone;
Feeling and watching my baby grow.

Each little movement and kick that I feel
Brings an endless smile to my face;
One that tells me my baby is real.

The constant smile tells how much I care
And that my love will never end;
For the times that baby and I share.

Each and every day, the changes that I see
Helps me to realize;
Just how much my baby means to me.

For everything in the world, I'd never trade
The love that I have,
For the beautiful baby you and I made.

When it comes time for me to see
The baby that I feel;
I'll never forget the precious moments just for me.

—Rhonda Lynn Thompson

TWO LOVES

Vowing . . . before God's altar, chosen, stand two;
Side by side 'til death us part . . . we are one.
Dreams bind our inner strengths, me and you;
    Happiness and love . . . together, each has won!

Mated . . . hope and home the bonding verves;
    Charitable and purposeful . . . two proceed.
Each copes with life's uncertain curves;
    One doer . . . one dreamer, both succeed.

Embraced . . . two succumb to touch and scent . . .
    Rhythms quicken . . . warmed of rapture's sun.
Eros flows . . . thrust, then of carnal bent;
    Now pools, serene . . . two lovers, we are one!

Maternal . . . one alone on womb's warm sea . . .
    Life's sustaining tether bonds yet two;
Feeble rolls and kicks . . . mere fetal glee,
    Prepare thy breast, we are one, me and you.

Celebrated . . . fresh egos send two to pasture,
    Old skills and tools no longer required.
Festive anniversaries . . . neither can demur,
    Memories lighten the load, albeit, mired!

Mortal . . . life's parting curfew sounds.
    One Soul seeks Light in the dark-alone . . .
The other's bliss . . . the heart confounds;
    Soon, two Souls unite . . . now Spirit prone!

—M. Donald Zartman

MOTHER

There were alot of things, I wanted to say,
while I was growing up, I didn't think you knew.
So I am writing this today, to explain it all to you.

I never could show you how much I cared,
but the love I have for you was always there.
I watched and stood by, when you went through
hell, love, loneliness and sorrow.
I stood there and saw when you thought
there would be no tomorrow.
You always stood by me, rather I was right or wrong,
And I will always stand by you,
so you will never walk alone.
Oh, words can not survey,
the Thank-You I would like to say.
I love you mom, more than you will ever know,
along with my heart, I gave you my soul.

— Denise Hutsen

A ROSE PRESSED IN SHAKESPEARE

I held it tenderly in my hand,
the art of Nature—a perfect rose.
It was unique and it was beautiful
with sweet scent and crimson glow.

I could have left it to die in dust
for none to notice, none to see
its pretty petals carried off
by winds that bore them, soft and free.

Its tendrils curling towards the heavens,
its petals opening to the sun;
Alas! its life would soon be over
ere it had but just begun!

And now 'twas not the Wind, but I,
that carried it from death to life.
I saved it from a darkened grave,
from being buried, yet alive.

I pulled a book from acorn shelves
when once again sweet home I met,
and—Oh! What sorrow!—crushed my rose
'twixt "Romeo and Juliet."

— Trilby Wheeler, Age 13

WITHOUT YOU

Winter wind from long ago,
Soon the air to fill with snow.
Here by the fire safe and cozy,
I sit and write of my sad story.

It was a bitter cold night back in seventy-two
When I sat and pondered on what to do.
Then, low and behold, before my eyes,
Appeared a dream in disguise.

I heard a whisper in my ear,
And turned to find you standing near.

Suddenly my heart, just like a frog,
Jumped out of my body and on to a log.
It caused a spark, which started a fire.
I felt its great warmth as it went higher and higher.

Do you remember our song and our laughter?
Late in December when no one else mattered.
But then spring came, all too soon;
Our morning-young love became late afternoon.

I've found a new love, yes, I've found someone new.
But nothing is the same without you.

— Lisa Ann Zimmerman

LOVING CARE

Virginia Fondren:
    When children are so small,
        You give them your all.
    With your face so bright,
        They know everything is all right.
    You give much more than your part,
        Which shows you have a big heart.
    All your loving emotions,
        Are shown with your strong devotions.
    The Lord will richly bless you each hour,
        Because you rely upon His power.

— Robin Carroll

SOUNDS IN A WINTER WOOD

Listen to the sounds in a winter wood
As the wind chills the bare-limbed trees.
Hark carefully or you'll miss the sighs
    Made by the passing breeze.

Soft sounds, approaching silence,
    May gently brush your ear
As the breezes still in the winter chill.
    You almost strain to hear.

The slate-gray sky grows heavy
And dark clouds burst their seams
    Spilling frozen flakes
    On the icy lakes,
The forest hills, and streams.

The earth first pales, and then grows white
    As its blanket thickens and spreads.
The woodland prepares for the coming night,
    As the creatures go to their beds.

Listen, now, for noise in the winter wood
While the falling snow mutes the sound.
The woods seem silent, and eerily good,
    As the flakes fall soft on the ground.

— Raymond F. Rogers

THE GIFT

When I look at you—
I know there is a God.
He must have heard my prayers.
He sent me a gift—
I will cherish forever,
For that gift was you.
I prayed for someone—
To be my friend—
To help me along the way.
He must have heard me,
Because you entered my life,
And now it is no longer the same.
He made every part of you—
With love and extra care.
He blessed you with many talents:
Your musical ability
And beautiful personality.
That love and extra care
Now shines in you.
I can see it shining in your eyes
And in your smile.
You laughter, like the bells of heaven—
Keeps a smile on my face and in my heart.
I'll see you in heaven
And in my dreams.
You—
My wonderful gift from God.

— Edith Lynn Stark

I LOVE YOU!

Your cheerful face is so kind,
When I see you in my mind.
You made me see right from wrong,
And helped me when the winds were strong.
You were gentle with your loving hands,
Even with your many demands.
Now may the world be kind and fair,
And keep you from sadness and despair.
For there is one thing I must say to you,
It is that I love you.

—Tina Johansen

TO MY WIFE, MY LIFE

There is but one woman in my life,
that my dear is you, my wife.
So very wonderful is she,
no luckier could one man be.
She's always there when I need her,
so fast sometimes like a blur.
There are no words worthy of her ways,
I'm just glad I have her the rest of my days.
We've been through a lot,
we always get through.
One thing's for sure,
our love is very true.

—C. David Brannan

COME UP HIGHER

I've been walking by faith on life's highway,
Trusting Jesus to lead all the way.
When I heard Him say, "Come up higher,"
"Take my hand, we need you today."

Then so softly, gently, we went higher,
Holding my hand in His all the way.
Now we sing, Praise God allelujah,
Allelujah to Jesus our King.

Oh the beauty words cannot describe it,
Voices blending as praises we sing.
Allelujah, praise God, allelujah,
Allelujah to Jesus our King.

Come up higher, higher, we need you,
Come up higher, higher and sing.
Blend your voice with the heavenly choir,
Praise the Lord, our Savior and King.

—Jennie M. Florence

ONE LOST FRIEND

His great laugh and smile,
I really used to like his style.
His eyes sparkled like the morning dew,
They were big, bright, and blue.

His hair glittered like golden rays,
Like the little boy within looking for praise.
His only flaw as a teen,
Was the rip in his jeans.

Life has just begun,
When he turned 21.
Spending the night with friends,
Little did he know life was about to end.

As we said our final good-byes,
I remember the light shining in his eyes.
It was on a special day,
My mom told me that God had taken him away.

—Diane R. Stouwie

I walk where once we walked,
I stand where once we stood.
I hear your golden voice raised high in
song.
I'd come to you in swiftest flight, if
only that I could.
It seems just yesterday that your hand
reached out to me —
So strong, so loving, and so kind —
guiding always that I might clearly see.
The treasured years just seemed to fly.
My grieving heart is left to cry.
I hear your step, I feel your
touch.
Your being gave me purpose and
always filled my life.
I miss you my love — so very
much —

—Hazel Meilstrup

THE OLD ROCKING CHAIR

There's an old rocking chair that sits in the hall
Not much to look at, but what memories I recall

For I remember when it shared a favorite room
with the floor kept clean by an old straw broom

While grandma rocked the babies and sang a song
It seemed like nothing could ever be wrong

Yes, the old rocking chair is silent now
No one cares that it's useless anyhow

For the children are grown and gone,
but the old rocker still lingers on

What a tale it could tell of gone by days
when its vivid colors caught the sun rays

Folks would clamber to sit there first
for the old rocking chair rocked as if to burst

Yes, the rocking chair now is still
with chipped paint and sagging seat with no fill

That old rocking chair when it was new
gave happiness to more than just a few

Yes, that old rocking chair that sits in the hall
Will always have memories for me to recall

—Fay A. Behlmer

THE GIFT OF GOD

Jesus went to the top of the hill
There His precious blood he shed; He did not spill
I am so glad he did this for me
If He hadn't, Where in this dark world would I be?

His cross was so heavy
Not just the cross of wood
But the sins of the whole world
That's why He shed His precious blood.

I can see Him hanging there between two thieves
He had never done anything to deserve such grief
He did not do this only for me
But for everyone, If they will only believe,

But the key to it all is Love
Given from Our Heavenly Father above
Jesus said, "Father, forgive them
They know not what they do"
I am so thankful for this gift
That God gave for me and you.

—Loma Stanley

THE RHODODENDRONS BLOOM

Have you walked among the rhododendrons?
They grow in such a lofty place.
They're set in high mountain crowns
To lend their beauty and their grace.

The mountain before me looms,
But beauty and fragrance calls,
"Come where the rhododendron blooms;
Up the dancing stream above the falls."

Thank you, God, for such beauty.
Thank you for the rhododendron.
Give me the ability to do duty
To all the loveliness I've come on.

Exalted by the incense of these flowers;
It is on holy ground I've trod.
In pale pink blossom-bearing flowers,
I kneel at earth's high altar of God.

—Elizabeth Wilkinson-Anderson

A WALK THROUGH A DIFFERENT WORLD

I find myself in a different world,
Walking on a path of gold.
Flowers seem to wave at me,
Of this land I've never been told.

Trees seem to smile and say "hello",
And leaves fall to my feet.
The green grass bows at my presence
Like wind blowing through a prairie of wheat.

Then the gold path leads to a castle,
And there a princess am I.
Suddenly appears a gallant white horse
With a handsome prince sitting high.

I am then sitting on a beautiful black stallion
As I catch the kiss the prince threw me.
We race the dolphins by the shore,
They jump up and dive back to the sea.

As we finish and win the race,
I am suddenly in a heaven of clouds and then . . .
I wake up in bed, full of disappointment,
But anxious for the next night, so I can be in my
    secret world again.

—Renata Ostrowicki, Age 12

A VISION OF MY MOTHER

I must search inside my mind
Until in thoughts I do find
A vision so dear and sweet to me

A vision like no other
A vision of my mother
Who on Earth was precious as could be

I will vision her once more
The way she always was before
before Death did close her eyes so blue

She and I will like a song
Enjoy life the whole day long
Having fun just the way we used to do

She will take me by the hand
And say to me "I understand"
Then upon her face will be a loving smile

I will then in vision see
My loving mother pray for me
And ask God to join us together in awhile

—Randall Williams

MICHAEL IN MY DREAMS

Some nights now I'll dream of you.
This child I gave birth to, held,
And then slowly and lovingly let go,
Is now a figment of my nocturnal imagination.

You come to me at all ages.
This child I directed, told
When to come and when to go,
Comes to me randomly now, three nights running
And then to Michael for long and lonely months.

And if I say you come to me,
Where do you come from?
Do you whirl about in black forever until
You appear inside my head?
When I awake, do I cast you back into the
Unimaginable void?

Or are you still forever in your oak and brass box
Down the road,
And am I the loving voodoo mother,
Making you walk again in my mind out of
Sheer force of love?

—Frances Greis

KELLIE'S SONG

Enchanting smiles and infectious laughter,
    only a daughter could bring.
The lively art of this twelve year old,
    oh how she loved to sing.
Living life to its fullest with never a care,
    was truly a daily game.
With a spirit so free my heart always felt,
    that her life would be filled with fame.
But suddenly snatched from this world,
    so quickly taken away.
This mother's heart is shattered,
    dear Lord, "Why couldn't she stay?"
Pain and sorrow have filled the days,
    two years of unbelief.
But God has promised another land,
    no tears, no sadness, only my relief.
This world is truly the loser
    when it lost that piece of art,
But she is singing in that unknown land,
    straight to my heart.

My Love Eternally,
Mom

—Joannie Kemling

A FRIGHTENED ONE

I roam the halls and windows
    looking in but never touching
Loneliness sets its side.
    Always looking in but wondering
    why they won't let me touch.
    Why I ache inside for love and gentleness
Scared like a frightened child abandoned by
    its mother.
Scared for my future, looking in
    but never touching,
    Never knowing what it feels like
to be close to be understood to be
        loved.
Wondering why the God above gave such
    ugliness to me, why insults hurt
    me so.
Wondering why but never knowing
    never touching what's inside.

—Stacey M. Boyd

61

A BLACKENED SUN

In a blackened sun I hide,
A medley of feeling restrained inside,
And yet amidst so much emotion,
Sits a void vast as an ocean,
Within this peculiar destitude,
A forming gap, so small and crude,
The ocean water soaking through,
Just as slight as morning dew,
As pressure builds around this cleft,
Less and less time is left,
Around the trickle appears a glow,
A little beam begins to show,
Unconscious now, I'm expelled,
Through the hollow that has swelled,
Overcome by brilliancy,
Are opened eyes that cannot see,
The answers before me now unfold,
The many secrets must be told,
Concluded now the timeless phase,
The blackened sun is a blaze.

—**Michelle Young**

AMOS, THE BASS BASSET

When Amos barks, we rejoice
To hear his deep, deep voice.
Other dogs may bark and annoy,
But this basset's bark, we enjoy.

A basset basso profundo,
He likes to bark for fun--low,
And practice sounding mournful:
Long barks, lonesome; or short, scornful.

Amos likes to talk and talk
At home or on his walk.
He plainly enjoys company
With voice to accompany.

Now Amos is moving away
To practice his deep notes each day
For his masters, once our neighbors,
And new listeners at their labors.

Amos, for us:
  "Sound Mournful."

  —**Ruth A. Hall**

What goes round, comes round
So I have heard it said.
Be careful what you wish for,
for it may come your way.

Take care in daytime dreaming,
for gold soon turns to grey.
Hope is swiftly stolen,
Happiness decays.

Guard carefully your joys,
Kind thoughts hold tightly close.
For like a thief comes silently,
so sadness does approach.

Give thanks for times of life and love,
Give thanks for times of peace,
Never take for granted,
a moment's worth of these.

They pass too quickly, fade too fast,
To ever waste a second.
The cold black pall of quiet death
Too soon draws up its coach and beckons.

  —**L.A. Jacob**

UNCONDITIONAL LOVE

What is unconditional love, you may ask.
Well, it's a love that's an almost impossible task.
Yet it's the way God loves all of us,
And He never complains or makes a fuss.
It's not hateful, jealous, vain, or cruel;
It's forgiving and refreshing like a sparkling pool.
For God loves us no matter what we say or do;
He sees the heart and looks inside at the real you.
Yes, we're all loved with an unconditional love.
We just have to accept it and realize it comes from the
Father above!

  —**Christine Sealock**

TAKE TIME

I intended today to write to a friend
Just to say I've had you on my mind.
But the house needed cleaning, the wash needed tending
And I just couldn't find the time.
Now the house is spotless, the clothes are clean
And everyone's shoes I have shined.
The days flew by, even weeks have passed
But today I will take the time.
So I called my friend only to learn
My precious dear loved one had died.
Then I realized I had missed the opportunity
To set a misunderstanding aright.
So now I shed bitter tears of regret
For words I could have spoken soft and kind.
Words I wanted to say to my friend
If only I had taken the time.

  —**Judy (Bell) Beasley**

WHERE'S YESTERDAY

Who would ever think that life would be this way,
So bold, so cold and that people would be so cruel,
We were taught to go by the golden rule and
        everything would go so smooth,

        WHERE'S YESTERDAY?

When a friend was a friend and stuck by you 'til
        the end,
No matter how much trouble you were in,
Now it's just a matter of speech, no longer do
        parents teach,

        WHERE'S YESTERDAY?

What ever happened to trust and belief?
It seems as if we're surrounded with sorrow and
        grief,
Jealousy plays its role from enviousness to
        heartless thief,

        WHERE'S YESTERDAY?

Has man lost his soul? Has woman forsaken the
        family mold?
What else will this world unfold?

        WHERE'S YESTERDAY?

When will the hand that fed me when I couldn't
        myself
Start nourishing the mind and bodies back to health?
And I long for the day when extending hand will once
        again
Mean good instead of evil to his fellow man,

        WHERE'S YESTERDAY?
        HAVE YOU GONE AWAY TO STAY?

  — **Windell Jones**

THE GIFT OF LOVE

It was the sparkle in the eye, the tremor from the touch
The glory of attainment that I loved so much.
The matches, rubbed together, caused the fatal fire
That burned at the hearts and couldn't expire.
I know I felt the heat before I saw the flame
I know I saw the burns before I placed the blame.
And yet here I lie in this bed full of ashes
With memories of the fire and pain from the gashes.
Knowing what might become of me I took my chance—
The fire and brimstone lust of planned circumstance.
I could see him in the fire basking in the heat
Bronzing his body to the rhythm of my defeat.
Bringing fire to my world with gentle trace
He was like a Titan god with all the mythic grace.
Knowing he singed me with the deepest passion
I felt only love in the most awkward fashion.
So here I await him in this tearful mire
Longing for Prometheus to bring me more fire.

      —Diane Kirsh

THE IRIS

This violet, sweet-smelling flower
  has always been my favorite.

    One glimpse of it—my own little sign
that winter is truly over and summer will
soon warm my soul.

    But . . . there is a sad mystery in this
flower. Its life, though filled with
incredible beauty, is short; It blooms and
is gone.

    It's hard to believe that this single
flower can fill me with such happiness
and leave me with such pain.

    But I go on . . .
and fill the long winter months with sweet
memories of my flower and know that when the
time is right, I will be blessed by its beauty
once again.

    —Lia Maree Bauer

REMEMBER THE HAPPY MOMENTS

Remember the happy moments.
  Remember the endless days.
Remember the times I have said
unto you I love you in many ways.

Remember a carefree evening.
Remember a song to sing.
Remember a break from sadness
alone when we have nothing to bring.

The life we live might seem
confusing at times.
The times we live might bring
on a new life, a new life.

The clouds float so gently,
among the shining stars.
The rain comes down
to the fields of the earth with its many charming charms.

The good seeds are our children
which grows from this love.
A flower of beauty sweetly
saying you are my beloved.

Remember the happy moments.
Remember the happy moments.

    —Gregory Kent Haynes

MID-WAY LOVE

I have so many things to tell you,
  So many things to share.
But I met you mid-way through my life,
And I don't know if there's time to spare.

For you have your old memories,
And I have mine as well.
We both know that it takes a lot
To really truly care.

To find and start a new love
Takes a lot of thought.
For you and I both know
A true love can't be bought.

I'll take that chance if you will,
And follow it on the wind.
For it's you and you alone, Bill
That I'll love till the very end!

    —Ms. Cary Deborn

SMILES ARE FOR FREE

It's easy to laugh and be pleasant,
  When life moves smoothly along.
But the man worthwhile,
Is the one with a smile.
When things are going wrong

By this I don't mean you should always,
Have a big silly grin on your face.
But a cheery word,
For your fellow man.
Can help someone who's losing life's race.

This crazy old planet we live on,
Just keeps spinning and whirling away.
You may be burdened with woe,
Cares and troubles, I know.
But remember, "Each dog has his day"

A philosopher I know I never can be,
For that's not my bag, or my style
But there's one thing I'll say,
As you live day by day.
It doesn't cost any money to smile.

    —George "Buddy" Filbert

TO MYSELF

Summer nights and quiet sighs
  Star light sparkles in my eyes
Moonbeams float upon my hair
And dance like pixies in the air!

Sunny days and gentle kisses
There is nothing my heart misses
I skip a stone on clear blue lakes
And watch the beauty that it makes

I sing the world a song of love
My soul is like a snow white dove
I open up my picket fence
For I am like the Little Prince

I'll never be left on a shelf
This is a poem to myself
I live on childhood memories
And whisper through the tall pine trees

I dwell within an antique world
Where sleepy kittens snuggle curled
A glassy pitcher keeps me whole
Filled with water of my soul!

    —Kendra Kay Springer

QUESTIONS

So many colors in the world today.
Black and white, or are they grey?
Look, the leaves on trees are so lovely
Put on earth by God for all to see,
Yet the questions of why they change
Is none-the-less quite strange.
When questions are left unknown
For people to meditate upon,
Then the colors of black and white
Will become shadows in the night
Making everything grey is all we see
But not an answer to our plea.
The questions answered in black and white
Separate the path between wrong and right,
And for the answers colored in grey
Are questions with answers gone astray.

—Theresa Worst

GOD KNOWS BEST

This world is full of trouble.
There is sorrow on every hand.
With hills to climb and rivers to cross,
In life's short earthly span.

There are some things that I've observed,
As I've walked this troublesome way.
After each bleak and trying hour,
There comes a brighter day.

For every sorrow there is a joy.
The sunshine follows the rain.
For every frown there is a smile.
In every loss I find some gain.

When I've crossed the turbulent river,
I see a beautiful shore.
After the storms have been raging,
I enjoy the sunshine much more.

When I weigh each situation,
I know that I'm perfectly blest.
Even though I might not see it right then,
Our loving God always knows best.

—Billie C. Burkett

THE HEART OF GOD

Who can tell me of the heart of God?
Who can know its response
            to pain

Who can touch its tenderness
        and claim its healing

Who can wrestle with sin's power
        and disappointment

and be forgiven
    washed clean
            by the washing
that comes straightway from
        the heart of God

Who can know the compassion
        of the heart of God

Who turns his own heart
    his own feet
            his own senses away
                from the heart of God?

Who?

—Isobel Ina Stein

MY INSPIRATION

Lord, You give me inspiration,
When to write a line or two,
A chirping bird, a gentle breeze,
As they give their praise to You.

The sun that rises in early morn
And warms the cool night air,
The quietness that You give your own
When they seek your face in prayer.

A peach tree laden in full spring bloom
The young tender grass so green,
Purple violets scattered about,
A good place to lie and dream.

But, Lord, of all the things your hands have done,
That inspire me most to write,
Was when You brought me out of darkness
Into your marvelous light!

—Brenda S. Jennings Fritts

BECAUSE

If Jesus knocked on your door
Would you make Him wait outside?
Because you weren't expecting Him
So there were things you had to hide.
        If Jesus called you on the phone
        Would you have to say "hold on?"
        Because your friends were much too loud
        At the party that was going on.
If Jesus would jump in your car
Would you feel your life's in danger?
Because you wouldn't read His word
So to you, He was a stranger
        If Jesus was to end this world
        Would you feel your heart get heavy?
        Because you weren't expecting Him
        Or because you just weren't ready
Would you know God if He'd come today?
And if you'd fail to pause
Would you ask Him why He passed you by
And would He have to say "Because."

—Shirley E. Hamilton

MY MORNING PRAYER

Lord, oh Lord, my Lord I pray,
Guide my feet as they travel through this day.
Let me not stumble, let me not fall.
Open my ears to your guiding call.
Lord, oh Lord, my Lord I pray,
Take the hurt from words I might say.
Let me speak with a gentle tongue.
Let me ask forgiveness for wrong I have done.
Hold these hands, give them the strength they need.
With your help oh Lord, they're sure to succeed.
Let their work be honest, holding onto what is good.
Let them not hurt a brother, but help as they should.
Let these eyes not accuse, ridicule, or condemn.
Let them shine with love, understanding, and compassion
From within.
It is said the eyes are the mirror of the soul.
Reflecting the image of all I should be, is my aim,
Is my goal.
Lord, oh Lord, my Lord I pray,
Help me with these requests all through the day.
Let this heart beat with undying love.
Let me be worthy of my home waiting above.
Lord, oh Lord, help me to pray.

—Carol Chamberlain

". . . dreams."

Age dreams of youth, and faraway lands,
of clear, twinkling eyes, and smooth, supple hands.
Age dreams of pastures, and running with the breeze,
gazing up at summer stars, and climbing into trees.

Youth dreams of age, of wisdom, and of truth,
of children, and of family; these seek the youth.
Youth dreams of country, of fighting, and of war,
or sitting on a barstool, "Bartender, one more."

Age dreams of youth, of romping with old Shep,
and having milk and cookies on Grandma's backdoor step.
Age dreams of youth with tear abrim its eye,
"If only to be young again, I know that I could fly."

Youth dreams of age, of making its great mark,
of writing some great novel, or teaching frogs to talk.
Youth dreams of age, impatient, needing more.
The dreams youth seeks are very close,
they're just beyond the door.

—Barry K. Dalton

(AN UNFINISHED POEM)

once i heard a nightingale sing sweetly
while the earth was unresponsive and covered
with the gloomy veil of night

its songs echoed throughout the darkened silence,
lashing against objects, only to be absorbed
and unnoticed

again and again songs of love and loneliness are
performed to an audience of none as this bird
remains calm and unconcerned of its undiscovered talent

i sit astonished by the beauty of each note
while these tunes fill the spaces in my
heart that were once open to suggestions

feelings nourished, refreshed, and somewhat sorrowful,
i take it upon myself to walk steadfastly
in the opposite direction, leaving the nightingale
alone to bare the burden of being neglected

as the sun paints light upon the morning sky
the nightingale vanishes . . .

—reneigh roberts

OUR HEAVENLY EARTH

Trees that loom into the sky;
Blades of grass caressing the earth;
Clouds billowing within the blue;
It must all have some heavenly worth!

An elephant with trunk at work;
A stalking feline upon its prey;
The birds cooing their morning song;
They must be in some heavenly play!

The wind blows gently upon my face;
Yet, destruction can be left in its wake;
Oceans of water surround our lands;
Must be for some heavenly sake!

The planet rotates around the sun;
Stars twinkle in the dark of night;
People live and people die;
Must all be for heavenly might!

Life exists in many forms;
I look about and see so much;
Yes, our world is still a wonder;
It must be that heavenly touch!

—Dee Dee McCoy

A MEMORY

When I was just a little girl
I loved my world so much.
Everything was beautiful —
Kittens, butterflies and such.

When my mother sent me to the store,
"Now, hurry — we need bread," she'd say.
But I had to stop beside the pond
To watch the tadpoles play.

Had to stop to hear the music
Of the red-winged black birds' chorus.
Had to watch the muskrats swimming.
All the things God made for us.

Many years have now flown by —
I must think of other things instead,
But today I wish I could go back
And fetch mama's loaf of bread.

—Carrie L. Swires

HOMEWARD BOUND.

The filled planes,
    The crowded trains;
The lonely pack horse
    On the plain,
Going home for Christmas.

Gayly wrapped bundles,
    Snow tugging at your heels;
Children all bundled,
    Music ringing in their ears;
Going home for Christmas.

Beautiful tree splendor,
    Porch lights brightly shine;
Mistletoe lonely hanging,
    Waiting for lips sublime;
Going home for Christmas.

Hello Mother, hello Father!
    Sister and brother too.
Neighbors and friends
    All gathered together,
Home for Christmas again.

—John Wodzanowski, Jr.

TO FLY

When Life's swift flow makes rest elude
And hectic times rush by,
I often think how great it is,
    How marvelous to fly.

To fly and view the earth's great realms
    above the strife and toil
Of millions who take little note
    of nature's ways they spoil.

To fly and see the silent world
    from miles above the ground,
To gaze in awe and humbleness
    At wonders that abound.

When I grow old and life becomes
    a pensive memory,
And days are filled with lots of time
    to ponder endlessly,

I'll think of times above the clouds
    When slipping through the winds,
I viewed the earth from far above
    Where beauty never ends.

—Harold A. Cross

LOST LOVE

In remembrance of days long past—
I think of a love that did not last,
A love as pure as the fallen snow—
With the dearest one I'll ever know.

Fun filled days so wild and free—
Moon-lit nights by the shining sea,
Memories linger of the love we once knew—
The happy days were all too few.

Now that our love has faded and gone—
I sit here and grieve all alone,
I think of our love and a long ago past,
We never dreamed it would not last.

New love comes and old love goes,
We can't fore-tell the future — only God knows,
As years roll on and heartache mends—
We can't be sweethearts "But let's be friends."

—Dee Mays

UNTOUCHABLE LOVE

Am I but an object displayed for you?
You must think I have no feelings at all
The way you treat me, if only you knew

The pain I feel over what you do
You grow so big while you keep me so small
Am I but an object displayed for you?

I do not have the courage to leave soon
I am trapped in an unbreakable wall
The way you treat me, if only you knew.

I want to go and start my life anew
Taking the first step is hardest of all
Am I but an object displayed for you?

You cannot just paste my heart back with glue
As if it were a broken China doll
The way you treat me, if only you knew.

Someday you will ask where I have gone to
Until then, I am at your beck and call
Am I but an object displayed for you?
The way you treat me, if only you knew.

—Jeneé Klemin

I'VE LEARNED

I've learned some things in life,
that a woman shouldn't have to learn.
I've felt love light as feathers,
and I've felt love ache and burn.

I've had endless nights of dreaming,
about a memory from long ago.
About a love that I once felt,
and a man I used to know.

I've been taught about true laughter.
And I've also learned how to cry.
I've found it inside myself to survive,
and how to accept goodbye.

I've learned to find the hope,
that I've needed when I was alone.
And learned how to stand up strong and tall,
when the ones I've loved had gone.

I've learned some things in life,
that a woman shouldn't have to learn.
I've felt love light as feathers,
and I've felt love ache and burn.

—Melissa A. Knight

LOVE, A SPIRITUAL MATTER

Someday I'll find you
And when I do,
This poem is for you.

Love in the waters of the world,
Peace in the silent night of forests,
On the road to the recovery,
Of shattered dreams and illusions of my love.

My heart, in a brilliant array
Of soft colors and sunsets,
Of truth and the search for dreams.
I know if I dream you're there, my dream is real.

My spirit flies so high above,
Thinking of my obscurities in life,
And realizing that the strengths of
My deepest hopes and dreams, are within myself.

—Janet Lee Charlton

SIGHTLESS, NOT BLIND

I love you dear, I really do
I would do anything for you
I know you can't see far through your eyes
But you have insight beyond the skies
I found out in the first few days
That you were special in many ways
I don't want you to feel alone
Even after you're on your own
As time goes by you cry on my shoulder
That shouldn't change because you get older
It doesn't matter what you can see
It's what's inside that matters to me
Nothing matters that the mean people say
Just overlook them and go on your way
I'll always be somewhere close by
Don't be afraid, give it a try
People like you are hard to find
You're the honest and thoughtful kind
Sight's not important when you have a clean heart
I knew you were special from the start

—Deborah Hannah

STRANGER OF LOVE

As I sit in the dark with nothing to spare
I can feel the heat and weight of your stare

I don't know whether to look around or just sit
I think that if I saw your face I'd know it

I think I'll leave not knowing what to do
I'll walk out of here feeling real blue

The sidewalk was just so cold and bare
I did things with you I didn't think I dare

Then all of a sudden there you were in your car
I couldn't move I felt like I was bottled up in a jar

You told me to get in and we'd go for a drive
After I got out I couldn't believe I was still alive

I went up the stairs and into my room
I felt like I was at my end and to my doom

I was looking around then the phone rang
I don't think that to this day I'll ever
forget the song you sang

So till the day that we first
met I was a stranger of
love

—Kiersten McNealy

OH, TO BE A BOY AGAIN

I'd like to be a boy again
And visit kith and kin,
To scuff my shins and brag of chin
With fuzz—a boy again.

I'd like to climb tall trees back where
The street lights never reached,
To jump and swing and loudly blare
My freedom there unleased.

I'd give a mint to dig that time,
a bygone year so dear:
The replay's lost, its cast once prime,
But recall's loud and clear.

Such thought ignites a steadfast gleam
Of sentimental yearning,
Which opens up a memory stream:
A boyhood crave still burning.

—Robert H. Hood

TODAY I WATCHED

Today I watched a boxing match, I wonder why
for a gladiator almost lost his eye.
I wasn't happy at what I saw,
my only thought —there ought to be a law.

Once was 24 — the other legs of 32
superficially asking what can I do?
Knowing what the result really would be
T'was only to satisfy a bloody curiosity.

From Olympians past we and the early Greeks
have responded to applause and publican shrieks
In the mistake of creating a healthy condition
of fierce, yet, friendly competition.

So, I watched and contributed to a state
from which only the minority can retaliate.
TODAY I WATCHED and did nothing about
the slaughter of my brother in a 12-round bout.

—Nick Chames

THE LOST DREAM

I remember that hot, sunny day he rode into town.
That was Mike on his Harley bike.

He stopped at the drug store and lit a fag,
And then told us all, "This town is a drag!"

Everyone's eyes were on old Mike,
As he started up the road with a big, wide grin.

This was the day I had to put Mike down.
Then I would be the talk of the town.

We met in a field with everyone there.
All wondering who would be more fierce than a bear.

I started my bike and gave it a rev,
And it sounded better than my '57 Chev.

The gun went off and we were into the turn,
Side by side, as the tires just burned.

Mike had the best of me the rest of the way,
And I never thought I'd live to see down this day.

The race was over. Mike won it fair and square.
He said, "Thanks alot," and pushed aside his long hair.

He left the town with the roar of his bike.
Some day I'll show up that good, old Mike.

—Jeffery C. Stefely

TIME-OUT

I've seen fields of green that have
gone on and into forever
Hey, I'm just like you, I've said
things that no one will remember
But when the end has met us, and
the stones been set afast
We'll all want to come running
back, and hope our number comes
up last . . .
For all we could have been, and
all we could have seen
For the good, for the bad, and some-
thing we call dreams
We've accepted time as a friend
and we never question why
For it's as much a thief of forgotten
dreams, don't let it pass you by

—Deborah A. Schalamon

LITTLE LEAGUE WINNERS

The ump called batter up
and Jeff steps to the plate.
He swung at two fast ones
and then he struck too late.

A big lad of about 5 feet
stepped up and eyed the ball.
He hit the very first one
right over left field wall.

It's the 9th inning, the game is tied at four.
Jeff's turn at bat once more.
We have a chance to beat them
If only he could score.

Jeff struck at two bad ones
and the next, a ball went through.
Then the 3rd one came to the plate
It sailed off into the blue.

Jeff had finally hit a homerun
His team would surely win.
Now the game is over
But Jeff wants to bat again!

—Ruth G. Chipman

THE OLD DRAGON

I was a dragon in a former life,
I knew no wrong, I ruled the night.
I had a mate, you would say a wife,
And whatever I did, it was always right.

Then age crept upon my wings,
My fire grew cold,
I felt the aches that time brings.
An old dragon, no longer bold.

No glory stalked my ever deed,
No fear, or trembling men now.
I became no more than a loathsome weed,
As feared as an aged cow.

My memory sung of glory spent,
Of times of youthful joy.
Now of my past there is no hint,
I am but a fable, a child's toy.

My dreams were dead,
My time was o're.
I went to bed,
And awoke on a golden shore.

—Ronald E. Taylor

WISHING SHE KNEW

Remembering the look in her eyes again,
Wishing that she knew.
That he loved her very much
And hoped she loved him too

Taking the ring from his pocket
And putting it in her hand.
Smiling back at the memories
Which he could barely stand.

Hoping she was thinking about him
And the memories they had shared
Praying to God above
That she knew he really cared.

A hand on his shoulder
As he silently looked away.
They soon would be together
Again some other day.

Wondering if she loved him
Wondering if she knows
Watching her pale young face.
As the casket was closed.

—Jennifer Sue Haskins, Age 15

ABORTION

We wonder at the beauty of
the rose bud in the Spring.
We thank the Lord for sharing
with us such a lovely thing.
But even as we lift our face
to catch the fragrance in the air,
our hand reaches out and takes a
bud to place within our hair.

Just as that bud in its first
splendor soon begins to die,
within my heart of heart's I have
to ask the question — WHY?
As that tiny bud plucked from
the bush is not allowed to bloom,
we pluck God's very own life bud
right from the mother's womb.

—Linda M. McClure

WHAT HAS LIFE BECOME?

The child is a wonderful work of art
With all he is able to do,
For he can search deep into your heart
And make you feel all new.

As you gaze into the sun-bright day,
Things will all seem to come to life,
For in the yards, the child will play
Until the day turns into night.

As the child enters the star-lit night,
Many can hear him release a great sigh,
For in his dreams, there is the fright
That there will be no more beautiful sky.

Man has made the child's life pure torture,
Like that of a soul lost in Hell,
For all the wars we have fought
Make the tears in his eyes swell.

The child is scared of the next day,
Now that it may never come,
For it is not quite easy to say
Exactly what life has become.

—Jason Monk, Age 17

ANSWER THE CALL

Let me live beside a mountain stream
where the spirit of man is free.
Let me sit beneath the whispering pine tree
and harken to the adventurer's dream.
Let me wander through a valley of green grasses
mid the daisies and violets sweet.
Let me listen to the meadow lark and answer the call,
to sit at nature's feet.

May I be blessed with vision to see
all the beauty there to be found.
Let me hear the hum of the honey bee,
and mentally record every sound.
Let me smell the fragrance of green growing heather,
of daffodils yellow and tall.
Let me heed the cry of fin, leaf, or feather.
And give me strength Lord
To answer the call.

—Helen Childs Johnson

DEATH KNOCKS

But give me just one more minute please,
Oh great Creator above, 'tis all that I ask,
The breath of life, like daylight it flees,
Black is death when you finally see his mask,
It troubles and pains me so to find,
Death knocks now and his face seems pale,
Pale before, but after the act not so unkind,
As to itself be blind as to whom to choose,
For a many splendored and permanent, dreamless snooze.
Why does death seem so cold so as to equate with black?
Maybe because 'tis a one way journey, fare paid full.
Once he knocks and steals away, there's no way back.
Many try to 'scape the unescapable grasp so tight,
They swear they'll not go without a fight,
The end of their life so grim to be,
Like the end of this poem that doesn't seem right.
Why not just accept it with joy and ask to be free?
Ask the One above to come into your heart and,
Free you will be, by the grace of His hand.

—Mike Jenkins

ABORTION

A warm feeling holds me tight;
I'm not blind, but I see no light.
I can't wait until the darkness is gone;
I'm anxious to see how life goes on!

I'm already attached to my soft home;
Yet, I feel isolated and alone.
I can't wait until I get out;
I'm anxious to see what life is about!

Even though I'm not much bigger than a dime;
I seem to be getting bigger all the time.
I can't wait until I've grown all the way;
I'm anxious to see life day by day!

Warmth from Mother and Father is what I feel,
I often wonder if this feeling is real.
I can't wait until I'm finally set free;
I'm anxious to see how life with Mother and
Father will be!

I shiver with fear for a coldness clutches my heart;
Silently falls a tear for something is pulling me apart.
I know now I'm taking my last breath.
I know now I won't see life but . . . . . death.

—Nicole "Nikki" Avera

THE BRIGHTEST STAR

One night you turned and looked at me
And asked about the stars
You said you like to look at them
And dream of where they are
You told me of this far off place
And how you'd love to go
To see the stars that shine so bright
And leave the earth below
I do not have a rocket ship
You know I cannot fly
But if I could, I'd find a way
To them stars in the sky
And take you there along with me
And make your dreams come true
Cause I would give the brightest star
To prove my love for you

—Alli

WHAT IS GOD?

What is God? I asked a child
"A perfect angel," my mother said.
Like Satan? my eyes searched her for truth
"Of course not, dear, now go to bed."
But what is God? I laid my head down
That I might die before I wake?

I know what God is, though it's hard to explain
He's not woman nor man, or shaped like an airplane.
Just infinite, perfect, without shape or form
That something that can be wherever it wants
In my earthly space or an unknown beyond
Seeing peace and great love, the only bond
Weaving its plume between there to here
For woman, for man, and small child like me.

Satan had God with him once on a time
In a world without death or a finite rhyme
But he took what he had and destroyed it with glee
Leaving all on the earth, including me
Confused about why I am and might be
But certain as Hell there's more than body.

—Carol Ann Lindsay

GOD LOVES AMERICA

Good morning America, how are you today. America
I love you, in so many ways.
I am so glad I live here, in this special place, where
the freedom for all, no matter what race.
America, you are the greatest place to live, in all the
land and you have truly been touched by God's loving
hand.
Yes, God has blessed you America. In so many ways and
Oh! how beautiful you are, as out the window I
gaze.
No place on this earth, can a person feel so
safe, as our beautiful America, kept in God's grace
I'm glad I live here, in God's favorite land and that
He holds us always, in his protective loving hand.
America you have always known God and his
love and that He watches over us from Heaven
above.
So when I say I love you America, It comes
from my heart and I know from God's love and
grace America must never depart.
This is why as Americans, God's people must
stand tall, because without God's love and
grace, there would be no America at all.

—Betty Hamar

Three words make the world go round
Through my heart delight is wound
A feeling that warms your heart
From these words we pray never part

I love you.

With her hand in mine we are one
Across the fields of life we run
Her sweet lips rest upon my face
Undying love makes my heart race

I love you.

This sensation words alone cannot express
Now I know, it is a true love I confess
An eternity of enchanting bliss
Love for one another we will never miss

I love you.

—John Wyzkiewicz

EVERY SUMMER'S LOVE AFFAIR

When I script sunshine in your heart
Though winter scenes are clearly there
I close my eyes and see the art . . .

Chaste will-less snow drifts alacarte
Then I feel like a millionaire
When I script sunshine in your heart.

Life's sweet perfume becomes a part
Of every summer's love affair;
I close my eyes and see the art . . .

Then suddenly a dove will dart
And lift its head in balmy air
When I script sunshine in your heart.

Strong stinging wind makes young flesh smart
As we stroll on our love to share;
I close my eyes and see the art . . .

In fantasy my lips impart
The rapture which lays this heart bare
When I script sunshine in your heart;
I close my eyes and see the art!

—Jessie L. Green

THE LIGHT, THE WORD, THE ONLY WAY

He is the light for us to seek,
Spread the word, it is to keep;
Follow Him, for He is the only way,
Read the Bible at least once a day.

Shine the light for others to follow,
Teach the word for others to learn;
Lead the way, make it not shallow,
Let your faith be not hollow.

Study the books, they'll give you light.
Learn the Word of God, it'll make you bright;
His blood was shed to cleanse away,
All our sins we have today.

The Priest, the Deacons, and Friends too,
Will teach the word through and through;
If you wonder or get lost,
Just remember the Lord gave what it cost.

The Light was bright that shone on the Lord,
Then came the Bible, the truly gospel word;
He was born to die for us this day,
He is the Light, the word, the only way.

—Jamie D. Ostland

DREAMS

Dreams are what keep people going,
  without dreams where would we be?
Dreams are what make things happen,
keep on dreaming, you'll see.
People who have no dreams have nothing,
you must have dreams to succeed.
For I have found that having dreams,
encourages what kind of life you'll lead.
Dreams of Michael Jordan fill my head,
inspiring me to be great.
Those who don't dream just sit and wait,
until it is too late.
You can do anything you put your mind to,
no matter how hard it seems.
Isn't that what it's all about, DREAMS?

—Niki Hulsey, age 14

RELEASE ME

See me,—
  For all I see is you:—
  The girl I always dreamed of,
  the girl I never knew.

Ease me,—
  And let me do the same.
  Tell me how you came to be,
  and let me know your name.

Touch me,—
  Release me from my fear.
  Tell me all you've ever known,
  and all you hold so dear.

And love me,—
  For all I do is cry.
  All I do is walk through life,
  and wonder when I'll die.

Then leave me,—
  My soul you can't redeem.
  I'll sit with you alone at night,
  but all I'll do is dream.

—William Dusty

FEELINGS

You have many ways to show,
  how you feel or what you know.

It may be a glance or smile,
  or a tear shed over many-a-mile.
You show a feeling,
  over most anything.
It can be over the loss of someone who,
  you cared about or really knew.
Or someone you want to spend the rest of
your life with,
  be it mystery, romance, or even myth.

You can send a card to show you care,
  wink your eye or toss your hair.
When someone you care about moves away,
  you miss them more everyday.
You show how you feel in the tone of your
voice,
  or words you may use by choice.
You can feel different everyday,
  but you show it in your own special way.
Just always try to remember,
  be your best January thru December.

—Judy Watson

LOVE DISTRAUGHT

Dusty shadows in the attic of my mind.
  Echoes of laughter leading the blind.
  All the patterns of withered leaves fallen.
The heart ache of love once they have gone.
  To such woe does the magic flame die.
  Leaving you lonely in the dark to cry.
  Mist of morning dew still left on the lawn.
  Birds with happy praise singing their song.
  Sunlight shining through your window shade.
  What happened to the life you hath made?
  Now in your soul the sun becomes clouds.
  The birds have forgotten all beautiful sounds.
And that mist of dew no longer lingers in the morning.
    HE SAID GOOD-BYE

—Renae L. Swanson

MY DEAREST LOVE . . .

. . . I write this with love
    I write this with care
I want you to know
I cherish all the Love — we do share

At times I seem so down
Then you come to me —
And turn my frown — around.
You look at me with great concern
And from the hard times — I've learned . . .

. . . Life is said to be precious
And I guess this is true,
but life itself, is not —
As precious as you!

While reading this, my love
I hope it touches you inside
For; my love for you
I don't want to hide!

Sealed with a kiss, And lots of love
To me — you're a prayer, answered from up-above

—Susie Steffey

BRANDED

Never a foot taken
  from the vague inch you gave;
Never was my soul so shaken
by every brief move you paved;
Paved, paved through the countless thoughts
of naive faith or mere wasted time—
The realism lies within the quest
    which is the sole tangible concept
    of our existence
Where thereupon you sought the flesh,
    yet I, I sought the bone
The very framework from which
    I had made such dreams upon which
    to build and create;
Yet most humanly to discover my true and
    intended nature—
And now that my search is nearly through
And I stand to peer my ascension
    of each educated step;
I have indeed found the basis
for this outpouring of emotion

In that, after all the mental violence
    you have instigated
I must succumb with the knowledge
    that I have once loved you.

—Alma Villacorta

70

PEACE

I wait, huddled in despair,
for someone to help me take away my cares.
A day seems like a moment, a moment like a year,
my laughter turns to sadness, my courage into fear.
Then, like a whisper, softly flowing to my heart,
He fills me with His Spirit and Peace that won't depart.
No longer to be burdened by endless cares of woe,
I'll wait upon the Lord, His blessings do I know,
A Peace to last forever, His promises ever true.
This life will bring some heartache,
His Peace will see me through.

—Darlene S. Noone

LIFE IS

Life is beautiful.
Like a flower it grows, it buds, it blooms
and it delights the eye.
Protect it.

Life is fragile
like delicate porcelain.
Handle it carefully
Lest it be broken.
Guard it.

Life is like a candle.
It is lighted.
It glows brightly for a time
then suddenly it is snuffed out.
Cherish it.

Life is precious —
a God given gift.
Protect it, Guard it, Cherish it,
Enjoy it.

Life is love —
Don't abuse it.

—Netta Miller

WHEN A CHILD TAKES WINGS

When a child takes wings and joins the Saints in the air
a child whoops and hollers, rolling among the clouds,
sweetly soaring to God on high.

A child takes wings painfree and restored, a child of
God's forever more. Floating, flying, and running pure
fun adventure in the air.

Our God, our Savior stands by smiling; angels of mirth
and angels of gaiety flow around the heavens, welcoming
this child who just took wings.

When a child takes wings, and joins the sweetness of
Jesus in the air, how they laugh, play, and delight
Jesus' heart, no memories of pain, no memories of
illness, a child just happily playing with the angels
and all the children in heaven.

When a child takes wings and joins the Holy of Holies,
he flies where he will, for no danger is there. Paul
and Moses run and play too, uniting the children for a
game or two. For when a child takes wings in heaven,
all heaven welcomes him there.

Matthew, Mark, and John play catch and volleyball with
a child on wing. Heaven welcomes them there and the
Holy God of the universe enjoys it all. For all give
pleasure to each other in heaven. Especially the child
who takes wings and soars over and above it all, straight
to the arms of God.

—Sonja Ruth Hunt

THE PINES

Through a chill November sunset
Snowflakes skittering sharp as wines
Stirring disconted murmurs
To wild screaming — for the pines,
Quick to sense erratic changes
Long before we ever know,
Have for hours sped the message
Of the coming of the snow.

How serene the stately pine trees
When the day is bright and fair,
Dark and gloomy we all call them
As their stewardship they bear.
Somber spires gird the northland
Blasted by its ice and snow
And least people shelter safely —
Forewarned by God's radio.

—Bess Barnum Halvorson

Break me down slowly Jesus,
My head's against the wall
feel the pain inside
As I take another fall
I know what you're doing now
And it ain't no crime
Break me down slowly Jesus,
My head's against the wall
One wish to be on the outside
One move to be in
I ain't seen one that could hold me now
Once the fire begins
Break me down slowly Jesus
My head's against the wall
Something started turning
But it ain't your fault
I've done all I could do
Only you know the cause
Break me down slowly Jesus
My head's against the wall

—Media Lynn Johnson

THE UPPER ROOM

There's a time in "all" our lives
to leave the ones we love

Adjust ourselves to our new room
with God who's up above

We never know when the time will come
the time of leaving here

Yet when it does, we can all be sure
of being with someone dear

We're all afraid of what's in store
for death's a natural fear

The upper room, you understand
is heaven up above

Where church bells ring and angels sing
and you greet the ones you love

There's nothing there for us to fear
for fear's a dreadful thing

So close your eyes and realize
that God will take you through

Those golden gates, that we all wait
till the day when we walk through

—jean gilliam

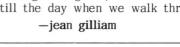

LOOKING UP

Oh, little bird sitting on the tree
Why did God make you to be so free?
Bouncing on the branch, singing a song,
Stay for a moment or stay so long.
I like to watch you do as you please,
Fly when it's calm or ride with a breeze.
Run from the noise or away from a fire,
It is you little bird that I most admire.
Come again, so I can enjoy you.
It cheers my heart whenever I'm blue.
Come again, soar through the sky,
Lifting my spirits again I'll ask why?
You can fly so far and never tire,
Yes, it's you little bird that I most admire.

—Patricia Anne Jackson

GOOD-BYE AND HELLO

It's not easy to say good-bye to the past
    and sail off towards an unknown fate.
Once you've gone, you can't go back
    the need to return comes too late.

Twenty years of being away from it all
    strange feelings of expectations not met.
Missing out on the fun of those years gone by
    yet, life's adventures are recalled, no regret.

Desires and encounters alter the soul
    no one remains quite the same.
Old friends disappear, as I did long ago,
    it's sad, going home, feeling to blame.

The rush of seasons, one to another
    turned youth to a memory remote.
Remember and forget, old times good and bad
    and look to the future on a good note.

Life events go forward, yesterday is lost
    keep memories, but live on with the quest.
A final good-bye to the irretrievable past
    a welcome hello to what's next.

—Elizabeth A. Mitchell

BEAUTIFUL BIRD

O'beautiful bird with broken wing
Unable to fly, too weak to sing

Tethered to the ground below
Cannot soar, cannot grow

Flailing midst the bush and seed
Searches sanctuary, seeking seed

Head tucked safely 'neath her wing
Protecting bird, who cannot sing

Nature stirs with morning light
Bird emerges, with lessened fright

Once again doth try her best
Against the odds of Nature's test

Little heart, thumping fast
Tries again, succeeds at last

Away she flies, above the trees
Knows the feeling, to be free

The untold journey begins anew
And having survived what she's been through

Now knows ahead what lies in store
Is far more special, than before.

—Lindy Leigh

A QUESTION OF FAITH

A loved one of yours has been suddenly
taken away,
And there really aren't any comforting
words anyone can say.
Your days ahead may be sad and unsure,
But for these feelings, I believe, time is the
best cure.
Your thoughts of him will not always make
you sad,
With time you'll remember the wonderful years
that you had.
The laughter, the tears, the special moments
you shared,
That special kind of love that cannot be
compared.
And though in your life he may no longer
be a part,
The memories you have will keep him close
to your heart.

—Kathy Leaver

BEACH WALK

The awe of being part of the continent's edge.

    Soft, warm sugary sand.
    Hard, damp gritty sand.

    The roar/then whisper of a rushing wave
    The lacy fringe as it fans out
        Fully spent.

    The squawks and shrills of gulls
    The squeals and thrills of children.

    Tiny shells, broken shells, clusters of mussel shells
        At rest.
    Brown seaglass, green seaglass, white seaglass
        Pounded smooth and dull.

    A playful breeze
        Lifts my hair
        Kisses my cheek.

The awe of being part of the continent's edge.

—Marie Martz Parry

THE FLAG NOW SPEAKS

My name is Old Glory,
Red, White, & Blue.
In service of my country,
    And, your country, too.

I am the flag, of today.
    America's freedom flag.
I am the flag for tomorrow.
    The youth of today's promise.

I wave ever so glorious, in the wind,
    As it breezes past my stars and stripes.
Whispering hope and peace and tranquility,
    For all America, to eternity.

My Country 'tis of thee,
    Sweet land of liberty.
These words are my hope . . .
    My privilege to carry.

Though, the wind may come,
    Though, the wind may go,
I will rise to fly always . . .
    To represent you. . . My People. . . My Land. . .
My Country. . . My Liberty.

—Robbin W. Barnes

FAMILIES

Family members need to grow and learn together.
Families should work, work and play together.
Parents must set good examples for their kids and teach.
They are to teach and play with their kids' and each.
Parents need to love their children but, be stern.
Parents must be kind but firm, so they will properly learn.
Children need and want proper limits to be set.
And proper enforcement of the bounds must be met.

—Jack W. Runyon

GRANDFATHER

Grandfather Benjamin sat with his cane
In a rocking chair made for the old and insane
Out a window he looked for the world
Thoughts came and went, in his head memories twirled.
Faces passed by, laughing and singing.
Sounds, disorganized, were soft, loud, ringing.
Within the moment a woman in white
Came carrying a tray and ready for the fight.
"Get away with it" he cried, "this food's not for me.
I wish for a cow and an orange tree."
"Now Benjamin," said the nurse "eat dinner and be still,
the days are gone when you were at your own will."

—Nancy B. Baker

MY GRANDMA

She is sitting in her room, all alone.
She is actively moving her arms.
She is holding cloth in her hands.
The sun is shimmering like a ball of fire.
She is wearing a vest as soft as a kitten;
She sits down.
Her sewing machine is as shiny as glass.
It shimmers as she starts to sew a ribbon in a
bow, on some lace; to make a collar for a
stuffed animal.
She forms the cloth and sews it so she can
stuff it.
She has created something wonderful.
When I see it, I think of my Grandma.

—Tammy A. Hansen, age 9

OUR GRANDPA

One big oak stands tall in our woods
his word is law and that's understood

He's the head of our family, the shelter from the storm
And he's loved everyone of us since the day we were born

His seeds have started the generations of kin
if it weren't for him we would have never been

His roots go deep, which makes him so strong
and we all know that he's never done any wrong

Yes he's a hell of a man, on that you can be sure
with his caring words and a heart so pure

He raised four good girls through the hardest of days
And tells his grandchildren of the right and wrong ways

When we were little he stood more than ten feet tall
And it wasn't just because we were all so small

Cause he's the pillar of strength in this family of ours
may his days be as many as a sky full of stars

I'm sure I don't have to say his name at all
if you don't know, it's Earl Scales, who we all call grandpa

—James Earl Swanner

LIGHTNING OR (MAN DELIVERED)

Light - dance on thy Heavenly stage;
Let loose, in the storm of thy rage,
    And be, with thunderous accordance,
The function to the Gods of sage.
Touch, with the wicked tentacles
Of such madly charged particles,
    All of the heads of decadence
Who blindly stare through opticales
Of a disillusioned vista.

Stealing thy way across the sky
In a herald of clouds twisted wry;
    From the primordial mixing
Thou hath created a life-sty;
And from this sty is genesis,
A starting of symbiosis;
    And from out of this fuss comes man,
An incoherent synthesis,
A forging of mind and matter.

—Michael Votsmier

DARK

The child
walks up to the hard,
grey
stone well.
She looks in the deep,
dark hole and listens.
The sound of water
is dripping
below.
She leans down further
to get a good look
at the ebony water.
The black water
seems to be
luring her in.
The child is not careful,
for she falls
in the coal-colored water.
She is not able to swim,
and the darkness now lurks inside of her.

—Karen Pugliese

TOO SOON, TOO SOON

We start our life in love and peace
Without a care or woe
Too soon we find our childhood gone
And we are in life's flow
Before we've had the chance to learn
How sweet childhood can be
We must progress to many things
That weary you and me
We do our best to stay away
From problems as we go
But there are times we trip and fall
O'er things we could not know
Somehow we seem to make our way
To happy times and then
We find that age is creeping up
And things that might have been
Are slowly fading from our thoughts
As too soon we pass beyond
To an unknown world
Where all before have gone
Too soon! Too soon!

—Grant W. John

73

From my heart, I sing to you.
My songs of love come from my inner-
most being.
I sing to life, the life I have found
through you.
You have shown me your song, a song
of love.
The melody of love comes from your
soul.
I listen as each note falls upon the
air.
As each wave strikes my ear,
I feel a surge of awe arising within
me.
Your song joins my song and the beat
becomes one.
The music in our breasts merges in our
passion for life,
And our song becomes the only song
there is.

—Barbara A. Martzen

PRAISE THE LORD
Writing away
at the sheet with the sword.
Writing and thinking
about every word.
Who will I please
in my poetry talk
and shall I write
about a cool summer walk?
Or shall I write
what I really feel
about the world around us
and what we think is real?
I wonder if this
will ever be read
or if my verses live
long after my death.
Lend me your eyes, your heart, your mind.
I will sing you a story
of a man who wrote poetry.
Praise the Lord!

—Guillermo H. Gonzalez, Jr.

HOME
This home is made of many hearts
It laughs and cries it is a part

Of growing years and child's play
Homes are meant to feel this way

Hear giggles so sweet in every room
Memories fill the space and consume

The tears that are shed do dry
For laughter hears this is why

It grows and builds this sense of home
Those feelings so tender to have known

A place so safe no pain is near
Just loving walls that hold you dear

It keeps the rain off of your face
Many memories you can't erase

Holidays of times passed
These thoughts of love are meant to last

"Home Sweet Home" you are to me
Within these walls you will see . . . . Love

—Anna L. Sorling

LIFE GOES ON
She knew that now she had to face the fact that
her grandmother has really passed away, and the
only thing that's left is the memories she
cherishes everyday.

She found that death was not as mysterious as
some people make it seem, but more less the
reality that is natural and not a dream.

Though she looks back on it now as an un-
forgettable experience, through which she
was shown, that mourning will be, but life
must continue on.

For Grandmommy
—Tanya Thornton

Stillness and serenity permeate the air
In the woods behind our barn.
Only the sounds of leaves falling . . .
Birds calling . . .
And the creatures going about their daily business
Disturb the air.

The old logging road is my path to thought.
I pass the ruins of an old house
I hear the murmur of the stream
And lo, and behold!
A yellow violet stands in my path.
The fresh, clear air of the woods is freshened only
By the cool breeze from the small cave nearby.

I think only of these things . . .
Not my problems or the world's
I realize what God meant by "peace on earth."
For here it is, if we but open our hearts,
The serenity, the grace, and the peace
Of the woods.

Ah, but my time is short,
I must return to go about my assigned tasks . . .
But this time,
I go with the peace of God.

—Steven Lynn Chitwood

HE LIFTED ME UP
I was walking along the beach one cool evening,
Watching the sun setting behind the trees, casting its
Shadows upon the water, a beautiful sight to see, when
All of a sudden he appeared upon the water, walking
Towards me. "This cannot be," I said to myself. So
Closing my eyes very tightly, I slowly opened them and
There was no one there.

Suddenly, a hand rested on my shoulder. I looked around
And no one was there. Then a soft, gentle, but firm
Voice said "Follow me, come on follow me." I will lift
You up and you will see, no more pain, tears or
Sorrow, only to be carefree. I looked around, but no
One was there, only his footprints in the sand. Come on
Follow me, I will lift you up and you will see.

He lifted me up and I did see a beautiful place that
Was so carefree. Animals and children playing and
Laughing. Friends, cousins, aunts, uncles. My
Grandparents who I never knew. My parents, niece,
Grandson, and my son who was made into a whole man
Again so happy and carefree.

He lifted me up and I did see all my loved ones who
Came here long before me.

Amen.

—Olga M. Halverson

COUNTRY KIDS

School's out and summer's here,
   For kids, 'twas the best time of year,
They could go barefoot, climb apple trees,
Or pick berries by the creek with ease.
They took a dip in the old swimming hole,
Or dared to shinny up that pole.
They valued each long, carefree day,
When after chores, they could play
With toys they'd made themselves,
Or read some books from the family shelves.
They'd help their Mom make jelly and jam,
And she'd even let them lick the pan!
When they measured themselves at the bathroom door,
They'd found that they'd grown some more;
But alas, then came those schoolday blues,
Their feet had gotten too big for their shoes!

            —Lillian DeKeno

MY FRIEND

Smile with me, laugh with me
   Stop me from crying
Talk me up when I'm feeling down
Don't ask too many questions
I need some secrets
Trust in me as I trust in you
I'm willing to listen
Anytime you must talk
Give me some room
Yet stay close beside
Accept my faults
Enjoy my strengths
Sometimes not present
I'll always be there to share your troubles
Freedom for me, freedom for you
A friend indeed
One who is true
Friendship is love
With that in mind
Be my friend?

            —TR3

THE OLD MAN

As the sun rose in the East and the tall aspen trees
   Quivered in the morning air,
A withered old man with silver hair
Sat beside a young boy on the front porch chair.

Each one, in pensive mood, thought of their lives
In connection with the outside world.
Then the young boy, with a voice as melancholy
As the midnight wind said:

"Sometimes I do dumb things to get attention."
"I know how you feel," the old man said.

"Sometimes I talk to ladybugs and butterflies,
And to myself, because everyone else is tired
Of listening to me."
"I know how you feel," the old man said.

"Sometimes I cry late at night when I'm feeling lonely."
"I know how you feel," the old man said.

"I don't like being alone, with no one to talk to,
It makes me sad."
"I know how you feel," the old man said,
"Yes, I know how you feel."

And the withered old man with silver hair, sat beside
The young boy on the front porch chair.

            —Alicen Perry

MY FAVORITE CHILD

While dining with a childless host
   He asked which child I loved the most
Lots of thoughts went through my head
I turned to him and then I said
I think it is my first born child
She warms my heart whene'er she smiles
On second thought my second one
Is my one and only son
But then again the third in line
Is always present in my mind
Again there is my baby girl
Who always keeps my head awhirl
But the child for whom I really mourn
Is the one who's away until he's home
And the child who makes my heart swell
Is the one who's ill until he's well

            —Ruth George

The Following Poem Is Dedicated In Memory Of George T. Grace, Grandpa . . .

The sands of time go by so fast,
   we must love one another while our
lives last.

   Through trials and troubles our
lives book draws to a close.

   The guardian angels come,
cries of mourning fill the air.

   But why I ask do we mourn so
late?
let us rejoice for his sake.

   His first chapter is over his
second is only beginning.

   We can only love each other with
all our hearts.
though at times we may seem far apart.

   Now, though you are so far away,
we have never been closer. For now I
carry you forever in my heart.

            —Robert Tingley

GRANDMA'S THOUGHTS

Children — Yes the number is eight
   Grandpa has been my only mate
Money — not much at all,
But riches are where we stand tall.

Grandchildren numbers now at twenty one
So wonderful healthy and full of fun
Yes, God has blessed us yes indeed
In time we know they will succeed.

Jesus loves them all we know
Because the Bible tells us so
With Christian love in their hearts
From God they will never want to part.

Exchange these riches from God above
For earthly things with out love
Never would I even consider
Exchanging these blessings, no not ever.

Through God's forgiveness I depend
That some day I will be without sin
Jesus died on the cross for me
And for all who will just believe.

            —Virginia Rogne

It was so beautiful
the time that was

I can't begin to explain
the pain and giving all at once

It overwhelms me like a new pillow case
quickly laid under my head

The smell is so extinct
the newness so rare

And I fear it will never last
like an hour glass

But it returns again around the rim
in a glow and sound like never before

And you wonder

Who's knocking at your door!

—Noel Stilphen

MY CHILDHOOD MEMORIES

Beautiful rememberances are mine
Lasting forever.
First thing at dawn I awake from sleep
of a warm summer night.
　　Smiling faces to greet at breakfast time.
Are my childhood memories good morning
to each Mom, Dad, sisters, and brothers,
seven in all.
　　Memories of all our secret plans for
this day.
After the morning chores are done,
　　Running through the cool of the fresh
morning air.
　　Before the heat of the sun.
Down to the creek to the cool of the water,
　　Splashing clean and fresh against the
rocks.
　　　Cooling my feet from the heat of the sand.
　　My childhood memories lasting forever.
　　　　Now cooling my heart, and my
soul, now & forever.
My lasting childhood memories.

—Deloris M. Lyons

A SONG IN MEMORY

As a flitting butterfly you
whisper to me in the rose garden
and together we soar in the
　　spirit of love.

And there you are in a jerky
　　elevator — insensitive and
indiscreet. Sadness pre-empts
　　reality over friendships lost.

In sleep you haunt my dreams
　　with bits and pieces of
hidden memory. Clouded truth
　　suggests we are siamese.

Staring out the kitchen window
　　my hands submerged in suds
you lecture me on altruistic ideals.
　　I listen and remember — for a while.

Driving by the sea you accompany me.
　　As dust is blown away in reminiscence
I am happily submissive; cognizant
　　that you eternalize my emotions.

—Betty A. Brown

IN ONLY A DAY
Her gown was afloat in shades of white,
The sun shone down upon her ever so bright,

The trickling water ran crisp and clear,
To the sound of sweet music that was soft and so dear,

They vowed to each other their love,
And looked up to watch a soaring dove,

Together is how they will always stay,
From this moment on to the very last day,

A lifetime of love a lifetime of joy,
This was not to be treated as merely a toy,

It was like a flower not yet a bloom,
It needed loving and caring to assure it no doom,

Thoughts of the future as much as they may,
Such great expectations in only a day.

—Kristina S. Hudson

LET THERE BE LIGHT

When the sun goes down in the city, only then is
the brilliance of the Lights made known.

To those who are inside, the Lights mean only
　　wealth and prosperity;
To the tired and destitute they only mean
　　increasing poverty.

But the ones who see Hope among the nightly blaze —
　　　　They are the special ones.
They see a chance to escape the slums and the
　　humiliation of begging for food or money.
They are the ones who will make a difference in
　　themselves and others.
　　　　For they have seen the Light.

Those who are on the other side of the Light,
　　inside the buildings,
　　　　　　will die in the dark —
　　for they never saw the brightness.
Those who lived in the darkness shall die
　　　　　　　illuminated.

These Lights are the beacons for the homeless.

—Kirsten Cauchy

LIGHT OF LOVE

The twinkling stars of the midnight sky
　　Shining on through space and time,
Have often been the inspiration
For music's melody and poetry's rhyme.

Watching those stars through lonely nights,
One wonders what they are,
and for what purpose they are there
To cast their light so far.

Yet far toward the eastern horizon,
A voice might be heard to say:
"In the great drama of God, my child,
I, too, have a role to play.

I guide the wandering traveler
Over desert, mountain, or sea;
Whether by land, sky, or ocean,
He can chart his course by me.

And twenty centuries have come and gone,
Since I led the Wise Men that night
To a manger that cradled a baby,
And the world's darkness is challenged by love's light."

—Virginia J. Lovett

HOW IT FEELS TO FLY

How does it feel to be above the clouds
And see stars and moon piercing night's shrouds?
How does it feel toward heaven to rise,
To feel the wings lift with surprise?
How does it feel to bank and ride
With engine throttled into a glide?

How does it feel to chandelle and roll
Such sensation and equilibria to unfold?
How does it feel toward the earth to dive,
Ground fast approaching--are you really alive?
How does it feel to rest between two wings?
To hear with satisfaction songs the engine sings?

How does it really feel to fly?
You'll never know till you try.
To know, come today and fly with me
The beauty of our world to see,
To experience the ecstasy of the sky.
Then you'll know how it feels to fly.

—Billy F. Andrews, Sr.

UNTITLED

Petal by petal
Leaf over thorn
To the roots of the reason for which it was born
To bloom and to grow
Yet to wither and die
To ask about rainbows
To ask how and why
To feel all emotions
Sometimes love
Sometimes pain
To learn about life
With knowledge to gain
Sandcastles in summer
Copper leaves in the fall
A snowman in winter
And spring rain, after all—
As we grow seasons change
In the heavens above
Bringing forth a new flower
For someone to love.

—Cindy Byrd

IF I ONLY COULD . . .

If I could deliver a message
To my beloved,
It would fly over rivers and mountains,
Whisper through trees
And whirl its way through storms
Only to lay softly on his shoulder.
It would curl around his fair hair
And in soft whispers,
Deliver my everlasting love and devotion.
It would then wrap itself around his sleeping body
To deliver him to me,
Carrying him above the mountains and canyons
To lay him to rest gently at my feet —
As tenderly as a mother would rest her newborn.
But I can't deliver such a message
And my beloved cannot come to me
On hushed replies.
For what we once had is long gone
And now we are both taken.
But our souls are forever joined
And our loving whispers echo forever in my mind.

—Lynette Pfahl

HIDDEN LOVE

We hide in the shadow of the night
Safe within the arms of darkness

Searching for love in candle lit corners
And the still of the deep dark forest

There is no need for bright light in our world
As our love shines through the darkness

The safety felt in the darkness of the night
Is reassured by the fire or our passion

—Toni C. Allard

FOUR MOST BEAUTIFUL THINGS

SPRING
Mother Nature said to herself one day,
I must get things into bloom,
Else the world will meet its doom,
I wonder when it starts, March, April, or May.

SUMMER
Summer days are fun days,
Full of laughter and rejoicing,
Pick a song of happiness,
You will surely have a choice in.

FALL
Fall, fall is never dull,
There is always joy to behold,
But with all the gold in the world,
Fall can never be sold.

WINTER
Hush, be still, spring is sleeping,
Walk quietly in the snow,
But when the sun is rising, creeping,
The flowers begin to grow.

—Jodie Harper, age 10

Life is soooo beautiful
Life is soooo beautiful with Love in it:

Alice in wonderland;
Memories of Ayn Rand;

The fountain of youth discovered;
The special secret of lovers;

Childhood dreams come true;
Boyhood wishes for you;

The sound of a plane overhead;
Thoughts of lovers in bed;

Fire in the night;
The fire is soooo bright;

So many stars in the sky;
Sun and moon and you and I;

A song of the South and the North;
A new time; a new coming forth;

A song of the West and the East;
A vision of everlasting peace;

A song of the cold and the warm;
A tumult, a throng, a multitude, a swarm;

A new day, newly begun,
When all are lovingly One;

Lightning and thunder and fun in the sun:
Two hearts—two souls—resolved into One.

—Paul Bollman, Jr.

LOVE

Love is something we can't understand
Probably because we're just a mere man
But Love is something we don't understand
Because it just happens in our everyday plan

Love is something you just have to feel
And somehow this really makes it seem real
Because it is something you learn just to feel
And the longer it lasts you know it is real

Love is something you can give away
If it comes from your heart everyday
But Love is something that will go away
If it is not nourished Day after Day

But Love is something that won't go away
If it is nourished from day to day
And True and Lasting Love won't go away
If it is nourished Day after Day

—Glenda Pulliam

AT THE FOUNTAIN

I didn't mean to wake you—
        you're so pretty when you're sleeping
I could watch you for an hour
        Breathing easily
        Your eyes move behind your eyelids;
are you dreaming of me?

I saw your face at the fountain
        as I looked beyond the ripples
        into the subtle water
Our voices carry from the top of the mountain
        and your laughter trickles
        into my thoughts tomorrow

Like rivers
        we'll run down to an ocean
and contemplate the sand
        I brush away
        some sand from your face
and your skin causes a tingling in my fingers
If only we could linger, here,
        until the sun comes around . . .

—Myk Clayton

THE TREE

The tree is planted, its roots take hold,
    the wind is constantly in flight.
Once rooted, the tree remains till it's old.
The wind continues both day and night.

The wind will travel from east to west
from north to south, over ocean and sea.
The tree remains, its roots at rest,
solid and firm, secure, not free.

The wind can gently caress the leaves
as it passes the tree on its way.
The branches can bend to sway with the breeze,
enjoying its touch while it may.

But just as gentle as the wind can be,
its careless fury can know no end.
And so it can needlessly uproot the tree
which is solid and cannot easily bend.

It took some time for me to see
that you are the wind with the need to be free.
Now you must realize what is meant to be
for I need security, I am the tree.

—Jo Gilmour

NIGHT VISION

Somewhere in the catacombs of solitude and fear
Arising from the fetid air of doom
A glimmer hovers near the heart
Of hope from this sealed tomb.

Icy lengths of streamers melt
As warmth begins to flow;
Shock recedes as on a wave
With tempo thick and slow.

The heart knows how to nourish pain;
The picture will not fade.
We must taste the fruit of all the trees
And feel the terror's blade.

Not pleasure nor the hippodrome
Nor beauty small or great
Can save us from the knowledge
That all must be our fate
Until we stand to face the truth
That love must conquer hate.

—Anita Sontz

I remember when, there were butterflies in the air
And the skies were fair.
When you could look up and aroun'
And not see any brown.
Perhaps a little here 'n' there
But n'ery a speck in the air.
I remember when the sea was clear blue, so clear
And the fish so plentiful and near.
When one could go to the bottom floor
And see all kinds of sites galore.
Those that wiggle and some that glow
Others that hop and even those that move slow.
Once down you go,
You realize they put on quite a show.
Plants small and short,
All of a various sort.
Others long, skinny, or thin,
Makes you wonder where you've been . . .

All of these, I remember when . . .
I think of them every now and again.

—Deanna Lee McMullen

NIGHT THOUGHTS

As I lie down upon my bed,
Can't stop the thoughts going thru my head!
Lord, let tomorrow be a better day—
Closing my eyes, I silently pray.

Thinking of all who took their leave—
Tears swell my eyes, as I still grieve!
Can't help but wonder, what will be my fate?
Wish I knew what I could anticipate!

Don't know why I even care
Sometimes I feel such despair!
There are so many close to my heart—
Praying that they won't soon depart!

Wish I could tranquilize my brain,
So some sleep I'd be able to gain!
My thoughts continue on into the night—
Lord, help me to do what is right!

All too soon, night turns into dawn—
As I wake sleepily, with a yawn.
Looking out the window at the sunshine—
I realize now, that all will be fine!

—Debby Laferriere

THE CLEAN SWEEP

(This poem is dedicated to my mother, who
has been in Heaven for six years. She used
to tell me this story when I was a little girl.)

My, my!
Our Heavenly Father's at it again —
Cleaning up the sky.

He's using His biggest brushes and brooms
To make room —
And to reorganize.

Some people say that they're cirrus clouds,
Just blown about by the wind.
But I know better and
Can't you see?

The strokes He's left behind
For all of mankind
Are His pathways for the angels above!

—Donna Gagne

THE WALL

I picked them up together
and gathered them in a pile.
I folded them all neatly
and stuck them safe inside
an envelope of anger,
the wall I built myself.

So as not to let them hurt me,
these emotions from bad times.
I shoved away my anger into
the envelope that was hid
inside a sturdy place in my mind.

I picked myself up and tried to stand alone,
and let all my happy feelings
escape swiftly through the doors
of another place
more open in my mind.

I filled myself of thoughts
of things I had to do
so as to fool my heart of feeling
what my mind had held in view.

—Jan Dishop

GENERATIONS

Over the years I've come to realize,
A feeling that I can't disguise.

How much like mom that I've become,
I always felt could not be done.

Now I have kids of my own,
Her words cut right to the bone.

Wait she said til it's your time,
You will go out of your mind.

As my kids begin to mature
Now I dream of their future.

They roll their eyes, give me that look
I almost feel like writing a book.

Of all the times I did the same,
Mom you see was to blame.

I look upon them with a smile,
And say, Mom's right just wait awhile.

In these eyes they soon will see
That they've become just like me.

—Gayla Bearden

THE CREATOR

The ocean rages from shore to shore
Never still or silent, always a roar.
In each billowing wave I hear God's voice
Beckoning unto me to make my choice
To follow Him and take my stand
To serve Him with a willing hand.

As I walk along the beach of sand
I can feel the touch of my Master's hand
Guiding me through the day and into the night
Teaching me what is right.
I tread in His footsteps all the way
A ransom for me, He has already paid.

God the creator of all
Loves us even if we are large or small.
He made all things with His mighty power
From the tallest mountain to the smallest flower,
Then He gave me the breath of life
To glorify Him without a strife.

—Clara Dean

THIS MAN THEY CALL THE SAVIOR

I stood looking into darkness,
I, in all my sin.
This man they call the Savior
Came and took me in.
The love flowed from His eyes,
And pierced through my lonely soul.
He took away any doubting
And hate running black as coal.
The night took on a light
That slowly grew into day.
I once was deep in sorrow
But He washed it all away.
Now when people ask me
What there is to look forward to,
I say, "He's coming back someday,
For His chosen few."
They may stand and wonder,
They can laugh if that's how they'll be,
Because inside I know what God has said
And a ransom was paid for me.

—Misty Paige

LET ME KNOW HEAVEN

I laid my pride-filled heart upon Thine altar,
My selfish will surrendered unto Thee;
Cleansed from my guilt, I drank life-giving water;
My heart grew like a calm and tranquil sea,
And I knew Eden!

Temptations came. Oh, Satan sorely pressed me!
Dear loved ones turned away from me in scorn;
Friends mocked. Life's burdens seemed to overwhelm me;
With Job. I cried, "Oh Lord, why was I born?"
And I knew Gethsemane!

Cruel scourgings of false rumor slashed and tore me;
Sharp thorns of sorrow pierced my aching brow;
I begged for strength to bear the cross of trial;
"Thy will within me work, Oh Lord, just now!"
And I knew Calvary!

The fury passed. God stilled the rolling water,
But beckons still along a stone-filled way;
"The goal is near! Ne'er let your footsteps falter!
The dawn bursts soon into a glorious day!"
Oh, let me know Heaven!

—Dorina M. Neal

It was cold today.
My thoughts swirl through my mind,
Never settling, never still —
Straying in new paths; leaving me behind,
So that in a wild frenzy, I,
Try to sort, to classify as they fly by.

It was cold today.
My patience is wearing thin, but I can't afford,
To let this, also, slip away
To fill the harmony of my life with swelling discord,
My problems are so many, yet so few,
Some abstract, some unheard, some untrue.

It was so cold today
They disappear one by one by one,
As sanity reaches out and touches them,
Leaving only the ones I can now understand,
They tick off like burdening weights,
Leaving clarity behind, with a hope for grace.

—JoAnne Bielke

LOSING A FRIEND

L ast week I was home for the ultimate bash,
Y our family and friends were pretty well trashed.
N ow we're together, where have you gone,
N ever again will we sing to our song.

F or days I've been meaning to communicate,
R ote a few letters, You're something I appreciate.
A nother day has passed without a reply,
N ext thing they tell me you're off in the sky.
C learly it's time to travel to Penn,
E veryone was helpful, I made some new friends.
S pruce and 42nd was indeed a tragic end.

A fter all is done, you made me so mad,
P arents I hope will be happy, not sad.
I can only pray that you'll wait for me,
C emeteries are places where we're finally free.
E verything has changed for me because of you,
L oving and caring are things I will do.
L astly, something good will come from this,
I know you so well, you're someone I'll miss.

—Thomas J. Denham

MY GUARDIAN ANGEL

H e is always there.
Sometimes in the back of my mind.
My Angel is my conscience.
He watches over me.

When I've been mischievous, or
slipped away to gain my independence
From all life's rules and regulations.

Somehow my conscience seems to
Keep popping up to remind myself
What life can be all about and
of who I really am.

There are times when I wonder
to myself — could I have chosen
a different path? could I have
lived this life differently?

Would my nagging, persistent angel
be more inclined to be proud of
me then? Instead of having to correct me.
Perhaps that is why I have my
guardian angel to watch over me.

—Theresa Anne Iacovelli

REMEMBERED

T he pretty young lady before you, you see,
I used to bounce upon my knee.
With little round face and chubby hands,
By my knee she would come and stand;
Until I would take her upon my knee
Where she would clap and laugh with glee.

We had so much fun, that child and me.
But now she has grown and gone away,
No longer little with me to play.
A husband she has and a child too,
With hair so blonde and eyes so blue.

Do you think she remembers you and me,
The fun we had, the games we played?
The little red duck and the cookies we made.
Will she take time for her child, like me?
And let him bounce upon her knee.

—Ann J. Hansen

SLEEPTIME

P ut your head down on Mommy's shoulder
Close your eyes and say good night
Put your head down on Mommy's shoulder
Go to sleep and sleep real tight

Say good night to all your friends
Say good night to all your toys
Say good night to Mommy and Daddy
Go to sleep and dream all night

Dream of new ways to spend your day
Dream of new things to do and say
Dream of things that make you happy
So when you wake up, you'll feel real snappy

Just remember how much we love you
Just remember how much we care
So when you wake up in the morning
You will know that we'll be there

Put your head down on Mommy's shoulder
Though it's sleeptime, please don't weep
Put your head down on Mommy's shoulder
There you'll stay until you sleep

—Georgianna Sedlacko

JENNIE'S HEART

A teacher is seldom remembered
In the memory of our mind,
Of things once taught from textbooks,
Now closed and lost through time.

But a teacher is often remembered
By what they say and do.
Some we gratefully recall,
While others we just bid adieu.

A voice of love still echoes
The halls of Woodburn High
Where sweet Jennie taught in classrooms
And left her love behind.

Her message, softly spoken,
Lay gently on our mind
Because it came from that grand old textbook,
From the land beyond the skies.

Her voice of love still echoes
The halls of Woodburn High,
Because the message softly spoken
Came straight from Jennie's heart.

—Gardner W. Jeffery

A PEACEFUL WORLD

I lie here filled with peacefulness not worrying
about the cruelness of the world outside,
Nothing is as threatening to me as when it's in
disguise,

I try to take a step forward but the barrier is
holding me in,
It's not wanting to let go of me, it won't let
life begin,

Finally the years are slowly passing, I'm growing
old each day,
I don't regret the barriers that held me, for
now I seek today,

I open the door as I walk outside the sun's rays
resting upon my face,
Oh, the freshness of the springtime, Oh, how I
missed this place.

—John P. Phipps

I almost lost my love one day
    To whom or where, I cannot say
I only know an emptiness
    where once I felt such happiness

I wake each day in wonderment
    where once I spoke, I'm hesitant
When will this hurt begin to cease
    So within my heart I'll have some peace

Each night I look upon his face
    Searching for love, just a trace
And as I fall asleep I wonder
    As teardrops fall, where did I blunder

But now tis Spring
    And I have hope
That with its warmth
    I can cope
With all life's joy
    And all its woe
That once again
    Our love will grow.

—Marie L. Palmesi

I can't stop thinking about you
    I see you everywhere
I can smell your cologne
I can hear your voice
Walk with me.

I feel your presence even when
you're not there — It's so real
I know you feel the same way
I can see it in your "windows of the soul"
Walk with me.

You touch my soul like no one ever has
It's so hard to explain
It feels like magic
Although I know it can never be
Walk with me.

Our connection is real
Our eyes hold many feelings
You are very important to me
Please be my friend
And walk with me.

—Maria L. Perrucci

WIDOW

Smoke curling from neglected cigarette,
    She sits so silently
Praying, to forget
What could not be.

Seconds creeping slowly, as if years,
    She wonders what to do
To stop the tears
From falling two by two.

Through cloudy panes she looks at stars above.
Remembering days and nights; (forever lost?)
Yet knowing that one cannot have true love
Without the willingness to pay the cost.

Time passes by diminishing the pain.
Soft memories turn her tears to gentle smiles.
But one small, cold, hard spot shall still remain,
Inside her heart, while traveling through life's miles.

—Raymond M. Venezia

Do you know how bad you hurt me?
    Telling me you loved me, that you cared
Yet forgetting me as soon as I am gone.
You told me I was special
And I, like a fool, believed you
Swept off my feet in just one night
By your "sincere" ways and honesty
Now that I'm gone, do you feel any emptiness?
For some strange reason, I doubt it
Easy enough to forget me knowing that someone else
    could easily take my place
I really thought that I loved you
But once I realized that I had been used
Even though you told me that wasn't true
It dawned on me — I hated you. True, deep hate.
Something I will carry with me forever
Finding it hard to trust anyone anymore.
But you did teach me one thing
Love does not happen on just one night.
And for the rest of my life
The same mistake will never happen again.

—Amy Mead

A MEMORY

We sat upon a patio of cobblestone and clay.
    Sunlight filtered thru an Autumn tree.
The Missouri River meandered by,
making a memory for — my daughter and me.

We ate our lunch in silence
upon a wrought iron table
and fenced about with brick and garden.
It felt nice that we were able
to be there together.

A train whistled by our moment,
just beyond the flower bed.
We savored all the sounds and smells
as we supped on tea and sourdough bread.

Our conversation was gentle
with hope in every word.
We enjoyed being there together
from things we tasted, felt, and heard.

We wrapped up a memory
and stored it deep within
to savour it another day
and remember where we've been.

—nola lloyd fulgham

WHAT GOD MEANS TO ME

God is there when I need help,
He loves, he cares, he lifts me out,
He also knows when I am down
And even smooths away my frowns.
His love is there for all to see
And I know, he cares for me.

No matter where my feet may stray
He walks beside me night and day.
I may cry out, "Oh Lord! help me",
His touch will always set me free.
If you believe with all your heart
Then God will never, ever part.

His touch is like an evening breeze
His goodness is for all to see.
I know, my friend, that he is there
Because he answers all my prayers.
If you have faith and you believe
Remember, this is, "What God Means To Me!"

—Erma J. Monroe

BLUE JESUS

I had a dream about Jesus last night.
Yes, it was Jesus, but something wasn't right.
He was kissed by the morning's dew But
his color and his clothes were Blue.
Yes, I dreamed of Blue Jesus last night.
I said, "Forgive me Lord, how I love You.
but, tell me Why are You so Blue?"
When I looked up he tried to Speak
But, down his face the tears did Streak.
Then, this is what Our Saviour had to Say.

He said, "Dear Son I know You're not the
only one Many men on earth have sinned.
But you see the End is near."
Then fell another tear.
"That's the reason I'm So Blue."
He then reached out a nail scarred hand.
"If I could, I'd do it all again."
But Now the rest is up to You.
For you See, I've already given
My Life for You."

—Rose Windham

GOD'S HANDIWORK

As the sun comes up o'er the horizon
I see the sky all amber hue;
I know it will be a beautiful morning,
and all the fields are kissed with dew.

The birds are singing in the tree tops
Giving thanks for another day,
It should be to remind us
To take time from our work to pray.

It costs us nothing to see the beauty
of the rising of the sun,
and makes us glad to be able to see it's sitting
When our day's work is done.

O, glad day it is to look up
and see the trees so grand and tall,
To see the miraculous changes
In the trees with the coming fall.

The colors change with such a beauty
That it's difficult to explain,
To know that God watches over all
And reigns each day and year the same.

—Rev. Rebecca Fogleman

WHITE CROSSES IN A FIELD OF GREEN

I stop along the road to see,
Where brave men rest, so silently;
Brave men who went to war and died,
And now they lie here, side by side.
I see a person, here and there,
With head bowed low in tearful prayer;
Tears for husbands, sons and brothers,
Tears from wives, sisters and mothers.
Across the field a great tree stands,
Its branches spread across the land,
A silhouette against the sky,
A sentry for those men who lie,
Beneath her arms and at her feet,
In silent, and, eternal sleep.
I look again, through blurry eyes,
Across the field, where brave men lie;
It is a sad, but lovely scene,
White crosses in a field of green.

—Wayne Wakley

THIS EARTH

This earth
Of such vast and immeasurable worth,
Constantly revolving, and ever evolving in space,
A complex marvel is this, our home, our place.

This planet,
Powerful and mighty, but gentle yet.
A living mass of alternating life,
Repetition in motion thru dark and light.

This world,
A masterpiece unfurled,
Providing abundant beauty all around.
Riches within it abound
There, in water, plants, animals, sky, and ground.

Glorious wonder is in everything everywhere!
It surrounds us
Close enough to see, to hear, to smell, to touch.
It gives so much.

We must be aware of it.
Then, we must take care of it.

—Sharon Maher Price

RAIN STORM

A swift gush of wind rustles dry, brown leaves
That crumble as a light step is on them.
The clouds overhead are dark and angry —
Grumbling about the fiery, orange mass
that has scorched the ground below.
Trees wave their long, strong hands in salute,
As a single, young child, with a
frenzied look in her eyes,
scurries to a place of safety
like a frightened mouse.
Lashing down in fierce anger,
the pounding beat of the furious,
cold rain reminds me of a song on the radio.
Thunder crackles wickedly,
followed by the flash of striking lightning
snapping against an old, rotten pine tree
causing a crack,
like that of an indignant whip.
I stare out the streaked window
And wait anxiously for the storm to pass.

—Cassidy René Molthan

MY TOWN

I walked through the town
Where I had spent my youth
Things were different, it had grown
It seemed foreign, to tell the truth

Once I had biked those paths
And met with friends each day
And in my youthful, carefree play
I wanted it to stay that way

Hardly a person did I know
My many friends had scattered so
In ten short years, a change so great
The memories caused a tear to escape

Emotion tossed, I struggled free
My thoughts transcended the altered scene
Though changed as human eye could see
In my heart, my town it would always be

—June Gruver

MORNING I

Awakening as i do
to the heat of the sun
glowing on my face
and the smell of freshly plowed dirt
                    in my nostrils . . .

The lingering night air
causing chill bumps on my flesh
while a splash of freshly drawn well water
chases all sleepiness
                    from my eyes . . .

Awakening as i do
in the Carolina countryside
                    reassures me
that no matter who or what i am
and who or what i am perceived to be
                    i am beautiful . . .

                    in the morning

—Franklin Deese

528 NORTH 38TH STREET

I remember:

    mulberry trees
    purples and blues
    dark grey shade
    the window to the world

I remember:

    clouds
    cool black
    billows of smoke
    the cover of nature's spring

I remember:

    round windows
    marching stained colors up the stairs
    not seeing through
    seeing forever

I remember:

    mom
    ironing and the smell of starch
    hot chocolate and graham crackers
    a good night kiss

—John P. Neal

COUNTRY SOUNDS

Country sounds make muted stabs
    at a peaceful, silent environment.
The muffled rhythmic beat of a hammer
    on a skeletal, unfinished shed.
Orchestrated concerts by nest-building birds.
The lazy hum of busy bees
    collecting nectar from the flowers.
A cow mooing in a nearby lot
    to her awkward, new-born calf.
A bored horse galloping determinedly
    around the enclosed field
        neighing in utter disdain
            at the chug-chug-chugging farm tractor
                who has replaced his mission in life.
The hammer ceases its muffled, rhythmic beat.
The satisfied cow stoically chews her cud,
    staring moodily at the horse
        who now stands silently watching
            the big, green farm tractor
                bringing the farmer home to lunch.

—Pauline W. Elswick

BLUE SKIES

Blue skies
dove cries; filling the sky above
It must be a sign of God's merciful love
Far and wide they climb
forever til the end of time
Bright and radiant a glowing array
Just looking at you makes me happy and gay
Oh what fun it would be
If we could just reach up and touch thee!
Holding the rulers of night and day
Guilding us in every way
As I think of this; a question arises within
I wonder, how long you have been
From the beginning of time of Adam and Eve
to the present day, people in despair . . . they grieve
This is one thing people can't explain
but this I know they must obtain
It had to be a God that made you
How else could you have lasted this long
Without ever being gone!

—Phadra Powell

THE LOOKING GLASS

Between plains of glass,
an overexposed Image Rails
through the Italian country side.
With a train of thought
Superimposing Its transparent self
over fields of grape
Sacrificing to the sun for wine,
and Roman aqueducts that watered the garden of empire
carry only dust of vestal statue and ruin
that suffers from the leprosy of stone.

    Past the bleeding
From broke village roofs
Their red terra cotta
Lying on fresh city cement.
Arriving at the final station,
the Image slowly turns the Venecians blind.
Leaving the mind to form mirrors
that will get caught between their reflections
a ladder of micro infinity
descending out of the window pane.

—Mario Raguz

YOU DEVIL, YOU!

Eat your heart out — you Devil, you
   There's members and visitors filling each pew.

And there's a feeling of love in the air
   One for the other — we show that we care.

The people are working and praying and planning,
   Singing and giving and learning and "telling."

The pastor, too, is doing his part,
   With a Spirit-filled message, that cuts to the heart.

You too, had a choice, you Devil, you
   But you spurned God's love, your own work to do.

But we decided each day that we live
   To completely surrender ourselves to Him.

So, get out from here, your work we won't do.
   Eat your heart out — you rascal, you!

                   —Marlene S. Jeffeaux

BREAD AND BUTTER

Eat the lobster — Boss said
I am a vegetarian — I said

'When you are in Rome, do as Romans do' — Boss said
'When we live, culture lives sir' — I said

'I am the Boss' — Boss said
'I am the culture' — I said
Because of the lobster, Boss fired me.
Because of the culture, I got fired.

"The knowledge and courage you gave me.
Here I am in America.
The culture you taught me
Here I am fired now.
O culture! What about my bread and butter?" —
I asked the culture, culturedly.

"The world doesn't end with lobster
knowledge and courage is bread and butter" —
Culture answered courageously.

Culture gave me courage
knowledge gave me job.

                   —Sundari Ramalingam (Abirami)

THE OLD FRANKSTOWN HUNT CLUB

On this cold dreary morning in late November.
In the old club house all alone I remember.
Thoughts of family, and of the friends here I had found.
Now they're tearing The Old Frankstown Hunt Club down.

No new generation will ever know of this place.
All grown up in weeds, despair, and disgrace.
No horses with riders, no more hunt horn will ever sound.
Now they're tearing The Old Frankstown Hunt Club down.

Oh how did we let this old landmark die?
She was so full of life, but time passed her by.
Across these fields no more hoof beats will pound.
Now they're tearing The Old Frankstown Hunt Club down.

It seems dear old hunt club, the years just flew by.
The memories you gave will live on, and not die.
The best years of my life were with you I have found.
Now they're tearing The Old Frankstown Hunt Club down.

This was the place where I learned how to ride.
We chased over fences where the foxes would hide.
The time that you gave us in our hearts will live on.
So dear old hunt club, you will never really be gone.

                   —Pamela De Rose

SUGAR

Faithful friend.
   Seeker of pats, kind words, and bones,
Welcoming me home.

Constant companion.
Ready for a walk or to listen to me
   talk,
Sleeping by my bed.

Chaser of sticks.
Sleeping in the doorway, or a paw
   in my lap,
Ready to play.

Never questioning.
Always accepting, warm eyes,
   eager tail,
Giver of love.

                   —JoElaine Vetor

MY BROTHER AND I

A child in teens it seems to me
Should show some signs of dignity
But my brother won't agree.
He laughs and says I put on airs
That that's just grown-up folks' affairs
And then runs whistling up the stairs.
His room's a mess of this and that
With here and there a coat and hat
And there and here a ball and bat.
He hasn't an artistic touch
He doesn't care for reading much
He just likes boats and cars and such
And when company comes around
He never asks them to sit down
But goes through antics like a clown.
I try my best to mend his ways
But often wonder if it pays
As this goes on for days and days.
But when my patience wears too thin
I'll just give up or I'll give in
Because with my brother I just can't win.

                   —Grace Keefe

FAIRIES

I've never seen a fairy
Maybe I never will
But I have seen their pictures
And I am wishing still.

I've heard they live inside of flowers
And there they play for many hours.
I peeked inside a buttercup;
Instead a little bug flew up.

On moonbeams they often ride at night
With wings of silvery white,
Waving their wands to and fro
Spreading their magic where'ere they go.

They bring in the morning dew
Making flowers pretty for me and you.
Before I get a glimpse so slight,
Quickly they vanish out of sight.

I've never met a fairy personally
But in my dreams they'll always be
Flittering and fluttering like butterflies,
And then I gently close my eyes.

                   —Rheba M. Moss

SUCCESS

Success is a dream
tied to a distant star.
Success is esteem
for yourself, just as you are.
For without respect for all that you do,
there can be no joy your whole life through.

—Edna May Hermann

From August through October
When summer is packing her cases to go,
And autumn is showing
Her bright and lovely face
Around each corner;
Something happens to each of us—
We realize we have lived another
Full season of life.
Look back—try to remember something—
A new friend, good times,
Life itself preserved—
Etched into our minds,
Memories.
These bring us together,
Gathered to reminisce and
Rearrange our memory books . . .

—Kate Andreas

Reach out your hand to me
I'm not the evil one they've told you
an iron curtain separates us
but it will fall as we march through

Your sun is poised to kill me
and I'm ready to take your life
but in the end it accomplishes nothing
only adding to the misery and strife

As faceless enemies it is easy to do battle
I must kill you to remain free
As brothers of the heart we'll wonder
why they didn't tell us how it could be

Reach out your hand to me
I'll help you break the chain
that holds you behind the curtain
then only freedom will remain

Reach out your hand to me, my brother . . .

—Charles F. Schwartz

FREEDOM

Freedom has come to me
A load has been lifted;
My eyes are clear to see
The beauty of life once more.
Like a bird—I can soar.
I am free to be me;

Not watched by angry eyes,
Not listening to the lies
Free to be me;
To make mistakes and learn from them
Not to be condemned for not being perfect.
When I feel free, I am also free to give,
Give love and warmth
To those for whom I care
Free to be aware of life's beauty.
Little things that I can share.
Like a caterpillar turned into a butterfly,
I am free.

—Judy Bowman

BLACK UNITY

I'm a Black-Man, and I know it—
So why should I let my hair grow long
Just to show it?

Yes I'm a Black-Man—as we all can plainly
see—
But the situation at hand, is Freedom and Equality.
Now if I let my hair grow long—as the
Black-Man want it to be—
Each root would cling together—in
Black-Unity.

—Issi Williams

The morning glare of sunshine fills my eyes
And from out of a dream I awake
to once again see your smile!
From my window I gaze to see the day
Oh how my vision takes me far.
And for a moment I drift away to find you
Through the sky I soar for you, just to
find that like the autumn breeze you're all around me!
Another day begins, a day full of you by
thoughts and dreams, only to once again be awakened
Through the sky I see your eyes
For they're all around me, such a pretty blue!
For they shine like the sun
So bright and full of life
It could never die
For that sun will rise for me until
the end of time!

—Mikel Woslager

THE SEEKER

I am a seeker,
I seek for life.
For I want to live in the riches of the Universe,
Among the ones who live and breathe
In the depths of truthfulness and love,
Who awake in the morning of knowledge,
Close their eyes in the eve of courage,
Die in the arms of the spirit.

Man is a seeker,
Man seeks for life.
Yet hastily he runs from death,
Not knowing that in it he will find the doorway to life,
For who knows the day or hour of his eternal bliss,
But man himself,
For he is the seeker,
And finder of life.

—Deborah Koorey

SUPERSTITION (?)

Three black cats, sittin' on a fence;
It really doesn't make much sense,
To me, lookin' out my window, here.
What are you really doin' there?
Is it just a place to catch the sun?
If I throw somethin' at you, will it make you run?
It's weird, I'm scared, you bring bad news;
And I've already had enough of those blues.
Lately, that is, with our income all spent,
And we can't even afford our rent!
So, go away and play, and start your roamin'
You look so innocent, but I fear you're an omen . . .
Mysteriously, you're gone; what a relief!
Have I been foolish, or will I find more grief?

—Jean Camelo Eckert

A flower sits alone in a field
Seeking, waiting
For another one to bloom

On the surface . . . it's a fantasy
Deep inside . . . it's a dream.

The thoughts of what could be.
You and I together.
Touching your hand,
Resting my head on your shoulder,
Gently touching your lips to mine.
Yet in reality it is only answered rawly.
Although the feelings are longing desperately to come
Out they are locked inside my dreams and only you
Hold the key.
I only hope that someday you will unlock the
Door.
But until then my prayers are answered only by a

Simple hello as you pass by.

—Rachel Angela Brown, age 14

A TALE TO TELL

The old house stood empty & high on a hill,
But clothed in majesty and dignity still.

Oh the stories it must long to tell,
Of the people it sheltered & loved so well.

Of the sound of a newborn baby's first cry,
And sobs for those who were about to die.

The romping of children on its winding stair,
The times when wedding bells filled the air.

There were warm roaring fires on a cold winter's night,
But the old house stood sturdy strong & tight.

Keeping all those within warm & secure in its fold,
Showing a love that could never be told.

When you see an old house so empty & still,
Whether or not it be high on a hill.

Just think of the tales it must long to tell
Of the people it loved and served so well.

—Viola M. Wurl

I AM, I AM

I am a side walk
For people to walk up and down on.

I am a door mat
For everyone to wipe their dirty feet on.

I am used
Every day of my life.

There is a sign around my neck
People read it,
Then they strangle me with their demands.

I am a chalkboard
When I am full of words
I am wiped off, then I wait for the next class to begin.

I am a bathroom tile
When I am full of dirt
I am washed clean to begin again.

I am,
I am,
I am used.

—April Virginia Look

COURAGE

A dream of mammoth waves
Crashing on the shore.
I cry to all SAVE YOURSELVES!
No one heeds the call.

Often times I cannot speak
Only shake in terror
Of impending doom
That will leave us all in peril.

I cannot cry for fear of images
Too frightening to believe
I know that if I lose you all
I was just too late to speak.

I pray for the day to speak my mind
Undaunted by your abandon
For it is better to be alone with truth
Than trapped in a crowd of phantoms.

—Lauri J. Rowell

MY FATHER'S SONG . . .

You know it seems times get too hard;
There's too much pain to keep inside,
My father's gone—he won't be back,
I'm left alone with tears to cry.
The situation's out of hand,
Too many lies to mask what's real—
His life just faded much too fast;
His life is gone, but I'm still here.
It feels that pain is not enough,
The anger burns within my heart—
The anger holds no comfort though,
It turns so cold now after dark.
I know the truth, and yes, he's gone;
But can the truth no longer free,
The bitter tears, the broken hearts,
The hurt of how things might have been?
Days come and go without much sense,
Why don't they stop—he can't be gone,
If he were, the world would stop,
Just long enough to sing his song . . .

—Teresa Lynch Collins

FOOTNOTE

I try to force your image from my brain
But you won't let me
Refreshing my every fantasy
With your smiles
Beams that pierce my core
Forcing the Flashback
        Centerstage

I want to reach out
But all my chains
Haven't been broken
I soar like an eagle
But my song . . . .
That of the caged bird

Shrill cries of desperate anger
Haunting lines of bridled rage
Vibrating throughout the
Plastic Chamber

As I desperately try
To turn the page of Love Lost
For here I am
Trapped within a footnote
Of my memories

—Bob Simpson

OLD MAN ON THE PORCH

Out on the porch, the old man sits,
Viewing his world in pieces and bits.
His eyes are dimmed, so he can't see far,
Not even to see the morning star.

His hands are gnarled and very work-worn
From days of toil, since early morn.
Though his hair is white and his back is bent,
He has no feeling of discontent.

He looks at the past without wishing it back,
No deep sighs of alas or alack.
He remembers the times that were so good,
And not the bad ones, that he had withstood.

So he sits in his rocker as time passes by,
Hoping, when he passes, no one will cry.
For when he leaves this mixed-up world,
His spirit, then, will be unfurled.

— Faye Robertson

GRANDPARENTS

You don't really know who they are.
All you know is, you want to go there.
They're the ones who play the games
That your parents don't want to.
They go the extra mile for you.
Making sure you're always safe.
All at once you grow up and realize then:
They are the two special people,
Who have watched you grow thru the years
The stories they tell of their lives.
God sure knew what he was doing
When he created grandparents.
The best thing about them is:
They are your very own.
There's something special about them
They're like a present you get year around.
I wouldn't trade mine, for the world
How about you? I didn't think so.
Just one last thing I can say.
I love you . . . my special grandparents.

— Michael J. Anderson

MY FATHER

As a child, I sat on his knee.
As a child, his face I loved to see.
As a child, I knew he loved me.
          My father.

As I became a teenager, he was a
    supervisor.
As I went to college, he was a
    mentor.
As I became an adult, he was an advisor,
    My father.

As he lay in the hospital dying,
    I tried to be cheerful.
As he accepted fate with dignity,
    I tried not to be fearful.
As he was laid to rest,
    I tried not to be tearful.
    My father.

As I remember him now, I am content.
As I know his ideas live on, I feel no resent.
As I know I will see him one day, I feel
    his life well spent.
    My father.

— Margaret Christine Massey Collier

A MASK OF MANY FACES

It is said that everyone has a mask,
A mask of many faces.
And the face you choose to wear each day
Depends on the people and places.

Many times you're a leader
Showing others what to do.
But other times it's them you follow
And you wish they'd notice you.

But then there are times when you can be yourself,
Anytime of anyday—
Because when you're with the ones you love,
You can put your mask away.

— Leanne Marie Cochran

MY CHILD

I teach you to always speak your mind —
    yet grumble when you disagree.
I ask you to be perfect,
    to become another me.

I tell you to be tolerant,
    yet with impatience in my voice
will make demands upon you
    without giving you a choice.

I teach you of democracy
    which you must abandon at our door;
For in our house, I am king
    and keep track of every chore.

You will learn that love is caring
    about what your loved ones do;
you will learn to accept me as I am
    to the degree that I accept you.

You will learn that I'm but human
    and will come to realize
there are some things that we must do,
    and that life is compromise.

— Karen Keegan Hutchinson

MY GRANDFATHER

My grandfather, I remember
Cancer struck him in September

It was a very sad moment for me
Thank God he passed away peacefully,

I remember all the things he has done
When I was with him I always had fun

My grandfather was very sweet
The things he did with me were very neat

He used to take me golfing
And sometimes even boating

My grandfather was very Italian
When he was little he loved the Black Stallion.

My grandfather's name was Ed
When I was little he would tuck me in bed

I remember his big boat
Until one night when it didn't stay afloat

I remember my grandfather's gray hair
When I asked him he would take me anywhere

My grandfather would watch me play ball
But when I didn't see him I would give him a call

I'm so sad that we are apart
But I always knew he had a great big heart!

— Michael Monahan

NATURE'S LOVE

Sweet dreams baby close your eyes
    And soon you'll wake to bright blue
       skies.
The birds will sing so cheerfully
Because you've come to play
And everything if big or small
Will always go your way.
The sky, the trees, the land, the seas
Are all in awe, some begging "Please"
We need your cheer
Your warmth sincere
We need your touch
And cleansing tear
For you are Nature's Little Love
That soars above the
       peacebound dove
Which no one else can rise above.

    —Robyn Cheshire

LOVE OUT OF TIME

I want to open myself up to you
    letting you pluck my heart strings
    until they burst into song
    filling you with love's spirit
    dancing in your mind long
    after I am gone

I want to share my laughter with you
    letting it ricochet off the trees of
    life surrounding us to knock us
    over again and again until our
    smiles touch and we stop to listen
    to the silence

I want to lay skin to skin with you
    erasing all thoughts of this and
    that leaving memory's stream
    filled only with our love juices
    and the quiet gentleness of bodies
    entwined in peaceful dreams . . .

But the song is trapped in a heart that cannot laugh
And the body in a time that is allowed no dreams.

    —Donna M. Fackler

WAVES OF ETERNITY

My eyes bled diamond tears
    Muffled in a flash of screaming navy
That lapped at my throat
And dragged at my bones

Endless motion enveloped strength
While thick crystal sheets were hurled
Caves of shaded glass glazed sunlight
From my whimpering eyes

Shattering cold gripped and pinched me
Wet sparks were flung wickedly
Gashing not my skin but my emotions
Violent thrashings tore at me

Flooded calls filled my ears
Air and water became one
My memories plunged into nothing
Fading movements controlled me

The lashes of piercing strength
Sagged against me
Survival's grip held me in safety
Leaving the waves of eternity behind.

    —Shelley Hoenle

PARENTS

Parents are here to comfort and share,
    To answer our questions, to give their care.
They're here to love
They're here to guide
My parents always take pride.
In the things I do
And the things that I say
My parents will love me in every possible way.

    —Carla Wing

FRIENDS

When the storms of life have surrounded us,
    And we feel our strength depleted,
We must then look towards others,
For the comfort that is needed.

Only in friends can we find,
The strength to carry on.
For a friend will always be there for you,
When the others have long since gone.

A friend will give you joy again,
Or lend a helping hand.
They'll listen to your troubled woes,
And they'll always understand.

They'll take the time to guide you through,
The hard times along the way.
They'll stand beside you all the while,
As your night turns into day.

True friends are treasures to be cherished,
For they are gifts that are the kind,
That are sought after and valued above all else,
But are the hardest of all to find.

    —Deborah M. Latke

TRUE FRIENDSHIP

When I look into your eyes,
    I can see the streaks of pain,
Oh please, tell me what is
            wrong, my friend,
So I can wash it away.

You see, you mean a lot to me,
No one else could mean the same,
You are my one true friend
            forever,
No one could ever take that
            away.

We've shared some good times
            and some bad.
That I still hold in my heart,
I finally realized why you are full
            of pain, my friend,
It is now our time to depart,

We have both grown up,
And now finally going our separate
            ways.
I hope you will never forget the
            love we shared each day,

You see, our friendship meant a lot
            to me,
And I hope it meant a lot to you,
I just want you to remember,
            my dearest friend,
I will never, ever forget you.

    —Patricia Gasper

UNTITLED

I walked upon a hill of dreams
To climb a mountain of hopes
And as I stood alone upon the mountaintop
I could see your eyes in the stars
I seemed to hear you softly singing far away
And I whispered your name to the wind
And though you stand upon a distant shore
Perhaps one day, as you walk alone
That gentle wind will find you
And you will hear my voice on the wind
Calling to you

—Tanya L. Marr

LIFE

Life is like a flower
blooming in Spring,
showing radiant colors to the world,
bringing happiness and joy to all who see it.
Then suddenly its petals droop
and the colors fade. It withers and dies
and its remains are blown away by the wind,
never to be seen again.
We must treasure our lives
like a gardener treasures a flower,
for our days are few and we only have
one life to live.

—Katie Vander Molen

STOPPED AT THE WOODS

The woods are silent, without depth
And tell of promises not kept.
The old stone walls are falling down.
The pastures moan with houses grown,
And on the wire, the cardinal, crow
Look down on progress here below.
The red fox finds the woodchucks' scarce
And looks for kittens in the grass.
The deer peek out at roadsides brown
For shelter, grass or bloodied brow.
Suburban spread has reached the wood
And touched the ancients where they stood;
Now boys and girls will laugh and clap
On pavement in a cul de sac.

—Susan E. Guilmain

LAND OF DREAMS

I have been through many lands,
And walked up to my knees in sand.
But these are not ordinary places
Nor are there the usual faces.

I do not get to them by ship.
Even an airplane couldn't make the trip.
They are far away,
In worlds sung of by lay.

The usual modes of transportation
Cannot give you a free vacation.
The best way is to use your mind,
Since dreams can create worlds of any kind.

Dreams don't cost anything,
But can give everything.
All you have to do
Is let yourself go through
The door between dreams and you.

—Kristine K. Stukerjurgen

PLEASE DON'T PLAY "THE GREEN BERET"

Please don't play "The Green Beret" —
Our boy just left with his troop today,
He doesn't need those wings on his chest,
To us, he was always "America's Best" . . . .

So please don't play that song today,
For we see our boy with his fearless wave —
The wings on his chest, for all to see
And the paratroopers emblem, upon his sleeve . . . .

It's just a song of America's brave,
And we loved to listen as the music played —
But now, with each word, our blood turns cold,
Our eyes fill with tears, as the story unfolds . . . .

So please don't play "The Green Beret" —
You see, our boy just left with his troop today,
He doesn't need "Silver Wings Upon His Chest"
To us, he was always "America's Best."

—Margaret Muirhead

AMERICAN

Always going non-forward, non-stop.
Always climbing to the top.
Proud of what we are,
And how we've come so far.

We made our way by sail.
We prayed to God we would not fail.
Then we saw the land;
We were guided by his hand.

We've liberated ourselves from a tyrant,
We've searched for freedom and we've found it.
We've fought our "mother" country for liberty.
We have become a nation that everyone could see.

We've welcomed people with unlocked doors.
We've triumphed in both World Wars.
We've fought back when we were wronged.
We have become a nation that is strong.

We've been through Hell and through war,
We're made up of rich and poor,
We're made up of black, white and tan,
We are proud, we are
AMERICAN

—Shane Joseph Lussier

MY AMERICAN DREAM

I dream to be a President of my country,
I dream to be a wealthy landholder,
I dream to have millions of dollars to spend,
I dream to have a beautiful home to keep warm,
I dream to look good in many clothing,
I dream to have a nice car to drive around,
I dream to be a businessman with profits,
I dream to travel around the world,
I dream to live at many places on this earth,
I dream to be in space exploring the universe,
I dream to make history on any accomplishment,
I dream to have many friends in my community,
I dream to have an appearance of good looks,
I dream to have numerous parties for fun,
I dream to have girlfriends to date them one by one,
I dream for a family who cares for one another,
I dream to be healthy so I'll live long,
I dream to be a good person rather than bad,
I dream to be happy rather than sad,
I dream My American Dream to come true.

—Kory Chavez

DAWN

Dawn breaks clear,
Over the sphere,
With sharp awareness,
Of splendor
And surrender,
As the many shades of pink and yellow intertwine;
In glory sublime.
Colors of the warmest,
Light up my heart this morn,

Then the sun,
At first shy,
Suddenly breaks forth;
To boast of its brilliant light
And sets its ray over all the peaceful morning tide;
Leaving my soul in breathless wonder,
At the beauty of the sight.

—Karon Greene

DAYS ENDED

My life is over,
My time is calling,
I heard it this morning,
In the song of a bird,

It's a chapter of memories,
Carelessly taken through time,
Like sunshine rolling upon streams,
Happy to see it pass,
But sad it's gone forever,

My heart's been so many times broken,
Why don't they want me?
The voice of my heart goes unspoken;
I cry once in a while.

But I'll miss the sea breeze,
I'll miss the tender mornings,
I'll miss being able to laugh,
And being able to cry.
I'll miss those who once loved me,
And never having a chance to just say goodbye.

—Eric Proescholdt

TOO OLD

Cursed at his birth in some shamble of pain
Beaten and cheated by some unkind fate
Fast chained by his dull, unknowing brain
To the gate of his master; Greed and Hate.
Is this poor creature the image of the Maker
This old, bent thing who begs a dime?
This derelict who waits for the undertaker
And who spends his last dime for wine?
Does God wander or starve on Skidrow
Because he's too old or cripple to work?
Or are all these old men that we know
Just lazy and professional shirks?
Today I talked with poor old Nick
Who came out here to the mines . . .
So handy was he with his pick
The boss raised his wages one time.
So eager was he for his master's goal
That he worked sixteen hours a day.
But he hurt his back lifting the coal
That's why he walks that way.
Is this God's image and likeness
So impatient and ready to go?
Half dead from life's sickness
I can't believe it's so . . . .

—Andrew Book

IN MEMORY OF MOTHER

Dear God, please help to ease my pain
I knew it couldn't last;
A bond that strong must end someday
The years went by so fast!

My love for her will never end
Nor will her love for me;
I miss her more and more each day
With her, I long to be.

I know You hold her gently
And safely in Your arms,
Her peaceful rest is well deserved
She's free from Earthly harm.

So, I'll live with precious memories
Of days that used to be,
I'll try to do Your will and hers
Until my soul is free.

—Phyllis C. Ransom

THE ESCAPE

I saw into the emptiness
Life itself started to sway
You were standing silent in darkness
My heart began to drift away
I cried and reached with all my might
As your darkness poured into me
Hoping, praying to retain some light
Though I knew it would not be
Engulfing my soul and twisting my psyche
I struggle to resist my thoughts
Imprisoned by the web you weaved for me
Finally catching a glimpse of what I've sought
I laugh because I made it out, I knew,
While countless others may not
The darkness recedes back to you
This encounter was mine, we'd fought, I'd won
Though I know I laugh in vain
For I'm no more than the mortal man
And you will greet me once again
With your icy outstretched hand

—Stuart Price

DROWNING

With eyes wide open,
He cannot see—

He's so consumed
With he and she!

All around him is a
raging sea.
The one in the middle
drowning is me!

I've given him
nineteen years of my life.
To have it erased with
one little swipe.

I've taught him and
nursed him and cuddled
and loved him.

She has erased all
his emotions for me.

Why can he not see?
The one, who is drowning is me!

His Mother
—Mary G. Nagel

SOMETHING I CAN'T SHARE

How can I say what's in my heart
How can I express my thoughts,
My heart is just an open book
That can be broke and tore apart.

I wonder if each tear I shed
Will ever heal the sores
I ponder this each day goes by
And then I wonder more and more

Heartaches come it seems to me
Like raindrops from the sky
Fast and quick they seem to be
As if they'll never dry.

But why should I to you complain
This is my cross to bear
And though it has a lot of pain
This is something I can't share

—Theda Fizer (deceased 7/22/89)

NATURE'S MASTERPIECE

Swinging in the breeze.
Hanging from one self-made
Strand
Like the pendulum
In my grandfather clock,
Eight legs scramble
To reach the top
Each one falling,
Gracefully,
One after another
Like a ballet dancer.
The crafty work
So skillfully patterned
Catches the sunlight
Glistening
Like the diamond on a newlywed ring finger.
But all the day's hard work
ruined
As the unsuspecting intruder
Prances through the masterpiece.

—Kirsten Hannawald

I . . . TRAVEL———

I . . . . .
Walk alone . . . . .
A traveler . . . . .
Away from home———

People . . . . .
All around . . . . .
I can't whisper . . . . .
Even a sound———

A friend . . . . .
I find one . . . . .
Yet times flies . . . . .
Then he is gone———

Unspoken . . . . .
Thoughts of home . . . . .
Now I whisper . . . . .
To the moon———

I . . . . .
Walk with the moon . . . . .
We're travelers . . . . .
Nearer to home.

—Zaleta Romano

TIME

Where am I going? Where have I been? Oh where has the time slipped away? It seems such a short time ago. I was skipping around with my hair in two long silky braids. Oh where has the time slipped away?

Now my hair is faded and streaked with gray. My steps are slower each day. Where did I come from? Where have I been? Oh where did the time slip away?

Now the face I see in my looking glass is faded wrinkled and old. For it was such a short time since I saw her there. So young and sweet pretty and fair.

Yes from second, to minutes. From minutes, to hours. From hours to weeks. From weeks to years. That's where she came from. Now where will I go? Forward the clock turns, and older I'll grow.

—Loretta Bice Austin

STAND UP

I wonder if anybody cares;
I wonder if anybody dares
to take a chance and really share.

The price is high to really let go;
Your feelings, thoughts and fears to show.
To allow your friends and foes
to see your high's and low's.

I wonder if anybody cares what I think,
or am I just a part of an anonymous link
who's chiseled in stone, or stamped in ink—
Like a robot . . . not supposed to think!

I wonder why everything has to be wrong or right;
Why can't you constructively disagree in full sight,
Still seeing that accepting light
As you lay your head on your pillow at night.

I wonder; surely, many care.
I know that many must dare
to take a chance and really share.
I fear, that maybe, there are few.

—Mary Ann Viator

STARLIGHT

To color my life with beauty strong
as within my dreams there is no wrong
my heart searches for the purest song
among the halls of loneliness.

There within a virtue I seek
chastised and framed among the weak
and frightened by the touch of cheek
among the fields of pleasures blessed.

Surely there are drums for all to see
the inner beauty that does not flee
from birth to death our passions plea
among the family within the nest.

Capture each silence in earthly sound
the cry of hope within each is bound
to wander in hunger as ancient hounds
among the timbers of the wilderness.

From waters edged with sands so dry
to mountain peaks that touch the sky
I seek the strength from which to fly
among the distant stars of promises.

—William R. Bowman, Sr.

THE DAWN OF AUTUMN

The mist of God's Breath surrounds the wood,
  blanketing, filling it with Life.
The trees, like sleeping children
with arms outstretched,
silently wait to be touched by the Hand of Morning.
Between Night and Day,
they are trapped
in another's dreamscape.
Untouching dimensions meet
and the Metamorphosis comes.
Colors blend and merge
and then grow vividly distinct
as the Spell is broken by the
first rays of the Autumn morning.
The tree children awaken and
once again assume their roles
as Purifiers of the Air,
but now carry with them
Color into the world.

—Ann Marie Dirsa

MORE THAN A CARPENTER

More than a babe in an oxen's stall,
  More than a lad with hammer and awl;
More than a carpenter who worked with wood
Helping Joseph as much as He could.

He amazed the scribes and Pharisees too
By His knowledge of scripture and things He could do.
He healed the sick, caused the lame to walk;
Restored sight to the blind, caused the dumb to talk.

More than a carpenter, this young Nazarene
Touched the lives of those who had seen
His great compassion for those that were lost
By witnessing His death upon the cross.

Poor blind souls who cannot see,
He's more than a carpenter, He's our destiny.
He's the promised Messiah, God's own Son;
He's the great "I Am", the Anointed One.
He's the Mighty Counselor, Saviour and King,
He's the Prince of Peace, He's our Everything.

—Doris B. Clearman

REFLECTION

They call a man a genius who can write at length
  And write convincingly of things that matter.
He writes because it is expected of him.
But few there are who read
And few who read
Who understand.

But take the simple man.
His life is nurtured by his surroundings—
His loves, sorrows, and joys
Fashion and mold the words
His pen jots down,

Be it prose or poetry.
You know him.
He is the man next door;
The teacher of sciences;
The peddler who cries his wares;
The beggar on the corner.
Yes, he is the simple man
Whose only art is to speak the words
That are in his heart.

—Ramona W. Leonard

ALL IN A DAY'S WORK

The dawn has come and duty calls,
  It brought the rain, the rain that falls.
And tiger lilies in their beds,
Through the rain had bowed their heads.
The rain has stopped,
Stillness disperses.
The lilies open,
Beauty emerges.
The sun, now shining, upon their faces,
The lilies stand at attention in their places.
The drops are reflectant upon the ground,
The lilies a new friend have found.
Through the storm, they withstood it all,
And then it came, it's called nightfall.
And now, that nightfall has come,
The lilies retire, their work done.

—Amy Lynn Wurzbach

A CLOUD

A cloud is but a fluff in space,
  Gathering moisture while it spans
The sky, we know for sure is an ace
That brings us luck, as more and more fans

The sky, and unite to bring us rain,
So man can raise his sugar cane.
They dance around and have such fun,
Scaring us, so to shelter we run.

When moisture content is too heavy, they roar
And moan and groan, and roar some more.
That is before they drop a load of hail,
You'd better seek shelter without fail.

After the rain is over the clouds float by
Gathering evaporated moisture on high
And zips in space to play and roam
Until they look like a ball of foam.

They float around as only clouds can
Until they pour water from their pan,
It is their work to help form a sky—
One of God's masterpieces from on high!

—Lois Flowers

THE DIFFERENT FACES OF LIFE

Overwhelmed with opportunities,
  Achieving goals, humanity, and challenges,
We are faced with CHOICES.

Watching lifelong friendships fade
As different courses of life are pursued,
We are faced with NEW RELATIONSHIPS.

Responsible for decisions,
Actions, mistakes, and failures,
Not as eager to get up after falling,
We are faced with STARTING OVER.

Achieving happiness through security
Rather than the recklessness of yesterday,
Falling into patterns rather than breaking them,
We are faced with MONOTONY.

Longing for what the years have taken away,
Leaving a void unfulfilled,
We are faced with ACCEPTING OURSELVES.

Although we long for it as a child,
We regret when it approaches,
We are faced with ADULTHOOD.

—Traci Nagy

TOMORROW

A sleeping cat,
A shining moon —
It is tonight!

A blink of eyes,
A streak of sunshine —
It is tomorrow!

—Samuel Ravenel Gaillard

YOU

You are my rock to lean on,
My lighthouse in a storm,
You are my fire when I'm
cold,
Your love keeps me warm!

I'd be lost in life without you,
Just wouldn't know what to do!

Say you'll always love me,
As I will always love you!!!!

—Jessie Cooper Owens

AWAY FROM YOU

Being away from you,
I miss you so much.
Your smile, gentle eyes,
    Your tender touch
So far away from me.
I hoped that I could have been
All that you wanted me to be,
All that you could ever need.
If I came back
Would we try again?
Can our love withstand another test?
Please, let us try our best.

—Heidi Hantsbarger, age 16

TO DAD

Dad is very nice.
If he was a toy, he would be
at a high price!

Dad is more than fantastic;
  he shares his love like
  elastic.

Dad is always true.
I know that he can make
people feel the way I do.

If Dad is last place,
  he doesn't care; just as
  long as he plays fair.

—Katherine Orloff

MY MARINE

Up in the air or down on the ground
Across the lands or out of town
Over there in other lands
Beached out on foreign sands
One day you'll find the mystery me
Then you'll be my marine.

—Ginnie J. McNally

BACKYARD HAPPINESS

Backyard Happiness
Flies in on wings
Flitters in the branches
Whispers to the leaves
"We love you"
"Protect our food"
"We love you"
"Morsels good"
"We love you"
They fly by
Backyard Happiness

—Jan Neville

PIANO RECITAL

Up and down my fingers go,
Not missing a single key.
Playing all the notes I know,
ABCDEFG.

Oh no! I hit the wrong note.
What am I going to do?
There's no time to stop and gloat.
Come on, I'm almost through!

Up and down my fingers go,
Wanting to stop, rest, or pause.
Now play the ending, take it slow.
Stand up and hear the applause!

—Christine Smith

HECETA HEAD

The wave batters
The long, low, cliff line,
Cascading, crescendo-like,
Making music from microscopic life
Sacrificed on the altar
That the shore creates
As an entrance
From infinity to life,
From inchoate mass
To a formal remembrance
That lasts.

Written at Heceta Head, Oregon, looking down from the mountainside to the sea.

—Nancy Terrell Yacher

94

MORNING ON THE WATERWAY

Coffee in hand, I glide outward to my deck
My chair same place I left it last evening.
Sky of powder blue, clouds like cotton
Trees of greens and browns.
Sounds of sea gulls, splashing mullets
Cranes white, like fresh snow.
Life is stirring,
As nature presents her outstanding free show . . .

—Vicky Vaughan Hobbs

Come my friend and go on a journey with me,
where only the minds eye can see.

Gently now, let us set our souls free, to
the pleasures beyond reality.

Ah my friend can you not smell the soft
scent of the flowers that bloomed so freely
in the fields where we played as children.

Feel the summer wind and listen as it
carried the birds sweet songs to our ears
when we so young and free.

Remember the water that flowed so freely
down the mountain stream, where we sat and
dreamed how wonderfully adventurous our
lives would turn out to be.

Feel the heat of the fire that warmed us as
the harsh winds of winter blew all around.

Such a world this is that only our minds eye
can see, so lovely and free.

Sadness touches us now as we journey back to
reality.

I leave all but one thing in my journey back
to reality, My shared friendship that I have
had for so many years with thee.

—D. B. Eccles

OUR AMERICA

God made our America
    Not just for you and me
He placed her proudly
    For all the world to see.

Gave her the love and freedom
    The respect for the rights of man
Brought her the down trodden masses
    Our people our promised land.

Taught her how to govern
    Our laws in constitution set
Boldly there in book is written
    Lest we e'er forget.

Proudly our banner still flying
    To show we love and do care
We may die for our trying
    Our freedoms still will be there.

Stand up and proudly be counted
    The strong the free and the brave
And prove to all our dead heroes
    The worth of their number and grave.

God made our America
    Not just for you and me
Fight to the last man to keep her
    The home of the brave and the free.

—Isabelle M. Wall

Like quiet pads of kitten feet
    Sleep crept into bed with me.
Like the soft caress of a lover's kiss
    It brushed my eyelids tenderly.

Sleep warmed my veins with soothing strokes
    And nudged me into an abyss
Of blackness cozy with the thoughts
    Of sweetest dreams of happiness.

Perchance to dream with joyous heart
    Of loved ones missed and far away—
But closer now because our hands
    Will lock together 'till next day.

Oh! Lovely sleep—please come with speed
    My loved ones wait impatiently—
To meet me in my world of dreams
    To laugh and love in sweet memory.

—Thelma G. Cremeans

TIP TOE TULIP TIME

They cautiously peek up thru the ground
    And spread their petals to look around,
A bluebird sings perched in a tree
Where budding leaves, finally free

Of frost, wave in the gentle breeze,
A babbling brook flows, after the freeze,
The old world becomes new, as a shower
Playing peek-a-boo with the sun, stirs the flower

And grass to life from a drowsy sleep
To refresh this world, as the hoppers leap,
The bees buzz around the ladened rose bower
while butterflies gracefully soar and flutter.

Who can be depressed at the arrival of Spring
When new life replaces the old in everything?
Our earth is recreated once each year,
No force can prevent the Masters' hand in gear.

—Della May Marsh

BUGGY RIDE

In an open buggy we did ride
One summer day, side by side

Through the village square.
We were quite a handsome pair.

The morning was sunny and bright,
Green was everything in sight

Except for the blue river and sky
And a sloping housetop we passed by.

We rode slowly on down the narrow lane
By the Clark's red barn and weather vane.

They were standing by the big round silo,
Smiling as we drove by; we waved hello.

Still further on and up a winding hill
By the O'Malley's house and windmill,

We crossed the arched bridge at the water wheel,
The general store where one can grind corn meal.

Time and breath stood instantly still
As we stopped on top of "Lovers' Hill."

The song of the mockingbird was clear
As the whispered words "I love you, dear."

Under the old oak tree, in the carriage
You softly asked for my hand in marriage.

—Bonnie McGill Cohn

SEASONS

We see fallen rose petals in
  the hot May sun.
Which tells us summer has
  slowly begun.
Fall comes in with brownish-
  red frills.
Then winter enters and gives us
  the chills.
After the coldness when spring is in
  all is renewed and we rebegin.
As you see the seasons all
  differ.
But if you really look you will
  see a surprise.
That all seasons change right before
  your eyes.

—Samantha Evard

A WORD OF THANKS

I thank Thee oh God that I can see
The beauty of nature surrounding me
The glorious stars and the raging sea

I thank You oh God that I can smell
The perfume of flowers I see in the dell
A freshly cut tree a woodsman doth fell

I thank Thee oh God that I can hear
The soft mellow tunes that catch my ear
The caressing words of a friend who's dear

I thank Thee oh God that I can touch
These animal friends I love so much
The strong hand of a friend and such

I thank Thee oh God that I can taste
The food that I eat though it's oft times in haste
Forgive me please for that which I waste

I thank Thee oh God for all things that are living
And for Thy bountiful blessings
On these days of Thanksgiving

—K. N. Nestor

SNOW

Snow is a wonderful thing
occasionally arriving from fall 'til spring,

It covers our yard of unwanted leaves
that had their turn and said goodbye to the trees,

Our house decorated like a big frosted cake
Ice showing at the back of the lake,

Windows displaying a light of glow
Front yard covered with layers of snow,

This truly is a wonderful scenery
replacing the summer and all its greenery,

So different as the night and day
each so perfect in its own way,

Then one day we see the sun
winter is over and spring has sprung,

We look foward to the showers
beauty and fragrance of the flowers,

We will miss you Mr. Bright
so perfect in your robe of white,

There's no other can take your place
you're truly a color of love and grace.

—Virginia McKinney

AMERICA THROUGH MY EYES

It's beautiful for its spacious skies,
through which our Air Force flies.
  And for the amber waves of grain,
that grow in our farmers' fields,
that we thrive on,
  because they keep us alive.
  For the purple mountains majesties,
above the fruited plains,
  that make us try so hard,
to do our best,
for all the rest.
  America, even though we sometimes
fall,
  you pick us up,
  and serve us a cup,
of your pride, hearts, and lands.
We praise you for each sunrise,
and sunset.

—Heidi Amber Googe

SILENT WHISPERS

There's a magic land where Unicorns play
Where Fairies and Elves whisper and say,
To the big people, saying, can you hear me?
Ha! Ha! Can you see me?
A sprinkle of glitter and off they go
Not caring for pain or trouble I know.

The Fairies have a jackpot of Leprechaun's gold
With other jewels and precious gems untold,
The Unicorns are white with colors of pearl
Their horns of a majestic golden twirl.

Is it so wrong to want this story to be real?
Maybe for children who don't know how they feel,
We have stars, suns, and moons that shine and
glitter
But a child can lose love and become so bitter,
Let them run around playing and saying,
Can you hear me, Ha! Ha! Can you see me.

—Karen Lee Hayes

THE SEAGULL

The early morning beach was desolate
except for the boy and I.

He loitered at some distance
kicking random rocks with one sneakered toe
skipping them across half-hearted waves.

My bare feet wrinkled in dismay at the surprise
of chilly water at the ocean's edge.

I saw him first
a blur of wings and bright excitement
in the sky
as though someone had told him some good news.
He was exultant in his soaring freedom
his bouyant grace.

And then it happened
the small sharp stone zinging through the air
with deadly accuracy

He faltered in the sunlight
wings in slow motion
drifting, drifting, toward the sea.

The splash made hardly any sound at all.

—Sister Maureen Thompson

GOLDEN ANNIVERSARY

Life is a game of give and take,
Love makes it all worthwhile.
There are problems and heartaches most every day,
    But Fran meets it all with a smile.

So we've walked together these 50 years,
    Sometimes the wind rose to a gale.
Fran stood tall with his head held high,
    As a shield for Ruth to walk through.

Then came the day life's price must be paid,
    Fran's body lies still and cold.
Strength comes from God as Ruth walks alone,
    The golden years are done.

Once more love shines through the gloom of life's tasks,
    Memories become very real.
Heaven is dearer than earth ever could be,
    Fran is at Home, and the latch string is out.

        —Ruth Burns

WHERE

All around, donkeys fly
Where cotton candy floats in the sky,
Where birds soar backwards through the air,
And fish have long, curly hair,
Where dogs say "moo," and cows go "tweet,"
Where snakes have ears and furry feet,
Where trees grow down from the clouds to the ground,
Where songs are sung without any sound,
Where statues become people, and pictures can talk,
Where a trip to the moon is just another walk,
Where strange things happen for no apparent reason,
Like snowfall and droughts all in the same season,
Where rainbows appear without first having rain,
Where nothing happens twice, and things are never
the same.
Where is this world, so odd and reversed,
Where first is second, and second is first?
Not on a different planet, your mind's your only
transportation.
This fun place is called your imagination!

        —Bridget Colleen Foley

COWBOYS HEART

They say that Cowboys are tough and raw,
    And seldom express what they're feelin.
They hardly ever talk about ma or pa,
And in love they won't be dealin.

To show that you might be soft and tender,
Could be a wound for funnin.
They might even question your own gender,
And Cowboys ain't for runnin.

So to play it safe they'll compose a poem,
And tell how they might feel.
They'll talk of things like home sweet home,
And other things that are real.

They'll mention things of family and life,
And things they might hold true.
They'll talk of children and their wife,
And they might even mention You.

But if they never show their love,
They still do have that part.
For we were all made by God above,
And He gave us all a heart.

        —Dave Knight

LAKE SUPERIOR

Its voice is ever-changing,
Its conversation never planned,
When it speaks to us in whispers
As it laps against the sand.
Then its whitecapped waves leap skyward
And it speaks with thunderous roar.
As if aroused with anger,
It attacks the rocky shore.
Our heartland's largest mirror
Can quite mesmerize the eye
When this liquid-ice volcano
Erupts against the sky.
From eons past, in timeless time,
Not ruled by gods or man,
Its innate beauty has survived —
A superior master-plan.

        —Marvin L. Nelson

UNHAILED PROTECTORS

The night is dark and still of sound,
    The good people are all asleep.
Unknown to them our safety is found
In commitment that runs deep.

In freezing cold and thunderstorms,
In heat no one could bare,
They steadfast hold to keep the peace
and villians from lurking there.

They know what price their job does take,
In family, self, and stress.
But dedicated to their beliefs
they stay to calm the unrest.

When we get caught for doing wrong
But think we're really right,
Remember please by not following the law,
We're endangering another person's life.

Thank you Officers for your strength,
And guarding us in our sleep.
We're glad you're here to do your job,
Happy Police Officers Week.

        —donna f. castillo

WISE LITTLE POLLYANNA

Pollyanna was her name —
    she had a gladful game,
of turning doom and gloom
into a happy day.

Her attitude to some
is deemed to be unwise;
but little do they know
what she learned from inside.

In her innocence and glee
she found an ancient truth —
perceptions create reality.
Such wisdom from a youth!

She saw perceptions play a part
in what one's life will be;
chosen feelings from the heart
enslave or set one free.

It's all in how one wants to see
what life is all about —
perceptions glad and happy
sure beat the down and out!

        —Sunshine Lahman

SIMPLY CREATION

Older than me they say,
   "Grow up, grow up today!"

The truth, the truth?
Creation is truth.

Create in your spirit
Immortal youth.

—Maria Lineker

HIDDEN BLESSINGS

O'er the rainbow we are told
   There may be a pot of gold . . .
Is it treasure Time's forgot;
Our God's truth to want not?
For a portion we will strive,
Thus the nature of being alive.
Too much wanting causes grief,
A heavy burden beyond belief!
Appreciate the while you have bliss,
The 'little comforts' you might miss . . .
Hidden blessings you will find
Is the joy of Peace of Mind.

—Sylvia Rosalita Kates

GOD'S LIGHT SHINES
ON YOU

Roses are Red
   Violets are Blue
I'm One of God's Children
And So Are You.

The Sun Shines So Bright
The Moon and Stars Too
This Lets You Know, God's Light
Is Always With You.

So when You feel You're
All Alone
Just Reach up to God
He's Always At Home.

He Hears Your Prayers
Both Day and Night
That's Why God's Light
Shines So Bright.

—Edith Jo Pettway

HIS GIFT

He was born, we rejoiced!
   In a small crude stable he lay.

He healed our wounds, we rejoiced!
His heart was filled with sorrow, for us.

He loved our children, he loved us.
And we rejoiced.

We stole,
We killed,
We hated,
We were idle . . .

He was killed,
By us,
He died,
For us,
He lives,

With us,
For us.

—Marian E. Drake

A PATTERN

There is a pattern, I am a part
   Of time and space there is a heart.
Mind formed this world and all about
   Mind formed this body within and without.

All things in consciousness continue
   Whether plant, fish, fowl or sinew.
O great Creator, is it true?
   I shall not be complete 'til I find You?

—Justine V. Circello

ENLIGHTENMENT

In the darkness of a dream, I am alone with a presence.
   There is no sound, nor any form of substance,
Just the knowledge that it is present and holy.
I am the one who breaks the silence
By boldly requesting a picture of God.
Instantly, there appears before me a frame
And I eagerly grasp it only to see
My own face reflected in a mirror.
Upon awakening, I am disturbed and confused.
But after awhile I am able to accept this visage,
For I remember that we all are made in His image.

—Anita-Goelz-Franke

ODE TO HISTORY

The one history book that teaches all
   is the Holy Bible which will never fall.
History isn't everyone's best, that's true,
but the Bible is the book that's read through and through.
The men in the Bible spoke with great strength,
and did mighty acts with torture at length.
A few of these men were martyrs in the end,
but that's when reward started and true life began.
The disciples were men who followed the Lord.
Never seemed tired, never seemed bored.
Stephen was stoned and left to die,
when the good Lord took him up to the sky.
Peter was crucified upside-down,
in hopes his soul to the devil would be bound.
The others were killed in the same fashion,
never doubting God's word or losing their passion.
Let these stories teach us a lesson:
Following God's word will surely be a blessing.

—Helen Malone

THERE'S NO HURRY

It's called the "Good Book" by many it seems
   And used at times to pray for our dreams
But it carries the rules, for man to live by.
And teaches how eternity can be ours when we die.

There are those who shout loud, times have changed, don't you see
The message no longer has values for me.
Man is king, live today, fun and frolic for now,
To greed and corruption and lust do we bow,
Life is short, we must play, take your Gospel away
I've no time for religion, maybe some other day.

We leave God in His Heaven, crying out, can't they see
The one hope for this world, is to turn now to Me.
But we lend a deaf ear, there is no need to hurry
And we run from the message, not a care nor a worry
I have time, maybe next year I'll listen, we'll see.
Fool, tonight your soul may be required of thee.

—June K. Montgomery

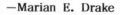

THE CAPTAIN AND SHE

Rubies and amethysts
Red mingles with blue,
As the sun takes its rest in the sea
Ablaze with reflection of light against night
Becoming a mirror for She.

Now the harbor is dark
And the wind gently blows
Through the rigs and the masts and the trees
Over 600 miles between Captain and She
He hears her bells toll in the breeze.

She is bound to him
Not by her choice, by her ropes
She awaits him secure in her hopes
The course that he takes is his pleasure to tell
She cares not but his wind's in her sail.

—Lila M. Fairbrother

PASSER BY

Passer by dont stand and weep
For my finest hours are well to keep
In the eyes of those and hands of many
My life has been full fantastic plenty

Passer by please tarry not
For I have loved to live and that a lot
The treasures of mine are now of those
Whose lives I have touched the beauty it shows

Passer by lead not a life
That possesses irony satire agony strife
Live day by day and vision the moment
The one of truth the one that has sent

This passer by please understand
That life has been clear wonderful grand
Walk past this moment and remember me not
That I too was a passer by but now forgot

—Stephen W. Yates

YOUR PRECIOUS LITTLE FEET

A pair of precious little feet one time
Walked boldy without much tact.
They stepped up, onto my knee,
Then crept slowly up my back.

Their steps were heard, as they crossed my mind,
Such a pronounced sound they made.
In search of quarry, but I knew not what
But, ahead I knew it still laid.

As they entered into my heart,
Their steps were precise and bold.
I knew then why they were there.
They were there in search of my soul.

Their tracks were deep and accurately placed.
It's the one thing I've guarded against.
Others had made the trip before,
But always away they were sent.

For when a person enters this place
And tracks up this hallow ground.
There's no way to smooth it over
And leave it as it was found.

For always the prints will remain
Because the steps were impressed too deep.
No one else could fill the impressions,
Made by your precious little feet.

—David L. Nelson

THE DOLEFUL CHILD

Woe, befallen Johnny, not brought to light,
Lies smothered in subconscience of the child.
His startled eyes and lonely heart, beguiled.
Tears, which have no place to go dim his sight.
His festered mind becomes malignant fright.
Worldly eyes are turned to him, as wild.
No spirit sees inside the covered bowl,
Nor feels the pain of torment in his mind.
There, worms are slowly eating at his soul,
To kill the cure he hopes so much to find.

We punish him! For what? He does not know.
And treat him in a much familiar way.
He grinds his stubborn teeth, gives us a show.
But where is comprehending at today?

—Jackie A. Larsen

KINSHIP

The ghost of mariner whisper to porpoise,
The bone marrow of kinship.
Kinship? Oh, Adam,
We are the fish that came out of the sea.

The sun's glance at a passing star,
And earth's bassoon murmur
Margined the cloud beginning the first day.
The garden, we never named it.
All trees and fruit that moved in forest and field
Were as one, all the same to us.

The baby antelope lay still
Blood---the rainbow spectrum red.

Awareness is not all
In the naming of name,
The word is prey, in the
Meld stone in mountain,
In the snake power, disguised in the totem
In the cat monolith elongate on the horizon.

And I looked at Adam, as Adam,
For the first time
As we stumbled out of the garden.

—Ernest J. Sneidman

JOHN

Why didn't you warn me
When you came to my door
That we were starting on
A roller coaster ride?

Why didn't you tell me
That after you
Every other lover would fall short
Of my expectations?

Why didn't I tell you "no"
All those years ago?
I think your tight jeans
Wouldn't let me.

Do you think I have forgotten?
Our time together surrounds me . . . .
Train whistles, pick-up trucks, parks, lawn
  mowers, hot baths, cold sheets, hard bodies . . . .
How could I forget?

Remember when we said good-bye (again)?
I planted a tree that day.
I wonder which of us will make it without you?
I'm betting on the tree . . . .

—Virginia Gilliland Cherry

99

WAVES

Icy foam crested waves
race each other to shore
smothering tiny pebbles
and shattered bits of speckled shells;
erasing tiny footprints
and magic fortresses skillfully molded from white
seaweed garnished granules, before becoming
one again with the sea.
Violent ones crash against jagged edged boulders
and thrash the sea wall with a mighty vengeance
spraying salted foam high into the sky.
Some calm, cool, mildly frothy edged,
roll swiftly, evenly,
touch white sand and slither back
with barely a ripple.

—Annemarie McPherson

ICE

She is cold and sealed above the sea
Heaving and swaying with every breeze.
Locks of snow encircle her head
Bringing light to what is dead.

Beneath the ice lies a gripping tale
Of silent worms and eyeless snails.
A walrus appears in silent form
And gropes the mud in a silent storm.

With green hair and violet eyes,
Crimson teeth and horny sides
A Sea Urchin is lifted and starts to float.
She drifts and falls down an icy moat

The rain of dust from the oozing sludge
Blocks out the light, and new creatures budge.
The Lantern Fish and the flying Skate
Slip in and out of the walrus' wake.

The walrus turns and rises up
To catch a breath and rest his sup.
He breaks his head through the frozen snow
And meets the spear of the Eskimo.

—James W. Farr

COMMISERATION FOR DALI

Clocks melting, torreadors hallucinating
Through the shadows of time.
Space makes way for another entity.

Abeyance of time, cogitation of man
Looking for the past through the future.
Open yourself to the truth of surrealism.

The numerous aspects of existence
Gnaw at the brain, screaming to be
Recognized, waiting to be avenged.

Delusions react inside your head,
Abrupt in form, coagulating into
An organism worthy of the name Id.

Eyes wander into the eighth dimension,
Images perceived as delirious invitations
To crucify the Almighty.

Waves of reality break into coalescence.
They reel through space as if enlightening
The ways of the elders.

Thoughts of violence seen in your face
Can be interpreted in only one way:
¡Vengo! ¡Esperadme!

—Mike Compo

WISDOM

Timeless treasure to thirsty minds am I.
Down through the dusty clods of crumbling Time
Across Fate's rocky breast of fickle rhyme
Blindly grope their aching roots ever nigh
My ample spring. They struggle, sweat, cry;
Wandering, winding, lunging toward sweetness sublime:
Then, having quaffed my milky fount, surely climb,
Steadily up their matted ladders ever high
Across that wobbly rock, rootless and worn,
And through the crumbled clods to the cool sod:
Sleeping buds swelling in the dew of morn;
Unfurling in Fortune's glow of journeys plod;
Raising leafy arms from uplifted souls reborn;
Gaily stroking the jewelled skies of Almighty God!

—Wayne M. Bushnell Jr.

KEY

All of life is a key
All keys need locks
With lock a key hole is needed
The Key without the Lock is dead

Master Key comes up every morning,
goes down every evening.
Major Key comes up every evening,
goes down every morning
Minor Keys join the Major Key every night
Sometimes, they are not seen,
rest assured, they are there.

Clouds gather to form their Key
in gathering, form a skeleton Key —
unlock rain, storms, hurricanes,
All Keys bathe the Earth
clothe with flowers, trees, grass, food, and water

Keys were made for man
Man himself is a Key
Universe and mankind is Key hole
God, the Lock

—Elizabeth Payne Broughton

TRANSATLANTIC MOOD

Alone I ran through wet fields of tall grain,
That rolled to the shore in the wind and rain.
I came to rest overlooking the sea,
and called out your name; heard only by me.

Pointing, I found where the sea meets the sky;
She's out there somewhere thought I with a sigh.

A transatlantic mood that's felt by two;
Yes, I wish you were me and I were you.
You'd know why I felt intimidation;
I'd know how you felt by my invasion.

The surf crashed loudly on the rocks and then,
Called out once more, but it came back again.

Yet, aside from all this I raised my eyes,
Finding gulls on the wing that filled the skies.
Descend those winds that keep you 'bove the sea,
And take a message to my love for me.

Tell her that even though we're far apart,
Through space and time with her I sent my heart.

But the gulls still circled in swirls of rain,
And I still stood there dripping with the pain.
I called out your name once more just the same,
And with a tear, went back from whence I came.

—Brent Allan Gilbertson

AUTUMN

The sun comes up a foot away
    from where it did the other day.
She sinks in gentle sloping arcs
that take the light, and give the dark.
I stand and watch the colors change
and feel the roots that do remain
pulsed with the sap that's downward bent
to flow inside the world who's spent
her energy in life and birth,
for now it's resting in the earth.
I feel transition moving through
my self, my feelings changing hue.
As cycles sink into the ground,
a whispered silence with the sound
of angels calling those who pause
to view their lives through veils of gauze.

—J. Robbins Walker

PORTRAIT OF BEGINNINGS

In the background, light in the blackness of space;
Fiery disturbance bestows the universe shock,
Where out of nothing God's creation takes place;
Dramas of lightning and burning liquid rock.

At the top, scenes give way to weather
Depicting restless winds giving turbulent clouds a ride;
Evidence from storms of winter and summer together
In the firmament where the breath of God abides.

On one side, droughts painted broad, brown, and deep;
On the other, floods of muddy waters having significance,
Render the beholder stark record to keep,
Showing the earth's inhabitants their impotence.

On the bottom lies the transition of time.
Some scenes painted present the newness of spring,
While others exhibit color after summer resigns.
All bare record of giving way to change.

The portrait still hangs in the gallery of space.
Its author still grasps the frame.
But until time's color has faded from its face,
Earth, weather, and seasons perform on the same.

—Jesse E. Nance

AUTUMN LEAVES

I walk, silent; among smooth stones, carved with letters
    of long ago. Maybe I'm not really alone,

as I walk here, through these past lives. My tired heart;
    emotionless, my soul had fled, when you moved here.

Was it not just yesterday you could run and speak,
    and gently breathe? Can't I speak and hear an answer,

echoing from beyond this time, Can't I hear your
    sweet soothing voice run over me, like fresh water?

Like fallen leaves
crumbled and brown
life slowly dies
and blows away
with a soft breeze.

Now under my sad, weary, feet, you are silent;
part of Nature, touched with the gift of Peaceful rest,

Spirit surrounding my body. Maybe my heart
will be warm once more, after all the pain has gone.

When I look to the endless sky, memories of-
    you linger on . . . .

—Elizabeth Grace Jeffords

OPEN EYES

Through my closed wings,
    Nothing comes in.
    I allow no help,
    Is that a sin?

    Should I love?
    Should I care?
    Why not shove?
    Do I Dare?

    The misery is felt,
    The memories fade.
    Whose fault is that?
    No one is made.

Through my open wings,
    I allow the help,
    And do not shove.
And in return, I learn to love.

—Kristen Alphin

GIFT

For I walked in a garden of friendship,
    music and laughter falling on my ears;
I shook the hand of pleasure,
    a smile and some tears.

Some flowers in the garden faded
    as many of them will,
But their lasting impressions are
    imbedded in me still.

The path is wide and endless,
    in a garden of this kind;
We must but look around
    and a precious gift we will find.

The garden gate is open,
    an out-stretched arm as well;
An unknown friend is waiting,
    as only you can tell.

Extend your arm without delay,
    for this garden grows
In such a friendly way!

—Marjorie Haller Kozak

THE DESERT SANDS

Mirages seen on desert sands
    Always seem to slip away,
And so it's been since time began
And will be til the final day.

Dunes of sand shift slowly along
Across the bleak, bare, lonely land,
Like giant white ghosts of ancient myths
Roves this silent band.

History is bound in those desert sands
Of empires that rose and fell,
Of tyrants and kings who reigned of old,
Oh, how much those sands could tell!

A shattered visage lies here and there
Or perhaps a trunk or leg of stone,
But all the rest has faded away
To blend itself with the unknown.

So all that remains is a sea of sand
Wooed by the wind's eerie song,
Moving in dunes across the land
Like a great majestic throng.

—Danny Paulk

TIME WAITS FOR NO MAN

For seven days and seven nights,
I stared into the sky;
In hope to see a sign above
But you kept passing by.

You never spoke, nor waved a hand
When I was standing near;
You kept your pace and stood your ground
As if you didn't hear.

I held the hand of Father time
To slow you down a bit;
But when I saw your fading smile,
I knew I had been tricked.

—Doris Alexander

OLD YOUNG MEN

They came from all walks of life
To answer their country's call,
Some of them returned home safely
And some of them gave their all.

Most were children when they went
But they changed, I know not when,
Though their tours were just a short while
They came back as old young men.

It's been years since the war
They were taught to fight and kill,
No one taught them when to stop
Some of them are fighting still.

They've tried to forget the past
But the memories remain,
They have turned to drugs and drink
In order to numb their brain.

I pray God that they find peace
For no matter where they've been,
They belong to you and me
These loved ones, our old young men.

—L.O. "Sal" Salinas

THE SILENT FRIEND

You see all kinds of people
When you go to the market place
But the one who stands out most is the
Farmer,
Because he's walking at a different pace

He looks real tired
As he strives across the lot
He has been busy plowing and planting
all week
And the sun was extra hot

But he made it into town
To get the supplies he needs
Because the next week may be harder
But that's the life he leads

He understands his place
But I wonder if others do
That without his hard work
There wouldn't be anything here for
me or you

So I say, "Give the Farmer a hand"
To show our appreciation
Because if he stops what he is doing
We would be in a bad situation

—Harry Lee McNeil

ALL HEAVENS ASTIR

All heavens astir, they're singing in glory
And praising the Father, for sending His Son
Another dear soul has their name written down,
Yes, written down in glory!
For they've come to the foot of the cross
And accepted the dear Saviour,
Who died for their sins, so gloriously!
Now they've been washed in the Lamb's shed blood
And made whiter than snow!
Yes, made whiter than snow, made whiter than snow!
And purer than wool.

Now all heavens astir, they're singing in glory
And praising the Father, for sending His Son!
And praising the Father, for sending His Son!

—Ronald A. Fegley

YOU ARE MY FRIEND, MY BUDDY, MY PAL

You tell me you're leaving, and to understand,
Please, tell me how?
You say it's part of God's plan,
But, oh, the pain, the hurt, the sorrow.
You tell me to have courage, be strong.
It's so hard, knowing you will be gone some tomorrow.
You've been my brother, and friend so long.
I hang on to the sound of your voice and laughter.
I want to remember the sound I'll miss
And I will remember long after
When you're here no longer to call me sis.
I'll hurt, I'll grieve
Long after you leave
But I'll always cherish the memory of you
And all you've meant to me.
I'll try to remember when the pain makes me blue
You said, "Everyone has to die."
But dear brother I can't say good-bye
Just that I'll miss you.

This poem was written for my brother-in-law, Billy Miller, who
died July 12, 1989, after long suffering of terminal cancer.

—Lois Miller

MY FATHER

To a beautiful person
whom I love so very much,

He's always been right there
by phone, or glance, or touch.

He has been there each time to
help out, however in any way he could,

My head is held proudly high
but without his love, I would not have even stood.

I am myself and very proud of it
and for this I give thanks and pray,

For he is my beloved father
and in my heart he will forever stay.

It does not seem enough to just say "I love you, dad",
for so many feelings are in it,

That as many times I've given thanks for you to God above,
a raindrop on my head has hit.

I leave you now and give you
all the love I can from your daughter,

Thank you Lord for giving to me
my friend, my dad, my father!

—Tina E. Clermont

WHERE DID IT GO

Empty eyes staring into nothing
gone are all the emotions that once were
so profound, the love that shined so
bright as you gazed at your love ones
was like an embrace, where did it go?

The sympathy you felt so deeply for others
less fortunate was natural anyone
could see it came from the heart.
We were once so close now we are
worlds apart, where did it go?

Eyes that showed a love for life
changing with each emotion are now
colorless. Void from love and concern,
gone are the smiles to light up your
eyes and the tears to wash away
your fears. Gone is the love you
felt for me taken for reasons I
cannot see, where did it go?

—Alpha J. Washington
**Dedicated to my mother, Doretha Dobie
(A Victim of Alzheimers)**

REMEMBERANCES OF EOLINE BYROM VOCKROTH

How can you explain the love in her eye
Transcending disappointments she was hurt by?
How do you stand up to her lofty life's goals?
Her honesty and fairness were her unwavering molds.
That social awareness she was dedicated to.
Was born of a thoughtfulness for me and for you.
A striving for excellence in all she'd do
Was perfection of sorts with a gentleness, too.
Selfishness was considered, just short of a sin.
Such practice to her was indeed a no win.
Born to silver and, they say, social royalty.
It remained unannounced, her manner claimed loyalty.
As a chosen profession of housewife and mother,
She succeeded at these, I'm sure as no other.
Most leaders are born, maybe some made
Some stand in the sun, she chose the shade.
A lady of ladies, an elegance to behold
Not stiffly paraded, she had too much soul.
Her "I love you so much," oft quietly spoken
Was returned, it seems now, only in token.

—George B Vockroth

WHAT YOU MEANT TO ME

Words could never express
What you truly meant to me.
We went through a lot together
Good times and bad. Sharing each
other's joy and easing one another's pain,

You were always by my side
You were the caring shoulder to lean on
Always smiling, never complaining.
Just whispering "Things will be O.K."

All the riches in the world
Could never begin to replace you.
You brought sunshine and rainbows
To all those who knew you.
Everyone misses you, I miss you too.

I regret never telling you
what you meant to me.
The time never seemed right.
Now it's too late, now you'll never know
What you meant to me.

—Jeri Frady

WITHIN

Stay within the confines you make
Make a world within the world to live
Live and learn all there is, and watch
Watch the lives and joys of others
Others that dared to live and laugh
Laugh within the world they made
Made without the walls of those alone
Alone because they fear to reach out
Out of their prison never to be free
Free of burdens heaped upon self
Self trapped within a sea of despair
Despair of life based of fear and doubt
Doubt of self worth, yet fully aware
Aware of the strengths within oneself
Oneself that no one will ever know

—I.M. Shafritz

WHY THE CHILD

It's not my call to question you
Or ever ask you why
So I'll accept and understand
As least my Lord, I'll try.

But if, just if I were allowed
One answer in despair
I might better understand
And really know you care.

Throughout the world we all can see
One force against another
The family structure broken and
It's brother versus brother.

I know from you it isn't so
Would seem an awesome price
To make the children pay for sins
As if a sacrifice.

To take the innocence of youth
How precious when it smiled
My one question now would be
"Why Lord, why the child?"

—James LaFayette Walker

OH — HOW I WISH

Oh how I wish that you were here
To hear the words, "I love you dear"
I wish that I had said them more
Before the final closing of the door

Now that you are gone
I will carry on
And do the things I must do
To keep my memory of you.

You taught me courage and taught me faith
You taught me not to be afraid.
You taught me I must be strong
And you taught me—it's allright—to be wrong

For all the things you gave to me
And all the things you made me see
I cannot thank you, dear, enough
You've smoothed a road — Oh so rough!

Yes! How I wish that you were here
To hear the words, "I love you dear"
And, oh—I wish I'd said them more—
Before the final closing of the door.

To my dear husband & friend————
—Dorothy Wiesler

WALK SLOWLY

Walk slowly.
The days are going by too fast.
Look closely.
Enjoy the roses while they last.

Think clearly.
Good thoughts enrich the cloudy mind.
Speak softly.
Let all your words be wise and kind.

Love deeply.
Love makes the world go 'round, they say.
Live fully.
'Tis only once we pass this way.

—Flo Bell

THE WAITING

As each day passes
I blend within the masses,
But my thoughts are afar —
Many hours and miles by car,
To that sweet love of mine
Patiently waiting in the blind,
Not knowing when it will be —
For neither of us can see
A short end of this tragic fate
That separates me from my mate.
Condolences could never relieve,
Nor express the feelings to believe
That love will have its say —
More than words can express
On that day.

—Carl London

FREE AGENCY

Free agency is the clay,
With which I mold my life each day.
Thought by thought,
and act by act;
I move forward,
but sometimes back.
Each thought and act,
start a chain;
Link by link
results to gain.
Mistakes are changed
one by one,
reforging the link
that's been undone.
I'm free to live life
like a dream
or flirt with death
and all between.
God would not take
from me my choices.
I'm free to hear
all the voices.
I can be swayed
I can be led
but only I choose
the way ahead.
Evil wants power
to control
the very essence of my soul.
Good wants only to inspire.
Help me stretch to fly higher.
I'll try to live the best I know
For I'll be reaping what I sow.

—Laurel W. Mickelson

THE BULLS

I got my favorite western duds out.
Washed the cow green from my boots.
Slipped my ten gallon hat on my head.
Headed to the city.
To ride the bull they do not let out to pasture.
Well the bull looked like a mean dude.
So I slipped a chew into my mouth, on I climbed.
Well the chew hit the inside of stomach.
Like a rock, I did not have time to chew.
Across the room I flew.
Well! Who ever worked the bull, knew how.
Cause I felt like a wreck.
I went home & hung up my duds.
I have worked the pasture bulls.
From now on I'll stick to the pasture bulls.
Cause if my boots don't slip in the green.
I can out run them.

—Madeline M. Queen

THE GREAT DEPRESSION OF 1990

The Great Depression of 1990 is weighing
upon the nation at last;
The stock market crashed one final time;
The booming economy at near full
employment is in the past.

What caused this great depression?
Stock market bubble? the federal debt and deficit?
If the nation as one but listen,
America was in a recession.

The rich were getting richer,
that global sorrow could not stand.
The poor were getting poorer.
Once more poverty and the homeless
were rising by the hand!

This is The Great Depression of 1990
that year after year
while in its stage, the depression's
disease is set;
Everyone of us must see and hear these
warnings we shouldn't dare forget!

—Felicia Johns

RETIRED WITH INTEREST

We retired in 1981 to have a business of our own
Aloe Vera seemed a good way to start
So Forever Living Products were purchased and shown
The move proved to be helpful and smart.

The 4 oz. bottles sold for $7.95 and a bargain at that
But someone gave me Eight and said, "Keep the change."
I thanked them kindly and put on my hat.
Went off to start another business to widen our range.

We went to Florida to get a car kit.
Bought a wrecked Pinto for parts to fit.
Worked hard for a year for the best car yet.
Colors of brown and yellow for Aloe, you bet.

We took our car and Aloe to parades.
Places for pleasure and also for trades.
Then a cloud came over us as I.R.S. said
All your debts have to be counted as profits, instead.

And now I'm in jail, no parades, nothing of that sort
No more success, my life a mess
All because I forgot to report
That darn Nickel to the I.R.S.

—Dorothy (Hammon) Kimball

A FRIEND FORGOTTEN

A face in the crowd,
       pulls at the strings of my memory.
I watch with puzzled emotions,
       at a familiar crooked smile.
Glimpses of the past return briefly,
       of a autumn night feathered in fog.
Laughter and young voices mingle,
       and startle a still night.
The horses pulling the wagon,
       nicker in response.
Hay clings to sweaty hands and faces,
       excitement embraces all.
A new friend shares secrets,
       we giggle with the experience.
The night ends and the years pass.
For a moment I smell sweet hay,
       he looks my way, but remembers me not.

       —Ree Ree Yewdall

MY FRIEND WITHIN

There's a kid I know, inside of me,
   Just like there's one inside of you,
Mine lets me see life differently,
And yours can see it too.

Life can be such a serious thing,
And we live it oh _so_ fast!
Rush here and there and everywhere,
Then before we know it — it's past.

One day I got so very tired
And I just wanted to give up,
When suddenly I heard a tiny voice,
Its message was so abrupt.

She said "You must relax and have some fun
Let's go outside and play,
Please walk and run and hold my hand,
I've got so much to say!"

We went to the beach and dug in the sand
We watched some trees and clouds
We laughed and cried and dreamed alot,
"Thanks God — of my new friend, I'm very proud."

       —Sandra Sue McBride

THE MUSICIAN

I was feeling sad and blue
A little down and lonely, too
I wandered into a local bar
And had a beer or two

The Piano Player began to play
And then he chased my blues away
He played the songs of long ago
When we were young and used to know

The memories came flooding fast
I told the man to fill my glass
My head was whirling in a spin
I gulped my beer and ordered GIN

The drink we toasted when we'd meet
The dreams we had, each one so sweet
So much in love those days were we
We thought that we would always be

I started home, it was so weird
My desolation had disappeared
And as I went I bounced along
And   REMEMBERED THE WORDS TO EVERY SONG!

       —Anne Issersohn

ALONE YET NEVER ALONE

Alone yet never alone
Paradox unfurled
within a dead beating heart
Strains of nothing
asundered in growth
Unwatered by life's memories
Within.
But Outside lay a vastland
Pretty lavander shades of evergreen
Timeless thoughts instill a commanding Presence
Alone yet never alone
Consider a flower, beauty unparalled
Yet with a step, it dissipates
Forgotten and lost?
Does its beauty then tarnish?
Or does it live on more beautiful than ever
Before

       —R. Cheo

ON PARTING

Oh night, who comes despite my vain attempt
To stay my rising fears, I thee address.
Let me forget the tears the day hath brought,
And rest in the haven of your darkness.

Let me forget the hour he did depart,
And sleep until my lover doth return.
I ache with longing for his gentle touch.
Remembered passions cause my heart to burn.

Eternal hours he hath been gone from me.
Will I forget the color of his eyes?
The way his hair curls 'round his muscled neck?
Those lines around his mouth that smiles disguise?

I will that he were here beside me now.
The coolness of his hand upon my face
To dry my tears while smiling at my fears.
Feverishly I long for his embrace.

Oh night, your endless time hath no pity.
Come forth with sleep and thus my pain allay.
I could not bear the strain of our parting
Were it longer than the hours of a day.

       —Pamela Surber

TIME

Hurry, scurry, flurry, worry,
Seconds, minutes, hours of time,
Constantly, reaching, seeking, searching,
For our existance sublime.
We rush, we tarry, we sink, we swim,
Should we put all our faith and trust in Him?

Do the crocus bloom every spring?
Are there not birds, forever present
       their songs to sing?
Do the trees still dress and undress their frames?
Are there not always little children
       to play at their games?

Why not rest a moment and
       --- pause ---
Lest our years fly by without any
       --- cause ---
Longing
       --- for one more hour ---
         to do or undo
          all the things
           we never had chance to.

       —Frances Alves

Cancer is such a ugly word.
It is one you wish you never heard.
Those who have it pay such a price.
It happens to those who are so nice.

How do you cope, how do you get thru the day?
You just hope and hope and hope and pray.
Loving the Lord like we do
You know that He will see you through.

Friends are so important in times like this.
You need that phone call, hug or kiss.
Why do we wait for tragedy to come
Before we show love to some?

Well, my dear, it is not too late.
Let us start from this very date
To look to God and show that we care.
Do what we can for others to share.

—Doris E. Estes

ONLY TO WONDER

As I stare out the great window,
I wonder what life has in store.

The window being struck by the raindrops,
sending me off in some sort of dreamscape from
which I can not awake.
The grey world dampened by the shower of
tears; but I do not wish to cry —
As I remember the times before, the pain
aches in me, and my shattered heart never to be
pieced together quite right, as before.

I wonder what life has in store —
As I watch the gentle petals of the rose fall—
into the puddle below with their glimmer of red
reflecting off of the water.
And for just that one moment the reflection
of the petals had disappeared and in its place ap-
peared the face of an angel in the water below—
Only a glimpse of her I caught over my shoulder.
But when I turned the hope was gone, reality
took over my dreams, and the petals of the rose
appeared once again.

I wonder what life has in store —
With this sorrow that has befallen me, and
tears streaming down both the window and my
sullen face as grey as the outside world.
As I remember the day under the dark sky
where I mourned the dead soul.
On my knees I prayed for his rebirth but I
knew it was futile.
As I layed a single rose on the black box, I
outlined the name on the stone which I knelt
before.
The stone carved in the lettering to match
that of the dog tags of war; around the neck of a
forgotten soldier.
The soldier who gave his life for a cause not
readily understood by he.
Each letter being colder than the next. I
trembled as I moved my hand across the stone.
And at the end of the name my hand stop-
ped. My mind could not grasp at enough hope, to
not believe that what lay before me was true.
Yet, my own name appeared before me.
As real as the stone it was carved upon.
As real as the petals of the rose.
As real as the rain which dampened the earth.
As real as you — As anyone.

—JO SO

MOUNTAIN BEAUTY

Dear God, for the beauty of this day
I bow in humble thanks to pray,
Thy wonders wrought in majesty,
In glorious grandeaur mountains high —
From cliffs to peaks encased in snow
Such silent beauty to behold!
For streams, and lakes, and babbling brooks
Resplendent with flowers in every nook.
No human kind could undertake
To create beauty — oh so great!
So thank you, God, for things conceived
For beauty, blessings, joy received.

—Ione W. Kendall

LITTLE ONE

Come to me my Little Love, my begotten,
Come and let me spoil you rotten.
Let me see your sweet little smile,
For you, Little One, I'd swim a mile,
In this river of my own salty tears;
Come, stay with me throughout the years.

Come and I'll hold you through the night.
But I promise, Little One, not to hold too tight.
For you need time and to grow up you must,
Come, and I'll teach you to love and to trust.

Come to us little boy or girl,
Come and brighten our world.
I promise to love you like no other,
For I promise to love you like . . . YOUR MOTHER.

—Patricia Scroggins Allison

MY THREE KIDS

When you have children, what emotions you
go through,
Everything in life is different, everything
is new.
Your outlook, your attitude, your priorities,
they're different now,
To Be a parent, you learn from
expierence, if you don't know how.
It is scary, raising children this day
and age,
Out of my mother's book, I could take
a page;
"You won't know what it's like, till you
have one of your own"
Now, I know what she means, now
that I'm grown.
The fears, the frustration, always wanting
to do what's right,
Wanting them to grow, but never wanting
them out of sight.
God has Blessed me with two girls,
and a boy,
And everyday I thank Him, for they
sure are a Joy.
The frustration, happiness, saddness,
and the fear,
It's all worth it, just to have them
near.
My Alex, she is five,
And makes me glad, I am alive
My Haley, she is not quite two,
She picks me up, when I'm feeling blue.
My Little L.A., well he is just two months,
And like the girls, I Love 'em a bunch!

—Teresa L. (Haight) Gore

A thundering 'BOOM' rolls through the park,
  setting trees afire.
  Buildings tumble in destruction, their ruins
pile higher and higher.
  People writhe helplessly in the streets,
screaming in terror and pain.
  All are begging for merciful Gods who will come
and stop the rain.
  The acidic rains that pour down, dropping
living things like flies.
  This is a cruel game called 'WAR' where
everybody dies.
  In the year 2000, mankind will start this
war,
  Then everybody will someday soon find death
knocking at their door.

—Tonya R. Ducksworth

CHEERS

You wake up today and gaze in the mirror
  But find yourself taking a few steps nearer
The vision is blurry, the mind's not as clear . . .
Happy Birthday as we welcome your 40th year !!!

That full length reflection brings quite a surprise
As you notice your midriff has dropped to your thighs
You realize that crumpled old pink negligee
Is your own wrinkled body, nude on display

Feeling tired and weary and over-the-hill
You decide it's now safe to skip the pill
You realize, at 40, the term having 'twins'
Refers to the birth of that new 'set of chins'

You shuffle along, your legs beg for a cane
You sit on the pot but unable to strain
You resort to 'the bottle', hoping nobody sees ya
Celebrate with a swig of Milk of Magnesia

While awaiting results, you mumble, "Oh, Lordie . . .
"What fool ever said 'LIFE BEGINS AT FORTY'?"
As you crawl back to bed, you'll realize that line
Was a quote by a fool who was still thirty-nine !!

—Carol A. Hardy

ONCE UPON A MATTRESS

Once upon a mattress
  High in a tree
There sat Santa Claus
As cute as can be.

A bundle of toys
Upon his back
But you know he isn't
there to take a nap.

Yelling for Donner
And Blitzen too
He's telling them all
He's got a job to do

And as he boards his sleigh
He always knows the right way
To get all the goodies too
Everyone including me and you

And as he goes on his yearly flight
I heard him say as he flew out of sight

Merry Christmas to all, And the whole year through
I'll see you next year with the same job to do.

—A.M.S

ANIMALS NEED TO LIVE

Don't kill animals no matter its size
  It doesn't matter if it walks or flys
Don't kill pigs for ham and bacon
Eat the cheese sandwich your mom is makin'
Don't kill seals for their skin
You know not to do that even then
Don't kill lambs for their chops
If you do I'll call the cops
Don't test make-up on a bunny
It's very sad and it's not funny
Don't kill calves for their veal
These things aren't fake they're very real
Tell this to friends and keep it in mind
If you do you will be kind

—Valerie Bauer, age 9

THE LITTLE GREEN FROG

Out in the meadow upon an ole log,
  Sat a loud-croaking little green frog
Waiting for a big, fat juicy bug
  to come by.
Hurry up, Mr. Bug, and head my way
So I can have my dinner today.

Mr. Bug darted from meadow to tree.
"He's not gonna' make a meal out of me,"
He said, as he flew from the tree
To the lily-pad pond to get himself a drink.
And, ssshlurrp he was gone, quick as a wink!
For Little Green Frog had gone for a swim.
Thinking to himself, I'll outfox him.

Now Little Green Frog is happy,
And Mr. Bug is gone.
So this will have to be,
The end of my song.

—Patricia Robertson Stem

ICE SKATING

Lacing your skates;
  Stepping onto the ice;
In front of the massive audience;
Clapping, cheering, more applause;
There was tremendous silence
all of a sudden;
The music began;
I glided one foot in front of the
other;
The spotlight followed me across
the rink;
As I leaped into the air;
I twisted for a triple-toe turn;
Then I landed with speed and
grace;
Just as a swan landing on a
still pond;
The crowd was awed with
delight and enthusiasm;
The spotlight the long flowing
gown, the silence hanging over the
rink;
It was said to be the most
magnificent performance ever performed;
I received a standing ovation;
Along with a Gold Medal at
Calgary.

—Melissa Ann Burns

HIGH PLAINS MURAL

clouds of cotton, towering, chaotic,
   from the Levelland
     spiked unto the blue
       by relentless winds.
         suddenly shredded
           by splitting fire
             from blue black booms
               into spiraling lints.
            giving flowering mexican hats
             and honeybees and soil
               halos of hope
             from the sienna earth
               scorching them with mortal's
                 first world herbicides,
                   insecticides,
                hydrocarbons.

        —Molly June

TEMPORARY SOLACE

Sometimes when I am worried
  I just want to run & hide
Where even shadows don't remain
Where trouble won't reside.

The place I find most satisfying
Cannot be found outside
For it's deep within my mind
A secret place that hasn't died.

Sometimes I want to stay there
While my problems fade away
But it's only a temporary solace
I know, soon, I'll face the day.

Perhaps I store my strength there
To pull me thru hard times
It lifts my heavy heart
And counsels me in rhymes.

In choosing to step out
To face my life head-on
I'm armoured with my secret strength
To tackle-yet-another dawn.

       —PRO

LIFE

Isn't life special,
  Isn't life so dear,
It's not always a bed of roses,
Nor should it always be lived in fear.

Each moment is priceless,
Never to reappear,
Hold on to its treasures,
Always keep them near.

Think of the many people,
Who do not take time to hear,
The echoes of their violence,
Or the children's helpless tears.

Is it that we do not listen,
Or that we do not want to hear?
My friend the world is changing,
I'm afraid the end is near!

When we see the angels,
In the Eastern skies,
We'll know his time has come,
Will we still try to run?

      —Amy F. Greene

ON LASTING IMPRESSIONS

How many days go by, a month, sometimes a year
  Before something happens and it's at once quite clear
This something new is so profound,
    We say in fond review.
I will always remember this and hold it very near.

And yet it may be a trifling thing —
    Your newborn's smile, your love's first kiss.
Again will bring a smile as you savour thoughts of this.
How sad we have few things truly worth remembering.

Fortunately, God in his grace,
    Sad memories subdue.
I know, for my part, I've had more than just a few.
    But the most lasting impressions
I have of heaven rife,
    Are your smiling eyes, your heaven scent —
    You have truly changed my life.

      —Dom A. Apikos

ENAMOR

Thine eyes mirror a soul tormented by love
  ever searching for a mate
hoping the master fate
will allow thine heart
to feel one special beat

Not just physical pleasure
but one who can mystically see thy treasures
gifts more precious than gold
one who can hold thy heart
against the world's cruel cold

Lifting thy spirit higher and higher with a fire
to finally know the special one came
when thy call went out to the reaches of the heavens
to know the peace and contentment
with the one who seeks the same
who makes thy heart and soul like the eagle to soar
it can also be felt like the sound of the lion's mighty roar
is this not the most exquisite jewel
in the realms of spirit and human desire?

    —Cecilia Venrick

BUILDING A WALL . . .
As you live this special day
Please stop, and pause along the way

So that, in years to come you may recall
The first stone laid to build the wall.

Today you set the stone in place
And etch your names upon its face

Where your wall will lead to, no one knows
You must find your own way, choose your own roads.

As the years wind on so will your wall
Some rocks will be large and some will be small

Some will be heavy and some will be light
Some will move without effort and some require might.

Up and down your wall will run
Sometimes in shadow, sometimes in sun

So remember the faces, the laughter, the tears
These special memories will see you through the long years.

And then, when it's time for your wedding day to depart
Tuck these remembrances away safely in your heart

Forsake not the vows that today you have made,
They're your marriage's foundation, the first stone laid.

    —Valerie Holmes

NATURE'S REFLECTION

To see solitude in the morning light
    strength in a twisted vine
life in a mountain stream
courage in a salmon's journey
struggle in a desert bush
sorrow in a thornbird's chest
beauty in a spider's web
silhouettes dancing in the moonlight
and your own reflection
    in a raindrop

—Marilyn Davis

BALLAD OF A LONELY PERSON

My pain is now to be done with.
    It's time to end my life.
To be released from this prison
With the help of one knife.

The scenery will then be red;
A horrid sight to see.
But that's how I want it to end.
I hate living with me.

I am leaving no one behind:
My friends and family,
Who could care less about my life,
Are living happily.

I will regret not knowing love.
My heart will be left black.
For the only feeling I've known
Is hate; for soul I lack.

My vision is now blurred . . . and red.
I am going to sleep.
My body falls down on my bed;
No memories I'll keep.

—Belinda Jo Soliz

LOOK IN THE MIRROR

Take a look in the mirror
    The way we fade with time
Broken hearts and past loves
The fears you can never hide
All the intake of memories and dreams
Watching it crumble all around
Finding something unexpected
To that your soul is bound
Some say it will never work
Too close to see the light
Should I find a place to run
Or stand and take the fight
Tired of playing to too many games
Looking for that last hand
God help me if I don't find it soon
For I'm sinking into the sand
Doesn't want a love that lasts
Can't take much more of this
I need to find someone who'll stay
It seems somehow I always miss
Just someone to hold and touch
To fill my waking hours
Whose strength I can lean on
Affection for me devours
Understanding and kindness too
Is all I'm looking for
It seems that all the guys I meet
On my love they slam the door

—Karen Elaine Huebner

WITH YOU FOREVER

How much longer can I hold on, my life is so empty
    now that you are gone.

You had something about you I can't replace I'd give my
life just to see your face.

We were so happy together in love, you're the only one I
ever think of.

Don't leave me here alone, I can't make it on my own.
Say you'll take me with you and we will always be together.
I'd take my life if I could be with you forever.

The day you died, so did my heart. I can't imagine us
being forever apart.

My days are like night, why should I put up a fight.
When my days are through, I'll be happy asleep with you.

—Kelly Rogers

COMPASSION BEAUTY ECSTASY

Comfortable
    Oblivion
Masterfully
Provided.
Always
So beautifully
Satisfied.
Intimately
Ours——
Nirvana,   Brilliant.
                       Ecstasy
                       Always
                       Unsurpassed.
                       Tempting
                       You   Eternally.
                                    Content.
                                    Sensually
                                    Tender.
                                    A
                                    Simple love.
                                    You.

—Lyna M. Gunderson

CHANCES GONE

Why don't you come to me, and be my lover?
    After loving me, you will never desire another.

Come with me to the dance, the dance that begins romance,
First glance, last chance.

Never think about it too long,
It doesn't last— the playing song.

Take me now or never,
Do you dare to endeavor?

To the immense, intense passion I can give,
Only when our souls unite, can we really start to live.

When love is offered, and it is right,
You must take it without any fright, or you might,
Not survive, being alive, without love,
When it is offered from above.

And at last,
Don't look to your past.

Don't go towards tomorrow,
With any kind of sorrow,
Of chances that are gone,
And left you all alone . . .

—Christy Shannon Parker

THE OCEAN IN MY LIFE

The beach is like my life in an odd sort of way
People pass through my life each day
They leave a part of them when they go
No one comes to see me in the snow

They leave their foot prints on my heart
My life changes when we're apart
My blood rushes cold through my veins
Sometimes I think I'll go insane

I need someone to take my sand
To love it and hold it in their hands
The sand is like my body in life
Trying to keep from getting washed out with the tide

The ocean is like my tears
Running down my face with the hurt through the years
Soon my life will be gone
But my spirit will live free as the beach is long

—Judy Mullen

MEMORIES

The full moon hung low over the sparkling water.
Its shimmering view cast a spell over the
two lovers standing on the shore.
Hand in hand they stood.
Remembering all the love they shared.
Remembering long ago when they first met.
The joys of things shared together, of poignant
Memories too sacred to forget.
As they stood hand in hand viewing the
silvery light dancing across the water, like
a stairway to the heavens, they knew
This moment so sweet, would last forever.
The magic spell was broken as the
clouds drifted across the moon.
All that remained was the slapping of the
waves against the rocks.
The water again became dark and brooding.
Only their memories remained.

—Edith Lindley

WITHOUT ME

The world   will   be   running.
 round   will   be   around
 and   ground   will be packed
                              WITHOUT ME _____
   clouds still will   be swinging
   and   mountains will be sleeping
             in a beautiful white snow
The world   will   have its noon
      and   people will   be drowning in fun
   God's   every kindness   will be   done
                              in   plenty
A   dog's   bark   will be   cutting
             spreading   darkness
                              WITHOUT ME____ ____
   Smiles   on   tender lips will flow and   flow
      A   frog   will be laughing   progressively.
   and a flag fly   will   touch   the sky
       and life's   bag will be   full of
                                    happiness
             like an overflowing mug of beer
                 WITHOUT ME _____

   doubt will be killed
        and shout   will   be ended

—Arvind K.

STORM

The moon rises over grey skies,
   Set like molten steel
Untouched by any setting sun,
   And clouds roll in,
   Black moods ready to explode,
   And vent their anger on
The unknowing world below;
   The sky erupts,
   Sending down bleak despair,
And releasing uncontrolled despondence
Onto a world that has lost all hope,
   And never, never will regain it.

—Rebekah Tedesco

IN LOVING MEMORY OF A FRIEND
Tim Rutledge

Tim was a very special man
and also a wonderful friend, May
the Good Lord comfort his family
my love and sympathy through this
poem I send.

Tim I thank you so much my dear
friend for the memories we shared,
And as one friend to another with
all my heart for you I cared.

Tim and Mary are both together
in heaven above, My memories of
them both are bound by love.

I feel so very lucky to have known
him, he always had something nice
to say, I remember crying about
Mary, Tim took me aside helped me
and really brightened up my day.

Tim's the lucky one no more
pain no more sorrow, He is with
God having a brighter and better
tomorrow.

—Dee Sorrento

THE OUTCAST

Here I sit   alone

   No one speaks to me
   And I speak to no one

Here I stand   alone

Everyone sees me
   And I see everyone

Here I walk   alone

No one walks by my side
   And I walk by no one's side

Here I am   alone

They are all there
   And there I am not

Here I live   alone

I live here on this earth
   And still I feel life escapes me

Here I die   alone

Now you all come to see my funeral
   And turn the soil over my coffin
      Forgetting me   forever

—Patricia Lynn Davis

111

THE WINDOW OF LIFE

Across the street from Grand Central Station
I sit relaxed full of the day's anticipation
I'm at ease with myself as I gaze thru
    the Window of Life
It's early Friday morn and a sea of humanity
    is walking by
On their way to work some wondering
    why
Most faces don't look happy
So serious with looks of much dismay
Why is it they look this way?
As for me each day is a celebration
A sea of joy with new creations
There are those times when I
    feel sad
But the joys of life overcome them
Why others don't show or feel this
    way I can't understand
As I gaze thru the Window of Life

    —Joseph C. Bednarik

NEVER SETTLE FOR LESS

There are times that the walls crumble
And I catch myself starting to stumble
I struggle to stand
Not let myself fall
On my feet I'll land
Take a deep breath, start a new day
Smile to myself, make a new way
I'll make it through the tough times
Smile through the hard
Cry only when I'm happy
And keep up my guard
I'll live for myself, not let myself down
Won't be put on a shelf, keep being the clown
Cherish good memories
Learn from the bad
Take in the scenery and never be sad
Living for my promise
No more lies
Never settle for less
Until the sun dies

    —Donna Strehler

A CONVERSATION BETWEEN THE SHUTTLE CREW

"They say it was human error!
We all feared Russia or Iran
Would bring on the wrath of terror;
The excuse to oppose the ban.

'The Valdez' should have been a warning,
Alaska paid the price for all.
We shook our heads, fingers pointing,
'Exxon's to blame, not our need for oil.'

While the West Germans protested
The War Heads on their land.
We criticized their naiveté; 'they'd be dead
Without NATO's Nuclear hand.'

Russia's poised ready to advance,
Imploring the West to reduce the arsenal,
Thus eliminating its powerful stance.
It was a deterrent, nothing personal.

But now that we know how it started,
It's so sad you have to laugh.
The safety checks so proudly touted,
Human error is now Earth's epitaph."

    —Linda J. Lawrence

GREATNESS

Has anyone stopped to think what remarkable
Greatness holds in life?
Greatness comes in all form and fashion.
One does not have to be great to recognize it,
    nor does one have to have the ability to achieve
it. Greatness comes with unusual ability that con-
    quers all things.
With Greatness, one may overcome negative and begin
    with positive images in life.
With Greatness one can strive for happiness and suc-
    cess in life.

    —Gelendy Carter

WARWICK CASTLE, ENGLAND

Crumbling with age and engulfed
In eager green moss
You stand, impervious to time as it creeps onward
Forever the ticking clock that counts years

How long have you watched?
And what have you seen?
I walk the same gravel path as the ironclad knight—
Eight hundred years before me!
Do you think we are very different?

We're just human beings
Who live our tenuous lives with bravado
Hoping to lay claim to greatness
In our time

But we die, and become a part of history
Vague, dusty, and eventually forgotten
And you still stand impassively—
Watching and watching
The new generations, hopeful and fresh
Who all come to admire your age

And wonder what you have seen.

    —Beth Del Colliano

ANYTHING

Anything is within reach
within the boundaries of your soul
reach for the highest you can
and your success will be the length you reached for

Grasp anything you'd like to possess
within the boundaries of your soul
partake in an open mind
and success shall be easier to find

Open your heart as wide as you can
open your heart, and pass around your hand

Always leave room for error
and if you should fail, try again
never give up on a plan for success
try and try again

Think positive, have a straight mind
thinking negative is very confusing
I think you'll find

Take one plan at a time
Firstly, the closest in your heart, the most important
make your life as carefree as it can possibly be
make your life a ladder
take one step at a time,
slowly and positively

Happy climbing. . .

    —Lindsey W. Noakes

HAPPY SIXTEENTH DANNY

Danny is now sixteen and almost a man,
With a very handsome body and a gorgeous tan,

He has many attributes which he cannot hide,
And therefore is just as beautiful on the inside,

He is a popular guy with many friends at hand,
And consequently found to be in great demand,

Danny is currently in high school with much to learn,
From computers to sports, who knows where he will turn,

Especially since the girls keep calling him each day,
When he should be studying instead of going astray,

What's in store for this young man only time will tell,
But we have faith in Danny and know he will do well,

So now we want to honor him on this special September day,
And wish him the very best that can possibly come his way,

We love you Danny, and will continue to hold you dear,
So to you a very Happy Birthday on your "sixteenth" year.

—Wanda E. Raggio

BIRTHDAY PROSE TO A TEENAGE FRIEND

My teenage years were tumultuous at best.
I often recall them as quite a test.

At the tender, young age between twelve and thirteen,
Behind the ears the color was green.

It's funny about what I most seemed to care,
Always pondering on what style to wear.

Gazing into the mirror I was apt to swear
While wasting good time say "I can't do a thing with my hair!"

I did my best to stay out of a fight;
Trying to figure the difference between wrong and right.

You learn from experience, always strive to grow.
It's amazing as time passes how much you'll come to know.

Discover what it is that makes you the best.
Then you'll stand out boldly among the rest.

Be guided by God in his masterful plan
And you're certain to grow into a fine young man.

—M. Cathleen Brown

To you a wild rose I give,
For that is what comes to my mind
With thoughts of you — the life you live,
Always searching for new ventures to find.

Your strength from within, we find,
Although fragile the outside reveals.
Your beauty stored in your heart and mind,
As so the inner beauty of the rose conceals,

My friend of many thoughts and acts,
Oh how your mind must turn.
Your acceptance of feelings not just the facts,
Your words, so gentle, but firm.

The wild rose so fragrant and free,
Needing of only a few things to live on —
The air, the sun, the rain, a feeling of need,
And the Master's hand of love.

So too as the wild rose may you now grow each day,
And unselfishly blossom so fragrant and mild.
For you shall be known not as a radiant, loud bouquet,
But as a simple rose, appealing to even the eyes of a child.

—SG

FRECKLES (my dog)

Freckles is sweet
But likes to eat
We try to play
While she nibbles away
She has big brown eyes
And very large thighs
She has four big spots
And lots of dots
Her bark is worse than her bite
But she doesn't like to fight
She turns her ears back
When she gets a smack
But I love my Freckles
Because she has so many speckles!

—Jessica R. Anderson

A MOMENT OF PASSION

Two lovers stand face to face
In a dark land.
Trembling hand meets trembling hand.

Silence surmounts.
The landscape lies still,
The wind whispers nothing,
The earth inspires with a hush . . .

They're swept into each others eyes
To a land of melting emotions
And entwining souls.

And then:
She breathes.

Their eyes blink,
Their hands twitch:
They've returned.
And they stand face to face
In a dark land.

—Leslie Bober

TO DAD ON HIS 82nd BIRTHDAY

Silvered hair in soft, soft
waves
cling like silk to a once
proud head.
Gentle eyes of sun
washed blue,
now seeing only into
the past.
Strong arms that once
tossed
a laughing child,
and catching her,
held her close;
Safe, protected,
loved.
Now she must hold
him close
and whisper o'er
and o'er,
I love you Dad,
I always have,
And pray the words
will cross
the years
and find a heart
that remembers.

—Radell Wade Settle

I TOUCHED GOD'S HAND

I touched God's hand today
Upon this mountain high!

A gentle flowing breeze
Crept softly from the sky;

It rustled in the trees,
And gently brushed my brow;
    I felt its soft sweet kiss,
    And just in passing by
        It ruffled up my hair!

I saw where God had walked
And left His footprints there;
I gazed in wondrous awe,
My soul enrapt with joy;
    And I reached out ————
        And touched God's hand!

—Bernice Lewis Anderson

GOD'S WAY

Life is hard
So I've been told
But turn it to God
And it can be gold

God hears all that calls
Holding them to His heart
Sometimes answering slowly
Sometimes right at the start

The world needs all to pray
To God in the heaven so blue
To bring us back to His way
And teach us to be true

His way is very simple
Follow it and rich is the pay
Love each other from birth till death
Because He did it this way

—Frances Roederer

THE MASTER PLAN

When God placed us here
        Upon this earth,
He had a plan for each
        To prove his worth.

He knew the trials
        We would know.
He knew how hard 'twould be
        For us to grow.

He also knew,
        That by His grace,
We each would find
        Our certain place.

To trust His plan
        Is what we must learn.
And know His favors
        We must truly earn.

He holds our hand —
        He leads the way.
Our path has been marked
        For each new day.

How can we doubt
        This strength from above.
When we feel so strongly
        His comforting love.

—Mini Rhea Calder

TIME

When you have some time you spend it,
    But you have no time to lend it
And sharing it sticks right in your craw.
You can save it and enslave it,
You can waste it and deprave it,
But time never loses in the draw.

Time is under-rated, and it's not that complicated
And you try to get more out of it someway;
You can steal it and abuse it, you can even try to lose it,
But time catches up with you someday.

Time can be your friend, it is with you 'til the end
And no matter how you treat it there's enough;
So use it while you can, try to help your fellow man . . . . .
Someday you will be told your time is up.

—Fenney Payne Derden

DIVORCE AND FORGIVENESS

By ourselves, it's not always easy to forgive.
    But because of Christ within, we can joyously live.
After a devastating divorce, my dad said to me,
"Patty, you must continue to pray for him."
I thought, "My chances of praying are mighty slim!"
Dad said, "He's the father of your children.
You must forgive, to make it more pleasant for you and them."
"But Pa, I have no more HEARTFELT prayers for their dad."
Pop replied, "Then pray anyway, and "act as if" you had.
God will heal, and soften your broken heart;
You can count on Him to do His part."
I was amazed by the change wrought by daily prayer.
I became serene, and full of nurturing care.
With Christ, it's easy to soar! . . .
And I remember sins and misdeeds no more. Amen!

—Patricia J. Berg

KENNETH WALSH
ARTIST

I'm just a simple person as you can see, just as simple as I
    can be.
But every morning when I arise, I thank my God and
        realize that I'm not small, and I'm not simple.

He gave me another day to use His temple,
To enjoy the world and make life simple,
To use my hands to ex-politic His temple,
To bring to knowledge the world around,
To show you things you've never seen, now
To make the world glow like a queen,
To let you know the things I have seen.

Yes, I am different, as through my art you can see,
I take the world as simple and free.
O what a great sculpture God must be
For he made everything here on Earth
For just you and me.

My mind is much different, my eyes you see,
Can see things much different than you can see.
I see the valleys, the skies and the trees,
As a magnificent sculpture of life so free.
I see the making of this Earth around me
As a beautiful picture of God's love for me.

And though I have searched my mind for thoughts,
I develop my canvas as though I was taught.
So look at my art with warmth and love,
For my only teacher is God from above.

—Kenneth Walsh

FIRE ON THE HILLTOP

Through the gleam of the morning sun
  Afar on the hilltop—why—I long to be,
  So deep into the pines have I run
Seeking a fire in vain, only to find my shadow and me;

  The heat so great, my limbs so lame
Racing so fast my heart flutters at what I feel,
  I know somewhere on the hilltop rages a flame
Faster and faster through the valleys, over the hills;

  The embers all around glowing on every stick
I grow so tired, I must go on I cannot stop,
  My body cries out, the air I breathe, so thick
Rest must I have, but not before I reach the top;

  Can only I put out these flames I cannot see
But if only there were someone to help — to lend a hand,
  Now atop the hill what is before me cannot be
No fire, no flame, only my love sitting in the sand;

  For the fire I felt, was a true love of mine
The heat, my longing to rekindle a love we once lost,
  Now I have found a helping hand so gentle and kind
And a "Fire on the Hilltop" will forever glow where we abide.

  —**James M. Ellis Jr.**

MY ROSE OF LOVE

One day while walking down life's lonely road, I found a
tiny seed.
  I planted it in the depths of my heart, and plucked away
each harmful weed.
  I watered daily this precious seed of mine, and nurtured it
with care.
  I placed my little seed outside in the bright sunshine, to
feel the cool spring air.

  As I watched my little seed, I saw that it was growing
more each day.
  And when it sprouted roots within my heart, I was
happier than words could say.
  Soon the once-fragile seed grew into the most beautiful
flower, a rose of love so rare.
  This was the most precious flower in the world to me,
and I prayed it would always be there.

  But then one day I noticed that the rose which was once so
bright and gay,
  Now was sadly wilting and its lovely color was slowly
fading away.
  Then too late I realized much to my heart's
dismay,
  That I had smothered the rose so much it could no longer
feel the sun's warm rays.

  I had selfishly tucked it away inside my heart, and kept
it from the world it once knew.
  I saw the skies, where ugly gray clouds were covering up
the blue.
  Is there any word that I can say, anything that I
can do
  That will remove the clouds of doubt, and let the
sun shine through?

  I don't want to lose this rose of love, for this rose, my dear,
is you.
  And even though you're far away, my heart is
still with you.
  They say that home is where the heart is, and now I
know it's true.
  For now that you, my rose of love are gone, I only want
to be with you.

  —**Wendy Turner Whitmire**

LOVE IS BLIND

Love is blind
  that's really true.
Just listen to this,
and you'll think so too.

He hugged me,
He kissed me, and told
me he loved me.

But now I know
it isn't true.
You married her, and
now I'm blue.

All I can say is,
that love is blind.
Because I know, you'll
never be mine.

I'm saying goodbye
It's for the best.
This one tear is the last, I'll shed,
Because I know our love is dead.

  —**Sharron Radcliffe**

EVERLASTING

A winding river flows,
Over this rigid ground.
Ever so smooth,
And so profound.

It whips like the wind,
In and about.
Mother Nature and Mother Earth,
In a constant bout.

Clear but blue,
Like the sky above.
Ripples of white
Like the flight of a dove.

A poem never ends . . .
In my estimation.
Such like a river,
With no destination.

  —**Todd Aren Blanchard**

TOGETHER

Before I met you
  It was only me.
Now I've found you,
It will always be we.

As two come together
As husband and wife,
It's a coupling, a joining,
A commitment for life.

There will be laughter,
Sorrows, joy and tears.
Also, dreams we build,
Together, despite our fears.

As seasons change and
Years go past,
Each day we discover that
Love is meant to last.

So, as we grow old,
Sharing our life,
We will always remember the
Day we became husband and wife.

  —**Bonnie L. Gaskins**

115

BEYOND LIFE'S GATEWAY

Do not weep for me
I've given my life to God
Somehow, this had to be
I fear not death's trod.

Do not moan for me
In God I still trust
Just open your heart to see
My faith in God was a must.

Do not cry for me
My hope is in God, today
Constant prayer is the key.
O God, that is the way.

Do not groan for me
In Christ, I am not dead
I will live in eternity,
In the Heaven above my head.

—James Louis Cohen

MY FATHERS

When I was a child,
    A very small lad,
My Father informed me
    Of another father I had.
High in the Heavens,
    Yet not far away
He loved me dearly, and
    I would meet Him someday.
I wondered of this father,
    As my love for him grew,
Then all of a sudden
    One day I knew
I didn't have to part
    From this wonderous earth
I didn't have to leave
    The father of my birth
To meet the Creator
    To talk with the Lord
All I needed to do
    Was open my heart!

—B. Smith

GOD

I am sorry, God,
    For I can not pray to Thee;
I have seen too much,
Of what there is to see.

The famine and the drought,
The anguish and the pain;
All those battles and wars,
Waged and fought in Your Name.

All the bloodshed and violence,
Carried on all these years;
Causing all this suffering,
And the birth of all these fears.

If Thou really were,
All of this would not be;
If Thou were as loving,
As Thou art supposed to be.

I hear the moaning, God,
The wails and the cries;
God, I will not pray to thee,
I don't pray to lies.

—David A. England

'BYE MA

Jesus died that we might have life and have it
    to the full.
Well, I'm afraid, my friends, I'm the exception
    to the rule.
For 'tho He is my Lord, and keeps me from the
    fiery cave,
He won't be giving me the life He fought so hard
    to save.
I won't have life as you do for it's written in
    the law,
That women can choose to rid their lives of every
    little flaw.
I'm sure that God will remember me when the doctor's
    job is through.
For I think Christ himself has said, "Before you're
    born I know you."
I'll be with God in Heaven today, as the hour's
    drawing near.
And I pray my mother's flawless when I'm no longer
    here.

—Maria DeMatteo-Forcucci

LOOKING FOR GOD.

One blissful night, O God, without a thought
    I flew on wings of Light, up past the earth,
Past twinkling stars, and felt the joy of heaven
Thrill my soul with joyful anticipation beyond earth's realm,
I shouted in triumphant joy, "I'm going Home."
Far beyond earth's dreary, plotting tread,
Whose eyes are ever downward, to the earth beneath:
See nothing but the muck, and mire of earthlings stumbling
Onward, to their destiny of Darkness.

As onward and upward I sped, faster than light, on wings of joy,——
    Reaching the gates of heavenly bliss.
Oh, God, You speak and all obey.———
The gates of God were shut to me.
With tears of disappointment I returned,
But with the knowledge, something must be done
And finished before the Gates of Glory will open eternally
Nevermore to close, and the serene joy of knowing
All is well. Death, sickness, sorrows of the earth
All gone, never to return, eternally in realms of LIGHT,
Where darkness never enters in.

—Tui Schnur

A CASEWORKER'S PRAYER

Give us wisdom deep and pure,
    Not eyes to see the outer man alone,
But eyes to penetrate protective armor,
To find goodness though obscure.

Give us tongues to speak
Not of the weakness we may see,
But tongues that help to mold,
A word of praise to strengthen,
The weakest of these.

Give us ears to hear a cry for help,
When pride holds back the voice before it asks.
Ears that hear a voiceless plea,
Hidden behind a stony mask.

Give us love, faith to give,
Strength to lend a helping hand held out.
So those who have a need,
Will know beyond a doubt.
That what we give was given first to us.
The reason we give, loving God we must.

—Virginia Ivester-Morgan

As the evening grows darker, into the night
And with morning comes, a new day's light

As a candle melts, around its burning flame
And the sun will share, a heated ray

As the rain in spring, will always fall
And the birds sing out, their awakening call

As the ocean roars, under powerful waves
And the sands on a beach, are left rearranged

As the wind will remove, leaves from its tree
And peace is given out, as a dove is set free

Deeper my love for you, will grow each day
And with you always, I plan to stay
—Carin A. Wilson

TIME

As the wind blows upon a new day,
The shadow of darkness starts casting away.
Slowly it leaves and it doesn't even mind,
Because all it takes is a small amount of time.

We begin the day with our usual roles,
By doing things to keep it from becoming cold.
That frigidness may be there, without us knowing it's near,
But as the day continues, it will suddenly disappear.

As the day continues, we will behold a smile,
On faces that have been vacant for quite a while.
Daylight and brightness all seem to come together,
And somewhere the sun shines, despite the weather.

As moments begin to linger away,
We begin to look forward to another day.
With the goods and the bads all left behind,
The day has vanished away in just a matter of time.

—Bernard Buster

MEMORIES OF YOU

Time comes and goes, but memories of you still haunt my
heart.
Time brings joy and hatred, for joy is being with
someone you care about and hatred is a burning
sensation that burns within yourself.

Words are spoken frequently with little or no meaning.
Words spoken through my lips express the way I feel.

You're the rose of the garden; I am the gardener with
you as my prized possession.
You're my rose and I care about you more than you will
ever realize.

When we are together, the stars shine for us and the
moon reflects your beauty.
When we are apart, the sun burns with a burning desire
and the moon is empty without you.

You're the star that guides me through the night.
You're the light of the sky that shines radiantly
in the day.

You're my star with me as your horizon, the star
of my horizon with the night as our setting.

You're like a drug and every day I want you more and
more for I have become addicted to you.
You're like a dream and every night I want you more
and more for that is all I think about.

—Rogelio Munoz

Only a Mother,
can feel this way.
About Her children,
She wants them to stay.

All of a sudden,
they're grown up you see.
She must release them.
It was meant to be.

Mother wants to hold,
Her children so.
Hug them, and kiss them
and not let them go.

But in the end,
She sets them free.
For this is the way,
It was meant to be.

—Elizabeth Shannon Manziano

GRANDMA'S HOUSE

Grandma's House,
How special it was
Filled to the brim,
With a special kind of love.
So many memories,
Precious each one.
Happy times, sad times,
So many gone by.
Just like the person,
Who worked to make it a home.

Grandma, I loved your home,
as much as I love you.
How I wish,
I could turn back the hands of time.
To bring you both back.

It's all gone now,
with death and a fire.
Like the house,
Age came too fast.
Both gone before your time.

—Angela Cullen-Newhouse

GRANDMA'S PATCHWORK QUILT

Relaxing in the evening,
Snuggled under a treasure,
But not that of wealth and greed,
This one is of love and pleasure.

You see, this treasure is to me
A remnant of the past.
The creator does no longer live,
But her memory will last.

Many years ago, with utmost care
The humble artist began.
Her stitches and her mastery
Made me her biggest fan.

She continued with the tribute,
And now it is a legend.
I vow to protect and cherish it,
So that the story will not end.

I keep it with my other antiques,
But it's the best of my collection.
I would not trade it for anything,
for it's my prized possession.

—Kathy Bonnarens

WRITER'S BLOCK

In the midst of a gray fog
My mind wanders
Drifting gently into a sea of
nothingness
Poetry runs through my mind
like a glassy brook
But cannot be translated into
written thought
Ideas blossom into beautiful
flowers
But cannot be put into words
Music dances through my
mind
But I can share the song with
no one.

　　　　—Autumn Crisp

THE MIGHTY ROCK

　 wonder how the rock was formed
　 How he became a stone.
Sure the rock is beautiful
but has a cold, hard, soul.

I'd rather be a flower
Just laughing in the sun.
I'd bring joy to the world,
I'd just please everyone.

Autumns certain death
Is springs rebirth.

The rock he asks us yearly
Tell me, what's your point?
You spring forth yearly just to die!
Why's your life so short.

You should be like me and
Last for ever.

Ages pass and flowers grow
And my numerous descendants thank,
For That mighty rock's a pebble now
On some lost river-bank.

　　　　—Allan May

YESTERDAY'S WIND

Sometimes I feel like
yesterday's wind

And where am I today
Did I stop long enough
to make some friends
along the way.
Or did I just pass by
everything in sight.
Not caring if it were
wrong or if it were right,
Can I go back, or is it too
late, should I have listened
to my heart or left it up
to fate.

All those yesterdays tomorrows
never to be. Am I the wind
that blows across the land
and gets tossed out to sea
The echoes of my travels fall
on deaf ears I'll just keep on
going and stop when I've
　　　　reached yesteryear.

　　　　—Valerie Pfaffenroth

INSIDE OF ME

Inside of me . . . .
Some places are like the storm wrack washed up on a shore,
Debris and memories through which I search once more.
Some places are frozen now like glaciers deep and old,
and I must walk among them through the biting cold.
There is an ancient forest somewhere inside of me,
And in it are the things I'm not allowed to see.
There are mountains in the distance reaching for the wind,
But empty like my arms 'till love is found again.

　　　　—Stefani K. Peterson

FEELINGS

Feelings, nothing more than feelings,
Lives crossing in the night,
Unsorted feelings, creeping into dreams,
Emotions held in conscious abeyance, not allowed to stray.

Confused — no, just uncertain of the choices,
Feelings revolving in a holding pattern, swirling in a
　　　　maelstrom,
A few moments of deep thought, set aside,
By the daily routine, necessities of life.

God leaves a sign, unrecognized but truly needed,
Emotions spill onto a tissue, a moment of relief, a moment of
　　　　settling;
Questions with more than one answer,
All answers are correct, yet not all are satisfactory.

Giving rainbows, receiving clouds,
That block the sunlight which nurtures the flower;
Nothing more than feelings, set aside, it's not a day for rai.
Emotions held in, not allowed to stray.

Freedom seems foreign, relief unknown,
Comfort stands in the shadows with an understanding smile;
Feelings, nothing more than feelings, crashing on Hell's gate,
　　　　flooding the catacombs,
Emotions released to the gentle waters of the flowing sea.

　　　　—Brian W. Feldon

GIFT OF THE SEA

An iceberg came to my beach.
It grew as the tide went out.
　 It got bigger and bigger and whiter and whiter until it sat
on the beach by itself.
　 The ice was shaped like a swan, with a shining blue heart.
　 I tasted the iceberg. It had none of the salt of the sea,
because it fell from the glacier that flowed from the cliffs by
the sea.
　 I watched my swan until sunset. I left it sitting in
moonlight.
　 In my dreams, I played on the swan.
　 I flew to the moon on its wings.
I danced while diamond lights shone all around.
　 I was a queen on a crystal throne,
　 A lily blooming in ice,
　 A frozen star lighting the night.
　 Just before dawn, I awoke and saw my swan floating away.
　 Like a white phantom ship, it sailed with the tide to the
place where icebergs go.
　 The swan left me a gift on the beach, a piece of itself, a
tiny, sparkling feather. It was clear, pure and white, as cold
and hard as the iceberg that it came from.
　 I put the feather in a glass and watched it melt.
　 It got smaller and smaller, the snowflakes, the diamonds,
the crystal, the lily, the star, all melting away into water.
　 Then I drank them.

　　　　—Lesley Croxton

MY SILENT PAIN

My lonely tears falling to the pages below,
Only this page knows all the love I bestow,

Leaving it scarred with memories of you,
My scalding tears ripping away these lines of blue,

Your shadows reach through me, beyond all of my defense,
Never once wondering about what our love really meant,

As the page smudging my tears from today, slowly leading them into tomorrow,
By the burning sterile whiteness leaving a trace of my sorrow,

With each passing second my tears start to gain,
Leaving the world unaltered to my silent pain,

From losing you while you are slipping away,
I've never once wondered why I love you still today!

    —Doris E. Phipps

SOMEONE SPECIAL

Being loved and held by someone special like you
Is the most wonderful feeling in the world
It's richer than all the money imaginable
And like having all your dreams combined and come true

Every moment that we gaze into each other's eyes
Laying in silence because we know it's obvious
That our relationship is an extraordinary one
Which makes my body hotter than melting ice

As we walk everywhere hand in hand
A radiant glow surrounds us
And strangers begin to look and stare
Feeling jealous of our mutual understanding

Before I would give up my love for you
I would give up my last saving breath
Just to prove how strong it really is
Because you're on my mind in everything I do

I always feel bubbly when we are together
It's when we are apart I start feeling sad
Only to regain my happiness once again
Remembering we can be this way forever.

    —Tina Marie

MY LOVE FOR YOU COULD NEVER CHANGE!
TO DARIN B.

Over the past few years I've watched myself grow and change an awful lot. But there have been a few things I've noticed to remain the same. And they are as this.

I need you like the stars,
need the moon at night.

I want you like a child,
wants a warm puppy to play with.

I need to see that special look in your eyes, that only two people can share when they know the love is there.

I need to feel the bond between two people, like when a mother and her new child are gazing contently into each other's eyes for the very first time.

I need to feel the passion between two lovers,
while they're making love to one another.

I need the strength that only you can give me when I'm feeling vulnerable or weak, for I know I can honestly trust you to be here for me when times are tough.

Most Importantly I Love you, like a dove loves to soar through the sky on a clear blue sunny day.

    —Danielle Na Veaux

There the leaves
  Are blown
Head for toe
Confetti strewn
By a seasoned breeze
Some hearty
Others plain
And gather there
Only to be reclaimed
Celebrated again
Up and down
And back across (the lawn)
Makes one imagine
Ol' Robert Frost
Oh child inside
Times past were best
I have had the time to hide
Leaves?
I'll miss them
When I go
Most I guess

    —J.N. O'Brien

In Memory Of My Departed Husband's Birthday Dec. 8th 1988

I thought I heard your footsteps
as from your work you came
  But when I listened closely it
was only falling rain.
  I thought I heard you calling
as your birthday drew near,
  I could only think of the last
one, the children made so dear.
  I thought I felt your hand
in mine, the warmth I always
cherished, but all too soon my
dream was gone.
  I'm all alone my dearest;
The six children that God gave
us, and trusted to our care,
  Have been my consolation,
since you had to leave me dear.
    Your devoted wife
    Irene.

    —Irene Clements

GOLDEN HEARTS

My spirit overflows with
Love for you
My dear, I really do!
For all the years we've
  Been at rest . . . . .
Now is the time to be our
  Best . . . .

My dear I pledge my
  Loyalty to you . . . . . .
I know that you'll be
  Faithful too.

So hand in hand
Let's tell the world
No one can break this
  Love we hold
To families we haven't told
That both our hearts . . . .
. . . Blended in gold!!!!!!!!
  (24K Solid Gold)

    —F C V

BY A BEACH

I am the coastline
sand which banks
sonic depth charges
calming and cool
as the neon navy pool
where fuel rods bask in tanks.

I wear a charm
bracelet of shells shocked
and scored by silent
implosions of pink
and white lines which link
and are rapidly interlocked.

And I'm lapped
and ebbed by memories
— narcotic bubbles
eroding my shore,
pulsed by the muted roar
of an underwater breeze.

—Diane K. Stewart

THE BUST OF A MIND

Why am I fondling,
This pit-ridden sculpture,
This stone-carved bust,
So lifeless —
It is still.
If I were to take it apart,
Just a little,
I'd have to chisel it for hours.
I'd begin with the forehead,
Stiff as an upper lip,
And as hard as a nail.
I'd hit it with a hammer,
And hope I don't miss.
I'd have to crack it open,
To see what's inside,
And then I'd pick,
Through the rubble,
Until I found,
One piece of mind.

—Lisa Lord

TIME

As I often sit alone,
I wonder, why does
Time flee so quickly?

Is he running to explore
The Future,
Or does he flee from
The Past?

What is in the Future,
Or in the Past,
For Time to flee so quickly?
Only Time can tell.

I often wish Time would
Slow down, or even stop
For a day, so that I might
Catch up to him.
But, alas, he does neither.

So our Time will continue
Running towards the Future,
Or from the Past.
Until, The End of Time.

—Danielle Bobzien

PICKING UP GARBAGE AND TRASH ON A SATURDAY MORNING

HEY BOY, DRUNK BOY, pick up garbage here and there,

Be the object of all who stare.

HEY BOY, DRUNK, TIRED BOY, may you still drive
 your car?

Must you walk home? How far, how far?

They don't know you're sick — drinking against your
 will.

Do you drink beer, and take a pill?

Place the garbage sacks in a line, neatly so,

Like ole empty soldiers, standing in a row.

Penalty for drinking, penalty for life;

Stigmatized for driving, your life — one
 of strife.

You broke a law, drunk boy. Will
 you forget it soon?

Look up, young man, or old,
 sing a new sweet tune ! !

HEY BOY, DRUNK BOY, don't be so down on YOU!
We give
Thanks for your community help.
We do — really, we do.

HEY SOBER GENTLEMAN, thanks for your concern —
Remember, we're just all on earth to L E A R N.

—Betty June Bradford

WHERE DID IT GET THEM?

They were led to believe that drugs were fun to use

They were told that it would be uncool to refuse

They did a little "coke"

Their families' hearts broke

They snorted some more and smoked crack

'Til they were poor; their brains out of whack

Little did they know that they were being ignorant, not brave

Little did they know that they were digging their own grave

They just kept doing more as they were told

And soon had the mentality of a five-year old

What had they done? Why did they do it?

It was supposed to be fun, but somebody blew it

And on that day it happened, the drugs had won

It was no longer a game of fun

They just silently stared, but did not wonder

Why the leader of the group was being put six feet under

They finally realized what had happened to their
"so-called" friend

Because of abusing drugs, his life tragically had to end

So why not get the message through your head

Or a gravestone with your name on it, is where you'll be led!

—Victoria Gaulrapp

OCTOBER SHORES

No longer upon the river's flow,
the mountainous pool or lake below,
no longer upon their pristine gleam
does autumn's evening solace beam.
They tremble with gray tumultuous skies
seldom now lit with ethereal eyes,
and woods so wistful for hissing leaves,
tender replies from oaken eaves.
Color has wholly this vista departed;
somber reflections are therefore imparted.
October shores, on the verge of November,
our walks together I here remember.
For the wind, the driftwood, the skeletal trees
of me are October's analogies.

—**Tim Keefe**

PEBBLES IN THE SAND

All the emotion conveyed in the brushing of two hands,
the accidental meeting of eyes, the sympathetic smile
All the fear when a stranger passing by
    hides her eyes and looks at the sky, beads scattered
    on the floor
All the love of whispered words

All the innocence of a small child singing, of an old woman
    crying
All the beauty of a gnarled tree, the mournful melodies of a
    dying swan
All the courage and cowardice in my heart coalesced to tie
    a knot in coherence
The anticipation of a fleeting touch, soon over but long
    remembered
The pain of a noble promise soon forgotten

All the desperate questions and lonely answers

Pebbles in the sand.

—**Robert Earl Behrman**

The silver sterling shining sea; stretches surprises in front
    of me . . .
The gilded golden rising sun, awakens upon my breast;
brandishing me . . .

Crystal sparkles into my eyes . . .
Wind through my tresses as it flies . . .

Velvet vessel on its side; colored sails flared full of
pride . . .
The waves it caresses, envelop gently and open wide;

Everknowing through the miles;
Glory echoes shivering mild.

Gliding by; gliding by.

The sterling silver shining sea; sighs silently in back of
me . . .
The gilded golden setting sun, yawns over my shoulder;
shadowing me . . .

Emerald reflection of my eyes . . .
Wind snuggled for sleepy havens lie . . .

Satin skyway rainbows ride; Brightly bobbing upon the ebbing
tide . . .
Emitting prisms smiling wide;

Widsom twinkling all the while;
Splendor answers dancing wild.

Gliding by; gliding by

—**Dawn M. Flowers**

SUMMER

As you awake one morning,
You notice a beautiful smell
In the new, crisp morning air.
Today, the day seems
Unexpectedly friendly . . .
You step outside —
And the world seems brighter.
The feeling of hope and exhilaration
Overcomes your not-so-weary body.
All your troubles seem to
Disappear with the fresh cool breeze.
It is then, that you realize
What all this means.
. . . Summer . . .
Once again it has come to
Rescue you from the world.

—**Laura Ann Rodrigues**

NOVEMBER DAYS

Glorious is the brisk new dawning
Of a bright November day,
O, what beauties there await us,
    As we rise to work and play.

Icy dewdrops hang like jewels,
    Glist'ning from each weed and grass,
Makes one feel a bit enchanted,
    Filled with wonder as you pass.

Leaves of every hue have fallen,
    Naked are the trees once more,
Busy are the hands of harvest
    Gathering for Winter's store.

Ghostly corn shocks stand reposing,
    Like staunch tepees 'midst the haze
Of a ling'ring autumn sunset,
    Golden time of harvest days.

Frosty breezes kiss the pumpkins
    Nestled 'mongst the amber corn,
Silky cobwebs draw the curtains
    Of the night, 'till dawns the morn.

—**Roberta R. Becker**

THE EAGLE & THE BUTTERFLY

The eagle, a symbol of power,
    strength, survival, freedom.
The eagle, the majestic ruler
    silently surveying his Kingdom.

The butterfly, a symbol of renewal,
    hope, survival, freedom.
The butterfly, the gentle giver
    of love, life, silent wisdom.

The eagle spreads his wings
    soaring high, a free spirit.
The butterfly spreads her wings
    fluttering softly, a free spirit.

You are the eagle, strong, proud,
    Lord and protector.
I am the butterfly, quietly, lovingly,
    feeding you love's nectar.

Your spirit and mine, inseparable,
    the two cannot be severed.
The eagle and the butterfly,
    two spirits, one, forever.

—**CJ Johnson**

FLOWERS OF SPRING

Spring is sprung, the
fresh flowers sprang from
the soft soil. The bees are humming
the birds are singing. The most
beautiful flower in my
garden was the Red Rose.
I watched it while I watered it
with my green hose.
I plucked it and put
it in my memory
book forever.

—Jenny Rynne

UNTOUCHED

Buttercups along our lane,
and flowering locust pink.
Tiny little cedar trees,
the birds put there; I think.
No landscape artist did this hill,
things just stayed and grew.
All green and colorful as if,
they just wanted to.
In this world of fenced in lots,
it's nice to see this place.
Where no one dared to spade it up,
and change its pretty face.

—Dorothy Thiel Geckler

SOUNDS AND SMELLS OF SUMMER

Sounds of thunder creeping,
rumbling, growling, lightning flashing,
crackling, across the sky —
Warm rain beginning to
fall, slowly, touching grassy
knolls, forming little streams
here and about, tapping gently,
window panes with their musical
pitter, patter.
Soothing to some,
frustrating to others, smells rise up
of fresh cut grass, mingle in
with the scent of the acid,
mineral odor of the summer
shower.
Then, as suddenly as it had
begun — The storm has passed —
Its evidence is there dew drops
glisten, like tiny diamonds on
blades of swaying grass.
Tires from passing cars make
their wet slip slopping sounds.
Children's laughter from puddle
jumping.
Umbrellas closed and set
down to dry —
Cats preening and
washing themselves, stretched out
patiently waiting for the return
of the sun.
Gentle breezes sway
calm and soothing. The storm has
passed —
Another summer's day
has unfolded — Showers and sun
have gone hand and hand once
more. Nature's way of sharing
The sounds and smells of summer.

—Dorothy J. Riley

A SUMMER FAREWELL

A few days now to summer's end
Till school begins and autumn too
I know they say, "fall is so beautiful"
It is, yes, but I still feel blue

Let's make that one more trip to lie in the sun,
And stay too long . . . .
At the ocean shore we'll share good times
and lounge amongst the summer throng

With suntan lotion still on our backs
We'll stop by the market to shop
Let's see, how about cold cuts, tomatoes,
And fresh cucumbers, and corn on the cob — a new crop!

Though I see by the shadows and the cold morning air
That summer is on its way out
As yet I cling to my lazy repose
Till the last precious days come about

Back to work, back to school, back to good common sense
None of summer's long, foolish, warm nights
Once again my good friends bid the season farewell
And to this sweet summer's delights!

—Shirley Westlie Orlando

HOLIDAY

I'm leaving on a holiday, to a place that's so serene.
I'm leaving on a holiday, to a place nobody's seen.
My trip will be long,
though I will not go far.
I'll need no money,
no bus, nor a car.
There'll be no traffic jams,
no construction, no detours.
No noise, or pollution,
no trouble, no wars.
Won't be no big cities,
or small country farms.
Any feelings, or emotions,
nor fun loving charms.
There'll be no time,
there'll be no seasons.
No one to believe in,
no need for reasons.
I'm leaving on a holiday, for such a long time.
I'm leaving on a holiday, into the world of rhyme . . .

—Philip D. Goguen

OUT THERE

Sometimes I look outside at the gray misty sky
and I see all the emotions I feel —
how many times is the sun going to come out and
raise my hopes and then disappear under a cloud of despair?

Is there a pot of dreams at the end of my rainbow?

All the shades of happiness, loneliness, and sadness,
are reflected in those colors of the prism.

Out there on the green fresh grass,
I sit and think of all my life
and how I can improve my outlook.

Then the sun comes shining through,
and the rain starts falling,
a gentle mist to refresh the world,
and my life —
the rainbow —
appears crisp and clear.

I'll be all right!
—Shani Lee Channell

AMERICAN GIRL

American girl, a glad whirl. Breaking into life for a first time.
American girl, a sad twirl. The heat of the world, dulls a shine.
American girl, a bad curl. Nothing to stop an anxious touch of a mind.
American girl, a mad hurl. Working into a newness, one that's mine.

—C. J. Morningstar

THE FOURTH OF JULY

The "Fourth of July", what does it mean to you? Is it more than
just picnics, fireworks and wearing red white and blue? And when
you hear, "The Battle Hymn of Republic", or "God Bless America"
sung--------or maybe "Onward Christian Soldiers", to the rhythm of
a drum, Does your heart fill with pride as the Flag passes by-----
and when you stand to salute it, does a lump come in your throat
and you're afraid you might cry?

On July 4th, 1776, The Declaration of Independence was signed, by the
foremost of leaders back in that time. Ben Franklin, it's recorded,
was one of the men and as he made the following statement he pleaded
desperately, Men we "must" hang together on this or we may "Hang"
separately. They didn't know what the future would bring, no more
than we do today, but they had the courage and foresight to reach
out and have their say.

So today we still have "Freedom", in this land of plenty, and we
should be so very thankful, even tho, laws we have many. Be proud
that you're an American, wave your flag tried and true, and remember
the men and women who fought and who died, and don't feel ashamed
should tears spill from your eyes.

Our country has made many mistakes, and we fuss and we fret-------
but as to my knowledge we're still the "BEST" country yet,
So go on a picnic, have a good time too-------just "remember" there
is much more to this holiday than just picnics, fireworks and wear-
ing red white and blue.

—Edna Weil

MY HEART LOOKS UP
Dedicated to "Tobie"
For our Fiftieth Wedding Anniversary
March 2, 1990

My heart looks up when I behold the sunrise in the sky.
So was it when my life began; so was it thus I became a man
So be it now I have grown old — or let me die.*

My eyes look up when I behold high noon was our wedding day.
    Our home a daughter and four sons, our periglobal moving van.
    From Georgia, Alabama, Pennsylvania, Maryland
        Always "Anchors Aweigh"!
    From New York, Minnesota, Tennessee
    From Pittsburgh to South Georgia our home where it began.

Our spirits look up when we behold sunshine in the sky.
    Four grandchildren in swimming ran, Gymnastics, Scouts and baseball fans
    We have learned the fun to give. We don't need much of such and such
    Lord, teach us how to live.
Our hearts look out when we behold a sunset in the sky
    So was it when our life began. So be it now, the world is grand.

Our souls look up when we behold a rainbow in the sky,
    Our covenant between God and man. So be it when we get the call
    From Diety in the sky
    the memories from all the lands will never let us die

Our brain wakes up when we behold snowflakes in the air.
    The smells of sprigs of Cedar, the aroma of Christmas dinner.
    The sleigh bells among the holly invite us to be jolly
        and celebrate our fiftieth year!

*Couplet credit for unknown to me historic thought
    in couplet: my heart looks up when I behold
        a rainbow in the sky.

—Robert Andrew Hingson

TRAVLIN' (June 20)

Trees and rocks
    The highway snakes
My thoughts drift
In and out, whiskers
Down the drain
And yet they turn
To you; always it
Seems. Trips with
You as my guide,
Copilot, friend—
Or not. Your face
Scrunched in anger
As we said goodbye.
Your eyes as beacons
Calling me back to
Wonder with you.
The pathways curl
And I wish you would
Share them with me.

—Douglas Serven

NEW JERSEY

New Jersey . . .
    Toxic waste
creeps up to shore
in summertime.
Pollution's murky soot
pales the brilliance
of autumn's
fire-filled rainbow.
Winter's white
is tarnished
greyblackbrown
by cold,
uncaring plows.
Acid rain
cries its poison,
and stifles
spring's renaissance.
My home state . . .
New Jersey.

—Meredith L. Kipp

THE YEARBOOK

Look at the pictures
    What do I see
All the old memories
staring back at me

As we take a walk
down memory lane
thinking of good times
thinking of pain

Remembering the way
we used to walk
Remembering the way
we used to talk

Then the day came
It was the end
It will never be
this way again

Now closing the book
a tear came to eye
Then I knew it
I was beginning to cry.

—Angela Michelle Hodge

COACH

What do I have to do
to make you see,
how hard I work
when will you notice me.

I work for hours on
all my skills,
but somehow my mountains
aren't becoming hills.

I wonder why I'm
treated this way,
I want to tell you but
don't know what to say.

When will you notice and
put me in to play,
will it ever be, could
it be, today?

—Rachael Marie Ettleman

ANIMALS

*''What would you do
If I could talk?''* asked the
Baby of the Man.

*''Didn't you know? I'm
Going to walk! Try to stop me,
If you can!''*

With that, the pink infant
Fell off the couch
And grandly stared into space.

''It's so simple,'' he thought,
*''To tease the old grouch, just
Look at the look on his face!''*

Well, not to be spoofed by
This tot so tart,
The Man became a Lion.

And, with one swift swat
Of his left front paw
Beheaded the babe, for tryin'.

—Carol Marie Magnuson

BLUE AND GRAY

Two neighbors lived up Longfork,
  Both prominent in their day.
One had worn the Union blue,
  The other Confederate gray.

Harper's Ferry was contested ground
  For which they both did fight,
Where Jackson of strategic fame
  Fought with valor and with might.

The boy in blue came home at last
  Through battles fierce and raw.
I am so glad he made it,
  For he was my own grandpa.

Both settled down as neighbors,
  At last became good friends.
Hostilities all had ended,
  Their fellowship did mend.

Their houses were joined together
  Long after their decease
As a symbol of Nation broken
  But united again in peace.

—Donald M. Howe

NO ONE UNDERSTANDS . . .

No one understands the heartache,
  no one understands the pain.

I keep dreaming my dreams, but it
seems like I'm just wasting my time.

I'm always taking chances on the
future . . .

No one ever sees my tears, feels the
pain I'm feeling, no one understands.

I try to run from my problems, I know
that's not the right thing to do, but
it'll have to do for now.

—Kristin Nicole Hurtig

SAND

As I walk on the beach
I see the sunset
    hanging from the sky like a curtain.
The breeze blows my thoughts along the quiet shore.
The moist sand
    still warm from the sizzling sun
      comforts my feet
        as they move along the fish-smelling land.

My feelings change along with the textures of the sand.
  Near the abandoned cave
    the sand is dusty . . . and blows easily into the wind
      like my thoughts
        when I am confused.

The sand in the center, where people pass their time
  is lumpy and uneven, like my thoughts
    as I try to make decisions.

As I lead my trail of identity
  into the foamy water
    I feel my identity being washed away.

No trace of who I am ...... or where I am going ....

—Pamela A. Raymond

WHERE IS LOVE?

I, have been all my life alone, searching here and there,
For a little bit of love, thinking that somewhere,
I will find the place, the land, for my heart to rest,
But the dam of hate and fear that stood in my way
                Was the heaviest.

I asked wizards, Magi and kings, that sit in high places,
To guide me where I can find it, but they with sad faces,
Shook their heads and crying loud, saying: 'There is none!
'Not a person in this world, who can tell you son, that
                The love is gone!

I climbed on a mountain, high, just to see the world.
Son against his father, Mother against daughter, servant
                against lord!
This was the tableau, the picture, that an ugly Hand
Drew before my eyes, and I thought: 'Isn't this supposed to be
                Our . . . Promised Land?'

I came down, my eyes were drowning in a sea of tears.
And I asked myself: 'Oh, when will I wake up from this cursed
                nightmare?'
I came to the cage, which I call-Home-, and lying on the bed,
I gave thoughts to what I've seen. My soul finds no rest again.

                For the love is dead!

Dedicated to the endless situation of terror
and fear that jeopardizes, every day, the lives
of many children in the Middle East.

—Sorin-Luciano, Mavian

124

FIRST BREATH

'Twas the sweetest sound I've ever heard
　　When our littlest angel came to earth, with delayed exploding cries.
A tiny being with a cherub face and big baby blue, wondering eyes.

Carried a month shorter than nature should prescribe
She was called a "preemie" fortunate to be alive.
We all prayed our tiny baby would be strong enough to survive.

For an eternity my heart stopped beating as I pleaded, "Breathe!"
As her little body seemed so frail, so pale, and a dusty shade of blue.
But then our little miracle wailed, and her color turned a rosy hue.

Breathing fine on her own, life support she did not need.
She was a perfect little darling, it was plain to see
And when her Daddy held her she looked around contentedly.

Jennifer was healthy and strong, though it was an effort to keep her warm.
I witnessed on that day the fine line between life and death,
And I will never take for granted again — a baby's first breath!

　　　　—Linda Stricker

THE TREE LIVES ON

Standing upright strong,
　　Its mighty trunk transfixed through eons long,

Or so it seemed to say;

Through winds which swept the very earth away,

And hotly scalded man — ironically with blasts like chilling arctic ice,

But with their bold yet bluffing hand did not intend or could not move that tree like dice.

And it stood on as shelter from the tempers of a bright and burning sun,
Which fed and nourished that tree with light.

That blazing candle showing its generous vital nature in the long run,
Something with which life could befriend as well as fight.

But as that furnace appeared less and less,
The mighty tree shed its vital leaves as if to guess,
That all was lost,
And as its trunk and outstretched arms began to seem devoid,
One mourned the greatness of the cost.
But then past cold sullen months our dear spheroid,
Turned to show that friend whose golden tresses deep,
Brought forth from that tree new leaves to show that it had not died — had only been asleep;
And that there was no reason for surprise,
For nature is not a fool but remains wise.

　　　　—John R. Lautzenheiser — age 17

"ALMOST HERE . . ."

I can almost feel Him now, the one I've been waiting for . . .
　　I have tied myself to this arid planet to search
　　for the one whose soul matches mine.
　　He is close now.

Since the dawn of this eighth sun . . .
　　my eyes have seen set but another century of loneliness.

It is time for Him to come to me . . .
　　for I have been as patient as a star which burns endlessly to light the
　　way of those who are lost at sea or within themselves.
　　It is time now.

He is to bring to me such love, such love . . .
　　that it will scorch my very being. My eyes that dance from memories of
　　past enchantments will go blind.
　　Go blind from His seeing.

I will put myself into His trusting hands and follow Him . . .
　　in the course He wishes to steer.
　　He is very close now.
　　He is almost here . . .

　　　　—Joell A. Carson

STORM OF FREEDOM

From the skies,
  A rain of tears,
For the freedom they wanted,
For the freedom they see.

Scared to leave,
Scared to stay,
Pushing on,
Trying to find their way.

The closer they are,
The further they are,
Trying, trying, trying.

In front of their eyes,
Their journey lags on,
With no end.

      —Lauren Rush

DEPARTED FRIEND

You don't acquire friends
  like materialistic wealth,
Display them like an
ornament
placed upon a shelf,
true friendship comes
from all of us within
and grows ever closer,
then even next of kin
If you live a lifetime,
and acquire a friend or two,
they grow within your
image and become a part
of you.
Death will teach its lesson
which makes it hard to part,
Memories everlasting
proceed to break your heart.
The hardest thing to learn
that you must now endeavor
'cause when you lose a friend
in death, it is now forever.

      —Lu Hagglund

REST EASY

Fear not the eve,
  It will soon pass,
And the monsters at lay,
Quietly rest.

There's only shadows.
No villian at wait.
You will be safe.
As it grows late.

The moon shines bright.
Not a cloud in the sky.
Only heavenly stars.
To catch your eye.

If in your sleep.
You start to frighten,
I will comfort you,
And my hold will tighten.

So sleep easy dear.
Do not cry,
For the sun will shine,
On you and I.

      —Misty Echols

MOTHER'S LAMENT

There was that time when life seemed to be
  Safe and happy, abundately fair,
I stood on high ground and watched
The events of my life flow by.
I did not recognize the hand that opened up the
floodgates
And washed away safe land;
But God—or Satan—some power I do not understand,
Drowned all my prayers of anguish,
And the one I loved slipped out of reach,
And I shall never feel safe again.

      —LaVera Yarish

THE GARDEN

Branches reach from out of the wall like the arms of drowning men
  My body lies in wait
The western sky burns an exquisite peach
The eastern sky in gray
A moment, unguarded, passes infinitely
The sentinel lies in sleep
Zion breathes behind its walls like a wounded soldier
Left alone to bleed
Demons dart in snaking trails
With their passion and their heat
Eating the flesh of happy men
And singing elegies

My body lies in wait

Dreamers throw their dying words into the milky pool
I stand and watch them turn to stone
And wait
For an exception to the rule
But never can they leave this state
And my body lies, alone
In wait

      —Jim Krueger

THE LITTLE GIRL

The little girl who lives inside my heart is always sad.
  Her pretty eyes are filled with tears,
her soul as if to hide.

Her tender heart was broken, oh, so many times;
and now she stands below the cliff
in mist and evening tide.

I ask this precious sad one, for whom she cries so long.
She looks at me with tear brimmed eyes and turns her head aside.

I point high up beyond the hill where sun shines long and bright.
Where flowers grow on meadow fair and birds go forth in flight.

Pray little one, go there and bide where love and hope abound.
Where children play and spend their days away from winter's storm.

Her deep, sad eyes slowly turn and gaze upon the sight.
And then she looks back to the sea as dusk turns into night.

Her tears begin to fall as rain upon the driven sand.
Oh, how alone and small she looks upon this barren land.
A child left here, year upon year, a lonely, hopeless plight.

Ah, what a shame, this little one, such heavy burden tows.
Who lay upon her grief and pain so very long ago?
For her all hope of love has gone.
Her tiny heart is cold.

She cares no more for promises, or that which might have been.
She waits throughout eternity for stormy tide and wind.
Her tears fall on dark waters and never, never end.

      —Grace R. Dalzell

THE ROAD OF LIFE

As we travel down this hilly, twisted, backwards road of life,
We find a mixed up interlude of happiness and strife.

The joy and pain and sorrow that accompany us on our way,
Are just the random, careless tune that marks each passing day.

The rain will come and soon the road is flooded with twisting streams,
Then the sun shines mercifully and dries out all our dreams.

Once again a storm may pass and wash all hope away,
But soon the storm is gone and we can face another day.

The final hill is climbed and soon is left many miles past,
Now the road is finished, and we can rest at last.

And only the wind, forever telling stories,
Is left to remember our lifelong struggle and eternal glory.

—**Emily Reines**

THE ADVANTAGES OF BEING 60

60 years old, sounds like a magnificent number
We should be getting smarter but I'm afraid we're getting dumber
Raising our kids to adulthood, we thought we did fine
But now when one asks for a favor, we fall for any line.

But age does have its advantage, we all think now
To do things we've never done is our vow
Fly across the ocean or cruise around a while
Wear out our shoes & our patience as we walk that last mile.

The air fares a little cheaper if you tell your honest age
Getting us to travel more must be the airlines gage
The best hotels don't bargain any as we try to get our kicks
But we do have a little advantage if we'll settle for Motel Six.

Medicare & Medicaid are drawing very near
AARP keeps trying to get our membership each year
Retirement enters the picture for most of us here
Hoping that social security stays solvent is an everyday fear.

Well, enough of this rambling around for tonight
I've loved the fellowship & I've taken longer than I might
Thank the Good Lord above for allowing this fun
May each of you wake tomorrow to the new day sun.

—**Wm. B. Davis**

MAMIE

I knew my grandmother well, I thought.

I remember her always wearing her blue dress
with little white flowers and a crooked hemline,
except on Sunday, when she wore her Sunday dress.

I wanted to ask why she always wore her favorite day dress
but I didn't.
Somehow I knew not to.

And when her birthday arrived, I told my mother,
"Let's buy Mamie a new dress."
She thought it was a good idea, too.

So we chose one that was green with little yellow flowers.
I knew Mamie would like it because she wore her blue one every day
and this was almost the same.

She liked it.

And then I knew.

Because after November she always wore her green dress
with the little yellow flowers and crooked hemline,
except on Sunday when she wore her Sunday dress.

—**Katie J. Brown**

ALL I AM

ALL I AM.
Is a speck of sand,
Drowning in a sea,
Of desert land;
Crying out for my own identity,
Crying out for all of man.

ALL I AM,
Is a single star,
Glowing amidst,
A galaxy;
Sharing my light with mankind,
Sharing my destiny.

With nothing except the will to communicate,
Break down the barriers,
Open doors that await;

I know I AM, ALL I AM.

—**Z.Zack**

SHE

She was small in size
stood about 4 ft. 11
you cannot meet her
you see, she's in heaven.
It's such a beautiful day
her favorite kind,
her memory is strong
today on my mind.
She had a hard life
done without many things
she was such a kind person
I know god gave her wings.
She wore her gray hair
in a tight knot on her head
o.h. how I loved her
no! she is not dead.
Her pale blue eyes
her hair white as snow,
she goes with me
wherever I go.

—**Jeanne Arnold**

HAPPINESS TO ME

Happiness is mine
Only if I make it.
Happiness is mine
Only if I take it.
Happiness is
A warm, sunny day,
A smile that just
Happens to be turned
My way.

Happiness is mine
Only if I make it.
Happiness is mine
Only if I take it.
Happiness to me is
My parents and brother,
Happiness to me is loving one
Another.
Happiness is mine
Only if I make it.
Happiness is mine,
I'm gonna reach out
And G R A B it!

—**Valerie Koehn**

CHILD OF GOD

Child of God,
Born of human need and divine love,
Accepted without reservation,
Where are you now?
In the prison of your body and mind,
Limited in your capabilities,
Crying for a chance
To be like all the others,
Where are you now?
Running through life
If only in your mind
Or simply being here,
Offering what you can of love,
Believe that you are wanted,
That you are needed,
Because you are,
Before all other things,
A child of God.

—Gayle Fruge

GOD'S HOUSE OF FAITH AND HOPE

On a hill in a lone valley,
Stands a lonely church building;
With weathered boards from age,
The paint peeling in the glaring sun,
And the foundation riddled with cracks.

The cross on top of the steeple
Points toward God in heaven;
And reminds us all
Of Jesus Christ's crucifixion
And His everlasting love.

God's house of faith and hope
Cries out to hear sermons again,
Preached Loud and Bold—
Ringing in the believer's ears
And piercing their hearts and souls.

Where God's glad tidings of salvation
Can be shared beneath the fir tree;
The shade bringing welcome relief
From the boldly shining sun,
As the wheat fields sway in the breeze.

—Pam Housden

COME INTO MY HEART!

How empty my life would be
If I didn't love Christ, My Lord!
There'd be no reason to awaken
If I couldn't hear His Loving Word!

My life would be total darkness
If I couldn't see "His Light!"
I need His Words to guide me,
To show me just what's right!

My heart would be quite empty
'Tho it would feel like lead;
I need God's Love to fill it,
Replacing my gloom instead!

So, I'm chasing out the sad things
That hang heavy on my soul,
And inviting in Christ Jesus
Who, indeed, has made me whole!

He will be my light forever!
He will do more than His Part!
So, I'll fling the doors wide open,
And let Jesus come into my heart!

—Bessie G. Brunson

GROWING LOVE

Love is like the growing of a baby leaf.
It grows stronger and stronger but sometimes it leaves.
You have to hold on and never let go.
And you have to have patience to let love know.
That with all of the happiness that love has to give.
In our hearts is where love lives.

—Stacia Ooten

GOD'S GREATEST GIFT
From I Corinthians 13

Though knowledge I have found, I'm an empty sound;
A vacuum spinning round if I have not love.
I could give away all I have today.
What's life worth anyway if I have not love?
Love is patient, kind, not jealous, meek of mind,
Unselfish, calm, refined. I wish for you that love!
Love forgives the wrongs you do; believes the best of you.
Brave, giving, loyal, true. May you know that love!
God's special gifts will end, except for love, my friend.
We cannot comprehend His perfect gift of love.
God gives to you and me faith, hope, and love, all three
Yet, through eternity, God's greatest gift is love!

—Patricia Cullen

THE TREES

How calmly you watch the years pass,
You — with centuries of growth, defier of tempests,
Sturdy and stately in your pride!
Do you think you are the one
From whose trunk a crib will be fashioned
             For the Christ-child?

How you tremble and sway in the soft wind,
You — with quivering torso bending low,
Tender, weepy, unhappy willow!
Do you think your pliable branches
Will make braided rods and scourge the shoulders
             Of our Lord?

And you — tallest of all, cloud-crowned with loneliness,
Remote and restless in your stark solitude!
Bend down through your thick foliage
And listen to the tales of lesser boughs,
They say you are being singled out
             For a Cross.

—Ruth B. Wilmot

LETTING GO

In your eyes I saw the skies of blue.
That was part of why I fell in love with you.
Your smile was the most beautiful smile I ever did see.
You said it was a reflection of the beauty you see in me.
When you tenderly embraced me in your strong arms,
I always felt safe and secure from any harm.

Then all of a sudden I turned around one day;
I looked into your eyes and the sky had turned to gray.
Day by day your beautiful smile begins to disappear,
But that does not matter, I will still be right here.
You can not embrace me like you used to could do.
Now I am the one who has to hold you.

As I seek God I begin to gain sight
And see I can no longer hold you so tight.
I have to accept God's answer I know.
It is just so hard to have to let go.
I have been with you for all of this time,
But I know now you are His and no longer mine.

—Maury Harnly

THE FUTURE

My grandson and I went to the museum
to see some of man's beautiful creations.
We saw sculptures of gods and goddesses
controlling nature and the universe around them.
There were paintings done in exquisite detail;
products of artists — masters of their surroundings.
Then, in the middle of the last room,
stood a work of infinite value and beauty.
Hundreds of people, touched by its magnificence,
surrounded the radiant exhibit.

I began to weep.

My grandson asked, "Grampa, why do you cry
looking at something so very beautiful?"
"My boy," I said, "there was a time,
many years ago, when you did not have
to go to a museum
to see a flower."

—Kevin Geiger

SISTERS

Some may rule with an iron hand.
Some may never take a stand.
Some will hold front and center stage.
Some may live to a ripe, old age.
Some may lead life's big parade.
Some may just sit in the shade.
Some may become Miss U. S. A.
Some will never do what they say.
Some may lead lives of mystery.
Some will go down in history.
Some will try but never win.
Some will take it on the chin.
Some are sweet, and some are good.
Some always do the things they should.
Some won't give you the time of day.
Some will keep the whole world at bay.
Some will stand beside you through thick and thin.
Some hope that you will always win.
Some are grand, and some are fine,
But there are none as great as mine.

—Jean Marie Downey

MY FAMILY

My family means a lot to me
Each one of them individually.
They bring me joy and happiness
Though along with this there comes the stress.

My father understands my feelings
And often uses his special healings.
He tells me not to worry or fret
The advice he gives is hard to forget.

My mother adds that special touch
That every child should want so much.
She gives me love and tender care
I depend on her to always be there.

My sister is always there to talk to
Trying to understand the things I do.
She helps me get through the rough places
With her laughing and smiling faces.

My family means a lot to me
Without them what would I be.
They love me in their own sweet ways
That help me get through all the days.

—Heather L. Stickley

SPRING TIME

I awoke this morning everything was so still
a robin was sitting on my windowsill
It sang so sweet and it seemed to say,
Spring is coming, it's on its way.
I ran to my window and what did I see,
Buttercups were blooming and smiling at me.
Green grass was sparkling and smiling too
and then I knew what the robin had meant
He was so glad of what God had sent

—Grace Monroe

GRANNY'S LITTLE PEANUT

Little peanut arrived in July,
Causing such a twinkle in our eye.
Five pounds, five ounces, twenty inches tall,
We shouted walking up and down the hall.
Big blue eyes and auburn hair,
Complexion to which, none could compare.
Papa and granny are proud as punch,
Sneaking in to have a peek, during lunch.
Growing fast, just like a weed,
Walking soon she'll be indeed.
To Papa she's something special,
And of course she's granny's little peanut.

(Dedicated to my first granddaughter, Christine Jean Knapp Born July 10th, 1988)
—Pauline J. (Carr) Smith

GRANDMOTHER

Leaving us with only our memories,
Whisked from our lives on a gentle breeze.
Tenderly carried on angel's wing —
On the final voyage to join the King.
To a place that knows no hurt or pain,
Only peace and love forever reign.
She touched our lives throughout each day
With love each time we passed her way.
Her smile, her love will forever be
A part of our hearts through eternity.
Her voice still whispers and stills our fears,
And calms our souls and dries our tears.
Her life was your example from moment of birth,
An angel in the midst of us on earth.
She's gone from us on that gentle breeze,
But will live forever in our memories.

—Marcia P. Englert

GRANDMA

My dear, old, sweet, and kind
Great Grandma May Grimes . . .
When I would go to her house
She would always put something in my mouth.

Whenever I would get in trouble
My Mom would make a fuss and grumble.
But my dear, old, Grandma Grimes
Would tell my Mom, "Just never mind!"

When I would go to Grandma Grimes,
She would always have a set of rhymes.
My Grandma also told us riddles—
That made us laugh and get the giggles.

My dear, Old Grandma Grimes passed away . . .
I just wish she would come back someday.
But everything will be just fine,
'Cause I remember my Great Grandma Grimes!

—Sean C. Fox

129

THE INTANGIBLE TOUCH OF TIME

Intangible time moving silently,
Changing the darkness to dawn,
There is no "now", for instantly
When brought to mind, it's gone.

We dream and we hope for tomorrow,
While our memory stores yesterday,
All so quickly, the days of our life go,
And to what end? No one can say.

Time the great equalizer . . . .
Touches all and leaves nothing unchanged,
Yet so often in remembering,
Past moments are re-arranged.

With passing time, days grow more dear.
Sadly, the only mark we leave behind,
Will be in someone's memory . . . . . .
Stored deep in the crevices of the mind,
Which when recalled,   will hopefully,
Bring a smile.

— **Patricia Ann Hopkins**

THE TREE AND ME.

Let me climb my family tree.
Let me find the beginning of me
Let me breathe my past in.
Let me find kin around each bend.
Let me search a face
To see if I fit in anyplace
Let me find an old grave
Whose life crossed an ocean wave.
Let me touch a hand
From a distant clan.
Let me hear a story
In times of old territory
Oh, the family tree.
All those kinfolks to be
Roots entangle me
Who, where, when?
Loved ones back then.
Then realizing that Adam and Eve
We are all family
Because they were the beginning of all men.

— **Lawanna Sue Craig**

In this busy world of ours
So much is left unsaid
We fill ourselves with nourishment
But the spirit goes unfed!

We hurry here and hurry there
And rush through every day
What will it take to slow us down
And smell the flowers along the way?

Why not try what I suggest
And when each day is through
Reflect on the happenings of the day
What thoughtful thing did YOU do?

It may take some practice
And a little effort too
But the good you do for others
Will come back ten fold to you!

So, try to make this world a better place
For everyone to live
The most important thing that you can do
Is be kind to each other, and GIVE!

— **Dee Dee Bowers (Diane)**

TEARDROP

Bottled pressure, emotions held-in
Discharging, it bubbles and fizzes when uncapped
Relieving pressure once confined
A tear sliding down your cheek
A moistened pathway, the droplet so sweet
A crystal so clear seeing a thought in each
Gently flowing letting it out
United body and soul, after you're cleansed

— **Larry LaPole**

LIFE

I've been through the valley of the shadow of death
I've felt death's icy stare.
I've known torment that tortures the soul,
But the Saviour met me there.
To comfort and soothe with His still sweet voice.
The tempest I couldn't bear.
In His own good time He brought me through
For His love was always there.
We struggle and strive and toss and groan.
The time seems endless and vain.
When we stood the test and weathered the storm,
He takes away the pain.
For He never leaves us completely alone.
His eyes never leave His own.

— **Evelyn Drewer Joy**

STRAIGHT FROM MY HEART

To Mom and Dad whom I love so much,
How could you raise a daughter as such?
You changed my diapers. You sent me to school.
You kept on loving me when I broke your rules.
You took me to church. You taught me to pray.
And that's why I'm writing this to you today.
I want you to know this is straight from my heart.
The Lord above knows you both did your part.
I hope that He is as proud as I,
To call you His own from way up high.
If everyone's parents were as special as you,
The world would be filled with love and truth.
I'd like to say I appreciate you a lot.
And thanks for being there when others were not.
I'm closing this letter. I've said quite enough.
Just remember your daughter sends forever her love.

— **Deborah Fowler**

OUR NIGHT

It was a beautiful night,
We made love under the stars,
Your love took me to great heights,
As we listened to soft music from the car.

A cool breeze flowing over us,
As we lay upon the grass,
We were lost in each others arms,
Hoping the night would never pass.

As the rain began to pour down,
It seemed to set us more on fire,
Our love making became more intense,
As we filled each others desires.

Thinking of that night still thrills my soul,
I can't believe it's been ten years,
Forever enjoying your slightest touch,
You are the only one . . . I'll ever hold so dear.

— **Sharon Swann**

ATHEISTIC COMMUNISM

The hammer's rhythmic pounds are sharp and strong
As the sickle nods to harvest the throng,
Upon hearing the sounds that smoothly roll
Secretly, from the aging Bamboo Wall.
The tanks move on to a savage call . . .
Each military step, a trample on a soul!

Like a wave of fire that hungrily consumes
Tangible objects into unpleasant fumes,
It comes to destroy and inflict great sores,
Transforms its subjects into nothing more
Than manless residue, a living corpse,
A slave of the soil and men who usurp.

The women, men and children are reduced
To godless ones, like machines that produce
Perishing earthly goods to satisfy
Swelling bellies that voraciously cry;
Unpacified, their greed for crooked power,
They spill the blood of patriots from the Tower.

—Inday Lombardi

NO POLITICAL STATEMENT

Politics is the definition of being unhappy.
We elect reasons already exhausted by formality.

Bright banners implode
Like the snap
Of hidden veins in upholstered armchairs;

Color,
Then band music descends the scale of satisfaction;
The new life assumes the old life.

With its threat
Of rapid random fire,
The false gold knick-knacks in illusions of living rooms,

Fumbled and moved through,

Perpetual rhetoric depositing us
Into the grip of soothing phrases,

Like babies sung asleep, like the dead

Thumbed shut by a prayer.

—Don Avery

THE MADDENING WALLS

These maddening walls that crush my soul
Hold me in a grip of pain
There's no way to escape the sorrow I feel
The humiliation, hunger and shame

Midnight black horses with eyes of red
And hooves of sharpened steel
Play a ceaseless pounding in my head
Can't accept that what's happening is real

An endless rain of blood that falls
Steadily from these eyes
I strain to reach hold of you yet you run
How can you not hear my cries?

A sharpened blade — a love gone wrong
A straight-jacket holding me still
To break free of this barrier and get close to you
Is my only love — my only will

Just a short time now I suffer
My mind screams and my icy heart calls
In this strained silence I hear my heart beating faster
The strained silence of four maddening walls

—Valerie Vincent

MISSING YOU

The day is done
The night is over
We look down to see the clover
Then we close our eyes to cry
For someone close to us has died
As we close our eyes to sleep
Someone else has closed their eyes to peace

—Cheryl J. Watts

PITCH BLACK NIGHT.

Pitch black night, with wind a howling
Blizzard surely blowing
A cozy fire
My chair pulled close
Kitten softly purring
My dogs lay stretched
Their tummies full
Content and dreaming dreams.
We're safe and warm
In God's sweet love
From winter's icy storm.

—Betty E. Bradford

PARTING WAVES

She waves goodbye and drives away
You think back to another day.
To the day that she was born
And lay as a bundle upon your arm
The years have gone by so fast
but for what more could you ask
Than to have a daughter go away
Knowing that she is with you everyday
For all the years that she was mine
I kept her close — did not loose the line
The memories of her happy face
Will always be there to take her place
So wave goodbye my darling child
For you must go many a mile
Tho life is not always good
do with it what you would.
For it is your life — that I know
So I wave goodbye as you go.

—Pat Dickens

SECOND CHANCES

All the days so filled with hope,
all the lonely nights with no end,
all the hours spent wondering if
the phone would ring, all the heart-
ache and confusion of trying to
figure out the reason why.

But never knowing the answer.

All the times my heart cried out to you,
but you never heard it.
The times my eyes were so filled with
love for you, you never looked in them.
When I held my hand out to you,
you refused it.

The times I tried to call, you never
answered the phone.
When I would drive by,
you never looked out the window at me.

What ever happened to second chances?

—Donna M. Fronduto

DREAMS OF TOMORROW

Deep inside the eyes
Of tomorrow's dreams
There lies the key to the opening
To what the future will bring
If you have the will
Then there will be the way

Because out in the opening there
Lies the key to wisdom
To accomplish, to succeed and for
You to make your future and not wait
For what the future will bring

So find that will, and you will have
Found the way and the golden key to
Your future to unlock any door that
Comes your way

—John K. Smiley

A SPECIAL ROSE

In a special garden set aside,
A flower is blooming there
A rose with so much beauty
It is beyond compare.

It was raised, with tender loving care,
Each petal, one by one;
It was watered by the tears of God,
It was nourished by the sun.

Early every morning,
It was blanketed with dew;
The sunbeams dancing on the rose,
Let its beauty shine anew.

God picked that special rose one day,
He touched it, tenderly
Making sure it was perfect,
He handed it to me.

God said, "protect and love this rose,"
"No matter what you do;"
I will do just that, because I know,
That special rose, is you!

—Bob Montey

THIS PLACE

Bubbles, bubbles all around
No other place can they be found;
Drifting in an endless space
Never breaking, floating lace.

In this vast and fanciful place
A world of soft and flowing grace
A world of love, a world for two
A world created for me and you.

Light song and whispers fill this place
Of peace and never ending grace;
Music heard from all around
Softly playing verse and sound.

Time is frozen in this place
In this realm of the mirrored face;
Fantasy painted on the dew
Images of love I have for you.

Bubbles, bubbles can all be found
In this place of mysterious sound;
A world of glitter, a world so new
A world of bubbles blown for two.

—Claudia Lumpert

THEIR HONOR

"God, grant me the strength" to live each day,
and, forever, be proud of the American way.
To always give "thanks" for our freedom, true,
and for young men and old, and the Red-White and Blue.
As I stand and look, as it waves — proud and free,
I realize, all the men . . . that aren't here with me.
My memory wanders, to where they fought and died—
with all of their hearts and their souls, they tried.
Their blood was smeared . . . upon the flag . . .
as their bodies were torn, by straying slag.
And, tho' they fell, with "unforgotten cries,"
and the tears are, still, in their Momma's eyes . . .
"Their Honor" remains, as the mark of a man,
that gave . . . his life . . . for the love of his land.

—Deborah Cooper

DREAMS

Thoughts of you are always on my mind—
Memories linger of a long ago time.
In younger days when our hearts were gay—
We were so happy before you went away.

We spent our days in the warm summer sun—
By the light of the moon our dreams were spun,
We dreamed of a cottage with a white picket fence—
We knew that dream was soon to commence.

Then your love for me withered and you went away—
Now my heart's filled with pain as I face each new day,
I hope you'll be happy in your home by the sea—
As you stroll on the sand "will you think of me?"

I'll always wonder "what might have been—"
If our dreams had come true way back then—
When our hearts were young and our dreams were new—
And we had hopes they would all come true.

—Elizabeth Jeffery

OUR LOVE WAS AUTUMN

When we met our lives should never have touched . . .
As Autumn grows cold, so our lives became
                                    separate . . .
As the blustery wind sweeps through the trees
          pulling the leaves from its branches
                    I swept you away from me . . .
Our lives turned from Summer to Autumn . . .
You should have left me long ago, but you chose
                              to hold onto me . . .
I fell in love with you giving all of myself I
    could give, you were the leaf, I was the wind . . .
Gentle at times and then I would twist and turn
                                            you . . .
You were the fragile leaf being torn from the
          protective branches of its Mother Tree . . .
And so our lives changed to Autumn . . .
I chose to separate us never taking us to spring
                    and warmth ever again . . .
As the Autumn starts to caress the earth, to
    take her life away, I have done this to you . . .
Slowly the petals fall from the flowers and the
                    flowers wither and die . . .
Only to be swept away by the cold wind . . .
  I have done this to you . . .
Autumn crept into our lives . . .
Our love was once a warm summer day . . .
Hopeful and bright, so happy at times, but
    Autumn was in the background waiting,
                              just waiting . . .

—Lisa Saladini

WHY I'M PROUD TO BE AN AMERICAN

I Was Born In America, And I'm Proud To Say,
I'd Die For America, To Keep It This Way;

Peacekeepers Of The World, That's How It Should Be,
The "Star Spangled Banner" Is The Song For Me;

When You Hear The Words, It Has A Message In Mind
It Couldn't Mean More, Than To Show Off Our Kind;

Stars and Stripes Forever, You Know That It's True,
Our Colors Don't Run, 'Cause They're Red, White and Blue;

We Stand For A Reason, To Strive For World Peace,
Hopefully The Conflicts Will One Day Cease;

America Is Beautiful, It's My Native Homeland,
And The American Way, Is Where I Make My Stand;

Like Martin Luther King, I Have A Dream Too,
To Keep The World At Peace, For Me and For You;

And That's The Reason, Why I'm Proud,
To Be An American, And Stand Out In A Crowd.

—Steve A. Taylor

BUNCH OF BIRTHDAYS

Birthdays are coming to me in a bunch,
That's why I have no money for lunch.
On April twelve my wife is the one,
But on the tenth see what she done.

First to come was Karen Ilene,
The very next year was Sheila Maureen.
In '56 and '57 the day was April ten,
Causing me to brag to all my kin.

As an old sailor I went to sea,
But learned about salt water with two girls on my knee.
And as a warrior it took awhile,
But I learned to change diapers with a smile.

Happy Birthday, Karen and Sheila too,
You girls are sweet and I love you.
But my special wishes are to the love of my life,
Happy Birthday, Judy, my darling wife.

—Jess Parker

FIRST DAY OF SCHOOL

The school bus arrives and the children are off,
one with a tear and one with a cough.
They run to their class to see what they will do,
but, the teacher is absent — she's at home with the flu.

They learn their letters and write them all too!
What they will do next though, they don't have a clue.
Then, the lunch bell rings, "Hey, it's time to eat,"
they go through the line and find them a seat.

Another bell rings and it's time for free play,
they laugh and have fun and wish they could stay.
But, it's time to go in; they line up single file,
then the boys start to push and end up in a pile.

They then do some spelling and then rest their heads,
'cause when this day is over, they'll welcome their beds.
Here comes the bus now, they step off with a song.
The cough is a little one and the tear is all gone.

So, the first day of school has come to an end
and tomorrow, we hope,
better things it will send.

—Lynn Rucker Holt

CHILDRENS SONG

I saw a boy smile today,
he couldn't have been more than ten.
All he wanted was to play
and then I saw him smile again.

I saw a boy cry today,
he couldn't have been more than two,
I saw his tears and had to pray
because he reminded me of you.

I saw the children of the earth
and smiled, because soon
this planet will be their turf
and they will sing a different tune!

—Djuna Z. Shultz

DID YOU KNOW?

When the forest is buried in snow
Little animals are dreaming
Did you know?

Not ice and snow
or chattering teeth
or chilly blue toes

But of blooming trees
pretty flowers
and running streams

Of nuts and berries
roots and seeds

All nice things
the sun shall bring

In burrows little animals sleep
Dreaming of snow? No!
But of spring and summer

Didn't you know?

—Wendy Jeanne

MY FRIEND, THE MAN

I had a friend, a jolly good man.
My best friend's name was Dan.

My friend Dan had a big sack,
it was used in case he had to pack.

Dan smoked a big pipe.
His face was so shiny it was his
face he liked to wipe.

My friend had a cane,
to hold him up if he was in pain.

Dan had a great big beard,
his great big beard looked sort
of weird.

My friend had a hat,
one time Dan stepped on it and it went
flat.

Dan went away,
on a trip to find clay

He said he'd back,
with his big sack.

I liked my friend,
throughout until the end.

That's all I have to say,
about my friend today.

—Ashu, age 8

133

TIME

We see time
Though not on a wall,
But from the brown leaves,
And cobwebs hanging in the hall.
We hear time
Though not from a twang,
But from the rocking of a chair,
And tapping of a cane.
We feel time
Though not through palm,
But from our children
And their bairn.

—Jason Marsocci

THE RECENT DAWN

As the tiny violets unlatch
their delicate hearts
to the rising sun,

The elegance of the first yawn
of the ever-so-fragrant
lily

Enlightens the path upon which
a fawn walks.

The trickling pond is streamed
with light which dances

On the small swells
of crisp water.

Pressed in my memory
is the gracefulness
of the recent dawn.

—Jennifer S. Baxter

AMERICA THIS IS YOUR SONG

The land that I live in;
the land that I share,
just wouldn't be the same,
if the people weren't there.
It's the home of the brave,
the free and the true;
America the beautiful,
how I love you.
America, that's where I belong,
America, this is your song.

There's trouble and famine,
you hear about it everyday;
from the north to the south,
and east of Bombay.
In Russia they're fighting,
their own little war.
Just give me America
it's my place I'm sure.
America, that's where I belong.
America, this is your song.

God gave us life,
and the power to be free.
His honor and love,
is in our country.
Things aren't so easy,
in the east or the west.
Just give me America,
I know it's the best.
America, that's where I belong,
America, this is your song.

—Holly Dawn Harwood

SHOOTING STARS

The motorcycle is the modern caballo
and the men that come riding are fearless of old
with their muscles agleam from the sun as they hold
silver reigns—and wicked grins of bandido.

Crashing came once men of silver spur along this same camino:
from the sheriffs well hid, the star-buttoning cold
brought from mountains to town for a fire of gold,
wild, daring men of black sombrero.

Motorcycle men on silver steeds flash through a dusty pueblo;
like mountain winds their engines roar and seeking spirits, bold
crack ope' a door and stand, their shirt sleeves rolled,
six-gun challenge in their eyes their arms akimbo . . .

—Aileen Dever

THE FLAG

The flag stands for freedom, under its stars and stripes many
brave men have fought and died. At the very thought of burning
it, you should be hog-tied!

Any American, who burns the flag, burns his heritage as well.
If his country means so little, maybe he should be shipped to
Russia or China or somewhere where there is no freedom. Then
the flag might become sacred to him.

Burning the flag to me is burning your birthright. The very
freedom the flag stands for goes up in smoke. Punishment should
be strict, loss of citizenship for a start. Listen to the words
I impart — Let freedom ring!

Fly the flag high and be proud an American to be, you could be
living in another country. The price for freedom was high. Now,
please don't black its eye! Long may its banner wave — America
the beautiful.

The price of communism is cheap, I don't know how you sleep, cause
to burn the flag, you must be a fag. Even yet, you're free to
be whatever you wish to be, the flag provides that freedom for
you and me. One nation for which it stands — Liberty and justice
for all!

—P. J. Morgan

MOUNTAIN STREAM

Sitting here by this mountain stream,
One can find peace and tranquility.
It will never be as magnificent as the sea,
Just the same, come and dream.

Hidden beneath the wind-breezed pine,
It babbles along, singing its own melody.
Over the rocks; it sounds like a good hard drink.
And I can't help wondering what its words might be,
It has its own language; listen carefully.

It can roar from the water fall,
Or trickle down the narrow ways,
It can have dancing sparkles from the moon,
Or catch the warmth from the sun's rays.
It is cushioned by the softness of the moss,
Or it is roughened until its waters against the banks are tossed.

In many ways it is like our lives,
It begins somewhere and gathers as it grows,
It survives all the seasons, the years,
Oh! If it could speak, would it tell of joy and tears?

It battles different conflicts the same as we do,
And when it is finished, the peace returns,
This cycle of living and loving; facing realities.
The mountain stream seems to whisper, "It's okay; go on."
There still is peace and tranquility.

—Ellen Hassinger

THE FORGOTTEN TREE

The tree appears to be so bare with its cover of leaves gone.
It looks to be so lost, it appears to be so all alone.
A different color shows today, though it stands just as tall.
It wonders who would miss its existence, if it decided to fall.
Some of us feel our lives at times, appear to be as that of the forgotten tree.
And we may wonder, "If I were not here, would anyone really miss me?"
The beauty of the tree is unnoticed as its golden leaves begin to go.
It may catch the eye as it's covered again with green leaves, or ice, or snow.
For some, perhaps the tree's bare existence now is symbolic of our days.
So often our true worth and importance is unnoticed in so many ways.
Once the leaves, ice and snow are gone, the tree's beauty will still remain.
But as before, its strength and dignity will be passed over again.
There are some who can be dressed to appear beautiful as the tree on a spring day.
Their ugliness and the many evil things that they do, get hidden away.
There are some who do good and their beauty is there for everyone to see.
But it goes unrecognized, like in winter, so often is the tree.
Wished there was someone who would sing of the tree's beauty to all.
Then perhaps, it would be appreciated summer, winter, spring, and fall!

—Marcella Battle

LONELINESS

The darkest shadow sweeps over my life. I can feel the tip of the sharpest knife.
It seems to fall straight through my heart. Where will it end? Where did it start?
Why does this knife seem to fall on me? Why do people fail to see?
I've done no harm to man nor beast, yet this loneliness continues to follow me.

The pain sometimes is hard to bear. Why does no one seem to care?
I try and try and try again, but still I am left without a friend.
I wish the world would open up its eyes and look not only out, but see what's inside.
I feel I am helpless, what can I do? I see no wrong I've done to you.

I know I must look to tomorrow, endlessly searching for hope, but I am finding it very hard to cope
with all of this pain and misery that God has somehow bestowed on me.
All things are said to be done for a reason. It seems to get harder with each passing season.
No love, no life, no one to share, all of these problems I alone must bear.

"Alone" is a small but monstrous word, I have prayed and prayed but God has not heard.
I continue to hope that someday this hurt will end, that someone will grasp my heart to mend.
I still have yet to find that someone, until then my quest will continue on.
I hope my Lord will someday see, one of his children is lost.
That child is me.

—Amalia Marie Liachames

THROUGH AGED EYES

In the days of my youth, when the world shone bright with the promise,
Of love and life, and sun and springtime,
    I passed the days without a care of what might come tomorrow,
Now I am old, the winter of my days hovers over like a shadow,
    Blotting out the sun,
My limbs now shiver with cold the sunshine cannot swallow,
    Memory like an old and cherished friend comes calling,
But even its comforting seems hollow.

    Gone now are my "salad" days when in youth's fickle grip,
I whiled away the hours in careless abandon,
    Gone too are the arms upon which I leaned while gayly rambling,
Now I lean upon the arms of one I hardly know,
    Taken places I'd rather not see.

    Yet even now, with death's icy breath on my neck there shines a ray of hope,
In the eyes of my grandchildren I can see the same bright promise,
    That once glittered and gleamed in these old tired eyes,
And for a time I am taken there again,
    Swept away by the fragrant winds of memory to my secret garden,
Where youth never fades and the mind stays sharp and clear,

    Oh, that I may ever dwell in that place where the hand of time,
Is stilled, And if only for a moment,
    I am young again.

—Jennie Varnam

HAPPINESS

You can allow yourself to be happy, if you really try,
Although it isn't always easy, there is a reason why.
You could have success, fame or fortune,
But if you aren't thankful for your health
What good are all your earthly treasures, or your monetary wealth?
For it is not the material value
That truly makes a king,
But rather patience, kindness and tolerance, that the humble man may bring.
The man who nods and says "Hello," as he passes by you on his way
May help to cheer you when you're feeling blue, and brighten up your day.
Or just a friendly smile from someone that you don't even know
Is a pleasant way for anyone to let their feelings show.
These little things can fast become forgotten, in our hectic daily rush,
But slow down a minute — and wish someone a nice day —
You will be surprised — the rewards to both are much.
These simple minor things, are often not thought about —
So take a moment to think of them — do one each day, and you'll feel good throughout.

Dedicated to Walter J. Donaldson, who always smiled, said "hello", wished
everyone a "Nice Day", who loved, was loved, and will always be missed.

—Linda D. Ferraro

INCIDENTALLY, ACCIDENTALLY

May I shake your hand?

Well, I certainly still shake deep inside.
This is always an uncomfortable time for both of us—do I use my right hand or my left?

Sinister (from the Latin stem—left), yes, since, sine, sinew, or just plain "sin?"
But no guilt complexes about God's retaliation—God, God-awful, and yes, so full of awe.

No, just in the wrong place at the wrong time: an accident, like has happened to others—
Much worse than I, you say, you think, and I do know that, you know.

And so the surgeon said: "One more time! for debrisment, just sign here."
But the paper said: "Possible amputation." And I did sign—again and again and again.

So, I'll be fitted for a prosthesis, which I'll then keep in a little box—
Smacking of a horror film or science fiction? Or is it an exquisite gem from my jewelry box?

So the brain's hemispheres adjusted—to adjust and adjust and adjust
The imbalance of the psychology of the physiology—the imbalance of life, day to day.

So the fingers of my right hand are gone—forever; they won't grow back, chameleon style,
But I will—as I am out of my shell, out of the closet!

And now, may I shake your hand?

—A. Lee Hamilton

"JUNIOR'S" PRIDE IN AMERICA

"Congratulations!" seem to be in order as we celebrate the anniversary of our 50th year;
"No, it didn't come to us that easy, you see many had to give that extra hand while
Raising a family or building a career!"

We are all young "Junior" women who will stand gratefully at your side;
Exclaiming what it means to be a member, shouting with love sincerity, devotion and pride!

Since we joined this organization, we vowed solemnly this pledge;
To always be justifiably proud of womanhood and our heritage!

The thrills of being a "Junior" are many, we must convey;
Just look what's been accomplished, we've built more confidence, and look at the future,
Sure looks brighter every day!

We are known as a freedom-loving people who have contributed significantly;
Whether social, cultural or economic development, to enrich this America, our country.

As God-fearing and hard-working women, with pride of the highest esteem,
We're ready for whatever lies ahead in search of the American dream.

We thank God for what we are able to contribute; the long hours, sweat and strife;
As we share to help create for many a happier, healthier, more beautiful life!

So now you know how we feel on what it means to be a member, everybody please join us,
We want to shout it out loud: "Thank God we live here in America, and we're active,
Yes, devoted "Junior" women, indeed we are proud!"

—Mrs. John Danczyk

DREAMS

A Nebraskan boy, who has never seen the sea,
walks through the wheat fields as it ripples at his knees.
Dreaming of the time of the sea he'll find.
As his young life slowly unwinds,
he shouts in a crying voice to the crows.
And dreams of the gulls flying low.

In time the day comes, he feels it, he knows.
He finished his school, so to the coast he goes.
He finds a place that looks so untouched.
For the beauty of this, he thanks God so much.
Now it's the water not the wheat at his knees.
He feels a love's warmth from the cool sea breeze.
He found a place he now calls home.
With his dream at hand, he'll never roam.

—Denise L. Dufresne

ROOT DREAMS

My father is the tallest, darkest,
Most deeply furrowed oak in our whole valley.
His powerful gnarled arms thrust upward and outward,
Sheltering the thin curving shrubs
And green grasses that look up to him.
His deep throated voice roars down the threatening winds
And his whole body quivers and groans
In his battle against the fisted rains.

I am just a small brown acorn here
Beneath his roof of leaves.
The rain never touches me
The wind only whistles at me
I have never seen the sky.

I want to grow tall and dark in the good black earth
My father prepared for me by his feet.
I want my bark to be sinewy and strong.
I want to join arms with my father and battle the wind and rain.
I want to see the sky.
But my father will not let me.
He cannot see the tree that's inside me.

—Michael A. Rice

SEAGULLS IN THE MIST

As I stood on the boardwalk, looking out toward the sea, I
saw him chasing seagulls in the mist, on a lonely stretch of
beach.

His brown eyes, flecked with dancing green light, were brimming
with laughter, as his joy rang out in sweet abandon at what he
was doing.

I've wished a thousand times over that I had a camera with me,
to try and catch for all eternity, the way he was that day.

Seeing the world through his eyes was seeing the world all
fresh and glowing—as if for the very first time.

Meeting him was finding the half that made me whole. So happy.
So carefree. Where did the little boy of my dreams go?

He's now so angry with not much joy in his heart. His laughter
hardly ever rings out on the crystal clear air.

Once in a while, when maybe he forgets himself, I can see the
carefree boy emerging from the angry young man, but he doesn't
stay for very long.

I wish he'd come back. The carefree little boy of my dreams.
I feel as though I've lost a part of my very soul. A part of
me that I may never get back. I miss him so.

—Kathryn Baker

IF SOCRATES KNEW TRUTH

If Socrates knew truth,
he gave it to the youth
whose ignorance denied
the things they could not hide.

If Darwin has his way,
the fittest had their day
for life is but a glance
of accidental chance.

If Newton gave us laws,
we while away the flaws
of why we're on the ground
instead of skyward bound.

If poetry shows grace,
then Einstein gave us space
to speculate in rhyme
and fly away in time.

—Cinda McCord

FOR A MOMENT

For a moment
I was there,
I touched the sky;
at the pinnacle of bliss,
at the height of happiness . . .
I was there.

For a moment
I was there,
and then it died;
the love we used to share
no longer meant the same.
Passion lost its flair,
devotion disappeared,
joy became despair;
hopelessly retracing
that which wasn't there.

But the memory will not fall,
forever I'll recall:
for a moment in my life
I was there.

—George Foss

WE SAY THE THINGS

We say the things
That have been said before,
Now turn that new engarniture
We listen, both
That evils might speak the word
That should unfetter
All that's sealed and dull,
And soon we tire of waiting,
That look, that quick expression,
Turn it as we may
Does not contain the
Hidden sense and secret
We had hoped.

It would seem that I was wrong
The answer does not lie
In the cool shadows of your
Aching brows;
So many voices
Have not spoken truth,
Perhaps the answer
Is not yet
A voice at all.

—Louis James

PEACE, DEAR MOTHER

Her gentle soul
is still
no more
does she fight her reality
she no longer clutches
for what will never be.

The curtain of her mind
she pulled
but still, the pain crept in—
withering, withdrawing
even still,
there was to be
no more,
no more fight,
all over now.

Peace, dear mother,
may peace touch you now.

—Nadine M. Hart

DEATH

The day you are born you
are one day closer to death,
Soon you grow and you feel
lifeless,
Your life fills with anger
and disappointments,
Everything you hoped for
has passed away,
You're alive only because
you survive,
The question is life: Is it
worth living?
You did everything you
wanted,
The time has come to say
goodbye,
Death at last, knocks at
your door,
At last, you REST . . . .

—Beth Holmes

OAK LEAF

Now clinging to its source
Upon a giant oak
An *omnifarious life
Is wavering in the wind

Below many have fallen
Instantly swept up in
A current of air only to be
Thrown into dungeons of darkness

Some come to rest
Upon a secluded pond
Gently landing
Awakening its still waters

Others are left lying
In heaps alongside a
Dirt trodden path
Life gone from within

Then the one lonely
Warrior drifts to its death
Leaving the towering
Oak bare and empty

* of all shapes, sizes & colors

— John W. McCarroll, Jr.

IN MY WORLD

Let me run! What's wrong with me that no one will touch me?
Where have all my friends gone? Why am I alone now!

Give me love, give me something to hang on. A place to belong.
Let me run to someplace far away in the woods. The trees will
not degrade me, for they cannot see to stare. And when the
cold comes I will fall on the ground and freeze like the leaves.
Body will follow soul. Beautiful as I can be, all wasted.
No one shares.

> You look at me and can't read. Because I'm broken too fine
> to see. Must I force myself on your company!

I feel so old and useless. But loneliness must have no age.
I should be young and free. I am young, someone include me.
Take me, don't let me stand here for show.

> Fill this empty basin. The water becomes my soul
> I promise it will all pour back to you, warmed as it flows

I see and know that warmth comes to some
But for me I'll just go on
Now my mind and spirit long to be free, a drug? . . . a dream?
Away from all that's real. So much pain with the living
breathing world.

—Jacqueline M. Whaley

LOSING CONTROL

Finding no meaning to this life I am leading.
This life is full of deception.
Dangerous, yet infinitely possessive.

I fear I am losing control,
if you do, you will pay.
The price you pay, is your life.

For life has no reality,
all has turned to an endless mass of inabilities to cope.
Seeking the escape, for what I seek,
nothing comes forth.

Leaving me blinded to the insanity,
that is lurking admidst me.
Finding no reason for this madness,
but madness has no reason.

Losing control has meant I have lost everything.
I have finally lost the sanity,
that I had held to me so precious.

I now welcome the voidless mass that now descends upon me.

—Dina Wright

TO DARYL, A DEAR FRIEND . . .

I'm lost in the moment.
The one you've just presented to me today,
as the long distance wires brought the news of your fate.
It was as though the nerve endings in my body were sliced in half.

Were you so lost that you could not find your way back?
Why didn't you drop pebbles, ones that would light your path,
in the darkness you must have found.

I reach out to touch you, then realize you're not there.

Something as precious as you were, gone from my life forever,
it's hard to absorb.

I'll miss you my friend,
one who believed in me.
One who helped me escape from the life that taunted me.

WHY DIDN'T YOU LET ME HELP YOU?

—Yanna Kay Phillips

FLEETING YOUTH

How sweet the sound of children
When they laugh and sing and play,
It fills my heart with sunshine,
And it brightens up my day.

It seems to me they grow so fast;
Much sooner than they should.
Why can't they just stay little;
The way I wish they could.

Time has a way of slipping by;
First babies — and then youth.
Why, before you know it;
It's time to turn them loose.

So folks, enjoy your little ones;
Their blightful happiness and joy.
One day you'll wake up all alone,
Missing all their cheerful noise.

—Nancy Ebbert

ARMS

Arms,
circling around, squeezing out
black crows flying
shrieking, cawing, diving.
Arms,
sinewy mass, bands of steel
protective shield
from the real and psychotic.
Arms,
gentle strength, puppy warmth
a sweet and saving caress,
harbor safe
against the raging storm.
Arms,
workman's skill, angel grace
loving touch.
Arms,
viselike grasp
yanks me from
the drowning pool
into sheltering safety.

—Jan T. Santoro

SINS OF THE FATHERS

Sometimes I wonder
in this world for sale,
Why bother to be true —
All pass through hell.

"The sins of the fathers
are sins of the sons."
The piano man knew
for he once was one.

In their anger and fear
they try to teach,
But the door is closed;
No sound will reach.

On the wheel turns
A shift in the weight,
The boy found out
how love turns to hate.

Be straight and true —
don't falter or bend,
But dad, you're you.
I'm not, the end.

—Ron Wright

WHEN TWILIGHT FADES

Darkness falls.
Lying in my bed I hear noises.
Noises of the night.
Images form on walls creating shapes
For which only the imagination can depict.
Shadows lurk somewhere in the darkness
Away from the eyes of those who worship reality,
And sounds that cannot be understood become objects of fear
For those of us who must have an explanation for everything.
The blissful hush (which some call peace)
Is not the result of the night hour's work,
But is merely a beginning for a new way of life
Which only the people of the night can understand;
While the people of reality are ignorant of anything
That lies beyond the sun.

—Kimberly Little

INNOCENCE

Up by the outhouse--------------- behind the chicken pen,
A special strip of yard--------- that smelled of laying hens.
Two little girls--------------------- dressed in dirty over-alls,
A singin' and a dancin'------------ and sittin' by the wall.
Just a makin' mud pies------------ to their heart's delight,
Oblivious to the flies-------------- that came to bite.
There were buckets and boxes----- and old fruit jars,
This house of pretend------------- a garage for a car.
They sat in the kitchen------------ on an old tin can,
Rolled out the mud---------------- with little dirty hands.
Baked the mud pies---------------- every shape and size,
They were playin' grown-up-------- you gotta' realize.
A lazy old hound-------------------- all droopy and sad,
Sprawled on the ground----------- licking fleas he had;
Watching and waiting-------------- for an old water pail,
But squirmed instead-------------- when they kicked his tail.
And in the pasture------------------ behind the fence,
A herd of cows---------------------- stood staring and tense,
With big solemn eyes--------------- just chewing their cud,
Watching two little girls----------- a playin' in the mud.

—Linda Louise Lung

HERE'S TO THE "KIDIOTS"

Here's to the "kidiots" — may Mother survive.

The givers of wrinkles, sponsors of headaches, artists of confusion, designers of stress, producers of tension, authors of conflict, and the unsurpassed, ultimate sources of all the loud noise God ever made.

The tattle-tellers, talk-backers, wall-smudgers, gum-smackers, swatters, biters, whiners, screamers, kickers, pinchers and spitters.

The anywhere-throw-it-downers, never-pick-it-uppers, always-leave-it-oners, won't-put-it-backers, never-close-a-doorers, under-the-bed-stuffers, toilet-won't-flushers, sticker-tongue-outters, I don't-want-toers, and won't-go-to-beders.

The pint-sized victims of magnetic mud puddles, aliens throwing dirt balls, imaginary friends, and made up monsters.

The unfortunate little owners of toys that break, clothes that crumple, bikes that skid, kites that crash, and bubble gum that wants to live in their hair forever.

So much the little dears have to do each day.
They never finish — try as they may.

And dare to ask them, "WHY?" "Why, my children do you do these THINGS that you do?"

"Gee, Mom, We don't know, I guess our brain just tells us to."

—Deborah O. Cantrell

THE MASTER'S HAND

The sands of time, washed gently by life's great tide
  Dotted here and there by shells of toil and care
Is held firmly in the Master's hand.
The great ocean of life
With its high tossing waves of strife,
White capped by troubles and tears,
Is shared by the Master, the One who cares.
He alone controls the wind
The storms that toss and seethe within,
He can calm the storm tossed heart
Remove the clouds and peace impart.
If you have not the peace that passeth understanding,
And the trials of life have become too demanding,
Wasted time — wasted hours — Searching, searching everywhere,
Just kneel at the Cross and leave your burdens there.
Seek no longer. The answer lies in this command,
The Master will take them firmly in His hand.

          —Catherine L. Scott

GRANDVIEW CEMETERY

From all the quarries on the continent
  They've brought these blocks of time-resistant rock
Here to this prairie place, and chiseled thereupon
The names by which men labeled the identity
Which each one bore that little wink of itme
He had between his birth and death.

Here lies Mary Able, immortal during the erosion-resistant
          span of pink qranite.
This tall white shaft tells any passerby that from 1847 to 1921
          John Johnson was Spirit manifest in flesh.
There beneath that highly polished sphere of mottled marble,
          all that's left of mortal McIlhenny Rests in Peace.

On these, the hardest rocks that he could find,
Man makes his last pathetic plea against annihilation.
"Remember me."
      "Remember me."
            "Remember me."
                  "Remember-----"

    —Alice Wilson

A WRITER'S LAMENT AND DILEMMA

Writers spout ideas and thoughts and convey emotion.
  Doodlers scribble letters to the editor at each notion.

The public demands sensibility and light. However, when does
that stroke of pen become might?

Reality in prose fashions a code, yet leaves a way open to
change the mode.

In non-fiction we garner fact, which when printed is rarely
exact.

Identical in poetry is the message we learn: that from
McLuhan the medium we must earn.

But why need the judging herd,
Beserk, create chaos wherever the word?

Writers excite and cause a stir,
But can realist and antagonist concur?

Thus ready to achieve results consequential,
The writer selects tools which are essential.

So sharpen pencils, and ready eraser,
It is time now to position paper.

Go access computer to state of address,
For the moment has arrived to probe and express.

        —Dr. David M. Silverstone

I'm on a roller coaster
One I can't stop
Just when I find I'm at the end
I look at you
or touch you
I buy another ticket
And the ride begins all over again

I pause
Let sanity take over
And guilt sits down beside me
I'll get off this time
I promise

The phone rings
You're there
And my stop goes by in a blur
I look back
Guilt shakes his head
And cries

        —C. L. Brook

CHAINED TO THE WORLD

If I was a rock
  would the world still
be harder than me?

If I was a tree,
would the world have any
mercy on me?

If I was a bird,
would they force me
not to fly?

But I am not any of these
and I am.

I am a rock that is forced
to crumble.
I am a tree that must die.
And I am the bird that
will never fly free.

      —Daniel Martinez, Jr.

BEATEN

The pain is great;
  It hurts, it's sore.
My body sinks slowly,
Slowly to the floor . . . .

Kicks at my left,
Kicks at my right —
I fall defenseless,
Alone in the night . . . .

A bruised cheek,
A twisted knee —
My body is numb,
Yet my mind is free . . . .

I ponder the hate,
The anger, the loss.
Consciousness fades,
My life this has cost . . . .

The pain is great,
It hurts, it's sore.
My body sinks slowly,
To rise nevermore.

      —Jennifer Lea Smith

LIKE A DREAM

Oh, my summer love.
Your eyes are as blue
as the sky above.
They're full of hope
and never-ending love.
Let our hearts soar
like kites.
while the days are as special
as the endless nights.
Just feel as I do
and love as I do
because I dream of being with you.
If we meet again
let us vow to never part.
Together, a new life we will start.

—Jenine Johnson, Age 15

A TEA PARTY

I looked up when what should I see,
but my daughter looking down at me.

She said, I'm bored, come play
with me, as I thought, it
seemed to me, a tea party,
was in need.

I told her, let's put on our
finest things and go inside
for some tea, just you and me.

Since it was such a warm day
we sat beneath a lovely shade tree,
with biscuits and jams and some
honey grahams and one lump and two
and then we were through.

My daughter turned to me and said
I love a tea party,
That's just with you and me.

—Yvonne Megnin

EMBRACED THROUGHOUT ETERNITY
Dedicated In Memory Of Jackie Dean Akridge 1-10-89

Our spirit cries
For our hearts must die
Sharing deepened secrets
With reasons of why

Loving and touching
With you in my arms
Reveals a destiny
With spirits so warm

Everlasting memories
Awaken our hearts
Soothing many emotions
When we're apart

I need to say
As time fades away
The spirit has time
For many more days

Through ages past
Our spirits will last
To a future place
With another face

When our bodies die
We must reply
What a peaceful journey
Just you and I.

—David E. Sommers

WHITE WATER

We all know error and we all know fear
as sunrise makes every option clear.
     — which one to pick?
     — is this the way?
     — shouldn't I go?
     — shouldn't I stay?

We all have visions and we all have dreams
     as they come floating by in endless streams.
     — I see it there!
     — I grab it fast!
     — I reach the shore!
     — It's mine at last!

We all can win it and we all can lose
     as we're wondering just what to choose.
     — which way is best?
     — is now the time?
Make up your mind!
Begin to climb!

—Tom Rezzuto

MAKE UP YOUR MIND

Do you love me or do you not?
You told me once but I forgot.
All I'm asking is how you feel,
I need to know if our love's real.
I told you I love you and yes I still do,
But what happens next is left up to you.
Look deep inside where the world can't see,
Sort out your feelings, what's it gonna be?
Is it over and are we through?
What's going on between me and you?
I just want some answers, the truth will do fine,
I wanna know if you're gonna be mine.
Do you plan to walk out and forget I exist?
Are you trying to tell me I wouldn't be missed?
I need to know if you plan to stay
If there's a chance? If there's a way?
Remember I care and think of the past,
I've gotta know if this love can last.
Look in your heart, see what you find,
Do you still love me? Make up your mind!

—Cathy M. Quinn

BONDING

This precious child that I hold in my arms now
Is like a fresh clean slate.
I want to help him become the best he can.
Will I affect his fate?

I hold my breath as I prepare to bathe him.
He loves the freedom so.
I change and feed and dress and lubricate him,
From soft spot head to toe.

And then he draws upon the food within me.
A quiet time I need.
For he is writing love songs on my pages,
This flower of my seed.

When filled and warm he turns again to sleeping.
I watch his eyelids close.
His gentle breath escapes between lips parted.
His mouth is like a rose.

I examine ears, nose, feet and fingers,
Tiny, perfect work of art.
A loving God's exquisite new creation,
We are bonded heart to heart.

—Gloria M. Meurant

PORTRAIT OF PATHOS

There's a soft faced Catholic schoolgirl
 In a virgin white dress,
Glowing with pristine purity.

She's tramping through the thick brown mud in the field.
The sludge grips her weak,
Velvet ankles.

The pointed heels of her silken slippers
Promptly pierce
The coldness of the ground.

And as the dark, wet blood
Creeps slowly from the hole,
It turns to black.

Then the young girl's precious smile,
Which would otherwise be beaming in her youthful venture,
Vanishes instantly,
As does her innocence.

So she begins to cry; what else can she do?
And I cry with her
Through the everlasting blackness of her night . . .

—George Griffith

FROM SOUL'S SLUMBER . . .

Sometimes the eye of the soul can remain closed
 You may not realize or even seem to notice
       but deep inside you do know — somewhere —
    The realization lies close and right before the
       first awakening
    You never knew you were dead until you
       started to come alive . . .

Why did you wait so long, soul of mine—almost too late . . .

Maybe you were lazy, not wanting to waste energy until
       you saw that I was finally ready and worthy of you
    Or did I keep the door bolted tight from fear of what
       I would find — until you made me see . . .

Maybe you knew you had to do something this time
    or you might end up in some other body
       —that of a donkey perhaps—

So, now I feel my spirit guide beckoning once again

    Where to now, my old friend?

—Alexis G. Robinson

YOU HOPE

The human soul is so delicate and fragile when it's low,
 If not handled with great care . . . it can weaken
just as the branches of a gigantic weeping willow,
Once the human soul is bruised in some way,
The healing process can take what appears to be
forever and a day,
Just as a bird with a broken wing can't take
off in flight,
A person with a broken spirit doesn't have the
strength to fight,
So holding on until the pain disappears,
And hoping that in time the turmoil and confusion
clears,
Is really all that we can do,
Until the clouds vanish and this storm in our
life is through,
You hope that once your heart mends,
That this devastating hurt also ends,
And that your heart and soul,
Will again be complete and whole!

—Cathy Tobey

SILENT INTROSPECTION

How are you feeling, friend?
 If you say nothing, I know nothing.
As you hide behind a closed door
are you keeping something in
or keeping something out?
There is so much noise in silence
it intimidates me with thoughts unspoken.
Silence speaks volumes.
Quiet, unknown silence
like darkness without light
strikes my soul with fear.
Communicate
Share your thoughts and feelings,
put them into words.
Who are you my friend?
Are you afraid to be known?
Speak
and find yourself.

—Florence Zielinski

IN THE STILLNESS OF THE NIGHT

The day has been long — and busy,
 And rightly it should be
For I have obligations now:
    to myself
    — and to others
But the day has departed for other lands,
And now the night has come
Bringing needed rest
    in the quiet
    — and stillness.
For a spell time has slowed her pace,
Allowing me space to think
And room to feel
    past pleasures
    — and pardoned pain.
In the lonely stillness of the night,
The musky odor of memory
Recalls the yesterdays
    of youth
    — and freedom
    . . . And the joys of loving you.

—Kathie L. Greer

SNOW DIAMONDS

On a cold winter night
 With a full moon in the sky,
The stars were shining bright
As the moon went sailing by.

The ground was all a blanket
Of newly fallen snow,
The full moon shining bright
Made millions of diamonds aglow.

They sparkled and glittered
Upon the newly fallen snow,
As long as the moon was high
And the sky was all aglow.

God made all of the stars
And He made the moonlight,
He made them so complete
They would give light at night.

God's wonderful creation to behold,
If the snow diamonds were real
They could be sold,
To help the homeless, hungry and cold.

—Ruby H. Anderson

Teachers are sweet,
they give you big treats.
They start your day,
with laughter and play.
Teachers are smart,
they teach you art,
They never make you sad,
but make you glad.
Now the day is over,
from laughter and play.
Hop in your bed and dream,
of the next day!

—Sobeth Collingsworth, age 10

SHORT AND SWEET

Sweet child with little lovely
faces,

Tiny smiles the hand of God
embraces,

How I long to slow the
time,

Which seems to follow close
behind,

And wisk away the treasured
moments it erases.

—Barbara Antonicello

MY PLAYMATES

To my playmates on behalf of
the good times that we've
shared.
Knowing and understanding
that you really cared.

I'll never forget the games we
used to play.
And the special prayers we
used to pray.

How could I forget the secrets
we held inside.
And what about the feelings we
were trying to hide.

I'll try not to forget my
playmates who encouraged me
to try.
But, I will never forget my
playmates who made me cry.

We had dreams we believed in.
We had victories we wanted
to win.

To my playmates I'm holding
on to a dream that seems so real.
And to a hope that one day will
be fulfilled.

I'm holding on to a desire
that won't let go
And to a fear I will one day
out grow.

Here's a token to my playmates
who outgrew the sun and the
season.
And here's a toast to them who
grew out of doubt and reason.

—Cynthia Ervin

LION?

Have you ever seen a tear fall from a lion's eye?
Felt a lion's sorrow, Heard his helpless cry?
Have you ever left a lion when fallen fast asleep?
Known his compassion for a lion cub in need?
Have you known his fury, Been made to suffer his rage?
Known his deep depression when confined to a cage?
You have known this lion well for he is deep within each one.
This lion is a man, the man, a boy, your son.

—Christy Lin Burton

THE MIRACLE OF LIFE

One night I was lying aside of my wife
when I felt the miracle of life
For the first time I felt you kick
While you were still inside Mommy's stomach
Mommy was beautiful and glowing on the outside
While you were growing ever so quickly on the inside
For nine months we waited with excitement and joy
Until that final day, God brought us a boy
I'll never forget the feeling that night
Of when you first came into my sight
Within my heart there was an empty place
But, when I laid my eyes on you, you filled up that space
And when I first heard you cry
The sound of you brought tears to my eyes
At that moment I knew you didn't have a clue
But, all I wanted to say was, I'm your Daddy and I love you

—Craig Sonon

OUR LITTLE BOY

On the day you came into this world, what happy parents
we were to see,
You were so little, with eyes so blue and hair so golden.
Does he look like his mom, or does he look more like dad?
You were beyond words, no matter what anyone else had said.
Now you're growing up, to be such a fine young man.
The time seems to pass so quickly, as we become your biggest
cheering fans.
As a child you made our hearts stop, every time you said, "I
Love You Both, forever and ever."
We can only try and teach you all that we can, Even though
we can't always fix the bumps and bruises, as you become a man.
We can only hope that someday you'll find someone to love
you forever and ever, as we do.
We may not always be right, but until the end of our time,
we shall always be, just mom and dad.

—Pamela K. Ulen

OUT OF CONTROL

Dodging hard-shelled beetles over a long brick road;
Running at the speed of light or in my own mode.

Passing mountains, bushes, rabbits living in holes.
Jumping through fire and tiptoeing over coals.

Time's running out!! What do I do? I'm about to go CRAZY!
Gotta lie down! Gotta take a rest! I feel so Gosh Darn Lazy . . .

Up those stairs! Down an alley where passageways are narrow.
Falling through clouds! Look out!! I just missed a sparrow!

The adventure's almost over. The Great Bowser awaits!
Trembling in my boots! What will be my fate?

Bowser's throwing hammers . . . Two, three, even four!
I duck! He's all confused. Now's the time to score!

Saving Princess Toadstool, I feel like yelling, "Fame!"
Mom's calling me to dinner! Gotta turn off my video game!!

—Billy Brill, age 13

"HUH?"

Cheerily I said this day is nice
She ignored me, so I said it twice
Then she whirled around frowning and said,
    Beat it you nitwit turkey! Drop dead!

On the crowded elevator, still cheerful, I say
    It's a beautiful morning. It's a great day!
Close to me a man standing stiff and grim
    Sneered, knock it off, boob, what's your problem.

Outside, I had an idea I thought was neat
    I'll help the old lady across the street
I took her arm, she shrieked in alarm
    I apologized and explained I meant no harm.

As the old woman scurried across the street
    I realized this day had not been neat
Rudely bumped into as I sadly turned away
    A voice bellowed, sorry! Have a nice day!

—W.M. Harrison

A FARM FAMILY'S DAUGHTER

The second of seven kids and the first daughter,
    To help do the chores that was an order.
Milk cows, do churning and gather eggs in,
Feed the dogs, cats, chickens and pigs in the pen.
Draw water, wash clothes with rub board and pat,
Hoe, pull fodder, pick cotton like it or not.
Make beds, scrub floors and help do the cooking,
Give kids bath from wash tub and in bed tuck them.
Get in wood, helping can and killing hogs,
Salt the meat down and boil out the lard.
Clothes starched, ironing, do dishes and mending,
For Sunday School and Church I'd be attending.
With feed sack dresses and hand me down shoes,
Long hair in pigtails that was the rule,
From a country school I got my learning,
Walking there and back each night and morning.
My reward was penny candy on Saturday night,
Grand Ole Opry on radio and kerosene oil lamp light.
All of this I am really so proud of,
For in this farm family there was also Love.

—Elizabeth Waters

TELL ME A RHYME WITH SILVERY CHIME

In the mystical dark of an ev'ning,
With the stars overhead shining bright,
    To sit all alone in the twilight,
Is my own special secret delight.

    I gaze in mute awe thro the darkness
At the stars that blink high overhead,
    And think of the people, in houses,
'Cept me, all a-dreaming in bed.

    I thoughtfully ponder the diff'rence,
When daylight with brightness is here;
    Then bells break the stillness with ringing,
Saying, "Hush, child, goodnight, and good cheer."

    Then I tiptoe upstairs to my own bed,
'Neath the covers I blissfully hide;
    Snuggling down, I wiggle still, deeper;
Feeling 'specially happy inside.

    "Ding-dong, ding-dong, ding-dong,"
Sweet and soft they sound thro the night,
    I hear the bells musical chiming,
Saying, "Hush, child, good cheer and good night."

—Red Hawk

LAST LIGHT

Toward this light we sure must go.
    This soft pale light can take control.
Leave the body, call the soul.
Toward this light there is an ease.
A silent feel of total peace.
Oh please! Oh please! don't go away
I got this far, don't turn away.
Now that I'm here, please can't I stay?
Oh no my child I will not sway
There's things I still must have you do.
Before my final call for you.
There'll be no problem, no more pain.
The hardships there won't have been in vain.
When your work on earth is finally through.
So I await with bated breath.
This pull I feel will never be less.
The wonderous light and glow I'll see.
This time I know will be for me.

—Shirley Winner

MIRACLE WIND

Catch me, if you can,
    hear my whispers chasing endless promises,
rustling break-through ears.
I'm traveling in speed on currents air,
floating to absolute trill, on fog cloud breezes.
I stir nature's vital creation,
intaking sea-shore voices crashing,
on salt mist waves.
Birds sing praises to my music,
played by invisible trumpets.
Trees clap their hands,
in soft tune harmony,
to my applause.
Touch my presence,
feel my pulse, against your face,
Dance with me,
along the way,
together we'll twirl under sunshine's ray.
Close your eyes, as we fly,
I'm miracle wind passing by.

—Raynette Vega

UNTIL THEN

You came into my life by such a surprise,
    You turned me around, opened my eyes
When I'm with you all my dreams come true
    I never knew what to say or do
Until I met you,

    If there's something that comes between us
I'll find the bridge and we'll cross it together.
    Bring me up when I'm feeling down,
Pick my head up and make our world go 'round.

Time rolls on
    People touch and then they're gone
I thought it would be different for you and me
    But who knew it was just gonna be . . . .

    When I'm with someone else
I dream about being with you once again
    Like I said many years ago
Someday we'll drift away together
    Someday soon, I don't know when
For now I'll keep on dreaming
    Until then.

—Joseph Sequino

OUR SYMBOL OF FREEDOM

She's red, She's white
She's a beautiful blue
She stands, for freedom
For me, and for you.

There are some who don't like her
So they're finding, a way
To destroy, and abuse her
In some, sort of way.

They tell you, to burn her
That's freedom, they say
Go ahead, express your feelings
In your own, personal way.

There are those, who shed their blood
On foreign, soil some where
So please don't let them, die, for naught
Let's show them, that we care.

—Ethel H. Perry

OLD GLORY

When I see "Old Glory" flying high
    above the houses and trees,
I know I'm still in America
    Where every man is Free;
We vote the way we feel is right
    And speak our minds with ease,
We work and play, go to Church
    We raise our families.

There's just something about that
    "Grand Old Flag" that sends chills
    all over me,
And tears start flowing down my cheeks
    When I see her flying Free;
I love the stars and stripes on her
    She is not a rag you see,
And when you tear her down, or
    burn her up,
You are doing the same to me.

—Wanda Wooten Baugess

CAMOUFLAGED
COMPETITION

My countrified fella gets
    crazy and acts sort of silly,
Known as a wanderer,
    Just a sweet hillbilly,

Like wine to a wine-o,
    Hunting is his addiction,
Even compared to his lady,
    I'm not any competition,

I'm told it's in his blood,
    That I'm in his heart,
He's tried to explain this,
    Right from the start,

In winter, it's coyotes and rabbits,
    Four legged deer in the fall,
In spring, it's turkeys and squirrels,
    But bow season's his favorite of all,

With a shot gun on his shoulder,
    A night's meal in his hand,
A content grin on his face,
    He feels like a fortunate man!

—Robbie

Tears . . . .
        —salted crystals of happiness and pain
        —bottled grieve's
        —explosion of a waterfall tumbling down
        —a never ending cry!

—Margo Férron

WAR

We are at war once again.
    This is a war we cannot win.

This is war where we are fighting each other.
Fighting among ourselves, with sisters and brothers.

We are hurting each other, hurting ourselves.
We are just like toy soldiers sitting on a shelf.

We are teaching our children how to hate,
One reason for the rising crime rate.

We teach our children how to use guns,
Until they go out and kill someone.

There are bullets now, flying in the air!
Would you shoot me, would you dare?

We are at war once again.
This is a war we cannot win.

—Rebekah Borders

ASHES

How cruel can somebody be,
    To burn the flag that set us free?
The flag that shall always stand
Against the enemy and protect our land.

But some people think this flag is awful.
While nine judges make burning the flag lawful.
Devastating, I do say,
What would make people act this way?

Just look around at veterans and you'll see,
People who helped this country be.
They fought for the flag and many lost their lives,
Away from their families, children and wives.

But the flag they died for,
Can now be burned.
I think our country
Has a lesson to be learned.

—Rebekah Steinmetz

GOD'S CALL

Life—what a precious gift to all
    It can be taken upon God's call.
God touches us and breathes life into our souls—
And stands beside us as we achieve our goals.
But someday, we must meet Him face to face—
And hope that we will be within His grace!
The call can come at anytime—
You may be rich or without a dime.
You can't run and hide when that time arrives.
He beckons everyone—children, husbands, wives.
We miss those who have gone before—
They have been called to pass through God's door.
They wait for us, watching with their loving eyes.
Sometimes you feel their hugs and their sighs.
Someday we'll be with them in heaven above
To share in their warmth and all of God's love!
No matter how we stumble, no matter how we fall—
Someday, we will all get God's final call.

—Cindy Slovacek

SUNDAY SILENCE

Sunday night — Stillness
Reflections on the day with you

Cool refreshing water filled your little pool
Splashes of water reflected your playfulness
Sunshine set the scene for a warm summer day
Gentle breezes ruffled your golden sun drenched hair
Soft easy breaths as you laid on the beach towel asleep

Once again you are asleep but
Day has flowed into night
Soft short breaths as you sleep in my lap
Your warm body fits snuggly with mine
Traces of sunshine and gentle breezes press softly against my nose
As your head nestles against my cheek
Suntanned arms extend beyond fire engine pajamas
Little legs dangle beyond my lap
Skin as smooth as finely sanded wooden spindles

Reflections on the day with you
Carry me through tomorrow.

—Lori A. Gohs

UNSPOKEN LOVE

As softly as the mountain stream, that ebbs its way to the valley
I hear my mind scream
Tormenting me, of my unspoken love for thee
Instilling insight into my yesterdays
Haunting me constantly, in so many ways
As brilliantly as a rose explodes its color in the morning dew
I experience the sensations of love through you
As the warm winds of summer caress my face
I become a whirlwind, to feel your embrace
As violently as the ocean roars to shore
The living memory of you, I'll adore
When star dust sprinkles its magic all over the place
I'll think of you, our steps I'll retrace
As snowflakes dance vividly on my window pane
Crystal clear reflections of you still remain
When the sun descends below the horizon in the West
Of all my friends, I'll love you the best
Though the world to me has no reason or rhyme
You will always be with me, throughout all of time
Unspoken love, a feeling so rare it eludes eternity

—Cindy K. Heath-Draper

THOUGH I DON'T KNOW YOU, I AIM TO BE YOUR FRIEND.

It's not my style to get hung up on first impressions. I won't judge you by your appearance alone nor by a fault or idiosyncrasy which happens to catch my attention. That wouldn't be fair, as your countless good qualities and innate talents will surface after I know you better.

I won't dwell on the fact that we're from different walks of life. Rather, I'll marvel at how we're both blessed with the gift of life. Each of us seeks peace, respect and fulfillment. We have our share of inadequacies and tribulations and a common fear of death.

To blame you for having a different viewpoint would be extremely unjust, as I haven't been faced with the same situations nor influenced by the same mentors. To fully understand you I would have to reflectively read your complete autobiography.

There's so much I can learn from you and share with you. We can exchange laughter, dreams and tears. As occasions arise, we can defend and comfort each other.

I promise I won't wait until you're gravely ill, shattered by a tragedy or snuffed out of life to compliment you, admit your value in my life and tell you that I love you.

—Heidi Hermine Godshall

A THOUGHT FROM THE HEART

If one has no lover,
then thou shall not be loved.
If trust is not found,
then thou shall be lost.
If passion needs searching,
then thou does not desire.
If faith one has not,
then thou does not deserve.

—Tami Jones

FEELINGS

Feelings are forever
That's the way that I feel.
I hope we're together for
a million years.

Friends may come,
Friends may go.
I hope we're together
Where ever we go.

Be brave and loyal
in years to come
And you'll never be hated
By the ones you love!

—Kelly Renae Boling

SISTERS

A sister is a friend
In so many ways;
They make the minutes
Seem like days.

There's never enough time
To say what we mean
And they're always there
Onto which I can lean.

Our quarrels are like the wind,
So eager to pass,
On all the empty spots,
They grow some grass.

To fill my bare personality
With creativity and more;
They fulfill my life
And open each new door.

—Laura K. Emery

THE ULTIMATE ELUSIVE DREAM

The peace and stillness of a
moon and starlit night;
Brings rest to a burdened soul
and quiet to a worried mind:
Soon the warmth of a newborn
sun shall rise;
Another day for us to tarry
while learning to be wise:
To walk a path of narrow which
has no dividing line;
Ending my journey only when
life is no longer mine:
In a place rich in beauty may
I wake to see;
To find my Lord has forgiven
and accepted me.

—Joseph Leroy Hartzfeld

I THANK THEE GOD

He walks beside me every day,
He holds my hand and leads the way,
My dear Jesus who is just,
Divine Savior whom I trust,
I place before thee many things,
Dear Lord and Master King of Kings,
You came to Earth to die for me,
So that from sin I might be free,
I thank thee God for everything,
For flowers, trees and birds that sing,
I thank thee for the morning sun,
The moon, the stars when day is done,
And when I go to sleep at night,
I pray thee Lord, please hold me tight,
If I should not awake next day,
My soul you'll take is what I pray.

—Emma Jane Klapproth

A MOTHER'S PLEA

Oh Dear Lord, this heart of mine
Is full of pain at this time
It's so hard for me to ask
Will you help me with the task

My little girl, you took for your own
and left me with pain I've never known
please help me to understand
as I reach out to take your hand

Oh Dear Lord, I'm falling apart
help me conquer my heavy heart
please help the memories go away
so I can keep from going astray

Help me find a better way
to deal with things every day
all my hopes, all my dreams
they're all gone, now it seems

Oh Dear Lord, hear my plea
Won't you give back my life to me
Don't keep her for your own
please Dear Lord, just send her home

—Linda Bessette

MADE BY GOD

My little eyes were made by God
He wanted me to see,
The beautiful world He created
For people just like me.

My little ears were made by God
He wanted me to hear,
The sounds of big and little things
Both far and very near.

My little feet were made by God
He wanted me to stand,
And feel the earth beneath my feet
That He made with His own hand.

My little hands were made by God
He wanted me to pray,
For peace, love and happiness
For those who pass my way.

I'm glad that I was made by God
He made these things for me,
So I can be the very best
Little me that I can be.

—Jean H. Mills

WILL SOMEONE CARE

I lay in my hospital bed and heard the cries of loneliness
from the other bed, yet not one came to care. My bedside
was full of laughter from spouse and children who held me
dear. As each one left they looked around a
curtain to a small and shrinking figure where no one
came to care. That evening I was moved to another
room because that small figure was growing
weaker, yet no one came to care. The next day I walked
past the room at noon and looked in hoping she knew
someone did care. When my doctor came he told me
that small person just passed away.
I slipped quietly out of bed and strolled unnoticed
to the room, and with a silent prayer thanked
him above because I knew he did care.
Life is so short for us not to love and care,
give each other love and remember the "Silent Prayer"

—Helene Cooper Guerrero

THE PICTURES ON MEMORIES WALL

I fancy a picture on memories wall,
All the treasures of childhood when we were so small.
The old fashioned farm house with the porch all around,
And the big country kitchen where the folks gathered 'round.
The big range gleams proudly; as if by magic it brings
The goodies to surprise us; oh such wonderful things!
Then I see mama's rocker, though it's empty today,
And my vision seems blurred as I wipe tears away.

The creek in the meadow still runs past the bog;
Skipping just as from childhood to the bridge made of logs.
The stream was perfect for fishing, and bathing as well.
How we romped in its shallows; more times than we'd tell!

The old One Roomed School House was a picturesque place,
Where mysterious lessons each day we must face.
Long summer vacations and holiday delights,
Easter baskets, Santa's stockings, and Christmas tree lights!

Have I glorified the moments so precious to me?
Magnified or revised them as I think they should be.
Perhaps it's not always so clear to recall,
When we repaint the pictures on memories wall.

—Ruth V. Shillito

THE LIGHT FROM ABOVE

I look out the bars of my cold, dark, cell.
The light from the sun comes in so well.
But all I can do is set within the light.
For one to know, what freedom that was.
Is not to be hailed a greater gift than of life.

But when freedom is gone I look to the sun.
A beam of light that which comes down from above.
For you see it is the only freedom in which I receive.
But it is the love of God and my friends that keeps me free.

So now I start a new book of life.
And to my good friends I wish a good life.
So remember one thing I give unto you.
It's your heart, of the ones that I love so true.

For this is the Freedom of which the light from above.
For which gives me the freedom in which I do love.
And to my friends— as long as there is a sun.
I will be in God's hands until light is there none.

Would you say a prayer for me if you know him.
And now I say good by my friends
Until the light comes down upon me again.

—Richard Green

ONLY SHADES OF GRAY

The day was without color,
Grass, sky, lakes and trees
Were only shades of gray.
The winding road was
Lined with ice-covered
Trees, greeting me one by one
Showing off crystal beads like
Chandeliers in a great
Ballroom,
Void of color nature shows
Art, displaying a vivid
Picture of this wintry day.
How easy it is to write of blue skies and green fields,
We capture them on camera, but seeing God's creation blend
Together with only shades of
Gray, Oh how beautiful a
Day!

—Nancy Hudson

MY TREASURE OF BEAUTIFUL SEEDS

Recently, I spoke of the seeds you have given to me
Let me tell you of how each is a special one.
The tiny, but yet so strong seed of renewed courage
That somehow I had lost or misplaced.
A colorful seed of change — the opportunity to grow
and change as Autumn leaves so often do.
You can't imagine the seed of happiness — it's my favorite.
For with it comes an inter-glow, much more than a smile —
but deep within my heart.
The seed of understanding — that only so few possess, it's
always there reaching out with a beautiful tender hand.
Yet one seed is still somewhat of a mystery, for I can see
its different changes of kindness, admiration, and sometimes
love.
But I won't question or disturb its growth, but consider
myself so very lucky to someday see its special bloom.
I sincerely thank you and hope you can see how beautiful my
garden grows with the seeds you have given to me.

—Margarita M. Campbell

METAMORPHOSE

Look back on your life with love and affection
Using it only to find new direction

Learn all that you can from what you have done
Let it slowly assist you to overcome

The state of confusion and total despair
Is sometimes a cushion while finding what's there

Don't stand still, don't run away
You must trudge down this road struggling each and every day

Panic and terror are part of the game
You cannot reject this, you must "walk through the pain"

Deep inside we are special in so many ways
Yet finding our talents does seem like a maze

As soon as you can, fulfill your big dream
Grab onto contentment, it's called self-esteem

Master courage and strength as each day goes by
Unending determination and yes, you can cry

Glance back for a moment gathering all that you know
You'll be getting closer to where you must go

I've been a wife and a mother you see
Now it is time for me to be ME . . .

—JoAnn Kelly

I DEDICATE THIS SONG

I love you more than I imagined
My love grows stronger every day
I wouldn't alter my affection
My faith in you remains unchanged.

In the past I had deceived you
I turned away in search of freedom.
But I realized I was mistaken
Now I turn to you in adoration.

Time and time again I wonder
Why it took so long for me to see
That no other love could ever free me
Not like the love you give to me

And so I dedicate this song
To you, I'll always belong
While others scorn your name
I'll never lose my trust in you.

—Carol Adamski

YOU

I have wandered many miles —
Almost around the world.
I've slept among the pine cones,
I've dived for precious pearls.

I've walked along the seashore,
And climbed the mountain high.
I've seen the beauty of the world
Beneath a blazing sky.

I have wandered many miles
And many things I've seen,
But when I reached my home again
T'was you fulfilled my dream.

You fulfilled the dream I had
of gems I'd one day own.
You fulfilled the dream I had
Of treasures, then unknown.

You fulfilled my every hope;
You made each dream come true.
There is no treasure anywhere
That I would trade for you.

—Doris D. McCombs

FAIRIES WALTZ

I sat upon a hill one day
to see a glade full of flowers.
where the sun shined bright.
I saw a waltz of moving colors;
Gold, blue, yellow, and creamy white.

A fairies waltz it had to be.
So filled with delight and glee,
I ran to tell my mother.

She said, "Butterflies they would be."
Then she patiently explained to me
about the caterpillar's odyssey.
Of how they make their own cocoons,
and hang in danger for many moons.
Then out they come
to a bright warming sun,
to dry their brilliant wings
and show to everyone.

Caterpillers and butterflies
they might be to my mother,
but fairies still would be my druther.

—Virginia Cook

STARS AND BARS

When plans were made to sew our flag—
God surely lent a hand.
He loaned us thirteen shining stars—
to wave above our land.

The bars of red and white He gave—
a sign that we were free.
To praise His name and worship Him—
for all the world to see.

As time went by He loaned more stars—
to brighten up our way.
Until at last all fifty shine—
by night as well as day.

Let's lift our nation up in prayer—
and praises to Him bring.
For loaning stars and breaking bars—
Christ Jesus is our King.

—Daisy Marie Mohorich

THE SILVER MIST

The Silver Mist floats above the valley,
 Ancient smoke signals from the ghosts of
long forgotten tribes,
Do you see the dust from the horses hooves
as they race across the sky?
See, just beyond the moon,
The Great Spirit has gathered all the stars
in His hands,
He tosses them one by one toward the
Silver Mist,
Where they become rivers and streams,
But in an instant, The Silver Mist
disappears,
The Horses no longer race across
the sky,
And the rivers and streams are
no more,
Was it millenium,
or was it just a dream?

—Lynn Kagan Price

KNOW GOD, OUTSIDE IN

God of creation, let me know Your heart
First take me from the dark unknowing
Reveal another way of greater truth
Your mystery and self invisible within
The heart of all creation, Spirit Divine

Show me trees from outside in
Show me streams flowing from within
Show me light increasing and pure
Show me children pure in breath
Show me first, the source in life

Take me by the hand, Oh God of love
Lead me past the obstacle of self
Shelter me against the storms of rage
Hide me in Your wings of gentle peace
Let me abide in Your knowing ways

Let my outer self submit with Grace
Let me bow my head to Thee within
Let this vessel serve the King
Let the outer me burn to ash
Let the outer dissolve in Thee

—Christine C. Van Dorn

GOD'S WORLD

There is a world of sunshine somewhere
 just waiting for someone to find,
Beautiful rivers and valleys
 that have been there since the beginning of time.

There's a blanket of grass on the hillside
 all wet from the falling dew.
It sparkles like millions of diamonds,
 It's there just waiting for you.

You can sit on the side of the mountain,
 Look down at the valley below,
There is a beautiful river
 With trees of all kinds in a row.

There was never a place quite so peaceful
 where you lay all your burdens aside,
Except in this beautiful valley,
 just left there by time and tide.

—Mary Murray

AS I WALK THE COUNTRY ROAD

As I walk down the country road, many
 sounds I hear. Such as the singing of a
snow white dove from the sky so high above.
 Oh, how sweet the smell the flowers send
as their petals blow through the wind.
 The scene is beyond comparison in sight,
such a peaceful sight.
 As I wander farther in time, farther down
that country road, night falls and the sounds
of darkness call. The winds of fate are
now blowing strong. As I continue to wander
on, I began to notice something wrong.
No doves are singing; the smell of flowers
have vanished along with the light of
the day.
 To travel this road, you must have faith,
faith deep down in your heart. This faith must
stay with you all of the way, never let it
depart, for this road is the road of life.

—Jennifer Ann Poole

DEAR GOD,

No matter what may come today,
 You're here to help me in every way.
When I want to crawl away and hide,
You're always right there by my side.
No matter what kind of trouble I'm in,
I know you'll stick closer than my kin.

When I've torn my heart in two,
By the mess I've turned things to,
You always know how best the problem to mend,
And will see it through 'till the end.

I can count on you to make things right,
Irregardless of my plight.

And when things don't go quite the way they should,
Because I thought I could,
I give them back to you
To do them as you would.

O, that I would trust your will,
Rather than my own,
And give back to you
All that I've taken as my own.

—Tonya Carper

HIM

It is his chair
His shoes
His earth.

It is his big strong hands that taught me gentleness and care.
His ideas and values that taught me real love.
His respect for the flowers and all the gentle creatures of
        the earth.
He is a bright candle in immortal darkness.
Born to bring hope to those who experience loneliness
He is love.

Now, that chair is empty
His shoes are bare
The earth tranquil.

The hands that once showed me understanding and love
        have disappeared.
But his radiant light shines in my heart
Never to be put out by the deluge of time.
He is love.

—Nancy Testagrossa

ALL MY LIFE, O LORD

All my life O LORD,
        I've sinned against THEE!
All my life O LORD,
        I just can't seem to win!
I have failed THEE, so utterly in my life!
And now I'm in the depths of deepest despair,
For so tragic and miserable HAS BEEN MY LIFE!!
Now I ask for THY loving gracious hand,
To forgive this wretched soul that I am!!
AND LEAD ME to that precious, promised land!
For I need THEE loving JESUS, in my life!!
To give me peace, not turmoil and strife!
For life without THEE O LORD, is ever so drear
So LORD JESUS, I HUMBLY ASK FOR THEE TO COME NEAR!
And I'll worship THEE O LORD!!, by THY grace
And save me I pray, for life's final day!!
        That I may see THY lovely sweet face,
        In that wonderful and glorious place!!
        WITH ALL MY BEING O LORD,
                I HAVE TO WIN THIS RACE!!!

—Jeannette C. Fegley

DECEMBER SONG

There was one man amongst the rest
    Who tried to love without regrets.
He'd hold the lady to his side—
        Though never ever to be his bride—
Yet, somehow wished he could be mine.

But, alas! From days gone by,
        The memories remain;
The one more time, for auld lang syne,
        She'll sing her sad refrain,
From love that could be thine.

She should have learned in forty years,
        She could have staved the pain and tears;
But having heart that would not die
        By his side she still would lie;
Surely, all else were loved in vain.

Never would there be that man: the one amongst the rest;
        One to take her to his heart, and give her all his best.
She is but a wilting vine,
        Still clinging to the dream divine—
Eternal is her shame.

—Carol Jean Weise

THIS DAY

Dear Friends how precious is
    this day! Most of all know this
one thing. It is the first
day of the rest of your
life! Yesterday is but
a dream, lost and gone forever.
No way can you bring it back
or make it different than
it was. Know also tomorrow
may never come. Tonight's
kind word and prayer
may be all there is. Knowing
this leaves only today.
For your life's sake please
do not waste your one and
only day
Give it to God and trust him.

—Quinn E. Wood

OUR HOUSE AT CHRISTMAS

This house holds many memories
    That I love to recall
But the memories of Christmas here
Are just the best of all!

This house once was my mother's
And we'd help her trim the tree
The tinsel and the twinkling lights
Were such a sight to see!

The table loaded down with food
And all our loved ones near
The Christmas spirit moved us when
Mom led us all in prayer.

Too soon the day had come and gone
And our good-byes were said
We knew with feelings that we shared
Our souls, too, had been fed.

So, I know if this house could talk
It would tell a tale of cheer
For never has there been a time
When love did not live here.

—Norma J. Meny

WHAT'S ON YO'R MIND?

What's on yo'r mind?
    Is it he?
Is it she?
What's on yo'r mind?

What's on yo'r mind?
Is it what he's got?
Is it what she's got?
What's on yo'r mind?

Wanta know what's on my mind?
It use ta be he
It use ta be she
That's what use ta be on my mind.

Wanta know what's on my mind?
It use ta be what he's got
It use ta be what she's got
That's what use ta be on my mind.

Today,
That's no longer true,
Today,
I've got the Lord on my mind.

—Elizabeth Partridge Godfrey

ALWAYS WITH ME

All the days we spent together,
All the days that were so tender.

You held me in your arms at night,
The touch of your hand felt just right.

The softness of your every kiss,
Something in which I'll always miss.

Softly you'd whisper in my ear,
Magic words I loved to hear.

The wonders of your blue, blue eyes,
Gazed meaningful into mine.

Your smile, your face, your warm embrace,
All parts of you never to erase.

Because far apart we may be,
But in my heart and mind,
You're always right here with me.

—Laura West

NAP TIME—SPECIAL TIME

All tired out, and gone to bed,
"Will you stay in here with me?"
    you said,
    "Read a book, or maybe two,
Then I know what you can do—
    Sing, Twinkle, Twinkle, Little Star
I know where you are.
    You're not in the sky today,
Mr. Sun chased you away!"
    The flowers on the windowsill
Are sitting very, very still.
    Fluttering from orange, pink
and white,
    The hummingbird is off in flight.
Sleepy brown eyes, look at me with love,
    The Lord above,
Knows, we have so much to share—
    And placed you in my tender care.

—Polly Poynor

THE DREAMER

Dreamer,
You are so self-deceived,
In your world of delusion,
Can you be believed,
Your life is based on illusion,
Dreamer, why don't you wake up
Put your shattered desires behind you,
And live your life right,
Dreamer,
Visions dance before your eyes at night,
But visions can deceive you,
Visions of happiness,
Visions of tenderness and love,
But you wake up to dream of reality,
And you live your dream,
Pretending your dream is your life,
Dreamer,
Let go of your dreams that have gone sour
Take hold of your life.
Dreamer, allow your life to flower,
Soon you will find
Your disappointments are out of mind,
And your life will seem
Oh, so much like a dream.

—Timothy Wittman

She walks along the sandy beach,
Her hair glistens in the pale moonlight.
She thinks about the pressures of today,
And the promises of tomorrow.
As the wind speaks to her through gusty blows,
She tries to interpret its vision of the world,
As she does the waves are crashing at her feet.
And then . . . . it becomes a bright new day,
While the sun tells her what the wind was trying to say.

—Kelley Freeman

ALL TOO QUICKLY

Blue skies and rainbows
That's what you said.
Visions of forever danced through my head.
But just like the sunshine that behind the cloud goes—
My visions of forever were just dreams I suppose.

You came into my life with love in your eyes.
The days filled with laughter, joy, and surprise.
But oh, all too quickly
It was all in the past.

For loving you darling just didn't last.

—Jo Blundell Rhett

SHIPWRECKED

Amidst the thrashing waves hailed my way
Also came the Master to be my constant stay.
Where once blown by the winds that caused me to bend,
Now reaches a hand, from a strong, loving Friend.
And each time the waters return to bury me
Jesus' eyes draw me nearer Himself to be.
No matter the wreckage, repeatedness or reason,
In repentance He forgives, in any state of mind or season,
His love everlasting, covers a multitude of sin;
His grace longsuffering, abounds once again.
The closer I walk, the more I desire
To please my dear Master, and be filled with His fire,
Of love, understanding, compassion and grace,
To become like Him, to look on His face.
So when someone is shipwrecked along life's shore,
Let me reach out my hand, as He did times before;
And gently bind wounds from being tossed by the sea
Let His oil of healing once again flow through me.

—Geraldine Ann Callaway

THE POOL OF LIFE

The crystal water trickles
    down the mountain
        Until at last it reaches
the Pool of Life . . . .

I have journeyed so far, and
fought so much pain
    Only to realize, my reflection
will not remain . . . . in the Pool of Life

I can only wonder Why? . . . .
    the Pool of Life will not
        let me die

I went far away and I returned . . . .
to the Pool of Life . . . .

My soul was free of any pain
    At last, my reflection will remain . . . .

                In the Pool of Life . . . .

—Derek Woessner

WALK WITH ME

Come and walk with me,
we shall scan the limpid earth
and a crescendo feeling of obscurity
will gradually overwhelm our eyes.
We'll make a trek among our fellow man,
we'll plummet among the vagrant people
miscast from a world they own.
Vassalage as for so long dissicate their life;
mimic and simulated ecstasy emerges reigning among their action.
You cry my friend to these adverse conditions,
fighting to undo what, for so long has been.
Man never left the comfort of his cradle
and not you nor I can speed its slowly growth.
We cannot see their hidden soul,
it resides into the alcarar of falseness and pleasure
and only time can destroy those walls.
You and I, will wait right here, offering them a
sheltered bay, where man will swim along free,
slowly realizing that truth and kindness
are important words, to a world that has to be.

— Gianvito Fagiolino

SWEAT LODGE CEREMONY

The sufferers come to the sweat lodge ceremony to pray
To the Creator asking for His healing power.
They lie down with friends and relatives in the darkness.
Their chants and the chants of the spiritual leader
Petition for an end for whatever ails them
Or the safe journey to spirit world.

Bright Cloud remembers the happy lessons of her youth.
The words of her father, the Ute tribal chief protected her.
His words, "Believe in your Creator, believe in Him,
Rely on that which is within and you can go through anything."
The teachings of her parents' religion kept her from the despair
Felt by so many of her Indian people.

Today when she needs His comforting help, Bright Cloud
Favors the Ute ceremonies over the complicated liturgy
Of the churches of the nearby reservation town.
She believes nothing can intercept the message
Between her heart and the Creator's as she lies down
Beside the other sufferers praying for His healing.
Out of the rising steam, the darkness and the chants
Believing in Him she feels sustained and cleansed.

— Charlotte Jones

ADVOCATE

He said it with a twinkle in his eye
As I gazed beyond him, out the window, at the autumn sky
And all the crispy, golden colors lying on the ground
All around, not making a sound
Like clusters and piles of my thoughts and emotions
Resting a bit from all the commotion of
Trying to be and become someone other than just who I am
He smiled some then
And repeated that phrase in various ways
While the picture in the window there
Grew brighter with its autumn flair
And as I sat across from his desk
My life didn't seem like such a mess
After all
And I think Fall is my favorite season
But that's not the reason I felt like laughter
Riding and hiding on clouds in that friendly sky of blue
It seems I heard him say,
"I think you'll be okay
Just by being you."

— Bethann Kramer

OLD MEMORIES

Why bother to go to a movie
or to see a picture show?

When all we have to do is let
our minds go —

Back to the times when we
let our true colors show —

Some will want to shout;
but they can't — you know?

They'll always be there
Waiting to be seen —

All it will take is for you
to turn on my mental t.v. screen

If I choose to let you
open me up —

Just listen — and I'll
tell you all about my first
little German Shepherd pup

— Gary L. Brewer

GOODNIGHT!
MOONLIGHT LADIES

For from the word moon
    She's a Lady
For from the stars up high
    She's a lover
For from the word feminine
    She'll always be there waiting
For from the day she left,
    She feared to be a teacher
And on the night you came,
You found:
    A Lady who waits by the full
        of the moon,
    Just to be your lover;
    And what she feared,
        became his fear,
    And thus had to admit
        he had learned!

— Nancy McFadzean

A CHILD'S MIND

A child's mind
Is something to treasure
So full of joy
So full of pleasure

It's something to cherish
Day after day
When their simple emotions
Are all that they say

What goes on
In a child's mind
To us may be confusing
To them is well defined

And as I look on
To watch them play
A child's mind changes
Every day

So as you sit there
Watching them grow
Just think of the memories
And how much more they will know

— Steven F. Haas, Jr.

153

SUMMER MOON RISE

The golden glow from the moon
Fills the sky with luminous light.
The dark clouds play hide and seek
With the moon tonight!
Now the white clouds go floating by
Shading the moon into a grayish white.
A soft glow soon fills the sky
Before the full moon slides into sight.
Its rays on the clouds turn silver and gold.
What a glorious sight!
Do you ever watch the moon on a summer's night?

—Esther Mehalow

MORNING

As the sun awoke from its rest,
There was nothing in sight
But a bird building her nest.
The morning dew lay on the ground
Like a sheet over a warm bed.

The sweet smell of flowers fills the air.
The sound of awakening animals breaks the silence.
Fog rides through the trees
Like a smoke coming from a fiery log
Cold as ice, yet warm as summer day.

I hope this wooded mass of land
Will be here through all Earth's day.

—Hunter M. Fulcher

MOCKINGBIRD MORNING

Each dawning I wake to a melodious song
that teases and pleases my work-weary soul;
undulations of tones that could only belong
to a mockingbird perched on a telephone pole.

Winging its way through my wide-open casement
the cascade of music brings happiness, tears;
my spirit is held in a blissful embracement
that speaks peace to my heart and quiets my fears.

Gone for the present the burdens of living,
suspended in time are little things that annoy;
I humbly accept what the moment is giving —
a precious and thrilling in-filling of joy.

What a wonderful way
to begin the new day!

—Marcellus Bosworth

AUTUMN LEAVES

The leaves have fallen to the ground
It's winter now and not a sound
Birds have all gone from trees for now
But squirrels will stay with us anyhow.

Leaves blow away when wind is strong
Not even a bird to sing a song
The trees are bare, the limbs they show
You can see them there in white of snow.

Leaves are falling, down they come
Big ones, small ones, there won't be none.
Beautiful colors made for us all
They won't be back until next fall.

We'll have to wait for the leaves again
Through long cold winter and through the rain
Down on the ground that's where they lay
But they'll be back when comes next May.

—Milton R. Cason

IN WAITING

It seems I am waiting, each day I arise.
For What? Whom? How?
A vision of answers to flash in my eyes.
Tomorrow? Next Year? Now?
I flow through the years in my usual way.
Yes? No? Maybe?
Pondering new people that I see every day.
Him? Her? She?
Driving along I view so many places.
Here? There? Afar?
Looking for answers or maybe some traces.
Land? Sea? A Star?
I know I should stop searching for things.
How? When? Why?
Because living for now is what happiness brings.
Sunshine? Music? Pecan Pie?
I think I'll stop thinking and waiting all day.
Oh Yeah? Really? To Be?
I don't want to regret questioning my life away.
Who, ... Me!!?

—Tamara Lynn

AN IMAGE, LIKE LIFE

Like a rose, life is a wondrous thing.
We never see the beauty of it
Until we take the time to,
Yet, we cannot only look,
but we must see
and we cannot only touch,
but we must feel —
and feel it with our hearts.
We must capture every moment
of its beauty while it is here,
enjoy it while we can,
for we never know just how long it will last.
When we receive a rose,
it's precious to us — so is our life.
But, it's up to us
to make our life more precious.
We must open our heart —
to see and to feel
while we still have a chance
to live and to love.

—Jennifer A. Zander

SEA, SAND, AND SALVATION

The salt smell in the air, the mist of
        ocean spray;
the beach at sunset is cool, calm, and
        peaceful.
Standing on a jetty, feel yourself, man
        and nature as one.
The swift nautical winds part your hair
        as the waves crash about you.

A seagull squalls, and the sound momentarily
        brings you back;
for you are drifting, drifting endlessly in
        all the splendour which surrounds you.
If all moments could be so fine, how wonderful
        life would be.
Thus, it is for such moments that we should
        live.

As the sun sets, you know it is time, you
        must be getting back.
Yet a smile peels across your face, for the
        sun will rise tomorrow.

—Robert Peppi, Jr.

HELPLESS LOVE

What happened between us
that set us all a whirl?
I know you'd like to think
I'm just a little girl.
Please don't make excuses
cause what I know is real.
It's not my fault that you're confused
and don't know what you feel.
Avoiding me will do no good
cause there I'll always be.
Every time you see me
you'll hear a silent plea.
I care about you truly,
but you may never know.
For you won't give a chance
for our relationship to grow.

—Candace C. Frese

MOTHER EARTH

Quite barren, the soil —
The dirt lay lonely in my yard.
A fence, a woodpile,
And one spruce standing guard.

How talkative the grass in breezes,
As they chatter blade to blade,
While the woodpile houses mice,
The great spruce offers its shade.

Pitying the ostracized patch,
I gladly lend a hand
For, the soil knows, as well as I —
Its only hope is man.

So I impregnated the soil with a seed
And nurtured Mother Earth.
When the following Spring commenced,
Our Mother, she gave birth.

How green with envy the grass —
For that patch of dirt now glows!
But how proud our Mother Earth —
As she boasts her new-born rose.

—Kristin Noél Reichey, age 16

ADVICE TO YOUTH

As the years have come and faded,
I have learned a thing or two;
It always pays to do what's right,
And to the Lord be true.

It took me many years to learn,
That when you meet the test;
The only way to beat the worst,
Is utilize the best.

You'll meet a lot of stumbling blocks,
There's mountains you must climb;
But an honest, Godly effort,
Will make the road sublime.

You'll find it takes more courage,
To turn the other cheek;
Than it does to flex your muscles,
Or loudly yell and shriek.

Learn wisdom from the wise man;
And meekness from the dove,
And use the fertilize of truth.
To grow the flowers of love.

—Wesley Yonts

DEAR SISTERS

You say life is not long,
Yet say not when I walk away like the ending of a song,
Slow I go and you care not for where I go.
"Just come back to me again," you say,
"You in my life is like the suns ray."
Proud and strong you stand for me.
So, Dear Sisters, true to you I'll be.
Think of me not as I was,
But as what I shall be,
Remember always, it is not for only me.
You are the source of light in my life,
And helped me to struggle against all my strifes.
So, Dear Sisters, remember you I will,
And what I say now, I shall always feel:
"To each of you, all my love I do give,
Because for each of you, I did live."

—Dawn Davis

LOST

A wary traveler pushing his way into the future
Living one day at a time

Looking from side to side, hesitating, turning the
curtain to see what's ahead.

It's so heavy at times, doesn't think he can move it

Seeing only the void he must fill in his life.

Are there too many mistakes in the past now to live with—

Unacceptance too great, can't forgive himself —

Do you know what he'll do since he's heavy laden

For a life he's been given and his energy spent?

Will he stumble alone on paths through his forest —

Walk ever carefully so as not to turn stones —

Will he trudge on, reach out, no matter how halting

For a chance, just a chance to live life again?

—J.M. Myhrman

WORDS ARE HARD TO SAY

You ask me a question, that I cannot answer
For mere words could not express, what's inside my heart
The beauty I see when I look into your face, is like a
shining glow
I see a man's heart that's filled with Love and made
of solid gold
I hear a man's voice that is full of laughter and his
joy overflows
I feel a man's touch that is soft and gentle against my
bare skin
A man whose eyes sparkle with tender kindness, for
everyone he meets
So in answer to your question, I'll do the best I can
because you are to me a very special man
I think of the wonderful times we'll always have
together
I think of your gentle touch I always long to feel
early in the morning and late at night in bed
I think of this happiness I feel deep inside, it's a warm
sensation I've never had
I think of the special Love I've always felt for you
and I know in my heart, you have felt that special
Love too
For beauty comes only from inside the soul
Not from the flesh or the shape of the mold . . .

—Darline Hall

SHE DIED LAST TUESDAY

The look in his eyes told tales of misunderstanding . . .
Clear and bright blue, surrounded by the redness of sorrow.
Standing there listening, I found myself suddenly inside his soul . . .
Screaming at the injustice of his life . . .
She said "John I'm dizzy," then bowed her head, and she was gone
Crying inside I say "don't worry, I'll fix your broken wedding ring . . . "
"Thanks" he said, "You know it wouldn't be so bad but my daughter
died of cancer just last year."
Searching for consolation, I feebly offer my apology . . .
Leaving he said, "I have to stop by the bookstore and buy a
Poor spellers dictionary. You see my wife was always winning
Spelling bee's when she was a girl and I'm lost when it comes to that."
Breaking into a laugh I say, "Yeah, me too . . . "
Turning to leave he said "goodbye . . . "
And from the depth of my heart I said "Go out and enjoy the sunshine . . . "
With that, he was gone . . .

Later I thought to myself, "Mighty is the strength of a man who walks alone . . . "

>—Daniel Leo Patriquin

"PLEASE LET ME LIVE"

Please Let Me Live, I Don't Want To Die
Just Let Me Enter Into This World, With A Strong, Loud Cry
    I Want To Feel You Hold Me Close For The Very First Time
And I Want to Hear You Say, "My Precious Little Darling, I'm So Glad You're Mine"
    I Want To Learn To Crawl, And Take My Very First Step
And I Want To Know That You'll Be There, If I Need Any Help
    I Want To Feel The Bright Sunshine On Me, When I Go Outside To Play
And When I Fall Down, I'll Know You'll Be There To Kiss The Hurt Away
Please Let Me Live, So That I'll Know What A Tear Feels Like, As It Trickles Down My Face
I Want To Feel Your Soft Skin Next to Mine, As You Hold Me, In A Warm Gentle Embrace
    I Want To Smell The Lovely Flowers, And Pick You A Beautiful Rose
I Want To Walk In The Rain, And Get Wet Through All My Clothes
    Just Let Me Live, So That I Can Go To School, And Learn The Golden Rule
There Are So Many Things That We Can Do Together, If You'll Just Let Me Live
Please Don't Take My Chance At Life Away, For I Have So Much Love To Give
    I Can Make You Happy, I Know That I Can
Just Let Me Grow Up To Become A Beautiful Young Woman, Or A Handsome Young Man
    But I Cannot Do Any Of These Things, If You Take My Life Away
Oh, Please Let Me Live, And I Promise You That You Will Be Proud Of Me Someday
Please Don't Put A Tear In Jesus' Eye, For If You Kill Me, Then He Will Surely Cry.

>—Janet Purser

I CALL YOUR NAME
(MARYANN)

The dream still occurs, endless are the nights without you!
Hot summer breezes flow silently through my window, and awaken me as they
Kiss my lips.

Tho you're not here to quench the arousal that I suffer,
I call your name, Maryann!
Temptation of a thousand fold lay before me now, and I wish to suckle you
As a babe would suckle its mother.

I hear your voice; soft!
As if it glides through a crystal windchime, and every note evokes my passion.
I call your name, Maryann!

I throw myself to the mercy of the darkness.
Sanity, where is your justice?
Taking the rose from the gardener, only to give it up to die!
Now all I have is the memory of how the rose felt between my fingers, against
My cheek, and in my heart.

Tenderness, capture me I pray once again, for I wait for you.
Eternity will see my face, for I wait for you until the end.
I call your name, Maryann!

>—John Quinn

ALL THINGS SACRED

I hold all things sacred
To this I do confess
The years I have in front of me
Are growing less and less.

I tried to be creative
All throughout my life
And never gave a second thought
To politics or strife.

I've learned that mother nature
Needs a helping hand
If we are to save ourselves
And our precious land.

My only main concern
is facing life and death
And holding all things sacred
With each and every breath.

—David Alan Nankin

LOST LAND

Through the morning and the night
Through things wrong and right
I find myself alone
Alone . . . away from home
No one is there for me
No one looks and see
That I, a mere child
Away from home in the wild
Is lost . . . lost forever
In a land too clever
For its own good
Not knowing truth from falsehood
Too blind to see the vision
Therefore causes collision
In a land of a thousand dreams
To them are supreme
If only they would awake
And see what they forsaked
Then maybe those dreams would
        come true
For me and for you.

—Diem Ngo

YESTERDAY TODAY AND TOMORROW

Do you remember yesterday
Today is almost gone
Tomorrow will soon be here
and time keeps flying on

Time stops for nothing
Regardless what we say
Don't put off until tomorrow
What you should do today

Don't take it for granted
Treasure every hour
For we do not know our destination
Only our Lord, we're in his power

Live each day to the fullest
helping others along the way
Give a smile not a frown
To help them make their day

Yesterday has already gone
Today is just beginning
Tomorrow we know not
Be thankful you're living

—Retha Reeves Smith

THE FLYING LESSON

I fell down and it went ouch,
The day I fell right off the couch.
I was jumping and bouncing high,
My mama said, 'Sit!', but I wanted to fly!
I yelled and I laughed and I went right on.
My mama said, 'Don't,' but by then I had flown.
I bounced right off and fell on my face,
I screamed and I cried all over the place.
I hit my belly when I fell on the floor,
I hit my shoulder and even more!
I hit my nose and all of my head.
It hurt so much, I thought I was dead!
I cried so loud I knew that wasn't true.
My mama hugged me and said, 'It's alright, baby, I love you.'

—Lauren Patton Roark

APPALACHIA, MY MOUNTAIN HOME

The cradle of my ancestors, Appalachia, cradles me;
She is a warm and generous mountain-mother who,
From the beginning through glacial ages to today,
Has been a shrine and sanctuary to all forms of life;
Lofty, she and her sisters extend from Canada to Georgia.

With her feet planted firmly upon the ground,
Her majesty rises far above the level of the sea;
There she stretches her loving arms for many miles,
Cradling her children in the cleavage of her bosom.

As you go up "Cripple Creek" by the "Wildwood Flower,"
There's tassled corn, half-runner beans, turnip greens,
Grape vine swings, leather breeches, and smoked hams;
Old time religion, hardwood benches, dinners-on-the-ground,
"Amazing Grace," creek baptisms, "Onward Christian Soldiers;"
Where else except in Appalachia, could all of this be found?

Southern Appalachia is my home, my mountain-mother;
Planted here by Scotch-Irish and German ancestors,
My roots grow deep, I thrive, and I will ever stay,
Secure in her fertile valleys, by cool rushing waters;
Appalachia is mine and I am Appalachia's!

—Carroll Lee Anderson

Tonight my love I'm lonely for you,
I'm a long way from home and very blue.
I boarded the train and headed west,
But to be in Michigan would suit me best.
My final destination I do not know,
But I'm sure I won't be walking in snow.
They say California is a nice state to be in,
But when they say that, I only grin,
Because down deep in my heart I know of a place much better,
That's the place you live, where I send every letter.
As I ride over mountain and through the dale,
I know my love for you will never fail.
The scenery is beautiful, loved ones so dear,
But I'd enjoy it much better if you were near.
It's hell to be going so far from home,
And I know when I get back I'll sure never roam.
I'm just one of the thousands of husbands you see
Who were chosen to fight for victory.
Why they picked me I don't understand,
But I am a number of this great band
Of Soldiers and Sailors, Coast Guards and Marines
Whose job is to fight in the battle scenes.
They say we are fighting for Uncle Sam,
But we're not, my darling, not by a damn,
We'll make the country better, just wait and see,
We're fighting for home folks, my family and me.

—Wayne Doyt Schaaf

158

UNTIMELY BORN

Silent, we left at night, or was it dawn?
There were three of us involved, the lovers
And me, the accomplice, who went along
To sit and wait among all the mothers.
And when the deed was done, we three explored
Our thoughts concerning the fourth, who was no more.

—Jennifer Ann Hancock

QUANTUM

There are moments neither measured nor explained,
and instants by some reason not the norm,
when time and space will seem to just relent,
and the stillmost hours pause before the dawn.
Dear one . . . perhaps a second thought,
that time and space are not unique,
for it was not so long ago I wandered
and placed myself beside you in your sleep.
Did you not spy me lurking in your shadows,
was not I for just a moment in your dreams,
and as you drew the folds of night so warm about you,
did you not feel that gentle touch upon your cheek . . .

—Bill Holler

romantic isolation

        he cried for things that should have been,
she cried for things that never were.
        his passion for the future dimmed,
her vision of the past was blurred.
        his aimless hopes pursued no course,
her heart's desires were oppressed.
        he suffered little save his remorse,
her gestures appeared quite rehearsed.
        his pain created for him a shell,
her expectations were torn to shreds.
        he was imprisoned forever in his cell,
she then expressed her depth of regret.

—Susan Dudley

THE ENERGY BUBBLE

Life goes astray like a wayward stream,
Mind, body, soul and a dream —
All — all out of control, yet within my skin . . .
"Take charge" — shouts a voice in resounding din.
"Be alive," it cries, "be radiant and bright,
In attitude more, than for people's sight —
Conquer whims — chase away moods;
There's nothing for one who sits and broods!"

I wake — yet something dulls my enthusiasm,
Not able to rise and feel the spasm,
Of existence — of life, that sometimes to me
Is like a hope or a link with memory,
That pulls me to act by strange forces,
With just enough energy as hay for horses.
In the song of silence, I hear His lyrics
For a moment, I become master, of time and spirits . . .

        Father, I turn to thee to quench my thirst,
        Do not deny me, rather settle this dust
        That trails the caravan of my thoughts
        This weary journey has had me lost,
        O sky, let me merge in thy blue range
        Lord, I cry for a spiritual change,
        I need to unload and feel set free,
        From a wild world and an existence earthly . . . !

—Mala Saxena

SHADOWS

I find myself in the shadows,
living on the dark and lonely side.
There is no light here,
No beacon in the night,
No star to guide me,
not even a candle to light my path.
I have no place to call home,
and no joy in my life.
It is cold, dark and lonely in my world.

As I lie here in the blackness of the night,
The shadows and the sorrow overtake me,
and the flood begins to erase me,
For a little while I am not here,
For, I truly wish I weren't.
I have found myself in the shadows,
and I know not why
or, how to get back into the light.
It is cold, dark and lonely in my world.
For I am trapped in the shadows.

—Mary A. Sturgill

LET ME IN

Mother, I'm trying to get to know you
        But you refuse to let me in

    I wish that I could hold you and
    wipe the tears from your chin

    I remember when I was little
    and you protected me every day

    I just want to pay it back to you
    Please help show me the way

    I would like to get close to you
    I would like to hold your hand

    Why can't you please help me
    Why can't you understand

    Mother I'm your daughter and
    and I need you to let me in

    And maybe then we could both
    open up and start all over again

—Ernette Pinkney

LOST SHEEP

I feel I'm on a circus ride,
Everything is going round and round.
I'm all so confused inside,
Even the mind is not too sound.

It's hard to see beyond today,
With these troubles on my mind.
And sorrow seems to sway,
What little hope I could find.

Sometimes I feel God has left me,
Shattered and hanging by a thread.
I should have more faith in Thee,
He wouldn't leave a lost sheep unfed.

Maybe the only way to find our soul,
Is to be lost among the herd.
Sharing others sorrow that life does hold,
And trusting more in God's word.

Many times I know I stumble and fall,
Knowing not what to do.
But one answer stands out among them all,
That is, God I always come back to You.

—Nita Hall

THE TOWER OF LOVE

The tower of love is
a special place to go,

You cannot see it, for it's not
there to show

It's a place in your heart
where all the love starts
and all of your secrets to be

And no one else but you holds
the key.

—Saree A. Cammisuli, age 13

MY IDEAL RELATIONSHIP

To have someone
That I can trust
To share my life
With full thrust

Someone to love me
As no one else can
To feel the joy
Of just holding hands

There's not a better feeling
Just to know
That there is someone
Who loves me so

One who shares my pain and joy
And really and truly understands
That I am not a mere toy
Or an old rusty tin can

Someone I can depend on
A real family man
Not one that is deceitful
On every hand

—Sufronia Pickett Thomas

LOVE'S RAIN

Teardrops staining my pillow
as they fall from the sky.
My mind so far away.
Fear bound as I cry,
Thunderstruck, lift me up, carry
me away
across the rough waters
come what may.
My heart like the rain
yearning to quench the ache
Missing your love as the
earth drinks its take.

—Annette Bayne

I AM

I am a hand for the weary
A help for their cry . . .
A refuge in the wilderness,
I hear the slightest sigh.

When the storms of life arise
I see your every need,
I feel your disappointments,
Don't walk away from Me.

For I'll help in time of trouble,
I'll show your feet the way,
I'll make your burden lighter
When you come to Me and pray.

—Karen S. Endsley

DOLORES

I loved her once not so very long ago.
How much I loved her, I was not ashamed to show.

My feelings were laid bare for all the world to see.
Yet in all that time I knew not if she cared for me.

So I thought about her and why I felt this way.
And found she's so much more than words could ever say.

True she has a pretty face and eyes of crystal blue.
A funny little laugh; a smile to match; all these things are
true.

And yet beneath it all lies a girl who's most sincere.
Whose true beauty is in her feelings and that's what I hold dear.

For only by her feelings can you know what she wants from life.
To raise a healthy family and be both Mom and wife.

And she makes me feel there's a chance someday she could be mine.
For this I loved her once, but once for all of time.

—Warren DiBernardo

FAITH IN YOURSELF

Faith is a virtue we all live by,
From the day of our birth until we die.
Without this unexcelling trait,
Progress in this world would have to wait.

Success would be a continual failing,
Ideas would be stifled before aborning.
Have faith in your own abilities,
And use your dreams like utilities.

Past knowledge gained by contemporaries do not scorn.
Seek information and with it adorn.
Be humble when any dicoveries you find,
Realizing those things were here before mankind,

This universe is like a cupboard supplied with plenty and more . . .
We only have to furnish the key to unlock her door.
That key is surely your dreams and ideas untold,
So give yourself a chance to let them unfold.
If you do this your life will have more happiness,
And you will find that elusive thing called unlimited success.

—Fred L. Minneman

MARRIAGE

He touches her — yet he does not.
He binds her — yet she is free.
He comes to her —yet not.

She touches him — yet she does not.
She binds him — yet he is free.
They merge — yet remain separate.

He has needs.
Some fulfilled,
Some finding fulfillment,
Some dead.

She has needs.
Some fulfilled,
Some finding a way,
Some dead.

But among the dead —
Are not some reflected in passing?

And in fulfillment of a long dead need,
Is not the death recompensed?

And is not life worth living?

—Nancy Anne Dornbos-Krueger

MERRY-GO-ROUND

Life is a merry-go-round
the things one says and does
we live and learn again and again
and dare to ask why just to hear, because . . . just because.

With so short a time it seems now
but not while in youth . . . forever
to love, to learn, to excel in this and that
no one knows all the answers, however.

Since I've met you
my life has been a merry-go-round
and here I go again, with you of course
round and round and round and round.

—Lisa Mignon' McEnery

A COWBOY'S LETTER

Dear Mama, you had me in the middle of the plain;
And I guess since then I give you nothing but pain;
You always wanted me to be a Lawyer or some such;
But I like herding cattle and for me that's enough;
You wanted me to be a gentleman but I'm a cowboy instead;
And while I ain't real respected, I 'bout always do get fed;
Mama, I am sorry if I upset you by being what I am;
Things changed me a lot while I fought the Rebs for Uncle Sam;
We're gittin' ready to drive the cattle up Charlie Goodnight's trail;
On up to Kansas City where there is a rail;
I'm riding for a Colonel Claybourne who owns the Circle C;
The Outfit's mostly Rebs but pay's plenty good to me;
When I get paid I'll likely spend down to almost my last dollar;
Then I'll likely spend a spell in jail and think of you, sweet Mama;
Fellar told me once that life is something that We all should enjoy;
Mama, I'm sorry but I'm happy too, Signed — your Son, the Cowboy;

—James William Cummings

ODE TO THE FAT WHITE PONY

Trit-trot, trit-trot, trit-trot.

There goes that fat, white pony again.

Trit-trot, trit-trot, trit-trot.

Trotting around the show ring with his nose out, ears forward,
and tail swishing in perfect rhythm.

Trit-trot, trit-trot, trit-trot.

Bouncing around lightly on those tiny little feet--looking for
the camera, videotape, and BIG BLUE RIBBON.

Trit-trot, trit-trot, trit-trot.

All of my life I have watched those fat white ponies take those
BIG BLUE RIBBONS. They are pre-ordained to win. Being
first is all they know.

Trit-trot, trit-trot, trit-trot.

All they have to do to win is be fat, white and there.
It's that easy.

Trit-trot, trit-trot, trit-trot.

Well, maybe add a bow to their mane and a cute little girl with a
pigtail——but I swear they could enter the show ring buck naked,
wearing bowling shoes and a calico bonnet,

And the judge would say, "What? Is that a fat, white pony trying
to disguise its cute little self?"

"Here, come quickly, Fat White Pony. Take this Big Blue Ribbon
before a real horse trys to claim it.

Trit-trot, trit-trot, trit-trot.

—Deborah O. Cantrell

THE DEER

There is a place with
a big blue sky, that is over
a forest, where the bears
walk and the birds fly.
In the forest, there is a
doe, surrounded by trees
high and low. Standing
by her there is a fawn,
with little wobbly legs
and eyes bright as dawn.

—Lisa Larson

SPRINGER SPANIEL

Longing for love
"Pet me please" eyes
Thick, fuzzy fur
Stubby tail tick-tocking
for attention
Pink, wet tongue finding
unprotected table scraps or
crumpled kleenex
Greets us with wild shakes,
wiggles, and woofs
Loves to be loved
Silly, stupid Daisy
Just a puppy at heart

—Molly Rebecca Youngstrom

ODE TO THE TELEPHONE ANSWERING MACHINE

Hi there friend,
And how are you?
I know that you're not there,
But I am here,
To let you know,
That friends like you are rare.
I'm glad you have,
A phone machine,
Or else you wouldn't know,
How much I'd like to see you,
And that I miss you so.
You can call me anytime,
I'm almost always home,
But if I'm not,
Then leave a message,
When you hear the tone.

—Teresa Coen Yarlott

TO CATCH A DRAGON

Up the hill,
Down the hill,
In my new blue wagon,
I'm going in to Dragonville
And catch a big fat dragon.

Up the street,
Down the street,
In my little wagon,
I chased a dog,
And caught a cat,
But could not find a dragon.

Up the hill,
Down the hill,
Back home in my wagon,
I found a dark blue dragonfly
Drinking from a flagon.

—Mrs. Guyneth Walker

SUNDAY MORNING

The fish were jumping right out of the sea,
On that beautiful morning at dawn.
The gulls were feasting and calling so loud.
They were trying to sing a sweet song.

The fishermen were casting out so far.
They wanted to catch their fill.
The snapper blues were close to shore.
It would be easy to make a kill.

An osprey was circling over head.
He dove straight down so fast.
He grabbed a fish and held on tight.
He had made his catch at last.

What a wonderful sight before my eyes.
There was so much to see.
As I looked out at the horizon,
Across that marvelous sea.

—Ann Gilmore Taylor

MY SONG

You are never cold,
Always warm within my ears.
Yet, you never tend to grow old.
The newness of your melody
Keeps me fresh and alive.

You follow me at all times,
Comforting my soul,
As the sound of windblown chimes.
My closest friend,
Who never leaves me alone.

For if you should leave me,
It would be impossible to find another.
I would search all land and sea.
My special song is not meant for others.
It is meant, and sung for me.

There are many different songs for many people.
I have my own, and they have theirs.
Mine is the song of life and love.
My song was not meant to be shared.
It is, my song.

—Lori-Conti-Sharapata

ALONE AGAIN

The frost of March, the flowers of May, the
Red leaves of September
In my mind the seasons pass
And I surely do remember

The love we had, the joy we shared,
The laughter and the sorrow.
But now that you have gone away,
I wonder 'bout to-morrow.

The memories are like music sweet,
I see the light and shadow.
I'm haunted by the "should have beens"
As the winds through shutters rattle.

The empty house, the lonely place,
The void in heart and life,
The reality of "on my own" goes
through me like a knife.

The frost of March, the flowers of May,
the red leaves of September
In my mind the seasons pass
And I surely do remember.

—Marilyn Whitaker

THE GRASS CUTTER'S DREAM

One of these days I'm gonna climb that mountain,
And walk up there amongst the clouds,
Where the weeds are high and the grass is growing,
And there will be no more lawns to mow.
With the sun beating down across that lawn,
I can see that old lawn mower and me.

—Marvin Rowe

THE TRIFLING WIND

The sullen sun in a moody sky
Looked askance at the passersby.
The wind walked by with an angry tread,
And gave all souls a nameless dread.
It shook the leaves like bits of sand,
And then came the strength of a strong, firm hand.
And soon the patter of falling rain
It settled the leaves now free of pain.
The sun peeked through with a crooked smile,
The curtain falls on the stage for a while.

—Cleo M. Cox

MY HEART WENT TO SCHOOL TODAY

Today's the day you start to school
And learn all about the Golden Rule.

You'll paint and color and play with toys
And make new friends of girls and boys.

Your nails are clean, your hair is neat
You skip along with wings on your feet.

I stand and wave, a little forlorn
Remembering so well when you were born.

I think God made my arms just right
Because you fit so well, for such a mite.

You were warm and cuddly and I knew that day
Something special had come my way.

I hope you didn't notice a tear or two
As I smoothed your dress and tied your shoe.

But darling, when you left today,
You took my heart all the way.

—Bernie Melcher

EVE OF INDECISION

I stand alone in the night of Doubt,
Frozen by the winds of Fear,
Caught by the barrier of the Unknown.

I know not whether to follow my heart or my mind,
And the Tide of Determination shifts
With every gust of deep, penetrating cold.

The time to decide has come
Yet I am irresolute,
Pulled in different directions by mind and soul.

Confusion becomes my master,
And the dread chill of the Eve of Indecision
Is come.

A light appears in the distance,
A beacon of encouragement . . .
But it is too late.

The whirlwind of Uncertainty has led me
Astray;
Its victim has been claimed.

—Terri Blissard

TURN THE PAGE VIETNAM VET

Finally — finally recognized, and no longer ostracized —
Buddies now memorialized, but still feeling victimized.
Turn the page; let it go, Vietnam Vet.
A new chapter can appear with a message loud and clear —
Can you hear it? Will you share it, Vietnam Vet?

Those who served before made the transition
To new beachheads on peaceful shores.
Let's not delay, or avoid attrition,
Pre-ordained members of an endless corps.
Turn the page; let it go, Vietnam Vet.

Others have been there and understand —
See their open arms, the outstretched hand.
We all must do what is there to do —
Come join with us; we've been there too.
Turn the page; let it go, Vietnam Vet!

—A. Lincoln Ames

MIDNIGHT FOR THE BLUE AND THE GRAY

From the Battle of Pea Ridge, Arkansas, March, 1862

By the light of the fire and the flaring lamp,
Midnight enters the Union camp.
With jerky gone and canteen dried,
They sleep like children, side by side.
The March frost clings to their dreaming sighs,
And they shiver, as one, as the fire dies.

A Confederate soldier beneath the trees
Grows weary of watching and slips to his knees.
His comrades sleep on the snowy ground.
Rebel ghosts drift all around.
Like honor guards the fallen roam,
And he slides into sleep, where he dreams of home.

The North's in the woods, and the South holds the Ridge,
And the midnight hour is the only bridge.
Soldiers, dreaming, search restlessly
For the arms of peace, where men ought to be.

—Carolyn Denise Wall

WAR

There is a place, in our minds, where peace must still
exist.
Yet to see the sorrow, that surrounds the place, and the
hatred that persist.

Like a child who's crying with agony, from the pain
that hurts so much!
And as her mother, is trying to crawl to her side,
so her child she can simply touch!

Yes just a touch of the little girl's hand, and the mother,
she begins to pray.
Yet the strength of the mother, is not strong enough,
to keep the child from slipping away.

As the mother is numb, laying in her tears, because her
daughter has just passed away!
She remembers a time somewhere in her mind, when she
heard, MOMMY LET'S PLAY !!!

Why? She cries as she cannot move from the pain that's
in her heart!
Why? Does the war continue?
Why? Did it ever start?

Yet while her pain is ending, her eyelids bead like rain,
And as her baby's hand, slips from her fingers

    that's two more lives in vain!!!

—Ronald G. Johnston

FURY

Masked in shadows of murky disuse
wrapped in tatters, layered thick
like rock strata, shielded from view
save for the intrusions roughly cutting
through stony silent flesh.
Pressure intense — building up steam
seething in caldrens of pulsing stone
spewing molten mixtures through veins
coursing in rivers of life/death
flux-liquid change.
Vents fuel the fire, stoking intensity
to critical mass — peaking, erupting
flooding torrents of lava,
spewing malignant spittle
cooling and clouding the jewel.

—Michael Robinson

UNTRIED FREEDOM

Speak not to me of
Freedom's tempting cry;
The thing to which we are born
And for which we may die.

Capricious freedom respects not
The passage of history's time.
Small losses, not counted,
Erode and make it less sublime.

No thing of marble or of iron cast
Can stand unchanged these times;
Guaranteeing future identical to past
And freedom unqualified.

Freedom exists until it is tried.
Some have it denied.
Still others have it from them pried.
What remains when we awake;
And freedom's died?

—Winston Bryant Odland

DEEP BLACK EYES

I need my deep black eyes
to hide my sorrow.
They become black soot hashish
to blanket our tomorrow.
All my life has been
an empty page of blankness,
and I'll never know why
the colors run
and make you fade away.

I wore those heavy years
like a drab, brown cloak
but now like a satin gown
it shimmers and slides from me,
shed like a snake skin on the ground.
How I long to reach for you
and cease this endless day.
To watch all the colors drown,
smothered by my cloak of brown.

You will be forever mine
in caverns underground.
We'll sink into a whirlpool
and like a fetus swim round and round.
All that will be left of us
is a tattered cloak of brown.
They'll wonder
why the colors ran
and made us fade away.

—Kathaleen Weiland

163

SNOWFLAKE
or Transformation

Alone and lovely snowflower,
Swirling, earthward bound —
Clings yet to another,
As it flutters to the ground.

Alas, it has to lose,
Its lovely symmetry,
Reluctant to surrender —
Its identity!

Blending, blinding, whiteness,
Sins seem to disappear
Covered for awhile
In redemption's bier —

Its Transformation unifies
And like a blade of grass,
Illusions to a ONENESS,
Forgets itself, at last!

— Grey, Lucille

A BIRD

Lightly touching
The green fresh earth
Sunshine exclaiming
Spring's birth
His head held high
With dignity and pride
His wings tucked
Firmly by his side
With the swell of hope
And flutter of flight
He took to the sky filled
With warm sunlight
Like a whisper in the wind
He was gone
Nothing left but silent
Memory of his song
Feeling of freedom disappeared
With a bird
Echoes of his cry
Can still be heard

— Dawn Gleason

NOSTALGIA

Thoughts, feelings, memories
from our past

A time of our lives gone all
too fast

Hopscotch, jumprope, marbles
and jacks

Fishing, picnics and races
in potato sacks
Yellowed pages in a scrapbook

Sorted momentos from our
past we took

A pressed corsage, a piece of
hair

Chosen photos of times to
share

Captured in our mind
forever

Stories of our life to treasure
— Anne Marie Coates

DEAR SHANE
(Dedication to my unborn son)

You started out as just a dream, it seems so long ago.
But as the months went passing by, I watched your outline grow.
I learned of you on May the 6th so joyous that I cried.
And then one day in late July, I felt you move inside.

I thought of you so often, son, as months went slowly past,
And dreamed so much about the day I'd cradle you at last.
You know not of the world as yet or of your life to be,
Nor of the love that waits for you from daddy and from me.

Your room is waiting for you here, arranged with pride and care,
and all the little things for you that daddy's check could spare.
I love your dad with all my heart, he's made my dream come true,
and with that love we have shared, we've now created you.

This world is not so great sometimes, you'll find that out one day.
But dad and I will be here, son, to help you on your way.
So grow and thrive and come out strong, for you need have no fear.
You'll have our love, that's all you'll need,
I'm sure you'll like it here!

— Kathy Leinenbach

LULLABY

O' roaring white foamed waves, you
crash against my body in a feverish
manner freezing my blood
in a fit of rage. I sink low
in a bed of sand, spitting salted
water from my mouth, and grit
from my lips. I shiver of cold,
but you come still, like a haunting
ghost, tormenting my body and
leaving only to haunt me again.
Pained watery eyes get no pity
from the sea salt,
the venom of the consistent mysterious
waters. Blackness, coming and going in a
hypnotic lull, causing my body to tire and
my muscles to relax in a deepening hole at
the mouth of the animal, foaming at the
lips. Eyes shut, no longer strained as the
body lies limp in the sands of the sea as
a wave crashes, closing the casket lid.

— Kymberly Rae

HEAVEN FELL DOWN

We've just seen the beginning of our walk through life.
We began with such simplicity, babbling one syllable words
then two, and taking our first shaky steps.
Then school begins and making friends,
no cares at all. Then we get our first bad grade,
and our first piece of heaven fell down.
We move on with less enthusiasm and a little more thought.
We learn and live with new experiences that each day brings.
We lose a first love and doubt we'll ever recover,
and one more piece of heaven fell down.
We heal, and others we do love.
We try new styles, new friends, some we like, some we don't,
some we wish we'd never tried. Still we age, as does family,
losing a loved one is the hardest time we may live through,
as when they die, a part of us does too.
We've seen yet another part of heaven fall down.
We do realize as time goes by, that life isn't as we first glimpsed.
We try to do the best we can to save ourselves and others,
To guide them as well as we may, and to be there for them,
when their heaven falls down.

— Rachelle Joann Asbury, age 14

A TEAR

A baby cries from hunger, wanting to be fed
Growing tired now, so you tuck them into bed.
A small child cries in the middle of the night,
Afraid of monsters, that growl and that bite.
A teenager cries for freedom, all he can get.
You give them a little, but they want more yet.
A parent cries, but no one's there to hear
Crying over things that you now hold so dear.
The sleepless nights you held your small child
To protect them from things crazy and wild —
A bump in the night, or one to their head
Someone called them names, their goldfish is dead.
No one loves them, they're ugly, or they're fat.
An old boyfriend or girlfriend is a stinkin' rat.
These days pass by faster than you think.
There's a tear in your eye, try not to blink.
Let it linger there a moment, savor that tear,
And think of the times you now hold so dear.

— **LuAnn (Rabenstein) Arnsparger**

WHAT THE CRUELTY OF MAN HAS DONE

I was walking along the Zimbabwe River,
When I looked across I noticed a shiver.
A large grey animal with long white tusk
Was hiding behind a tree at the hour of dusk.

To see fear in an animal so large and great,
I had to go ask him what disturbed his fate.
But as I went up and as I drew near,
One glance at me, and he ran with great fear.

The ground beneath me trembled and shook,
It happened so fast I didn't get a second look.
I looked around me to see what he feared,
To see what dangerous animal appeared.

I looked to my left and then to my right.
I searched all day and all night.
I saw nothing to stir such a fright.

So there was only one reason why he had to flee,
Because of a human — because of me.

— **Kathy Cook, Age 18**

I'M STILL NUMBER 1

I'm right at the top of your list, I know
Right after turkey hunting, or shooting a crow.

After going fishing with your buddy each chance
You get and here at home patiently I sit.

I'm after the car has had an overhaul
After your friend has given you a 2 hour call.

After the lawnmower has been painted and fixed
And the rototiller's oil has been mixed.

After the dogs have been watered and fed
After the parakeet has been patted on the head.

After the winter wood is stacked in place
After you've cut your hair and shaved your face.

After the news is off and Johnny Carson comes on
You fall asleep on the couch alone.

After the fingernails have been chewed to the bone
After all the snacking food is gone.

After the boat has its yearly inspection from you too
And there is absolutely nothing else to do.

But I know I'm still number one in your life
What? Who am I? Well I'm your wife.

— **Jean Palmer**

THE CHILDHOOD BOOKWORM

I looked at them
and they seemed to look back at me

And, it occurred to me that
maybe they had something to say

So, I tried them
and fell in love

And, now I move through one or two each week.

— **Ralph Hogges**

TO A SOLDIER SON

Your picture is in my living room
And on my dresser too.
In loving memory of you
There's a star hanging in the window
Saying you are away.
Yet your face is always before me
As if you were home today.

I pray each dawn as I awake
That now this war is over
You, my son, will be sailing from a foreign shore
And when I set the table
I can see you sitting there
Instead of looking at the only empty chair.

Your plate is in its place dear
Just as it was before
And I'm praying that
Soon dear you will be home with us once more.

— **Ruth Goddard Finch**

LONELY LAND

I always wish it was you and me alone on a
silent sea.
Sailing away to another land where no one else
would be.
Alone we'd sit for hours staring at the stars,
listening, sharing everything from moons
to wild flowers.
You would put your arms around me and
keep me warm at night.
Then you'd kiss me and hold me very, very
tight.
After the moon was out and the stars were
shone bright, we'd begin our most
wonderful and loving night.
We would make love and show each other
just how much we care.
We would share everything in this land
and we'd be very fair.
Then you'd give me a wedding band on this
cold and lonely land and tell me that you
love me and that you want to be my man.
I'd accept and with no doubt and there
we'd be, you and me with no one else to
see.
We would live our life together on this
barren land.
We would share everything and walk
around hand in hand.
As we sat in the sand our love would never
end and we'd care forever, until we both
passed away,
But even then we'd always be together on
this cold and lonely land.

— **Jill A. Weber**

SILENCE

Silence is so cold and dark,
That no one wants to violate,
This silence so deep and dark,
Even with a spark.

Is it like a prowling cat,
Who stalks its wary prey?
Is it an arrow red,
Piercing the calm of the day?

No matter what the answer is,
This, believe, is true.
Silence lives the shortest life,
Then flees into the blue.

—Sherrona Wood

ALONE AT NIGHT

My granite seat
is surrounded by pines.
Their drying needles
carpet the dusty earth.
I am alone, until
I look up
and know I am not.
The moon, round and pale,
towers above, as a conductor
before the night's black curtain.
An audience of a thousand stars
gathers about him.
They seem to dance and sway
to the melody of nature's orchestra.
The bowing of violins heard
in the cricket's song,
the fluting of an owl, and
the river's beating percussion
fill the night.

—Janet Barton

APART

In early morn,
    a cool grey mist
        hovers undisturbed.

The returning blue from
    the disbonded sand granule
        reiterates

without incline
    or angle, but,
        for life.

To deepen your depths
    and extend your feel—
        to change!

As God's daughter
    you are loved
        and abused.

In your troubled salty body
    and endless nourishment
        lives hope.

How long my dry
    surface thirsts for
        your seething touch;

to be held, moved
    and changed,
till we part again.

                for: Heidi
            —Dennis Sullivan

Rivers cutting deep like a knife cutting flesh
And confusion like a whirlwind out of control
Driving rain beating down like the raining of shells
From a gun accidentally fired at a non-existing target,
Barren, empty as my open hand.
Rushing water, drowning me in an endless sea.
Fire as cold as ice, burning inside of me.
A lone eagle, proud and revered, soaring overhead.
Nothing but the shrill cry of the wind blowing through the pines.
Desolation. Depression. Dying as the silence overcomes me,
Drowning out my silent cries, for nature's silence is more
Powerful than mine.
For now, the silence is overwhelming, broken only by an
Occasional cry from someone else, but my own silence is
Not affected, for I am all alone, drowning in the
Screaming silence which surrounds me.

—Melissa Parson

FOR MOTHER

Think, if you can, what it would be like
To have never loved another human being.
People's problems, people's joys, to your eyes, unseeing.
You say you're afraid of heartache.
Of men tearing and crushing, quite aware.
So you run from your feelings and say you don't care.
Think how you'll feel sitting alone in old age.
No photographs to look through. No memories in page after page.
No children to sigh upon, whether in joy or grief.
No help to be attempted, no trust, or belief.
So you that never loved, you say you missed the pain.
But you haven't found happiness,
so what have you gained?
And you that have loved, and failed, so you think.
You say the pain surmounts the happiness.
And now it's swim alone or sink.
I ask you, have you children?
Well think of them. Chances are they'll help you swim.
Another question I wish to bring to your mind.
What is better? The heart abused, or the heart unused?

—Kathaleen B. Torres

GRANDMA

Grandma turned eighty years old last February,
But she doesn't seem that old to me.
She's worked hard all her life,
But she has aged quite gracefully.

She was widowed in 1936, when she was only forty.
Grandma never remarried, and raised her two kids alone.
She supported her family by selling Avon,
Though the years were rough, she cared for her children and home.

She's lived alone since 1953, when Mom married Dad.
And she's done some traveling — even to New York by plane,
That was an adventure for her, she'll tell it if you ask,
Because it stormed and thundered and rained.

Last winter Grandma moved to a new apartment,
She'd been waiting on this for three years.
She was so excited and happy,
That when I saw her I had to hold back the tears.

She is an amazing person with wonderful traits,
I enjoy seeing and talking with her too,
But the thing I want to say right now is,
Grandma, I love you.

**(This poem was written in 1977 — and is lovingly dedicated
    to "Grandma" who passed away in 1984)**
            —Brenda Finicle

YELLOW HEADS IN THE MEADOW

A gentle wind caresses the meadow.
Their yellow heads, tipsy, swing back and forth
and side from side.
They gyrate in joyous rhapsody.
Aeons past, Maenad would have succumbed in envy.
Their vast numbers reach as far as the horizon
Where the cerulean sky hugs the golden surface.
When the curtain of darkness falls over the meadow
A stream of glowing eyes embraces the clear sky above.

  —Mr. Mahdy Y. Khaiyat

WHY

Why must we go on living this way
In a world where no one cares
Where there are homeless and poverty everywhere
In a world where there is no hope or any dreams left
Why must we live where violence is a way of life
Where people's hearts are filled with fear
I have but one solution we must stand up to our fears
We must prove to ourselves that this earth still has a chance
We must all stand up and start to care

  —Bryan Ball

OUR WEDDING DAY

(Written for my husband on our 41st wedding anniversary)
'Twas three days after Christmas, in balmy "spring" weather,
We promised to love and to cherish forever.
"I pledge thee my troth," said we two on that day,
And we asked God to bless us, and to show us the way.

We were happy and young, and we knew that our love
Was a gift from our God, in the heavens above.

We stood side by side, as we solemnly said,
While reciting our vows, "With this ring I thee wed."
And since God blessed our marriage, there's very small wonder,
We feel as we do — "Let no man put asunder."

I love you, my Dear, all the days of my life,
For you are my husband and I am your wife.
I love you, my Dear, with all of my heart.
My love is forever, "Till death do us part."

So a toast to our marriage of forty years plus --
A healthy and happy Anniversary to us!

  —Eileen S. Hutton

OUT OF PLACE . . . OUT OF TIME

You must go your way, and I must go mine;
For we met out of context . . . out of place, out of time!

We've known love together, too good to be true;
And put aside for the moment . . . what we already knew!

Life shared together, so much laughter and fun;
Gave a radiant glow . . . to our place in the sun!

Loving, and playing, and walking the beach;
And sharing love too . . . for pet creature, named "Creech."

The plans made together, can just never be;
And in spite of our love . . . I must set you free!

I must be the strong one, and turn you away;
But remember I'll love you . . . just as today!

For as I grow older, and you are still young;
We'll cherish the memories . . . of our place in the sun!

For now just go your way, so I can go mine;
Til we meet up in heaven . . . in place . . . and in time!

  —Betty Karkutt Pace, Dedicated to RNH

ALL ALONE

Alone,
All alone,
Floating in a quickening sea —
  just me.

Alone,
All alone,
Imagination running wild —
  foolish child.

Alone,
All alone,
Dreaming dreams that will never be —
  dear me.

Alone,
All alone,
Children leave till there are none —
  work's done.

Alone,
All alone,
Sitting here in shock and grief —
  no relief

Alone,
All alone,
Creeping round at a snail's pace —
  lost grace.

Alone,
All alone,
Soaring toward a ray of light —
  end's flight.

  —Blinda Cline Doty

The cold steel of sadness
Runs its sharp blade
through the soul,
Keeping the hopeless dreamer awake.
As if knowing the same cold,
harsh world will wait for dawn.

Steal a few precious moments
of dream state.
Dream about a land where
wishes come true,
fate is controlled by the
dreamer, and truth is
everyday.

Grab and hold tight to fantasies
of sleep, cherish them and
pray never to wake, for the
end of sleep is the beginning
of reality and reality is all
around.
Ready to bare its sharp claws
and tear the soul. Leave in
shreds all held dear and loved

Don't give up or abandon
hope.
All that's left is the small
chance that tomorrow's
dreams will someday crash
the barriers and conquer
reality.
And the souls of all free
spirits and dreamers will
dwell in the sweet serenity
of their fantasies.

  —Thomas E. Smith

A FATHER'S LOVE

My Father's love for me
was more precious than silver or gold,
And his memory of love and laughter
In my heart shall never grow old.

As a child he was known as "Daddy,"
As I grew he became my "Dad"
and as years passed by I soon realized,
That a true friend I also had.

We did so many things together
as Father, Daughter & Friend,
He gave everything such meaning,
Until the very end.

My Father is no longer with me,
He has since been called away,
But the sharing will go on forever
Like Yesterday, Tomorrow and Today.

—Anne Marie Lima-Jackson

MY SON

God entrusted in my care
A baby boy with golden hair,
Endowed me with a loving heart
To proudly mold His work of Art.

I filled his baby heart with love
For man and beast and God above,
And sowed a seed of charity
For all less fortunate than he.

He was receptive to my touch
And out of love responded much.
I molded gently year by year,
That I might fail, my only fear.

I shared his hopes, ideals and dreams.
Swift eighteen years, a day it seems,
And watched him grow to man from birth.
What greater blessing found on earth.

—Mildred R. Catterton

RETIRED SENIOR VOLUNTEER PROGRAM

Retired
    We are not asleep
    And way down deep
    We have a lot of gumption
    Truly want to function

Senior
    Sometimes have a fear
    Of being scorned and unwanted
    We sometimes shed a silent tear
    But perseverance makes it clear
    We can still do a thing or two

Volunteer
    We don't hesitate
    Never think it too late
    Our fingers and steps
    May not be as nimble
    Even though we tremble
    By thunder
    We sure do wonders

Program
    Is very diversified
    Gives us all a chance
    To do our stuff
    This is not just a bluff

—Lydia Braf

THE BLACK TULIP

You are as rare as the black tulip
A beauty to gently hold, to passionately behold.
And like the honey bee that visits
I want to delicately separate your petals
And draw the sweet nectar from deep within your stem.

—S.C. (Syd) Comer

PAW PAW

Tonight I thought of you
and I realized how sick you really are.
I have my whole life ahead of me
but you may not have a tomorrow.
I really regret all the time we never had
and all the things we could have shared.
All the times I never showed you
or told you how much I really cared.
Paw Paw, I love you.
And you'll always be in my heart.
I wish we could have been closer
and not lived so far apart.
I could have written more
or spent more time with you when you were here.
I love you, Paw Paw
and in my heart, I'll always hold you near.

—Carol Holland

LIFE AFTER SIXTY

We'd like our hair fixed like the models do,
But our hair's too fine and we've got too few.
We need a style that will hide our scalp,
A real good Beautician now does help!

We can't eat the food we used to eat,
They need to chop the veggies and grind the meat.
We'd like to wear high heels and be in style,
But we're not as steady now, we might land in a pile.

Our skins got wrinkled not nice and smooth,
Most of it we can cover, this our ego soothes.
Our youthful figure has gone and went,
But our feelings now are easier to vent.

The Lord is with us to guide our way,
This keeps us going, trusting Him each day.
Being old's not bad, if we're not owing,
And when we die, we know where we are going.

—Coleen Mae Roberts

RETIREMENT

Retirement means so many different things
Relaxation and put off flings
No set schedule to keep or meet
Sleep late, eat whenever hungry, rest tired feet

Get to meet new friends and socialize
So many hobbies, travel dances and even a prize
There's no excuse to be bored
Help with taxes, problems — you're not ignored

Friendly people with a great big smile
Bingo, pool, cards — stay a while
Every day of the working week
A hot meal, interesting talks and the medical aid you seek

Active people from the 50's to the 90's you'll find
Talented, sociable, helpful and very kind
Congratulations and hail our many seniors
Full of pep and vigor — model for our juniors

—Blanche M. Krystyniak

MYSTERIES OF LIFE

Many of us seek,
 Many of us find.
But life has no
Secrets if we learn
But only to survive.
Nature is the key that
Will open up the door.
Peace will be the prize
That we all can endure.

—Nelson A. Grant

FREE SPIRIT

I sail with memories of the past;
 Days of wooden ships,
clouds of canvas on their masts.
 Ghosts stand by my side,
From the time 'ere I was born;
Ghosts of the men,
Who sailed 'round the Horn.
 I sense them near me
and a feeling comes,
of being home — of being free.

—Larry Lee Roney

TALL TALES

My Grandpa tells me stories,
 Or what you'd call Tall Tales,
Usually about his childhood
 or about the Duke of Wales.
Some of them are funny.
 Others are so scary.
My favorite ones are the tales
 that are joyful and so merry.
My Grandpa tells me all of them.
 every tale he knows,
About all the people
 or places where he goes.
Tall Tales about the animals,
 or even some on plants:
My Grandpa's favorite tale
 is the tale about the ants.
My Grandpa tells me all the tales.
 It takes a lot of time.
Every one of those Tall Tales
 falls completely into rhyme.

—Paula Bell

DEAR GHOSTS

Dear ghosts
 For only one day
Will you let me join you
On Halloween

To say the truth
I'm sick of the human world
Tied up with duties
Chased by time
Tortured by human bondage
Such a world
I cannot tolerate anymore

In order to join you
What should I do, please tell me
Holding your hand
I want to fly around freely
In the world of fantasy
Even just for one day

—Harumi Williams

DOG-WOLF

A little snow had fallen, the moon was bright,
 I could hear a wolf howling, on this cold wintery night.
It slept in a haystack not far away.
I had to walk to school the next day.
I walked fast! Then I'd run,
I'd sing and try to hum.
I was six years old, and had been told to be brave,
Study hard! And do behave!
A guardian angel, I knew I had,
And many the time, I was ever so glad.
When up ahead I saw tracks in the snow!
A dog? A wolf? Which way did it go?
When right behind me, there came a sound,
With a quick jerk I turned around.
It stood there snarling! Its teeth were long and gray,
I stamped my foot, and shouted, "Go away"
Its hair stood straight up, its growling grew worse!
Just then a man appeared on a big black horse,
Click—click—and bang—went his gun!
I smiled, but it wasn't fun.

—Dolly M. Dowd

NATURE'S CONCERT

The Great Maestro lifts His baton
 To direct a chorus of birds in song.
With voices lifted, they herald in the Spring,
 As fervently as seedlings are never asked to sing.

The seasonal prelude of the Summer lies
 In the thunder and rain from darkened skies.
The crescendo of the frogs, as they begin to croak,
 Is as deafening as the silence of the rainbow's sign of hope.

The Fall rendition begins with rustling leaves,
 While whistling winds replace with Summer's breeze.
Proudly the Maestro conducts this symphony,
 As the earth changes colors in perfect harmony.

The Grand Finale has been chosen well.
 Snowflakes mound in a great hushed swell.
The concert is now complete without one discordant note.
 Only a repeat performance fills the air with hope.

—Gayle Hollis Phillips

HALLOWEEN NIGHT

Dad brings home a pumpkin, and carves a funny face.
 Hollows out the middle, and a candle takes its place.
Now the pumpkin's sitting on the porch rail way up high,
 So little children see it as they go walking by.

Halloween's exciting when it is your first time,
 Picking out a costume and a mask to hide behind.
Don't forget your little bag, to put your many treats,
 And please be very careful, when crossing those dark streets.

Go to people's houses with the porch lights that are on,
 Ring the door bell once or twice, Be sure your mask is on.
When the party answers, They'll tell you to come in.
 They'll look you over head to toe, and ask you with a grin,
Do you live next door to us? Is your brother Jim?
 Do you live around the block? Are you Tom or Tim?

If you answer no to these, Then you must abide,
 Remove the mask that's on your face, Now you don't have to hide.
Just open up your little bag, I'll drop in things to eat,
 For that is how the game is played, And it's called trick or treat.

A heartfelt thanks to those who gave, as you walk out the door,
 With mask in place you start back out, To Halloween some more.

—Sandra L. Snyder

MAMA CITA

Mama Cita is a cat that stopped by one day,
She liked it so well she decided to stay.
Mama Cita is dark grey with two spots of white,
To survive she has always had to fight.
It's been over twelve years since she came,
One litter after another was how she got her name.
People and other animals treated her unkind,
We had her spayed to give her peace of mind.
We try to give her a life of happiness,
But she doesn't completely trust us I guess.
She lives in our garage but she isn't tame,
We can't touch or pet her, but we love her all the same.
You say cats are only dumb animals anyway,
But Mama Cita, understands everything we say.
She comes to the house and up the walk,
And all the while she is trying to talk.
On Dorothy, and me she has come to depend,
Because she knows we are her friend.

—Nino Colo

THE SOJOURN

With stratospheric sullenness
She blankets the sky with darkness,
And the earth begins to quiver
Beneath her cannonade of menace.
With impetuous fury she unleashes tempestuous turbulence.
Leaves overturn in defiance
Against her bullets of betrayal.
Saplings grow weary
As they dodge relentless torrents.
Streams struggle past her gauntlet of debris,
Twisting and bending in desperation.
Faint flickers of fulminating brightness
Conclude a self-gratifying performance,
And her breath whispers of a truce.
She summons her iridescent aura to swiftly follow
Her combustible haze as it tarnishes the silver horizon,
And the scattered glitter upon the earth
Reminds us of her frivolous farewell.

—Cindy Lee Powell

MOTHER NATURE

Everything from it teaches the truth
Mother Nature is the most beautiful treasure of all
We can not live without it

Mother Nature does not teach us selfishness
Everything it supplies to us is important
But, most of us do not know how to appreciate

How many of us sometimes say
Thanks for everything Mother Nature
Your sunlight, moonlight, air and water just to name a few

Yes, let's learn together
And teach our Children Mother Nature's beauty
The beauty of our "UNIVERSE"

Let's teach them that without air and water
Our World would not be what it is now
And all living matters use them in some way or the other

And some time, some day, we will return to Mother Nature
Doctors will say: Without air our Patients can not live

Engineers will say: Without air, water or sunlight,
We can not produce electricity and other important things

Thanks to You, "MOTHER NATURE."

—Emmanuel Serge Frasier

THE WALL

As much as you'd allow, I cared;
Loving you wholly as much as I dared,
Always, always there came between,
Impenetrable and unseen,
        A wall.

Bricks of silence, mortar of doubt
Kept you away, and kept me out.
When, rarely, a ray of hope I caught
And eagerly reached across — to naught,
        I wept.

Across that wall, across the years,
Our love outlasted all my fears . . .
Yet often, in vain, I try to recall
Which of us had built that wall,
        And why.

—Winifred T. Neville

BEYOND YOUTH

Innocence is stripped away,
Eroded by a place
That snubs the core that laughs aloud
And marches with a different pace.

Hold tight, dear child, the ride is wild;
The bumps abound and then,
Expected to endure and smile,
You're pressured not to bend

Away from sanity; facades must last;
The veneer remaining tight.
Bruised, discouraged, weak or drained,
Go with what you feel is right

For your heart's rays are all you'll have
To judge your judgements by
And if at times the going's hard
They may not hear your cry.

So look within and hope so hard
We managed when you were small
To sprinkle in your spirit's base
The elements to make you tall.

—Mary J. Moura

THE ADVENT OF FALL

FALL — it's here!
A general coolness prevails,
And the crickets are ready
For their seasonal raids.

Farmers are saying:
"Yep, think we had a frost,"
As their eyes glance
O'er gardens that are lost.

But everyone is thankful
For the peas, limas, and corn
Already lying frozen in deep freezes
For the winter's fare alone.

How wonderful that man
Can successfully adjust
To life's ups and downs
And comes out a better person!

So, with the advent of fall
Get ready for those scenic walks
Among crimson, yellow, and bronze leaves
Beckoning in our lovely fall.

—Cecile W. Aylor

SILENT LOVE

Silent as a rose that's growing
Tranquil as a river flowing
Majestic as the towering mountains
Subdued like a whisper is our love.

Peaceful as a spring breeze blowing
Quiet as a moonbeam glowing
A silent love that cannot die
A love between just you and I.

—Becky Scicolone, Age 13

TOGETHER

Someone is Waiting
Waiting for You
You are the One
One of only Two

Two thoughts in Vision
Vision drives them Through
Through all the Troubles
Troubles old and New

New scenes are Growing
Growing in our Eyes
Eyes see the Future
Future holds our Cries

Cries and sighs of Wisdom
Wisdom gray and Bold
Bold with our Comfort
Comfort together Old.

—Mary Herlacher

MY LOVE

My love — I need your arms
To hold me tight . . . .
To give me strength
In my daily fight—

Without your arms
I feel so weak—
Without your arms
I feel life's defeat—

I feel so lonely . . . .
I need your love!
To help me keep going
In my darkest hour—

My cup has run over—
I feel the end—
Love— don't let me fall!
Hold me in your arms.

—Julia Grosberg

Love is a stranger
Someone I
shall never know
I see his face
all around me
but he doesn't know my name.
Sometimes I
tap him on the shoulder—
he looks at me
with strange eyes,
and in them I see
the cold, familiar truth—
that Love
is a stranger.

—Christie D. Cole

WITHIN YOU

I wish we could all stay warm in an emotional bliss:
Loving and caring—sensitive—understanding
For emotions are not to be taken advantage of.
Emotions need attention and demand strength;
They involve "feeling" to survive.
To be a better human being, we <u>all</u> must strive.

Just follow your heart:
It leads to the path where all your dreams are in reach!
We must learn "trust" in order to be set free.
Acceptance and love become "keys" in unlocking who we are.

But most of all,
JUST BE YOU;
And no matter how it goes,
You just can't lose!!!!!!!

—Robin Lovich-Segermeister

BEAUTY AND THE BEAST

Beauty: her face was as white as a first fallen snow;
          her eyes were pools of blue and green hue;
          her body was as delicate as crystal;
          her heart pounded in search of the prince in her dreams.

Beast: his face was covered with scars and bumps;
         his eyes were a piercing brown mist;
         his body hunched over in a slump;
         his heart pounded at the Beauty in his dreams.

Beauty gazed at the beast with horror.
His every scar and bump was Beauty's internalized questions;
The brown mist in his eyes was Beauty's inability to grow;
His hunched body was Beauty's refusal to see life clearly.

Beauty was the Beast.

Their faces fused together in warm cream.
Their eyes locked, hazel depths emerging;
Their bodies intertwined and rooted;
Their hearts pounded in rhythm.
Beauty kissed the Beast.

The Beast was Beauty.

—Karen Josephine Germano

BEAUTY AND THE BEAST

I sit alone each day and visualize your charms,
          and wonder what in me it is you see
                    that keeps you in my arms.

          Your tenderness, your thoughtfulness,
                    your warm and loving ways,
They are you see, the destiny
                    that helps me through the days.

Your body moves so gracefully,
                    like a blade through a butter's ease.
          Your hair blows free, and beckons to me
                    like trees in a whirling breeze.

Your eyes, your smile, your heart,
                    even your golden touch,
          Brings to me a bit of reality, and
                    I know you are far too much.

Your warm embrace, your gentle kiss,
                    all of which I do upon feast.

For to me, I want you to see,
                    you are the Beauty,
                              and I the Beast.

—Duayne Albert Hoolapa

THE BLESSINGS OF LIFE

God gave us the four seasons, spring, summer, fall and winter.
  Each one has its beauty.
This time is the greatest of all the year,
    More love is expressed, good will, happiness and cheer.

On Christmas morn was the day of our Savior's birth.
    For about 33 years He was on this earth
He went about healing the sick, giving sight to the blind,
    And teaching a better life to all mankind.

Over one thousand years have passed,
    The wonders He did on earth will always last.
Our heavenly Father in His great love,
    Sent His only Son from heaven above.

To everyone who believes, a great blessing you will receive.
    In all this turmoil and strife,
I thank you dear Lord,
    For all the blessings of this great Life.

—Etta Mae Harrell

She gazed at the trust in her small withered child,
    And the guilt in her mind was driving her wild.
"The party is finally over," she said.
And she thanked the good Lord that her child was not dead.

"How could this have happened?" she thought once again.
"I was just doing things that were cool with my friends."
"A joint wouldn't hurt me or a snort now and then.
These were the things I must do to fit in."

"I wasn't an addict, I could quit any time."
"It's just when I took it I knew I could shine.
I was the life of the party, the belle of the ball!
No one could stop me cause I had it all."

"I found out too late, when reality set in,
And I got a good look at the shape I was in,
I'd sold out my soul to the Devil, you see.
And he took his revenge on my little baby."

"If anything good comes from the evil I've done,
If I can save anybody, if even just one,
From becoming the creature that I used to be,
The Lord just might give back my baby to me."

—Teresa L. Philbeck

HOW DO I FEEL?

How does it feel to be locked inside
With anger, hurt and pain; wondering what's real
And what's been denied over and over again?
How does one deal with all that is tied
To the anger, the hurt, and the pain?

Lock the door! Keep it sealed! And hope that you've died.
If not, I just might go insane. Just be the ideal,
So perfect that I'd never, no never complain.
Who cares how you feel? Who wants to reveal
Your existence? What would it gain? Who cares that we've lied;
Your appeals we've defied — Come! Celebrate! More champagne?

Who cares if we steal her life? She's not cried!
Her rage remains restrained. How would it feel
To be taken outside? Or would it all be in vain?
What will we reveal? Will it be like the tide
Of history's worst hurricane? I think not! Her appeal
Is that of a bride whose joy is unrestrained.

Maybe we'll heal the child locked inside —
Pain, anger, and hurt all slain. Just tell me.
How do I feel?

—Beverly Townsend Cooper

TAKE TIME

Take time to work
    Take time to Play
Take time to be happy
Take time to Pray.

Take time
  a helping hand
      to lend someone along the way
Take time
  a kind word to someone say.

Take time
  a worthy task to do
Take time my friend
before time takes you.

—Joyce Butler

OUTWARD BOUND

It's an end that's inevitable,
  A beginning that's slow to start.
The reunion of the spirits,
The souls that drift apart.

Cycles that are working,
returning to the heart.

All things are closing quickly,
The future's right at hand.
It keeps me in boundaries,
I don't know where I stand.

It's time for the coming,
I hear the heavenly band.

The crashing sounds of cymbals,
The harsh noise of horns.
All announcing the end,
This time . . . no need for thorns.

And yet, the worst is over,
for I am the newly born!

—Theresa Hovind

FORGET ME NOT

There's a very special lady,
  To me, life's greatest friend.
She gave to me this pleasant thought
    To you, from me, to send.

It says to always be thankful
    For everything there is,
Someday, something may fade away,
    Someone you'll really miss.

The thought's to be patient and kind
    And always to believe,
And someday down the rugged road
    One day you will achieve.

My grandma, with her words so wise
    Did not say this to me,
But in her precious, loving way
    She gave me this, you see.

She gave to me, from all her heart
    The gentle, blowing breeze.
She touched my life as forever
    Like sunshine in the trees.

Now Lord has taken grandma
    Because he too did know,
How much she gave to all of us,
    And how we love her so!

—Lynda Clothier

TWO WORLDS

One is yours, the other is mine.
So different, yet the same.
Striving for the top,
Passing worlds of confusion on the way.
Wondering if it really is worth it;
The pain, for all the glory.
Feeling so lonely,
Wondering if the person lying next to you in bed
Is really the one
Or is it the one in your dreams?
Wondering if you're really making a difference.
Realizing that taking one day at a time
Isn't the easiest of all tasks.
But still smiling, for everyone else's sake.
Two Worlds
One is yours, the other is mine.
So different, yet the same.
We can only pray
Someday they will collide.

—Rosa Maria Cavazos

THE WILLOW

The massive willow stood in a place,
crowded with brush and feeling disgraced.
It cried for vacancy next to the brook,
but it seemed the spaces were already took.
Oh well, it would be content and fine,
as long as the birds flew by and he was alive.
Even through the rainy days he stood tall,
and danced in the wind, not afraid to fall.
One day standing gallant and proud,
a mighty gust came and blew him down.
The inhabitants of the forest all cried,
for such a mighty thing had died.
No more birds would sing,
from his once dangling limbs.
Squirrels could no longer run and play,
and since his death, they were bored all day.
It's a shame he never saw the brook,
and how his life from him was took.
How unimportant a tree may seem,
even massive willows have dreams!

—Steven J. Reed

A COINCIDENCE

"I'm going to be married," he softly said,
She looked up in swift surprise.
The color from out of her bright face fled,
The light grew dim in her eyes.

"You're going to be married?" she echoed low,
Her voice kept a steady tone;
"I hope you'll be happy wherever you go,"
A cough hid a little moan.

"Your bride will be good and true!
I know you could have no other."
She steadily looked in his eyes, dark blue,
"I wish you much joy, my brother."

"I'm going to be married—that is, I hope
To be, though I hardly know—"
"Dear love, shall I longer pine and mope?
I tremble for fear of 'no'."

Then color that out of her face had fled,
Came back with a deeper hue,
"Why, isn't it funny," she shyly said,
"That I'm to be married, too?"

—"Bobbie" Boyd

MOM and the FALLING STAR

When we were so close in distance,
The distance seemed so far.
You just wanted to better me,
While I wanted to chase a star.

But you knew it was a falling star,
And the path that it would lead.
For long ago you traveled that road,
The warnings you never did heed.

And now that I have watched you thru the years,
I am understanding the wisdom of your ways.
All the times I thought you shot my star down,
You were helping me thru life's treacherous maze.

So now I would like to thank you mom,
The distance is not as far.
Though there are many miles between us,
You are my shining star.

—Stacey Grajczyk

LAUGHTER

Laughter is the magic ingredient
That helps me rise above circumstance.
It's the ability to laugh with someone
Or at myself.

Laughter relieves tension
And reduces mountains into molehills.
It reaffirms my belief in tomorrow
And yesterday.

Laughter ripples with promise
Of another chance to get it right.
It carries rejuvenation and the reminder
This, too, will pass.

In laughter there is hope
Problems will go away and be forgotten.
It helps me survive everyday disappointments
Without it I am hollow.

Laughter releases natural painkillers
Thus I have learned how to manage chronic pain.
When I laugh out loud at a unique wit I
Forget pain for a few moments.

—Gala Mae

OUR PATHS MAY NEVER CROSS

The time has come for us to part
And go our separate ways,
But before you walk out of my life
There is something that I must say.

Most of our time was spent apart
And there were promises we could never fulfill.
Though our paths may never cross again
Someday our hearts will.

Saying good-bye is the hardest thing
We'll ever have to do,
Since the love we thought would change our world
Never came shining thru.

We had our chances to make it work
But I guess the timing just wasn't right.
Instead of our love growing stronger each day
It would always disappear in the night.

So someday when you're all alone
And you feel that familiar pain,
Please don't worry, it's just our hearts
Crossing their paths again.

—John C. Stringer

ONE WISH

One day when I was walking, I looked up in the sky
My mind began to wonder what it's like, if we could fly
The beauty of the world, below for all to see
The distance we could travel would be our fantasy

I'd soar throughout the heavens, my wings so open wide
I'd take in all the beauty of stars that clouds can hide
I'd sit upon a rainbow, then down to earth I'd slide
I'd catch a star and sparkle, to be seen from earth, with pride

I think if I had wings, I'd stay up in the sky
I'd have no wish to roam the earth, with all that space so high
So if I had one wish to make, and know it would come true
I'd like to have a pair of wings, and fly above with you

> **Dedicated to John**
> **—Barbara V. Olson**

FREEDOM THAT COMES FROM A FALLEN RAIN

Sometimes the feelings of emptiness go so deep within my inner
    core . . . and so much more
The moment after he goes, the wind blows on a silent plain of
    never more
The loneliness aches within my heart . . . This is only the start . . .
Part of me is missing
Tears fall from a broken heart and a lonely soul
Oh such sadness in letting go . . . Both of us must grow

Love holds no barriers . . . It bonds
Love is letting one's soul have wings to fly from bondage
Fly, little eaglet, from your nest . . . but know that love awaits in
    the comfort of your mother's breast

Eaglet or Eagle . . . it matters not . . .
The softness of a gentle caress . . . The comfort of a mother's
    bosom . . . that's where you'll find rest . . .
The love of a mother is as sure as falling rain . . .
It always remains.

Eaglet, spread your tender wings and fly high as the Eagle flies,
    close to the master's eye.
Soar to heights above, Eagle, bask in God's love.

Tears of sadness . . . Tears of joy . . . You are no longer a boy
The sadness of love and freedom remains . . .
The freedom that comes from a fallen rain.

> **—Lizabeth Jackson**

LOST FRIEND

It was during the monsoons,
I had my orders I was going home soon.
The weather and war I would leave behind,
Once again I would have freedom of mind.

The enemy had other plans for me,
Attacking my unit vigorously.
My sanity was leaving my very soul,
All those attacks were taking their toll.

The Commander ordered, "2nd squad, go out on patrol."
Find the Viet-Congs blow up their holes.
I got sick so my best friend took my place,
He was killed in action, I never again saw his smiling face.

To this very day the burden of guilt weighs heavy on my mind,
It should have been me who died from that mine.
I look skyward often seeing his smile,
Just beyond the gray colored clouds.

A part of me was left behind,
In a God Forsaken place at an unpopular time.
A part of me is in Arlington Cemetery, under the headstone etched,
with the name "GARY."

> **—Calvin Ken Eger**

Parked on a night street
    Watching bare tree barnacles
Harvest the snowfall.

> **—Kelly Jorgenson**

MISGUIDED

A life entwined,
    With drugs and mind.

Lonely illusions
Of a world not mine.

Whispered thoughts of insanity;
Self destruction I long to see.

I live my life no meaning at all;
Just there to be,
Just there to fall.

Endless thoughts intrude the mind,
Broken off, then left behind.

Never to be solved;
Never to be found;

Never to live,
A life so sound.

> **—Christopher Kurt Miller**

ANOTHER ONE

this sudden poetic roll
is quickly taking its toll
every minute a new verse
yesterday seemed quite reverse
poems derived from loving you
anxious feelings ever true
inexplicable surges
uncontrollable urges
quickly losing all senses
and living on pretenses
memories alive and real
flashbacks of the sweet ordeal
loving and wanting much more
feeling your death to the core
foolish in magical bliss
with just a word, and a kiss
every day is quite unreal
and the clouds my poems do steal

> **—Inez C. Eisazadeh (ice)**

BOUQUET OF MEMORIES

I picked a bouquet today
not of flowers,
but, of memories.
I was thinking of the time
we were together
for the first time.
The fun we had,
the love we shared.
The big Christmas tree
we cut.
The good times we shared.
There is no flower
to compare
to sweet memory.
If you have a sad
or a blue day.
Pick a good memory
out of your bouquet
one that makes you smile.

> **—Peggy Sue Dempsey**

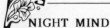

NIGHT MIND

There's something that I'm thinking of
That's coming from down deep
I don't know really what it is
But it's keeping me from sleep.

As I ponder the world a bit
The clock ticks on and on
For I really don't know what to say
And soon it will be down.

But as I think of moments past
And soon I see the light
I think of things that are to come
And hope they will be alright.

So now I wander off to sleep
And dream of life and fun
For tomorrow I know I will awake
And greet the rising sun.

—Christian Michael

THE VIVALDI

A song is a picture,
Artistically painted.
Fine and pure,
A dream recreated.

A piano is a color,
Brilliant and bright.
A violin yet another,
Both lovely in sight.

Two sisters of one family
The artists so fine,
Played the Vivaldi,
A composer of long ago time

They took their colors in their hands,
The audience fell still and silent.
Then pure as the whitest sands,
Came their picture and all that it meant.

Two sisters now much closer,
Through the colors of a painting.
Two sisters now more loving,
Because their dream was recreating.

— Kerilee Grames

JUST AROUND THE BEND

You feel you can't take any more
And think the road will never end,
But you'll find what you're looking for,
Just around the bend.

Whether it's a season or a holiday
A dream or a friend,
Be patient and wait,
They're just around the bend.

The time may seem so far away
And the excitement a little too great,
But stop to cherish the present day,
For the future will always be late.

The minute you start to lose your breath
And ask yourself "when?"
Take a moment out to rest,
And then move on again.

Another mile or another week,
Both road and calendar have an end.
You have my word that what you seek,
Is just around the bend.

— Nicholas D'Andrea, Jr.

THE REKINDLED FLAME

When we were together the flame was strong,
But then we broke up now the flame is gone.
Now it's time for the flame to be renewed,
But to do this we need caring people, like me and you.
The flame is not just a word to you and me,
The flame keeps us warm inside you see.
This flame that is present when we are together,
Is a flame that will protect us through all kinds of weather.
What we must do is create the sparks.
What you must do is open your heart.
Together we can do it, if we try.
We can let the loneliness and pain to die.
So let's do it now, give a spark and see.
Rekindle the flame for you and for me.

—D.J. Jerome

CAVERNS OF THE HEART

I close my eyes and glide into the still caverns of my deepest heart.
And there he waits for me—my secret lover on the other side of reality.
I feel his presence come to life, as my armor of defenses abandons me.
The tears of his compassion wash away my sorrows.
The tenderness of his care soothes my restless soul,
His love surrounds me like a fortress—while his strength and courage I absorb.
I see his eyes like fire in the reflections of my heart.
His passion fills me with warmth—but never burns.
I long to join him as one, but he tells me I must go.
He slides away into darkness leaving his forever burning glow.
For his perfect love has healed me, and from this magic
I emerge so serene and whole.
To know the love and beauty of perfection of the soul.
To this life once more—forever with the key to open up the gate to the other side of reality.

—Linda Simpson Obit

A CHANCE TO CHOOSE

If I had the chance to choose where I may belong,
Or where my home is to be in the days to come;
There would be no search in thought of the places I
    have been,
For I would choose only one place, and this one I would
    call home.

If I had the chance to choose one person to wake up to,
To share a fresh morning with, in special talks;
I would want to choose the one I cherish my time with,
And one I could hold hands with, in special walks.

If I had the chance to choose one to share my day,
In work or pleasure, whatever it may be;
I would want to choose a friend I enjoy to have near,
To make good memories together, of each day we may see.

If I had the chance the choose one to share my whole
    life,
On this earth as trials may bear upon my way;
I would want to choose one who could comfort me then,
And share my burdens to ease the pains each day.

If I had the chance to choose and the power of my
    choice,
I would choose you to share each moment in my life;
For it is you, I would trust to make my life complete,
And keep happiness in our home, even through days of
    strife.

—E. M. Burson

176

FRIENDS FOR LIFE
ARE
FRIENDS FOREVER

When things go wrong or when you have a
problem, it's always nice to have someone there
to listen. Someone who might understand and
even if they don't they just lend an ear,
and when they do there is no fear.

When you lend a hand it doesn't always
have to be a helping hand, sometime just a
simple gesture that lets one know you care,
which will let each other know they will
always try to be there.

And even if life does deal us a hand which
we feel is unfair, it's always nice to know that
you have a friend, who when you need them
just might be there.

—Richard P. Micallef, Jr.

HANGIN' ON

Turn on the Beatles and yesterday,
Oh I wish it would go away, the feeling's back,
can't shake it from my memory.
See you laughing there in the sun,
see you happy and having fun, but not with me,
those days are dead and gone.
Your new lover seems real nice,
please excuse me if I'm like ice, I don't know him,
but then you're a stranger too.
You seem so confident and in control,
do you wonder about your soul, where will it be,
for all eternity.
The impressions you try to make,
are like the icing on a cake, they look so good,
but they melt in the sun.
Please excuse me if I'm not polite,
I'm having trouble sleeping nights, letting go,
ain't as easy for me.
Still I keep hangin on, to the feeling inside,
I keep hangin on, God knows I tried.

—Wesley D. Meyer

CHOICES

We have a choice to serve or not;
Each is responsible and casts his lot.

Each heart is filled with love from God;
Which we pass out as on earth we trod.

Free will within us reigns supreme;
Upon awakening, we discover the dream.

Intent on serving and doing our best,
One day we come to that final rest.

And knowing back to God we go,
We joyfully give up this life of woe.

For even the wonders we experience on earth
Will pale in comparison after re-birth.

Future lives we have yet in store;
For always we will need to learn more.

And back we return and choose once again;
The cycle repeats and seems without end.

So let us be conscious in our daily affairs,
And not make those choices as if unaware.

The more we choose wisely, the more we can grow;
With each daily lesson, toward perfection we go.

—Shari Reeves Whalen

SOMEDAY WE'LL MEET AGAIN

Someday we'll meet again my dear.
Maybe next week, next month, next year.
Tho I think not. Not for a while.
I'll keep inside your loving smile.

So that I may face eternity
My love with you, your smile with me.
And think not that I've gone to stay,
For we'll meet again somewhere, someway.

I'll miss so much your skin so fair,
And the sweet perfumes that fill your hair.
You'll see someday that you were wrong
By telling yourself that I didn't belong.

I'll be back your way again. You'll see.
Another time . . . Another me . . .
And when it's time for me to go
We'll meet again—in love—I know.

—Debbie Henry

JULY 20, 1989

Its ancient dust still, its great craters, like
dim eyeless sockets, staring down at Earth,
the Moon will grace this evening in July
with a full pallor countless other months,
in countless other years, have seen entice

Man's growing mind, from prehistoric caves
to modern corridors, and yet tonight
the spectacle will be as it has been
for only twenty years, since human feet
first touched Diana's guarded purity.

The footprints, the flag, the Eagle's claws
remain where silent darkness meets the edge
of a far deeper darkness, in which live
broad shadows curling up their monstrous tails
and hiding from all sight behind large rocks

That point to other worlds, and other times,
more distant than imagination knows,
whose conquest man has not begun, but whose
shores lie beyond each step, as certain as
man's first explosive moment taming fire.

—William Glover

THROUGH A NOVEL DREAMING

We are shadows of our former selves
Storing pictures full of meaning
Now and then we delve
As through a novel dreaming

Personal demons make us cower
From adventures in the hidden mind
Along with other powers
There but hard to find

Dark pictures hurt and blind our sight
And make us fear to tread
But when exposed to light
Leave us none to dread

Truth makes life secure; lies make all unreal
They do not stand to scrutiny
Nor do they heal
But perpetuate a false reality

A philosopher said of responsibility
Do not blame others or look to fate
Look to your mind to find serenity
A great adventure waits.

—Marcia Sebby Winborne

DESTINY

With great majesty the Eagle does fly
O'er this country ever so high.

In freedom he soars.
To him there are no closed doors.

Nothing has he to prove.
The mountains he can move.

He knows his place.
And so — gives no cause for case.

He protects his domain.
And we all do the same.

Is it not God that created this great beast?
Well then, the same must be true of even the
least.

— **Judith M. Alden**

FIVE MORE MINUTES

Be gentle, my love, in leaving me —
Don't rush away too hastily.
Give me fair warning that you would go,
You know how I do need you so.

And as you head towards the door,
Your presence longer I will implore.
Be not surprised when you shall hear
This familiar refrain whispered in your ear —

Give me five more minutes of your time,
Five more minutes that I can call mine.
For just five minutes tarry, Dear.
Linger five more minutes and hold me near.

A wealth of memories I shall collect,
As we always so gently disconnect.
Throughout our life to you I'll cleave
Until the last time that you take leave.

And when your time on Earth has passed
And God does call you home at last,
I shall request one final repast —
"Just five more minutes, Lord," I'll ask.

— **Sharon O'Reilly**

LIFT YOUR HANDS WITH TENDERNESS

Lift your hands with tenderness . . .
A presence forms from formlessness,
Universe's song of endless possibility . . .
Caress the world with downward curving lids;
Tentative fingers. . . cradling arms
Evoke a strange and shaping glory

Shadow and light,
Song and its silence
Play in their colors. . .
Urge upward in dance

Shadow and silence
Drift into blackness;
Light and tonalties,
Merge. . . and entrance

Light sings to light;
The harmony dies. . .
The light now is blinding,
It forces your eyes. . .
Gaze firmly. . . stand fearless,
No need for your fleeing —
The God you have fashioned
Has refashioned your being.

— **H. Robert Cohen**

A POEM

Poems are special in every way. Some make
you happy and laugh. Some make you sad and cry.
You always feel something for a poem.

Poems come in different styles, and different
subjects. Some styles are: haiku, limericks, and
lots more. Some subjects may be about people or
animals.

The author of a poem may decease but the
poem will never die with him. Once a poem is
written it will always be alive.

— **Amy Jo Huntley**

CHRISTIAN FEELINGS

Church, to me, is a place I can go,
When my spirits are down and my feelings are low,
Jesus is there, and He always will be
A Savior for you, and also for me,
The choir sings such meaningful songs
We are fast becoming a God-Centered throng,
The youth of the church are growing up fast
And will soon enter into the world so vast,
Our parents will have to learn to let go
'Cause with Jesus to guide us, they already know,
Although we all make some mistakes,
In the end, with Jesus, A Christian we'll make.

— **Misty Morris**

WE ARE NOT ALONE

With the vigor of youth and strong in our pride
Up the road of life with purpose we stride,
Secure in the fact that no one but we
Can achieve the goals of our destiny.
These goals of power, wealth and fame,
By our own strength alone we'll attain;
And having attained we'll not have to share
For we alone will have gotten us there.
The road before us is shining and bright
But shorter now that the end is in sight.
Then slowly we see and we understand,
That we were guided by an unseen hand.
We didn't achieve all our goals alone;
With His own hand He has guided us home,
And all along we have had to share
For it is by His hand we have gotten there.

— **Leo J. Gougeon**

JESUS IS

Jesus is the Way, the Truth, and the Light.
Since meeting Him I've received my sight.
Before I met Him was like walking in the night
Now that He is with me everything is all right
I praise Him and thank Him with all of my might
Yes, with Him in control there is no need to fight
There is no more fright
Because His love is greater than the greatest height
Only Jesus can turn a pimp to a preacher
He can turn a thief into a Sunday School teacher
It's Him who gives divine protection
Only Jesus gives supernatural direction
He leads me and guides me in all of my ways
With Jesus as my Shepherd my soul never strays
When you listen to Jesus it always pays
The Holy Ghost in me always prays
If you obey His commandments you live longer days.

— **Torin Bowers**
452 Market St. #6
Williamsport, PA 17703

PATIENCE

Patience is a virtue, for the Bible tells me so.
  Because I had no patience, in this way I had to grow.
And so I went right to the Lord and handed Him my plight.
I knew that I would get an answer almost overnight.

But days had passed and still I got no answer from above.
I said, "My God, Your time is up. You sure had long enough!"
He said, "My child, can you not see the reason I am late?
You're growing in your patience by my causing you to wait."

      —Randall Alan Disharoon

OUT OF THE MOUTH OF BABES

Silent whisper, hear my cry. Don't let them take me I don't
want to die. I know I haven't been here long, but a life's a
life be it right or wrong. Please show compassion for I'm
a part of you. I do understand what you're going through.
I too need a chance to see the sun, your life is nearly over
but mine has just begun. Inside I keep growing, getting bigger
and stronger. Just a few more months, it won't be much longer.
You'll stand there in silence, rejoice in my birth this is God's
greatest miracle, the grandest on earth. When my journey's
over and I've come this long long way. My eyes will say
thanks for listening to the words I had to say. Inside your
mind you'll wonder why you ever kept this kid, but believe me
when I tell you I'm certainly glad you did.

      —Karoline Bethea

CREATIONS

I look upward to the heaven, in the morning part of day,
And I see the many clouds as they go floating on their way.

I look into the heaven with the coming of the night,
And I see a million stars looking down and twinkling bright,

I see the flowers blooming, radiant with color,
Adding beauty to the land, with an unforgettable fragrance,
As I hold them in my hand.

I see the dew of morning as it glistens on the grass,
Knowing that with the coming of the sun,
All drops will quickly pass.

I see the rainbow after rain, and know with sun and showers,
It will come again.

These things are created for us to share,
And kept like us, in the Lord's tender care.

      —Darlene M. Cordrey

A TRIBUTE TO GRANDAD

Although some think I never cared,
  I think of you often as I sit and stare.
Remembering the way you held me tight,
  And played child's games in the early night.
I remember your whiskers that tickled when you'd touch
  my cheek,
  And the tenderness your voice had when you would speak.
Every time I see your chair,
  I always see you sitting there.
Oh, Grandad, I can never forget;
  The way my eyes ne'er did get wet.
I loved you so,
  I could never let you go.
And even though some think I never cared,
  I always wish that you were still there.
It's a little late for tears to come,
  But I check my cheek and there are some.
Oh Grandad, how can I let you know;
  How much I cared and loved you so?

      —Dawn Haywood

PAIN

Most terrible Lord of Man
  Singing through the Night,
Pleasures of sleep overwhelmed
Waking moments under siege,

Destroyer of lives
Liken a knife slicing through,
Sharp edges, dull throbs
Agony unfathomed,

Rages, swells and burns
Flaming reds to somber grays,
Flashing and glowing
Thinking and feeling gone awry,

When moments stretch toward eternity
Lose yourself in the Pain,
Drink of the vessel, and die of thirst
Untold burden, lifted free.

      —S. J. Hoff

GRANDPA

See the years upon his face,
  the wisdom in his eyes,

The smile that time cannot erase,
  the spirit that never dies.

For all the roads he has walked,
  The miles number many.

For all the conversations talked,
  forgetting not any.

He's brought with him the experience
  of life,

With time engraved across his looks,

Something not given . . . just liven,

His knowledge beyond the books.

What a blessing from Heaven and God
  Divine,

That shares with us this survivor
  of mankind.

      —J. LEE

JOURNEY'S END

Man appears to self though grand
  Flesh withers like grass on land.
Labors hard for fame he yearns
Soon but fades the name he earns.

From the time man breathes his last
Pride and beauty things of past.
Flesh he knows returns to dust,
Yet he spends his life in lust.

Trees have hope there is no doubt,
Break and cut them still they sprout,
Water's scent revives the roots
And the stem brings forth new shoots.

Man lies down but rises not,
Soul departs, then flesh is nought,
When it meets a pit or pyre
Gets consumed by sand or fire.

Common yard, in fact, does greet
His remains for last retreat.
If the flesh thus ends in ditch
Why then brag the proud and rich?

      —P. M. Verghese

THE OLD GRAY HOUSE

There was an old gray house, that sat
 on top of the hill.
It sat there so quietly, lonely and still.
The house was once filled with a lot of laughter
that was so loud it rang from the rafters.
The noise came from the couple and
children who lived inside.
And when it came time the couple
got old, and the children grew up, then
they pushed the old gray house aside.
Now the old gray house sets all alone;
until someone comes by, and calls it
their own.
But someday there might be another
couple who passes by, and they may
happen to look, and wander inside.
Maybe a couple will live there once
more, and then the old gray house
won't have to be lonely anymore.

—Linda Gordon

THE MOON

Mistress Moon,
 don't be shy and hide
behind your fickle sweetheart.
Come out,
and let the world below
bask in your lustrous glow.
Let your friend, the sailor,
steer his ship safely,
by your guiding splendor.
With your glittering light,
Cast a spell over the sleeping countryside.
Princess of the Dark,
present your gift of silver moonbeams
to the earth below,
so each creature of the night
may find its way.
Come out of hiding,
Queen of Night,
so all may see
your heavenly form.

—Wendy Nelson

I DON'T CARE

I don't care for you, you say
 Don't show my love in any way;
Don't buy you gold or lace or rings,
I remember giving you all those things.
Don't take you out at night to dine,
Can't ever seem to find the time,
Many times I recall us doing that;
And still you say that I don't care.
You must have forgotten all the morns
When I tramped through grass and weeds
And thorns all wet with dew, and
Picked wildflowers, just for you,
I gave you bouquets many times, and
'Twould have been simpler to visit that
Florist there
I guess I did that because I didn't care.
There are many ways of expressing love
And I wonder if it has ever occurred to you,
My way is not in things I say;
But in the little things I do,
For you.

—Floyd E. Byrd

MY JOURNEY

Once in my peopled world, I moved like a small brook
 with courage.
The sun shore warm on the current of my memories.
As I traveled further, the bright beginning faded.
I fought against the oncoming storm,
 smashing my troubled waters against rock-sides,
 jumping banks in a tide of fury,
 drowning everyone in my flood, leaving only
 debris.
After, like the deepest river, bitterly cold and silent,
 I felt the rain from a gray sky falling on me.
My heart lay still and dark along my river-floor.
But now I know that no other storm must grasp me,
 no rocks force me.
I continue to flow toward the infinite sea.
I will lead my journey alone,
and like a river,
I won't look back.

—Megan J. O'Connell

CALIFORNIA

California, the land of milk and honey
 where the blood is booze and the soul is money

A shiny land of glass and chrome
with purple-tinted grass on plastic loam

The land of a million questing queens
and funky freaks in faded blue jeans

Bleached-out kids running everywhere
with two mamas here and three daddys there

Where the glaring lights destroy the night
and fifty million cars scream out their might

And an old man dies in a dollar-a-day hotel
while ten thousand people wish Elizabeth Taylor well

California, the land of golden dreams
where nothing is impossible it seems

Where night and day they laugh and play
too busy to ever hear what lifes gotta say

—James R. Prince

DREAMS OF GREATNESS

A daisy, a sailboat, an inkblot, a poodle—
 At a loss for words, I find instead
Crawling across my page idle doodles
That betray no clue of the thoughts in my head.

My mind starts to wander, as often it will
And visions of greatness dance into my dreams
Emotions swirl to a crescendo until
Words flow from my pen in opulent streams.

I see my name carved in stone in the annals of Time
Boz to my left, Saki on my right
I hear Shakespeare applauding our kinship in rhyme
And Dickinson admiring my gifted insight.

I awake with a start and see looking down
Crumpled rejects lying cold round my feet
No longer a writer of timeless renown
Oh, that vision and reality one day could meet!

With a weary resolve I reach for my pen
From which ink will flow but words will not
And press it to paper once again
To form a daisy, a sailboat, a lovely inkblot.

—Karin Beuerlein

180

EARTHEN GREEN

The earthen green rises anew today
  With worn reproving promise in rebirth.
Gone are the remnants of old decay
Compounded back into relenting earth.
Through tight gnarled black limbs ancient winds
    thrust and spend
To find their way on plains where whispers
    stay.
The wind calls the day as it were to blend
As soft it blows and all work summons play.
There is a raw hint of deity that shows
Now in every glade where prairies deign the plow.
Wonders stay the wind, poke past lasting snows,
And set the ardent force that wills our now.
There metaphors no words or thoughts for long
That bridges real and reason, in this song.

—Robert Oakes Jordan

IF EYES COULD TALK

Playing on the shores
  Having some fun
When all of a sudden
I couldn't see the sun
My feet slipped away from me
Everything went grey
I knew in a moment
This was not supposed to be part of my day.

The water was cloudy
And not easy to see
But thank you dear God
For sending my Grandma to me.

With heaven soon to be mine
There was an anesthetist right by my side
In a boat we go headed for shore
Grandpa called for an ambulance
And it was there ready to roar.

In the hospital I stay day after day
With my parents beside me and the Lord
    there to guide me
I want everyone to know, "I am not letting go!"

—Lynne Marie Johnson

SPRINGTIME

When all the branches are proudly sprouting,
  Their green and tender leaves afore,
And winter says farewell in parting,
Then Spring will open every door.

The sunrays, they are shining brightly.
You can see the sunshine everywhere.
The birds are chirping songs so lively,
And everything looks so nice out there.

The buds are coming out in spring,
And out there everything turns green.
Everyone should enjoy this time in Spring,
When blooming flowers can be seen.

With children playing in many places.
There is a flower fragrance everywhere.
They sing their songs with smiling faces,
And are happy in this beautiful spring air.

You feel free and easy in your thinking,
And collect new courage for the year,
And thank the Lord for all this blessing,
For the most wonderful time of the year.

—Peter Kraemer

DREAMS

Close your eyes and dream of a day,
  With castles, fairies, and knights
faraway.

Where flowers and trees sway in
the wind,

And no one ever, tries to offend.

Close your eyes and dream,
Of elves, dragons, and queens.
Where peasants are happy and shout with glee,
Where everyone and everything are free.

Close your eyes and dream,
Of places and things that gleam.
Dreams are many, and never few,
And will always be with you.

—Rachel D. Erwin

EVOCATION

At the shore, with joy,
      I watch the seagulls' wingéd flight,
against the azure sky
      curving paths of flowing white,
with quality of grace that's magical,
      sheer delight.

So hauntingly beautiful,
      poetry in motion,
ballet dancers creating a mood or emotion—
their backdrop the tow'ring surf,
      their stage the wild ocean—
evocative of great nostalgia.
      I, too, would be a child,
caught in a game of half-remembered dreams,
      free to run and slide,

wing-borne,
      beautiful,
            joyously free.

—Dorothy A. Hamann

MY PRECIOUS "SNOWFLAKE"

The snow is beautifully falling on the frozen,
  sleeping land,

    An assuring sign that the pain of winter—
    like the ache within my heart—is now at hand.

But look! Jewel-shaped flakes are dancing and
skipping through the crisp air,

    Frolicking on the earth, imitating a once
    living, loving, canine "Snowflake" so rare.

Oh, yes! Happily will I welcome the arrival of
each snowy day, and have no fear,

    For every time a gentle, diamond-crystal
    rushes to lap my face and rests so near,

Gratefully will I smile and, with joy, recall
as a sweet embrace,

    The loving presence of a pet who often
    washed my tearful face;

An endearing animal-friend, of color pure as
snow, who once calmed my every fear,

    And now, ever remains my precious,
    well-beloved "Snowflake" so dear!

—Anna L.E. Gonzales

SON-IN-LAW

You bore the legal title "Son-in-Law,"
    but my heart called you — "my son,"
I miss your smile and joking way
    you had of teasing me,
I'm glad I said, "I love you"
    although you seemed so shy,
I was proud of your achievements
    you made while here with us,
But, my Son, there was one
    you never knew about,
Henry, you made us all so proud
    especially me — your "Mother-in-Law,"
For the medal they presented
    was presented for "my son,"
There will be no more birthdays
    for you have gone on home,
Yet memories will remain
    until we meet again.
        —Dorothy Ann Bilton

THE LIE

We went out berry-picking
    In the vacant lot next door.
The flies and mosquitoes had already
    found
A place to rest in the not-so-early morning
As the buzzing of a chain saw flew
    around our ears.
Reaching for a blue cluster high up,
My daughter asks, "What's white on them?"
Smoke from the coke plant in the
    valley rose up
And blew our way like a wind sock
Over the berries,
Over the trees that held their fruit tightly,
Over the joys and chick-a-dees and bats
With their Peter Pan attitudes.
I said, "I don't know,
But I'm sure they're OK."
Someday I hope she'll believe that.
        —Carol Adams

MELANCHOLY MOTHERS

Silver chimes and golden rhymes
    The daylight rings, the morning climbs
Voices sing in high pitched notes
While their children play with plastic boats.

The breeze sways high
The clouds drift by
The sea churns and the waves rush in
Another day of wonder is about to begin.

Lovely ladies basking in the sun
Daydreaming of days still more pleasant
    when life was full of fun
Like their young children, carefree as can be
Free as the wind and restless as the sea.

Out of the blue the heavens turn to gray
Now the raindrops come out to play
Young children raise their eyes in wonder
To the sound of morning thunder.

Golden notes and rusty chimes
Dreams can change with the times
Now you are what you always wanted to be
And all you desperately desire is to be free!
        —Kevin J. Cronin

SOLITUDE

Solitude stands by the window,
    Staring into the cold, winter night
Her cloak of darkness surrounding her,
Never letting through the light.
The rain slides down the window,
Like streaming tears
The moon illuminates her somber frown
Showing her unspoken fears.
Sadness glistens in her eyes
Her heart yearns for someone to take away the pain,
But still she stares through the window,
Her expression always stays the same.
        —Amanda Terry Moore

THE FORFEITURE

Now close your eyes
    and journey to
the land of instant smiles;
where circumstance allows forgiveness
and soothes the searing heart.
erase the tattered dreams,
then throat parched from
the little lies will bleed
till pressure's done.
one step, and then
another.
up and over;
obstacles jointly braved
and conquered.
yet, in this leaving,
each step is four,
and soon the distance
is much too far for memory
to remain.
adieu.
        —Stephen K. Wallenmeyer

RETURNING HOME—CHEYENNE AUTUMN

(A tribute to Mari Sandoz' book, Cheyenne Autumn, which tells the story of the Cheyennes' attempt to flee the hunger and sickness of their imprisonment in Oklahoma.)

the ghost of the night drums
in the warriors' minds, like
chants of the ancient Sweet Medicine
foretelling the little ones' cries.

the lone wolf is chasing the smell of the bawling calf.
winds blow the trills from the sacred flute.

the hollow tone falls deftly
on worn, rising dust.
red blood flows from
slaughtered cattle.
the sweet smell taunts the sacred arrows.

the hungry Indian children will be quieted.
clouds spread like the tails of flying horses.

Beaver lies dead, unavenged,
grey-coated soldiers beat
their fine steeds' hooves
on arrowheads driven deep
into scars with blood
long since dried and cracked.

the women cut their thighs and wrists.
blood flows thin as sinew, binding the Cheyenne.

Run now, harder than ever, blood is on The People.
        —Gail Henik

A CHRISTMAS REMEMBRANCE

It was the night of Christmas as we all gathered around
the table, in joyous celebration of that event which happen-
ed so long age in a stable. As we clasped our hands together
and bowed our heads to pray, I gave thanks, and recalled
precious memories of by-gone days. Going back one year, who
would have thought that in a short time we'd lose two ones
very dear. I can see my grandma cooking in the kitchen now —
three kettles on the wood stove and the oven filled with home-
made cookies and bread. Cooking was really one of grandma's
gifts, for she fixed and fussed, for times were many when we
ate in shifts. Yet, when all were finished and done, there was
still plenty of food in case another would come. We loved her
dear, and thinking of her now brings a tear. For grandma pass-
ed away on an early March morn leaving all of our hearts torn.
Grandpa seemed to take it well, and likewise precious memories
of him I can tell. I hold them both very close in my heart,
and with their precious memories I'll never part. And as we
bow our heads to pray, we will all be with you again some day.

—Deb Donat

IN FIELDS OF GREENERY

A step or two ahead of us our father's arms await us,
ever watching, for he knows what lies ahead.
He blesses us with roots — roots that know no bounds:
parents to nurture us,
grandparents to spoil us.
We play and laugh in fields of sunshine and greenery;
in pure meadows we plant our seeds, harvesting crops.
Fall blows in with thoughts of days spent doing fonder things.
Winter hits with fury as the master's blueprints are laid.
We grow from childhood to adulthood apprehensively, yet
knowing this is our path.
Sadness fills our hearts as heaven's door opens,
forcing us to say goodbye to you.
Then we will walk hand-in-hand with God
until that precious day
we can play in fields of greenery again.

—Rose Faux Fowler

GOD IN EVERYTHING

I sat down beside the pond
When my work was done
Like a thousand diamonds
It sparkled in the sun
And as I beheld its beauty
I saw God in every one.

I looked up into the sky
So clean and so blue
Covering the vast wide world
Clouds were but a few
And in the beauty of this sight
I saw God there, too.

I looked across the open field
To the budding trees
With their lovely branches
Swaying in the breeze
And as I beheld their beauty
I saw God in these.

I silently sat listening
To the songbirds sing
And the many other sounds
That tell us that it's spring
And O, how marvelous to hear
God in everything.

—Jeanetta DeBoef

There is a simple beauty,
that I wish to obtain.
It can't be bought for money,
for it is not that tame.
Shall I ever be so pure of heart,
for this I would be fain.

It is an inner beauty,
that shines forth from the soul.
While living God's will daily,
thou shall never be a troll.
And finding peace within thyself,
while living on this knoll.

—Mrs. Jil Muller

SINCE THE LORD JESUS CAME

Once when I began to smile
It all was kind of strange
for I felt my whole mind and
soul
go through a spiritual change.

My body was light, careful and
free.
My mind calm and controlled
I didn't understand — this was
not me
But the Lord had come and
patrolled.

He whispered, "child, you are
mine
Please let me come in
For you are one of those
special kind
I want without any sin."

I sat and cried, happy as
could be
that this unexplainable thing
was happening to me.
Someone wanted to be my friend
to actually stop and let me
come in.

I can't quite tell you, my
friend
how now I'm not the same
For I now feel an inner
peace
Since the Lord Jesus came

—Tracy Elaine Jefferson

GOD'S CREATIVE HAND

God has helped me through
and through,
Sweet and fresh like the
morning dew.
He guides me like a pure
white dove,
When I'm down and cannot
feel love.
He helps me through my
prayers,
And keeps me in His
care.
God's love is like a
supporting hand,
Giving me the strength
to stand.

—Jennifer J. Hartman, age 11

FATHER

I awoke at the break of dawn,
to bring your morning paper and coffee.
That was our last,
as father and daughter.
What I found was you lying there,
with no life left in you.
You have left me, no more pain for you,
my pain has just begun from the loss of you.
You were still so young,
and so much ahead of you.
I never got a chance,
to make you proud of your little girl.
I will follow in your footsteps,
and keep your name alive.
You made yourself a legend,
in my eyes.
As the greatest,
understanding person, teacher, and most of all my father.

—Brenda Kathrine Greer

Rush, rush, rush, do this, do that,
Can't find my homework, where is my hat?
Here comes the schoolbus, run, run, run.
Thank goodness he made it, my day has begun.

There are beds to be made, dishes to do,
Clothes to be washed, ironing, too!
Christmas is near, there are cookies to bake,
How about dinner? Stew, hash or steak?

Answer the phone, or was that the door?
Cupcakes for the P.T.A., twenty-four or more.
How about Christmas cards, did I forget the Roes?
Oh, dear, here comes the schoolbus,
The day is near it's close.

Now it's time for Father, his day's work is done.
It's tough to be a man, he says,
Man works from sun to sun.
Women sure have it easy, nothing to do all day,
But watch T.V. and kaffeeklatsch and attend the P.T.A.

—Maybelle Hollocker

MOTHER'S DAY

Mothers are soft and clean and pure
They are the one thing of which you can be sure
There to love and give advice
To bake a cake and add some spice

To soothe a burn or add a patch
Upon the smallest little scratch
To talk to when you are scared
And for your life she'll get you prepared

Mothers are honest and true forever
They are also smart and very clever
She'll hold you tight as she can all day
And remember all the nice things to say

So today when she smiles that trusty smile
Why not stop and linger awhile
Tell her Happy Mother's Day
And thank her for all the prayers she will say

I love you mother, so very much
I love your smile and your gentle touch
So when I talk to God tonite
I'll ask Him to keep my mother alright
I love you, my mother.

—Robert D. Barber

MY MOTHER

I could search this world over
A thousand times, it's true,
And never find a mother
Who'd measure up to you.

You bring a lot of sunshine
To a world that's filled with rain.
You bring relief and comfort
To every heart that's filled with pain.

God said "Love thy neighbor as thyself,"
And this you surely do.
And I know there is a special place
In the heart of God for you.

All the things that Love is
Is what you are, you see.
And I'm so thankful, mother,
That God gave you to me.

—Janette Gruver

MY JEWELS

Life has given me jewels
More precious than a sapphire or pearl,
They are my boys and my girl . . .

As I have gathered my jewels
And watched them sparkle and glow,
It has brought me such great happiness
As only a Mother could know . . .

I have jealously guarded my jewels
Have called them my own through the years,
And I'll always have the memories
Of their baby laughter and tears . . .

Other settings will hold my jewels
And other hands will help and guide,
But I have had the happiness
Of walking by their side . . .

I have loved and guided them
And no matter where they roam,
They will never forget the setting,
Of their Mother, of love, and home.

—Christina Miller

A MOTHER'S LOVE

Son, I love you dearly,
you have been
the rainbow of my life

The years slip by,
like vapors toward the sky . . .

I thank God for trusting me,
to guide you through
life's rocky roads

Remember no matter where
you may roam,
you will never be alone

With a Mother's arms wide open,
to greet you back home . . .

There is nothing so awful
that together our prayers
and hearts can't mend

There is always something so very special,
a Mother's love for her Son,
that will never end.

—Bonnie Duke

BELOVED

I know not where I stand on earth;
I know not why I came henceforth—
I came from far to claim my berth,
Was I hear before or after birth?

The realms of time that span the earth
Contain the answers, to quench my thirst—
The realm I'm in has beckoned me
To live this span as part of eternity—

In this vast space rotates a world
of human love in hearts of gold—
I thank the one who sent me here,
To live and feel in a human mold—

This earth of his goes beyond our minds
a perfect orb — a perfect time—
I give him praise, I give him love,
    In his pure heart we are
        all from above.

    —Mildred Michel

CONFUSION

You play tug-of-war with your emotions
    and the feelings build up deep inside.
You try to think of something else but
    there is no place to hide.
Your mind becomes twisted with the
    thoughts of right and wrong.
Your body tense has given up but
    you know you must go on.
Confusion takes over and you feel
    that you can only cry.
An unanswered question is all you
    ask, the reasons for "why."
Pain and misery, hand and hand,
    break your fragile heart.
Pressure and worry, side by side,
    tear the beat apart.
Can you win, can you survive,
    a chance you'll have to take.
But in the end, what you decide,
    lies in the hand of fate.

    —Phyllis Norman

MAKING IT TILL TOMORROW

We were very hungry and very cold as
    we struggled down the street
    And we walked so slowly 'cause for
several days we couldn't find food to eat.
    A can of soup, a slice of bread,
mostly spoiled fruits or molded cheese
    Not nearly enough, but for days we
ate only such as these.
    We haven't had much food to
eat — barely a shelter over our heads
    But we've done a lot better than
some we've known; we're hungry but
we're not dead.
    The sun is sinking far in the
west and we need some place to sleep
    So we'll try this old car with the
broken door to rest our body and tired feet
    Maybe tomorrow will be warmer, and
maybe a little more to eat.
    But makin it 'till tomorrow will
be one remarkable feat.

    —Willie Stine Gonzalez

Standing by the towering pillar I think
    how small we are
Like being up in an airplane over a city
I've lived in all my life and not being
able to see my own neighborhood . . . anything
    that is familiar . . .
or looking up at the stars
on a night when there are no clouds
and thinking . . .
some of that starlight has been traveling
for hundreds of years
and I've only lived for sixteen.

    —Mamatha Kamath

Elusive image in absent may past,
    Sweet time when I first held thee — and the last —
Before me. You were fair and lovely then,
One who I will never gaze at again!
I miss your arms immeasurable sweep
And the quiet, unfathomable deep
Of your alluring, grey eyes that held sway
Over my path . . . but the turning away
Is surging across me, holding fast
All joy of memory desired to last.
I wondered, in a moment of frailty,
If ever you longingly remember me.

    —Renae Kelley

LIKE ONE

I used to feel so close to you — like one,
But now I'm beginning to wonder — like one.
I still think of you as my lover — like one.
    Please, I ask of you — like one,
Don't leave me — like one!
    You're like one of the keys to my heart — like one.
I don't mean to be mean, but I'm beginning to die —
    like a rose.

This little rose is now laid down waiting for your last word.
    But before I go, I just thought you should know,
I love you very much. If it weren't for you, I don't think
    I could have lasted. Thanks for all the fun, the talks,
and everything. I'll never forget you. I'll always have
    a part of you in me, always!

This is my last farewell — like one.
    Now I'm just like I used to be — JUST ONE!!!!!!
    —Precious Alls

THE WONDER OF YOU

I watched him at the dance last night
    As he conjured up drive, to blend with their plight.
Mostly in wheelchairs, he felt their pain.
They've lost so much, What could they gain?

Suddenly, he began to flourish, and extended his hand.
As he spun her chair closer, she was in awe of his plan!
He charmed her being, as he made her chair dance!
She felt valued and worthy!
With her evening enhanced!
As evident as it was, that some grief was masked:
His enjoyment was strained, as his eyes still asked:
"Confined to pain and wheelchairs, in bodies so lame;
What difference could 'I' make? What could they gain?"
My eyes responded, from across the floor:
"They're gaining the "wonder of you" . . . .
As you give more and more!"

    Dedicated to James Cardinal
    —Nancy Falzone

SILENT CRIES

How great the span that reaches out,
far away and out of sight
   into nothingness.

You cry out and the echo that is suppose to ring
   is lost somewhere in this great space.
You feel there's nothing there,
   just the quiet and the air.

Far off . . the cry of a bird
   he calls to you
and nothing's heard.

A ray of sun is warm and real
   why oh why then can't I feel,
the glow of all
   the bird . . its call.

—Shirley Lamphere Rachiski

UNKNOWN

You wake up in the morning,
   You look at your face,
You're staring real hard,
But you don't see the trace,
The burns from the fire,
The cuts of a knife,
Allowing other people to control your life.

Do you think you have a say in the routine?
You go by day by day.
How much do you really control?
When is the pressure gonna take its toll?

When you talk does no one hear you?
Moving up but you don't appear to.
Do you know what it's like to be unknown?

You always seem to lose, no matter what you try,
You barely make enough money to get by.
With a dead end job, it ain't for you,
You're so far gone you don't know what to do.

It's time to break free, time to move on.
You gotta take the time, before the time is gone.
Break the chains that have kept you tied,
Your life's worth nothing till you're satisfied.

—Jeffrey Lamar Yancy

LIFE

As the century comes
   To its last decade
It's time to take a look
At things that we have made

From birth we hardly knew
What it was we had to do
We crawled and we walked
We also learned to talk

Adolescence brought out the best
Rebellious nature never the less
A touch of discipline was what was needed
Where oh where were the words to be heeded

Young adulthood came at last
From trekking jungles to student unrest
We came, we saw, we conquered all
Met the challenge and defied them all

Now as our days come to a close
We sit and ponder without regret
For after all we did our best
We love and die for eternal rest.

—Alfred G. Araiza

LET ME RUN

Let me run, 'til the day I die.
   Let me jog 'neath the open sky,
In quiet, green fields with the heavens above.
This is the life that a man can love.
Let me feel the wind so free,
And breathe the air that was meant for me.
With forest beyond, and meadows before,
I'll run and run, 'til I run no more.
Mockers fuss, and black birds call;
I love each one, and I love them all.
Dandelion and clover too
Dance in the breeze, as I pass through.
They accept me now as nature's friend,
But I know someday it will have to end.
Someday beneath the ground I'll lie,
But I love the sun, the wind, the sky,
So let me run 'til the day I die.

—Fred Thompson

SHILOH

A mother's two sons marched off to war,
   one Dreary Winter Day. One proudly wore
his coat of blue the other his of grey.

At Shiloh they would meet again, and
each would be the foe, and each would
take his brother's life, though neither one
would know.
   One's grave stands neatly in a Row,
marked with white marble Stone.
   The other's in a common trench
where all grey coats were thrown.

   Now once again the peach trees Bloom,
the trees are all in Bud. And
Bloody pond is clear at last, not
stained by Brother Blood.

   The Bell of Shiloh Church is heard,
Its notes ring loud and clear.
And on the green spring grass there falls,
A lonely mother's tear.

—Roy J. Vines

STOPPING TO REST

I stop to drink,
   parched are my lips,
soon the blood of my own will quench them.

My rifle uncleansed,
for the bullets it holds,
has pierced the hearts of many.

The smell of death is in the air,
bodies without movement surround me.

Wounded are my friends.
Warped are our minds.

Happy thoughts never occur,
memories of my other life have faded.

No longer do I consider myself human.
Just another animal,
seeking to kill.

My obligation is to paint the earth red.

There is no time of day in this world I'm in,
it's just a never ending day of destruction.

Continue into the battle I must,
for my moment of rest is over.

—Michele Hall

OUR LITTLE ANGEL

Sandy; you weren't with us very long.
You never got to call me "Papa,"
like Chris, David, Lucas, Josh and Mike.
But you touched our hearts, Grandma's
and mine, and we will remember
you forever!
When you were found there by your Mom,
in a sleep from which you never awoke.
The feeling of helplessness we had was
just, just terrible.
But the night was made a little brighter
by a new little star, and Heaven opened
its doors for a new little angel, Our
little angel.
We miss you, Sandy, and we love
you and we will never forget you!

This poem was written for our little granddaughter who
died of crib death, 3 months after the death of her father,
from an auto accident.
She was 2 months old at the time of her death.

—Norman Suydam

DUSTY SHELVES

A cluster of dolls and warm memories
of them too
Sitting ever so nicely and neatly
in view
These are my dearest friends of
so long ago
Dusty filled shelves that are
hardly visited today
You sit there so pretty even though
I no longer long to play
but cluster of dollies another year
passes on
I very seldom come to see you anymore
but I'll never break our special bond
I'll still pass my dusty shelves
of dolls once in a while
Remembering sweet loving imagination
of a loving mommie and her
pretend baby child

Dedicated to my sister,
Bernadette Csik Bush
—Barbara Ann Csik Stadvec

MY BUDDY

My Buddy, my dog, my pal,
He is always by my side.
If my day is going well,
Or my patience being tried!

Makes no difference who's around
Or where in this great land we're at,
All it takes to keep him happy
Are a few loving pats.

He likes to go for walks,
And he likes to go for rides,
But most of all the "frisbee,"
Is the "apple" of his eyes.

He jumps and barks and persistantly waits
And will stand, and stand, and stand,
Because he really loves to play,
When he sees the frisbee in your hand.

My Buddy, my dog, my pal,
I hope he will always be there.
Because when things aren't going well,
I always know, "He" cares.

—Carmen Matter

FEELINGS

I gave you the pictures in the path of my own weakness,
only to find I wept your life away.

In the awakeness of my mirrors, I found myself
reflecting your reflections;

So nice it is to say, "I am still a man"
and proud of it!

—DMK

THE OTHER YEARS

I have known the joy of a trusting little blue eyed girl.
In her heart she seems to love the whole world.
I take her hand in mine and we explore.
Things she sees, I've never seen before.
I love what I see in the eyes of a trusting child.
Cares of the day are forgotten for awhile.
The rain and pretty leaves that fall to the ground.
In her world, beauty is everywhere to be found.
With my hand in hers, the sunset we saw.
And I, in my heart, love being that special Grandma.

—Lou Simpson

LISTEN TO THE CHILDREN

We've got to listen to our children,
and heed what they got to say.
We've got to listen to our children,
each and every day—They need our love.
We've got to listen to our children,
so they'll never have to stray—in search of Love.
We have to care about the children—
no matter who they are.
As long as we care for our children,
they can reach their shining star—They need our Love—
This world has a future—
And it's up to you and me,
So let's all stick together—
And they'll have it all to see.
Show them Love and inspiration—
In everything they do.
With a little kind persuasion—
We'll see their dreams come true.

—Adolfo Bernald Vera "Lobo"

TO MY MOTHER
If I Only Would Have Known

If I only would have known . . .

how much my parents really did know, I would have
listened to them more often.

how soon I was going to hurt, I would have been
more compassionate when I saw others hurting.

how truly serious life is, I would have watched
more closely the steps that I took.

how fast children do grow up, I would have grasped
more memorable times with them.

how special my family means to me, I would
have recognized their place as a purpose in my life.

how close a Mother feels to her daughter, I would
have spent more time with you.

how wonderful it is to be hugged and to hear "I
love you" and "I'm sorry," I would have said
them more.

Love,
Your Daughter
—Lisa M. Ahlswede

IMAGES

Whisper of the leaves — singing of bird friends,
Morning music, amid crisp air it sends.
This early rise, to a Smoky Mountain dew,
Radiates spirit, in God's breathless view.
To mirror in deep sigh,
Thereupon ascending, to a natural high.

—Gloria M. Kovalik

UNFORGETTABLES

I hear a low rumble and
        can't forget,
Christ bearing his cross up Calvary.
I see the sky lightning-streaked and
        can't forget,
The multitude at Golgatha.
I hear the storm's increases and
        can't forget,
The ring of nails being driven.
I see a bolt of lightning split the sky and
        can't forget,
A cross lifted, dropped into the hole.
I'm spellbound by a spring thunderstorm's Passion Play and
        can't forget,
Christ's agonizing death for me.

—Anita Neuhauser

EMPTY UNTIL WHEN

If possibility ever became reality,
   one would think of oneself as
   being completely full.
But if the reality is there, then the possibility is gone.

You were my possibility for fullness in this life.
It was as though I had some sort of loyalty
to the possibility of having you, holding you, loving you
   for more than a day or an hour.

Remaining loyal to these thoughts brought hope that they
   would soon become reality.
Only then, would my entire being be fulfilled.

Now you are gone.
Never will I know that if the reality of you were here,
Would I still yearn for yet another possibility.

My soul remains empty until when.

—Theresa Elaine Ailey

GOD FOR US

God had a million little paintbrushes;
   God had a trillion minutes to paint the
Beautiful trees and grass and flowers.
But He didn't need so long
To brush the gorgeous colors on and spray perfume.
He loosed a billion, billion raindrops to freshen
The rivers, trees, and flowers and all His other plants.
God lighted a million, million comets and planets,
The sun and stars and all the many moons.
He formed oceans and rivers rushing to the seas
Making homes for billions of fishes, crabs and turtles.
God dressed many, many birds in spectacular colors.
God raised great mountains for us to climb.
We see God's handiwork everywhere.
He uses His lightning-fast fingers for us.
Do we praise Him and thank Him everyday?
Best of all He gives us His undying love
And hope of eternity.

—Ruth Rector Farrar

GOD IS IN CHARGE

If in times of sickness or sorrow
   There seems to be no hope at all,
We can always look to tomorrow
And know . . . God is in charge.

When financial worries come our way,
Where's the money coming from?
We can look forward to a better day . . .
With God in charge.

From babes to teens in such a short span,
We may often wonder what to do
To best help this young girl or man?
Teach them — God is in charge.

—Dennie Vogler Essic

THE DROUTH

The heat shimmers fields and roads
   It's a bad year for crops and people
Daily we have a clear sky
We wonder why,
Clouds of rain don't come

Yet there is a hope for tomorrow
That the skies will drop us much
needed rain.
New hope, New days, more lasting showers
God's plan for us is often not ours

—Nelda Zeller

THE GATEWAY

The Gateway to heaven
   is shown by love.
The staircase to heaven
   goes far up above.
The Master that awaits,
   is at the gate.
The angels you see
   are there for you and me.
The Sinners all forgiven
   by the streams of flowing blood.
The path that is so led
   goes toward peace and serenity of deeds.
The Lord will be there, just wait and see.
   The gates are wide open, without a key.
The only thing he asks, is to Believeth
unto Me.

—Ethel J. Morsey

THE MAN OF GOD

Who is there when wedding vows,
   Are said to two in love?
Who is there when Children arrive,
Their lives to be blessed from above?

Who is there when problems arise,
And things seem all wrong?
Who is there when Christian life calls,
To baptize, and read the covenant song?

And who is there when sickness comes,
To comfort and call the Master Physician?
Who is there when death bells toll,
To remind us of the Lord's position?

Who is there? — The Man of God,
He's around whenever you call,
So today we pause to say our thanks,
To him, his family and all.

—Otis C. Polk, Jr.

ROADTRIP

You lead me down a road paved
with your friendship.
A road that comforts me and
gives me support when things
go wrong.
A road that is not filled with
the danger of desertion
but by the joy of
everlasting companionship.
A road that is accessible by all
paths: reachable to all the
ends of this earth and beyond.
A road in which I wish to
travel with you always.

—Angela DeMario

ENCASED

I've built a shell around me
To help keep people out
It protects me
From feeling
Which can be good
For I feel no pain
But it is also very bad
For I don't feel.
I miss life.
It's like a glass egg
And I'm the chicken
Trying to get out.
Usually this shell is gone
But sometimes unexpectedly
It goes up around me.
I want to take a hammer
And smash this glass shell
I'm ready to feel
To accept the love and pain
So help me shatter my glass shell
And I'll help you shatter yours.

—Kathleen McDaniel, age 19

PEN PALS

Years of writing
across the seas,
have sistered our souls
a bond with no key

The stories, the singers,
of those times have long past,
but the dreams and the wishes
survived in stone cast

Our thoughts of our futures
we've shared back and forth,
I've prayed to your angel
He knows of your worth

The likes of your soul
there has never been better,
I knew I've been blessed
from your very first letter

The years, they've gone by
but the letters are still there,
from the distant pen pals
the ones that still care

I love you, my pen pal
you know that I care,
of our friendship that's distant
but a friendship that's there.

—C.E. Januszkiewicz

MY DESTINY

In the mist of dreamland, we held hands,
And talked of our lives since we last saw each other.
The good times, the bad times, and we looked into
Each other's eyes and without a spoken word, we asked
What happened to us?
Then, I awoke and looked at the man beside me and it wasn't you.
And at that moment I understood. My destiny was this man here
with me now. You were a moment in time, a helper, along the way
To my destiny.

—Anita L. Safford

THE TREATMENT

Cross the chasms of life's despair with the chains of mortal love
Bind the wounds of discontent with rays from the sun above

Treat those hurting memories with a cheerful note of hope
And help a friendless passerby with a hand so he can cope

II

We each must bear our burdens, we each must carry our load
But life can be much better with a friend along the road

Sometimes the cost is heavy, sometimes we feel the strain
But there's always a new tomorrow when the sun replaces the rain

III

For no one is really an island, no one can stand alone
We all need a friend or helper even though we stand on our own

So when your pain is the greatest, reach out and help another
The cure is love and friendship, a medicine like no other

IV

The keys to each day's happiness are kindness, help and love
The things we share with others flow back from up above

So rise and face the sunrise, confident in each day
The key to a great tomorrow is in sharing your love today

—Stanley N. Searles, Sr.

A MILLION MILES FROM HOME

I look over these wicked trees, gazing into the haze of a
setting sun.

Standing on this distant hill I look back at the war
warped castle from which my journeys begun.

I searched for the unknown, for an eternity it did seem.

Finding untold treasures that are only revealed in distant
dreams.

My thoughts though they are tired, look back at the mystery
only my eyes have seen.

But we all share the beauty and sorcery that show the good,
kind, wicked, and mean.

Now as the fog lifts off my mind, I see into my weary past.

Of the shady but clearly seen travels I journeyed from,
my start to the last.

Death seems as good to what my restless soul has been through.

For I have felt the horrid wind, forever the dry breeze blew.

Now my spirit feels the calm breeze flowing through the
valley of my soul.

I now feel the warmth of the light, it makes me warm, it makes
me whole.

My journeys were far and wide not only on this land, but
deep inside myself.

—Thomas Snyder, age 17

LET ME LIVE

I want to live to watch the glow of a Sunset,
as it appears in the late afternoon.
   I want to live to see the moon,
I wouldn't be a burden to you soon.
   I am just a tiny seed,
depending on you for my needs.
   You believe you can't afford me,
so you want to abort me.
   If you could hear me,
you would know, that I too want a chance to grow.
   I want to live to see the stars,
to climb the bars in the park.
   I want to live to see night and day,
to run about and play.
   I want to live to see land and sea,
and to make you proud of me.
   My eyes are sore with scalding tears,
Let me live will you, please?!
   God will satisfy our needs.

     —Yinka Sabree

MY FRIEND

Open my eyes that I may see
a more complete image of thee.
The one I hope in day or night
to lead me through this dreary plight.
Just to have you at my side
makes all my doubts and fears subside.
I want no other one but thee
to stay so close right next to me.
I cannot think of anyone who,
has loved me more than perfect you.
Imperfect from the start you see
you came into my life to set me free.
   Free from all my doubts and fears,
free from pain of mounting years;
Free from guilt, hurt, and despair,
Free from all with your loving care;
I love you more than words can say
and hope within me you'll always stay.
   There could never be anyone else who could suffice
but you, my loving, Jesus Christ.

     —Donna L. (Guire) Reed

YOUR CHOICE

Here you stand, in the midst of the currents
shall you watch, or be watched?
     The power of the mind at your grasp
the horizons and endless space in focus

Only for awhile shall you remain in tune
     for the moment you hesitate, all is lost
so while the mind lay ready, you will arise

And what do you say to the mind
     when it yearns to be more than just a thought
and when it nags you to open it and travel?

As the grass grows through the cement
     against all odds, you have overcome the waves
in the breaking forth of dawn lives an example
     as it sheds light upon the darkness, consistently

You have the light of life within thy abode
     shall you prefer the darkness of night?
As it too holds a key and a gift

But you be not a servant of two
     for one master is loved and the other despised
and what good is the light without the darkness?

     —David King

HIS WORD

Once I stood by the side of a loved one
And my heart was oh so alone.
Then I felt the hand of my Savior,
Who gave me peace and a song.

Now I sing of joy and His promise
That His Word is life and peace.
He lifts every burden from us
If we will but only trust.

Yes, He gives us this assurance
That His Word heals our broken hearts;
Makes our bodies well and fills us
With hope all the days of our lives.

He's my hope, my peace, and promise;
He'll protect me from all harm;
So, I'll trust Him through each trial,
Resting safely in His arms.

     —Alene Bullard

I lived a life of lust and greed.
My Savior's love I did not need.
While in my heart my soul did plead,
for His saving grace to change my creed.

Holy Jesus set me free.
Holy Jesus hear my plea.
Holy Spirit my guide be.
You're all I have take care of me.

At last my sin convicted me.
Its burden drove me to my knees.
I felt the breaking of my heart,
that's how my christian life did start.

Now I'm tired of living in this world.
where satan's poison darts are hurled.
It breaks my heart so when I sin,
knowing how I've let Him down again.

And when one day my rest shall come.
I'll stand before the judging one.
He'll ask me how that I have come,
I'll tell Him through His loving Son.

     —Don W. Gauer

ESSENTIAL TRANSFORMATION

Faith in Goodness is Omnipresent Wisdom
activated by Inner Conscience —
to create equilibrium

Attachment and vanity brings confusion
of unbalanced passions and desires —
weeds from fields of darkness
promoting destructions and sadness

When Mind and Spirit in daily Communion
are united — Wonders always happen —
Everyone can change themselves
thru this Supreme Power
from lower frequency of materialism

Blessed ones with Trust of Eternity
they are not afraid of anything
raised in Higher Consciousness —
over evil-producing vibrations
which practice disharmony and disasters

Happiness is in a Spiritual Atoms
Energy of Love in Action —
Essential Transformation

     —Victor Tajan

RUNAWAY

You travel all over the country,
You travel from near and far,
You call and sometimes write, to say
you're fine just where you are.

From East to West and North to South,
no matter where you roam;
You'll never find it anywhere else,

It's a place in your heart called
Home.

—Peggy Harr

A MOMENT IN TIME

For one fleeting moment
I saw it in your eyes;
It was so sudden, so unexpected,
it gave me a surprise.

I thought that I could see
the heavens in your eyes;
As they each reflect the golden light
of the sullen, moonlit skies.

For we must share if we should keep
that blessing from above;
For ceasing to give, we cease to have,
such are the laws of love.

—Mark Harrison

TOMORROW

Today we see the star filled sky
and trees, above which birds will fly
and flowers that sprout from the ground
and creatures that run all around
today we feel the heat of the sun
and dance and sing and have lots of fun
but tomorrow will come
sad is it may be
rockets in the air is all we will see
then the skies will be dark
and all will be lost
unless people love people
at any cost.

—Kristina Erickson

MYTHICAL

I can breathe fire and travel space
I am a rebel without a cause
Enduring pain to run the race
I am a tiger without claws.
And when I reach to touch the stars
I am the Jupiter and the Mars
I can replace the love you lost
Give you back your lust for life
In early spring, I am the frost
That comes with darkness of the night.
I will protect you from the storm
Feet on the ground and standing tall
I'll make you glad you were born
And pull you back if you should fall.

This is the strength of make-believe
To bring you back to reality
To live the life that you conceive
Give you confidence, set you free
This is the end of your respite
Come walk within the light.

—Bonnie Navicki

IN MEMORY OF: RODNEY ALLEN STITT

The road we chose has lost its way
it all the sudden changed one day
They say all good things must come to an end
I should just be glad we had some time to spend
All these lonesome memories I cannot bear
spring turned into the summer we never would share
Now when twilight dims the sky above
I can't help recalling the thrills of our love
And when I remember all the days gone by
a flood of tears fall from my eyes
We had such happiness when we were together
I still can't believe that it's now gone forever
Time carries on, I guess it always will,
but deep in my heart, time will forever stand still.

—Jamey S. Dykes

ALONE OUT HERE

I need to reach out, to feel, to touch
Someone who understands.
Who'll realize the pride, yet the pressure I undergo.
For we're alone out here.

In this world, conflicts rule.
Tension caps our Earth.
Will one find peace, as the next battle continues?
I can't foresee 'cause all I know is,
We're alone out here.

With all the madness, murders, and crime,
Is happiness a word that exists?

You see the news, you read the paper,
Is it all you can do to sit and be a spectator?
Make a stand! Speak out! Don't let our world crumble!
Will anyone do as I say?

I can't foresee 'cause all I know is,
We're alone out here.

—Megan Diane Mills

QUIET MOMENTS

The clock chimes two a.m. as I quietly sit in the dark
In the distance, crickets chirp and dogs bark

Watching as my child slowly breathes in and out
Eyelids fluttering and lips forming a pout

Thinking of what you might be when you grow so tall
A painter, a musician, or a doctor always on call

Wondering, too, if I can ever really let you go
Yet, knowing that only then will my love for you show

Wishing I could always hold you and calm your fears
Kiss away your hurts and dry your tears

Loving you so much that it hurts inside
Growing stronger each day as I watch you with pride

Then as if you know I am near
You begin to stir and my name I hear

Those piercing eyes look through the dark at me
And the magic of love is so easy to see

Holding you tightly to my breast
I thank God that through you I have
been blessed

An angel in the form of a child
Giving meaning to life in that toothless smile

Nestling close, you slowly drift back to sleep
And inside my heart I know this moment forever I will keep

—Geri C. Smith
Dedicated to my five beautiful children: Steve, Jason, Clare, Parker and Peyton

FOREVER HAS AN END

The words we whispered quietly on a moonlit night,
The promise that we lived by, which seemed so very right,

Everything has been displaced, the love has been upset,
And yet there's a painful yearning, it seems I can't forget,

The plans we made are all erased, no more dreams of us together,
And now that we're apart, tell me what happened to forever?

—Pamela S. Phipps

TIME

Though it is most watched it is never seen,
It changes you without being felt,
Slowly ticking by, no one caring,
Only those who need more time do.
This time is with you all your life,
You can only change it in your mind,
But your heart knows the time,
It tells you when it is time for sleep,
And when it is time to eat,
Never will your heart let you forget the time,
It will always remember, Until it has no time either . . . .

—Patrick J. Calhoun

LONELINESS

In the middle of the night, when all is hushed and still,
I can hear the sad refrain of the lonely whippoorwill . . . .

crying out his mourning to the quiet emptiness,
heedless of the ear that hears and answers his distress.

"Whip-poor-will . . . poor will," he cries as if his chastisement
would rid the world of all the woes inciting his lament.

I tell you, little bird, that you are not to blame
for the torments of this earth which fill our hearts with shame;

but, the tears that fill these eyes at the chanting of your name
well up from a heart that bursts with the fullness of its pain.

Sing on! . . . your song gives solace to the solitary soul,
for, in you it finds expression which itself could not have told.

—DMShaw

ARE WE NOT

Though years have passed, has our zealousness been retarded
by some unseen foe;

Are we not still king marching with his pacifist glow;

Are we not the two students that were killed in a Jackson
State University dorm;

Or does our goal somehow elude us as we retreat into our homes?

Where are the sandals, dashikis, and the wearing of the African
robes?

Though this is not the sixties, are our goals still not the same?

Are we not the four innocent girls killed in the bombing of a
Birmingham Church,

Are we not Malcolm, Medgar, and many that died the violent death;

Are we not the ebony children that have had to do battle with
bigotry's theme;

Are we not the proud people who have climbed from the abyss
hoping to fulfill that impossible dream;

Or do we try to forget our past, and that we are in many people's
debt?

Becoming like Ellison's Man Invisible.

—Rob Barbee

CLOWNING AROUND
(Emmett at the Children's Hospital)

Clown around and fool around
There's always more to give—
These saddened little faces
. . . Need the will to live!

Look around and walk around
But don't forget the smile—
These happy little faces
. . . Need you for awhile!

Joke around and poke around
Some kids are full of fear—
Suddenly you see,
. . . A clown within a tear!

Clown around and fool around
There's so much more to give—
These precious little faces
. . . Have found the will to live!

—Virginia A. Carruthers

DEW IN THE GARDEN

When morning dew is glistening
on the freshly opened rose,
daily my feet go wandering
just following my nose.
A tiny chirping cricket
sits on a blade of grass
singing his happy little song
as I aimlessly wander past.
A robin skips and hops along
while blue jays take wing,
Bees buzz in the flowers
while making do their thing.
God sends the morning wonder
for all man to survey,
and marvel how such a miracle
could be placed this way.
When I've seen my last dew
and in death quietly sleep,
Remember heaven has a garden
and for me do not weep.

—Willard Lee Skelton

THE LEGACY OF CHERNOBYL

As nuclei burst from liars
Isotopes fractionize the sin
Of a long-forgotten virus;
Lethal breath again is the wind.

But now a fallout of patience
Radiates on wavy spectrums,
To sweep across the nations
The cry of a resurrection.

While the keepers of the fissile
Deny the new revelation,
They know the flux of a missile
Penetrates the false equation.

For they worship the holy birth,
Baptised in annihilation;
Righteously forced upon the earth:
The doctrine of the infection.

So again futility mutates,
Resultant of our own free will;
Unborn horror elucidates
The legacy of Chernobyl.

—Ian O'Steen

CHERISHED FOREVER

I will cherish forever
My memories of you and me
Together as one,
Even though it may not
Have lasted long, we
Had our moments, and
Those moments are kept
Deep within my heart.
To be brought up and
Remembered, making me
Wonder: How are things
Going for you? What have
You been up to? And sometimes
Even — was it a mistake for
What we had to end?

One thing I do know is
That the love we have
Shared will be cherished
Forever . . .

—Velvet Cutting

WHAT IF?

What if there was no sunshine
    to follow the rain?
What if there was no relief
    to follow the pain?
What if there was no wave
 to follow the one before it
    in the sea?
What if there was no God?
Where would any of us be?
What if we were all the same
    color?
And there was no such thing
    as the word races
Would this put a frown or
    smile on our faces?
Only God has the answer
To each and every "What if?"
Because everything that we
    possess
Is from Him a precious gift.

—Dorothy Clarke

THE SPIRIT OF LOVE

There are feelings
    That wish to be expressed.
They must be held back,
Denied their chance for freedom.

A freedom that could bring
Pleasure, happiness
But could also bring
Pain, sadness.

Should the risk be taken?
Can the pain of the past
Be forgotten?
Will it forever cause uncertainty?

The time has come
To take that chance,
To live life
with its pleasures, its pains.

A time to share
Each day as it comes.
To swell in the spirit of life,
The spirit of love.

—Annette Aguilar

PATCHES

Heedless of the icy patches of the road, I skipped like a child
down the street of life.
Oatmeal face pale and pudgy, a smile beaming where there had
not been in ages
When once there was a time you worried not about looks or beaming
smiles
Things taken for granted only a short time before lay heavy on the soul.
Reminds me of a children's game, "Red Rover."
Now how does it go? Send someone right over?
Today is a good day, after a million of bad ones.
Remission, Submission, Omission which mission are you?
It takes so little — can you spare a smile and a kind word?
So little for you — means so very much to others.
For in my mind I am heedless of the icy patches of life —
because in my dreams I do skip like a child.
Because someone like you spared me a smile.

—Judye Deavers Coleman

THROUGH MY EYES

A brilliant orange sun sends streaks of fire red, royal purple,
and orange across the sky. What a wonderful sight to see
through my eyes.

A flower garden filled with flowers of all colors and sizes.
Such a pleasing sight to see through my eyes.

A golden colored doe plays gently with her tiny fawn, enjoying
the time they spend together. What a beautiful sight to see
through my eyes.

A walk through the woods to smell the fragrance of the woods,
enjoy the falling leaves, and listen to the sounds of nature.
What a refreshing sight to see through my eyes.

A cold winter's night snow falls silently from the sky covering
the ground with a soft blanket of crystal snow. What a great
sight to see through my eyes.

A couple holding hands and gazing into each other's eyes. What a
loving sight to see through my eyes.

A man who is gentle, kind, loving, compassionate, truthful,
happy, passionate, tender hearted, fun loving, and caring is
hard to find . . . this is how I see you through my eyes.

—Cheryl Eller

PRECIOUS PILGRIMAGE
To The Brave Knight Who Seeks Access To My Heart

Run now, lest ye be strong of heart and stalwart of soul.
For the portal to my heart is shielded by a fierce animal.
A dragon, a demon
Of the worst kind. He is fear.
Consternation of all that is utterly good and wonderful to me.

Don no armor, for the purpose of the long and narrow walk.
It won't protect you from the beast. It will only screen you
From the beauty and wonder of discovery.
Only those genuine of intention along with being capable of
Giving and receiving profound piety can gain entry.

Enter softly and quietly lest you awaken the dragon.
Slowly walk the blind, treacherous path to the core of my heart.
You may fall and be trampled by the foreboding dragon,
Hot on your heels.
Stay fast and true, my ancient prophesy.

Moment by moment you reach the dawn, the light of united
Abysmal ardor. Closer and closer you come, until you can no longer
Endure it. Then you feel it, the warmth and joy of true love.
Now run with open arms and meet me, for I and the beauty of love
Forever await you. It is our Destiny!

—Holly Marie Payne Bliss

SANCTUARY

The willow branches hold hands in the quiet before the storm.

In the cold blue grey of dawn
I am lonely
for what might have been:
the love, the passion
the healing words and touches
the simple friendship promised
that I dared not accept
the nights spent talking or crying or understanding
the days spent in laughter and sun
the times spent wrapped inside each other
because I could give what I saw you want

But beyond all that you must know
that I loved you
in a way different than I had ever known
that I wanted you
and trembled slightly thinking so
and that I treasured you most of all
for not asking too many questions.

—Patricia L. Vanriette

MEMORIES, BITTER-SWEET

I sit in silence, looking at pictures of you.
Memories of a time that once was,
Of a time I wish could be again.
I read an old letter and smile,
Remembering the first time you said you loved me,
Remembering our first kiss, our first fight,
Remembering when the love we felt was for each other.
Pictures never lie,
I see your smile, and must smile also.
Your laughter lingers in my ear.
A time when happiness was all I knew.
Now in the past, just a memory.
Memories so bitter-sweet.
Bitter because they are of a place in time that is now no more,
A time that may never be again.
Sweet because they are memories of you,
A time when you used to say "I love you."

—Rodney B. Greene

WORDS FROM THE HEART

If you listen, you will hear.
The cry of a little one, so innocent and dear.
If you look, you will see.
A new day born, in all its beauty.

I didn't have the time, to listen or to see.
I just worked hard, to be all that I could be.
The days of my life, went by so fast.
Then I awoke to find myself old, looking back at my past.

So now I strive each day, to make a difference.
To touch the hearts, of everyone I know.
For love is what really makes the difference.
It is what makes us grow.

It's not just the love of others, that I seek.
But the love of life, that is so unique.
How do I put into words, something that is felt so deep inside.
It isn't just love I feel, but happiness and pride.

For I have finally realized, what true happiness is.
I now can see, all that I have missed.
The answer is caring, and being cared for.
It is truly the answer, for happiness ever more.

—Linda Richardson

MY LOVE

Dappled shadows on the lawn.
Memories of days gone by.
Sweet are the patterns where
the sun breaks thru
Like our lives, just me and you!

If time is a healer, golden
memories I see.
Sun thru the leaves and branches
Your love for me.

Dappled shadows on the lawn,
In heaven again I'll see.

—Alta Lida Tuttle Lugar

TO ALL MY FRIENDS

To all the friends I've ever had
I'm sorry
for I have doubted but not done
wanted but not won
fought yet not felt
talked some but not trusted
I thought I knew what love was
but I thought not
I knew not
I understood not
I'm sorry
for I have loved you all
Hidden deep within my shell
I have visited the wishing well
and almost drowned
but I have swam away
and I will swim again
For I can Love

—Bruce Hardy

MEMORIES

I wish I could turn back the time,
To the day I gave birth to you;
There you were, so little and new,
We were so proud of you.

Even though you're only five,
You say you'll soon be six;
There are so many wonderful
things inside,
That beautiful head of yours.

You have a memory that is quite
uncanny,
For remembering things long ago;
Music and books are a part of my
life,
You have shown that you love
them, too.

When the first day of Kindergarten
finally came,
You couldn't wait for the bus;
The smile you flashed just before
you got on,
Will always stay with us.

The years will pass so
quickly,
You'll soon be all grown up;
But we'll treasure the
precious memories we have,
Of the days when you were
young.

—Jan Aimee Frederick

195

FEELINGS

When I gaze into my dreams at night,
I think of you as a light;
A light that shines all for me,
That no one else can ever see.

I begin to feel as never before.
I have something very special;
Feelings of such great galore,
As to follow, so that I can adore.

Adore the looks that have abound;
To see, but not a sound.
A voice will seek so to hear,
I gleam to listen with no fear.

—Jimmy Baker

TEACHERS

A teacher is a special friend,
they care, they guide and mold you.
At times they may seem hard and mean,
the homework never ending.

Believe me though — they know what's best,
expand your mind and listen.
For you are growing day to day,
with knowledge you had missing.

They try their best to fill your minds,
with all you need to know.
Of how to live your life and find,
your dreams and watch them grow.

So please remember and be kind,
they want to help you grow.
Each one of you will someday find,
what teachers often know.

That everyone is special,
in different things they do.
And teachers know you're not the same,
so they make the time for you.

—D. J. Preble

WHAT DO YOU DO

What do you do when someone's got
        a problem you can't reach
When you want to tell them to
        practice what they preach?
If you know they're throwing their
        life away
And you're the one who'll remember
        the day
You didn't help, you couldn't help; you
        knew exactly what they'd say.

What do you do when you cry out for
        help for you to cope.
And there's no one there to give you hope?
Pray to God for a helping hand
And pray for wisdom to understand.

But then what do you do if you're
        too late
And the problem has become much more
        great?
Can you wait and watch time go by?
Just sit back and watch them die?
Take heed and help them through.
Don't sit around and wonder — What
        Do You Do.

—Heather Kitchens

SHARE

I want you to hold me in your arms
And soothe my worries with your charms
Seduce me without convictions
And love me without restrictions.

I need to feel your presence about
That what we have is special, without a doubt
I need to know you will always care
And our special love is something we will always share.

—Gordana

I'm not going to tell you that I know just how you feel.
I'm not going to tell you that in time the pain will heal.
I won't say, "Don't be sad," or whisper softly, "Please
        don't cry."
Or explain with awesome wisdom that his
        time had come to die.
I won't say that tomorrow will begin a fresh
        new day,
But I'll hold you in your sorrow, and I'll kiss
        your tears away.

—Kirianne Weaver

A DAUGHTER'S EXPLANATION

I ran inside my mind today
Through my thoughts, my love, my fears
I found something I have found before
Minutes lasting years
The caves inside this head of mine
Are longing for someone
I keep saying to give it time
Until the pain is gone
But how long must I wait
To wipe out the memories
The time we spent together once meant the world to me
So many times I ask myself
Should I still hang on
Hang on to a painted dream when tomorrow it may be gone
I know your definition of love
I know your needs I'm not meeting
But who am I compared to you
Just another dreamer who is dreaming . . .

—Chrisann B. Ferris

TWILIGHT DREAMS

My dreams; crystal jasmine scented,
Expansion of thoughts
Dream of dreams.
Immense fields with tall, cool blades of grass
Touch my body, while a lusterous moon reflects in the dew.

Moist, Glowing, Intricate.

Alone with my universe, my eyes gaze up at a sky
Full of silvery stars.
I ponder the thought if they were all to suddenly
        Drop
As if no longer suspended in time,
Drift into a slow descent —
And then land softly in the grass
Like giant fireflies.
My dreams; such explosive stars
Soft flickers of hope . . .
Twilight dappled with melting diamonds
        and you,
        always you . . .
Dream of Dreams.

—Marcia McCreary

JUST OUT OF REACH

Love that runs away from me, dreams that just won't
Let me be, blues that keep on bothering me, chains that
just won't set me free, too far away from you and all your
charms. Just out of reach of my two open arms.

Each night in dreams I see your face memories
time cannot erase, then I awake and find you gone, I'm so
blue and left all alone. So far away from lips so sweet
and warm, just out of reach of my two open arms. If you
need me I'll be near I'll be faithful never fear.
I'll think of you both night and day, so close and
yet so far away: I pray the Lord to keep you
from all harm just out of reach of my open
arms. That lonesome feeling all the time,
knowing you cannot be mine, dreams that
hurt me in my sleep, vows that we could
never keep too far away from lips so sweet
and warm, just out of reach of my two
open arms.

—Penny Coy

LAURA D'LYNN

You are gone.
I cannot believe it is true.
You were in my body, my soul,
        so full of life, so eager to grow.

And then He needed His precious Angel again.
For you were to bless me with your presence
        for only six short months.

But oh, what you taught me.
You taught me how strong I am.
I endured the most horrifying pain of my life.
I lost you—the precious little girl I always wanted.
I wanted to dress you up and fix bows in your hair.
Oh, how beautiful you must look in God's glorious heaven.

The day we lay your body to rest it is supposed to snow.
Will you be the little Angel kissing each snowflake
        that melts against my tear stained face?
Will you be kissing your Mommy good-bye?

I love you, my Angel Laura D'Lynn,
and I am looking forward to seeing you again.

—Lisa Fullwood

MY FRIEND

Our paths crossed in time and space
I was in pain, but I felt your grace
When our eyes met I saw an instant friend
One whose caring would never end

Your words were gentle and kind to my ear
They helped erase pain and overwhelming fear
They started the healing of a broken heart
The mending of a dream that was shattered apart

My moment of darkness was filled with prayer
Asking that help and guidance would soon be there
I closed my eyes and journeyed my nightmare alone
Battling my ego and pride as I tried to travel home

Your call of my name awakened me from my dream
Your presence silenced my anguished scream
With compassion and understanding you showed me the way
To hope and faith in a brighter day

You taught me so much in a short moment in time
To believe in myself when I have mountains to climb
I know God sent you in answer to my prayer
I thank you, My Friend, and God for being there

—Trish Pratte

TIME TO SHINE

Cold dark waves, that seem to warn
A dreadful caution of a powerful storm
Fierce winds blow, clouds move fast
A storm has brewed, a spell is cast
Covered skies in a cloak of black
Sharpened lines of lightning crack
Thunder roars in anguished pain
Sorrowed clouds cry angry rain
Raindrops fall with mighty force
A storm roams free
No charted course
Now the storm was ended
Dangers past
Through tainted clouds
Sunshine at last

—Ralph M. Monk

RISE UP

Go on rise up, you sweet child
So tenderly and oh so mild
For in just a short while
You will be able to walk that mile
That mile to stardom
Something that's seldom accomplished
In this world of confusion
But if you have the mind
You can put those obstacles behind
Be kind patient and with a willing mind
you will be able to accomplish
what few dare to start
Be smart, nothing is too hard
Instead of saying Oh No! No!
I Can't, Say and Believe with assurance
Yes, Yes I Can
So go ahead accomplish that Dream
With Spirit in Hand, Mind, Body and Soul
You can, You Can

—Mrs. Helen Benson

A POEM FOR VICKY

I wish that I could be a bird
and coast upon the air
I'd soar among the tree tops
and never have a care.

I'd dance upon the phone lines
and sing a joyous song,
and call to all creation
to come and sing along!

Oh, the world would look so small
way down upon the ground.
I'd perch upon the chimney tops
and never would come down . . .

Except to lunch with the other birds
at the feeder in my yard.
I'd have no fears or worries
For my dog is standing guard.

And when the evening comes,
I'll fly into my bed, where
I'll chirp a bedtime prayer and
lay down my little head.

It seems such a grand life
to be a bird, you see . . .
and maybe you could wish to fly
and come along with me.

—John P. Riley

SACRIFICE

Conscience beckons with distant calling
Shimmering fingers shot through with pain
Look inward, seek the dusky valley
Examine the numbness of the mind within

Youth is faceted through shrouded slumber
Webbed and faint from the darkest din
Courage the remnant that sheds its light
To see the creation formed in sin

Life gasps as it beholds the picture
The fallowed land that youth walks in
Fragments of past illusions conjured
Vain death laid bare the bones of him

The summit glimmers with tainted solace
Crystals pristine, hard and bold
Youth served up as the silver platter
Resposing upon him the gift of win

—Katharina E. Greenberg

LIFE — A PERPETUAL TEST

The waiting has ended,
The moment is here.
Relieved expectations,
Joy, laughter and tears.

A new beginning: a whole new life,
It comes to meaning between man and wife.
Abundance of love and plentiful sorrows,
They come and go and start fresh tomorrows.

Years of learning the good and bad,
Everything happens through mom and dad.
Sometimes happy, sometimes sad,
Memories suspended; all of them glad.

All grown; a family
Looking back on those days,
When young and untarnished,
It all seems a maze.

Mothers and fathers,
A career at best.
A continual process;
A perpetual test.

—Susan M. Buck

MY PRAYER

Take me by the hand, my Lord,
and guide me with Your Light,
Walk with me, my Saving Lord,
down the road of life.

Richly bless me, my Sweet Lord,
from Your Royal Throne above,
As you teach me daily, Lord,
the proper way for me to love.

Please protect me always, Lord,
from Satan's evil slaves,
As you greatly make me, Lord,
one of Heaven's strongest braves.

Jesus, You are my Lord and God,
You are my Holy King,
Your Mighty Hand made Heaven and Earth,
and all that is within.

So as I kneel for you today,
and with these words that I pray,
my voice will echo praise Great King,
through this little song I sing.

—David T. McGinnis, Jr.

GOD'S HOUSE

Once again we assembled in thy house dear Lord,
We trust with every heart in one accord.
Once again thy message in song we sang
And the reading of thy word through the building rang.

Once again spiritual food for our soul we received
And the week's heavy tension on our heart is relieved.
There was no condemning voice to try to still
As the empty place in the pew did fill.

Once again we worshiped our children by our side
And the love of God our soul satisfied.
No fear for the future overshadowed our way
As we worshiped our Lord in his house today.

May the time in our life never come dear Lord,
When we fail to assemble in one accord.
When we fail to find in this world of strife,
Our hearts still hungry for the "Bread of Life."

—Mrs. Annie P. Sherrod

CLOSE

Here I lay beside you, near you,
Watching your chest rise and fall.
Closer to you now, I am not close enough.
Your name I want to call to wake you from this sleep,
But disturb you, I will not.

If inside you, I
would not be close enough.
Beside you
would not fulfill me,
Satisfy my need, my hunger for you,
For everything of you
I need.

It is not by chance that we
have come to be.
No longer two, But one.
A part of each, each a part.
Without you I am lost.
Watching your chest rise and fall
I will never be close enough.

—Sandy Urbanowski

PILOTS

To lift above the earthbound plain
To soar and glide without restrain
Man dreamed of flight, with heart and soul
For thousands of years, it was his goal.

One day God smiled upon the land
He gave man wings to join his band
Soaring high he heard the eagle cry;
Man has joined us, he can fly!

Man flew in peace and died in war
and the earth was covered by an ugly scar
Freedom and liberty, the right to be wrong
To fly with a purpose, the urge is still strong.

The pioneers that carved the way
Are not forgotten to this day
We hope they see us reaching for the stars
and gently and slowly cover earthly scars.

God help us to preserve this precious gift of flight
Let us come nearer heaven to see your light
So shed your earthly bonds and look toward the sky
Your body and soul will follow to a new high.

—Karl Heinz Schiller

LOOK IN MY EYES

Look in my eyes.
What do you see?
Look in my eyes.
What do they say?
When you look in my eyes,
They should say I love you!
Look in my eyes.
How do you feel?
Do you feel the warmth
that I feel for you?
When I look in your eyes,
I see you looking back in mine.
What should I feel
when I look in your eyes?
Should I feel that I love
you or that you love me?
Look in my eyes!

—Kristen

JOLLY AND MAGICAL BOY

I will tell you about a little boy.
His name is like little boy blue,
Which is Rene, Rene, Rene.
The sound of a little lamb.

Call out to see if we can see,
The cry of help for me.
Come help! Come help! Come help,
The call of come to me.

I need, I need, I need,
The bandage for my knee.
I am lonely now and then.
I want your company.

I'm happy when you are here.
I don't want you to go.
Promise me my friend,
You will come to me, although.

You see, you see, you see,
The presence of yourself.
I'm smiling with such glee,
Because you are an elf.

—Carmen Delgado

UNSPOKEN

A knowing glance
A fleeting smile
Dare we chance
    To talk awhile?

Our eyes have met
    And said so much
Dare we let
    Our hands now touch?

The social spies
    Are everywhere
They criticize
    The words we share.

Can we be
    As people do
The ones we are
    Just me and You?

To just be friends
    As you now see
Assumes the ends
    In poetry

—Ernest E. McClellan

BRAVERY IN MIDLIFE

Bravery in midlife is generally misjudged.
It bursts upon the world's deafness and blindness.
Some call it impetuousness, foolishness, wanton disregard
        in the face of obligation.
Few recognize the integrity of the courageous soul.
        Bravery in life's crucial decade receives little praise.

It is easier to be brave in youth.
The inner turmoil hasn't had as much time to develop.
Taking chances is encouraged.
Failure and indecision are acceptable and excusable.
Youth is not required to explain its choices in any great detail.
        Action is applauded.

Courage is born of disappointment and grief.

Center your thoughts on the fullness of Life that is yet to come.

Let your strength of character propel you forward.

—Elizabeth Jensen McConnell

ESPECIALLY FOR BID WHIST AND ALL OTHER GAME PLAYERS

After reviewing the initial rules in the game of love
You married me and agreed to play.
Strategically glancing at my hand I called my trump — hearts;
        you already knew
You may have had some, but not many, I thought
Winning was to be my ulterior motive — after all no one wants
        to lose
Smooth at first, but then you began to constantly play out of
        turn.

You slipped, made a mistake, "reneged" it's called
When you spent the night with the queen of spades instead of
        coming home to your ace of hearts
So a trip to Boston I did take to file for my divorce
My lawyer got it all for me, the house, the kids, the car,
        alimony and child support
I WON — didn't I???
Bid made or was I set?

—Tanya Williams

THE VOICE ON THE LINE

"Mom this is Jack," oh the sweetness of the tone.
It makes my heart swell up inside, this voice on the phone.
It seems like only yesterday that he was just a boy, sitting on
his mom's lap and playing with his toys.
As he grew up so handsomely I knew the day would come, when he
would start to venture out and I would miss my son.
MY son's been overseas a year, his duties to complete. Because my
little boy is now a United States Marine.
Now the day has finally come and home again he'll be. His coming
will be wonderful, a very loving scene.

—Jessie Scarborough

THE YOUNGER WOMAN

I looked in the mirror and what did I see?
An old wrinkled grey haired woman staring back at me
As I stared in the mirror I said to myself—this just can't be!
I got into my car without a sound
I put the pedal to the metal and made it to town.
I bought some dye for my hair and cream for my face
I hit every store, I went every place
To find me some makeup, some new clothes and shoes to match
With a spring in my step, his eye I did catch
Now when I look in the mirror, what do I see?
A new woman looking ten years younger than she used to be

—Lottie L. Adams

The question
such a circular subject,
the end,
Seemingly the same as
the beginning.
The line always straight,
yet curving,
a-r-o-u-n-d circle,
No matter how you try,
Never a hollow existence.
You'll always see
something in the
        center of that
            circle,
                don't you?
The question.

—Debbie Elisco

STRIFE AND LIFE

The men in Blue
are full of Blood
run rough shod
over the innocent flood

The guns are silent.
So are the Bodies.
The living ask why
Need the thousands die?

We wanted peace
But the soldiers released
Our blood upon the Street
The living stare in disbelief

A generation lost
To the despots
Anger rises
With the reprises

Silent no more
Carry the Cry
From shore to shore
Our brothers live
Forever more

Dedicated to the Student movement in China
—Matt Hartman

MIRROR IMAGE

I look in the mirror
And what do I see?
A wrinkled old hag
That just can't be me!

But turning away
From this horrible sight,
I find a solution
That may be just right.

The face may be wrinkled
And hair Oh, so grey —
But thoughts are not wrinkled
And smiles are not grey!

Will a smile on my lips
And a gleam in my eye
Make me look better
If I really try?

Yes, forget that sad image
That gave me a start!
My years may be many
But joy's in my heart!

—Beatrice B. Turner

THE POET'S PALATE

He rejects the concept of billowing clouds
and looks for the taste of the sky. He'll
    make you listen to ice cream, or see the wind;
        he'll help you find the smell of a sidewalk.
            The poet's eyes are those of an eagle, soaring
                above those of mortals.
His senses can rival the greatest of predators;
    the keenness is unsurpassed. The painter blends
        colors and the musician sounds, but the poet blends
            feelings and categorizes in words and phrases. The
                painter and musician have the whole spectrum of color
                    and sound, but the palate of the poet is confined to
                        the ineffectuality of words.

—Theresa Lang

INTEGRITY

Did you read the 'Obit' for integrity today?
Honesty? and Ethics? "What are they?" the children say.
You can hear the lack of scruples, on the TV News each night,
squeezed in between the murders, and the tales of urban blight.
You can find it while you're shopping, "Bait and Switch,"
the salesman's spiel,
Yet you say you don't believe it? That the problem isn't real?

You can see it in the Senate, You can see it in the House,
out of twenty politicians, maybe one is not a louse.
They are lining all their pockets with our hard-earned cash today
But it must be with our blessings, 'cause we vote them in to stay.

They could be anyone you know, your boss, your child, your mate
I may be optimistic, but I don't think it's too late
to end the vicious cycle of dishonesty and fear
Remember, as you tuck your children in their beds tonight,
the importance of integrity, should be taught right here!

—Catherine T. Miller

GRADUATION

This is how I see this very special night

Graduation is not just an end of twelve long years of hard work,
but it is turning over a new leaf in life that will lead us into a
different journey. I know that everyone of you is sitting there
feeling a little nervous and scared, wondering of what tomorrow
will bring. One thing is for certain, as you look around and see
those special faces that made these years complete. One thing that
everyone of us will have to do is say those words that bring tears
to our eyes "Good-bye." "Good-bye" is just a word that we say
practically everyday of our lives, but now it seems so hard to
say. They say friends are forever and in a sense this is true. The
heart is a place where memories never die, not feelings nor friends.
Friends may not stay together forever and may even be thousands of
miles away, but in their hearts friendship is very near. All of us
are happy that tonight has finally come, but you have to admit that
a bit of sadness is also felt. This is Graduation and it certainly
is special. After this occasion is over and the time to say
"Good-bye" has come, take a deep breath and smile and remember
"Good-bye" is for now, but not forever.

—Carolyn Trevino, G.

Why do artificial people buy real trees, real fruit, real jewels
Why not fake parts
Fake art
A lot of saran wrap
To place on a fake frappe
Never to look at nature
Never to enjoy the sun
Maybe to them, this would be fun

—Ann Daniel

HOMECOMING

The rusty, crusty cargo ship,
  Coaxed by a single tug,
Abruptly slid into its slip,
  And nestled safe and snug.

The sky was gray, the pavement wet,
  As lines were all made fast,
And only husky dockhands met
  The soldiers, home at last.

The war had ended months before,
  And memories are short.
There was no crowd, with welcome's roar,
  To jam the ship's home port.

A thousand men came home that day,
  All thoughts of glory past.
A thousand men came home to stay,
  And flags flew at half-mast.

—Merrill Edward Holden

I READ THAT BOOK

I read that book,
  It took me far away,
To lands and people unknown.

I camped by their destinies,
Looked and listened as they grew,
Watch out, the plot has thickened.

Deeper they go into the story,
People speak, their words mean something,
See, there is love hiding in the shadow.

Conflict has come, conflict will go,
Where fate stops nobody knows,
Will the writer give us a clue?

Lover greets lover again and a day,
They came together,
Even though they have distant thoughts.

The moment of truth has come,
Pages of the book will now reveal,
No dragon ever defeated a good knight.

—K. J. Lambson

BOARDWALK AT NIGHT

Swoosh! Crash!
  Surrounded by a somber pitch.
Alone, with nothing
but dank wooden planks beneath my feet.

the Thunder rolls under and sprays
as the icy wind taps on my shoulder
like an old, forgotten enemy,
chilling my sodden form.

I gaze into this boundless obscurity,
scarcely distinguishing black from blacker,
As the mighty thunder rolls on.

Contemplating danger,
I think of parting my safe haven
to slowly sink my naked toes
into the swiftly sliding sand.

Illusory hands now grasp my soul
and tow it away and o'er the sea
as I unite with nautical spirits,

Ebbing to ebony,

Until the peace of morning comes.

—Tina Urso

DADDY

I never got to tell you, exactly how I feel.
  Sometimes, I even wondered, if you were really real.
There were times, when it was me you didn't come to see.
And, with you, is where I only wanted to be,
Then there were promises, you never kept.
Half the time, I didn't even know where you slept.
But in my mind, you were always there.
Those thoughts, someday, I hoped we'd share.
I know there were things you hated to miss.
Like making things all better, with just a kiss.
I wanted you to know, that it's you I love.
Even though you're with, our God above.
I can't say, I really understand
What happened between my mother
And, that very special man
Somethings, I guess, I'll never really know.
But, my love for you, will never stop to grow.
About the past, I really don't care.
I just wish, the rest of my life, with you I could share!

—Donna Schott

A BROKEN HEART

He died of a broken heart for you and me
  Not for the scorn and misery of Calvary's tree.
Father forgive me for breaking His heart
For clutching on to my sins and refusing to depart.
The lust of the flesh and the pride of life
All the world had to offer with all its strife.
I grasped it all to my sin scarred face until—
I met my Savior face to face.
I wasted so many long precious years,
Serving satan and his world and all its fears.
But never again from you will I ever depart,
For I know you died for me of a broken heart.
The Creator on the cross . . . . Even the sun hid
its face in shame, The stones cried out, "Who in the
world is to blame?"
But the grave could not hold your wounded bleeding heart,
For from this sin sick world the Creator did depart.
I am watching and longing for thy return,
My Savior of the broken heart
Whose love I once spurned.

—Anonymous

SEPARATING

The deep rumble of the elevated train
  broke the silence between us.
My thoughts were as bare and colorless
as the late November trees
that stood shadowless at the edge of the muddy park.
We sat at opposite ends of an old bench.
At first we said nothing.
Then you brushed aside strands of your brown hair
that fluttered in your face,
bit your lower lip and asked: "Do you love me?"
Not sure of my answer, I stood up and walked away,
stepping suddenly into a carousel of wind and flying leaves.

Now, months later, I stand and stare out
of the frosted windows of my little apartment,
watching the endless white speckles of snow falling.
I dream again of the park bench and sitting close to you.
But winter has set in,
and my thoughts cannot thaw and resolve into words.
The words are too late and somehow lost—
buried like those leaves long dead beneath the snow.

—John D. Healy

SEASONS

Hot sun warms the earth,
Cool breezes fill the air,
Sunsets of gold light up the heavens,
Smiles and laughter on all chilren's faces.
This is the season of warmth and fun; this is summer.
Raindrops from clouds fall to the earth,
Rainbows of color fill the sky,
Umbrellas, like flowers, bloom with the rain.
All new life joins together.
This is the season of joy and rebirth; this is spring.
Colorful leaves fall from the trees,
Warm smells fill the air,
Children hurry, ready for school,
Memories of summer blow away.
This is the season to prepare for the cold; this is fall.
Snowflakes like lace fall from above,
Mittens and gloves warm tiny hands,
Temperatures below freezing warn people to stay.
Thoughts of the summer are the nicest of all.
This is the season of cold and snow; this is winter.

—Stacey Monahan

LOVE AND LIFE

Love and life. Two words that are easy to say yet not so
    easy to understand because their meanings can be,
    if not already, virtually endless
Love and life. Simple, innocent words but both can bring
    down the world with much noise
Love and life. Everyone sees them in a different way. Yet
    I believe that everyone agrees both can be either
    the highest pinnacle of happiness or the deepest
    fathom of sorrow
Love and life. Both are one and yet neither is either.
    You love to live and you live to love, complex in
    thought but simple in action
Love and life. You must face it, I must face it, everyone
    must face it sometime. So maybe you let life be a
    a jar and try to fill it with love
Love and life. Two words that are easy to say yet not so
    easy to understand

—Michael Anthony Ftacnik

IF THIS IS LOVE

Why do you make me do things that make me feel like dirt?

Why do you make me slave and do all the work?

I try to please you, in every way I can, but on the floor
    you throw the pots and pans.

You make me get on my knees and beg you to stop,

You threaten me if I try to call the cops.

If this is a phase, Will it ever go away?

I can't go through this, every minute of the day.

Do you have a heart?

You were once in mine, but now far apart.

Because of you, I don't think I'll ever love again, I thought
    you were my love and my friend.

You beat me and push me around all the time, And then you
    ask me, if I'm fine.

How would you feel if you were constantly used, To live a
    life, of painful abuse.

If this is love, I shall never love once more,

You are not the love, I loved before.

—Cassandra Octivia West

I HOLD THE LIGHTNING

I hold the lightning in my hand,
Upon the mountain top.
I summon here the valiant band,
And I bid the darkness stop.

For seven times a thousand years,
Darkness covered the world.
But now we cry happy tears,
As the kings banners we unfurled.

Behold, Oh darkness! I am he!
The one who wears the ring.
I hold it high for the world to see,
Let every voice now sing!

Let all creatures behold the sun,
Let there be no mournful cry.
For the mighty unicorn has returned,
And the darkness now shall die!

Let the people praise with one voice,
The greatest champion ever known.
Let the faithful now rejoice,
For the king is on his throne!

—Ivan E. Eberhardt

STARCHILD

And she lingers in twilight sleep
a stardust queen
with nothing to live for
but velvet dreams

While her kingdom's in trouble
her knights
fall and fade to day
and she is left in anger
so she leaves her lovers
and digs their graves

Amongst the isles of dreams
she wanders
and spreads her wings
and the satin clouds welcome her
so she slowly begins to sing

While all of earth's tender children lay
curled in their gentle beds
a stardust widow soars
over them and drops dreams into
their settled heads . . .

—Cassandra

FRIENDS

Here's to friends, to each their own,
Be they near or far from home.
Some may dwell within our hearts,
Others stay, but too soon depart.

Here to share our precious days,
And accept us for our separate ways.
Some to share laughter, joys and tears,
Others to quiet our innermost fears.

So I say to the friends,
    Whether or not.
Lessons are learned,
    Some are forgot.

Hold on fiercely,
    to each living day.
Fear not the tomorrows,
    or their unseen ways.

—Elizabeth Kyer

LIFE

Time,
    Life's most precious gift
Love,
    Life's best feeling
Friendship,
    Life's most valuable possession
Without time,
    All is lost
Without love,
    Who cares
Without friendship,
    Nothing matters
Time, love, friendship
    The elements of life.

        —Melissa Bathrick

HIDDEN TREASURE

Grandmother, so small and fragile
like crystal,
yet so strong in many other
    ways.
Her eyes begin to gleam, "Now,
    let me tell you dear,
    When I was fifteen — "
Then the tales of hard times
    and good.
Almost forgotten tears and faded
    lace.
Stories of lazy summer picnics by
    the lake,
One room schools and kinder simpler
    ways.
Life is renewed while thinking on
    the past.
As I bend to kiss grandmother
    good-bye, I breathe,
"Thank you God my world's not
    too fast,"
To slow down and see all the
    treasure
Hidden behind those beautiful eighty
    year old eyes.

        —Wanda Draeger

LETTERS, ROSES, & MILES

Let my letters bring you love,
My roses bring you smiles,
If only in my thoughts,
I span the endless miles.

My letters are not but words,
Engraved upon a page,
But phrases that grow in meaning,
Ever mellowing with age.

My roses are lovers hope,
As clinging petals part,
Distance unfolds the beauty,
Flourishing from the heart.

Miles stand between us,
Impregnable so they seem,
But surely you know I'm with you,
When you close your eyes and dream.

So let my letters bring you love,
Red roses bring you smiles,
If only in my thoughts,
I can span the endless miles.

        —Betty Fick

Who would weep for me should I die today?
Would the clouds cry tears at my passing?
Would the winds whisper a tale of a fallen warrior?
Would the birds above sing a dirge in my honor?
Would a woman place a rose at my grave?

Who would mourn for me should I pass away?

Would the minister pray for my immortal soul?
Would my parents know how to grieve a lost child?
Would my friends eulogize me of what happened in years past?
Would my enemies pay last respects to so great a foe?

Who would weep and mourn for me should I die this day?
I fear that I know not for I have gone away.

        —Eric Shoars

THE LAST WILL AND TESTAMENT

I sit here — drinking the sorrows of the world in.
Looking at a face that fled this world many years ago.
Pondering on what the future holds for me.
As I look I see only a blank sheet of paper with a small cut.
A knife lay in front of me —
the cold blade of reality stares back at me
I mope and sigh and touch the sharp edge —
It is cold.
I breathe and feel the dull metal and nothingness of my life.
The stone of society sharpens the blade.
All life has already been sucked out of me by depression.
A final cut is to be made.
I wish you all to see it and
To remember it well.

        —Frank Perlmutter

THE WEEK OF THE LILAC

Commencing with a color to make one stop and stare
then swelling with an aroma to fill the air
which lingers like a sweet love that will always be there

A Purple straining her way through Natures' every day green
calling out with her sweet smell to be seen
like a lost lover making his final scream

At last nature must take her away
something so beautiful must never stay
but her memory will never fade away

If her memory is strong and her beauty really there
Nature will bring her back so one can stop and stare
and linger with a love that will always be there

        —Josette R. Collier

LIFE IS LIKE A COMPARISON OF A STREAM

Behind imaginary dreams, is a world full of bright colors,
Laughter, and crystal clear streams.
Like life, like water, they both flow along.
When the current gets too rough, life and water splashes
Against rocks that are rugged and tough.
When the current slows down then everything is great.
Life attends to have its ups and downs, unfortunately
Some of us do not get back to a level position, but
A stream always makes its way back.
Nothing stands in its way.
It will either splash over a rock and make its way into
Pure, white drops of tears or beat under a rock like
A beautiful butterfly hanging from under a pink petal.
Why does everything get in the way of life and not a stream?
Maybe because a stream lives its own way and life lives us.
Maybe we'll never know the answers to those mysterious
Questions. Maybe we are not meant to know them.

        —Angel Griggs

OF BEING A DREAMER

The wandering soul of a dreamer extends with fervent arms . . . . unceasing, absorbing every moment that graces its depth.

Fear has no voice to the dauntless ears of a dreamer. The rapturous whispering of what awaits ever lures the dreamer to journeys others less attentive shall ever know.

—Maura Ometz Burd

THE ROSES

I study them, like I study your eyes
And the contrast between red and green makes me
    realize
That this gift of love, this gift from him
was to pressure the guilt I feel within.
And I study them, like I study your face
hoping to find some message inside the vase.
Searching for some thought, some emotion
but feelings were lost in all the commotion
Still, I study them like I study your eyes
and suddenly I begin to fantasize
that I could do what my heart wants to
and how I wish the roses were from you.

—Jennifer L. TenBarge

WHAT MUST I DO?

I live, I love, I laugh, I cry. As time goes on, I too must die. The feeling of falling, I'm feeling I'll fail. I do my best. But, to no avail. What must I do to put my life together again? I sing, I dance, I do my part. Loving and caring from the depths of my heart. I listen, I help, and I pray real good. But I'm let down, I'm put down, I'm misunderstood. What must I do to put my life together again? The road that I follow is long dark and hallow but I try so Hard to be strong. The stories I tell have their own sets and morals. Delivering a sad lonely song. I'm reaching my peak, I'm achieving my goals, I'm living, I'm loving, I'm free. All of my life, I've tried oh so Hard. Never to forget about me. What must I do? How will I do? That was the name of my song. My life is worth living. My faith has returned. But, besides all of this I am strong!

—Monique Carroll

MEMORIES

Springtime is here
Love flows through the air
But I'm saddened without you
Please don't go, I know you care

We had so much going for us
The trips through life's amusements and despairs
Holding tightly to each other
It was as if the world was just you and me
    Until we glimpse at those who stare

Oh how I cry myself to sleep at night
Suddenly reaching out
Telling you no more lonely days
But you're not there and I'm filled with doubt

You'll only be a thought in my head
I'll never be able to feel your strong embrace
But I know I'm strong enough to go on
It's just that I wish some memories could be erased.

—Linda Heasley Miller

CHRISTINA

Why cry little one?
Gentle waves swell in windowed blue.
Has someone lessoned you?
Cared a bit, then laughingly run
        Away?

        Stay.
Arms to enfold, chair a-rocking,
Songs of sorrow, shared warmth of sun.
Head pressed to breast, scarce hears a knocking
Door's summons to play. Laughingly run
        Away.

—DAH

I KNOW ABOUT FEELINGS

I know that it must be very hard for you to just hear about the things that are important in your life. Never to be there to see them happen. Or to only have a picture to look at and nothing to hold on to.

To live off the memories of all your yesterdays. To live for the "What If" dreams of tomorrow. I know of the sorrows, the fears of emptiness. The sadness of being lonely, the longest of days. The hurt of empty arms, the false kisses of dreams that walk in the night.

I cry for all the you's and me's when I think of all the time wasted, that the space between us has taken away from us never to be given back.

        So you see
        I know about feelings

—Becky McCann

ILLUSIONS WITH YOU

Did you ever have a fantasy come true?
I'd like to share my experience with you.

Lying on the beach with someone I love,
Looking beyond the clouds into heaven above.

The air filled with whispers that only we,
could hear,
He says the place for him was always in my
arms, as he pulls me near.

As the wind blew it brought the softness of
his touch,
To see his warm smile when I'd say I loved
him so much.

Of the special moments that had gone by, we
reminisce,
As the moonlight shine upon us, we shared a
tender kiss.

Together we wished on a falling star,
To always stay close and never somewhere far.

For this memory to forever cherish and lock
within our heart,
And never to forget this night when we are
separated and torn apart.

Silently; we gazed into the midnight sky,
As I turned to him, a tear fell from my eye.

The blur from this tear had caused his
reflection to fade,
But it was all an illusion, my mind had made!

—Monique Patino

The sea mimes the relic and the stone.
  Like the feline monument of ages past,
Time watches.
And waves created, crash upon the shore
In submission to the power
And the glory of fallen deities.

—K. M. Woodbury

LIFE

Life is too short, to worry about tomorrow,
  Live each day the best we can.
  Yesterdays are past and filled with sorrow,
Filled with things done and left undone.

When we waken in the morning light,
The minds are clear of the doubts and fears.
  Of yesterday's worry, pain and woe,
  We know GOD'S promises are here.

Love is a very precious thing,
  Given to man by God.
    Cannot be traded, bought or sold,
    It fills our hearts with Joy untold.

—Mrs. Edith McElroy

ANGELA

As graceful as the willow in a summer
  breeze,
The very light of heaven in her smile;
Her eyes — reflecting pools of peace and
  joy within,
Her words reveal a child-like lack of
  guile.

Her voice — the cooing of the dove,
Her laughter like the ripple of a mountain
  stream;
A vision lovely as a day in May,
Intoxicating essence of a pleasant dream.

Her heart is warm with love of life,
Compassion lit by heaven's fire;
A jewel in the crown of womanhood,
The very height and depth of any man's
  desire.

—Nancy Love

A CHILD'S PLEA

Please listen Mommy and Daddy
  I'm depending on you,
to teach me and show me
just what I should do.
I have no one else
I'd like to look up to,
So I say what you say
and I do what you do.

Let your love be as sunshine
and your care as the rain,
let me grow through your praises
with no need to complain.
Please take a little time out
to teach me right from wrong,
give me love and guidance
So I'll always feel strong.

Help lift me up and turn me around
Help me to feel I'm on solid ground,
Make me know you believe in me,
Mommy and Daddy, this is "A Child's Plea"

—Phyllis L. Gibbs

LOVE, LOVE

LOVE, LOVE . . . is a bundle of hearts put together
  LOVE, LOVE . . . is a world full of nice people
LOVE, LOVE . . . is all around us
LOVE, LOVE . . . is everything that exists
LOVE, LOVE . . . lives in the beautiful sky
WHAT IS LOVE???

                    . . .
                GOD!!!

—Shelly Lynne Pratte

THE FUNNIEST MOVIE I'VE EVER SEEN

The funniest movie I've ever seen
  Took place on my old movie screen.
It all began with an old church bus
That our pigs rode in instead of us.
They looked out the window
And sat in their seats
As they took a wrong turn and got lost in the streets.
Then up ahead they saw a butcher shop
"Lets get some roast beef" they said as they stopped.
We looked at them and they looked at us
As they drove away in that old church bus.

—Rachael Pridgeon

AS . . .

As the sunset dims behind the haze,
  I sit upon this lifeguard tower,
    Pondering the joy of previous days,
      Wondering where you are this hour.

As the seagulls soar with beauty and grace —
  Higher and higher they fly.
    I wish you were with me at this place,
      As I struggle to conceal a tearful cry.

As our footprints are no longer in the sand,
  A walk along the beach brings a shedding tear.
    I reach out and cannot find your hand,
      But in my heart I know you're near.

As this day ends I prepare to go —
  Reflecting upon this tranquil day.
    I hope we may continue to grow,
      And share future sunsets our own special way!

—D. A. Blackwell

ONE — BUT NEVER ALONE

Here alone I lay in solitude;
  Dormantly staring at a candle;
Melodic tunes entertain my aloneness;
Glimmering brightly through the darkness;
The flame stands alone as it flickers;
Gradually, observing a beautiful sight;
Uniquely, the flame did not stand alone;
But, secretly flickered in three parts;
At the beginning of the flame,
It glowed ever so brightly;
The middle, just a dimmer hue;
At the bottom, a soothing soft blue;
But, glowing at the tip of the wick;
This rare and special sight;
A dainty little red heart;
Had found a resting place;
Realizing, the flame never stood alone;
Just as I am never alone;
Because, forever in my heart abides,
The Heavenly Father, Jesus Christ, and the Holy Spirit.

—Mona Lisa Smiley-Hallums

THE BECKON

Oft I've thought of New England to leave, to tread the far
places, of spires and mounts to climb;
    But then alas, there's spring in New England, with greens,
and ferns, and life renewed.
Oft I've thought to dance on palace floors, of kings, of glitter
and gold;
    But then there's summer in New England, with roses and flowers,
crickets and children.
Oft I've thought to sail; of Isles and sea, of sun and mystery.
    But then there's fall in new England, with reds and yellows,
with ancient walls, and wooded paths beckoning home.
Oft I've thought to stand on arid sands, of pyramids tall, of
pagan steps and hidden crypts.
    But then there's winter in New England, with barren Oaks,
of gleaming ice, and silent snows, of reverent solitude whispering,
this is home.

        —John F. Burnett

COMMUNION

A fresh spring morning, the smell of flowers in the air,
I come to our special place, and find You already there.
You're always there before me, You'd sit and wait all day,
Hoping that I might come to ask, "Lord, which way today?"
You long to give me direction, and power for what I must do,
All You ask is that I'd come and humble myself before You,
This time is so very special, without You I stumble and fall,
So I give these first moments of day to make You Lord over all.

Your holiness overwhelms me and the way You know my needs,

You fill every longing of my soul, if to Your voice I'll Heed,
Now the time has come to rise, I ask You to take my hand,
And walk along beside me, to show me this day Your plan,
For You alone are able to sustain me in everything,
I offer a prayer of thanksgiving, my sacrifice of praise I bring.

You are the Lord of my life, all other kingdoms will fall,
You are my Master Designer, and You're my all in all.

        —Dixie McDaniel

MUSIC SUCH AS SOOTHES THE SOUL

She lives in an oasis of secluded, quiet halls
With greenery in places, and a cockatiel makes calls
To the music of Vivaldi that vivifies the air
And breaks the somber silence and the sense of lonely there.

The years gone by have brought her into a wilderness
Of time alone that's taught her to live in loneliness,
Aging in her daydreams, she takes a long, deep breath,
And listening to the whispering sound, lets her thoughts drift off
to death.

The rocking chair is Grandma's world; she doesn't care to leave.
Farms to cities have unfurled, and she just does not believe
There's anything for her out there, at least not anymore.
She just waits in her oasis till someone visits at her door.

Then she hears the sound of laughter coming nearer in the night.
A child come running after. Tears of joy run from her sight
To see a grandchild in growing years; five have come and gone.
A melody of life she hears as the child bursts out in song.

 She reaches down to the whirlwind child; for a time she does
embrace
And holds her to linger there awhile to feel the softness of her
face.
The grandchild chatters constantly, a song of the giving kind,
Music such as soothes the soul and brings living to the mind.

        —Karen Morse

SPRING PROMISE

A raindrop fell on a leaf
it slid slowly downward
'til it became a teardrop
then fell again to the ground
where it nestled next to
a daisy seed
and made promises for spring

—Mary Elizabeth Sanders

THE LEAF

Sitting by the stream
Warming by the sun,
Back at the homestead
No work is being done.

Watching the water flowing
A leaf gently floating,
Little leaf wish you tell
When did you fall,
Where are you going.

—Jean Antonacci

A NOTE OF GRATITUDE

To You
  who
    sparkles the stars
    shines the sun
    lights the moon

To You
  who
    rains the showers
    waves the water
    slicks the ice

To You
  who
    colors the flowers
    dances the wind
    sweeps the sand

To You:
    Thank you!

—Sister Margaret Halaska, OSF

WITH SPRING TO SPARE

Though the winter is bleak
All frozen and cold,
How sanguine my heart
  In my garden's threshold.

It seems not to matter
  The spirit-winds chill.
Gone is the dayspring,
  Yet, a robin doth trill.

The hum of snow falling
  sends thrills up my spine.
Cold is snow's fleecing,
  It's nature's opine.

One must be bold
  In the scald of the wind,
Yet, a robin is perched
  with a song to rend.

How clear the trill
  in the robin's lair.
He's winter's refuge
  with Spring to spare.

—Bert Knowles

I AM AN AMERICAN

I am an American,
   Thus forever let me stand
Never defender of another
   But my own native land.

On her soil I have fed
   My soul upon her creed,
Asking and receiving justice
   For my smallest need.

I will repay with loyalty,
   It is the least I can do,
By living each new day
   A worthy citizen and true.

Shall I dream of other lands
   Washed by a foreign sea?
Oh no, I have enough
   Reality in America for me.

—Vi Dykins

SORROW

We met as the cold of
   A winter day
Shimmered from the
   Distant sun dogs
And entered your heart.

Our meeting was caught
   In a web of frosting
Of cake uneaten
   Footprints on barren ground
All held in silent misery.

Slowly came a separation
   A timely divorce
Between the bonds of steel
   That held us
And you thought to be free

But suddenly —
   Out of a soft moonlit night
I seized you unaware
   And we walk together
In full-blown agony!

—Dorothy Ranstrom

OLD GLORY

I see Old Glory waving
   And think of those who died,
Who on the field of battle
   Defended her with pride.

Most did not seek the battle,
   But they received the call,
So to defend this banner
   They gave to her their all.

Some served her on the waters,
   And others in the air,
But it was for Old Glory
   They served and perished there.

And when she flies at half-mast,
   I know that one has gone
Who loved and served this banner,
   So we must carry on.

So let us fly Old Glory
   And proudly let her wave.
Remember unsung heroes,
   Who all they had, they gave!

—Harold W. Smithson

SILENCE WHISPER

War, Death, Anger . . . . I have stood beside it all.
   And all too close like my family on Sundays
Commemorating behind the breakfast table,
As laughter rose throughout the dining room.
And I walked away in silence . . . . unpronounced.
For I knew why they laugh so warm heartedly . . . . Which,
Sounded like antique muskets fired at closed range.
And I took hold of my eyes filling the palms of my hands,
Hoping not to remember.
Not to remember the war, the anger, deaths I have never seen
But those feelings I have felt when Grandpa cried
And his eyes would burn as fire, and Grandpa would shiver.
And I would often hold his hands to comfort him,
But soon Grandpa would be asleep, asleep
To a world he carries long since yesterday.

—Stephen A. Forbes

CHILD ABUSE

C — Is for the CRITICISM, he sometimes had to take,
   You know, the insults and threats, parents like to make.
H — Is for the HITTING, he soon learned to expect,
   Just another little way to teach that boy respect.
I — Is for his INNOCENCE, when you asked him not to tell,
   "Let's just say to Grandma, Little Johnny fell."
L — Is for his LONELINESS, empty feelings of despair,
   A Doctor can set a broken bone, but a heart he can't repair.
D — Is for the DAMAGE, you did that fatal day,
   With one hard blow/ you took his life away.

A — Is for the ANGER, burning you inside,
   It must burn cooler now since Little Johnny died.
B — Is for the BURIAL, of a boy six years old,
   You can put away his body, but can't confine his soul.
U — Is for the UNDERTAKER, who must put him in the grave,
   Just another little guy, no one tried to save.
S — Is for the SENTENCE, the Judge and Jury filed,
   May you serve every day, for killing your own child.
E — Is for ETERNITY, where God now keeps your Son,
   Don't you feel remorse for the awful thing you've done?

—Shirley Jo Redmond

THE CHALLENGER SEVEN

Oh we have touched the heavens, left the real world behind;
   Never to return again in body or in mind.

We gave our lives to our country, our country did us wrong;
A human fatal error, and now we are gone.

Unbeknown to us the o-rings were disordered;
The problem was never solved, the mission should've been aborted.

The cover-up had happened, none of us were told;
The 28th had dawned, clear and crisp and cold.

We got into the van, traveled out to the pad;
Boarded the shuttle, and the countdown began.

The smoke had already started right on the pad;
We couldn't sense it, but their cameras had.

We blasted off to no-man's land;
73 seconds later the horror began.

Mike's last words were "uh-oh," then the fireball came;
Two minutes later we felt no more pain.

Our lives are over now, the hierarchy knew;
It was us against them, there was nothing we could do.

Our hearts and souls are still in the heavens;
For we were the crew, The Challenger Seven.

   TO THE MEMORY OF THE CHALLENGER CREW
—Kathryn S. O'Leary

LIGHT

Lost in the darkness of my thoughts
I wonder when there will be light
Light to guide me through the path of tranquility
Stop the hurt, stop the loneliness
Make me open my eyes to what has been in front of me all along
The light of hope within me

—Lillian Fabian

IT'S NOT WHAT YOU SAY, IT'S THE WAY THAT YOU SAY IT?

Some things are only skin deep
And that's the way they are to be
Not to be picked apart
And examined thoroughly.

Some things just mean what they say
No less, no more
So next time just listen
And don't even try to explore.

Some things are drawn or painted.
Sculpted or even designed
It was done for that specific reason
With nothing else in mind.

So you see, it's just what I say
Not how I react in these modern days.
You must suspect the obvious with some things
With some things, but not always.

—Cameron

A MYSTERY TO ME

Before you were a mystery to me.
I never knew you or what you were like.
I used to wonder about you and where you were.
Wondering if you thought about me or what I was
like, what I was doing, or did I think of you.

Before you were a mystery to me.
I couldn't picture you in my mind, because
I was so small when you left. I grew up with my
mother, brother, and my sister. In the back of my mind
I always wondered where you went.

Before, you were a mystery to me.
Now, you are still a mystery to me.
You are just waiting to be solved.
I know where you are, they told me.
They also told me some things about you.
They say that you are still the same.
What same?

Now, you are still a mystery to me.
A mystery I am afraid of solving. I don't know
what to expect if I solve the mystery and come
to see you. I don't know how it will affect my life.

Now you are still a mystery to me.
What will happen if I solve you?
My life's mystery of wondering about you.
Will I come to see you and that is it, or will
we get to know each other and see each other now and then?

Now, you are still a mystery to me.
There are so many questions I would like to
ask you. So many things about you I would
like to know. I am afraid to ask. Afraid to
start thinking of what it is going to be like, and
then be disappointed by them not happening.

YOU ARE STILL A MYSTERY TO ME.

—Teresa Groff

THE WONDER OF IT ALL

The rain falling softly on
the roof above.
The sound of the river
flowing, winding,
running along.
The night comes alive with
sounds only the
darkness hides.
Warm breezes blowing,
gently bringing to our
senses the smells of
the night.
Our senses are alive with
the wonder of it all,
always wondering
yet never knowing
what tomorrow
will bring.

—Kelly Rice

LOVE IS LIKE A FRAGILE FLOWER

I had a dream last night
I had you here
But you turned away from me
I shed a tear.

That tiny little drop
Fell into my palm
I became calm.

I closed my eyes and opened them
And what did I behold
A single perfect flower
One single red rose.

Love is fragile like a flower
So delicate, so bold
Or strong as the earth
on which its roots take hold.

I stared upon this flower
My heart in disarray
But my thoughts are elsewhere
Since you walked away.

—Brad Ellin

HOPE

As I go to sleep each night
I feel you come to life
reviving in me memories
that some think best to hide.

It's hard to separate the thought
which flashes through my mind
as I fall back into the past
and as you come alive.

I know the past is all but dead
and should be left behind
but I still need those memories
to love her in my mind.

It's difficult for me to say
what love I have for you
I fear the past will come again
and this time, I'll lose you.

I ask that you should understand
your difference is in name —
for she gave us our memories
and you shall do the same.

—Marie C. Gray

ONCE

Once I could see you.
I felt the softness of your hair . . .
I felt it gently touch my neck
As though you were really there.

Once I saw your eyes;
And I saw your loving smile.
In my heart I heard your laughter
That made life worthwhile.

Once I heard your whisper
In the darkness of the night.
Once I thought my heart would break
When you forgot to call —

Then I realized it wasn't love at all.
Just a figment of my imagination
And just a passing dream,
That seemed to end all at once.

—Monique A. Pritchard

BRIDGING THE MILES

Close your eyes and think of me.
Asking why? To wonder how it would be.
Thoughts of us within your smile,
As you pause to dream for a while.

If only you could feel my heart glow,
To fully understand how I miss you so.
Wishing to hold you, I really do,
Tears from my heart weep for you.

Close your eyes and think of me.
Is it real? Can it be?
Close your eyes and believe it's true,
We're hard to explain, me and you.
Yet so simple, I Love You.

Far is the distance between us now,
Directions to find somewhere, somehow.
My feeling is lonely, and yes it's true,
There is hope for tomorrow, but today,
I Miss You.

—Bobby Maskew

THE MOUNTAIN TOP LIBRARY

I go there to meet new people, a book
a marvelous place to look
at citizen old, young and in between
who want to know more, now and then
no doubt it is also apparent
that they are not average in appearance;
It's so easy to start up a conversation
they are practically in communication;
with the written word as a friend
see you as a allied kind
and don't mind
to be entertained,
manners too, are refined.
Hearing easily
first names faster than usually
(also birthdays quick and casually)
even though female or geriatric,
the smiles are true, not fanatic.

There am I searching for the printed call
and find myself involved in talk
for a small story to tell
the librarian belle
a tale as well.

—John M. Piser

FRIENDS

I'm taking a walk with nothing to do, but hide the
hurt I can't show you, 'cause you see I don't have
friends like others, who are as close as brothers,
friends are there when you are down or mad, friends
are there with you through thick, and thin even if
you have a hard time trying to grin, if you let them
help you through the trouble times, then you've made
it you're home free, that's why friends do good for you.
and me so the next time you're feeling down, or blue
just remember the message I told you.

—Jeff Conover

if i tell you' it's only 'cause i love you
after all, that's what friends are for
if i'm persistent, it's only 'cause i have faith in you
and wish that you can believe in yourself
like i believe in you
if i nudge you along
it's because time is of the essence
in this life we have
it's because i learn faith/ trust/ persistence
and all that is necessary for me to carry on in this life
from watchin' you

—Jaki-Terry

OUR CHILDREN

We cry, we laugh, we live.
We worry, we save, we give.
We pray our children will succeed
And hope we've given them what they need.

Our children are born, so fragile, so sweet;
Each day a new challenge for them to meet.
They crawl, they walk, and then they run,
Their eyes filled with wonder, their lives just begun!

We watch with pride and are amazed
At just how much of ourselves we see
In our children while they play,
And wonder what they'll grow to be.

We love, we hate, we regret.
We work, we play, and oft forget
That children come first above all others;
And they depend on fathers and mothers.

—Bonnie Buchanan

YOUTH

Youth is the need for bonds and friendships,
yet it is the need for independence of one's self.
It's the need to feel the authority of an adult,
but it's the need to rebel against adult ideas.
It's the need to have fun and adventure;
it's also the need for loneliness and boredom.

To be youthful is to be everchanging,
but constantly the same.
To be youthful is to be always questioning,
but never wanting to carry the load of the answers.
To be youthful, one must be simple,
yet complex.
To be youthful, one must be easy to understand,
yet misunderstood.
To be youthful, one must laugh as he cries;
he must dance as he sits;
And he must learn as he grows.

—Jeffrey Brian Collins

AZTEC CELEBRATION

When the corn had tasseled
the women loosened their hair
to honor the goddess Xilonen:
a priest carried on his shoulders a young slave girl,
a personification of the goddess:
later they cut her head off, a ceremony
depicting the severing of the green corncob
from its stalk. Then there was a feast
during which the new corn was eaten
for the first time that year.

—Carolyn Martha Neubauer

STATUS QUO

Blind to the Vision of others;
Unaware of the consequences of their sight;
Forever distanced from another perspective;
For always having stood behind the eyes of our lives.
Better we accept that
They see what they say
And feel what they tell us,
Because in their place
We could only see their life through our eyes;
Wholly neglecting the images of their minds.

—Susan Marston

JUST TWO LITTLE BOXES

All people carry two little boxes with them
One to hold hopes, the other dreams
Poor people can live forever with these two things
Just two little boxes of hopes and dreams

Take them away and they may die
Or just turn into hollow people who cry inside
Don't laugh at these people, for it's all they have
Just two little boxes — without them they are dead

A sad day in May, I went outside and into the sun
With tears in my eyes, lifted both covers
Hopes and dreams flew away, the world had won
A poor person died — a poor person is done

Keep these two litte boxes near your heart
With your hopes and dreams may you never part
Open two small covers, hopes and dreams shall fly away
Without them near you — inside you too may die

—Rex Wiley

WHEN COMES HAPPINESS

You were so gentle and kind spoken
now here I am with the heart broken
My baby said good-bye, what am I to do but cry
I try to go on, but it's so hard alone
as the tears roll down my cheeks
it's the heartache that reaps
A hard feeling of emptiness
Oh when comes happiness?
I've loved too often, and been burned
guess I should have learned.
I'm feeling sorry now for myself
saying there will be no one else
I've said this many times before
then with one look, it can open the door
to love and it starts all over again
relationships you think will never end
Then the saying good-byes
tears that fill the eyes
feelings of emptiness
Oh when comes Happiness?

—Diana Pick

THE HALO AROUND ME

The light shined on me
it came from deep within,
It started on its journey to
reach every part of my body,
until it worked its way out
to enclose my entire outer self.
It formed a halo around and inside of me.
It was always there,
I just didn't see it.

—Natasha

PORTRAITS ON THE SHELF

There sit still a parade of pictures,
in line upon the shelf;
Only I knew the story they told,
For each could not speak for itself.

Looking through the tiny eyes,
I saw his future tears,
Changed much from infant tears,
As life unfolded the years.

The resemblance there in stature,
Not conforming with emotional change,
Cannot tell of the tender years,
From innocence to adult man.

A smile upon the tiny lips,
The eager eyes shine bright,
Not revealed by the man portrait,
Who has seen the dark of night.

His head is straight, his eyes pierce deep,
A world that taught him much;
His stern silhouette shows the discipline,
Learned from a sterner touch.

—Gloria Frazier Lee

OPTIC

Reason eludes no mind with order,
Strike a blow of pain then laugh;
Brutal centuries of wanton slaughter,
   Law of the Jungle's infant daughter;
Persistant dominance fellowman,
   Caging millions to bar a chance;
Greed and pestilence allies in suffering,
   Paid for by a hammered spike;
Mercy Sister, I awake to softness,
   Gentle touch, calm, and comfort;
Secure and warm the breath of life,
   Mortal wounds that heal with care;
Raging nightmares, drowning sweats,
   Heated fever left no sight;
Hear the pleasant words of whisper,
   Limbs forever function severed;
Take me up before I wither,
   Return again when I shiver;
Fast is how we soon forget,
   But never found a replacement yet;
Burning rays of light dismember,
   Caught in planes of time and thought;
Visions quest for distant closeness,
   Searching loves for something lost;
Single moments burn a path,
   Find yourself and lose your tross;
Search the chaos all uncommon,
   And expect the answer true;
Crawl, walk, fly past Pluto's photo,
   Sentence Man into the mist.

—Scott Anthony

I heard a whisper in the wind,
    the stream's murmuring,
    a tree-swaying sigh

And they sang to me
    of far-off things
    which we would know

Before we die.

—Nancy Rutenber

SHARING TOGETHER

Share your thoughts
    Share your dreams
Sharing it together
Share what it seems
Share your hopes
Share your plans
From state to state
To land by land
Share your ideas
To the community
We'll be together
From unity to unity
Share the love and joy
Let this war cease
So that the world
Shall live in peace
Let's do it America
From day to day
Sharing together
That's the way!

—Michael Youngblood

TAKE HOLD

Of body and soul, take hold.
    Comfort me from the cold.

To feel your touch is of such.

I reach out for you,
and you seem so far.
I wish upon that lonely star.

Hoping you'll come to my door.
As if you're on another shore.

I think of you as I ponder
and stop.
Looking upon hollow novelty
shops.

Wanting you to know how much
I care.
Holding back the burden I
bear.

My heart gladdens when you are
near.
Distanced, in my eyes you've
seen the tears.

Your inner and outer beauty
surpasses all.
To this I attribute my endless
fall.

Yet there is no reason for
alarm.
I will ascend embraced in
your loving arms.

Of body and soul, take hold.
I do not wish to be bold.

—Steven Gerard Kilner

THE PIRATE SHE

As each boy reaches manhood, sets out on the sea of life;
    He's told he's only half a man, without a thing called wife.
    So out he goes in search of SHE, the other half of HE;
    Unaware that what he seeks is only half of She . . .

She will give her half to make him whole, but never give her all,
The half she gives is only bait, to make that sailor fall.
    From his deck he spies a ship, run by Pirate She;
    Her sails are full, her course is set for intercepting He.

Not knowing of the danger on life's open sea,
He soon becomes a victim of The Pirate She.
    She sinks his ship and steals his gold out on life's open sea
    She ties him fast onto her mast and will not set him free.

Her sails are full, her course is set across life's open sea.
    The sailor boy becomes a man . . . A slave to The Pirate She.

—T. R. Bloom

GENTLEMAN IN DISGUISE

On the morning of a bright new day, I took a drive in my
    brand new Porsche, like I do every other day.

On my way, I saw a man looking for a ride, so I stopped by
him, and picked him up. He looked at me, I looked at him,
and he knew I was a lady.

The way he was dressed, wasn't my kind. I asked him where
he wanted to go. The words he used, the way he spoke, which
might make him,
    A Gentleman in Disguise!
    How do I know a gentleman in disguise.

I took him where he wanted to go, and he took my hand, gave
a kiss, and he told me that he wished to see me soon.

I am a lady, but he's no gentleman. I don't understand why
he's dressed like that, and why he wants to see me soon.
He must be,
    A Gentleman in Disguise!

—Jesse Centeno

MARIE

Hark, it's only the orbe of peace and solitude, this rude raven
    that lurks and cries the night, begone you winged demon vile
and spite.

Against the sad mournful wind you cry as though to tell to
all my secret tis deed that I've done this night.

Ah poor beloved Marie, my only love, my last love, sheltered in
death's rapture's white linen on Her death bed.

Marie, my so beloved Marie, tis the story of love gained and
love so soured so unsettled like a rude smoker's mist.

With me only as a fool to snatch and snarl until I was Hers
only, ah but She was not mine.

Hark you raven, will you tell of Marie's beguildance to place
many others in our bed so to be so cruel thine?

Spious raven will you tell how I came home early from my absence
to find Marie coveted and laid with another, will you tell?

Oh bitter wind that ghostly raptures the shutterings will you also
tell the world how in my hurt and anger how I killed them both
with my gun to feed Her lover to the dogs and to lay Her to tis
night and so days so long that Her body lays spoiled beneath its
shroud and swollen with death's sickening putrid odors.

    Ah cry the raven.
    Cry the Wind.
    Marie my so beloved.

—James Odell Caldwell

VIC

You came to me quietly, without warning.
  Touched my life and I became free.
The fear slipped away, replaced by courage to find the
love and peace you offered me.
Now we begin and should remember these moments, how
illusive they can become.
I give you my life and all that I am and together we'll
reach beyond.

—Carol Morelli

THRESHOLD TO BEAUTY

A vision of beauty entered my domain
  Her name of Lynn is in for a long reign
Her appearance radiates charm and grace
With touches of blush on her lovely face
Eyes that glitter like stars in the night
Can awaken a dark forest to a glowing light
    She's one to be compared to the Goddesses of Greece,
Helen of Troy, the awe of the Golden Fleece.
    Forever, and ever I could go on, because being
With you makes life a song.
    However at this point I will subside
and patiently remain by your side.
Until you finish reading this and reward the poet
With a great big kiss.

—Donald Clay Campbell

A FLOWER

A flower was delivered in class yesterday;
    A card . . . A poem . . .
    Something sweet to say.
  A tug at my heart, a sparkling eye . . .
    (And a thought!!!) . . .
    Too much time's gone by!
  I'm arrogant, thoughtless, and selfish I know,
    Out of the blue!!,
    A great time to show;
  Thoughts rarely surfaced with such style and grace.
  A flower . . . A poem . . . A smile on your face.
A butterfly in your stomach, a tear in your eye . . .
    And a rush of that feeling, never to die.
  It's always there, although sometimes repressed;
  And pounding so strong, down deep in my chest.
As you gaze at this flower, partake of its scent . . .
  Reflect on the years, and what they have meant.

—Arthur D. Harrison

A POEM FOR MARK

I walk upon the sandy beach and the wind
  blew around me
as it knew as I turn to see, what manner of
person is this, that moves my spirit to care
I turn around and you were there
I could not find the reason why, nor could I explain
the feeling that reach the deepest part of my
inner being inside
I turn again and you were here
I ponder all the day and ponder nights
I could not seem to get you out of my thoughts
the more I try, the more I care
afraid to turn around and find not to see you anywhere
Sadness move upon me, for one cannot hold the tide in
so I send happiness to wherever you are
then I turn around and move on as the wind
along the beach I walk.

—Sheryl Galloway

SOMEDAY

Perhaps someday . . . . .
    by chance,
    a glance, a smile, a kiss, an embrace.

Perhaps someday the chance to use,
    those two for the price of one coupons,
    two for the price of one dinners,
    a pair of pillows,
    his 'n hers towels.
Perhaps someday . . . . .

—Celia Garcia

MY MOTHER'S ARMS

My mother's arms are open to greet me
  when I come home from another
tiring day at school.

Her arms are there when I need her
hug to wash away my sorrow.

My mother's arms are full of
Kindness only she could give.

Without this blessing my life would
fall before me.

—Tanieka Sanders, age 10

PERSONAL FORGIVENESS

I look at the glass and see my
  reflection,
    Old memories come to mind with
new resurrection.
    Faces and voices crowd my head.
    Things I wished I'd done, things
that should've been left unsaid.
    Regrets too many, relationships too
few;
    Infatuation too often, too many
lies I thought were true.
    But all my mistakes are buried
in the past,
    and the things that were first
before are now second to last.

—Ane Southward

THE GARDEN

Singers and teachers,
  Artists and priests,
Affluence is gained
With so much for the least.

We need to live long
For the faith that is strong.
And the reasons we share
Until the end of our song.

If life is to give us
The right to compare
The love that we give,
So many can share,

Then cling and believe
In the lessons we learn,
And the hope we embrace
Will forever return.

No matter the clouds
That came and have been,
The sun will return
For the flowers again.

—Gilbert Marcus Woten "Marc"

The blue skies whisking,
   The grass growing from the lands
and the leaf's blowing away.

—Dominic M. DiBenedetto

LOOKING AT LOVE
Behold the beauty of the rose
   And so it is with love;
Beautiful in all its splendor
   But hurting just the same.
Doesn't it make you feel grand
   When someone you love holds your
                              hand?
   Doesn't it make you feel fine
      knowing somebody loves you?
   But love can cut you like a knife
And make you bleed,
   Helpless it does render.
The red, ruby lips are to kiss,
   When mine touch yours, the deeper
I grow in your love.

—Nancy Grim

MEMORIES
We moved the mountains as a youth
   We rode the seven seas
We traveled down the lonely trails
And laughed with every breeze.

We lived each moment of the day
That youth can only live
We rode the currents of the time
And give all we had to give.

Ah! Youth is a wonderful thing they say
We know — because we've been there
But the years are adding one by one
And our cheeks aren't quite so fair.

But memories are made like this
And treasures we've tucked away
We'll have them all to look upon
When our Hair is Silver Gray.

—Jenny Clark

Two as one
   Will be forever.
Two as two,
Together never.

Love that's true
Will never die.
Love that's false
Will always fly.

Love's confused
As rippling water.
Love's as sure
As hands of a potter.

Love is lonely
As flowers in winter.
Love is together
As words to a printer.

Love is all blue;
Yet quietly green.
Love is all hues
That ever were seen.

—Jennisen McCardel

WE
What is it that you hear?
   The sound that whispers above all.

What is it that I fear?
Your words seem to fall.

When at first I sought light in your eyes,
I saw it gleaming over the sun.

When at first I saw darkness in your heart,
I hurt my eyes looking so deep within.

There's no love that can hold
anything but sorrow and joy.
There's no difference I'm told
for any girl and boy.

So, why is it strange for you and me?
   Why is it we?
 Instead of you alone
      and me.

—A. Winegar

LOVE TO CALL MY OWN
I knew from the beginning that you were
   just a flirt.
But yet I fell in love with you knowing
I'd be hurt.
I thought I could tie you down and make
you love just one,
But how can I do something no one else
has ever done.
I know you'll never love me, and I'm
trying not to cry.
For I must find the strength, somehow
to kiss your lips goodbye.
When you ask for me again, you'll find
I won't be there.
I want a love to call my own, not one
I'd have to share.
So I'll hide my broken heart beneath
my laughing face,
And though you think I never cared
no one else can take your place.

—Angela Mustica

JUST YOU AND ME
There is something happening in my life
   Like a small spark that will ignite
A burning fire in my heart
Something I thought would never start

Having you as a friend in the past
Has shown me qualities that cannot be surpassed
I am so attracted to you in every way
That sometimes I run out of things to say
But usually there is only one thing on my mind
And that is that someday in time
You will come to me and say
That you are attracted to me in every way

There are great distances between you and I
That even I cannot deny
Would make it hard for a relationship to last
But time apart will go by fast
For if this was to work itself out
You know that there would be no doubt
You and I were meant to be
Together forever, Just You and Me
To Stacy with all my love, Mike.

—Michael Kimble

215

MEMORIES

Memories — like tapestries —
Are woven in the mind.
Fragments of time long gone
Return like empty phantoms
Lingering on in broken rhymes.
Colors fade, as faces do,
People, they come and go,
But memories — like tapestries —
Are pieces woven in time.

—Richard Youghn

TRANCE
(to Marshall)

The red light glows
and here I am
asleep to life
Alive only
in the beauty
of my own dreams
hearing the strings
of angels' harps

The white flame flickers
and here I am
lost in dreams
of life asleep
with my desires
Hearing angels
strumming harps

And here I am

—Katya Sousa

LITTLE WILD PONY

Little Wild Pony
was born in the Spring
Little Wild Pony
wanted just one thing
Little Wild Pony
liked to play and have fun
Little Wild Pony
could run and run and run

Little Wild Pony
was abused by a man
Little Wild Pony
ran and ran and ran
Little Wild Pony
was frightened and scared
Little Wild Pony
thought that nobody cared

Little Wild Pony
found a place to play
Little Wild Pony
found a place to stay
Little Wild Pony
was graceful with style
Little Wild Pony
was happy for a while

Little Wild Pony
was loved by a man
Little Wild Pony
was one of the clan
Little Wild Pony
was delivered and spared
Little Wild Pony
knows that somebody cared

—Glenn Lechniak

BELLE

Resting quietly against an adobe wall, she waits for me.
Light blue eyes reflect a starlight within.
Lips the color of grenache,
hair light brown with streaks of fire,
skin a golden brown, a tribute to the worship of Apollo.
Wearing a long sleeve white dress, fluttering against heat-hazy air.
But I am afraid of a perfect beauty and its lasting embrace.
Sadly I turn from her beckoning smile.
Realizing that as a dreamer I long to hold her,
but facing the mirror of reality I must turn away.

—Phillip T. Cochran

A DEAR DAD

He brought sunshine into an otherwise cloudy day.
The wishes and desires of others took precedence over his own.
He wore his concern morning, noon and night.
The enthusiasm and interest he shared manifested itself daily.

His compacted schedule was not too full;
The complexities of childrearing were not too much;
He created time to read to us and time to share.
The daily cares of life encircled his fulltime role as Dad.

His face gleamed when he saw me, and I knew.
The furrow of his brow disappeared when he saw me, and I knew.
His entire body radiated when he saw me, and I knew.
The love he had was real.

—B. H. Lee

YOU'RE ODD

Your lens is out of focus and your song is out of tune.
Your beat is never quite in step and your winter starts in June.
Your paisley pants and plaid shirt just never match your socks.
They say you are the peg that never fits the box.
You break dance to Mozart and hang your wash out in the rain.
And though they often hurt your pride you never feel the pain.
Your taste they say is so bizzare, cartoons can make you cry.
You say goodnight to all your plants and wait for their reply.
But what they cannot see in you, I find I love the best!
The thing that makes you special is you're different from the rest.
Your heart's the size of Texas, and you always find the time,
to see that all my puzzles fit and make my poems all rhyme.
I'll kiss away your sorrows and brace you if you fall.
I'll stay yours forever cause you're perfect after all.

—Cheryl Lea Bridget Baker Brecunier

BOAR'S NEST BATCHER

I'm holdin down the boar's nest, an a-cookin for myself;
A chunk of sow hangs from a nail, the lick can's on the shelf.
The prunes is schwivelled up so hard they take two days to
boil. I'm outa baking powder an I'm outa lantern oil.
My coffee pot has sprung a leak; the gravy that I make
Would float a two pound biskit, an my pepper can won't shake
I set beans on at sun-up, with a hot fire in the grates —
I dish em out for supper, an they rattle in the plate.
I've studied through four catalogs, wore out two almanacs
Till knowledge bulges out my ears about them kind of facts,
By day I doctor screw worms, an I ride the lonely bogs;
By night I snore and dream of things thats in them catalogs.
I'm batchin in the Boar's Nest—my chair's a staple keg;
Jest the thought of canned tomatoes makes my paunch set up
an beg. The coyote howls an hears his kind respond acrost the drawl
and even my old ponies has each other's necks to chaw—
But if I squall—no answers but the bull bats lonesome tune,
Or a skeered mouse on the table knockin off a dirty spoon
I ain't no hand for fancy chuck, I don't like crowds too well,
But batchin in the Boar's Nest get lonesomer than hell.

—Mary French

THE MISSING PIECE

As I have gone through my life
Trying to put the puzzle together,
I thought this one piece would be missing forever.
Through the years it brought me many tears.
When I finally surrendered and gave up my search
Like a bird, you flew into my life
And made my heart your forever perch.
Now I hope to one day be your wife,
For I know our love will never cease.
Because you are the missing piece.

—Tonya Reneé Pruitt

FEELINGS

Nothing is greater for a husband and wife,
To add their first child into their life;
Whether a boy or girl it just doesn't matter.
It's exciting to hear the noise and the clatter.

Crawling and sprawling all over the place,
Moving around as if in a race;
Fumbling and tumbling with little or no grace,
Feelings of happiness to see your child's face.

Their cute little smiles, their sad little face,
you knew that instant they found their place:
How precious and tiny, but full of might,
Feed them, bathe them, they put up a fight.

Altogether as a happy family;
Feelings of love that's the way it should be.

—Jeanine Ostland

PROCRASTINATION

Old Rafe Collins sat on his porch, rockin'
to and fro,
Shakin' his head, lamentin' his life and
wishin' it just weren't so.

"When I was young, I vowed, the finer things
in life I'd taste,
I'm an old poor man now, my life's been
naught but a waste."

"Ah, but if I could only return, to those days
gone long before,
I'd make somethin' of my life, I'd certain
not be sittin' here munchin' an apple core."
"If I could only return, to start my life
anew,

Why, I'd work from morn to night to make
my dreams come true."
"But — the panes in my windows are gone,
the paint on my walls is peelin'
There's holes in the floor, cracks in the wall
and spider webs on my ceilin'."
"Rafe, Rafe Collins, 'tis your wife here
a speakin',
The rain's comin' hard and the ceilin's
a leakin'."

"Stuff the hole with paper, Woman, and stop
that dreadful leak,
Can't you see I'm busy now, I'll fix the
leak next week."

Who can ponder those who have suffered
a change in life's station,
From careless living in the dreadful state of
procrastination.

—Linda Sellers

GOD'S GIFT OF MORNING

The powdered wings of a butterfly
Dance in summer sun.
Morning's breath of dew
Kisses roses one by one.

God's rainbow of bright colors
Is splashed across the sky,
Like a painting on a canvas
So perfect to my eye.

The breeze is so gentle
As if He's whispering in my ear:
"This is My gift of morning.
I am always near."

I look all around
As far as the eye can see,
And I realize the beauty of morning
Is God's gift to me.

—Teresa Mae Friskney

AUTUMN

Autumn is a lovely time,
The leaves are colored,
Oh, so fine,
With their brilliant colors
raining down,
Falling softly without a sound.

The pretty fall flowers dressed
in yellow and gold,
Oh, what beauty we behold!
The pumpkins ready for the pies,
The jack-o'-lanterns smiling with
big mouth and eyes.

The little squirrels scurry,
With bushy tail and packed jaws,
Up one tree and down the other.
They are always in a hurry.

The air is crisp,
The children brisk,
While they try to catch the leaves,
As they drift down from the trees.

—Pat Bell

NATURE

The river passes slowly
The trees, with wind, do shake
The Hand of GOD reaches lowly
The life of man to shape

His nature all about us
Brings special moments when
The works of GOD reaches out
To touch the hearts of men

A peace upon us settles
So much a part we seem
GOD blesses all of nature
With His love which is supreme

The Blessings show around us
In the most precious little things
The first tree buds, a robin's egg,
The movement of a stream

We are part of all this beauty
That GOD made for us to share
And all He asks us in return
Is that we take the time to care

—Roanna M. Walters

LETTER TO AN ELDERLY FRIEND

To talk about the past, we must
since we are friends
traveling on a dead end street
and running out of years,
while everything we did before
descends on us
like a shrouded mist
not quite within our grasp,
and so we seem to live a double life,
to reminisce
on days of eager youth
when rhapsody of blues and melody
accompanied our evenings out,
and search for answers
strained the carefree thoughts,
a time when nuclear was an unknown quantity,
HOME movies,
entertainment for the future.

—Jane Murray Seip

BUTTERFLY SUMMER

I recall the summers of my youth
When I tried to be a grown-up
And the falls and winters of my adult years
When I wished I was a child
Nowadays, I watch the children
As they play in the park
Catching butterflies with green nets
And the joy they discover upon setting it free.
"It's one of God's creatures,"
They exclaim, watching it fly away
How often I have dreamed
Of doing just that
Of not having to care, who pays the bills,
What time to fix dinner,
Does my slip show at the bottom of my dress?
It was a hot August morning
I sat in my backyard on the edge of the deck
Watching a Monarch fly from flower to flower
My hands around my coffee cup
And I was a child again
Chasing Butterflies

—Christine D. Sterling

NOW, DADDY'S GONE!

Their home, now empty, is falling down:
Tangles and snarls all cover the ground.
There! signs that flowers once did abound
And, glimpses of eloquence can still be found.

A swing is poised as if waiting in play.
The small house in back, now invaded by rain,
Was once where children played and sang —
It's walls with innocent laughter rang.

A peek inside and, there's a glance —
The place small feet once merrily danced.
A little girl had twirled and pranced.
The mirror's now cold — it's sorrow enhanced.

Living room windows are dark and bleak —
They're staring back, as if to speak.
The family's now gone as new lives they seek,
In times when the world — finds them weak.

Here, they held on tightly to a string:
Ties which bound them, provided a dream.
There! an old, broken gum ball machine.
Encouraged, enhanced — they used to sing.

—Carol Marie Darling

A MOTHER'S TEAR FROM A SON'S EYE

Mother sweet Mother so caring and kind,
Always arriving just in time.
With remedies, answers, and a whole lot of love
It's all for you Mother, I thank the lord above.
Your silent strength, your helping hand;
Making the worst times seem like they were grand.
It is you mother I hold in my heart.
Not in an eternity's time will we ever part.

—Paul R. Carlson

SABLE ON FIRE

In the lackluster pitchy sky
the clouds danced in the starlight
Abruptly, the sable was ablaze
illuminated by the beautiful meteorite.

Plunging out of the heavens
scorching into vibrant tones of orange and cinnabar;
and abbreviated existence in the atmosphere
proves toxic for this shooting star.

For the doomed satellite
set the night aglow with its fire;
come radiate my darkness
with your brilliance and grace to admire.

**For Sharon whom I love with all my heart,
all my soul, all that I am.**
—Kevin O. Mulholland

DIAMONDS

Diamonds are a girl's best friend 'tis true
The colors, yellow, black or sapphire blue

A gift to wear that leads to the heart
Anyone who gives a diamond is usually very smart

True love grows from year to year
Recalling the ones we hold dear

Diamonds, like love, should last forever and ever
Giving out light that will dim never

Our lives should be filled with love for one another,
like a diamond's sparkling light
That radiates as a streak of lightning for all to see,
be it day or night.

So as we go fleeting down life's highway
May our diamonds sparkle with love from day to day.

—Roberta Petermann

ORCHARD IN THE EVENING

Their shadows blanket and cool the dry ground.
Tall and sturdy, hardly a sound.

The wind exercises its limbs and the tired fall;
Nevertheless, others soon will be installed.

Full bloom or naked a wondrous sight to behold.
So vital and sacred in Earth always mold.

My head leans against the stern breast, I breathe.
Immediately, I feel life indeed.

Oh, the mysteries you must keep!
So, so ancient no soul can peep.

Give me a hint or even a sign.
Maybe whenever the wind whistles by.

Touching my ears, then I can perceive.
All the knowledge, you hold I believe.

—Amy McRae

WRITER'S FRUSTRATION

He needs to find something,
A way to create,
A way to express.
but the words will not come.
The frustration weighs too heavy.
If only . . .
But no!
The imagination runs dry.
What to do?
He cannot find the clue to the writer's dream.
The masterpiece is lost.
He pays the cost that the searching brings,
like bells that ring,
forgotten.
Still, he keeps trying to weave magic of golden words.
Maybe someday, some way the magic will unfold,
the story that is still untold.
Only then will be the end to the writer's frustration.

— Noelle Tennant

THEY PAVED THE ROAD

There was a country road,
Where long ago, I walked barefoot
In the soft, warm, brown dirt.
It was quiet and peaceful.

A few cars — drove slowly by.
If one met another,
Someone had to pull over
To let the other pass.

Everyone you saw — said "hello."
Beside the road — wildflowers bloomed,
Small animals played,
And after a rain — tiny rivers flowed by its side.

Then one day,
People came with machines.
They paved the road!

Now it's noisy and hurried,
Cars whiz by, no one speaks,
The wildflowers and animals are gone;
It's just a hard, cold, black piece of asphalt.

— Natalie Golin

COAL MINERS

Deep 'neath the mountain in a black sweaty hole
Where staunch, daring miners dig the black coal
Where the view of a sunrise, before work begins
May be the last sight of these lusty brave men

On their faces a look of unconquerable pride
That no coat of grit and coal dust can hide
Yet deep in their hearts hidden from men's eyes
Lies a fear that no more may they see the blue skies

They live in dread of that awful sound
That earth shaking rumble deep underground
The cracking of timbers as they feel the shock
Of the pressing and shifting of the mountain tops

The thing that brings fear to the bravest of men
A name unanswered, when the tunnel caves in
There's a tear in their eyes, they cannot hide
Shed for their friends, still trapped inside

When this back breaking toil, their strength has drained
They still face each day with a faith unchanged
Their thoughts are heartwarming as the spring sunshine
As they dream of the days spent down in the mines

— Carl Williams

THE AGONY AND ECSTACY OF WRITING

Writers are sensitive spirits
Saturated with worldly pain
With a little pen and paper
They sit down to explain

The reality of life "As Is"
Unearthed beneath the glittering dreams
For each one of us has a truth
Concealed in his heart's seams

"Don't quit yet" — They say
Pen is mightier than sword
They had their share of heartaches
May be one more they could afford

Still — writing is fulfillment
Writing is a spiritual quest
Once you get the taste of it
You simply cannot rest.

— Mrs. Sudha Goyal

THE CYCLE

CRACK!
The light breaks through, leaving
Spots upon my naked form. My eyes
Soon open to see a blurry shape — then
Suddenly forms an outline. From
Darkness to cloudy and then — Mother

THERE! Now, I may survive.
Air gives a sense of Freedom.
— A feeling that seems to make me
Soar until reaching the heights of unlimited
Emptiness. There! There is my Existence.
I take it and feel strong.

The atmosphere brings a cloud of doom.
PCHOOOO! —— POOOMPH!
The piercing plunge of a foreign body
Enters my body and thus my soul.
I feel myself weakening as I slip through the
Fingers of the Hand of the Wind.

My Existence ceases. I am no more.

— David G. Dover

SOMETIMES POETRY HAPPENS

Some poets can write
from reflected experience
referring back to what was written.

Others need to be there,
in full view of their subject,
opening up to what's being given.

Sometimes poetry happens between the two.

It's then you don't really write the poem.
It writes you!
You just put it down on paper.

When you see it there,
You've captured it.
Or, rather, it's captured you.

What really happened between the two?

To explore that space
between you and me
Is to discover who we are.

For deep within, at the source of the gap
lie the togetherness of the three —
the seer, the seen, and the poetry in between.

— Kenneth Chawkin

GONE

Remember not me
When I am gone,
Yet if you must,
Remember just
A grain of sand
In the ocean spray
Upon your shore
That washed away.

—Peggy M. Smith

WOMEN DO IT ALL

Stops children crying
Grocery buying

Bills to pay
Finds dogs that run away

Mopping floors
Closing doors

Stays up all night
Referee brother-sister fights

Cooking lunch
Sunday brunch

Mending clothes
Wiping noses

Teaching morals
Beauty palors

Showing love
Killing bugs

It's expected
So nothing's neglected

—Barbara Richardson Jackson

BAD DAY: MOM

Phoning to hear another adult voice
Being able to talk about subject of
choice
Cat trapped in pantry, kids have her
pinned in
Water boils out while making formula,
baby drools down her chin
Sister eating brother's donut an he
lets out a scream
They're playing Humpty Dumpty off the
furniture; "Yes" this is real not a
dream

Walking out of bathroom, one comes
pants twisted to knees
She wonders "What's next?" Will they
hang from trees?
With gum in mouth, another gets bored
On house, on another's clothing, and in
hair, gum is stored
Baby's still cranky, crying on and on
The others are fighting, only five
minutes gone
Here comes the "Whys" and "I had that
first"

Within the very next sentence they're
dying of thirst
Finally getting close for some of
them's nap
A very "BAD DAY", baby still on
her lap

—Lou Pinter

CHILDHOOD

Over meadow, hill, and pathways
How we played and played!
In and out our forests,
In the sun and shade.

Tasks, we had in plenty,
But after work was done
Off for swim and fishing.
Oh, it was such fun.

There were sun perch in the deep pools,
There were tadpoles in the sand,
And berries in the fence rows—
It was a pleasant land.

From birth Until adolescence,
How we played and played,
In the springtime of our lives
Through the sun and shade.

—Enola H. Martin

THE SANDS OF TIME

The sands of time may wash away every fear;
But God can wash away each tear.
Minute by minute the day ticks by . . .
But God is always there to help us find the way.

To feel the cool chilly waters of God
Sweeping over us!
To feel His presence nearby . . .
Drinking from the Eternal Fountain . . .
To know God!

Feasting on Him and His love,
What could be dearer?
Drinking from His fountain;
Feasting from His supply
Of eternal food!

God be near us;
God help us.
Our strength is Your strength
O, Lord!
Walk daily by our side . . .
Talk with us daily.

—Wanda F. Davis

OCEAN CROSSING

The Pacific's waters are running swift
With winds so strong and free,
Billowing out the Clipper's sails
As we plow through choppy seas.

The sky has turned a greyish blue
Dark clouds are gathering high,
Makes the art of sailing ships
Challenging to those who try.

The trenches of the ocean's swells
Puts the crew to the test,
When the great ship slips and rides
Upon white foamy crests.

I stand here on the windy deck
With the wheel in my firm hands,
As my hardy shipmates aloft
Set sails for distant lands.

There's nothing like that solid bond
Between sailors and their ships,
While sailing the restless oceans
On their adventurous trips.

—John Shaw

SUMMER STORM

The smell of fresh mown hay is strong and sweet.

I hear the low, far off rumble of an impending storm.

See the corn?
It seems to be lifting its mighty leaves to the ever darkening skies
And applauds the ever needed rain, the rain of a summer storm.

—Jane Piercy

ROOTS

We all have roots, but what exactly are they?
Anchors holding our memories, so in our minds the past stays.
Sometimes roots hold us tightly; moving is misery.
Sometimes they hang in tatters, too weak to imprison me.
If strong, it tortures; if weak, just slight regret.
Slowly roots weave a tight, tangled net!

—Marisa Kim Clayton

DUNGEONS

Stuck inside my many dungeons trying to control my cries, with
my dreams of falling how can I learn to fly? Oh damn my eyes,
damn my eyes for refusing to see, Whispers from Phantoms al-
ways mocking me. Climbing the ladder of life finding there's no
place to go, Back to my dungeon with my wandering soul. Tear
these eyes from their sockets and no blinder could I be! You
locking all the stairways despite all of my pleas. Am I just
your lap dog with oh so many fleas? You open doors, your kind-
ness spreads the light
But my dreams are shattered by the lonely night
My mouth is so useless because the words it speaks
And sometimes I worry that my mind is growing weak.

—Bill Higgs

I AM A NIGHTMARE

The fear of nothingness took me by surprise, as the
coldness surrounded me. Silence was everywhere, Darkness all
around me. For when death came upon me and stared straight in
my face I didn't quiver — I realized I stared back.

The darkness came upon the earth, the moon became fully
bright and shiny casting shadows, from the Cross before the moon.
Eerie sweat was dripping from my face — death was before me. My
nerves stopped shaking, I remembered I was here before.

As I woke up from my nighmare the darkness came before
my door. I opened my top lid, and as I raised from my coffin and
leaving it behind for the night. I stalked the dreary night,
in my black cape as I suddenly had the hunger for blood. My fangs
out to settle the urge for my hunger.

"I AM THE NIGHTMARE!"

—Michelle R. Desrosiers

BLOWING THE COBWEBS AWAY

She wasn't forced to leave him
as he slowly slipped into sleep last night.
Again, she wasn't away when he awoke, just a few hours later.
Form and features unforgotten, her face danced,
just inches out of reach.
Remnants of her slight rasp resounded
about the rooms and hallways of his imagination,
releasing deadbolts long ago left locked.
Now he's a child, awaiting the clowns of a circus parade;
the brass band making its way, marching up Main Street,
sends seas of excitement surging through his body.
Now a teenager, hungrily awaiting the wildness of summer,
as the final seconds of the spring semester lumber away.
Finally a man, set free in his passion, just waiting to see her again.

—Joseph Tait

Peace
for my heart
A sigh,
A sign of Love
in the dark
rain rain hard,
hard rain
It feels Like
pain.
Somewhere,
Somewhere out there
We are
I know
it's not far
Standing hihg,
Standing high in a tree
Look at me!
I just want to be

free!

To Laurie Frank
—Barry R. Collins

Field of green
that's what you are
rippling wheat
that moves and
sighs —
torn by wind, sun
and rain
frost that weaves itself
on window panes
leaves that curl and
spiral to hard ground —
then dance and rustle with
whispered sound
— curl around the earth to
die
muted shapes everchanging
death defy —
and born again
with each new spring
heralding life and the hope
it brings.

—Lillian Sturm

LOCKED IN A STORM

A treasure was shared
In loves' vast chambers
This thing beyond dreaming
It was real, yet not there

An ocean of time
A forest of waning
Cold are the depths
Of funneled despair

Clean yet despondent
Depressed and forlorn
I reached for a moment
The locks of her hair

The key was all rusted
The lock was not there
I found in its place
The place to nowhere

If beyond this is dreaming
If beyond this I care
A dead world is living
Enormous, unfair

—R. L. Williams

SUMMER MISCHIEF

After a summer rain
    the puddles
    are still.

Then sounds of laughter
    and splashes
    are everywhere.

I look at my son — wet
from head to toe — and say,
"Out of the puddle!"

A sudden look
    then that smile
    what mischief
    he must feel inside.

I'm taken back to distant days —
    the mud between my toes
    and splashes way up high —

What mischief I felt inside.

—Randall K. Anderson

AFTER THE BOMB

Where are the cats,
    the dogs,
    the birds,
    the frogs?
Where are the people,
    the child,
    the horses,
    running wild?
Where is the love,
    the pain,
    the anger,
    the day?
    the night . . .
Where are we?
What have we done?
What happened to the ocean,
    the land,
    the Earth
    that was so grand?
After the bomb . . .   Why?

—"Pie", age 15

FIRST TASTE OF ECSTASY

You'll know it on one warm day
    The first part of some spring —
Rosebuds will be coming out
To hear the songbirds sing.

The debut of the daffodils
Will dazzle and soon be gone —
Crocuses that came to drink of rain
Will thrill, then drift slowly on.

Some later day you'll search in vain
For metaphor or seldom used cliché —
To tell all the world's young lovers
How they'll feel that first magic day.

But poets cannot depict it,
Nor sonnets show the way —
The bliss is yours ineffable,
One first warm, ecstatic day.

So welcome back each springtime,
Knowing it's always meant for thee —
As all young things so much in love
First taste of ecstasy.

—Wayman Grant

EARTH

I'm like a kitten asleep after a warm bowl of milk;
    I'm as cuddly as a newborn puppy;
    I'm as soft as a rabbit's fur;
I can be as mean as a grizzly awoke from a long winter's nap;
    I can be nice as Santa on Christmas Eve;
    I am the Earth that you stand on!

—Cal D. Grote

DUST

I always feel guilty whenever I dust.
    I fear there's a little pixie somewhere
in the house crying.
As I wipe away a week's worth of her hard work,
it seems to me she must have put
every piece, every tiny speck in a specific place.
She laid it all out "just so" — just so I could see
exactly how small my tiny nephew's hands are.

—Elizabeth A. Cullen

SEPTEMBER STORM

To sleep by the fire on a Persian rug
    With the rain coming down outside
To drowse under cover of green/gold silk
And feel the warmth in my heart
To hear the echo of music once known
The stillness of beauty once seen
The sweetness of silence that smiles from dark worlds
Into ripples of soft shining laughter
To wait for my love in the mystery of
Sound and silence and rain and flame

—Elizabeth Alleyn

WATER

Water, the precious commodity from Heaven's golden hand,
    and, a survival existance source, for mammal, and the man.

We take it for granted, and don't treat it as we orta,
the Master made it pure, let's help Him clean our water.

Two-thirds of the Globe, so there's plenty for us all,
the oceans, streams, and rivers, it's there when we call.

For fishermen, swimmers, and drinkers, coast to the border,
contaminants have no place, within our precious water.

Commercialism and greed spills, in their awful haste,
killing our real wealth, much more dear than their waste.

Clean clear water, is a concern, shut down the hoarder,
active detergent for cleanliness, is made by our water . . . .

—Al Jones

THE SONG

The song inside yearns to be sung
and my body aches to be played

As an unseen hand hesitantly strokes the first notes
it comes out haltingly at first
tripping over my ineffectual human instrument
quickly it gains strength
becoming louder, stronger, truer

Escaping from earthly ties
it illuminates the heavens
as it slowly encompasses the planets, the galaxy, the universe
mixing with the spatial music of the stars
my song of love changes, is adapted
and is now an astral rhythm
unique yet universal

—Mary E. Stephens

NOVEMBER MELODY

November air so cool and crisp . . .
The leaves are beautiful colors, with mist.
A November Birthday is here . . .
A time to celebrate another year of life, just kissed.
November trees all bare of leaves, and the
      smell of the sweet soft breeze.
November is a melody that will sing all over
      the earth, for this is the month of your
      wonderful birth!
Happy Birth-Day my dearest!!!

      —Jennifer Prince

LEAVING HOME

Oh parents my parents why can't you see,
    the pain in my eyes you have given to me.

Oh parents my parents don't turn your backs,
    the path I must follow has arrived at last.
    Your approval I seek, so don't close your ears.
    Please hear the words I must reveal.

Oh parents my parents don't give me that look,
    I know where it comes from, I know what it means.
    Don't open new wounds that can never heal.

Oh parents my parents just give me a smile, a hug,
    a nod, oh don't cry out loud.

I love you please know that, but I still must plea;
    permit me my life, please set me free!

      —Peggy M. Flinn

LEAVING

The set has dissolved . . .
    The players have quieted . . .
The abrupt shoals before the fog . . .
Coolly we disintegrate into absence, into solitude,
Silenced by the perspective of time.

Your well-timed alliance with distance I respect.
Your innocent idiosyncrasies I like.
My grace in acceptance is now my virtue.
But still, your presence, our days of diligent ease,
I miss.

And as I sit here in this room,
I see the success in my effort, my admittance of an end.
It is only because of my virtuous acceptance,
and of your time ago presence,
no longer ghostlike, that the past is forgotten.

      —Susan E. Vecho

YOUTH CONTEMPLATING DEATH

Sometimes, I wonder

    Who will be at my funeral when I die?

Will I die an admirable figure
With many friends, or will I die quietly,
A nobody?

Will I die having achieved
All my lifetime goals,
Or will I die never having reached them?

Will I "pass away" in sixty years,
Leaving my children and grandchildren to grieve, or
Will I "go" tomorrow, leaving my predecessors to mourn?

After I'm gone, who will remember me?

Sometimes, I wonder.

      —Wendy Riegel, age 19

SUMMER SOUNDS

I will always remember that night,
    The old swing, the fireflies, the moonlight,
The frogs softly croaking by the lake —
Your words of goodby.
Why could you not hear my heart break?

      —Jean Brenningmeyer

REFLECTIONS

My eyes grow dim
    on the image of you —
a ripple on memory's pool of dreams.
In my search through waters deep,
reflections tempt me
to sleep with the coldness.
The deceit, the trickery
must soon end,
and my eyes be dried with reality.
Gasping for air am I,
yet always yearning for another swim . . .
a swim, a touch, a kiss
beneath waters cold
and sombre and dark
shall I eternally covet.

      —Thomas Chadwick Horne

MISSING YOU . . .

If you woke up one morning
    And the sun was no longer there,
If you smelled the misty rose
    With no scent to fill the air,
If you have listened for the morning bird
    And did not hear his call,
If the honey that once tasted so sweet
    Now had no flavor at all,
If you had to say goodbye
    To someone you care deeply for,
If the parting was so difficult
    You felt you could bear no more,
If you understand these feelings
    As I hope you really do,
Then you know what the words mean
    When I say I'm missing you.

Dedicated to: David Gue
      —Michelle Underwood

Grandma you are the greatest.
    You mean the world to me.
There is no way to show you.
    Of just how much you see.
There was a time, I took for granted.
    The way you show your love.
But now it means a lot to me.
    As much as heaven above.
The phrase they say, "He broke the mold."
    Is oh, so true for you.
Because my dearest grandma.
    There's no one else like you.
This poem is to let you know.
    That I really love you.
With all my heart, and all my soul —
    It's everything about you.
So keep this poem — read it twice.
    It may often bring a tear.
When you think of me, remember this:
    I love you, oh, so dear.

**This poem was written and dedicated
to my grandma — Lavina C. Sappington.**
      —Yvonne R. Gordon

LEAVES

Leaves fall softly to the ground,
To sleep through winter safe and sound,
Brilliantly blinding the human eye,
As they tilt their colors to the sky,
Slowly, softly tumbling down,
While making a quiet whispering sound.

—Jill Harper, age 12

A MASK

How could anyone ever know
the direction the girl would go?
She was so young and the night was cold
as her story began to unfold.
In the desk of her bare room
hid a mask of total doom.
The mask was cold, its mouth was wide.
Too big a voice to try and hide.
She felt alone and so full of pain.
Her happy life ceased to remain.
Life got harder for her every day.
Putting the mask on seemed the best way.
A coldness was felt on her head.
The answer there, no peace, instead
the mask and her soul began to wither
the second after she pulled its trigger.

—Kathrine A. Machacek

THE TREASURE OF THE BEACHCOMB

Peering through the circling tide,
Sandpipers quickly find the treasure.
With their ever-probing beaks
Striking side to side . . . .

The treasure is the perfect shell
Of the legendary sand dollar.
Found in the aftermath of rain
When the tide flows out; no ocean swell.

As fragments found along the sand
Pieces picked with hungry vigor
Or precious treasures found unbroken
Come to rest upon the land.

Sandpipers find them a delicacy,
A gift from the ocean.
Sweet nectar for them
A treasure for me . . . .

—Linda Rawlings Steyding

THE ABC'S

The ABC's just aren't
the ABC's any more.
    At one time, seems so long ago,
that we had to know all the ABC's
We had to be able to count, to divide,
to read. Oh, those stories we read of
Tom, Susan and the dog. How they
jump and ran for the ball, see how the
ball, the big ball could bounce.
    They would give us a page with a picture
of money on it, to see if we could count the
money, nickels, dimes, quarters.
    They gave us, pictures of colors to see if
we knew, blue from yellow.
    The only sports we played then was
tag, or stick ball in the playground at
breaktime, some had footballs they would
play on one end of the playground.

—Joyce Smith

FOREBODING

Gnarled old hands clutching at the sky
        disappear at the crack of a whip
    only to claw upward again to
        grasp at their black oppressive tormentor.
Blue distorted fingers slash out
        raking deep across the dark face
    creating a new deformed figure
Only to be snatched back as a
        threatening rumble breaks the
    eerie fear-laden silence and
        grows to become a dreadful rage-filled roar
        releasing a torrent of suppressed fury
    and a dire warning of the eminent
                    Rain.

—Angela L. Gray

DEFIANT LIONS

Sinews rippled in sensuous fire
Living flesh sculpted fine and hard
Taut and lean from thigh to jaw
Blazing under the beating sun . . . his sun

A kingdom falls, a crown tumbles to the dust
The lions roar and circle the prey
The bloodlust hot burns in their eyes
Like the roaring throat of a volcano's spasm

A wicked gleam suspended in time
The prey hostage now to defiant claws
Proud nations like great stags fall, too
Without mercy in the eyes of their wanton God

The defiant lions, drunk on the blood, dance
Awash in the ecstasy of their kill,
Ignorant brutes blinded to the sight
Recognizing not that they and their victim are one.

—W. Robert Kirbo

ODE TO THE BROWN THRUSH

In early morn I hear this bird outside my break-
fast nook;
He wakes the robin and the bluebird in the piney
wood.
    Why he comes here to sing, I'll never know.
But in my simple ignorance, I suppose
    The Self-same Power that brought him to sing
Brought me to listen.
    In the moth hour of morn, he sings from a yellow
spray,
On the forsythia tree that boldly grows.
    He surveys the orchard in song.
And often draws the watch of hungry cats with lone
dismay.
    He hears the doves coo when long their lovers
stray.
He hears the lark and linnet that sprinkle dew
    In honeysuckle lane or bosky avenue.
Whatever the robin or bluebird dreams,
    This bird can say.
Down he drops, scratches a leaf, hops along the yard
fence,
    Picks up a cricket, sings a song, flies to the box-
wood,
Hides himself, and to his art again.
    Dear science, this riddle please explain;
How could the death of that noisy cricket be the life,
Of yon Caruso in the forsythia tree?

—J. H. O'Stephenson

NURSES

AH!, there seem to be so few
Maybe that's our cue
I think we should review
And see what we can do
To make something new
For YOU, YOU, and YOU!
Because, I think there should definitely be more than two
Or else these hospitals are going to be like a zoo!
Without more Nurses too!

—David John Schneider, Jr.

TO A FRIEND

The night is black, and I'm feeling blue;
but the moon has come out, while thinking of you.
No time is too rough, or moments too drear;
for with you as a friend, they all disappear.
Though the miles are between us, just let me say
I'm there if you need me, just a phone call away.
I've got my shortcomings, I'm just a man.
I'm also your friend; I'll do what I can.
Like you've done for me; I just want the chance
to make your spirits soar and dance.

—Robert S. Sutton

Who is always in my corner,
when I'm down and need a hand?
Who gives the love and understanding,
of more than just a friend?

Who is last to criticize,
or question what I've done?
When asked who still Loves me,
who stands together proudly, and answers one by one?

Who is second only to God, in forgiving,
when I've gone astray?
Who will be there waiting,
while I, the price do pay?

No man has more to treasure,
Than that which God has given me.
Life, Liberty, and Happiness,
I have it all, I have my
"Family."

—Clayton

MY MOTHER

Thank you God for a Mother as sweet as mine,
And for a Mother who was so kind.
Thank you God for a Mother with a gentle touch,
And for a Mother who loved me so much.

Thank You for guiding her along life's way,
And for helping her to trust in You day by day.
Thank You for letting her live to be old,
And for the memories more precious than gold.

Thank You for a Mother whose love always shone through,
And for a Mother who cared enough to guide me, too.
In a lifetime there is only ONE who is our Mother,
And the love of her surpasses that of any other.

Thank You God for a Mother as sweet as mine,
And for a Mother who was so kind.
Thank you God for a Mother with a gentle touch,
And for a Mother who loved me so much.

**Written in loving memory of my
Mother, Mrs. Mary Cleo Taylor
who died March 15, 1974**
—Eva Taylor Moody

THE QUESTION, "WHY?"

To the question, "Why?"
The answer's many times exempted.
It's often with a sigh
When any answer is attempted.

—Lu Ann W. Shaw

HEALING

The healing's come; the hurt is gone,
I think I've learned to carry on
Without those constant thoughts of you
Pervading everything I do.

I've learned to think again and smile
And even dared to dream a while,
Although I feared I'd cry anew
O'er thoughts of you.

I didn't though; I'm proud of me;
I've learned to face reality.
I know you're gone; you won't come back;
You are the love I'll always lack —

The world goes on; the sun still shines,
And poets still make foolish rhymes,
I live again; I've lost my fear . . .
Oh, damn it all, here comes a tear.

—Tony Imbruglio

No shoes for my feet,
food, so long ago.
Then you came and rescued me,
from the pain and famine of the times.

Grateful was I and my brothers, too,
the price we paid no one knew.
All equal in this land, or mostly so,
all alive, but surely not well.

You gave us food and clothing,
our fires burn through winter's cold.
We gave you all we could,
then you took our spirit, too.

Proud were we so long ago,
living, caring, working hard.
Now we're shells, our spirit gone,
falling deeper daily into despair.

Comments on Communism
—Kenneth H. Schwieder

OCTOBER

This time of year
confounds me —
rising through
all its little dyings
there's the dream
taking hold again
to root anew,
to strive, to grow . . .
. . . and so I think of you.

Shiny red magnolia seeds
that seem
to glisten
in among the fallen leaves
like ruby teardrops —
in my heart I see
tender blossoms
on a glorious tree . . .
. . . I wonder if you ever think of me.

—Sandra Sena

SUMMER

Summer is time to get in a pool
A pool that is cool, cool, cool.
There are flower blossoms
and cute little opossums.
There are horses eating grass
while little ants pass.
There are birds flying in the sky
never saying good-bye.
Summer is the time to rest
that's what I like best!

—Dusti Smith

LIFE'S JOLTS

Life is like a bucking bronc.
It has its ups and downs,
its twists and turns
and rough rope burns.
Sometimes you feel like giving up,
it's hard to take the jolts
and all the slammin' around.
Sometimes you hit the ground,
but there is always another chance
to ride the tough times down.

—Rita Kelly, age 19

My lovely dove
Fly away
from here
Forget not
your song of mortality
Banish my whimsical fear
Sing to the sea
A sweet lullaby
Follow my image
to a hidden beach
Listen to my
silent soliloquy
Hide my dreams
Within my reach
And do not wander,
or flee
from my grasping hands
to drown in the
restless sea

—Jessica Caum

DELAWARE BEACHES

Best do I love your shores
at low tide
When their magnificent sands
lay exposed,
Displaying the subtle beauty
and loveliness
Of glimmering sand specks,
and the muted
Color shades of shell and rock —
yellow, blue, brown
And purple and black.
May all who visit you
truly respect you,
For otherwise your present majesty
truly will fade
And you, like others before,
will be part of the Past —
No longer to be enjoyed, but
only to be longed for.

—Terry M. Fontaine

OBSESSED WITH LOVE

Fickle love comes and goes like the
Noon day sun,

Yet within there is a real love which
Lasts for eternity,

Probed by the complete embodiment of
Another's spirit.

It grows full like leaves of branches

But it never withers; never dries up.

—Sharif Atkins

LITTLE BILLY BROWN

The notes of jazz blasted strong and wild
For Little Billy Brown played with such pizzazz.
Notes from his sax came winding down
Through the mystical mountain and into town.
The father of Billy heard his cry
And beat a rhythm from the heart into the sky.
In this way the father of Billy also sang
But Billy sang with a voice of brass and reed.
Upon that mystical mountain away from town
The notes of jazz blast strong and wild
For Little Billy Brown played with such pizzazz!

—John Pennington

YOU KILLED MY QUEEN

Hey, Lee why don't you come back down,
I hear you're the sweetest girl that was around.
I have some small dreams that I want to spend,
why don't you just be my friend,
for just a little while.

The last time I saw you, was when you went to New Orleans,
you became the victim, I was the king and I had no more queen.
There had been better moves with the moods,
and it is harder to think of the styles,
when you're gone for a while;
what can I do?

KcHratishae I had to be with you!
You traveled around the board and we made our ways,
I never once forgot the way I felt that day,
that you had passed away!

Now I think that I am ready to play my rook,
I just wanted to be your knight in shining armor;
and now I know that will be hard to do.
Oh KcHratishae I was so in love with you!

I've been a wondering man since you left the game,
I can't castle; so now I don't know how
I'm ever going to survive the next play?
Oh GOD, please don't put me in check this way.
KcHratishae, don't you go away!

I've been searching for the right piece to move
for such a long, long time.
Now I'm going to let you know what I have on my mind.
The pawn takes the queen for the very first time to the LORD,
and the piece is slowly, but surely moved off the board.
The king was left a lonely man.

Lee, I don't want to live my life without you.
There were times when I could cry and get you off my mind.
You were the girl of my dreams, KcHratishae.
Sometimes I find myself calling your name out loud and,
Lee . . . I want you but, the opponent took you off the board,
and I'm going to need you to help me finish the game.

CHECKMATE! He calls out, as the LORD took his move!

—Chad Baugus

injurious

At the time of healing or laboring
for the miracle cure, every troubled area
is the latest unprotected.
touching seems to coincide with imperfection
and just how best to be.
such a narrow, well-hidden, much travelled doorway
that hell and heaven shares. the shoulders stay turned
for strength or passing glance because its squared shoulders
that are fooled by initial location and one-sighted determination.
healing is a miracle.
when it arrives at the door that we gave it
then follows our miscalculated directions to the next.

—Matthew Tracy Hallman

THANK YOU GOD, FOR MY GRANDPA

My grandpa has taught me a lot through his sickness;
He taught me hope, love, trust, patience, and even kindness;
Sometimes, when I went to visit him, I would wonder if it
was worthwhile; But I was always reassured, when I could
get him to smile; And when I would leave, I could see a
twinkle in grandpa's eye as I stood at the door; He
seemed to know more than we gave him credit for;
And I think of all of his years that were wasted in vain;
When he struggled endlessly and suffered with pain;
For in heaven is where my grandpa will stay;
"Lord take him home," is what I had prayed.

**Note: This poem is written in memory of my grandpa who
had spent many years of his life in a nursing home.**

—Holly Heser

A BIRTHDAY

It's Christmas! What more can we say
As we contemplate the approach of this Holy Day?
Hearts are grateful for happy childhood days past
As we conjure up feelings which we know cannot last —
Gay times, fun, and magic of this wonderful day.
Impatiently we waited for the exciting mirage
When Santa's sleigh would be parked in our elongated garage —
Then with toys and gifts he would jump from his sleigh
And then into our chimney with a hey, hey, hey.

Today we commune with our ghosts of days gone by
Continually wishing on that great star in the sky
For the joy replacing happiness, Christ's joy in living,
When we are filled by his power with a love worth giving.

—Kathleen Gore Chandler

COMING OF AGE

Once the dawning of a new day filled me with enthusiasm
for life . . .

But in my Summer, I gazed upon my self.

I beheld the tiny lines of mystery etched around my eyes
and on my forehead.

Coarse gray strands now intermingle with the mousiness
of my natural shades.

They are, I've been told, birth marks.

But I say no. 'Tis the touchings of age. The result
of wisdom far beyond my years and the scars from the cruelties of
living.

Tarnished by life, I have known disgrace and its punish-
ments.

And the prematurity of Winter has left me old in mind and
body, and inflicted in spirit, though I still be young of age.

—Kimberly K. Burgess

COMFORT

"The world breaks everyone and afterwards
many are strong at the broken places."
                                        Ernest Hemingway

Sure
I'll sit with you for a while
the others have gone off
to chat and smoke
The stories you tell
only I will know
Perhaps I'll pass them on
or forget them   I don't know
In the end they'll only matter
to you and me
And you won't be there
Go ahead I'll sit
with you for a while longer
Of course I'll hold your hand
You still have
that grip.

—Keith Pearson

WE DANCED TOGETHER

An eternal fire,
burning in my heart.

A taste of love,
right from the start.

A magic touch,
melting my emotions.

Those glowing eyes,
with fiery devotion.

A glint of summer,
that warmed up the night.

The luminous heavens,
with its bodily light.

I lived and died,
that night and forever.

That one blessed moment,
we danced together.

—Jennifer Richardson, age 15

A FANTASY, SIR?

A fantasy you say is the
cause of my plight.
I know you are wrong
    I feel too much fright.

I cannot relay how I
    deep down feel.
But I know my terror and
    anger are real.

Would a fantasy make me
    shake and dream?
Would a fantasy make me
    cry and scream?

Some day I'll remember and
    you'll see the light.
You'll see you are wrong,
    a fantasy's not right.

But if I die from this
    awful disease.
Will you then say I died
    from my fantasies?

—Ann Baxter

How special you are,
What an impact you've made
In our lives and hearts
You could never be replaced.
I was talking with Grandma
About the joy you have brought
She told me how Grandpa
Would smile, just by your thought.
How your little frown
Made us laugh inside
That smile like a clown
Made us boast with pride.
It's so very true
You're loved whoever you meet
I'm proud to know you
This boy at my feet.

—Gary Wayne Dees

MEMORIES

Walks on the beach
Relieve my mind.
Of all the memories
I leave behind.

Time after time
I seem to wonder.
If I should forget
Or even ponder.

Listening to the waves
Rushing against the shore.
Thinking, do I love him
Or even more?

Watching the sunset
Viewing so quietly.
Thinking of the past
So does he.

Waiting patiently
In the mist.
Wondering . . .
Will he ever be missed?

—Laura -Lynn

A BEAUTIFUL RAINBOW

Today when the heavy
rains and the sun
met,
Not long before the sun
was going to set.
Off in the distance
sky was a beautiful
rainbow,
With its red, oranges,
green and blue aglow.
It's one of God's special
wonders,
That many people just
stare in amazement
and ponder.
Ever since I was a
young girl, I was
told,
At the end of the rain-
bow is a pot of gold.
Until the next beautiful
rainbow fades apart.
Let your dreams always
be in your heart.

—Nancy Smith

THE SECRET

There is a secret part of me that climbs the tallest tree,
a sand castle builder amongst the reeds, against the frothy sea.

Who sits by the banks of the river and clucks;
Bringing scurrying hordes of fine feathered ducks.

My feet cover trails, in green mountains I go;
Flowers in the Forest, while the blue sea is below.

And now one can imagine the secret part of me;
To seek and nourish this, is how a life should be.

—Terri Regan

A MUTUAL TRUST

Today I asked God why I even deserve you as a friend.
Why have I been blessed with someone so understanding,
so giving, so caring in my life?
Someone who laughs when I laugh,
Someone who isn't afraid to share himself totally
and completely with me,
Someone who can tell whether I'm up or down without
me saying a word,
Someone who is willing to put up with all my crazy whims,
And someone who is always there to calm my fears and to
reassure me of my self worth.
God looked down and his answer was crystal clear when he said:
"My son, this morning your brother asked me the very same thing."

—Michael R. Shreffler

CAN IT BE FAIR?

My heart is breaking, another life has been taken.
How can this be fair, all this misery and despair?
A mother calls for her son, but soon she'll realize,
his life ran out because of a gun.
Can it be fair that you look at my skin or hair?
Instead, you should look inside and care.
Can it be fair that you love another and another,
and can't stand your brother?
Can it be fair, a baby has to have drugs,
because of the mother's cocaine loves?
Can it be fair a life with so much to give has been killed?
How can it be fair? Save me from this misery and despair.
Would anyone care if I pulled out a gun and prepared.
"No!", a voice in me shouts
Life is filled with despair, pain, and doubt.

—Kennith L. Mitchell

WHAT IS THE REASON FOR CRUELTY

I want to know the reason
for cruelty
Not just cruelty to people,
but to animals
Why must we hunt
And always get what we want
Why do we perform
experiments on animals
Why do we hurt the seagulls
Why do we do all these awful
things

People care when a person dies
But why don't they care
about animals
When animals suffer
When they die
I don't know the reason why
Because we are not the only
ones who cry

—Lisa Schwenk, age 13

THE SCHOLAR

The Flowers Have Come To Their Bloom And
  Soon
The Journey Begins To Find Peace And Relinquish
  All Sins
Along My Side A Man Of Logic, Curious To What
  Makes Him Tick
He Has Become A Scholar Of His Own Choice
  Going To The Land Of Rejoyce
His Voice Speaks Out Bold And Strong, Lashes Out
  In Burst Of Song
Mouth Like A Cherry Of Deepest Red His Thoughts
  Wander Into What's Ahead
He Says Ride For Freedom Of All Given Sins
  Traveling With A Power From Within
A Man Of His Breed Is Kind With A Smart Mind
Who Is Intelligent, Generous To Everyone Willing
  To Give Up His Last Cent
The Man Wears A Shirt Of White With A
  Protected Insight
Wears Boots Of Fine Leather And On His Cap A
  Bluejay's Feather
He Believes That All Men Should Learn And Never
  Make A Wrong Turn
Man Of Many Skills Only Riding At His Own Free
  Will
And Yet, By Heaven I Feel My Love As Strong, As
  Any He Overwhelms With Nothing Wrong
The Scholar; A Man Who Will Not Give A Speech
  But Gladly In Return Teach.

—Brenda Lee Jordan

THE PIONEER

What a beautiful little ship she is with her
  white sails against the pale, blue sky!
Along the shore, people greet her warmly as she
  majestically passes by.
Oh Pioneer! Oh Pioneer!
You are such an enchanting little thing,
Oh the joys and lovely memories you will surely
  bring!

Her captain steers her carefully from port on a
  cool, dry breeze.
On the East River she gently sails, cutting the
  water with such ease.
The passengers aboard the deck delighted with the
  New York sites do strain to look both far and
  near,
So it's not surprising to hear the remark, this trip
  makes all things seem wonderful and dear.

Her guests for the day can relax and enjoy
  themselves without a care,
As their smiling faces soak up the sun and they
  revel in the saltly air.
And when the cruise is over and the sailors are
  asleep,
The moonlight makes a silver blanket 'round her in
  the deep.
Our little ship so safe in port rocks contently in
  the velvet night,
And dreams happily of the voyage to come with
  the rays of the morning light.

—Michelle Stevens

AROUND THE BEND

I can't see what's around the bend—
A birth, a death, an unknown friend.
It's surely good that I cannot,
else I might never leave this spot;
Or ever strive to reach a goal,
to use the faith within my soul.
I can't see what's around the bend—
Perhaps some fences I must mend;
Many things that I may fear,
Around the bend, what will appear?
This I do know, when curves draw nigh,
We'll round that turn, my Lord and I.
He's omnipresent 'til the end.
God holds my hand, around the bend.

—Virginia L. Foster

OLD LOVE

If we perchance should have to meet,
If we should pass upon the street,
Would you turn and walk away
Or would you stop with words to say?
Life has taken us both far
In word and mind and who we are.
I hope that time has passed away
Any anger from that day,
And reasons now more understood;
I tried to do what's right and good.
So should we pass some time, some day
I hope you'll nod and give, "Good day."
"Good day, good day," and again to you
Old love now passed and faded blue.

—Terrilynn Krampetz

SCRAPBOOK

Because it is precious to me
I would save this day
This moment; here, with you
as a flower pressed in a book
That I may in some year yet to come
turn through the pages of yesterday
and discover it again.

I know that then
as with all things reverently tucked away
and dusted with time
It will have faded a little;
the details will not be nearly so sharp
nor the colors quite so clear
but the feeling will remain the same.

—Marty Medley

Thank you oh Heavenly Father
For

Our bread our wine
Our family and friends
Our tears of joy
And hope within

Thank you oh Heavenly Father
For

Our house in which we live
Our happiness which we share
The wonderful world that we live on
And the hope in the air

Thank you oh Heavenly Father
What a loving God you are.

—Crystal King, age 11

MY FOREVER DIET

Dieting and exercise is such a bore;
Bending and stretching until my body is sore;

Dieting is such a terrible drag;
growling and moaning my poor stomach nags;

I will have a beautiful body, is my continuous song;
unless I die from starvation before too long;

The thought that I ponder and wonder if it's my nitch,
To be a happy little chubby, or a slim,
svelt, bitch.

—Sharon Gail Walker

If it's true that there are angels,
then I know she is one.
Her angelic smile and rosy glow
always cheer and warm me.
Her laughter is like the tinkle of chimes,
it brightens even the worst of times.
But today she started school
and it was like part of me was lost.
I looked this way and I looked that way,
then soon she was there with smiles and a hug.
And I was reassured that nothing had changed at all,
I love you my daughter, I love you my child.

—Regina Wingo

DEAR SANTA,

I cannot talk, nor can I write.
So mommy helped me, to do this tonight.
She said, "Christmas is for giving," and getting gifts too!
But no one will give a gift, to jolly old you.
This is my first Christmas, so I don't understand.
Why you don't get gifts, when you give all you can.
So here is my gift, that I am giving to you.
You can ring it for Christmas, or for whatever you do.
I know little about Christmas, so little it seems.
And little I know, about everything.
But I keep on trying, I try to understand.
Just what's going on, in this crazy new land.
A place of glitter, and merry ho-ho's.
From a jolly old fat man, that I don't even know.
As mommy would say, "Merry Christmas Tonight."
And Thank you for making, my first Christmas so bright!

—Faith Ann Brannigan

LITTLE DRUMMER GIRL

This is a story 'bout a special girl,
Who enters, this year, in "Jr. High" world.

In Jr. High, you get to play in the band,
And, you've chosen the drums — now isn't that grand?
Keep practicing hard — you'll be the best in the land!

I know that you can do it cause you ain't dumb,
This, I know, cause you've chosen the drum.
I can hardly wait to hear your "rummy-tum-tum."

I also know it cause you're just a special one,
So, while you're learning drums, hope you'll also have fun!
Wonder if you'll give us a "concert" when the job is done?
I'll come from Arkansas, to hear it, in a run.
But, even if not, you're always grandchild, number one!

With your drums, you may not go here and there,
But your <u>family</u> will applaud when you play that snare!

Oh, perhaps, you'll never be a Ringo Starr,
But, Little Drummer Girl, we love who you are!

—Glynda Edwards

SHORT, BUT FINE

Even though I'm so far away,
My Love for you will never stray,
For the thought of you fills my mind,
Our time was short, but ever so fine,

I will never forget my time spent with you,
For it was one of my wildest of dreams come true,
I never thought you would love me so,
Then the time came and I had to go,

We said our goodbyes and talked of my return,
For that was our life, so we learned,
Even though our homes are so far apart,
You will always be the only one in my heart.

—Dynamo Dan Hembree

TRUE LOVE

Love is beautiful — Especially when new
But it takes many years to know that it's true.

It takes working together — day by day
To wither the storms that will come your way.

To the defects and failures — Be a trifle blind
Be understanding, patient and kind.

Make Truth and Trust a firm foundation
Built without walls, that tear down a relation.

Share your dreams and hopes and fears
You will also weep each others tears.

As the years go by — Your love will grow
And you'll know it's True — cause you made it so.

—Mabel Mae Kelley Crown

VIOLATED

The pain, the hurt, the inside cries
The sense of loss, the part that dies

The guilt, the sorrow, the hidden frustration
The feeling of numbness and manipulation

The nightmares, the cheapness, the look on that face
The fright of knowing the strength out of place

The worry, the slander, the revenge as a goal
The hatred that's burning deep in the soul

The loneliness, the scars, the question of why
The invented to bury the unknown lie

The courage, the healing, the real true test
The swallowing of pride and putting to rest

—Gina D. Carriveau

"TO MOM: HAPPY BIRTHDAY"

To wish them well in life and love
is to show your unselfish love
To comfort them during pain and fearful moments,
is to give them a sense of security
To understand them when they themselves are not
sure how to understand, is to show trust
in their judgment
To stand beside them when only they know for sure
of their innocence, is to show them that
at least for you they are not alone
To let them go, when a tug at your heart says,
"Hold on," is to accept their individuality
and trust their ability to live
And for all this they give you the title
"Mother."

—Jan Deborah Davis

STARS

The stars in the sky are like diamonds,
On a satin dress of blue.
I like to watch them twinkle,
And I know that you do too.

When the sun goes down and the moon comes up,
The stars put on a show.
They dance and sing the whole night through,
As they brightly glow.

—Shannon Mary-Lynn Robison

A BOYHOOD WALK

Dark green moss cushioned footsteps . . .
The sounds of the stream and birds . . .
High domed lapis lazuli . . .
A lack of laughter and words . . .
The scent of pine; blossomed tree . . .
The bothersome spider's thread . . .
Strong heat of the midday sun . . .
Straw of the little bird's bed . . .
The distant cry of a fox . . .
The chicken hawk's frozen flight . . .

All this calm a sort of key,
Unlocks the gate of delight.

—Jason Stephen Smith

THE DEBT OF LOVE

Why can't I say I love you?
The words get in the way.
I wish I could explain the way I feel.
Do you hear what I'm trying to say?

I'm trying to say I love you,
I love you with all of my heart.
But until I can tell you face to face,
my world is falling apart.

When I think of all you've given me,
I feel so ashamed and small.
Because of all the special things I've received,
I've given you nothing in return at all.

So as I try to return your love,
just remember these words I've had to say.
Because of the debt of love I owe
to you, I will repay.

—Barbie Martin

MOM AND DAD

There are some parents that are good and bad
But there's no one more special
Than my mom and dad

It takes understanding and listening
To make a good kid
And I have proof my parents did
And that is me
They have both made my life very happy

Now that I am grown up and gone
They're still there to listen to me
When something goes wrong

I could not ask for better parents than you two
Who show they love their children as
Much as you do
I hope to be a great parent like you two
So my child will love me
As much as I love you

—Rosemary Quiroz

GOD IS IN CONTROL

The earth is the Lord's and the fulness
   Thereof.
He owns the land, animals and trees,
   even the birds and bees.
He allow Hugo to come, at his command.
What a mighty storm. So much of ours
he has destroyed, with no regard for our lives,
houses and land.
People let's return whole-heartedly to
our God. He does whatsoever He will.
In Love and Judgement He does chasten.
But with love and kindness toward
us, His hand is stretched out still.
Let's humble ourselves before Him in prayer,
He resides in everyone, no matter where.
These words that are written by my hand.
Let them comfort you, for it is God's command.
Christ is within every living soul, and God is
definitely in control.

      —Mrs. Louise Cohen

WINTER LEAVES IN WHITE

It seems our friends have long since gone
  Tis only you and I who hold tenaciously to life
A duet of winter leaves in white
Upon this withered bough

Remember the rapture of springtime?
How we danced with every breeze
Green leaves we were, in blue skies

But as of late my love, I am oh so tired
and the tugging of the breeze seems to
mock me, saying, "You are Old."

Last night I saw a shooting star
When its brilliant flame shot heavenward
I couldn't help but wonder, if I too let go
Would I glide majestic in the crisp winter wind.

It may comfort you to know, I feel no fear of
Destiny, but only hope and peace.
You have saved me the last dance as promised
Farewell my Silver Love.

      —Debra Simcheck

MY LITTLE OWL CLOCK

There are tales about the Grandfather clocks
  That stand in halls of fame,
But mine is about a little brown owl
That runs by a weight and chain.

He ticks and ticks as he rolls his eyes
Looking this way and that,
Grasping the higher and more noble things—
Not one time does he look back.

If somehow he could but talk to me,
I think he would, you see,
In his own "wise-owl" way
Tell me all about the Japanese.

He came from an island far away—
The "Rising Sun" so fair.
He could tell me of the people
And their customs over there.

But he cannot talk and tell to me
The ways of Japan at all,
So I must keep on wondering
While he just ticks on the wall.

      —Capitola Clapp

A FRIENDSHIP BLOOMS

Together they laughed and talked and played,
  But deep inside each one was afraid.
Feelings were warm and a friendship made,
But if romance began would the friendship fade?
They searched their minds and their thoughts
were weighed.
And again they laughed and they talked and they
played.

With snow on the ground during a colder season,
Taking a chance was their logic and reason.
Their soft warm bodies touched one night,
And a friendship blooms like a dove in flight . . .

      —Gary Brandenburg

HIS PLAN

The sun inches slowly down into the west,
  One more day towards the end of my quest.
I thank the Lord for this day He made,
As I watch the colors of sunset fade.

Of course there's more 'til the work is finished;
when self is gone and my soul's unblemished.
Praise God for His glory, mercy, and grace!
His spirit that moves at His perfect pace.

You see,

Time is not measured by minutes and hours,
His design is His word, our prayers, and His power!
We speak His peace, of which love is the essence.
We are moved by the power of His very presence.

      —Jan Moore

PROUD HERITAGE

I am one of the proud. One of the bold. I
am from all nations. All tribes. I was a free
spirit with the grace of a chaste doe and the
strength of the mighty black bear.

   I harmed no man until he took unjustly of my
birthrights. All I asked was to live in the
serenity of my land. But my soul bares the scars
of the hatred for my people.

   He raped my land and took until there was no
more to be taken and still longs for more. What
is now left, he shall never gain because my
dignity shall remain steadfast forever. And I am
still one of the proud. One of the bold . . . . an
Indian!

      —Kathy Ruth Black

SONNET 33

Why must the bonding tie of hearts be test?
So strong but yet so fragile--stretched too far
Results that turned out worse but done for best
  Leave on your heart a sore, unhealing scar.

  Gone within a blink of a cat's dark eye
  Was an unspoken thought unknown to me.
Gone were your feelings true . . . locked up inside,
  Forced to be forgot as thought it should be.

Why must thou cast aside thy feelings true?
Pushed from the center true honesty's housed
  Unseen like the sand in the ocean blue
Lost among millions when the floor is roused.

Mistake not true meaning of friend's joined hearts,
  The bond will shatter leaving both apart.

      —Nichole Anderson

A squirrel sat on the woodpile as still as still could be,
And as I sat and stared at him, I thought of you and me

I thought of when I was little and the sno-cone man would come
And how I'd run up to you and say, "Awe Mom, c'mon!"
Then you would start a smilin' and say "Get me one too"
And we'd have to taste each others; I remember that of you

As I got a little older and I thought I was "It"
You'd laugh at me and I'd get mad and then I'd have a fit
But it never seemed to matter, so long as you were there
No matter just how bad I was, you always seemed to care

Although when I was younger, I was too blind to see
But I just had to let you know how much you mean to me

  —Rebecca Arko

WHAT IS THIS
What is this, so precious to me,
 That moves so swiftly, I cannot see?
What is this that gives me my friends,
 Then with a whisper, it takes them away again?

What is this phenomenon that brings us into existence,
 Then deteriorates our lives with unyielding persistence?
It solves my problems, both large and small,
 It heals my wounds when it hears me call.

It turns the entire world, but never too fast,
 It was here in the beginning and will forever last.
It embraces the universe and the sky so blue,
 What is this that takes so much TIME for me and you?

  —Carl M. Love

COLOSSAL RED
Oh why, oh why, can't I be red,
 Like the new red tractor in Mr. Springfield's shed?

It overtakes me with awe inside,
This big red tractor, I'd love to ride!

Red is bright, shiny, it's out-a-sight,
Red is colossal, stupendous, it's dynamite!

Red must be important, why it's in the flag,
It's the color of the fire truck and my mother's handbag!

And what about Santa? He likes red too,
Who'd second-guess Santa? Not me, would you?

Yes, I'd love to be red just like that farm thing,
But instead, I'll have to be Howard P. Ling.

  —Kathy Parsons Robison

SEI . . . GRAY
Poetic rhythms glide around them as they stay suspended,
 in tranquil waters.
Beautiful voices utter rememberable verses . . .
so magnificent, so colorful, so shy.
Picturesque motions as a ballerina would do . . .
jumps, leaps, twists, so skillful are they . . .
so very skillful.
Their soft silhouettes against the fading sun.
Their forms so sleek, muscular, and bold.
How can they be so shy?
Why are they so calm and serene?
This strong and gentle animal of ancient time,
who could ever really know their true beauty?
It would be hard to imagine for me not to see,
this gracefulness that makes me cry.
It will forever remain in my mind.
This is the story of the whales.
  —Shelly L. Peter

Oh my child
 How I love you so
But you will never know
How strong my love does hold
Until you have grown
And maybe children of your own.

  —Bev Jensen

BEHIND THE WISHES
She'd make a pilot,
 want to return from his skies.
She'd make a sailor,
come home from the seas.
She'd make the cowboy ride,
in from the lonely, dusty plain.

But she can't get him
to call her on the phone.

Knowing that the pilot,
the sailor, and the cowboy;
are things that I've wished
I could be.
I guess somewhere inside,
I've wished I could be
the voice that she wants to hear.

  —Larry A. Turnbull

JUST ME
It's dark in here
 But you seem so near.
Can't you see?
It's just me.
Long halls
Tall walls
Doors all about
To take me in and out.
Why am I here?
Trapped in fear.
Will it go away?
Or will it stay?
Can't you see?
It's just me.
I'll soon find
It's all in my mind.
Just a dream
It would seem.

  —Michelle Hoggle

HEART SUMMER
Somewhere a hill
 Where daisies grow
With a meadow
Serene below
Smelling of hay
New-mown and still —
A golden sun
Smiling and gay —
And bees humming
Up and away —
Somewhere from out
Of a bright past
A summery day
Vividly comes —
I feel its warmth,
Its perfumes smell,
Where once I was
 Again I dwell.

  —Eula May Lutzenhiser

LOVE, LOVE, LOVE

Know I the redundancy
Of language little.

A rooted foreshadow,
A numb fool's fiddle.

Lest we long the allure
Of a masquerading middle.

How I lurch at that riddle
Of language little.

—Leighton J. Aronson

Last impressions are
usually more accurate
than the first
i've found since knowing
you and it
pains
me
to reach out for
shadows though substance
becomes more and
more difficult to find
because i'm not searching
for direction
anymore . . .

—Ruth Jehlen

THE TRYST

An hour stolen,
hidden away.
some time together,
a warm summer's day.

a patch of sunlight,
the rustle of trees,
a blanket to sit on.
a soft cool breeze.

a table for two,
under bright blue skies.
fleecy white clouds,
the warmth of your eyes.

This hour, like initials
carved into trees,
will forever remain,
in my memory.

—Corby Hawkins

A MIDSUMMER DREAM

Salzburg, Vienna
The waltz and Mozart
Coffee not too sweet
Chocolate sundae treat

Laughter, tingling joy
Crisp, cold snow
Lovely aroma
Of the sea air glow

crackling cadence
Of a fiery flame
White lace dresses
Pretty shoes, fancy names
Girls with shiny hair
Eyes black as the night

A wild stallion to ride
Miles and miles tonight.

—Anjali Viswanathan

THE FLAME OF A DREAM

As a rookie cop, he's young and energetic actually thinking a change he can make.

He studies hard, works and plans knowing someday he'll make his mark.

Knowing someday society will respect and support his badge and suit of armor, keeps him going day in and out, blindly following the flame of a dream.

Through the years he trips and falls and instead of staying down, he jumps back up to try again, the flame begins to flicker.

He must be dumb this rookie cop, now many years since past, dumb because the dream he had, a flicker does still last.

The years and time have taken their toll, the rookie's dream is shattered. The badge once shiny now is dull and the armor now is spattered.

A rookie's dream is hard to hold, someday the light will flicker. And when it does, hold fast the flame and pass the dream to another.

—John A. Corder

CAMERA OF THE HEART

Take a picture with your heart and capture precious moments;
Be sure to focus well, they fly by ever so fast.
Store them deep within the pages of your memory,
Cherish every single one, do all you can to make them last.

Take time to smell the roses each and every day,
For life is short and minutes so very few.
Make the most of every fleeting second;
Look to each day as something wondrous and new.

Don't waste any time with regrets and "if only's."
Life is such a beautiful gift sent from above,
So share it with others, make someone laugh, say a kind word,
Reach out to those in need, spend more time with the ones you love.

It is by giving ourselves, in any way we can,
That we shoot the scenes of life we can always treasure.
Let go and release the love within you, show it to everyone.
And it will be returned in ways that can't be measured.

Make up for past mistakes, show someone how much you care;
You may not get another chance and it's never too late to start.
Only too soon our time on earth is gone, the times with those you love,
So save those precious memories—Take a picture with your heart!

—Barbara Ann Hopkins

THE SUMMER OF EIGHTY-SEVEN

I have a bell I'll never ring   I speak a love I rarely sing

We're miles apart	New England's land
There she is found	New Hampshire's strand
My home I leave	the Midwest I part
I went to her	to present my heart

Our eyes they met	our voices wove
We hid within	nostalgia's cove
With time I saw	and clearly knew
Love 'twas a dream	my eyes teared blue

I have a bell I've often rung   I hold a love I never sung

Yes, her I left	with feelings bound
She never heard	my heartbeat sound
Although I cried	my heart was free
New souls to seek	true love to plea

Retracing steps	the many miles
Returning home	to Maggie's smiles
A love so close	so true and dear
These miles caused	blind eyes to hear

I shake my bell the clamber sounds   My heart shall tell true love abounds

—Lee O. Detwiler

GET OUT AND VOTE

Some people say the times are bad, The economic outlook sad;
That prices rise and wages drop, The present party is a flop.
That taxes rise eternally and politicians dance with glee
to see the little fellow down, where they can trod him in the ground.

They say the White House is a nest where robbers; hidden beneath the
breast of government; work day and night to see if they can wrong
"OUR RIGHTS."
But these same people, you will note, when election time comes 'round
don't vote.
They had their chance; They can't deny they made the bed in which
they lie.

—Hector J. Burke

GATHERING OF THE CLAN

The Clansman's call is sounding, yet none hear the bugle blow,
To others there's but silence, we're the only ones who know.
Even as the trumpet calls, we answer to a man,
To rally round, one and all for the gathering of the clan.

When there's need, our clan is ready to share in joy, in love or pain,
as one, our force is awesome as we stand together, yet again.
Many times the call has sounded, still we come from far and near,
Many times we know will follow because we hold our kinship dear.

Though separate, we're united — one hurts, the other cries,
One pains, the other sorrows — one is born, another dies.
We share our strife and triumph, our laughter and our tears,
Sharing love for one another, we are timeless through the years.

We're not great, nor are we mighty, but our force is strong and sure,
Being bred for generations with the strength which will endure.
Mountain people, proud but humble, sharing but a simple creed,
Blessed by all who passed before us, passing all to those we leave.

When ere the clan is gathered, be it now, or days of yore,
We pass on our proud tradition, as one we stand forevermore.
So if times there seems one missing, not according to our plan,
Even absent, yet so present, at the gathering of the clan.

—Iona Quillen

THROUGH MY MOTHER'S EYES

Reflecting on her life as she looked back over years
only treasured memories could bring this sort of tear.

Not a tear of joy nor sorrow
but a tear filled with yesterdays and tomorrow.

Once a child bride to the man she still loves
her life became filled with things she never dreamed of.

Together they have stood side by side
and as each day passed they brought meaning to each other's lives.

In a world filled with people they couldn't been more alone
but they found all they needed in the warmth of each other's arms.

The odds stayed against them right from the start
but the strength of their love blazed deep within their hearts.

Life never was easy as they struggled to make a home
things got even harder as their three children came along.

Hard work continued as the years drifted by
sacrifices began to show deep within their eyes.

Looking back past all the ups and the downs
it is oh so clear what she had found.

The love she always had for this one special man
she can still feel with a simple touch from his hand.

She realizes now her destiny has already been made
for she owns a life full of treasured memories she would never trade.

—Penny Ann DuBroc

I see you in my dreams
Most each and every night,
Always being there
As big and bright as life.
You whisper to me
The things I love to hear,
The sound of your voice
So sweet to my ear.
Then I wake up
Find out it's only a dream,
That you're so far away
Not as close as you seem.

—Lindsay A. Squires

LIGHTNING

Once there was a streak
of lightning
i thought it was
   beautiful
the way it was full
   of anger
it called friends and
family all around
and i just fell
asleep and i awoke
   in the sun

—Ariana Hollenberg

YOU & ME

Your hair is brown,
So is mine.
Mine is curly,
Yours is fine.

You are dark complected,
I am light.
I think of you,
All day and night.

I am short,
While you are tall.
Nothing will stop our love,
Nothing at all.

You are taken,
While I am free.
That doesn't matter 'cuz,
Our love is meant to be.

—April D. Schafer, age 15

THE HANDS OF LOVE

Calloused and rough,
Weathered and worn,
A father's hands of love;
Now they are gone.

Gone from this real world
But not from my mind,
Their touch lingers there,
For his love stayed behind.

A touch very fleeting
But more precious than gold.
It conveyed words unspoken;
No need they be told.

Calloused and worn,
Weathered and rough,
The memory of these hands
Must now be enough.

—Anne Gillis Lawrence

THE QUIET

Listen to the quiet — out in the woods.
Small creatures run about, squirrels,
Chipmunks and birds. How so much better
Than to be where there are many words!
You can get your thoughts together,
And your dreams, and really, as you're
Quiet there it seems that God is there.
And you know that is true.
He's waiting there, and just to talk to you.

—Mattie Davis

IN THE YUKON

Is Sally still in the Yukon
My first and only date;
Would I still get some miners hot tips
Down the trail of ninety-eight.

How are my dear old pals in the Yukon?
I'm shouting to goldpan Joe
As I grab the arm of my buddy
Please! Tell me, I want to know.
I then clamp my left arm to his shoulder
Right hands we solidly clasp,
My eyes plead warmly for answers
And intensely I then gasp —

Do the jack-pines still soar in the Yukon?
Do the young lads grow as tall?
Do their northern lights still shine as bright?
Do they miss me there at all?
Do they break the ice for the caribou
When the lake's a frozen sheet?
Do they miss me, dear old buddy?
Do they miss me on the street?

Oh! I long to return to the Yukon
Risking the blizzards and snow;
Sharing my love in the dancehalls
A part of the northern glow.

—Sophie Barton

TEXAS TWILIGHT

Long ago and faraway,
Are the golden hours of yesterday,
When a barefoot boy, and a redhaired lass,
Found buttercups in the dew-wet grass.

Brother and sister, hand in hand,
Wandered into a magic land,
Where whip-poor-will his sad tale moaned,
And Leprechauns and Fairies roamed.

Bare feet bathed in the shallow stream,
A time to pause, to listen, to dream,
Young minds gripped in twilight's soft glow,
Mystic moment for the soul to grow.

Bluebonnets covered the gentle hills,
Indian paintbrush added its thrills,
Of vivid shades of yellow and red,
In the meadow grass, by cool springs fed.

Faraway, in time's length span,
Is the childhood magic,
Of that Texas land.

—Onie Slabaugh

NIGHT

The stars shine bright at night,
as if a bird in flight.
The sunset stretches across the land.
On a beach a shell lays in the sand.
The lake glimmers like a diamond in the moonlight.
The grass glistens as the gemmy dew comes down.
The sun rises in the east,

but do not frown . . .
Morning brings even more beauty;
this the least.
Night is a wonderful magical time.

—Carrie Lynn Anderson, age 11

THE DECISION

Watching the wind lift it higher,
Following its swirling motion with my eyes.
Wishing I could hold it, clasp it,
As it disappeared into the endless skies.

Saying nothing, as I stumbled
Searching for the courage that I could not find.
I just waited for someone else
To shout out what I was screaming in my mind.

My eyes burned in anger and in shame
As I looked at the charred and smoldering grave.
I laid a flower on the spot
Where a flag was burned . . . instead of proudly waved.

—Lynn Campbell Warren

STORM CLOUDS

When I awoke I was filled with fear
Then I remembered, the storm clouds were here
Stay close by Father, strengthen me so
I can face the day and can onward go
At first thought, oh why did I awake
These trials are too much for me to take
But too we know as we turn and bend
With the trials and sorrows that on us descend
Comfort and relief down deep inside
And with arms of comfort with us He will abide
And we strengthen and grow and our roots go deep
And no task will seem so steep
Thank you Father, stay close by
I need you — I need you — is my cry.

—Mrs. Della Hoggatt

SEASONS

Winter is cold it is
So beautiful outside
and it's fun to have
snowball fights.

Spring is so colorful.
The birds are singing
and the grass is growing
and the flowers are blooming.

Summer is so hot.
Some people like to
go swimming and some
like to get a tan.

Autumn is so nice.
Leaves are falling
and the leaves are
red, yellow, brown, and orange.

So everyone likes different seasons but I like 'em all.

—Julie DeJesus

SUMMER DAY

In the morning, when I opened my eyes,
Mother Nature seemed to have a surprise.
Spring was all gone, the summer was here,
It is the very best time of the year.
I rushed out of bed, and ran through my door,
I was so excited, I wanted to see more.
The morning was bright, and I paused to look around,
Today would be great, no rain on the ground.
I stayed out all day, playing, while it was bright,
Wishing for it to always be light.
It was so wonderful, but then, all too soon,
That summer day was gone, with the rising moon.

—Kirsten Helseth, age 10

UNIVERSE

Our earth so great, beneath our feet
The space we want, is ours to keep.
The colorful rainbow, after a rainstorm
Brightens our life, as it glows in splendor.
The sun as it peaks, beyond the lake
Shows the beginning, of a bright new day.
Our dreams are so dear, that we often fear
The future ahead, in this hemisphere.
We are all surrounded, by human beings
Who have learned to survive, amongst those fears.
No one can show us, the easy way
So we struggle each day, come what may.

—Mary M. Franceschina

SOMETHING IN THE DESERT

She wolves
in winter white
know the step of mating
in harsh dry lands
that move inward
on her dwindling species.

Time shifts
and howling still
on hot red clay
she calls her thirst
to the missing mate
from canyon bluffs

overlooking nothing.

—Dee Ferguson-Martinez

LISTEN LITTLE CHILDREN

Listen little children to your Father
He is always there to call on
Even when you're sick or bothered
Our GOD is always there to call on

GOD IS ALWAYS THERE
GOD WILL ALWAYS CARE
HE WILL HELP YOU OVER
EVERYTHING THAT YOU ARE UNDER IF YOU TRUST HIM

Talk little children to your Father
He will always hear you when you call
Tell HIM your problems big or little
And HE will always answer when you call

Listen little children to this song
What GOD wrote can't be wrong
Read daily your BIBLE
There will be a great REVIVAL
If you'll do GOD'S WILL

—Andrew R. Rice

REGATTA

Sails of white slide by;
Regatta on sky blue sea.
Hoist the sail! Blow, wind!
Spray whips the straining faces,
Bright jerseys, salty hair, suntanned legs.

—Joann Ball

OCEAN SINGING

My name is like the ocean
singing to the clouds.
My name is a forest of redwoods
touching the sky.
My name is a dove flying
through the air,
a child singing in a field of horses.
My name is a leaf floating
in the air
A squirrel running up and down a tree
My name is me.

—Jessica Anne-Lynne Holden, age 11

THE FORTUNE OF THOMAS PLANT

He built his castle in the air
away up high within the clouds
which sun burned off on clearer days
so he could see the lake below
stretching out to farther shores.
And money was no object then . . .
he had enough, nor wanted more.
Yet to protect what he had left,
he took the matter to his friends
who told him what and where to buy,
and careful plans were so well laid.
Yet fortunes made can disappear
as in the life of Thomas Plant,
who died with only memories
and borrowed for his final rest
a simple coffin which his friends
provided for the man who had
at one time bid them come to see
his castle in the clouded skies.

—Steven Rembold

THE SEASONS

We saw a tree by the river
Her branches were green and free
The breeze caressed them lightly
Her blossoms were filled with bees

Again we came to the river
And noticed the bees had fled
In her branches the fruit had ripened
We will harvest her fruits we said

In Autumn her leaves had fallen
She was planning, though looking drear
We could see new buds were forming
In hope for another year

Then in the late of winter
We broke a path through the snow
A beaver was gnawing her tree trunk
Thus showing a young one how

In spring we returned to the river
Our tree was then in a jam
She had fallen alas for the critters
And was part of a beaver dam

—Dorthy Burroughs

BETIMES

To conquer life minutely every day
Hold small wonder for long moments
Breathefully, seeing what's before me long
And for what it is without
Getting lost in yesterday or tomorrow
Will there be always, once I wait
And see now

—Adrienne E. Hall

EYES OF A CHILD

They tell so much, those beautiful eyes.
They say things will be okay
when you have had a bad day.
They find so much beauty in little things,
the things we take for granted
or just pass by.
They have so much hope
and give so much more.
So, when you see those little eyes
be sure you look inside.
Beauty is in the eyes of a child.

—Amy Michelle Baldwin

CRICKETS IN HIS EARS

I suppose he had a lot of thoughts,
but nobody seemed to care.
Sitting at the end of his worn-out couch
with crickets in his ears.

Ten was his only contribution,
but they just strayed away.
"There ain't no more confusion."
I guess that's what he'd say.

He took with a bad cold,
in the beginning of the summer.
Donna knew he was getting old,
and he was so glad to hear from her.

So she left her kids and husband,
went down the two-laned road.
Christmas cards were not enough,
so she sadly took the load.

In the middle of the front room,
with his "air" by the bed.
Anson knew his luck would run out soon.
"Not long," the doctor said.

Florence had an awful feelin',
but she could hold her pain.
She regretted that she hadn't seen him,
but she saw him in the picture frame.

St. Francis was rough that day,
I knew she felt it comin'.
And with that he passed away,
early that morning.

Seven came and three were scared
to pay their last goodbye
"Grandaddy, you know I really cared,"
but, I couldn't even cry.

I suppose he had a lot of thoughts,
but nobody seemed to care.
Sittin' at the end of his worn-out
    couch,
with crickets in his ears.

**Written in memory of Anson Martin
    Hudgens, Sr.**
—Nikki Campbell Costilow

ARTIST

I can't draw you with lines,
but I can paint you with words,
    —A lover, a friend
    —A goofy little girl,
    —A mature sensitive woman,
    —A cute little doll,
    —A sexy irresistable "thang,"
    —A girl who needs attention,
    —Who strives to keep her identity,
    —Someone who makes me happy, by letting me in.
I can't draw you with lines,
but I can paint you with words . . . . .

—Paul Gianesin

WILL BE TOGETHER

As I sit by your bed and watching you struggle
for each breath.
Feeling so helpless. Thinking if only you
could get some rest.

When you got so sick I told you so many
lies.
I couldn't tell you that you were going
to die.

At the end I had to tell you, "It was alright
to let go.
Someday we will be together, and I love
you so."

—Karen Buak

PICTURE BLACK AND BLUE

In a child's world there is no wrong,
(I see and feel the red rain come down on me.)

but in the mind of some men, there is evil, (silent pain)

and at times, children,

are, are the victims of this silent pain in man,
(Picture black and blue)

without cries or words the helpless children surrender,

surrender to the fists of angry men,

one like you and I, will never understand,
(Picture black and blue)

so if you can, picture black and blue.

—Paul Silva

INSCRIPTION

As such, are the numbers inscribed in the book,
With ultimate meanings . . . to those who will look:

#1 — The number of "The Eminent,"
#2 — Resembles "Government,"
#3 — The symbol of "Making known,"
#4 — The mark of "Temptation" shown;
#5 — The sign for "Unmerited favor,"
#6 — The "Humanistic" savor,
#7 — "Completion" of an art,
#8 — "New beginnings" start;
#9 — "Made known by Divinity,"
#10— "Human responsibility,"
#11— Is "He, beside a one,"
#12— The "Perfect rule," begun . . .

And so on — the numbers inscribed in the book —
With ultimate meanings . . . to those who will look.

—Cynthia Hinkle

BENEATH THE FIG TREE

Beneath the fig tree in a circle of sand
Morning sun attends in sacred repetition;
Curling my toes I consider the gardeners ageless hands
The old bones made brightly perfect in position.

The chorus of the rake on whipoorwill's cry,
The motion of the leaves in shadow's lace,
And where be more contentment in the eye
Of nature and a man in his place?

Fine for me to see my father's face among
The apricots (knowing which to pluck, which not)
To see that line from him to me re-strung
Some ages hence in some new mystery spot.

—Charles H. Seaver

THE GIFT OF CHILD

Yielding from the heart's infinite hollows
    Spotlighting moments from time distantly past
Swelling the intrigue of a yearning soul
    Sharing spectral reflections with dauntless heed
Nurturing the tiny matters in floral detail
    Embracing daily growth and change progressively
Preserving truths without regret or blame
    Taking responsibility of injury ungrudgingly
Sheltering fears with powers of silent strength
    Caressing loneliness and insecurity adventurously
Frolicing the ride of moods and color
    Accepting disappointments with gladness
Conquering the unimaginable with hope
    Giving from the heart without measure.

—Mary Ann Moseley

For a curly-haired boy on a shiny red bike
I bought some new toys I knew he would like.
He always did well in school, honors meant so much
It seemed that in all subjects he had a magic touch.
But he grew up so fast.

He excelled in sports, there were none he couldn't do
He captained his team, the girls loved him too.
He loved his first job — worked hard for the place
A quitter, a drop-out just wasn't his case.
But he grew up so fast.

Now he's in college, a PhD is his goal
He surely will get it, of that I've been told.
His future is bright and I am so proud
But over it all there is still one dark cloud
He grew up so fast.

—Barbara Boggiatto

BRANDON

Brandon is his name,
a blonde haired lad I hold forever dear.
His days are spent between chair and bed,
'cause useless legs won't hold him up.
His back is forever bent, his small hands
hold no toy; his voice I'll never hear.
In his head, the soft white mass
a damaged vessel where
consciousness and volition are exiled from here.
Blue clear eyes stare up toward Light with calm enduring
I pledge my faithful allegiance to thee
thou brave and courageous soul.
I salute you laddie
for all your silent suffering,
you inspire me, my precious son!

—Nancy Ellen Nelson

DIANE

I once had a garden
with flowers bright.
A lawn to mow day and night.
The flowers died, the lawn to blight.
No lawn for me, no flowers bright;
brick and mortar will be my plight.
Wait, reseed, reseed and wait.
A new garden, a flower bright.
It stands above the blight.
Green eyes soft petals and gentle to sight.
I once had a garden in a flower bright.

—Thomas A. Burke

MOMENT IN MARCH

Burden-sated I trudged through
Streets, still splattered with snow.
Suddenly an acrobatic squirrel
Scampered across a slatted fence
And in surged Spring, all at once:

A redwing missiled across the sky
Lemon sunshine softly warmed
Budding blades of green
Winged wisps of hyacinth fragrance
Made wonder rampant and in a trice
One heart soared to meet the redwing's!

—S. Gale Gilburt

MY PLAYGROUND

Sitting on a rock, breathing sips of light
flowing from our life-force river.
without an ounce of conscious duality.

Relax, I'm relaxing in bliss, in
    a present moment of love, with
Spiritual responsibility, (a golden rule), for
    the child in me.

Saying, numbing, my body
                bouncing like a ball.
    I pretend to have many friends
playing all around. I absorb the sky
                through the cricket's sound.

Meteor showers race, with all our eyes
    in sparkling glee. Moments burning up
        in space, and in our hearts
                    from what was seen.

—Craig Peterson

ME

My bones are tired and somewhat weary
My eyes are weak and often teary

My legs ache and often cramp
My underthings are sometimes damp

My hands are old, wrinkled and rough
And so is my skin; but I'm tough!

My hair is gray and also thinning
But my hair dresser and I are winning

My tummy is big and fairly round
But underneath it, I'm sound

Although I'm getting on in years
God has kept me well, and I know
                    "He" hears
A youngster you can tell I may not be
But I've been very, very happy.

—Gerrie Forgey

NEGLECTED

Dreary colored
         sunken faces
lifeless disposition,
   r o b o t   speed
scrambled thoughts
         ragged,
                  tossed out.

—Kimmela O. Boyd

THOUGHTS

It would certainly
   Be a comfort
   To be captured
      Within
The mountains again.
   I would let
      All of my
      Thoughts
   Rumble throughout
Their caverns and valleys
      Then gently,
   As they came back
      I would
      Listen.

—Leann M. Wallace

DESPISE

The fire of lies
   And hearts beating fast
   Her stare is the secret
it will always last

   A feather in her cap
is what I am
   Tossed aside
   Eternally damned

   With hate on her mind
The truth is her shield
   She has no money
She will never yield

Forever tormented
   Her morbid eyes
Did you know, that
   her name was Despise?

—Osvaldo Cruz III

AS WHEN I BELIEVED

I will not
be the same
as I was—
when I believed.

I will not
behold the magic
of special wonder
without your Spirit.

I will not
feel the eternity
of sweet Eternity
the dreaming Child.

I will never
know my destiny
unless I suffer
for it.

—Marcelle Jones

DREAMING OF LIFE

The waves wash me over the beach
   Hitting the sand with a deafening roar
I lay on my back to see the sky and feel the sun
The wind blows softly, gently caressing my face
   Like a lover's hand
The beach is wet and my body's weight sinks into it
Mermaids, who have died have become the foam at my feet
The warm sun splashes onto my body—giving me energy, giving me life
The sun, the waves and the wind uplift me, fill me
Raise me to the sky
O, to die and to be reborn on the beach!
There is no pain, no noise
Just life

—Kimberly Anne Morris

THE BETRAYAL

Enclosed in a home I came to call my own;
now, it is a hiding place from an enemy who seeks to destroy me.

For in it, I once found comfort and contentment; a treasured safeness. Lock and key could never hold me as this haven which I came to know as my world.

But then came the decision. A decision to end my dreams and my future. Don't I deserve to live my life, as you do, mother?

There are only days left. It must be true—one lives alone and one dies alone.

The salt burns with unrelenting vengeance; the knife breathlessly sharp. Does a mother hear the cries of her unborn child? No; she pretends this is an acceptable method of alleviating an unplanned burden.

The pain is unbearable.

The one who was to shelter me within; as part of her very being; has betrayed me.

So, this is your goodbye, mother?

In just a whisper, I bid you farewell also . . .

"Now I lay me down to sleep; I pray thee, Lord,
my soul to keep . . ."

—Kathleen M. Wilson

THE WALL:
A Marine Remembers

Black marble wings that vanish in the mist,
I fall to my knees and begin to read the list.
Sensing a deep feeling of comradeship and joy, to be a part,
As each name burns itself into my heart.

To many this symbol brings pain,
But for me, the effect does not seem to be the same.
I do not quiver from its touch as I kneel,
But rather, I am drawn to it as a magnet draws a piece of steel.

I am drawn to its strong silent embrace,
Feeling a warm flush, a beam of light upon my face.
A living monument to those who fell,
It calls, it beckons, "Come out, come out of your shell."

But is it the wall, the thing itself, that calls,
Or is it the collective voice of those inscribed upon the wall?
"Come, bask in my light and allow your pain to be relieved.
Come, allow yourself to be healed so as to finally be free."

To be sure, this is indeed the majesty of the wall.
To hear the soothing voice of those 58,000 plus who fell.
They tell me, "Weep not, carry on and walk straight and proud.
For through the deafening silence of this wall
Shall the greatest chorus of triumph, praise and remembrance sound."

—Daniel W. Kavala

Cold, wet drizzle
On the window pane.
A little boy peers through the other
side,
Looking through me
At something I can't see.
He traces little boy dreams
On big clean window panes.
An art
                    invaluable
because what I see on the other side
was once me.
I seem to have run out of time
for something
money can't give me.
I ran out of time for
Cold, wet, musty rain
And drawing dreams on window panes.

—Sarah Masi

S-T-R-E-S-S

Stress is everywhere today.
In our work and in our play,
In our attitudes and what we say.
It takes the zest out in everyway.

Stress causes people to fret and stew,
It affects teachers and students too!
Nations have it and let it brew,
Blow their top and slay a few.

It's in our family life, day by day,
Get up tight over what we say.
The factory has become a ho-hum place,
Workers grumble and slow the pace.

People drive like in a race,
Cut you off, then give chase.
Honk the horn and motors race!
Yell at others, get no place.

Stress is terrible, it kills a few.
It is curable, it is true.
Instead of fuming over what others do
Consider how really lucky are you?

—Morris Eldon Ward

QUANTUM WORLD: QUANTUM VIEW

I wonder: will I ever
Know the universe within?
I'm lost within enigma's maze,
And cacophony's din.

Within-without; the coin's two sides,
I: paradox of one;
Diffusion through osmosis,
And shadow cast?   There's none.

A time-warp, wrapped in skin and bone,
Conflicting properties;
I wrest my little universe,
The ah ha! point to seize.

Until infinity is turned,
Collapsing inner space;
I hurtle into nothingness,
An outcast, with no place.

Alright then; back to square one;
Life's gauge is set on zero;
Humanity continues,
To track down moment's Hero.

—Diane Gerber Baugh

AIRPLANE VIEWING OF CITY NIGHT LIGHTS

Black velvet is the backdrop of the night covered with
Zircons, rhinestones and fake colored jewels
Glittering and dazzling gaudily below,
Flickering in patterns left and right to and fro.

Floodlights spraying misty halos of luminary globes
About them, as if shimmering from a giant atomizer.

Gold and silver headlights from cars look like fireflies
marching in never-ending formations row by row.

Streetlights decorate each tree for a year-long holiday
With glistening gold dust and stars twinkling away.

This iridescent painting of the world below creates
A peep-show, everchanging in flashes of light — at night —
Seen through an airplane window.

        —Muriel (Easton) Chreist

POP FLIES

There is one way to look at you and I.
Mama, just as a pop fly!

This shouldn't have been a pop fly.
We should've gave it, at least one more try!

Now, the way things fall.
It has turned into a foul ball!

They say, you got to wait on the good things.
Only, the good might of already came!

I don't expect it to always be an out.
It's time for a home run, or about!

I'm tired of always being called out for a pop fly.
I want to be in the game too bad, to say bye!

        —Billy E. Bruce

JUST ONCE

This is a poem about a nice man.
Now he not dare walk nor stand.
He died many years before his day,
But now he is gone he's passed away.

He used drugs just once that night.
It gave his family quite a fright.
They called the hospital to send a truck,
But I guess that night they were down on their luck.

He died 2 hours later on.
He said no goodbyes and now he is gone.
His falling star that night had fell,
So when you use drugs you're headed for hell.

        —Brandi Kate McManus

HELL . . .

Burning . . . tormenting . . . . raging within . . . .
A pitiful prison just to be in,
Where darkness is welcomed and light is shunned,
    While shadows dance recklessly in wild abandon.

Wailing and shrieking those hell's restless souls;
    Whoremongers and wrongdoers taking their toll.
Entangled in darkness, they weep and they cry;
    To live is a misery, never to die.

Minutes like hours, and hours like days;
    For vast worldly treasures and pleasures they pay.
"Have mercy upon us!" to Death they do plead;
    But Death turns his head and refuses to heed.
In Hell's ugly stench, nothing else can avail;
    Their terrible fate does always prevail.

        —Grace O. Acoba Untalan

WHO KNOWS

The walls talk,
  Talking and taking it all in.
Telling of the hemming and the hawing
and the humming.
Whispering rude suggestions,
Spreading rumors,
Bluntly showing
Right there on the walls.
No one knows.
Now one knows what I know . . .
Except the walls.

—Leslie Pedrak

HOMEWARD BOUND

Through the window, fluffy clouds
  Paint shadows on the ground.
That majestic snowcapped mountain
  From here is but a mound.

All I see about me moves so slowly
  To my eyes.
Yet I know we are swiftly flying
  Through endless, awesome, skies.

Going home, going home, it's
  Where I want to be.
Where I can see your smiling face
  And you are close to me.

So many miles, so many days;
  Too far, too long apart.
Each mile, each day, a wicked knife
  Thrust deeply in my heart.

The Bible says, where our treasure is;
  That's where our heart is found.
I'm heading for my treasure,
  For now I'm homeward bound.

—Don Perry

FLAMES OF FIRE

Fire, fire, rising higher,
  In your flames I know there is
    power;
But what I see in you are these
That remind me of a power higher
    than yours can tower;

Red flames remind me of the
    blood Jesus shed;
Yellow flames remind me of the
    crown of thorns upon His head;
White flames remind me of His soul
    as pure as the lily that unfolds,
    on the day that He arose.
The blue flames remind me that we
    too can conquer death and be made
    anew.

Beams of light I can see flicking
    back their tongues at me.
I can add to your flames or I can
    take from your coals and lower
    your great heat.

But on a night like this
As cool and crisp as first winter's
    night,
I'll roll in my blanket warm
    and snug 'til morning's light.

—Jimmie Donnell

NIGHT CONQUEST

Night pours and trickles across the dim landscape,
  covering and enveloping all and growing until its
conquest is complete.
Then do the night creatures stir, once more exploring
their dark realm.
The beautiful solitude and undisputed silence ensue
and are uninterrupted save for the hushed chirps of
the wandering cricket.
And while these peaceful creatures do wish for eternal
darkness, still comes the sunrise and dashes the quiet
night with its soft rays as a falling leaf upon a pond.
And the night pours and trickles away to the place
from whence it came and waits for the time when it
may again conquer.

—Gregory K. Baxter, Jr., age 14

I HAVE SET YOU FREE

Come to the table prepared for you,
  Body and blood are given to you.
Do this and remember my living and my dying
I give salvation that is soul-satisfying.

Everyone come now and kneel in prayer
Give thanks for the love I ask you to share
Let your love shine brightly all over the land
Till the day you see that my kingdom is at hand.

As I fed my flock so shall my lambs be gathered in,
No more pain and sorrow, my death was for your sins.
  I come to bring new life, rejoice and follow me,
Come lift your voices high, for I have set you free.
Come lift your voices high, for I have set you free.

—Patty B. Clement

THE FLOWERING TREE

So beautiful is the flowering tree
  And around it busy at work is the honey bee
The tree is so beautiful to see
And so sweet is the necter produced by the honey bee
So many different colors and shades
And to take care of them
Some people dig around them
With shovels or spades
And after the flower comes the leaf
Which brings to us the shade for relief
And many of them a fruit we can eat
Beside the shade to protect us from the heat
There are no other trees that can compare
For it gives us all three to share

—Donald W. Dutcher

CAREFREE DAYS

Back to the days of Christopher Robin and Pooh,
  When you were young and so was I.
The carefree, troublesome days of long ago,
I had my dolls and you had your cars.
Now they're packed far away.
Though the memories of those days remain,
You've gone your way and I've gone mine.
Out into the world of reality,
Fantasy far away.
Working from day to day,
Striving and seeking more and more each day.
When things aren't going right,
We may return to the days of Christopher Robin and Pooh
Lost in the fantasies of a child for an hour or two.

—Sheila M. Stirmel

MY DEAREST FRIEND

No one heard my cry.
No one felt my pain.
Sad and all alone was I, having lost at love again.
There was no one to run to.
No place where I could go
To escape the mounting, deep despair of the love that failed to grow.
Then one night in silence
like the wind He came to me.
He said, "I'll never leave you. I love you — just believe."
My mind was filled with doubt.
Confusion veiled my sight,
but as I clung to Him in trust, He clothed me in His light.
Since that day when He embraced me
He has never left my side.
He carries me through all the pain; He is my strength and guide.
And now I am an open book
to the One Who holds the pen.
He is my Lord and Savior
Jesus Christ — My Dearest Friend.

—Meganne K. Winder

MAN COULD ONLY FLY IN FAIRY TALES

When the rain has wet the world and the clouds connect in circles
and catch like feathers on the wind, when sun and stars are
strangled beneath a sky of evening haze, and the sight beyond
your windowpane grows dark and sullen with each yearning of the
heart; do not weaken. The only certain crime is when the fancy
fails. Centuries ago, man could only fly in fairy tales.

Sparrows darting over rooftops, lovers holding hands.
O tempora, O mores, I have no doubts, I am merely undevout.
The blood of disbelief is thick when left too long unbled.
Speak no more of what must be said, just quench this simple
thirst within me.

Standing outside, in full view of life, the moon is high and the
breeze is howling melodies.
Strange, wide earth you are.
With each new darkness that descends upon me comes to rest a
newfound sight — our thoughts are not unlike the music brought by
morning birds in flight.
All I say is trust the mind's ability, when confidences fail.
Centuries ago, man could only fly in fairy tales . . .

—Kimberly A. Robinson

STARTING OVER

The wide open spaces of forests, deserts and mountains
Is where my God reigns.
The beautiful places with rivers, trees and fountains
Still un-marred by chemical stains.

I'm always in awe of the simple things like the birds that flutter by,
While singing their mating call,
Or the intricate patterns on the wings of the passing butterfly,
As I lean against my cabin wall.

Give me always this life of freedom, fresh air and peace,
Of hunting, fishing and feast.
Give me a wife to share this kingdom of beauty without cease,
And we'll exist with this land of tree and beast.

The multitudes can have their cities of endless hurry,
Of pain and power madness.
They're deserving of all our pities and useless worry,
And the feelings of our sadness.

There will be no TV to corrupt our children's minds,
With ideas of hate or love's imitations.
We'll re-discover the wealth of nature's greatest finds,
And shun man-made desolations.

—Gurney Buckles

A LOST MEMORY

Not afraid of actual death
Afraid to be forgotten
Immortality achieved when
we are remembered
we die when we are forgotten
this is my greatest fear
Our souls dwell in hearts
Our lives in memories
Memories in records

—Mark Holcombe

THE FUTURE

The future lies before us,
We fear that vast unknown,
But we believe God's promise,
That we'll never be alone.
Because He holds the future,
We trust to him our lives,
Content to have him lead us,
With hope that satisfies.
We need not fear the journey,
If we keep him in our sight,
For He protects and guides us,
With his everlasting light.

—Mae O'Bryan Stallard

WALK

Walk with the sea
and discover its shore
don't stop now
there is still more.

Walk through a forest
and hear the trees
so full of spirit
swaying to the breeze.

Walk down a path
'til you reach its end
turn around
and walk it again.

Walk each day
and LIVE your dreams
there's more to life
than what it seems.

—Jeanie Kenow

MIRACLES

God's gift to man
Newborn baby's cry
Healing painful hearts
Touching joy to faces
Sunsets on the horizon
Morning glories after a snow
Children playing together
Love between two people
Laughter in people's hearts
Singing in the rain
Animals sleeping peaceful
Birds flying south for winter
Life in his hands
Joy in our souls
His belief we'll survive
Our tears for lost ones
The memories of days past
Lasting friendship forever
His miracles to us

—Wanda Lee Myers

PROMISES KEPT, PROMISES BROKEN

You give me friendship, the true and genuine kind
You give your love, even though I don't give mine

You give me contentment, which means so much to me
You give your devotion, and let me know you need me

You give me encouragement, to face the world each day
You give your concern, and do your best to light my way

You give me strength, to begin each day of living
You give me comfort, in knowing you'll keep on giving

You give me hope, just to know someone still cares
You give me peace, in knowing you'll always be there

You give your all to me, even though I haven't earned it
For all you give I thank you God, someday, I promise, I will return it!

—Jack C. Sherouse

BOXES OF MEMORIES TIED WITH RIBBONS OF LOVE

What is this feeling stirring within my heart?
It feels almost as painful as two lovers when they part.

One son off to school, one off to marriage to a blue-eyed girl so fair.
Wasn't it just yesterday they took their first steps up the stairs?

As I look around the rooms seeing memories from years gone by,
The quietness and emptiness bring from my lips a sigh.

In one room I still see posters from floor to ceiling.
They've been replaced with blank walls — no character revealing.

In another room uncluttered shelves and no gadgets within its border,
Makes my heart pine for just a little disorder.

Memories all boxed nice and neat and put away,
Tied with ribbons of love greater than I can say.

No boyish laughter or wrestling with a friend,
Makes me realize that all "good" things must end.

You yell and scream and worry how you'll make it through;
Now the time is here and you realize those years were few.

But we must go on to the next phase of our lives,
And pray to God that we can still help "when asked" with their strifes.

—Jean Wilson

ODE TO DELIVERANCE FROM ADDICTION
(alternatively titled "Edna St. Vincent's Malaise")

I burn my candle at both ends, an all consuming fire;
Born forth from sin, this flame ascends, to light my funeral pyre;

The knowledge of this world I sought, in hopes that I would find;
Deliv'rance premised on a thought, a rest wrought by my mind;
As lust's begotten heir is sin, this child I did entreat;
Its pleasures made of paraffin melt now before the heat;

Fix not your eyes upon the world, I cried amidst the din;
Toward hell mankind itself has hurled, creation steeped in sin;
But as I spoke this somber truth, hypocrisy laid claim;
For I who'd chastised flaming youth, stood guilty just the same;

In quiet desperation's night, I slumbered unawares;
That death knelt willing to requite the sorrows I did bear;
The amber beacon that had led me onward towards my tomb;
Casts shadows as my sins are wed, and darkness lights the womb;

I burn my candle at both ends, an all consuming fire;
Born forth from sin this flame ascends, to light my funeral pyre;

Oh, hear my words, all those who search, take heed this sinner's plea;
Climb down this moment from your perch, perchance that you may see;
His grace our conscience to amaze, these hardened hearts to turn;

Golgotha's luminescent blaze, forevermore to burn.

—Andrew Todhunter

FATHERS

According to the calendar,
there's a special day —
dedicated just for you!
Reflect and be aware of
the stablizing stronghold
that you possess and
look ahead for success
through good communication,
understanding and happiness.
Values are assimulated.

—Marilyn M. Turner

EXPECTATIONS

Wishes and hopes
Of children and old
Become mankind's legends
In stories retold.

Thoughts and ideas
Of woman and man
Combine into history
A record to stand.

Oceans and tides
Of moon and man
Envelope and glide
Like water and sand.

—Russell Wiltse

RECIPE FOR LIFE

A handful of happiness
and four cups of dreams
an ounce of believing
what no one else sees,
Add much confusion,
rebellion, and such,
a spoonful of tears,
and the wind's gentle touch
a pinch of pain,
a tad of sorrow,
and hope to keep reaching
for a better tomorrow,
Mix well, sprinkle in
a few very good friends
and hope that the best
will turn out in the end.

—S. E. Weber

TRUST IN ME

Let go of your fears
And come into my arms,
For I will let nothing
Cause you trouble or harm.

Tell me what caused you
Such sorrow and pain,
And together we'll work
To make you happy again.

I won't ridicule you
Or laugh at your sorrow;
I will just offer hope
For a better tomorrow.

We can have friendship
And happy we'll be,
If you will only
Trust in me.

—Cindy L. Godwin

Are there words
that can feel?
So full of color of
    a blowing autumn
        evening . . . . .
Black clouds edged
    with the fire of setting sun —
Leaves, torn loose,
    flung high . . . .
Color so vivid, that
    my being flows into
And rides with the
    autumn wind . . . . .
into the setting sun.

—Mary F. Munneke

A HEARTY BREAKFAST TREAT

Come early
In the morning,
We will be
A perfect match:

You will be
The pancakes,
And I will be
The syrup.

With loving care:

I will pour myself
All over you
And fill you up
With my sweetness.

As one:

We will chase
Away hunger,
And be
Very much
Satisfied.

—C Jackson

AURORA BOREALIS

Aurora dreams,
Plasma streams,
Fluorescent beams.

Plasma dashes,
Fluorescent flashes,
Celestial splashes.

Sunspot ejects,
Van Allen collects,
Ionosphere projects.

Solar flares,
Ionosphere glares,
Eyes stare.

Pulses of light fly,
On earth's magnetic ply,
Illuminating the night sky.

Night sky brightening,
Cloudless lightning,
From gods, frightening.

Mother earth's halo,
A nocturnal rainbow,
In excelsis deo.

Gaia's aura shows,
When Aurora glows.

—Randy Hirschey

AS I WALK

As I walk, feel the breeze, hear it brush through the trees.
As I walk, a grasshopper jumps, off and on of grassy clumps.
As I walk, the sun shines high, a little yellow ball in a great big sky.
As I walk, smell the fresh air, walking just walking without a care.

As I walk, the flowers bloom, smelling like a sweet perfume.
As I walk, river water rushes, against the muddy banks it brushes.
As I walk, some birds fly by, they swoop down low then soar up high.
As I walk, animals are aware, walking just walking without a care.

—David T. Ebert, age 12

SAXOPHONE SONG

Hearing the swanky, slanky, slick sound,
of a saxophone, I have found,
Is a relaxing way to pass the day
With my head lying on the ground.

Hearing the loud, lovely, low tune,
of this instrument morn, night and noon
does make my feet dance, they will not keep their stance
as I lie on the floor of my room.

Hearing the soft, sweet lullaby song
of my friend as we say, "so long"
will put me to sleep, I will sleep oh so deep
with my saxophone song singing strong.

—Michelle Jean Wisener

IF I HAD HAD A DIFFERENT HUSBAND

I wouldn't have had so many different dancing partners.
What a blessing, he was gone for weeks at a time.
A whirl here, a twirl there, hair flowing in the breeze.
I had the best of two worlds, envy of all the girls.
What if he had been a town man/
Years and years of sameness.
Wash, iron, scrub, care for crying children.
To a man whose ego was as large as the ocean.
The only reward you received was a grunt.
Who thought of you as a runt.
Thank God I was spared that fate.
There was a little diversion in my life.
"Goodbye, dear, see you next week. Be careful on the road.
Or you might turn into a toad."

—Eleanore V. Urban

I'M A SOUTHPAW — SO WHAT?

So, you are a southpaw, how unfortunate they say,
To have to go through all your life, in the left-handed way.
To some, we may a little awkward look,
But, no matter, you can't find a book, to prove that
We left-handers can't do,
Everything our right-handed friends try to.

History tells us that we have had four left-
handed presidents — namely Garfield, Truman, Ford and Bush.
What causes a great person to use his left hand?
Could it be inherited? Maybe, it is so,
But these four presidents, for example, great prestige
did and do show.

Now medical science states that the right-handed
person uses the left side of his brain.
While the left-handed person, the right side of his
brain does use and train.

So, you see, we southpaws are the only ones using
our right mind!
Can anyone out there, a better answer find
To the superiority of a left-hander's mind?

—Mrs. Grace Freestone

DEAR FRIENDS

We must suffer patiently the hardships of life . . . .
To bear without resistance and tolerate our strife . . . .
Friends can help that burden they'll be there all the way . . . .
To help you see the dawning of a bright new day . . . .
When that day's approaching with all its trials come . . . .
The patience that God gives us through Jesus Christ His Son . . . .
So as each day glides swiftly by with trials of its own . . . .
Remember "dear friends" — God will never leave you alone . . . .
He walks right beside you every step of every day . . . .
And carries you through the valleys till your tears are washed away . . . . . .
Then with hope inside your heart — a gift God will send, to help you through
The troubled times . . . .
This gift you know as FRIENDS . . . .

—Vicki M. Kidder

ONE VIEW

The one's at the top,
   Are only hypocrites dictating to the people.
And they will never stop
Until the "real" common man is speaking from a universal steeple.

In our blindness for a free nation,
The people have stopped caring.
The world has become selfish,
Only to one day realize the doom facing the future generation.

We send our young away to face the world.
Trained only to see things from one point of view,
And not as a whole.
For the aftermath, we don't realize, will one day haunt us.

They blame other countries for our drug dependancy.
But they ignore the fact that we are a free nation.
So that most have chosen their destination,
And that is to dream while the politicians prove their hypocrisy.

Until we get to the heart and soul of the problem as a whole,
Our officials will never solve the unending nightmare.
For, we, the people, have to accept the fact that the world is to share
Among different colors and cultures because the world is our soul.

—Maria Paula Goncalves

FORTITUDE OF AN INVALID

The young man had the misfortune of being born with bad genes
   His acute muscular dystrophy escalated in his teens.

As time progressed, crutches helped him to get aroun'
   He worked at a concession stand selling goods downtown.

He never thought he'd marry because his eyesight was so poor
   But along came a wonderful girl who gave him something to live for.

Even though they were both legally blind
   Love and the need for family life is what they had in mind.

Many discouraged the couple from having a baby urging them to wait
   But the man and his loving wife did not hesitate.

Against all odds this happily married dual
   Have raised a healthy boy and girl in spite of ridicule.

His daughter now a Brownie, his son an active scout
   The invalid and his wife haven't the time to pout.

Unshaken and undaunted by the challenge that persists
   His family adds a new dimension to the life that now exists.

And even though in wheelchair and barely able to see
   This courageous man still finds time to laugh with glee.

Although the M.D. has taken its toll now and reached its bitter crest
   At least the invalid will know he's given life his best.

Dedicated to: Ben and Julie
   —Angeline Kotarac

HAPPINESS

The trees are waving
   in the breeze,
While I hear the leaves
   crackle under me.
The birds are singing
   in me
And I feel happy.

—Timothy Patterson

TIME

   Time
   is all, I sought
   to see, lost is
   mine, taught
   to be believed
   eye to eye
   we cry
   we fall
   all is time
while none is all . . .

—Lisa S. Eland

THE QUIET RAIN

The quiet rain
   drops
dripping softly
   on my window

Washing slowly
   through my life
leaving sparkles
   in cobwebs

Words from voices
   dropping around me
Apart and yet here
   so much of my life

And meaning emerges
   only when
I look for it
   but seldom alone

—Kate Cook

JUST CALL

Who am I,
   but one man,
among many.

With just two hands,
but ready,
to help many.

A hand I lend,
to you,
my friend.

Not from pity,
do I lend,
but deep within I send,
love abound.

To lend you,
from the bottom
to the top.

And if you stumble,
and fall,
just give,
me a call.

—S. D. Galvin

AN OCEAN APART

Though oceans and
    miles may keep us
        apart
I shall always hold
        you close to my heart
You gave my life joy
        when your path crossed
            with mine
I pray that again they
        will soon intertwine.

—Tammy Jo Madison

TIME

If all the time
    Was yours and mine,
And all the world was free;
Then we would live
To share and give
Our love as it should be.

All will be right
Within the light
Forever and again;
And grow we will
From now until
Time starts over again!

—Mark Dale Irvin

ABSTRACT PORTRAIT

Clear and Candid
expressing the truth

Not to be an eyesore
disgrace to hide
something taught to fear

Not to confuse a mind
upset concrete
that lies in us all
firm and forever still

Here to behold
honored honesty
the imagination
beauty within

Grace present throughout
Color and Character.

—D.R. Williams

A DREAM

Reach out and touch,
    Reach out and take hold,
Make believe you can touch
That pot of gold.

Wander to places beyond
Yonder river and hill,
Go one step further,
Find one more thrill.

Do the unusual,
Be daring and bold,
Try to be unafraid,
Gather all you can hold.

Stride across fields,
Step across the next stream,
Grab the gold ring,
Take hold of A DREAM.

—Dale L. Burkett

AGES OF MAN

A distance of lavender colored mountains
    Straight forward, ahead . . . . how grand!

Pioneers of long ago, back in time, as our
        Forefathers wrote by hand.
Dried, wooden wheels squeaked as horse hooves
        Clumped in the sand.
In the heat of noon's blinding light pioneers
Had to stop in search for water in the cactus
        Sprouting all over the land.

Sounds of howling wolves echoing nightly
        Throughout the valleys and the hills.
Then mornings came with a strong
Wind . . . cooling the new day and bringing some
            Slight chills.

Fading . . . then . . . into the sunset of a golden ray
The weather beaten covered wagons continued.
                    Yes.
Legended by pin and quills.

—Sharon Pelate

A PLEA TO MLK

Your dreams of the world
    And your dreams of peace,
Were lost when you left.
        I wish you were here to show me the light.
To give me hope, for I've lost my faith.
        To show me love can conquer hate.
To show me kindness is better than a gun,
        And not only me but all the young,
It's with them you have to start.
        For the old have let their dreams disappear,
Where ours are just beginning.
        But my dreams are already starting to fade.
Watching men kill each other day after day.
        When you live with hate,
Peace just isn't a reality you can comprehend.
        I need you to help me believe,
To pick up where you left off.
        And not only me but everyone,
From the old to the young.

—Rebecca Gangl, age 15

IF I COULD NEVER PRAY

I often wonder what I would do, if I
    could never pray, and ask God to guide my
way,
To lead my footsteps every day.
The night would be o' so dark if His light
could not shine.
I could not sleep, because fear would fill
this heart of mine.
A song my heart would never sing, I would
be so sad and all alone. If I could never
pray to God, and claim Him as my own.
But I shall never have a fear, because my burdens
He will share.
Just a low whisper, and He hears my every prayer,
He will always walk beside me, that I may never
fall.
By my hand He will lead me, "Jesus my Savior,"
the God of all.
Sometimes my night may be dark, but God's love
will always shine.
I can sleep in peace, and never have a
fear, because I know God my Savior is always
near.

—Mary Lucy Moore

MORNING STAR

Life and love is what you are.
Truth and understanding is what you are.
I feel so good with the warmth of your light.
The morning star is so bright.
There is nothing else in sight.
You are like the rainbow in the sky.
Teach me how to fly.
Not a worry or a care can there be.
For you are everything I could ever want,
    and see.

—Brent Kyrk

I'LL LOVE YOU—ALWAYS

While sitting by my window,
My thoughts were filled of you,
The cool, cool breeze came floating in,
And seemed to whisper low—
I love you, love you very much,
And always will, I know.
For each bright star up in the sky
A wish is often made,
And if that wish be quite sincere,
True faith will never fade.
I wish tonight for just one thing,
And know you wish it, too,
Happiness and lasting love—for me and you!

—Louise Struthers Bernoski

THE INN

On the outside looking in
I could remember my time there with him.
The memories have not grown dim,
Nor has the love I feel deep within.
Yes, deep within my soul you see
I love him, and that's the key.
If only I could see my own destiny
and be sure his faithfulness was only to me.
I would surround myself in glee
and walk hand in hand with him toward the sea
Letting our hearts and souls live in eternity.
Together you see,
Me for him and
Him for me.
Growing in our love and also separately.
Alas! For now I am free Mon Ami.

—Lynn Devereux

NOBLE CONQUEST?

Forever the lofty peak of Everest —
So far up, so unreachably tall —
For mountain climbers provides a test,
A challenge to their skill, an irresistible call.

With undaunted courage of body and soul,
Defying all dangers, they with stubborness seek,
With persistent effort, to reach their goal,
To answer the call of the challenging peak.

O climber, with nerves as strong as steel,
With stubborn determination, courage and pride.
What is it that you truly feel
While laboriously ascending the mountainside?

Is it an answer to a noble quest,
Or just a feat of do-and-dare —
Just to accomplish another conquest?
To defy the peak "just because it's there"?

—Michael S. Koch

MY SON

When the doctor said, "it's a boy"
My heart filled with pride
To see this little bundle of joy
That wiggled, kicked and cried.

To bring him home
Out of the winter chill,
And tuck in his crib
With blanket, pillow and little toys
That I so longed to fill.

To feed him and hold him
And before my eyes I see,
The little bundle of joy I hold
Looks more and more like me.

To see him laugh and crawl and walk
No better could I have done
To hold him high for all to see,
"Hey everybody! This is my son!"

—Tom Davis

TO MY LOVE

In the silence that comes like sleep
You come to me
In whispered words
Warm
As a desert kiss.

In the calm that settles like sand
You come to me
With ivory hands
Soft
As a summer moon —

In the love that spreads like Spring
You come to me
With hands
    and words
Pure
As your smile
    at dawn.

—'Ian' John Lennon McKay II

SWEET THINGS

Have you ever sucked on sweet grass
As you stripped it through your lips?

Have you ever savored birch bark?
Carried hay upon your hips?

Did you ever note a warbler's song
Or cry of Mourning Dove?

Did you ever see a Weeping Tree
That sang of Dying Love?

—Heléna Willett

LIFE IS . . . .

Life is like a dancing song,
All you can do is sing-along.

If you let the beat go on and wait,
Something will catch you it is called
fate.

Life is not always fair but do not fret,
There are some who care.

Life just goes round and round.
Same song, same dance, same sound.

—A.M. Thiessen

249

NATURAL BRIDGE

The Natural Bridge:
Nature's wonder,
Virginia's rock,
Place to ponder.

Unnatural bridge:
Not like another,
Not man made,
Not put together.

Awesome sight:
Beauty to behold,
Refresh the spirit,
Revive the soul.

Gladys S. Formby

REFLECTIONS

But for the night
I cease to be,
aimlessly looking
in search of me.

Images mirrored
for those who see.
Does vanity win
to set them free?

For all of time
reflections remain,
for all of those
who are so vain . . .

Susan Vinzant Thomson

THE POET'S EPITAPH

Expressing what
I cannot say
aloud I write
these letters black
on paper white.

When I have gone
your lips will breathe
new life through words
a dead man wrote.

You read and find
my secret self,
the feelings I
once had for you,
this love inscribed
on paper white.

Peter M. Schweighofer

CASTLES

I saw a child
Kneeling in the
Grass.

Curious, I asked
Him what was Lost.

"Nothing," he
Replied.
"But I found
A castle."

I looked where
His stubby finger
Pointed
And saw
The anthill.

Michelle S. Hodge

CHALLENGER

Reaching above and beyond earth's control;
Seventy-three seconds in flight, seven heroes relinquished their souls.

The world wept for those who tragically died;
Americans wept, too, for we are a nation built with pride.

Technicians, pilots, and a teacher trained with dedication and devotion;
God in Heaven has rendered thee your final promotion.

Blasting off to the heavens, seeking educational wisdom;
Challenger's astronauts have achieved the purest form of freedom.

Engines roared as Challenger streaked upward with noise so loud;
All nations watched as you made America so proud.

1969, NASA achieves the ultimate goal, landing men on the moon;
Shuttle missions, beyond the horizon, orchestrate America's finest tune.

Americans look for direction and guidance in the stars;
Astronauts, a chosen few, will be the only ones to reach so far.

Supreme Commander resting behind the gates of Heaven;
God shows love, because earth has surrendered to Him the magnificent seven.

—**Joey Parker**

THE EAGLE BOTTOM FIDDLE PLAYER

The Eagle Bottom fiddle player, Bass Tate was his name.
Making country and mountain music was his call to fame.
The fiddle player really liked his music, he'd play it both night and day,
And when he'd start a fix'n to leave, the people would ask him to stay.
Please Mr. Fiddle Player, won't you play one more?
Won't you please step back inside? Won't you shut the door?
Please Mr. Fiddle Player, won't you pretty please?
So the fiddle player would sit back down and put them at their ease.
And then there was music, music all the long, long while.
The fiddle player was something else, the man really had some style.
And there was dance'n, dance'n all across the floor.
And when the fiddle player would stop, they'd all ask for more.
The Eagle Bottom fiddle player, he's not with us now,
Cause he's in the sky above, taking one last bow.
But he's looking down on us, wish'n us all well.
The Eagle Bottom fiddle player was really something swell.
The Eagle Bottom fiddle player, he's not with us today,
Because the Eagle Bottom fiddle player, "Bass Tate" has passed away.

Written in memory of Bass Tate
—**Albert Bruckelmeyer II**

FATHER, COME QUICKLY

Father, come quickly. They have captured your son!
YES, I KNOW. I SPOKE WITH HIM LAST NIGHT IN THE GARDEN.
But, Father, what shall we do?
NOTHING.

Father, come quickly. They are mocking your son!
YES, THOSE WHO LOVED HIM ARE TURNING AWAY.
But, Father, tell them who he is.
I CANNOT.

Father, come quickly. They want to kill your son!
YES, I HEAR THE CHANT OF THE PEOPLE.
But, Father, doesn't it make you angry?
NO, IT BREAKS MY HEART.

Father, come quickly. They are crucifying your son!
YES, I HEAR HIM CALLING TO ME.
But, Father, can't you go to him?
NO, NOT YET.

Father, oh Father, come quickly. They have killed your son!
YES, IT IS FINISHED.
But, Father, why did he have to die?
TO SAVE THE WORLD.

—**Jane Campbell McIntyre**

DAD, WHY DIDN'T YOU?

Why didn't you throw a football with me,
 or show me how to climb a tree?
Why didn't you teach me to fly a kite,
 or read bedtime stories to me at night?
Why didn't you teach me to tie my shoes,
 or to throw a baseball, just like you?

Did you think time wouldn't pass along,
 that I'd be little for so long?
There was no need to spend time with me,
 that I'd be small eternally?

Well, now I'm grown and I can't find time for you,
 to do the things we didn't do.
I spend my spare time with my little ones,
 just teaching them things and having fun.
I wish things had turned out differently,
 but Dad, why didn't you throw a football with me?

 —Charmaine W. Cole

MY TENDER LOVE

We have known each other for a very short time,
 Yet when together we are, then life is sublime;
She's young and she's tender, She's my Olga divine;
She brings happiness in abundance for she's all mine.

A beauty she is all loving and tender,
And my heart to her I would gladly surrender;
She is a mother of two yet a spinster at heart,
She's the one I should have met right from the start.

Together we are one and apart we do fret,
Success is ours together on this anything I'd bet;
Olga's a woman and a mother, she's my young hearted lover,
She is a blessing from above to hold and keep forever.

'Tis sad her first marriage was such a wholesome mess,
Though I hope our union does not undergo the same stress;
If make it we must then each other we shall fully trust,
And let not our caring for even a moment rust.

Her kisses are so sweet and her caresses Oh! So tender,
My shoulder, in her hour of need, I'd gladly lend her;
One day soon she will be completely free,
And together we shall fulfill our every need.

 —Stanislaus R.C. Moss

BITS AND PIECES

A little bit of love, a piece of pain
 Today I felt that hurt again.
I come home to see your bags all packed
with intentions of leaving, never looking back.

Maybe time alone will ease your mind
You'll realize what you're leaving behind
Here sits a girl with love so true
And a mind that wonders if I'll ever have you.

You sit in silence, wonder where to begin
"But don't worry babe, it'll never happen again"
Only this time those words weren't spoken
Guess there are no words for a heart that's broken.

Now I sit confused as you put things away
Still not knowing if you're here to stay
Seems you can't feel love when times are bad
You walk away, and I gave all I had.

It's the Bits and Pieces that now remain
that you must put together again.
But if you must throw this good love away
Always remember, I even loved you today.

 —Nita Randolph "(Nete)"

SUNSET

The sun in the evening sky
 Shadows the earth below.
With the golden sun rays disappearing
Drowsy darkness begins to show.

Beyond the horizon the sun descends
Into a secret sea of sleep;
Daily duty and regal role forgotten,
There he is nothing, but there is peace.

 —Maude Sumner Campbell

TRUTH

Truth
 Is
Like a small piece of sculpture
Carved from a large piece of granite.
The truth-seeker
Chips away at the granite,
Heaving away huge chunks of useless rock
Until
What is left
Is
Truth.

 —Dozier Cade

REMEMBERING OUR WEDDING DAY

It has been one short year,
 Since that day I hold so dear.
The day that started our new life,
To love each other as man and wife.

In our home, we married that day—
And as a family I know we'll stay.
Laughter, sorrow, come what may,
Past or future won't stand in our way.

A February day, oh, so cold,
Three lives together, we promised to mold.
One child we had, but soon was told
We would have one more to hold.

When repeating my vows, I cried a tear,
But you should never, ever fear.
For love and joy filled my heart,
For I knew we would never, ever, part.

 —Judy England Ray

SPRING BEAUTY

Dainty rosebuds . . .
 Fill the garden;
Tender buds . . .
 Fragile and pale;
Symbols of early Spring . . .
 Burst into splendor;
Color and fragrance . . .
 Fill the air.

 —Heather Eileen Burdette

OF AN ARTIST-MUSICIAN LOVED ONE

Heaven will be more beautiful
 Now that her new home is up there.
The joys her talents gave this earth
Prevailed in hearts throughout her sphere.
Sunsets will reveal her deft touch
In her new realm in places higher!
And surely golden streets will ring
With music from her own new lyre!

 —Mrs. Harriet S. Eckles

FLIGHT

Not out of moments
But of years,
Fire of desire,
Flame of pain;
In the embers of the heart
The tempered soul is forged.
What price the soaring spirit!

—Enola Mangelson

SOMETIMES

You are,
Sometimes imperfect.
Sometimes Impossible.

Still you are
the only one in this world
to make me feel at home.

Although I am,
Sometimes imperfect.
Sometimes impossible.

—LeAnne M. Emery

EAGLES OF PAIR

Peace within Dream;
Given Hope.
Awakening Eyes;
Direction of upward sky.
Seen above and beyond;
Beautifully they soar.
Two Eagles in flight;
Wings of a pair.
The Lord's presence known;
Spoken identity unfolds.
Given two names;
"The Eagles of Pair."

—Rebecca Lynne Chaput

QUESTION OF PATRIOTISM

In a Land that's bold,
I want the gold.

In a Land I fight,
To do what's right.

In a Land called home,
Like an enemy I Roam.

In a Land of Liberty,
was killed my sensitivity.

In a Land I Live,
my Life should I give?

—Mark A. Sercye

ABORTION

I am going to be killed
I don't know why
What did I ever do
to deserve to die.
Does my father know?
What's going on!!
They're going to kill his baby.
A daughter or a son
She doesn't want me to live
My mother doesn't care
I guess to her
I'm just a nightmare

—Edward (LaLo) Martinez

THE LITTLE BOY'S PRAYER

The other night I heard a prayer, from such a little boy.
He was asking God some questions, in his voice there was no joy.

He prayed about his mother, how his little heart was torn.
When he said, "I never met her Lord; she died when I was born."

As his voice began to quiver, he said, "Lord, tell me true,
Was she, my mom, a Christian, did she live her life for you?"

The little boy was crying now, it was hard for him to speak.
He dried his tears and raised his head, his voice so ever weak.

He said, "Lord, if she wasn't, maybe I could do,
Twice as much here on earth, my share and her share, too."

"Oh Lord, I'll work so very hard, just watch and You will see.
If only You will introduce my mom one time to me."

I knew his prayer had ended, when I heard him say, "Amen."
Now both of us were crying, and here's what happened then.

Everything got very quiet, as another voice did say,
"My child, your mother's here with Me, as you too will be, someday."

—Cindy Masino

FREEDOM

Freedom, it is just a word. But in this simple word there
is power, a strength. Freedom, such as an eagle, who but spreads
his mighty wings, and begins to fly. Freedom, like the wind,
whose breeze fills the sail of a ship and sends it almost
effortlessly across a calm sea. Freedom, like a man who is
shackled to reality for too long, that whenever he discovers
miracles really do happen is released from his bonds. We
sometimes wonder where it is to be found, this strange but
friendly freedom? We look all around, we escape, and for awhile
we find it, only for it to slip away once again. Then we
realize, that though we were looking for this freedom, we were
blind for freedom is all around us. It is in the sun, which
casts its rays upon the cool dawn and brings warmth. It is in
the flow of a mountain spring, which is forever moving toward
its ocean home. It is in the stars of night which never cease
to reflect their magnificent glow. But, freedom is also found
in the most beautiful and unexpected place of all, ourselves.
For we are a part of everything around us, and we share its same
breath. So, we stop looking, and we just simply live, for now
we realize what freedom truly is!

—John R. Murphy

IS DEATH TO DIE???

We walk under the great Elms and Oaks;
Finding comfort from the sun —
In their shadows they invoke.

We walk beside the gigantic skyscrapers,
For what it is worth;
And are cast in their shadows —
Feeling serenity, strength and character
As the shadows hang like draperies
Over the windows of the earth.

We ride the roads of the beautiful countryside.
While the shadows from the large trucks and vans
Pass over us as the movement of the wheels
Go safely by the roads' divide.

We learn from this that Shadows never hurt us!
In death, we do not die but simply walk through —
The valley of the shadow of death and on the
Other side of the divide we find life eternal.
The serenity of heaven, the greatness of God
And the strength of perfection.

Death is simply the shadow of passing from one life to a greater one.

—Shirley Lee Spivey

CATERPILLAR TO BUTTERFLY

I am a . . .
Yes . . . a caterpillar
In motion across the burning pavement
Of a journey to branches
On the other side of life

I am but one of many
Soon to become dancing beautifully,
As beautiful as my looks

Two figure eights,
One smaller than the other,
Can be seen on me
In different colorful forms

I am a butterfly
As beautiful as can be

Yes . . . a butterfly —
Ah, a butterfly finally!

—Debbie Budnick

SNOWFLAKE

As the night wind grows still,
The snow silently falls to earth.
I catch a snowflake in my hand,
And look at it with care.

That snowflake reminds me of you,
There's not another one like it.
Its beauty shines through
Much like yours does.
Its fragileness is so great,
But strong enough to last the fall.
The snowflake is special
Because it brings me warmth,
That warm feeling I get
Whenever I'm near you.

As much as you are like the snowflake,
There is a difference.
The snowflake will melt away,
But you never will.

—Billy Dowdy

UNTITLED

When everything appears lost
And you're all alone,
Unleash the mind and unharnass
Emotions to roam.

Study defeat and what makes failure.
Seek and struggle with your foes.
From failure comes wisdom,
From wisdom comes sight.

The struggle of good versus evil
Goes on through the pages of time,
Sometimes following a well worn path
Sometimes twisting through the mind.

I wonder what the price is we pay
For the destruction that is wrought.
In the future, there will come a day
to review the battles that were fought.

It will be learned that all lost.
There are no winners in struggle.
Not just war, but any dispute,
Every rift shows lack of cooperation.

—Thomas K. Ferrell

BENEATH DEPRESSION

Depression is like a piece of glass.
Fragile, yet sharp and clear. Some
can see through it, while others
believe it too clear to exist. If
you can see through it, you can
change it. But, if you are unable
to clearly see through it, you will
drop it, and it will shatter in
many pieces.
     Pieces you feel cannot be put
together again.
     The glass has slipped from my
hands many times, and as I
bend down to pick up the pieces,
I cry as they cut my fingers.
     But wounds, I'm told, however
deep, can be healed in time. Just
as that useless piece of broken glass
can be swept up and tossed away.

—Tamera Roe

REMEMBERING

Midnight breezes carrying memories,
A young life, long lived.
Birth to sunrise,
Youth to wildlife,
Death to darkness.
Enveloped forever in immortality;
Back to beginning, memories.

—Andalynn Hansen

I HAD TO GO TO TOWN TODAY

I had to go to Town Today
Tho sorrow and despair
had me held tight — as if to Stay
this Mournful Deed I fear.

With heartstrings taut to breaking point
and eyes so full of tears,
I could not see beyond my grief;
Just back to Better Years.

I had to go to Town Today,
and forever the pain will Keep
tucked Deep Inside life's Memory Book:
When I put my Pet to Sleep!

—Sherrill A. Brooks

MY EPITAPH

I hope that when they come
To write "Finis" beside my name,
I'll have proved to one and all
That life was more than just a game.

I hope I'll leave a record,
Carved on stone — not in wet sand;
Something to show what I accomplished,
While I was present on the land.

That when it's time — they'll say,
She was kind — not filled with hate;
And the color of one's skin,
In friendship — she did not debate.

And maybe when my time does come,
And they lower the coffin into the
     grave;
People gathered round may say,
She didn't take more than she gave.

—Patricia D. G. Otake

LIFE

Life is like a candle,
lit for the very first time.
The flame jumps about,
earning strength and power,
as its bold flame burns on.
Slowly, it fades away,
until the flames, burn no more.

Life is like a story,
Starting out with a beginning.
And as you read on, the story gets
stronger.
The farther you read, it gets better.
Until it nears the end, the story
becomes weaker.
The story ends and you wish
it would continue.

Life, it has a beginning and an end,
but the best times, are in the middle.

—Courtney C. Pace

CAN I HELP IT?

Can I help it if I love you,
   when you mean so much to me?
Can I help it if I run to you,
   with every cry and plea?
Can I help myself from falling
at your feet when e'er you're near?
Can I help it for admiring you,
   for you make all things clear.

You've changed my life completely,
   and I thank you every day.
And for your love and friendship,
   I never fail to pray.
A rainbow you've created,
   bringing color to grey space.
 you have become a perfect rose,
   among the thorns I face.
So, really can I help it,
   when I feel the way I do?
For you're the one who introduced me,
   To a love that's true.

—Julie Lynne Pifer

A BUNDLE FROM HEAVEN

The years have passed so quickly,
   since the day that you were born,
when I heard your healthy cry so loud,
just a little before the dawn.

As I held you close, with tears of joy
just trickling down my face,
I knew that very moment,
nothing else could take your place.

I gazed into your eyes today,
and thought of years gone by,
and hoped you loved me just as much
as the day you just turned five.

I thought of how I wiped your tears,
when you were sick or sad,
and held you till the morning
when your dreams were really bad.

I thought of how you ran to me,
with little tiny flowers,
and hoped you needed me just as much
as the day we called you ours!

—Nancy A. Dureault

MY SON—MY SAILOR

When I was only twenty, I had a baby boy!
Happy were my days, you brought me so much joy!
Sometimes you were rowdy, like little boys can be,
But I took care of that with a little hickory tea!

Two little blackbirds sitting on a hill, one's named
Jack, one's named Jill. Fly away Jack, fly away Jill.
Come back Jack, come back Jill . . . . I picked you up at
Nursery school you told this poem to me. I thought it
Was so cute, 'cause you were only three!

I really can't remember the day you got your bike, I just
Know you rode it morning, noon, and night! You'd ride it
To Bob's house, and down to Granny's too. You'd ride it to
The store and Bear would follow you!

It wasn't to be mean, when we took your car away, we had to
Make you study so you would pass your grade. It didn't take
Too long, a couple of months I guess, of riding on your thumb
To make you do your best.

And now you've joined the navy, you'll be going far away,
I'll say a prayer for you each and every day, always do what's
Right and if ever you're in doubt, the Bible that Dean gave to
You, would surely help you out!

—Bobbie Hight

SPRING HAS SPRUNG

Birds are singing.
Bells are ringing,
and a sweet smelling baby is born.

Flowers are popping.
Bunnies are hopping,
The child opens its eyes so blue as the morning skies,
and life is full of bumble bees and sweet cherry pies.

The children are playing.
Old folks are praying,
and sap is flowing new life into the trees.
Soon the world will burst into new splendor,
fireworks of color, joy, and emotions so tender.

Wonderful spring with all your wonder
come! Bring us new life and thoughts much fonder.

—Traude DiCerchio

AUTUMN

As I walk near the lake, next to our Summer home;
seeing the late Autumn, a strange feeling comes over me.
I am lost and lonely, the whole world is empty, except
for me.

Nothing is important; all my problems disappear,
roving thoughts turn toward the lake; I see the deep
blue waters, with its capped peaks rolling to the white
glistening sand, then moving back to nothingness.

I hear the humming motor of a motor boat, disappearing
over the horizon.

Huge Maple and Oak leaves herald the beginning of
Autumn, turning gold, rust bleeding red, fiery orange
and tan.

I hear the crackling of leaves beneath my feet;
Suddenly a golden leaf, tumbles to earth with the
precision of an expert acrobat.

I wander to the cottage and smell the smoldering leaves;
and stand there to stare into the flames and wonder
what God has in store for me.

—Marilyn P. Holleback

HEARTFELT

My heart is like a little boy,
Full of fun and filled with joy!
Sometimes shiny-clean and bright
Or shady if things aren't right;
But deep within, there's something proud
Because YOU ARE AN AMERICAN MADE BY GOD!

—Jenna V. Ownbey

LET ME BE ALONE

Open thine eyes; Take heed . . . . BEWARE!
A mixed up world in despair
The lies, The wars, I'll not condone
I'll find an island to be alone.

Tis but a dream, yet it shall be
An isle of peace, I yearn to see.
I ask thee Lord, guide my way
Toward peace, serenity . . . . Come what may.

Oh thank you God, this isle you give
Is just the place I want to live.
Just love; No ills; Not even hate
Let this isle then, be my fate.

—John J. Dalessio

THE HOUR

In the twilight of the hour.
In my mind just passing by.
All the things that use to matter.
Of the things between you and I.

Though the years have gone by quickly.
The memories of you still linger on.
Sometimes often I still hear
your laughter and I miss you in
my life.

I know your spirit's
soaring in the world of God's
divine. And I am still here
on earth.

Waiting for the reunion of you and I.

—Carmen F. Young

THE FARMER'S PRAYER

Dear "Lord," I know it's been awhile,
Since I spoke these thoughts of mine,
But lately I've been so busy,
    They just slipped away with time.

"Lord," I don't have a fancy place,
    To share my thoughts with "you,"
But I don't suppose that matters much,
    So I guess this log will do.

Most of all "Lord," it's the "Love" I feel,
    When I rock my Babes at night,
And my Heart, well it seems to overflow,
    When I hold my Sweetheart tight.

Well "Lord" that's about it, I guess,
    It's almost supper time,
Just "you" and me here, so I'll wipe these tears,
    Since a Man ain't supposed to cry."

I betrayed no sign that I had heard.
    For fear I'd break the spell,
But "Lord," I wish, oh how I wish,
    I could say it half as well.

—Maxine Morris

ASH WEDNESDAY

Ash Wednesday.
The start of another Lenten Season
Of repentance and atonement,
Suffering for our sins,
To free our souls
From the heavy chains
That bind us,
Preparing for the salvation
Of Easter time.

This Lenten season
Is made all the more poignant
By the self examination
Imposed by the crisis
I wish we could share together.
But I know
Part of our purgatory
Is to examine our lives
Apart from each other —
Separated, alone, and depressed.

—E. Michael Schoonmaker

FRIENDS

Just how many are there
That we can call true friends?
Is it one, two or maybe three
Who loves us to the end?
Look around you and count them
The ones you can tell your troubles to;
Can cry upon their shoulders
And know they still love you
One who will listen, but never criticize
No matter how things may seem.
They make you realize
On them you can really lean.
They are always ready with words
Of comfort, love and praise;
And tells how Jesus loves us
And strengthens all our days.
How He died upon a cruel cross
Our sins all to forgive,
To bear the shame for you and me
And with Him in eternity live.

—Leota Mills

I WILL LIVE THE WAY I PRAY

I knelt to pray when day was
done,
And prayed "O Lord, bless everyone,
Lift from each saddened heart
The pain,
And let the sick be well again"
And then I awake another day,
And carelessly went on my way.
The whole day long I did not try
To wipe the tear from another's
eye;
I did not try to share the load
of anybody on my road;
I did not even go to see
The sick man just next door to me.
I prayed "O Lord, bless everyone . . .
God sweetest blessing always
go to hands that serve him here
below"
But let me see another day.
And I will live the way I pray

—Estelle Hughes

MY GRANDMA

I see my precious grandma
As she plucks a rose for me,
Her flower garden is her palace,
Her favorite, the rose especially.
I love my grandma dearly,
Her life is a pattern in bloom,
She tenderly cares for her garden,
The rose and its sweet perfume.
One day she laid down her burdens,
To go to Heaven above,
Now she's in God's flower garden,
A rose in the bloom of His love.

—Flossie Cramer

BYE, GRANDMA

You are the comfort of any easy
chair; the dream in our sleep; the
play in our game.

You are the plot of our story; the
laughter of our jokes; the weep of
our mourns.

You are the blue in the sky; the stars
at night; the sun that shines so
bright.

You are the anchor of our ship; the
collar that hugs our necks.

You are the color of our rainbow, and
at the end your golden heart lies
peacefully.

You are everything to this family
and more, much more! You are
my Grandma, and I send my love
with you. Bye Grandma, I love you.

—Reid Phifer

EMOTIONS OF A WEEPING BIRCH

Must I weep
When the heart of me captures
The fanciful raptures
Of Spring?

May I laugh
When gay breezes that fill me
With ecstacy thrill me
To dance?

May I smile
When I see 'neath my tresses
The fond, sweet caresses
Of love?

May I love
When I press to my breast
Tender young of the oriole's
Nest?

May I sleep
And dream that my foundlings
Will always their rendezvous
Keep?

I awake
I am sad and bereft
For my dear ones have left
My arms with an empty ache
I weep.

—Grace Young Y. Hadfield

THORNS OF LOVE

There's a thorn in my heart
From the rose of your love
Scarlet tears wet the wings
Of the dead song bird
Can you see I'm dying?
Can't you remove the thorn?
Or will ignorance leave me cold and empty?

—Jill E. Church

MORNING

Surf between my toes
Salty breezes in my hair
Golden pink and purple clouds
Rise out of the ocean far away
The sun slowly rises and shoots its laser beams
Rimming the clouds with halos of light
I breath in deeply
Hold the morning air deep within me
And then slowly let it go
I am one with God
All's right with my world

—Pauline Browne

GRANDPA'S TIME

My life is almost through,
I feel empty, But I have lived to fullfill
my destiny.
I feel sad, yet I'm happy for I have achieved.
All of a sudden I get a chill, and though I try
hard not to, I close my eyes for it has ended,
God's greatest gift to mankind.

Now I will see what I have only dared to dream.

I have reached what I have most feared. But, I
have achieved and done the best I could.
Now I have received my reward:
Heaven instead of Hell.

No more hurting and no more fears.
Just the feeling of Peace and tranquility in
the silver lining of Heaven.

I Love you Grandpa . . . .

—Bobette Lee Lemke

There is so much pain in this world of ours.
There is so much grief and sorrow.
There are so many things we have to fear.
There are so many dreary tomorrows.

Every morning when the sun rises,
I dread the coming day.
Because with each day, new pain is born
That will never go away.

Ignore her words, and they mean nothing.
Let your mind wander to some other place.
Because when you listen and grasp the meaning,
The hurt can never be erased.

The pain when she tells me she hates me—
The scorn and fury she directs at me—
The constant stream of terrible insults
That she uses so ruthlessly.

She wishes that I'd never been born.
It's what she's always said,
And that's one thing we both agree on.
We both wish that I was dead.

—Priscilla Chapa

SUICIDE

My life is nothing but an endless cry,
As I sit in my room, waiting to die,
And my bleeding heart nailed to the grave,
Betrays the love I cannot save,
With fallen angels upon my breath,
I find myself alone with death,
And though I bless what is a fraud,
I do not fear my life with God,
So ignore not all that I have said,
Or some day soon you will find me dead.

—Andy Behr

LONELY SYMPHONY

Today I heard a mockingbird sing
In the early morning as daylight
Slowly pushed away the darkness,
Causing my thoughts to turn homeward where
The song of a mockingbird
Is familiar and welcome
And very endearing
To those who know the singer and the song.

The sound of that symphony flooded
My memory with pictures of places
Where other songsters had voiced concerts
So sweet that the notes ringing in my ears
Became a throb that increased
Until it was a deep ache
In my heart, a longing
For sights and sounds and people I love . . . home.

—Shirley Barnett Barr

FINAL MOMENTS

My life leaps from my chest
Like a crimson flower, between my fingers.

My breath like perfume,
Escapes my breast in a final sigh.
Good-bye, good-bye.

Over my eyes slips a filmy veil of grey.
My life escapes.
Away, away.

—Matthew C. Tiffany

THE YELL OF AFRICA CRY

I heard a yell in my African land.
The cry of freedom for boy and man?
My mountains are high and my children low
I hear their yell as freedom goes
Three young boys of different tribes
Two killed one and there he died
But before he closed his eyes to death
He gave out a yell for Africa health
Two went back and one was left
O, Africa, Africa, heal thyself
I hear the moans in the valley below
And I hear the cry at death open door
My children are crying for Africa tonight
They're yelling for freedom to make things right
Free my man and suffice my child
Comfort my mothers, for I hear their howl
There's a fog coming in over Africa today
O, Africa, Africa, what can I say
I heard the yell of Africa cry
Two came back and one did die

—Bessie M. Miller

SUICIDE

The Withering Weeping willow gave
a Voiceless Scream
Frantically Struggling to Evoke a
Traceable Cry before Expiring
from a Lack of Nourishment

—Kristin Queen

Don't do drugs
Cause they are bad for you.
If you don't stop they will kill you.

I knew this old man,
His name was Dan
He took drugs cause he didn't understand.

Taking drugs is very suicidal
But not taking drugs is very, very vital.

When doing drugs
Don't expect to live,
Truly your life's
The only thing you give.

Funerals aren't very fun
But you might be part of one.

—James Neff

IF I SHOUD DIE BEFORE THE DAWN

If I should die before the dawn
Do not cry, but sing a song.
If I don't last through the night
Know that my soul has taken flight.
My body is dead, but my soul is free
Living in God's light is where I'll be.
Don't cry anymore
I've reached the shore.
Don't shed another tear
I'll always be near.
Although I may seem far away,
Everything will be okay.
What wasn't perfect on the earth
Is now complete in my new birth.
So do not cry, but sing a song
If I should die before the dawn,
And one day you'll see
That together we'll live in eternity.

—Mary Catherine Spencer

TIME

There's a time to live.
    There's a time to die.

A time to laugh.

A time to cry.

When life leaves you but few options,

You struggle with your innermost self.

What is there left?

Where to go?

What should I do?

What should I know?

Only through our experiences and life's
    teachings;

Can we know the answer.

—Ron Cunningham

REFLECTIONS

I gaze into a maze of yesterdays
And pause to ponder, also to wonder
About past times and of what might have been.
Although more days have gone than those to come,
It's not old Father Time I dread, instead,
The friends I've missed, the ones I never kissed,
Kind words unsaid, an extra mile unwalked.
Oh Lord, don't let my final thoughts be filled
With yesterdays and of what might have been.

—Lyn Sanderford

WISHES

Fiery red, yellow, orange;
I watch the sun set and think of you.
I haven't seen you in so long.
My memories of you are beginning to fade,
Like the dying light of the sun.
Twilight sets in, and a sigh escapes me.
I miss you so much.
A tear like a brightly shining star slips down
        my cheek.
I wish you were here.
Star light, star bright,
The first star I see tonight . . .

—Priscilla Chapa

LOVING YOU!

Loving you is like eating sweet, wild honey;
For you, are a taste like no other.

Loving you is like holding a big bunch of vibrant
balloons; As your colors splash into my every day!

Loving you is like making the first prints in new
fallen snow; Those prints that for just a moment
say, "The world is mine!"

Loving you is like finding the first bloom of violets
in early spring; That bloom which gives fresh
courage, bolder strength, and new hope.

Loving you is like singing on an outdoor stage;
Where one's voice gently caresses the sky.

Loving you is a toast to love and life;
A life that brings me exciting new experience in
Love . . .

—Susan Snavely

Me and
You
Forever.
Apart, but still
Together.
Hearts and hands
Entertwined.
Remember?

You are the best father that you could be
The best to Lynn, Craig and me.
I'm not very good at making a rhyme.
But maybe you could give me a little time.

OK, here goes.

Never forget about the "Hot Does"
Or any of the other stupid things I've said.
Or any of the wonderful places you have me led.
Maybe my grammar isn't the best,
But you, Dad, are better than all the rest.

—Amy E. Smith

PROUD TO BE A TARHEEL

I am glad I am a tarheel,
The love for my state is real.
I wouldn't take a dime,
To live on the Great Rhine.
From San Antonio to Manteo,
There are many sights to see,
But the great Old North State
Is the only one for me.
The pine trees so green,
They are the prettiest I have seen.
From the east to the west,
North Carolina is the best!

—Sarah Measamer

I TREASURE LEZH'AR

I treasure my leisure for pleasure.
When I'm busy all day
I love to steal far away
to laugh, or to dance, or to play!
Or to just lie and dream
by some shaded stream
where a stray sunbeam
might glide through the trees
to tease the half-day by the ease
of it winging, bringing there <u>gold</u>
to lighten the singing
of the glass-twinkling brook.

With a wonderful book,
I would need no genii
to make new worlds lie at my feet.
My tiny retreat would be quite replete
with the wealth of the whole universe.
And I might fare worse
than to often rehearse
in my mind the joy that I find
when I leave care behind
to treasure fair leisure for pleasure!

—Phebe Alden Tisdale

UNSOUND

The sound of silence is deafening
As it falls around my ears,
No more do I hear their squabbles
Which ended up in tears.

The house is deathly quiet
Their toys are all picked up,
No happy teasing and playing
No yapping from their pup.

No running up the flight of stairs
To see who'd be the last.
And sliding down the bannister
Is all left in the past.

No water fights or kickball
Once played upon the lawn,
Like puff blows of the dandelion
All too soon are gone!

I long to tuck them in their beds
And listen to their prayers,
To fill my life with all their noise
And know somebody cares.

The sound of silence is deafening
When once the family's grown,
The noise and toys are packed away.
With Mom and Dad at home.

—Ethel K. Davis

LOVE — A VALENTINE'S DAY POEM

Love, — is it a theory or is it real?
Is it something you can feel?
Does it bring your spirits up and
does it lift you high?
Does it take you soaring, way up through
the sky?
   It doesn't matter how, and it doesn't
matter when,
It only matters that you feel it time
and time again.

   —Sarah Jean Bibeau

MESSAGE IN THE MIST

The mist came rolling up the hill.
It rolled past shadows, past the mill.

It made its way up through the vines,
the ones around this house of mine.

I knew without a doubt this was
the wraith that goes where no one does.

A shadow on its way through time,
it had a message so sublime:

Make all your hopes and dreams come true
for someday soon this will be you.

   —Joanne M. Costa

I dropped the plate and
   it shattered
Tiny shards of pale pink glass
   surround me
Every step I take cuts my
   feet
I look to the archway in front of me
   and wonder
Can I make it to the door
   and still survive
My mind blocks out the pain but
   I still feel it
When I look up to the doorway again
   You're there
But you won't help me and
   I don't even ask
The look in your eyes makes me turn around
   and walk back to where I began

   —Gina Hall

I HEAR LAUGHTER

I hear laughter in my mind.
or, is it coming from behind?
Veiled in darkness, hidden from all;
   Laughter is heard across the hall.

Satin reminders of secret times.
   Seductive shadows of past crimes.
I hear laughter not far away.
   Perhaps they're mocking things we say.

Closet ghost and haunting dreams,
   Keep us awake with silent screams.
Second glances we must take;
   For I hear laughter that we make.

Turning heads and alibis;
   Clever stories laced with lies.
Laughter is heard close at hand.
   Now, I'm sure they understand.

   —Christine Lenzner

CATHY

You set my heart adrift
on an endless deep blue sea
My soul soared high like a nightingale
   when you simply smiled at me.
My mind raced like a mustang
   running across the land
My breath was quickend inside of me
   when you simply touched my hand.
I felt a peace inside of me
   like the cooing of a dove
A joy I hadn't known existed before
   until you simply gave me your love.

   —Larry Baker

GOLDEN BAND

This golden band is growing old
   All through the years.
It shed many tears.
It also had many fears.
This golden band holds memories and
secrets it's true.
Through the years it led happiness and
sadness too.
Love knew the years would last.
Love knows best and be at rest.
Love shows and tells all.
This golden band is my wedding band.

   —Mrs. Ruthann Beninsky

Though I can not share your sorrow.
   I've tried to understand
The loss you've feeling deep inside,
The emptiness within.

But please, try to remember,
That through God's great gift of love,
We will all meet again
In heaven up above.

There will be no pain, no sorrow,
Only happiness complete.
Let good memories sustain us
'Til once again we meet.

   —Anna-Patricia DeCosta

THE SCARED CROW

A pimp kills a whore
And a soldier asks for more
While a junkie shoots and O.D.'s
The mother stands and begs No PLEASE

There's a scared crow
That wanders the forest
Ripping and tearing
It cries when it kills
Strong of heart and weak of brain

When nuclear missile blows
It easily melts Arctic snows
So cold I soldiers marching in my town
And none of my friends have I found

There's a scared crow
That wanders the forest
Ripping and tearing
It cries when it kills
Strong of heart and weak of brain

Are we all insane?

   —David Knight

TRANQUILITY

Beautiful are thine eyes that see
Things of beauty God made for me
Hills of wild flowers, and gentle flowing streams
Where we sit, ponder and slowly dream.
These things of beauty that we see
Cannot be bought they are free.

—Joseph J. Patti

SALUTE TO FREEDOM

Courageous and valiant our Lady stands,
A symbol of Liberty that men fought and
died for at others' hands.
Silent and bold against the sky,
Daring any and all to question "Why?"

Men across the years have gazed upon this
Lady with Hope in their hearts,
Determining that from these principles
and values America will never part.

Stand up for right! Prevent the wrong!
She seems to say,
Her flame symbolizing Hope as a shining ray!
Stand secure, forever endure, Precious Lady.
We salute You!

Dedicated to Richard Coxen
—Shirley Coxen

FREEDOM

FREEDOM! — so precious you are!
You make living so worthwhile —
You open wide the gates of opportunities,
Enable people explore life's possibilities.

In search for you calls for sacrifice;
For your sake, patriots pledge their lives —
You offer hope and spiritual rebirth,
You bring a piece of heaven on earth.

Above and beyond the price to pay
Freedom lovers take the challenge willingly;
With heroes in mind to emulate —
To gain freedom is the prize, ultimate.

FREEDOM! — when your bell resoundingly rings,
The sound echoes deep within —
With happy faces and smiles that can't hide
All freemen stand tall with great pride!

—Carmen Orodio Weist

THE UNIVERSE

The universe, deep, immense and far,
Shines with the lights of many a star.
Luminous, mysterious, unable to conceive,
What little our natural eyes can see.

Planets revolving round and round,
Seemingly to float, never touching the ground.
Regions and regions of space to explore,
Scientists everyday, are learning more.

Mystery, illusion, comet's delight,
Streaking by, out of sight.
The Milky Way and the great black hole,
Are the universe's very soul.

Rockets and satellites, we send out in space,
Feeding information to the human race.
Territories unexplored, forever will be,
Unconquered, imaginative land, for you and me.

—Joyce Faye Pierce

TO THE MORNING GLORY

Has anyone ever noticed
This mysterious little flower?
Who winds and creeps on any bower
Inch by inch, and then a flower.
Every morning so heavenly blue
Then, when eve comes, curls up
To sleep and wait for the morning dew.

—Cathy Dowling

OPEN UP THE WORLD

Open up the world,
Read a book to a child.
Sit on a front porch swing,
During a summer, warm and mild.
Catch the sight of a fawn,
As it scampers through the trees.
Taste the salt on your lips,
Kissed by the calm of an ocean breeze.
Lift your eyes to the heavens,
Open your heart and let it sing,
Feel the glory of the universe,
Cherish the wonders life can bring

—Kitten

The piercing blade slowly digs
into me further and further inward.
Unlike an animal who can ward
off its enemy, I have no way
of fighting back.
No harm to the environment for
I am nature. For my food, no
distraction to others it is
only but what is in the
air around me.
As my long slender body falls
to the ground, I can only ask
myself why? Yet never understand
my rival's thoughts.
I hope I have made him
happy — for now he will have
more land to build on, and I,
nothing but a stump for a
young child to stand upon.

—Dawn Munno

MEMORIAL TO A SAILOR

How <u>can</u> they know —
The youth today,
What the plaque on your grave
Is trying to say?
Your name and rank, your span of life,
World War Two, and to be specific
The last line reads
"South and North Pacific."
It cannot tell
Of the hours of fright
As the enemy planes
Attacked day and night,
It cannot tell
How you willingly gave
Four years of your life
Our freedom to save.
On the edge of your plaque
Old Glory waves tall —
More words are not needed,
The flag tells it all!

—Lucille Williquette

ARIZONA MOUNTAINS
Mountains move by light,
Shadow dancing in their flight
From dawn to dark night.

—S.G. Crecelius

WORLD PEACE
Someday the world will have peace
The world will be quiet and still
All the wars will cease
And no one will have to kill

On that glad day
All will be friends
The children will all play
All hard feelings will mend

Everyone will be treated the same
All will have their place
Trouble will be no one's blame
You'll know all's face

Our hearts will hold the key
Our friendship will never cease
Someday the world will see
World Peace

—Teresa Duncan

WAITING
I heard your voice the other day
All the darkness went away
The sun came shining through
I'm sure you know I still love you.

Though many years kept us apart
You are forever in my heart
My empty arms yearn for you so
Oh! Why did I let you go?

Won't you return into my world
And make it bright again, girl?
Our love story has no end
All twigs sometime must bend

Let us wish on our own bright star
Although it is so very far
I know it will hear our plea
And from this heartache set us free.

—James Barataris

PEACE
It's time that we as nations,
At last might sheathe the sword;
And to dwell for once unfettered,
To strive for peace, accord.

And to banish want and hunger,
Like we as humans should;
To dispel all greed and hatred,
With all evil turned to good.

That we might share together,
Yes, the mighty and the meek;
And tender those a helping hand,
Whose quest for freedom seek.

All of this mankind can do,
Grant it soon may come to pass;
That true freedom will prevail,
With peace on earth at last.

—Stephen H. Fagg

THE GREAT ERASER
My blackboard was the soft white sand,
Which stretched out far on every hand.
I searched and found,
An empty shell,
And wrote out words that I can spell.
But waves dash on the sand to play,
And washed my letters all away.
And that is how I got the notion —
A great eraser is the ocean.

—Lynne Wester

AMAZON
Breath of Life that we need,
Take it for granted the daily seed;

Ocean that covers us derive from our flora,
Wanton destruction in a single hora;

Source of Life as we know it,
Complete disregard for those to follow;

Temperate Zone without renewal,
Destroy its bed for Mother Earth's funeral.

—Scott Anthony

FEDERATED WOMAN'S CLUB
On the first Wednesday of
the month
Members of Federated Woman's
Club meet
Our friends we are so glad to greet.

Our program materials are fine
Just happen in, most any time.
Book reviews, different kinds of art
Of everything, we are a part.
We help students, support the blind,
Our members work together fine.
When our town celebrates, we do too
We make a float, tho' we can't gloat.
It's so much fun, the togetherness
Talking, laughing — but working
none the less.
The Woman's Club gave us the mood
To belong, to care, to serve the best we could.

—Matilda Nordyke Seyb

AN AMERICAN'S LAMENT — 1989
America! O America!
I weep, I cry, I mourn for you!
I ask, what has become of your
Promise to the world?
You told the world to give you its
Tired, its poor, its oppressed, its homeless.
But now, now you have become a
Country that rocks in limbo.
I see the elderly sleeping in your cities' streets.
I see a mother and her children living in
  an abandoned car.
I see runaway teenagers selling themselves
For money and drugs.
America! O America!
What has made your promise to the
World become empty and void?
For now, all I see around me is apathy, cynicism,
And mindless greed.
America! O America!
Please, awake before it's too late!

—Juanita Campbell

SOMETHING OF MY OWN

This is my world,
   And you can't invade it,
You're a stranger here,
With no way to explain it.

Try to understand,
Logic's off hand,
If you don't feel the beat,
Go—move your seat.

You don't belong here,
Logic is my world,
I have it wrapped tight,
Silliness changed its height.

I won't let you in,
You must be disciplined,
Shaping rhythmic patterns,
Listening and blending in.

You wanna share My world with me?

   —Mirna Edith Parker

A MORNING WISH

The morning light is breaking
   The dew still on a rose
A breeze is gently blowing
The world in a lazy doze
Two doves are softly exchanging
Love calls in the valley below
And I sit here in wonder
as I watch a young buck and doe
If I listen very carefully
I hear the chatter of a squirrel
In my mind I see him scampering
up a tree in his playful world
The pleasant sound of a babbling brook
Plays softly in my ear
as I let my mind appreciate
All the things that I hold dear
And all this peace and loveliness
Fills my heart with love "This Day"
I long for all the simple joys
We've lost somewhere along life's way

   —Jodie Eadon

BASEBALL!

Whoever thought a ball so round
   Could cause so much excitement
In our little Cherokee town?

We had the most winning team
Of all the schools around
We'd win again and again, it seemed.

Some players have moved on
And left this hallowed spot
But when we talk of baseball
Your names are not forgot.

We loved you and you know it
So when you think of home
Defend your alma mater. Show it
Wherever you may roam.

You were and still are Number One
So we will always cherish
Your record, our dear sons.
At CVHS we'll forever embellish.

Good luck and may God always bless.

   —Bobby Adams

The darkness envelopes her.
   She bumps into walls.
Her body is battered and bruised.
   Her nose drips crimson pearls.
She tries to dodge the hands that grab for her,
   out of the murky depths of her imagination.

   —Holly Kroh

WHY AM I ALONE?

Why am I alone?
   It's been too long.
I tried to remember all the faces
Because I've been to a few places.
   Learning to take life in stride,
I've adjusted my time.
In the Bible, it says "It's a blessing
   to be alone."
      But, once again, I pick up the phone.

   —Wanda Yvette White

DISCOVERIES

A flash of dream lift in between
   A spark of thought left unseen
A twist of flame withered by an autumn breeze
A burst of bud on blossoming trees
A shift of cloud on a windy day
A yearn from a child left with nothing to say
A scream from a gull deep in the night
A screech from a hawk high in piercing flight
A soft gentle tear from a heartbroken lover
A belief in which we shall discover

   —Catherine L Schuermeyer

LAST WORD

You look upon your loved one's face
   Perhaps a million times or more
Each time the same as always,
Expressions same as before.
What would your words be,
if somehow you only knew,
that until the end of eternity
these were the last words he would speak to you?
If you knew for sure that
Death would take this he or she,
Have you ever thought my Friend,
What would your last words be?

   —Don E. Dumond

SILENT TEARS

Silent tears you never see
   Silent tears for you and me
Behind the smile where no one sees
Are the silent tears that belong to me.

If you know who I am,
If you care, like I care,
Then you know the silent tears
Are for all the dreams and fears.

Never asked for very much
A hug, a kiss, or a gentle touch.
Never shouted, yelled, or hit
All I needed was to quietly sit.

All the silent tears are here
Behind the silent smile,
The sorrow will only be known by one
Unless there is a true bonding of two into one.

   —Eunice P. Anderson

REALITY

In the early morning hours
is it in my power
to drive you from reality,
only to face you once again
in the tranquil peace of night.
Even in sleep there's no escape,
as the last flicker of consciousness
leaves my body,
thoughts of you steal into my dreams.

—Norma Jones

TIME TRAVEL

The silvery river of my mind
    flows over those dark rocks.
Some made light by the
    silvery light of the Unicorn's horn.
Others the light refuses to touch.

This river flows free through time
    touching all with its inner glow.

Such are memories.

—Sarah K. Mitchell

I came from my meeting and
drove up the hill,
Oh, it was much too dark,
What can I say?
It was much too quiet
As I walked in the house,
Where are all the noises?
the TV, stereo, radio and
the squabbles from the den,
It was much too empty now,
I walked up the stairs
to the bedrooms where
beds were neat and tidy, with
no dirty sneakers and
clothes on the floor,
This mother was suffering to the gills
from empty nest illness,
Didn't know that it was
her children she missed until
her eyes became mist.

—Martha D. Mehlhaff

TO MY GRANDSON ON HIS "18th BIRTHDAY"

Now that you are a "Macho Man,"
    The girls are out there to get
you if they can.
They see your good looks, and
charming ways, and the way
you dance when the band plays.
"Eighteen" was a wonderful age
as I recall,
I thought at that time I knew
it all!
Before you are 21 you will have
Many more "Obstacles" to over come.
Have a "Goal" and always
aim "High."
Maybe you will become "President"
by and by?
"Happy Birthday" to a fine young man,
From your next door neighbor
your Old Gram.

—Nellie Tyler

B-DAY 18

I didn't want to grow up this way.
The sight of blood, the cries of friends,
The silence stalking the bush.
The friend is my enemy, the enemy my friend.
Here in this jungle I became a man.
I didn't want to grow up this way.

—Cameron Fox

We became good friends
    That seemed would last forever
Not once
Has two people as close as us
Stayed less than friends
We became more
Now the friendship is lost
Because you wanted something
I felt I couldn't give to you
Though I wanted to I wasn't ready
Now it is over but remember
We were friends to begin with
And again I would like to be
So let us start all over again
This time we know that our friendship was all
That was meant to be.

—Lynette Holmes

A LESSON IN COEXISTENCE

The Sahuaro stands with arms uplifted
    A voiceless sentry for the desert.
Its hulking body sways an inch or less
In the breezes that blow at 2 PM.

Birds seek sanctuary within its flesh
Leaving holes of expression for its face.
Ants scramble at will up and down its ribs,
Yet the Sahuaro remains compliant.

Bees persist to attack its flower crown
Ravaging pollen from unspoiled petals.
The burning, sun rays strike it from all sides
Sucking moisture from the Sahuaro's form.

Snakes and lizards tunnel around its roots.
Indians take its fruit and plant its seed.
The Sahuaro is stoic through it all;
For hundreds of years, this has been its life.

—Pam Schmidt

BURN BUNDY BURN?

Then the tragedy of all crime is told
    As all bad news sooner gets old
People drain their evil side dry
And bring out the ugly with wry

So soon you look and there's no queen
The prettiest face made to look mean
It is then you know the man kind of crime
The way nothing will make you feel in time

They have left a poor widow wrenched!
They did make her loose her wench
So at number one hundred they must pay
We've drawn the line; This time it is our way.

Then come time to pay in kind
Same pretty queen we may not find
But we know another won't from him run
Because now we can say Burn Bundy Burn!

—Joel E. Kalle

WATCH YOUR HAPPY HOME!

Old Satan is always working in your home.
You may look around and someday your
Old man may be gone.

There're too many women
and not enough men.

When the road gets rough,
love your old man anyway.

You'll have to pray
that the women won't
come and take him away.

Although you may think that he's too old,
there's always some woman waiting
to take control.

You'll have to pray that the Holy Ghost
will make your old man stay at home
or you may look around and he may be gone.

Watch your happy home!

—Sarah West

DEAR MOTHER

Mother, dear Mother, the years have been long,
Since I last listened to your lullaby song.
Sing them and unto my soul it shall seem,
Womanhood's years have been only a dream.
Clasped to your heart in a loving embrace,
With your light lashes just sweeping my face,
Never hereafter to wake or to weep,
Rock me to sleep, Mother, rock me to sleep.

—Matthew Swift, age 11

MOTHER'S DAY POEM

You'll lead us through special times.
From our first step to the Senior Prom,
Yet only one day a year,
We put aside to honor Mom.

On that day Mom is flooded
With flowers and poems that say:
"I love you," "You're the best,"
"Have a happy Mother's Day!"

All of this is nice
And I'm sure she thinks it's dear,
But take a little time to say the same
Each day of the year!

—Darlene L. Posey

MOTHER

On this day I want to tell you
I love you in many other ways
You brought out the love you showed for me
All these years through.

For I praise the gift of beauty on you,
For years ago, you once said to your mother —
Out of the kindness of your heart
I love you, because you've been so generous
through the years.

So, I'm telling you how much I love you
More and more each day
My love is growing like a flower just for you
But the easiest thing to say, Mom,
I Love You Dearly!

—Kelly Albert

PICTURE

This morn, the lake is a mirror
Reflecting beauty in power,
Nothing is moving,
Just quiet stillness.
Not even a duck stirring.
A picture —
In a frame of loveliness.

—Helen Morley

MOTHERS

According to the calendar,
there is a special day . . . .
dedicated to you.
However, all the time, your
concern, never ending lessons
that are imparted to all —
bring hope, peace, understanding
and proper growth — as
Mothers are the ones who
nurture, and thus cause
maturity.

—Marilyn M. Turner

I met her years ago
When I first came to be
A very special friend
That's done so much for me
She's helped me through the hardships
That I've had through out the years
Like skinned up knees, shattered
Dreams and frightened baby tears
She shared in fun and games
When the teen years came about
Just where she found the time
Is hard to figure out
She watched me go from infant
To child and then to man
She's always been beside me
Ever since my life began
I love her very dearly
She's as good as they can come
And I'm very proud to say
That this woman is my mom

—John L. Williams

MOTHER

My mother is a memory,
But oh I loved her so,
Her face seems to follow me
Everywhere I go.

There was a sweet contentment
A look that seemed to say,
Please don't grieve for me dear
ones.
I am content, and my work is done.

My earthly body was sick, and weak,
My mind was failing fast.
My fight for endurance reached
its peak,
And I am in my father's arms at
Last.

My only thought is for you dear ones
And, I hope that you will see
If you live your life for Jesus,
You will someday be with me.

—Ferne V. Hessong

A SHINING STAR

A very bright and shining star,
The Wisemen sighted from afar.
They used the star to find the way
Where Baby Jesus gently lay.
And, Lo! They beheld and adored
A Baby who would be our Lord
From that day on and ever since,
The little baby has been "The Prince."

—Regina Gollihugh, Age 15

WHEN I WAKE UP

As I wake up I hear
the birds chirp with joy and love.
I walk through the green
grass and the autumn leaves
falling down on the ground.
I sit under a tree of many
colors to rest.
I see a river of sparkling
water flowing gently by.
I arise and walk home to
return to my place of rest.

—Marcy M. Hurlocker

UNDERSTANDING GOD'S LOVE

Understanding God's great love,
can only happen from above!
There is no way that we can show,
the depth and height that it will go!

He loves us when we're far from good,
and lets us know He's understood!
He loves us when we're doing right,
and shows we're precious in His sight!

He sends His spirit in each life,
and gives us peace in times of strife!
He lets us know He's very near,
what more to drive away our fear!

His love goes far beyond our measure,
a love that all of us can treasure!
To understand it, we cannot,
it's just the greatest gift we've got!

—Jimmie R. Smith

IT'S CHRISTMAS

A brightly shining star
Beams a message near and far.
The mellow rays of sun and moon
Proclaim that soon

IT'S CHRISTMAS

Golden bells are ringing
Celestial angels singing
Their voices sweet and clear
For all the world to hear

IT'S CHRISTMAS

Hold fast to your dream and prayer
hold fast
That "PEACE ON EARTH" will come
at last.
With happy voices singing
Joy bells ringing

IT'S CHRISTMAS
BEAUTIFUL BEAUTIFUL CHRISTMAS.

—Ruth R. Ripper

STAR OVER BETHLEHEM

Star over Bethlehem
Three wise men follow a Star
To Jerusalem then to Bethlehem
Christmas Day in a Manger a Baby
Three wise men follow a Star to
Bethlehem with Gold Frankincense and Myrrh
Silent night Holy night
follow a Star over Bethlehem
Remember the Christ Child.

—Stephen John McCarthy

THE WIND

The wind passed by me so gently
Carrying with it my most inner thoughts
And they too will blow so gently
And come to rest in your heart.

We are separated by distance
But our hearts are chained together
By the gentle breezes of life.

Wherever the breezes of life take you
I will be there in the wind.

Feel my presence upon your face as
it softly touches you.

Hear my voice speak in the wind
And know I will forever be near.

—Linda McKee

OUR CHILDREN CRY

Oh, mighty forest so awesome
so wild.

What treasures are we yet to find?

Will our children know of the
beauty you hold?

Or will you be broken and crushed?

Will your teardrops cease to caress
the faces of the land so far and wide?

Or will the children wake to your
mournful cry?

And, rush to greet, your teardrops
on their faces!

Please Help save our Rain Forest.

—Rose Darling

MOMENTS

Time has a tendency to slip away.
When you're awaiting an important day.

Time moves forward, then time moves
back, and sometimes stays in the middle.
Reaching out and touching a time, in
our mind, how—is still a riddle.

There are times to remember, and
times to forget, and times just not to care.
What matters the most, and always
will, we did these things, and we were there.

As the sky would move and my
eyes would follow,
My thoughts lingered on yesterday
and rushed to tomorrow.
"for Storm, my miracle"

—Beverly Snow

ALONE

The light in my brain has stopped
the ardor fell down my mouth.
I tried to drown it with my spittle
but it was still burning.
I gave it to you through a kiss,
and now you are shining.

The light is now gone for me.
I have no need to turn it on
I have no need to see it.
When it comes close it threatens
to burn my words and my paper.
It threatens to burn my memories.

The tears you cried were heavy
you cried them just for me.
Now you are so far away
I forget you are shining.
We were so close — we didn't
know whose heart . . . . .

—Helene Emborg

A NEW STRENGTH

There are times in every life
when we feel hurt or alone . . .
    But I believe that these times
when we feel lost
    And all around us seems
to be falling apart
are really bridges of growth.
    We struggle and try to recapture
the security of what was,
but almost in spite of ourselves . . .
    We emerge on the other side
with a new understanding,
a new awareness,
A NEW STRENGTH.
    It is almost as though
we must go through the pain
and the struggle
in order to grow
    and reach new heights.

—Robert T. Williams

HOMEWORK

"Tonight there's company coming,"
    My parents used to say.
Meant we scurried to the kitchen
    Studied lessons without play.

We tackled math and history
  (Munched on sugar cookies too)
While reading "Idylls of the King"
  Tried to be the first one through.

The oilcloth-covered table
  was a desk for big or small
Till scattered books we neatly piled
  And we said goodnight to all.

Now, homework's sort o'different
  Seems there's company all the time
TV's blasting out a western
  A talk show or a crime.

The radio or hi-fi
  With recordings and the phone —
The way kids do their homework now
  They never are alone.

—Gertrude C. Stoltz

MATURITY

Why did I lose my way today?
    My compass must have gone askew.
The ground unsteady seems to sway.
To do? The options left are few.
Consult an oracle some say.
Gracefully grown maturity,
A batch of insecurity;
A gaze at Polaris brings hope.
Alas! There is my horoscope.
Did someone say I could not cope?

—Manuel F. Llaguno

TOGETHER

If I stood alone,
    The wind would sting my cheek.
The empty sky would shed its lifeless light
    On vistas dull and grey.
The barren shore would hide
    The treasures I would seek.

But with you at my side,
    Your hand to hold.
The sandy shore will bare
    Its gifts upon the sparkling tide.
The gull will cry.
    The sun will warm our souls.
The shells will dance
    And seek our secret spots.
A sand dollar for your thoughts.

—William C. Herman

SEPARATION

So quiet, never thought could be,
    this house I call my home.
No bikes, no toy-strewn hallways,
    no tugging at my knees.

And morning breaks through sun-bleached curtains,
    asleep and fast to be,
My early morning wake up missing,
    "I need a Ba Ba, please."

The perfume scented bathroom pales
    with walls of mildew gray.
My family since departed,
    I wish that they had stayed.

And evening comes so peacefully and still
    the quiet sky,
    With blanket and my "Teddy,"
    I'll hold them close tonight.

—Michael S. Velko

SETTING SUN

Look to the sun as it sets in the West
    And you shall know the joy of light.
Take heed of the heat in its yellow chest,
Read the sky as day turns into night.
If a tear bathes your eye then let it fall
And stain the earth with salty wet
And think of evenings long past
And of evenings come not yet
And know that life is taking leave
For short hours of darkened silence
Until the sun cracks through the leaves
Of trees and rises in ragged defiance.
Use the new light to cleanse your soul
And the dusky light to make you whole.

—Greg Corrao

DEVASTATION

The howling wind with giant stride
  Came stomping down the countryside,
Beneath its ruthless tracks lays scarred
A tranquil path forever marred,
It shrieked against a blackened sky,
With gnashing teeth while passing by
It crushed to shreds, in fiendish glee,
The best of all, my old pine tree.

—Gertrude Dole

BREAD CRUMBS

She sat there like a tattered little bird,
  Her misery unmasked.
Little bird claw hands wringing in her lap.

Gently, the tattered feathers were preened.
Her little face reflected gratitude for the
mercy shown.
The little claw hands relaxed.

As the years passed, the tattered little
bird returned
Seeking mercy like bread crumbs.
Always grateful.

—Edna H. McCaleb

INCIDENT ON NINTH STREET

The trees — the trees are gone.
  And the afternoon air is astir
with an inclement industry
spitting and screaming through spinning teeth.

Witness the wonder that once
with a spiritual innocence
scrapped the underside of the sky
lying wasted on the shattered sidewalk.

But do not long search
for some visible sanity in this matter.
This all requires no rhyme or reason.
Just cut the damn things down.

And now to the east endless blue
displays a disturbing emptiness
and tomorrow the sun
will rise unobstructed.

—Mark Bradley Sanderson

THE FARMER'S LAMENT

Under the hot, humid summer sun
  The grass of the plains goes into ruin
The wheat withers as it breaks through the soil
No rain today, the drought is having its way
Row after row, the corn in total ruin
Scorched in the sweltering sun
Hope fading from his half-closed eyes
Realizing the days ahead are ones to dread
No rain today, the drought is having its way
The watering hole is only a foot deep
He tosses, turns, he can't sleep
Where will the cattle drink, where will they eat
The banker called again
No rain today, the drought is having its way
Next year, things will be just fine
He says with pride, family by his side
We'll make it through, like always
No rain today, that's okay —

—Rayford Woodall, Sr.

CAMEO OF LIFE

Today is a cameo of life
  A day of meeting,
        of learning,
            of sharing,
                and revealing.
  A moment of wonder
            and a delight.
  A pleasant memory shaped.
  A blissful moment from everyday strife.
Yes, truly,
    Today is a cameo of life.

—Donna Juffer Williams

LITTLE BOY IN THE SANDBOX

Little boy in the sandbox,
  an imaginary world of his own
What is going to become of him,
  when he is all grown?

He's building magic castles,
  and excavating make-believe roads.
As the sun beats on his forehead,
  his trucks carry heavy loads.

It's only a matter of time,
  until his make-believe world becomes real.
Full of decisions and choices,
  with which he will have to deal.

As I watch him from the window,
  a tear flows down my cheek.
I pray that life is good to him,
  for the future won't allow me to peek.

Sometimes I wish that I could stop,
  the hands from turning on the clocks.
For only then could I preserve,
  Little Boy In The Sandbox.

—Andrea Reed

MY ROOMER — BETSY ROBINSKY

A sweet young thing stood at my door,
  And asked for a place to stay,
I wasn't ready for a roomer just then,
  But I couldn't send her away.
She stood there, so neatly dressed,
  In her little gray suit and perky
  red vest.
So she lived at my house, and day by day,
  We became close friends, in an unusual
  way;
I would offer her food, but she ate like
  bird, though never any complaint was
  heard.
She loved to stroll in my garden, which
  was a puzzle to me,
For there really wasn't anything out
  there for her to see;
So I watched her one day, and as I quietly
  waited,
She pulled up a WORM, and then she ate it!
Now two of her children have moved in with
  her,
And that nest on my porch is quite an
  eyesore,
But her song in the morning makes up for
  all that,
And I'm so glad that she's safe from the
  neighbor's bad cat!

—Beulah E. Lenze

HOPELESS BAY

Now the water is quiet and calm.
A look of solemn elegance perhaps to one
    not knowing the true sight they are seeing.
At its glory, hidden behind the mask of
    darkness, the water brakes and russels
    against the shore.
Beckoning to all who is beautiful and clean
    and full of thought to come and partake
    in its splender.
To solve a problem, to ease a sorrow, to
    dream of being free.
The water holds unto its own whatever
    the eye may see.

—Raymond P Glessner

LITTLE MAPLE SEED

If they could speak we could ask:
Little maple seed where have you been?
Pray tell, where are you going?
Hidden in the cold ground 'till May,
With soft white snow for a quilt;
With the first rays of spring sunshine;
With the fragrance of lilacs for company
I awaken to a bright world renewed.
Mother nature gently, gently shakes me.
The soft earth is my haven of rest.
Back to the ground from whence I came.
Weep not, it is not a sad occasion at all,
For you see, life for me will commence
all over again — a second chance.

—Ann Bobik Clark

THE OLD PLANT AND ME

This old plant and me have been friends a long
    Time. Existing together, a lot of tears, a lot of
Joy, a lot of special moments . . . it's been here
To make me appreciate the sunshine in the
Window and cast its magical glow after the
Storm clouds have left . . . it's brought life
To many a house making it a home, letting the
Boy and me feel welcome.
All this happy little mass of leaves asks of me
Is a glass of water now and then, and to look
Outside, its only hope is for space to grow. . .
No more then any other living thing asks for.
I'm glad I bought it to fill the empty
Space in the staircase years ago, it's filled
Much more than the staircase.

—Gail Taylor Johnson

ALWAYS

A knitted lace pocket
That used to carry love
Slipped on sharp rocks
Tiny threads weren't strong enough
Torn valentines fell into a valley
Over and over
In nightmares
My eyes miss the light
Soft silk on my neck
I struggle to breathe
And try to forget
Having been wrapped around you like a bangle
Always I know
You'll tell me forever
To love is always to strangle.

—Cheryl L. Alden

LATE BLOOMER

Tall and thin
    With only a wren,
Others have given
What should be taken.

But wait!
I see buds — what did it take?
There must be some mistake.
The others are almost done aching
From having their branches hanging.

Oh my, you are ready to give
And I am ready to take.
It certainly was no mistake,
You are among the beautifullest to live.

—J.J. Perez

SHADOW OF A MISFIT

Dancing in the bright light was a
    beautiful girl flowing within her dreams.
    Dancing in the darkness of night was
a shadow, a misfit it seems.
    Misfits are always behind and they never
do anything right, that's why they have to
dance in the darkness of night.
    There are no dreams for misfits, just
punishment by embarrassment and sorrow,
not caring to live to dance in the shadow
of tomorrow.
    But one day for the beautiful dancer, her
light's not gonna be lit, it's gonna be shining
on the real star, the shadow of the misfit.

—Penni Davis, age 16

LET ME IN

I sit on the bandstands,
    Hands on my lap,
Waiting . . . .
i see You All out there,
    Hand in hand,
Relating . . . .
What's wrong with me?
    Why won't You let me in?
Is it something i've said?
    Or maybe something i haven't?
i'm probably ostentatious for saying so,
    But i think i've got something to offer.
All i want is a friend.
Please let me in.

—Jess W.L. Stuart

FRIENDS

I thought of you today,
    When the winds began to blow.
I felt the love that we once held,
When I read the letters you once wrote.
I cried when I felt the freedom,
The freedom we had,
Walking hand in hand on the edge of
tomorrow.
I think of the times we spent together,
The time I cherish now.
Life will be so different without you
here.
I know now that I have the thoughts, feelings,
and the tears all in one.
As I think of yesterday.

—Connie J. Searles

TRAVELER'S-RESPITE; TOURIST'S—DELIGHT.

The best trips made are those seen
in Geographic Magazine.

—George H. Ziegler
Ton Son Nuit,
Saigon, Vietnam
1966

A child . . .
laid to rest, in Potter's field
t'was on the news today . . .
one of many infants
to be buried there, they say . . .

Each in a tiny numbered box
no one was there to mourn them
no one to cry a single tear,
not even those, who bore them . . .

Sweet little spirits of the dawn
we lay you now to sleep,
Heaven's smallest treasures
your wings . . . so soon . . . to keep.

I scribe you this remembrance
each time a church bell rings . . .
a prayer . . . for the children
of Potter's field,
now held . . .
               by the King of kings . . .

—M$_{E_K}$

FREEDOM

People cry for freedom.
Martin Luther King cried—
Freedom for blacks—
Patrick Henry cried
Freedom for a New Nation.

People fight for freedom.
Blacks were spurred on by
Equal rights.
America was spurred on by
A New Nation.

We cry for freedom from sin.

We fight for freedom—we are spurred
On by Christ.

—Rebecca Rogers

SEASONS OF FAITH

How could Spring
Know the joy of coming
Had not wintry winds
Turned to warmer drifts
        How could shoots
        Know to rise and blossom
        Lest melting snow
        Invade the soil and cliffs
You might wonder too
How God could love us mortals
With all our lowly feelings
And our faults
        But He understands, forgives
        and prays we may see
        The light and love
        In which we could exalt
                —Gerre DeLongis

IN THE HEAVENS: A NIGHT VISION

One moonlit night as I was gazing at the sky
I saw a thousand twinkling objects passing by
Like happy little shining stars,
Or playful lightning bugs in giant celestial jars.
Suddenly an illumined sign held by two doves
was reared.
On its surface two lines of script appeared:
"Home of the aborted and the unborn,
The battered babes, the lonely and forlorn."
It was a wondrous fleeting sight!
I never shall forget that night.

—Eddie Lee Sutton

Last night was a dark and stormy night
And thunder rumbled around the sky
Several trains whistled in the distance
And then came passing by
And in between each pleasant sound
Came another still
A moaning, whistling wind, cavorting
Around our window sill
Now that was a nice night, we love nights
Like, this that your worries take.
Because we love to cuddle up and listen to
The beautiful sounds—that only God can make

—J.C. Beard

MAY 25th 1988

Thank you for coming,
and sharing our day.

As we dine,
and dance in May.

How many words are those,
of Love, Peace, and Joy to say?

For those who couldn't be here
and keeping us in their thoughts of the day.

The Holy Spirit dwells within
and guides us on our way.

Twenty-five years together
and many more we pray.

Theresa and Jule thank you again
for making us happy today.

—Theresa Torba Helbling

HOW THE KNIGHT BECAME KING

The Knight said to The Lord,
"Come quickly, and bring a sword."
The Lord said to The Knight,
"I'll give you a sword, so that you can fight."
The Knight, who was a marvelous sight,
In his shining armor,
Slew a dragon,
Which was attacking The Queen,
And which did alarm her,
And was trying to harm her.
The Queen gave The Knight,
The privilege and the right,
To live in the castle with her.
The Queen called him "Sir."
And he enchanted and charmed her.
The Knight became King.
And he enjoyed all of the luxuries,
That life in the middle ages could bring.

—Kenneth B. Fischer

THE LOVE THAT KEPT THEM TOGETHER

The love that kept them together
was so strong no one could pull them apart
the love that they had for each other
came from deep inside their hearts

The love that kept them together
throughout the many years
was far more overpowering
than the crying and the tears

The love that kept them together
until that very last day.
When all of a sudden with no expectation
one of them passed away

—Jennifer F. Czelusniak

TO: JOHN

How do I love thee?
There are countless ways . . .
Your tender soul, your passionate gaze.
You fill me with hope and build my dreams.
We can do anything no matter how impossible it seems.
You are my strength and my reason for living.
You make dreams worth sharing and kindness worth giving.
Our roads have been rough and days sometimes bleak . . .
But our love kept us going. It's never been weak.
Thank you, my darling, for all your love and care.
You always lift my spirits when life is too much to bear.
You've given me sensations I've never known before.
I will love you now and forever more.

—Laura Michelle Moore

TIME

Coming and going without even a clue
Seconds, minutes, hours an endless stream
Will there ever be time to try something new?
Look to the future to live out your dream

Time never sleeps, runs or walks
But ticks on never a beginning, never an end
Pays no heed to season, sunrise or clocks
Cannot be bought, cannot be sold but daily is spent

O to be captured, frozen in time
Reflect on the past our only control
Divided again and again our reason, our rhyme
Time forces age to collect its toll

—Gabriel Royal Robinson

LOVE'S PROMISE

Take time to tell me you love me,
Set aside time each day.
Show the way you care,
Choosing carefully the words you say.
Be with me when I need you,
Never hasten or delay.
Make me your friend before all other friends
Of today and yesterday.
Give me something to believe in,
Promise me you'll never stray.
Find compassion for broken dreams,
Learning together in a loving way.
Share with me our future,
Being equal in our parts to play.
Be honest to me always,
For the liar's price is high to pay.

—Twyla D. Herold

HELLO

Hello, my parent,
one who gave me life.
You of human body,
who gave birth to my metal one.
You who destroyed your world,
allowing mine to begin.
You built me with knowledge of the brain,
but also with love of the heart.
I called you God,
and now you lay buried in the past.
Hello, my friend,
you who I wish was here.

—Scott B. Gibson

FRIENDSHIP

Love is the greatest gift of all
A special present which never can fall
Remember true friendships are based on love
Friendship a great gift from the above

When true friendship is your goal
Listen to your heart and to your soul
Remember always the heart is not blind,
And a true friend you will surely find.

A friend who sees not with the eyes
A friend so true, who never tells lies,
A friend who is truly smart,
A friend who sees with the heart!

—Deirdre Marie-Daly

DEVOTION

For what I'd give my only breath
my last heartbeat on a single word
My only life taken to be understood
all words echo,
but only one heard.
Years must pass in a single hour
the winter's night,
an eternal day
All roads will wind through my
broken heart
on which path will I choose my way?
My life will lie in an endless kiss —
truth,
at the brink of day
all hope will cease on the edge of night
by the sword on which my body
lay.

—Elizabeth Muldowney

I LOVE YOU

I love you.
You are the heart and soul of me,
That beats so cautiously,
Lest I might tread upon and hurt
The very heart of you.

I love you.
You are all the dreams worth the memory
When I wake at dawn's first light.
And hold you near,
Accepting the reality of you.

I love you.
You are the future's bright endearing ways,
When you and you alone
Complete the ideal,
The perfection of life, for me.

—Charlene Bramell

Color: beautiful, shadowy, sensual,
       emotional, timeless, illusive,
       abstract and void if not for
         mind recognition.

      —Jay

Keep what you have,
  hold on with all strength
for one will try to take it
and he will only destroy.

Cherish your everyday,
fill it with love
and all the sunshine possible,
for you may never be there again.

Strive to be what you are,
not what others want to make you.
For in the long run
nothing will be true.

Protect your loved ones from harm
that some will try to inflict upon them.
Show special ones your feelings
or maybe next time they will
          not be there,
      to touch, to tell to their ear
      I love you . . .
          say it today.

      —Karla McClure

TIME LOST

People will come, and then will go,
  Times are sure to change.
But love's found once, then never lost
    For true love will remain.
A friend is there to share the times
    That you cherish most.
To ride a bike, or climb a tree,
    Or just to get some coke.
To help you learn, and make you laugh,
    To share a stupid joke.
Let you drink, but never drive.
    They walk you when you're low.
Hold your hand, and kiss your cheek,
    Hug you when you're sad.
Cry with you, and feel the pain
When relationships go bad.
A friend will come, and never go.
They're always in your heart.

      —Trent Fryar

THE HEALING TOUCH

Belonging is the sharing
  Of all life's pain and joys
Love mutes the blaring
Of life's unbearable noise.

Loving is the caring
When all life's work is lost
Touching dims the glaring
Of dreams so recklessly tossed.

Touching is the spirit
That heals and speeds the pace
Healing shades the hurting
Fades the grimace from the face.

The healing touch, the greatest cure
Resides in love, so rare, so dear.

      —Maria Coleman Barker

PRINCESS

Impervious to threats and bribes; she walks
 Alone against a thousand enemies; she stalks.
A stinging bee she dances round;
A dust ball makes her leave the ground.

Yet, when I am low and sad,
She comes to me on silent pad,
Rubs her head against my hand
And willing she makes me stand.

Impervious to threats and bribes, I walk

      —Maggie Costello

NATURE'S BEAUTY

A forest of trees is arched over the ground
  where a flower garden
  is speckled with color.

The blue sky can be seen
  through the big oak trees
  where the sea and land meet.

Many seashells can be found
  on the hot, dusty sand
  glistening with beige and brown.

Many white seagulls
  sail in the dusk.

It's a most quiet sight.

      —Kristin N. Roberts, age 8

SUCH WISDOM IN GIVING

Can the child, of all my offspring,
  One I thought would frustrate my space,
And design to make my life's complaints
So impossible to face;
Can this child who shares my talents,
This beauty who often quotes me
And follows my every lead
And learns all offered at my knee;
Be the unborn that I dreaded,
The embryo that became my plight;
The baby I feigned to nurture
But has become my soul's delight?
How did Heaven know I'd love her
And know of her bond to me?
Who but the wisest creator
Such a blessing could foresee?

      —Lindy Oelrich

MEMORIES OF GOLDEN SUNLIGHT

The warmth doesn't come at daylight
  But creeps up through the hours.
By noon it is bright and golden
On the ripening fruit and the flowers.
The bees hang aloft o'er the meadow,
The birds gather fast into flocks.
They know that the warm days are numbered.
They have natural calendars and clocks.
I sit and soak up the sunshine,
I, too, must have things that I store;
My memories of sunshine and warmness
Must last me a season or more.
Remembering last winter's desolation
When snow filled each cranny and nook,
I'll keep my memories beside me
As I settle down with a book.

      —Bertha M. Soske

I AM MY OWN ENEMY

I am but a face in the crowd,
                              or am I someone?
I am hollow. Just a figure with no insides,
for they are all around me, dancing like puppets
on a string.
So enchanting; they lure every eye; determined
to show the real me. Or, do they intend to
hide me in the entrance of a bottomless pit,
awaiting my fall? Their dance draws the audience
closely, closely, so close, so tight that
my breath breaks into a beaded necklace! Sharp,
painful breaths I take! Their voices, they
taunt me, echoing inside my head!
I grab to hang on
                              but I have slipped.
Sweet, sharp razor,
                    lead the way!!!!!
—Lisa Marie Martin, age 16

LONELINESS

Empty halls. Dim faces.
A man moans from his pit of confusion.
A cold wind blows through the barren trees
A dog whimpers with hunger.
A coin drops in a tin cup.
The lights shut off at dawn.
Another piece of coal is added to the dying ashes.
It's damp . . . and moldy.
The bed creaks as the dead take their last breath.
Heads turn away without a single word;
Ears are closed, never listening to the pain.
Tears form and fall,
Leaving hope and faith behind.
—Tiffni Y. Baxley, age 19

DID YOU SLEEP?

That beautiful day, while I was sleeping
  I felt a strange light that laughed
And when I awoke, I looked at the sky
And the light was still there
I went out, I looked around, but still it laughed
I looked for it in the colorful sunrise, but it ran fast
I looked for it in the biggest rainbow, and it grew larger
When I returned, I still didn't know what I felt
But when I saw you in bed, you were asleep
And surprised, I watched a beauty shine in your hair
And I couldn't believe it
But when I remained by your side
That strange light, didn't laugh . . . . . . anymore.
—Rudy Faverio

ODE TO A DYING WINDMILL

You pumped the water for house and stock
  for many years around the clock.
The kids climbed high to catch a sight
  of creek and pasture — to their delight.
The well gave out, but you lingered still—
  through fire and storms, hot winds, and chill.
A faithful sentinel you have stood,
  pointing winds' directions as none else could.
With resounding crash you fell to earth,
  remains were viewed with little mirth.
And now you will be laid to rest—
  you served us well and did your best.
In days to come, how will we know
  which way the winds will choose to blow?
—Sylvia Gilbert

BROKEN GLASS

If eyes were windows
  To the soul's nights and days,
  Your curtains opened,
Would I find you, like me
  Picking up the shattered pieces
  Of our tomorrow from the floor
Clutching each broken moment?

Will I find how to
  Stop the sound of breaking
While I tend, piece by piece
  Day by day the way to live?
—Charlotte Stonestreet

The time has come
  after sixteen years of waiting,
searching for someone like me.
He understands me. He is me.
I finally found my freedom,
My outlet.
I know I am no longer alone.
I am not one of a kind now, but two.
Fate has brought us together—
I hope it never tears us apart.
My flame was getting old and tired
of burning alone.
Now it is eternal.
—Deborah Glicklich

STOLEN LIFE

Gone is the life of a love one.
Gone is the passion of love.

Softly it comes. Stealing a life so dear.
Leaving one crying how could death be
so cruel!
Yet, we know that love is a maybe.
Hope is for the future.
And, death is always.

Angrily, I say why.

Didn't he conform to rules?
Didn't he reach out and touch someone,
so that he could have a better day?

With silence unbroken a life steals away
leaving behind memory.
—Ardella M. Thomas

OILED WINGS

The loons cried long with covered wings
  To somewhere miles distant
Please save them from waters they love
That's been transformed and sent

Into a living hell of blackness
No more days they'll fly
Grounded by oil a half foot thick
It's chosen them to die

Along with friends and family
From many miles around
No humans could tell them to leave
A slowly dying sound

There was no interpreter
To wave them east or north
Communications between species
Drown beneath the shore
—David Bacher

MY WONDERFUL FRIEND

I have a friend, her name is "May"
She sure knows how to brighten my day
When I am down and feeling so blue
She picks me up and makes me feel like new

Her loving eyes, her beautiful smile
Just to see these, I'd walk a mile
She's always there, especially for me
And never once has asked or expected a fee

She comes over every day, just to check on me
We'll visit, have coffee or a pot of tea
What can I do for you today, she'll say
To help you out on this beautiful day?

My spirits are lifted by this woman so gifted
She knows what to do and just what to say
To make this just another perfect day
I wish everyone in the world could know and see
This wonderful, dear friend, I call Mrs. P.

—Josephine Lamitina Johnson

I LOVE YOU, HAVE A GOOD DAY

As I leave each morning on my way
I wave to my 5 year old and say, "I love you,
    have a good day"
And as I drive away — I see her wave and watch
    her smile
I know that's my baby — and she's only going to
    be mine a little while.

Kindergarten will be starting soon
I'll have to move over and give my daughter the
    room
To go out into the world and to make her own
    way
And pray that God stands by her each and every
    day.

Today, as I look into the past
I can still hear my mama say, "I love you, have
    a good day"
Those words, softly spoken, were a very useful
    tool
They were a stepping stone for me and will be
    through all her days of school.

As I look into the future
I see my daughter who
With guidance, love, and patience will grow up
    too —

She'll make a good mother
She'll be a good friend
Each morning she'll say, "I love you, have a good
    day"
Which will be the best start in the kindest of
    ways.

—Donna R. Dalton

ONCE IN A LIFETIME

Once in a lifetime
You find the right one
Who makes you happy
Fills your life with fun.
    Once in a lifetime
He's rare to find
I thought he wasn't there
I must've been blind.
    Looking back now, I can see
All the others, What
they've done to me.
    You're the best —
I want you to know.
Please give me a chance —
    please don't go.

—Christina Leuenberger, age 13

YESTERYEARS

There is a time for learning and a time for
love, when the soul soars light and free:
    And a time for thought and a time to muse
o'er the weave of memory

A time to tread the hills and vales with a
pace both free and strong,
    And a time to remember footsteps from the
past, to retreat from the burgeoning throng.

A time to look up to the rock-ribbed hills,
their eternity only a myth,
    And contemplate the gradeur of the land God
left us with.

A time to feel the comfort of the lakes and
the watercourse,
    To wonder at the stream of life as we
wander to and forth.

A time to see the blossoming flowers, to
ponder their form and their hue:
    To lie in the shade of the forest green and
be blessed by the skies of blue.

A time to gaze on the works of man, to ask
as we tarry there:
    If the wonders he wro't on the face of the
land, can pay for what he laid bare.

A time to enter the temple-place, dedicated
by man to his God,
    But ask yourself, is he really pleased by the
ritual we applaud.

A time to ask if it may be true, that he
who God forswears:
    He first makes man and on the land their
souls he then lays bare.

And a time to study well, what memory
gives to you and linger long on the vistas seen in
pleasant yesteryears:
    Be not abashed by times inroads nor the
sins that others say, but rather smile upon God's
land, it vanishes tears away.

—Richard B. Rypma

ETERNITY

The little boy sits on the green
Admiring a seeding dandelion
While eating a chocolate treat.
A butterfly dances by.
In a blink of an eye the boy wonders,
"Where did it come from,
Where will it go?"
Then goes back to eating his treat.

—Sonja Jones

IF . . .

If one does not wish to die . . .
One must not be born.
For at birth we die with our first
breath and cry.
But as we must live, to make it
bearable, one must revel . . .
In serenity and inner peace and not
travel the body so fast,
That the soul is lost.

—Nancy Gwynne

A FINAL TAUNT

Upon a hill, he stood aloof.
The sky above, a starless roof.
Into the breeze he softly sighed.
His reveries had been denied,
and urged to court with suicide.
Subdued beneath some devil's hoof.

In longing for his endless dream,
his lips produced an anguished scream.
Some shrieking foreign voice returned,
and pleaded for the death it yearned.
Such troubled thoughts forever burned,
beside some river's ebon stream.

His wretched soul, in shock took wing,
toward the water's shaded spring,
and then beheld with moistened eyes,
the cause of all his hopes demise.
There daemons mimicked lonely cries,
laced with an evil mocking ring.

—Stuart Edgar

REPRIMAND

I literally slink down the
hall,
   Humiliation, anger
            total frustration
God, that I could crawl
into a corner and
assume a fetal position.
I try to be professional
accept with grace and
apologize
   — a weak defense
thank God —
         there is positive reinforcement
Whatever little perception
there be of me
   He tries to soften the
   blow.
Three years of hopes
plans, and work in one
moment
   seem totally smashed and shattered.

—Catherine A. Waldron

LUCILLE BALL

Heaven must be a brighter place today,
For in her company angels will be gay.
Her legacy "Joy, to share hereafter"
Her gift was one of hope and laughter.
Her glorious manner of acting befuddled,
Eased hearts and the sorely troubled.
Mischief she gave like a present,
Her personality was more than pleasant.
God knows, she did her best with fun,
Her banter seemed to please everyone.

—Margaret M. Viret

FOR FIFTEEN YEARS NOW

World rulers have played with the antichrist
For fifteen long years by now —
With treasonists, pornographists, abortionists.
The lust for great power wows.

Sure! We have detectives, policemen.
Sure! And we always have had!
Until fifteen years ago we had such peace —
Next door were mostly law-loving lads.

For fifteen years now, though, we've had right next door
Terrorists who us harrass —
Yet our leaders — they tell us now that we have peace,
Will not the terrorism pass?

—Katherine W. Shelton

WHO'S RIGHT?/WHO'S WRONG?

Who's right?
Who's wrong?

There are NO blacks or whites to disagreements.
Just GREY!

There are NO browns or whites in difficult
situations.
Just BEIGE!

There are NO reds or whites in affairs of the
heart.
Just PINK!

So if everyone sees things differently,
Through a spectrum of the rainbow;

Who's right?
Who's wrong?

—Traci-Lei Sein

ANGEL FROM HELL

Like an angel from the sky she fell.
"Angel" promised heaven but gave hell.
In and out "Angel" went like dust,
Year of 72 "Angel" made her bust.

The scene was changed from flowers to knives.
"Angel" took with her more than few lives.
Violence and barbarism became the real.
Her effects she left were all part of the deal.

It was to her you surrendered control,
Your mind is beyond with no patrol.
Messages sent to the brain only deceived;
Back towards your body their nor received.

Your body becomes beside itself with isolation.
"Angel" leaves body and soul in desolation.
She turns dreams without hopes into nightmares.
It is in phencyclidine "Angel's" name bares.

—Blick

MEMORIES

Stretching earnestly to recapture
What once was a reality.
Caught in a warp of time and feeling
Longing to recall and hold on
To the pictures of your mind.

—Amy Jones

MORNING IN THE VALLEY

Mountain tops caress the Ohio valley
sleeping far below.
Fog raising like a soft white veil
putting on a show.

Spiderwebs criss-cross the trees
sparkling with the morning dew,
appearing as a net of jewels just
waiting here for you.

A red-tailed hawk flys swiftly by
surveying his domain,
a place time has forgotten and things
remain the same.

The mighty Ohio River laying soft
on the valleys face,
twisting and turning about like a
beautiful piece of lace.

—Lorena Orchard

DAYS GONE BY

We cannot dwell on days gone by
even tho we often do
Remember places, friends, events
that made us, me and you

The past is part of future
as well as what's today
It's why we see the things we see
and say the things we say

Each person finds along the way
a storehouse full of reasons
For standing tall and bearing up
to all the coming seasons

We cannot go back to days gone by
so let's tuck them in a drawer
And when we need a boost or lift
they'll be with us evermore

—Linda J. Wilson

NEW BEGINNINGS

Today two very special people
will start a new beginning.

May your new beginning bring
happiness and hope,
laughter and joy.

Today brings a great bond. May
this bond withstand any hardship
and pain that may come your way.

May the warmth of your love
protect from the cold.

And may the unity of your souls
for heaven's sake never break.

Take these words to heart,
they come from deep within.

—Jessica L. Terry

As the sun rises
Slowly, over the horizon
And the moon retreats
For a peaceful slumber
I am stunned by the majestic
Force which crashes
Rythmically, against the shore
What dark emotions must fill the soul of Nature,
For her to create such violent beauty?

—Jeanie Elizabeth Walters

SPRINGTIME

Spring is the sweetest time of all to me
I skip with all the white lambs as they play.
I flow with all the small creeks flowing free,
And fly with wild birds at the break of day.

I blossom with the flowers as they break
The bonds of Earth to show their brightest hue.
I chuck with woodchucks—rattle with a snake
And watch foxfire shine in the nightwatch dew.

I bless this time that brings its fairy glow.
I hide with rabbits in the stubbled field.
I see ahead the bursting crops and know
Before it's time the summer's heavy yield.

I would forego the heaven that I never
Have seen if time like this could last forever.

—Bonnie F. Mooney

TRUTH vs. KNOWLEDGE

What passes for knowledge today,
tomorrow is obsolete;
But Truth lasts forever,
and in Itself is complete.
Ignore Truth in search of knowledge,
and destruction will surely follow.
Build nuclear bombs with knowledge—
leave out Truth and have a heart that is hollow.
This path away from Truth
has brought only pain.
There is nothing in knowledge alone
that we can use for gain.
Only Truth can conquer evils
caused by knowledge abused.
And Truth will judge how well
knowledge alone has been used.

—Sharon Goodwin

I feel the meaning rush deep through my soul
The words I whisper come out too slow
To say that I love you is hardly the way
To express all the happiness you brought me today

Deep down inside it makes me cry
I want to hold you in my arms until we die
I want the memories that bring the pain
To open my eyes and see the rain

The longing to cling to you scares me
Though love is blind I still see
The ocean in your eyes that washed me away
The tide that brought me back to stay

The moon was made for us to share
Though miles apart I know you're there
I touched the stars with a kiss I blew
And somehow I know the stars kissed Michael too!

—Ramona Sleeseman

FLOWERS

Delicate petals dripping with dew,
Red, pink, yellow, and sometimes blue,
Their long delicate stems of green,
Make a very beautiful scene,
They all have different names,
Not a one is the same,
Some are wild and free,
While others are tame as can be,
All are loved,
Like the stars above,
All are lovely as can be.
And they are something great to see.

—Cathy Homan

SUMMER

The season changes, the days grow long,
The sun shines bright, hot, and hazy,
Birds, crickets, and frogs sing their song,
Humid, warm weather makes us lazy.

Swimming, camping, baseball, and riding bikes,
Picnics, hot dogs, reunions, visiting with relatives,
Vacations, sight-seeing, and going on hikes,
Summer's the season that everything lives.

Soon it will be gone, the season will change,
The trees will relax and shed their leaves,
School will begin, schedules rearranged,
Fall, winter and spring, go by quickly, please!

—Meliss Moran, age 14

SAND, WAVE, SUN, GULL, AND I

Sand soothes my racing mind.
Sun tans my skin.
Wave caresses my legs.
Seagull screams and reels, annoyed.

Sand settles.
Wave, angered, slaps at my legs.
Tired sun sinks low in the sky.
Seagull, quiet now, preens.

Sand jumps into the sky to shine.
Sun is replaced by moon.
Wave is impressed and reflects the scene.
Seagull dozes . . .

    . . . as do I, unaware of nature's moods.

—Lisa Faye Nelson, age 13

GOOD MORNING!

Our world, aorist asleep, thunder booms loud;
rumbling, echoing from a Milky Way.

Bolts of chevron-shaped lights, announce a birth;
followed by trumpeting, "Will the Sky Fall?"

Calmness and darkness, bring deafening shrouds,
decreasing visibility . . . blind foray.

Silence, interrupting a heavenly mirth
offering peace, love, serenity to all.

Vernal sun burns off sulphur-colored clouds,
as night, mysteriously, drifts into day.

Minuscule dew stars caress on cold earth,
granting animals and plants, a 'wake up' call.

—Steve Reisen

SEPTEMBER

September brought you to me
A friend from out of my past
September brought us closer
Friendship turned to love at last
Another September left me crying
As we parted and said good-bye
We may meet again some September
When the leaves began to die
But if all my Septembers shall pass me by
And your face I shall not see
I'll wait for you in Heaven
And save you a place by me

—Stella Inez Crawford

SPRING

God lays His Almighty hand
On the frozen earth.
The snow melts, and the
Ice leaves its wintry home.
Bushes sprout and trees show
evidence of new life.
Leaves start showing green,
Flowers push their tiny
Heads through the hard winter worn soil.
The days get longer,
The nights get shorter,
My heart sings — IT'S SPRING!

—Esther Koechel Nering

AUTUMN

Autumn, tell me where you've been;
I'm so glad you're back again.
Winter came and stole you boldly,
Took the warmth and left us coldly —
All alone,
Feelings gone,
Where were you?

Brilliant now the world beholds
All your russets, browns, and golds
Blowing round in chilly air;
Beauty causing me to stare.
Lost in awe,
Silent I,
Sit and gaze.

—Kelly E. Rawlings

SUMMER'S DAY

Oh, to be a child again,
To run, to sing and play,
Happy and carefree, was I then,
On a beautiful summer's day.

With my brother, at my side,
Through fields of clover, we did roam,
Sailing boats in muddy streams,
With nar' a thought of going home.

Catching turtles and butterflies,
Picking wild berries, too,
Heads tossed back, scanning the sky,
What a glorious shade of blue!

Weary, smudged and barefoot now,
Homeward bound, are we,
With thoughts of a tomorrow,
More wonders, for to see.

—Gloria W. Squires

MY GRANDPARENTS

My dearest Dears:

At night back at home
I have dreams that are unknown.
I scream and cry,
But when I look at my side
I can feel and see
The warmth and care
of my grandparents there.

Thank you my Dears.

—Ethan Atwood, age 10

LIFE OR LUXURY?

Mink, fox, rabbit, and seal
on a fur coat, in the store down the street.
Soft, warm, beautiful, and real
on sale too, at a price you can't beat.

How could this be? Why is it so cheap?
People know now, beauty is only skin deep.

For an animal belongs in its original coat,
not to be killed for style or fashion,
but to live freely near its stream or its moat,
and not as the object of someone's greedy passion.

So before you buy that mink, fox, rabbit, or seal,
think about the life you're going to steal.

—Nicole M. Sezov

THE FARM

The farm is such a peaceful place,
    With many animals there.
No traffic, no cars, no trucks, nor noise,
    Just the neighing mare.

With fleecy sheep that run around
    In a verdant pasture green,
They run about and chase and baa
    Playing their games so keen.

The chickens are roosting or walking about
    In their clumsy fluttery way.
The cows are chewing their cuds in the
        shade
    For this is a balmy day.

—Lisa Kerber

YARD OF FLOWERS

The evergreens are young, yet old.
    The day echoes life, yet is silent
They are so near, yet so far,
Seems like yesterday, yet tomorrow,
Death comes so soon, yet arrives so late,
Always present, always past,
Have you sin? or have you faith?
Have you sin? or have you faith?
The flowers are sweet, yet bitter
Strong as one's love for another, yet
    they wither,
In one's eyes forever tears will fall
    like rain,
Yet another's remains so dry,
For one brief moment, the heavens will
    shower
It has yet to rain in the yard of
    flowers.

—Kevin Nolan

NIGHT HUNTER

Softly the kitten is purring to me
Softly it says come see come see!
I walk to the window and look through
    the night
To see a dead mouse in the pale moon-
    light
Well done I say
Well done indeed
And with her soft eyes she gently does
    plead
To hear more praise for this is her need
    well done I say
        Well done indeed.

—Katie Plumley

GRANDPA'S CAR

The old car sat in the driveway
    Polished with special care.
The windows were washed and shining
Grandpa always kept it that way.
The model was not the fashion.
The interior was out of style,
But the running board came in handy
When grandpa got in to drive.
Lovingly he touched the fender,
Rubbed his elbow across the mirror.
Slowly he got in the driver's seat
Daydreaming of trips gone by.
These were the only trips he took now.
He wasn't allowed to drive anymore.

—Coleen Myers Anderson

SENIOR CITIZEN'S DANCE HALL

Huge Christmas bells glued to the ceiling
    In August
Humid air permeated with stale sweat
And cloying perfume
A rickety man playing on a rickety piano
The strains of the Missouri waltz
In heart-patient tempo
Gnarled hands clasped together
Boney arms around boney backs
Shallow breathing, asthmatic wheezing
AND YET
The beaming faces and beatific smiles
Betokens an intimate man-woman relationship
And dreams of a romantic past
As they sway together

—Charles H. Fish

RUSH-HOUR

We fight our way through the rush-hour
traffic on Broad Street swimming upstream
like nervous city salmon.
We exchange signs in a language
only partly understood
—like anxious initiates
and ask ourselves just why
we are here . . .
You make me smile.
Our hands meet halfway and for a moment
we're in a field-stone house
tending the hearth fire . . .
Outside there are children and wildflowers;
ocean waves, prayers
and memories . . .

—J. Kevin White

278

PARADOXICALLY YOURS

Absorbent white,
Reflective black,
Color molded together
As one in Nature Mother.
Parading as a Zebra,
Giving reinforcement
To muffled hearts that listen
To the desperate whisperings
Sung by the Universal Soul
In search of a colorful vacation resort
For Lost Legacies

—Peggy Hernandez

HUSBAND

Oh, your eyes
          so dark and deep
The secrets of my heart do keep
Igniting a steady burning flame
With each soft whisper of my name
That holds me fast forever long
The invisible force
          so gentle, so strong
Whose vows I'll keep until my death
Whose kiss I'll crave till my last breath
The kind of love that set me free
My love for you
          and yours for me.

—Marcia Nelson Perone

DEEP INSIDE

Deep inside there is a feeling,
one I can't explain,
without you it would cease
and cause pain.
It fills me with sheer happiness,
whenever I'm with you,
and there's nothing in this world,
for you I wouldn't do.
For you, my heart pours out a song
of a sweet melody,
it's because your smile, to me, is
so heavenly.
My dearest, eternity, is how long
we'll be together,
for this feeling, deep inside of me,
is forever.

—Mala Lucretia Wright

MY LOVE

Eve-ning shadows make me
blue. When each weary day is
done. How I long to be with
you. My love every day I
reminisce dreaming of your
tender kiss. Always thinking
how I miss you my love. It
seems a million years have
gone by since we shared
our love and our dreams.
But I'll hold you again. There
will be no more blue memories
then my love. Whether
skies are gray or blue any
place on earth will do.
Just as long as I'm with
you my love.

—James Vincaro

THE WEDDING

Swans, geese and peacocks
Elegant and eloquent
Birds of paradise and other beauties
     Love in its endless bounty
Dissolving walls of resistance
     Oneness in the atmosphere
Reverberations of unsung
     Yet unknown prose.

—Nabil R. Ghawi

LOVE IS . . .

Love is caring through it all
And sharing when you want it all.

Love is giving from your heart
And receiving every part.

Love is needing that special hug
And fulfilling without a shrug.

Love is crying over something small,
Yet laughing and having a ball.

Love is trying to make it worthwhile
And accomplishing through trial.

Love is everything from your heart.

—Michelle DuBose-Yeager

LOSS

Did I love him?
          Yes.
Was the future planned around this?
          Yes.
What changed it, why didn't it happen?
          Fear.
          Fear of what?
          Letting go . . .
          Pride . . .
          Not Trusting . . .
Could it have been different?
          No.
          Why?
Because no one was strong enough.
          Why not?
          Fear.

—Christel Morgan

A WEDDING PRAYER

Lord smile upon Your children
Kneeling at the altar now
Pledging to one another
And to You a sacred vow;
Thankful that You answered prayer
Gave this wedding joy to share.

Hear from these two happy hearts
Tender love, devotion deep,
Promises of faithfulness
Confidence they'll always keep
Though rich or poor, health or pain,
True commitment will remain.

Two precious lives now are one
Dedicated Lord to You,
Guide in Your ways step by step
Keeping love's pledge firm and true,
Give courage, strength and laughter,
Bless today, all days after.
                              Amen.

—Pauline B. Surpless

WHY?

Everyone used to have an American dream,
But due to all the riots, it would seem;
That now the only time you dare to dream,
Is with your eyes wide open while you scream.

The flag our veterans now fly with pride,
Seems to be used for a criminal to hide;
They can now burn it and let the ashes lie,
While proud Americans just sit quietly and cry.

I'm glad I'm an American and that I'm free,
Where I have the right to just be me;
I'm proud my children also have the right to see,
Exactly what they would choose to be.

—Brenda J. Roberts

LIFE'S JIGSAW JUMBLES

When times do come, or slip away,
last or fade, through night or day,
to have a love or hate to know,
your feelings for to hide or show.
I wonder who did set the tides,
of all of life's regrets and prides;
from whence did come the tapestry
of all of life's ambiguities,
to cast upon creation's loom
the uncertainty which fate calls doom.
While time should bring us peace of mind,
and cast life's pieces all in line,
it never does quite get in place,
the jigsaw jumbles of our race.

—David Drake

WHAT IS A MOTHER

A mother is the cream of the crop,
A mother is a lady that is the tops
When you need her,
Like any true friend she'll be there
She always stands by you,
With a hand that is steady and a love that is true
Without a question or doubt,
A mother will always help you out
Mom will always lend a hand,
She will do whatever she can
She is a true friend,
With loving advice to always lend
But one thing I know is true,
There is no mom in this world as special as you.
To my Mother with all my love.
—Barbara (Spaar) Ockenhouse

SYMPHONIC SONNET

It lies in quiet rest upon its stand
As disharmonious sounds consume the air,
The master takes it now into his hand
and taps it on the podium with a flair.

The silence now, it sears the darkness vast
It echoes in the ears of all around,
A pressure splits the skull, resounding blast
Anticipation strains to hear a sound.

The time has come for tensions to be loosed
As lips are pursed and fingers tightly bent,
The first note wakes and exits from its roost
And wings its flight as from the page it's sent.

Stresses float away with unseen grace
And leave instead the warmth of an embrace . . .
—Darrin Hull

A SISTER'S CONTEMPLATION

Why do I care so much?
She only uses it.
Why do I try so hard?
She won't appreciate it.
Why do I worry so much?
Isn't that what she wants?
Why have we grown apart?
She doesn't seem to mind.
Why does it hurt so much?
Maybe I shouldn't think about it.
Why can't I leave her behind?
Maybe because I care.

—Robin A. Bradley

BABY

The baby you're expecting
will sometimes cry and fuss and fight,
And that may keep you on edge
For the first couple of nights.

Still, your baby will be special
And you'll love it through and through
And the love you give will be returned —
From the baby unto you.

Now you both have a second job —
Not just being husband and wife,
You have to be loving parents
For the rest of your baby's life.

—Jessica Morissette, age 11

CUSTODY

This is a bedroom? Are you kidding me?
Wall-to-wall stuff, piled precariously,
A living carpet of dangerous traps,
Things that rev, rumble, tumble and snap.

A model airplane with a remote device,
A Freddy Kreuger doll, real nails, how nice.
A wooden frame to build a club house.
A personal computer complete with a mouse.

Fast moving cars and durable soldier dolls,
Tees, clubs, padding, mitts, bats and balls.
All that's missing from the blur of toys
Are the players themselves,
my lost little boys.

—Susan A. Sager

MY LITTLE WEASEL

He was a cute little guy
As I was fishing on the shore
He scampered along upon the rocks
A couple of hours or more.

I talked to him while I fished
As he scampered around in fun,
And every time I fished there
I'd see this fascinating one.

One day while I was fishing
It was quite a surprise,
He scampered over to my feet
And looked me in the eyes.

Then one day I went fishing there
Oh buddy, where did you go?
But he never scampered around again
Little guy, I miss you so.

—Ellen Quinn

POOR CHOICES

Some might say this is poverty:
That I choose to live within my means,
Which I do, eating mostly cabbage, rice and beans.

Three kerosene lamps, light my way,
Electric power, not me, no-way.
Every winter I take off,
Without any trip to the welfare office.

I've chose a life that's plenty fine,
Blessed with know-how and a working mind.
Of these poor choices I am free.
Lots of notes like some folks tote,
Keeps 'em working, and they still be broke.

—Tamra Chavis

CLASS OF '27

With wrinkled hands clasped together
He raises a glass to his love
And in his twinkling eyes
She becomes sixteen again.

As she returns his admiring glance
A jaunty youth re-emerges
Crackling the crusts of time
As though its river stilled.

And in that private, precious moment
Linked by loving memory
A young man and his lady
Kiss in the moonlight.

—Kathleen Ouellette

It is hard to believe how the years have gone past
How my friends have grown older, while I seem to last
Their faces have wrinkles, the men's heads are bare
Some girls have grown lumps, and changed here and there
At times they will squint and strain when they look
Reach out at arms length, to read a good book
My case is much different, my skin is more fair
And where it's discolored, it's just natural wear
My hair's slightly thinner and now snowy white
'Twas the natural result of a hat worn to tight
When my legs jump and jiggle at night in my bed
It's caused by strong muscles, I hear it's been said
At times I'm amazed at the difference I see
How all my friends changed while I'm the same me.

—Keith A. Magee

CADENCE

Someone will bring tea
That steams up ghosts
Of summer afternoons
when arabesques of laughter
went spinning through the air.

But now her chair remains,
Wheels locked in place,
and only beads of rain
Spin in the windy air outside.

A life-line of get well cards
Pulls her mind back to room 304,
    Arctic white
except for the shawl her daughter made,
    soft wool in gold.
    like sunlight through closed eyelids.

—John Bolinger
Fifth Place Award Winner

OF FEELINGS

When I look into your eyes. I see
pain mirrored there.
As I reach with a touch to reassure,
You cringe as if seared by a live-hot
coal.
We sit, the silence creating a gulf
between us.
Numbness slowly, seeps through
raw nerve endings.
Finally, a sigh escapes, diffusing
the hurt.
The ache remains—a reminder
of misery past.

—Mary Jo Sweeney

REUNION

Tis twenty ago we met,
Tis twenty since we've seen,
Seems like yesterday but,
Twas a lifetime between.

Twas youthful arms we embraced,
Twas unlined eyes we looked,
Seems so difficult to remember,
Such deep emotions that shook.

Such promises were made,
Such lies we knew not then,
Seems painful to relinquish,
Kept images of you my friend.

—Debra E. Leonard

LIFE

Thru the sadness and tears;
Don't look at life in terms of years.

Take each day one by one;
Think of the good things that are fun.

Learn to accept and look over your sorrow;
Remember there is a tomorrow.

You can always look back and reminisce;
But don't tarry on things you have missed.

Stop! Don't think and worry;
Life slips by us in such a hurry.

—Gwen Miller

WAY BACK WHEN

It seems so many years ago
when I was but a lad
I think of all the things we did
and all the fun we had.

The simple things we did back then,
were nothing like today
our marble bag was close at hand
many games we had to play.

We'd spend our days down in the woods
a cabin we would build
and if we saved a dime or two,
oh we'd be so thrilled.

But now today I look around
and see what our young must face
I'm glad I'm not a kid today
I'll stay right in my place.

—Robert E. Clark

281

HOMELESS OR IMMIGRANTS

Today we speak of homeless ones
And see them on our streets.
They do not know or do not care.
Their homes You will prepare.
What homes we buy won't satisfy
Because we're passing through.
We're immigrants to lands beyond.
The homes on earth we've found.
What is the fare for over there?
How do we qualify?
God's word is clear. Accept His Son
To enter there — the only One!

— Carol Knopp

I'M HOMELESS

I have no home.
I can only roam
from sea to sea,
from sidewalk to sidewalk.
Yes, being alone is a sad thing to be.
You may see me somewhere.
I'm an old lady.
Not meaning to stare
I'm so lonely.
Nowhere to go.
I live in a cardboard box.
I'm all alone.

—Lizzi Bozzi, age 10

I DIABETIC

The pain in her eyes is so real,
Yet a smile is able to cross
her face.
What she must endure to make a
step through today so she can
make it through tomorrow,
Makes my heart yearn to trade
her places.
She never runs away from the
pain, she faces it with courage
each time.
The day becomes night as I
cradle her into a deep sleep
Hoping tomorrow they'll find a
cure or maybe just lessen
the pain.

—Margaret Weddle

LOST? OR HIDING?

The cat, not mine, it's lost again!
Where is he hiding now?
We said we'd watch him for three weeks.
It's been a job, and how!

Come on, you kids, let's look once more!
The cat, I'm sure, is near —
It seems a hopeless quest, I know,
to find the silly dear!

Let's try the shrubs. Now, here we go.
It looks a likely place.
What would we give for just one sign,
for just one tiny trace?

Well, there he is, the little toad.
He looks so smug and fit.
I'll bet he's thinking he's the best!
It makes one want to spit!

—Elsie V. Angell

LONELY PEOPLE

There are so many Lonely People;
Their bodies are racked with pain.
In their hearts they know they will
Never walk again.
And so — they sit by the
Window — and watch as you go by.
Wishing **so** much you would stop —
and just say Hi!
It only takes a minute — but what
a change 'twould be —
A smile would light their face
For all to see —
To know you loved and cared —
and a minute of your time you shared.

—Lillian Wells Payne, R.N.

CRUEL WORLD

Goodbye, cruel world,
I've closed the door on you.
So it's time for me now,
To open the new.

All of my life I've been wondering who,
Held in my own shell and longing for you.
Now it's my chance to see a new side,
A side of longing, a side of pride.

So, goodbye, cruel world,
To all of you,
who made my life wrong,
Who made my life blue.

—Amy Mansur

NEVER BY MY SIDE

Where were you in the darkness,
When I was frightened deep inside?
Where were you when my hopes were low?
You were never by my side.

Where have you been when tears fell,
Or when I needed a friend's advice?
Or just a friend to give me a hug,
You were never by my side.

Maybe I needed you to help me,
Or just talk for a little while,
Well maybe now it's a little too late,
You were never by my side.

—Crystal Andrews

BURNING HOUSE

The little house stands all alone,
shivering in the night.
Tho the flames soar very high,
the sparks shoot out of sight.
People standing very near, if you
look you'll find they're not hot, but
very cold, a shiver up their spine.
For this house I feel so sad, for
all its glass and panes
If I pray a little harder, maybe it
will rain.
If this house belongs to you, a
tear comes to your eye.
With your hand you wipe your
face and watch the burning house die.

—Theresa M. Christy

THE RIDE TO TOWN

Younger men live in them now,
These monuments to endurance
From the days when a man's arms grew
With his firewood and lumber piles.

There is something inequitable about it.

They come from New York, New Jersey, Connecticut,
Rhode Island.
Their money is green,
but their backs are not strong.
Their faces are not leathered from sun or wind,
and their children will not remember or care
who felled the trees that put them there.

—Patience Bouchard

A letter from the north has come this morn'
As autumn's chill, crisp air awakens sense.
And rosy reds the poet's cheeks adorn
While small, moist puffs display the breath as mist.
The sky, a huge, domed canopy of blue,
Admits one lone inhabitant, the sun,
Whose rays, like cloaks, with warmth the earth endue,
And wind is still, its unseen course is run.
Across the way the trees in autumn dress
Present themselves in multi-shaded hues,
While geese above to south their way do press
As if some unseen Spirit gives them cue.
And, if we mortals would this Spirit hear,
We, too, would walk in autumn's time of year.

—Michael Toland

THE NIGHT OF THE UNIVERSE

So beautiful it is, As beautiful
as the sunset on the ocean.
So fearless it is, As fearless
as a little puppy.
So fearful it is, As fearful
as a savage beast.
So peaceful it is, As peaceful as
the calm ocean.
It is beautiful,
It is fearless,
It is fearful,
It is peaceful,
It is the darkness that surrounds you.
It is the night in the universe!

—Lynette Silverfox

THE WEIGHTLIFTER

He may be doing it for Friday night
When the fans are cheering ready for a fight
Or to build his muscles big and strong
So he can pose all day and all night long
To impress the girls that he may see
Or (maybe) to impress you and me
He could be a wrestler to pin his foe
Ready to play from the word go

No matter what his trade may be
If you go and watch him then you'll see
That he's doing the best that he can
To prove to his coach that he is a man
To prove to everyone that he can take it
And when he plays he won't have to fake it
Because life is tough and the world is cruel
He's making his body a sellable tool

—Brady Redus

MORNING

The sun starts to wake up
the stars have gone to sleep,
All I hear are soft sweet birds
and a little peep.
The sun's sweet glare
and the morning air,
waken you from sleep.
The sun that glows
helps you know
that morning's here again.

—Shannon Carraher

MOONLIGHT ON THE SNOW

I ventured out of doors tonight,
And there was a light upon the snow;
Then I looked up into the winter sky
And saw the stars and moon a'glow.
"How beautiful," I said to God,
As there was no one else around;
And in that eerie stillness,
I could not hear a sound.
I think He heard my comment —
How could any mortal know?
But, His presence was most evident
In that moonlight on the snow.

—Robert R. McEllhiney

WHISPER OF THE WIND

A whisper of the wind
That's what you've been
A brilliant second in time
In this dreary life of mine.

A warm glow in the dark night
That's what knowing you has been like
The sparkle in those golden brown eyes
touched by a smile.

But now you've gone away
While only your memory stays
And the word "Darlin' "
On my mind.

But you'll always be my dear friend
And remembered very fondly
Whenever there's a whisper of the wind.

—Maggie Burrow

WILLOWY BREEZE

Blow willowy waking breeze,
Display your softness upon the trees.
Rustle sweetly autumn leaves,
And kiss the waves upon the seas.

Sweep across the mountain tops,
Touch the blossoms of the crops.
Blow across the valleys wide,
And carry my lover to my side.

Blow as nothing else should dare,
Clustered whispers on the air.
Run your fingers through my hair,
And caress the heart of my love so fair.

Kiss the early morning dew,
And carry the planes that ride with you.
Blow beautiful breezes do,
And I shall not cease to follow you.

—Barbarayn Faircloth Filippetta

THE MAN WITH THE PIN . . . .

You've called again . . . and why?
   Aren't we just playing the fool's games; the
   endless teasing, the taunting names?
Don't you know if this persists — you'll hurt me
   once again in this?
My tender heart continuously aches for you, I've
   no choice — these matters always bear a
   heavy price.
I will abstain and refrain; to cause not even you
   the heartache nor the pain. This torment's
   great indeed for me, I must move on and set
   you free.
Please, don't take me lightly in all of this . . . I
   do hurt, I do love, I do wonder for endless
   moments on, "when will this charade desist?"
   Will anything just come out of this?
I want to be good, I want to be right . . . but
   then again and again; I'm wishing you here
   beside me by night. WHY?
I want to let go, I want to hold on . . . my mind
   and my heart just keep tugging along. One
   going this way and one going that. Do you
   feel the same? Or have I been truly alone or
   surely to blame?
Just tell me this, dear Sir without shame . . .
   what gives?
Is it me? Is it your name? Or, is all of this just
   insane?
Please answer . . . from within — Oh, Man with
   the Pin . . . .

   —Jasmin Peña

DREAMS—EBB AND FLOW

The waves roll in with new promises.
   Each one holds a dream; a dream of freedom
   with you.
You and I, this is where we began.
You and I, walking hand in hand, listening to the
   sounds of freedom.
Listening to the constant rush of the sea, waiting
   for treasures in the sand.

You chose the place, I chose the time.
Together we would face the dreams and pain.
We knew we were wrong, because we shared a
   love that was forbidden.
At the time, we were sure that like the waves, we
   could hold the dream.
We were sure that we could hold on to what was
   real.

Storms blew in and darkened our shore, and
   treasures rolled in no more.
As the waves rolled away, our dreams vanished,
   too.
What else can we do—you remain in our place, and
   I, I must be strong to face the remains of the
   storms.
I walk alone now on our shore, with memories of
   you.

Memories of sunsets, moonlit walks on the beach,
   and laughter in the sun.
Our hearts will always know that the love will
   forever show;
But only in our dreams, as the waves carry them
   away.

   —Martha L. Londeree

The bird's wings spread
   As it lifts off
Into the night's powerful stillness.
The stars continue
To sing their song
While the bird flies on
Into the powerful stillness of the night.

   —Sarah Rodgers, age 12

WINDFALL

In my isolated kingdom of martyrdom I endure
tight-lipped season after season. Never do I
shriek profanely towards my antagonist. Because
I languish the refining of my tarnished armor,
so that I may overcome this pure immersing agony.
Oh patience and courage be my pillow tonight.
Health-giving slumber do pour out upon me.

   The fear of death! Why do I feel the opening
of Pandora's Box upon my soul? The coldness
of death masquerades inside my empty heart.

   In the darkest part of my mind's eye; a flight
of love came down the oracle of God chanting
in a radiant breeze — "Peace."

   How lovely the sound of my empty heart
being filled. Filling my soul with brilliance and
splendor; the gentle spirit reaches out and warms
my very soul and tenderly strums my heart stings.

   Oh how the flame of the spirit burns through-
out my dust encompassing my lamenting mind.
Holy fire purify my mind; ignite the blaze with
my contrite tears.

   Oh celestial spirit pour balm upon my wounds
and heal my faculties; for I know the purity of
the mind is given freely from you through peace.
Indeed, it is receivable to all gentlemen who will
humble themselves and simply ask for it.

   —Terry S. Chambliss

MISSING THINGS RIGHT IN FRONT OF YOU.

Although I'm awoke I'm still
asleep, because I'm missing
things right in front of me.

Things important are in front of
   me, clear as day. But I don't
see them and I walk the other way.

I went to sleep at night but
   didn't wake up. I look well
and alive, but that's what you
   thought.

I see, but I don't see the
   world and how it lies. I
don't see because I'm looking
   with a natural eye.

Close the natural eye and
   open the eye of the mind,
And see how much more you will
   find.

   —Kesha Broady

About The Authors

Authors are listed in alphabetical order by name or pen name.

Kristen Alphin

Mrs. Mabel Amsden

Dixie Lynn Anderson

Dom A. Apikos

JEANNE ARNOLD was born May 17, 1934, in Harlan County, KY. Her education includes two years business college. She is owner and operator of Jeannes Antiques, 11610 Leitchfield Rd., Cecilia, KY 42724, and is married to Verne Arnold. **Dedication:** In memory of my Grandmother Narcissus Irvin Middeleton.. 127

Jeanne Arnold and her husband Verne

SHARIF ATKINS was born Jan. 29, 1975, in Pittsburgh, PA. He is a 9th grade student at Whitney Young High School in Chicago, IL, and a member of the USTA Tennis Association. This is his first published piece. **His comments:** I truly love writing, not just poetry but speeches and stories. God has blessed me with the ability to write and I do use it wisely. I remember a year ago, after giving my valedictory speech, the applause and the smiling faces. . . from that moment I knew my writing was a blessing........................ 226

Sharif Atkins

DONALD MAURICE AVERY was born May 14, 1953, in Miami Beach, FL. He graduated from School of Visual Arts, 1979; won Humanities Award that year; BA in Fine Arts. He is a musician-poet. **His comments:** Just write about my times and survival of 80's.. 131

CECILE W. AYLOR was born May 18, 1923, in Brightwood, VA. Her education includes: high school, 1940; Mary Washington College, 1944; University of Virginia, M.ED., 1962. She never married. Her memberships are: Alpha Phi Sigma (honorary); AARP; Queen Esther Chap. 14; Brightwood "Happy" Homemakers. From 1981 to 1989 she was published in weekly newspaper **Eagle**, Madison, VA: **Brightwood Hi-lights**, social visitation news; and poetry under **Owl's Corner** at the present time. **Her comments:** Highlight for me was having my editor publish my poem in weekly county newspaper. Writing poetry since retirement has afforded me a way to "keep busy" and happy at the same time!.. 171

Cecile W. Aylor

JIMMY BAKER was born June 25, 1977, in Effingham, IL. He is in the 7th grade at Newton Central Grade School in Newton, IL, and is 12 years old. **His comments:** I have been writing stories and poetry for 2 years. Someday I hope to become a writer. I woke up in the middle of the night with the words to **Feelings** running through my mind, so I put them down on paper right away.. 196

Jimmy Baker

NANCY BENTON BAKER was born Dec. 30, 1963, in Baltimore, MD. She is a student. **Her comments:** I know we have a very real problem today with old people and the illnesses they have to face. They can be so alive inside even though they're crippled or feeble. I tried to express what aging people face and what they wish even though these opportunities may not be available to them...... 73

Nancy Benton Baker

J. SOPHIE BARTON was born in Saskatchewan, Canada. Her education includes one year high school and one year business college, Success Regina Sask. She is retired, and her husband, William, is deceased. Her poetry and lyrics were published in Nanaimo, B.C., in 1983 (Book 1) and 1985 (Book 2). **River's End and My Old Guitar** received a small award in the sixties in the Scribes Column, Cowichan Leader, Duncan, B.C. **Her comments:** The sources of my inspiration are no doubt my fondness for poetry and moving a great deal in western Canada. In latter years I have travelled extensively in distant countries—viz: Hawaii, southern U.S.A., British Isles, south Africa, New Zealand, Costa Rica, twice, as well as Montreal and Toronto in Eastern Canada...... 236

J. Sophie Barton

MELISSA BATHRICK was born October 4, 1974, in Northern Dutchess Hospital, Rhinebeck, NY 12572. She is a sophomore at Red Hook High School, Red Hook, NY 12571...... 204

Melissa Bathrick

WANDA WOOTEN BAUGESS was born Jan. 27, 1932, in Richardson, KY. She attended high school in Louisa, KY, and is a cashier for Luby's Cafeterias, Inc. She married James S. Baugess on August 21, 1969, and is a member of East Texas Song Writers Assoc. **Sonshine of My Life** (10 songs, one tape) was produced by Al Petty, Love Concept Studio, Overton, TX, in 1989. She received the Harmonious Honor Award from New York Pro/AM Song Jubilee, 1986. **Her comments:** Most of my works are put to music. "God and My Country" are my inspirations. I hear a statement, see a beautiful mountain, or flowers and I can see a whole verse of poetry or song. I have written 32 songs and over 50 poems...... 146

PAULA DIANE BELL was born March 31, 1976 in Hermiston, OR. She is currently in the 8th grade at Echo Jr. High. She has received School Athletic Awards in volleyball, basketball and track in 1987 and 1988...... 170

Paula Diane Bell

MARCELLUS BOSWORTH was born Jan. 22, 1906, in E. St. Louis, IL. He has a high school education, and is retired from the Post Office. He married his wife, Irene, on June 6, 1926. He is a member of Ft. Worth Poetry Society. His publications include **Sit A Spell** published in Osage Beach, MO, 1974; **Forward Is Forever**, Osage Beach, MO, 1975; **Third Time Around**, Ft. Worth, TX, 1986. He received the Truman Medallion in 1975 and a Citation from the Missouri Senate in 1974. In 1975 he was named Poet Laureate of Osage Beach (Mo.). **His comments:** I had own poetry column in 2 weekly newspapers for 8 years in Osage Beach, Mo. area pertaining to beauty of Nature, humanity's failures and achievements, humor, tragedy. Also, a series of poems entitled **Vanishing America** recalling things of the Past. Over 450 poems... 155

Marcellus Bosworth

LILIAN P. BRINTON (Mrs. Hugh) was born Sept. 20, 1905, in Raleigh, NC. She received an MA—Sociology from UNC, Chapel Hill, 1930, and an M.S.— Social Work, Catholic University, 1943. She is a housewife and a widow, married June 12, 1928. Her memberships include WILPF - AAUW; NARFE. Her awards include First Prize, District #8, N.C. Federation of Women's Clubs, 1989.. 13

Lilian P. Brinton

RACHEL ANGELA BROWN was born July 13, 1975, in Charlestown, Carolina. Her education includes Narragansett Elementary, South Kingstown Junior High, Coventry Jr. High. Her memberships include Washington County cheerleading. **The Kite** was published in **Merlyn's Pen**, 1987. **Her comments:** My poetry reflects my perspective on life. The way I see other people as well as how I feel myself.. 87

Rachel Angela Brown

MAURA OMETZ BURD was born March 23, 1962, in Pittsburgh, PA. Her education includes Mars High School, Mars, PA, and Robert Morris College, Pittsburgh, PA. She married her husband, Randell, in 1985. Her publications include **Touch** in **Poetic Voices**, 1989. She received the Golden Poet Award from World of Poetry in 1985. **Her comments:** I believe writing is a positive approach to understanding one's inner feelings. My inspiration most often comes from spiritual and emotional experiences that have touched my life.. 205

Maura Ometz Burd

HECTOR J. BURKE was born Aug. 26, 1913, in New Brunswick, Canada. He has an education through 4th Grade, and is a retired Electronic Technician. He married his wife, Ann Marie, on July 3, 1932. His memberships include 4th Degree K of C... 235

Hector J. Burke

CHRISTY LIN BURTON was born Feb. 22, 1972, in Grenada, Miss. Her education includes Iuka High School graduate, Iuka Junior High, Olive Branch Middle School, Water Valley Elementary School, Smithville Kindergarten. She is a member of Southern Poetry Assoc. Her publications include **Breaking My Reality** in **Southern Poetry Review,** 1987, and **You Promised Me Love** in **Poems to Remember,** 1988. Her awards include Featured Writer in Response to Life, 1988... 144

Christy Lin Burton

JESSIE HOLDEN BUTTRAM was born May 31, 1933, in McDonald, TN. She received a BA in special education in the area of visual impairment and taught briefly in a classroom situation for the visually impaired before moving to a city where there was no such program. She married H. Jeff Buttram, Jr. (now deceased) on Dec. 22, 1958. Her work **Mostly My Going Is Up** was published in 1982. **Her comments:** I do not write about what happens to me but about how to react to and handle what happens to me. I am a close observer of others, and many of my poems are not personal but reflect my interpretation of their reactions to situations... 15

DONALD CLAY CAMPBELL was born Jan. 8, 1959, in Cleveland, Ohio. His education includes high school—John Marshall; college—Cuyahoga Community College Associate's Degree Business Management. He is a Production Supervisor and married Lynn Marie Campbell on Aug. 2, 1986. **His comments: Threshold to beauty** was simply a poem derived from the meeting and courtship of my now wife Lynn. This poetic work reflects that physical appearance is only the beginning to behold. One must then look beyond the threshold and discover the beauty of one's heart and soul.. 213

Donald Clay Campbell

ROBIN LYNN CARROLL was born Dec. 7, 1958, in Eupora, Miss. She graduated from Eupora High School, Mississippi State University and worked on Masters Degree at Miss. State University. She is a Certified Lighting Consultant and owner of Lighting Showroom. She married Larry Carroll on April 22, 1984. **Her comments:** I write poetry when I feel certain emotions about people or things. I usually write them in about ten minutes. I have only given one other poem to someone. I gave it to my mother who is a very special person. I write poetry when I sometimes cannot put into words how I feel... 59

Robin Carroll

SUE HUNT CARTER was born April 1, 1936, in Menard, Texas. Her education includes Wichita Falls (Texas) Sr. High School, Wichita Falls Draughon's Business College; private painting classes (won 24 ribbons with "Artist of the Year" California); private lessons in music and piano; performing at the Danville Etude Academy, California. She is an Artist and Business Manager of their own Roofing Consulting Firm. She married Guy Ross Carter on Nov. 22, 1956. She is a candidate for DAR (existing line established) and a member of NSWA (Nat. Songwriters West. Assoc.), and San Jose Real Estate Board (Ca.). She received awards for her paintings **Barn Scene,** 1976; **Covered Bridge,** 1974; **Aspens,** 1973. **Her comments:** My inspiration comes when I am of a quiet mind. In turn I reflect on feelings or happenings which are not spoken very often but are important to me. Then I find my pen and paper and record them usually just for me, but on occasion I share the words. I think good feelings shared in the form of words on paper feels like a warm warm hug... 28

Sue Hunt Carter

JESSE CENTENO was born Nov. 26, 1950 in Port Lavaca, Texas and graduated 1970 from Holland High School, attended 3½ years at Grand Rapids Junior College, and is not married. Publications include: **A Place of Beauty** published by **American Poetry Assoc.,** 1989; **To Fear** published by **The Poetry Center,** 1989; **The Composer** in **N. Mentor Magazine,** 1982; **Love Me No More** published in **Cambridge,** 1988. Jesse received awards for **A Place of Beauty,** July 1989; **To Fear,** Sept. 1989; **The Composer,** March 1982. **Comments:** Words of poems express the feelings through a person's heart. Poetry brings out the inner self beyond our comprehension.. 212

KORY CHAVEZ was born March 9, 1951, in Waimea, Kauai, Hawaii. He has an Associate in Science Degree and is an Administration Clerk. His memberships include International Longshoresmen Warehouse Union Mixed Bowling League. **His comments:** This poem is about an american daydreamer thinking of the social rewards of success for his futuristic living. The author describes the wants and personality traits of wishing the dreams to come true.. 90

Kory Chavez

CHARMAINE WHITE COLE was born Jan. 22, 1956, in Baxley, Georgia. Her education includes Appling Co. High School; Waycross Jr. College for Real Estate. She is a Bookkeeper-Secretary part time, and married Michael A. Cole on June 27, 1981. **Her comments:** I have written poetry since grade school. It is a form of therapy for me since I usually feel myself relax after I begin a new poem.. 251

Charmaine White Cole

MARY KATHLEEN COOK was born Feb. 6, 1971 in Norfolk, VA. She is working on her G.E.D.; went to Vero Beach Senior High, quit in 11th grade. Her memberships include Key Club, Save Dolphins, National Geographic, World, Wildlife. **Her comments:** Poetry to me is a mood. I can't just sit down and write a poem. I have to be in a cheerful, sad, curious or really just any kind of mood. When I get into a mood I sit down and then there is a new poem... 165

DEBORAH COOPER was born Jan. 27, 1953, in Graham, Texas. She has a high school education, and is a Song Writer, Poem Writer, Mother and Housewife. She married Tom Cooper on March 27, 1979. **Her comments:** The love that I have and feel for my husband, Tom, and children—Mark, Angela and Kelley, gives me an insight of life that I will forever appreciate, and my love and compassion for people will always reach to the inner-most depths of my heart... my feelings are my words.. 132

Deborah Cooper and husband Tom

FLOSSIE CRAMER was born Jan. 22, 1898 to Lucy and James Higgins near Willow Hill, IL. She attended Willow Hill High School, Teachers State College, Charleston, IL; Teachers College, Danville, IN; and the University of Michigan, Ann Arbor, MI. She taught school twenty years and served as Assistant County Superintendent of Jasper County Schools in the office of her husband for twelve years. Since she has retired she has written poetry as a hobby. She had one book published—**Poems For Pleasure and Treasure Verses.** She is in **Who's Who and the Poet's Hall of Fame** published by National Society of Published Poets. She has received 108 awards from many contests and poetry societies. In 1987 she received The Golden Award from The World of Poetry. She just received word that she has been nominated for this award for 1989.. 256

Flossie Cramer

BRANDY ROSE CUMMINGS was born Nov. 14, 1975, in Evansville, IL. She is presently a student in the 8th Grade at North Junior High School in Henderson, KY. Her poem, **My Grandma,** was published in 1989.......................... 44

Brandy Rose Cummings

GRACE R. DALZELL was born December 2, 1936, in Mexico City, D.F. **Her comments:** Writing has been my first love for more years than I can remember. Fortunately, the course of my life has endowed me with a vast storehouse of experiences, memories and feelings from which many of my poems are born. To me, writing poetry is spiritual in that I am somehow redefined and recreated in each of my works.. 126

Grace R. Dalzell

PENNI DAVIS was born August 5, 1973, in Memphis, TN. She is a Junior in High School. Her memberships include National Roller Skater in 1981 to '86, cheerleader her sophomore year, French Club. **Her comments:** No matter where you go, there are people treated unfair and don't fit in. If you are one of these people my advice to you is to always keep your head high for which if things are at its worst, the best is yet to come........... 269

Penni Davis

JULIE DeJESUS was born May 16, 1979, in Brooklyn, NY. She is a grade school student. She received a certificate plus cash prize in Sebring Lake Poets' Student Contest for **A Flower** on May 11, 1989..................................... 236

Julie DeJesus

CARMEN DELGADO was born Dec. 5, 1944, in Edinburg, TX. Her education includes High School and Beauty College. She is a Cosmetologist. **Her comments:** My inspiration was the behavior of a child, my mixed emotions towards a special friend and the sadness of a betrayed one............... 200

Carmen Delgado

Gerre DeLongis

GERRE DeLONGIS was born June 1, 1940, in Floral Park, New York. She is Community News Columnist for **Smithtown News** and married her husband, Bill, Aug. 27, 1966. Her memberships include: Smithtown Township Arts Council; secretary, Smithtown Writer's Guild; editor, SEPTA Newsletter named **The Advocate. Her comments:** I have written poetry since my teens. The following poem, **A Writer's Prayer,** explains the way "I am inspired to write":

```
Show us the way
  With words, oh Lord
    So that our writings will
    Enlighten, brighten, minds in numbers
    Give hope to hearts once still.
If just one word or sentence
Just one page or chapter small
    Makes another living being, feel
    Alive, worthwhile—in awe
Then lead us to write great novels
Children's stories, poems unending
    For we know the words
    We speak and write
Are gifts that you are sending.
```
...... 270

Angela Marie DeMario

ANGELA MARIE DeMARIO was born March 31, 1969, in Norwalk, CT. She is presently attending Sarah Lawrence College, and plans to be a future writer and counselor. **Her comments:** My dreams are just beginning! Thanks to Mom and Dad for believing in me and to my sister for her encouragement. Special thanks to Frank for taking me on the "Roadtrip" and to my Chucky, who continues to be my source of inspiration. I love you all 190

Deb Donat

DEB DONAT (FRIE) was born July 4, 1962, in St. Paul, MN. Her education includes Woodbury High School, Woodbury, MN, and Lakewood Community College, White Bean Lake, MN. She is a Registered Nurse, and married Al Donat on Aug. 18, 1984. **Her comments:** Inspired with many fond memories of my paternal grandparents, I wrote this poem shortly after they passed away. My poetry writing includes one other poem...... 183

Penny Ann DuBroc

PENNY ANN DuBROC was born July 28, 1961, in New Orleans, LA. She is a student at N.H.C.C. of Houston, TX, graduating in December 1990. **Her comments:** My inspiration to write comes from my family, heart-felt emotions and personal experiences...... 235

Mrs. Harriet S. Eckles

MRS. HARRIET S. ECKLES was born Jan. 21 in Hot Springs, AR. She attended high school and two years of University of Missouri, Columbia, MO. She is retired and widowed. She married Harry Fabron Garard Oct. 1, 1944, and William C. Eckles, Feb. 17, 1980. Her memberships include: Daughters of the American Revolution, Daughters of the American Colonists, United Daughters of the Confederacy, Charity's 20th Century Club of Missouri, Extension Homemakers of Boone County, Missouri. She has a certificate of award from the Missouri Writers' Guild, Columbia, MO, certifying that she received recognition April 30, 1977 for the poem published in this an-

(Continued on next page)

thology. **Her comments:** When I heard of the death of my cousin, Miss Frances Cornelia Hardin of Hot Springs, Arkansas, who was an accomplished musician and artist, I shed tears as I wrote my little poem, and would love to have it published in memory of Cousin Fannie...................... 251

JAMES M. ELLIS, JR. was born Sept. 29, 1959, in Hollis, Harmon Co., OK. He attended Arnett of Hollis, small country school for all of the twelve years, graduating in 1977 with honors. He is a tonsorial artist and striving writer. He married Lisa Marie Ellis on July 28, 1986, and is a devoted member of the National Rifle Association; active member of the community; loving father. He was named Grade School Valedictorian in 1973. **His comments:** The majority of all inspiration is purely from the heart, reflections of past experience, some of wondrous joy and other of sorrowful memories. All of which translated together becomes the fountain for my pen.................... 115

James M. Ellis, Jr.

LILLY ERICKSON was born Dec. 6, 1910, in South Dakota. She is a retired seamstress, and married John Erickson on Oct. 22, 1988. She is a member of Elim Lutheran Church and American Legion Auxiliary. **Her comments:** I wrote mostly about people and just for pleasure... 26

Lilly Erickson

LILLIAN FABIAN was born Oct. 18, 1954, in Newark, N.J. She is a graduate of Harrison High School and has a certificate in non-fiction writing at NYU. She is an administrative assistant. **Her comments:** This is my first poem and it was written during a sad period in my life. The message is: There's always hope no matter how bad things seem.. 209

Lillian Fabian

NANCY LUISA FALZONE was born Feb. 23, 1955, in Springfield, MA. She is employed at a hospital for chronic-care residents, and also is involved with mentally ill participants as a Community Integration Specialist. **Her comments:** I write poems about what touches my own soul, and about what I witness as touching the soul of others. Realistic joy and pains; giving, and sharing; is my inspiration in this world so beautiful, yet so tragic............. 186

Nancy Luisa Falzone

DEE FERGUSON-MARTINEZ was born Sept. 9, 1952, in Florida. She attended high school in Del Rio, Texas and attended college (Texas Southmost) in Brownsville, Texas. She is a former high school drama teacher, and married her husband, Peter Robert, in 1972. They have three children. **Her comments:** I write poetry to set free the highest spirit from within. We are all poets; all people are touched by the muse. It is as fundamental as breath.. 237

Dee Ferguson-Martinez

LINDA D. FERRARO was born Dec. 31 (Capricorn) in Bronx, NY. Her education includes: Licensed Medical Technician, Registered Nurse, Bachelor of Science in Nursing, Clinical Nurse Practitioner, Medical Social Worker. She is self-employed as owner of "The Faded Rose" Used Clothing and Knick Knack Shop. She married the late John Ciccone on Nov. 27, 1970. Her memberships include: National League of Nursing, American Nursing Association, American Association of Psych. Nurses, Life Member Utility Workers Union of America Local 1&2, Life Member National Rifle Association, Wm. H. Morton Fire Co. Ladies Auxiliary, Hunka (Relative) St. Joseph's Indian School Vision Quest. Her publications include **Gratitude** in **Golden Treassury of Great Poems**, 1988; **Yesterday, Today and Tomorrow** in **Great Poems Vol. II**, 1989; **Nature's Mysteries** in **Great Poems of the Western World Vol. II**, 1990. She received the Golden Poet Award in 1988 and 1989; Honourable Mention Award of Merit Certificates March 1988, June 1988, October 1988, November 1988, January 1989. **Her comments:** My life experiences, people I've met and known, a love of nature, all have inspired me. I originally started out when I was younger writing verses for greeting cards for Price Advertising Agency in the Bronx. I have to "feel" a poem, and the verses come spontaneously, I can't just sit down and say "I'm going to write a poem.".. 136

RUTH GODDARD FINCH was born Sept. 20, 1906 in Boston, MA. She has an eighth grade education, and is a housewife. She married William B. Finch (deceased) on Feb. 10, 1924. Her memberships include Veterans of Foreign Wars Auxiliary 161, Tri States Country Music Association, Country Music Association of Nashville. **Turn Back** was published in **World Poetry Anthology,** 1988. She received an award for **The Mountain** in 1987. **Her comments:** Started writing poetry at age 11. Inspirational and activities around me. Personal—regarding friends and relatives.. 165

Ruth G. Finch

EMMANUEL SERGE FRASIER SR. was born in Haiti. He attended Staten Island Community College of New York, and is an engineer. He married M-Gladys on June 7, 1973. His publications include **Mother Nature**, published in U.S.A. 1989. **His comments:** My source of inspiration: The Bible, my childhood and time I used to spend in the wood. My occupation...................... 171

Emmanuel Serge Frasier Sr.

Lisa Fullwood

LISA STEWMAN FULLWOOD was born May 5, 1959, in Abilene, TX. She is a high school graduate of Highland I.S.D. and attended Texas Tech University. She is a housewife/rancher/farmer/aerobics instructor, and married Scott Fullwood on August 5, 1978. Her memberships include Nolan Co. Farm Bureau Young Farmers and Ranchers, Roscoe Church of Christ, American Breeders Assoc. **Her comments:** My husband's Aunt is a very dear friend to me. When she was 6½ months pregnant the baby died. The doctors had to induce labor a week later. The whole experience was so traumatic. I was filled with empathy. Sometimes my emotions and feelings run so deep— the only way to express them is to read them and weep. And yes, it did snow on that very sad day. My husband and I have 3 sons, Jake 9, Zach 6, and Cole 2. One of my goals in life is to "Author" and illustrate children's books. I'm working on the illustrations for two I have written. My main objective with any of my writings, is to entertain—touch—demand thoughts—and somehow get inside the reader and share their feelings... 197

Danita Elaine Gibson

DANITA ELAINE GIBSON was born March 18, 1967 in Columbus, GA. Her education includes Hardaway High School, '85, Advanced College Preparatory Curriculum; Clemson University, '89, B.A. English; Columbia University, '90, M.S. Journalism. She is a free lance writer and student. Her memberships include National Association of Black Journalists, New York Association of Black Journalists, Society of Professional Journalists, Blue Key Honor Fraternity, Delta Sigma Theta Sorority, Sigma Tau Delta English Honorary Society, Omicron Delta Kappa Leadership Honorary, Order of Omega Greek Honorary Society, Alpha Psi Omega Honorary Dramatics Society. She has received numerous oratorical and speaker awards, plus Brunswick Yarns Theater Excellence Award, 1988; Who's Who Among American College Students, 1989; Outstanding College Students of America, 1989; Outstanding Young Women of America, 1989. **Her comments:** Writing is a cathartic experience for me. Through writing, I am better able to understand myself and those things I love: my family, friends, my people, life in general. Also, I am able to reconcile some of the inherent contradictions of life and realize that there are just some things that God never intended for us to understand. Yet, I am still able to question those things through my writing, and for that opportunity to write, I am a freer, more intuned, uninhibited person (at least on paper)...................................... 42

Mabel D. Gilmore

MABEL D. GILMORE was born Oct. 12, 1909, in Hundred, WV. Education: Elementary and High School, Hundred, WV, graduated 1927; West Virginia University, Morgantown, WV—AB, 1931; Geo. Peabody College for Teachers (now Vanderbilt), Nashville, TN—MA, 1938; Post Graduate Work: West Virginia University; Morris Harvey College (now Charleston University) and Mason School of Fine Arts and Music, Morgantown and Charleston, WV respectively. Occupation: Taught in secondary schools for 36 years (Hundred High School; Scott High School, Madison, WV; Chestertown High School, Chestertown, MD; Magnolia High School, New Martinsville, WV). For one year after finishing her AB she did secretarial work for her father, H.B. Mayne, who was Field Foreman for Columbia Gas Co. She owned and operated "The Old Hundred Art Shop" in hometown. After teaching her last year at Magnolia High School, she retired 1974. Date of marriage: March 31, 1939. Spouse's name Delbert E. Gilmore (now deceased since 1975). Memberships in professional and social organizations: county, state and national teachers' organizations; Phi Epsilon Phi (honorary botany fraternity); Theta Upsilon (college sorority); Delta Kappa Gamma and Alpha Delta Kappa (two international honoraries for women educators); West Virginia Garden Club, Trillium Garden Club of New Martinsville; West Virginia Writers, Inc.; Wheeling Garden Center, Wheeling, WV; Friends of the Library, New Martinsville, WV; Order of Eastern Star; member of First Christian Church (Disciples of Christ), New Martinsville, WV. Publications: **Poetic Potpourri** (a volume of original poems) 1983; theme poem from this volume, **Poetic Potpourri** in **Poetic Voices of America** (1987); **Master Artist** in **Poetic Voices of America** (1988); **In Due Time** in **Treasured Poems of America** (1989); **Winterized** in **Treasured Poems of America** (1990) this volume; **Always, With Love** (dedicated to my husband) winner of Golden Poet Award, World of Poetry and published in **Great American Poetry Anthology** (1987); **West Virginia Whiskers** in **Down The Road** (1985); **Cleaning Time** and **Verse Pains** in **Best of Hill and Valley** (1985). Awards: **Look Up and Sing** Holiday Contest of World of Poetry 1987, Golden Poet Award for **Always, With Love** 1987 received at World of Poetry Convention, 1987 in Las Vegas, NV; Honorable Mention for **Priceless Sky Art** in the New American Contest, 1987; Fourth Place for **Fastidious Summer** in Goddess of Love Contest, 1987; and Honorable Mention for **Paid in Full** in New Golden Contest, 1987. Several awards for oils, water colors, charcoals, woodblock prints etc. entered in exhibits in West Virginia. Selected as West Virginia Biology Teacher of the Year 1973. **Her comments:** Since my poetry is so much a part of me, I like to share it with others. Having taught biology, science, physical education and art, I associated with many interesting teach-

(Continued on next page)

295

ers and students. Since I now live alone since 1975, I often read my "pennings" to friends who will listen and criticize. Willing ones become my "sounding boards." Other sources of inspiration come from varied activities: church, painting, crafts, volunteer work, clubs, travel, nature study. When I can no longer contain my ideas, I jot them down. My retirement from teaching has been anything but dull. I am busy and happy. Giving readings is fun.. 18

grace g. glaros was born Oct. 10, 1916, in Pittsburgh, PA. Her education includes High School and Art and Ceramic Courses at Carnegie Tech. She is a Home maker and Secretary, married to E. Michael Glaros on Aug. 13, 1938. **Her comments:** No penchant toward poetry ever surfaced in my life until 1972, when I was miraculously reborn. I began to be awakened before daybreak by the sound of words in my mind, accompanied by a compulsion to put them on paper, securing for me my family's title: "The Night Writer." I wholeheartedly believe that it is a gift from "- - - - God my maker, who giveth songs in the night" (Job 35:10)... 48

grace g. glaros

RAYMOND P GLESSNER was born Oct. 17, 1966, in Ashland, PA. He is currently in his freshman year at Penn State's Schuylkill Campus..................... 269

Raymond P Glessner

ELIZABETH P. GODFREY was born June 17, 1951 in Greenville, GA. Her education includes: high school diploma, Greenville High; B.S. degree from Morris Brown College in Atlanta and Medical College of GA in Augusta, GA; post-baccalaureate, GA State University in Atlanta, GA. She is a Dental Office Manager, and married Dr. Grier Godfrey on August 25, 1971. Her memberships include Friend of Library of Newton County, Newton County Historical Society, Hospital Auxiliary of Newton Co., Habitat for Humanity, Education Committee Chairman at Bethlehem Baptist Church, Usher Board, and Missionary member. She organized the Youth Summer Feeding and Enrichment Program at Bethlehem Baptist Church. Her publications are: **Garland Hillman Made Historical Footprints in the Sands of Newton County** in **Atlanta**

Elizabeth P. Godrey

Daily World newspaper, 1987; **Garland Hillman Honored for Black History Month** (essentially the same article) in **Covington News**, 1989; **Family History of Dr. Grier Godfrey** in **History of Newton County**, 1988; **Education, Our Personal Responsibility,** an article listed as a letter to the editor in **Covington News**, 1987. She has received "applauses, standing ovations, but, no awards yet!!" **Her comments:** My poem(s) are written to inspire, encourage, and motivate. The poem, **What's on Yo'r Mind?,** is an overcoming experience in my life of worrying about trivial issues. I have written a play (30 min. performance approx.) which is in the process of publication... 151

ANNA L. E. GONZALES was born July 3 in Boston, MA. Her education includes A.B.—History; M.A.—European History; M.A.—Spanish Linguistics and Literature. She is an educator by profession, and a member of Massachusetts Society for the Prevention of Cruelty to Animals; Animal Rescue League of Boston—active member. **Her comments:** Inspiration comes from the beauty reflected in ordinary people and ordinary circumstances of life. All animals, large and small, are of special interest and concern... 181

Anna L. E. Gonzales

NELSON ALEXANDER GRANT was born Dec. 31, 1951, in New York City, NY. He is a graduate of St. Augustines College. His education was done in the U.S. and in the Bahamas. He is employed by the U.S. Postal Service and the U.S. Air Force; also a notary. He married his wife, Donna M., on May 9, 1973, and is a member of National Association of Letter Carriers and Non-Commission Officers Association. His awards include Mechanical Engineering, City and Guilds of London, 1971. **His comments:** I was inspired to write this poem due to the many events of today where man has tended not to use common sense and pushed nature aside. If this trend isn't corrected in time man will undoubtedly destroy himself... 170

Nelson Alexander Grant

MARIE C GRAY was born June 6, 1962, in Newark, NJ. She received a BA in English from Montclair State College, January 1989, and is a Network Marketeer. She married Thomas F. Gray on July 8, 1984, and is a member of MIDS (Miscarriage, Infant Death and Stillbirth Support Group). Her publications include: **When Someone Dies**, published October 1989; **The Wall**, November 1989; **A Sonnet for Tommy**, October 1989; **Thoughts in Limbo**, October 1989. **Her comments:** I have been writing both music and poetry since I was twelve years old. My themes have matured and basically focus on my family and children. My primary inspiration was one of healing after the death of my daughter Melissa Marie, (11-05-85—01-10-86) who died of SIDS, also my son Thomas Francis Jr. (11-10-86) and daughter Deirdre Elisabeth (02-19-89). My writing emits both therapy and love for these children..209

BESS BARNUM HALVORSON was born Feb. 14, 1904, in Eldora, Iowa. She attended grade school, high school, and two terms of college. She is a teacher, and married Almer Halvorson on June 2, 1926. Her memberships include church and social clubs. Her publications are: **Snow Angels** in **Cappers**, 1969; **The Enigma** in **Cappers**, 1988; **In Supplication** in **World of Poetry**, 1989; **Spring Magic** in **Cappers**, 1987. Her awards include: Award of Merit Certificate, 1989; Heart Songs, a book of poems, 1986, Cappers. **Her comments on her sources of inspiration:** Things that stir me as: babies, human and of the wild; a beautiful day, birds singing, wildflowers, meeting an old friend, the unkindness I read about against other races, etc........................ 71

Bess Barnum Halvorson

BETTY HAMAR was born Jan. 4, 1939, in South Georgia. Her education includes 12th grade; Beauty College. Her occupation is housewife, gospel singer, songwriter and poetry. She married Vernon Hamar on April 11, 1970. She has written over 200 poems and songs, some of which she has recorded. Her publications include: **God Loves America;** a 45 record, **Precious Memories of Elvis,** January 1979; an album, **Special Ways I Love You,** 1985. **Her comments:** I have been writing poetry since January 1976. It is a God given talent. I received this gift after dedicating my life to the Lord Jesus Christ. I am inspired by things I see and hear. I may be riding down the road. I may be awakened in the middle of the night. My most beautiful and best poems, were written, when my heart and mind was on Jesus. I am a gospel singer, songwriter and recording artist also. For what I am, or ever hope to be, I owe it all to my Lord and Savior Jesus Christ. I give Him all the glory.. 69

Betty Hamar

W.M. HARRISON was born April 18, 1904, in Arkansas, and has a high school education. She is retired, and her husband is deceased. **Her comments:** Since I don't have a recent picture I'm sending one a few years ago as I am now 85+ years old. I've always scribbled limericks but no serious poetry. My inspiration is Art Buchwald.. 145

W. M. Harrison

CINDY K. HEATH-DRAPER was born May 23, 1950, in Rockford, IL. She graduated from Millikan High School, Long Beach, CA, and received an AA Degree from Long Beach City College, Long Beach, CA. She is Sales Secretary for the Clock Tower Resort & Conference Center, Rockford, IL, and married James W. Draper on April 12, 1974. She is a member of Mahabarata (sorority) and Mothers of Multiples (twin's club). **Her comments:** My inspiration comes from my relationships with my husband, children, family and friends. This poem was written for my husband and a very special friend. I'll cherish their love and friendship forever. Love comes in many forms. I love all of you.. 147

Cindy K. Heath-Draper

RANDY CHAL HOLBROOK was born Jan. 29, 1965, in Winston-Salem, NC. He has an A.A.S. in Electronic Technology from Surry Community College, Dobson, NC. He is an Electronic Technician and married Judith Holbrook on Sept. 8, 1984. **His comments:** The poem was based on my marriage proposal. I have hundreds of poems but I have never taken the time to submit them. I believe the art of rhyme is dead and simple thoughts have replaced an art form... 25

Randy Chal Holbrook

DR. REX DERDEN HOLT was born Nov. 8, 1958, in Ellijay, GA. He has a BSA from University of Georgia and a DVM from University of Georgia College of Veterinary Medicine. He is a veterinarian, and married his wife, Kristin, on Feb. 21, 1987. His awards include Writer's Refinery Best of Blurbs, 1988. **His comments:** The inspiration for my poetry comes from life. The inspiration for my life lies in two beautiful and gracious ladies. Without my mother, Mrs. N.B. Holt, and my Significant Other, Dr. Kristin A Green, neither my life or poems would exist.. 36

Dr. Rex Derden Holt

ESTELLE HUGHES was born Sept. 31, 1938, in Maben, MS. She has a twelfth grade education and is a writer. She married Manville Hughes on June 22, 1960, and is a member of Church of God In Christ, in Eupora, MS. Her publications include **I Will Live The Way I Pray** in **Treasured Poems of America**, 1990. **Her comments:** What inspires me was that I love to write poems and because I love God.. 255

Estelle Hughes

KAREN KEEGAN HUTCHINSON spends busy days raising four children in the quaint New England town of Londonderry, NH. While supporting her family as president of a Real Estate Firm, her true love is for her family, community through civic involvement and writing. Her poetry reflects the joy of home and children; the pain of love and divorce, and the ironies of life in modern America... 88

Karen Keegan Hutchinson

THERESA ANN IACOVELLI was born Dec. 21, 1964, in Bridgeport, CT. She earned a high school diploma in Gainesville, FL, and is a mother and amateur writer. Her publications include **My Guardian Angel. Her comments:** I would like to become a known writer someday.................................... 81

Theresa Ann Iacovelli

JAKI-TERRY is the pen name of **LORRAINE J. TERRY**, who was born Aug. 13, 1956, in Wichita Falls, TX. Her education includes: Durham Technical Institute, Durham, NC (Business Administration); Hillside H.S., Durham, NC; Mergenthaler Voc.-Tech H.S., Baltimore, MD. She is a poet, and a member of American Society of Prof. & Executive Women; NAFE, Greenpeace. **Her comments:** Since I was 16, poetry has been a very special connection between me and Infinite Intelligence. I try to relate to simple things as my own inspiration dictates. In exposing myself to myself I'm better able to relate to humanity around me, and how much we need to regard each other........................... 210

ELIZABETH GRACE JEFFORDS was born Dec. 31, 1970, in Kearny, NJ. Her education includes Kearny High School; she is going to night school now. She is a secretary and aspiring writer. Her publications include: **Rose** in **Great Poems of the Western World**, 1989; **Money** in **A Time to be Free**, 1989. She received Honorable Mention for **John** in 1988, **Rose** in 1989, and **Autumn Leaves** in 1988. **Her comments:** Poetry is written emotion.. 101

TRISHA LeANN JENSEN was born March 13, 1974, in Emmett, ID. She is a sophomore in high school, and received an award in All High School Poetry Contest, 1988... 40

Trisha LeAnn Jensen

CJ JOHNSON was born Feb. 16, 1952, in Louisville, KY. She attended South Gate High, South Gate, CA, and Mohave Community College, Kingman, AZ. She is a Secretary/Bookkeeper, and married Allen J. Johnson on Aug. 17, 1985. **Her comments:** This poem was written for my husband who is a police officer. The inspiration for all my poetry comes from the Lord Jesus Christ and my love for my family.. 121

CJ Johnson

HELEN CHILDS JOHNSON was born April 1, 1922, in Louisiana. She is a teacher of arts and crafts, and a thirty-year member of the Fraternal Order of the Eastern Star. **Her comments:** Most of my works are drawn from memories of childhood and my love of nature, of my relationship with the creator of all, and a very strong desire to contribute something as tribute to one who lived.............. 68

JOSEPHINE LAMITINA JOHNSON was born March 2, 1923, in Rock Glen, New York (a small rural community, in western New York). She is a housewife, married to Robert P. Johnson. Her publications include **Just For Me** in **Poetic Voices of America 1988** and **My Brother** in **Treasured Poems of America 1989. Her comments:** Dedication: To Mrs. Charles (Marilyn Miller) Pasquale, of Leroy, NY, my wonderful and dear friend and neighbor. For all the big things and little things she has done for me. For all the love and compassion and for always being there for me. "Thank you, my dear friend." This is for you "Mrs. P.", with a heart full of love and gratitude........ 274

Josephine Lamitina Johnson

LYNNE MARIE JOHNSON was born in St. Paul, MN. She is a Reservation Agent/Northwest Airlines. **Her comments:** My poem was inspired by my little friend Ryan, who nearly drowned in the St. Croix River the summer of 1989. Welcome home, Ryan!................................. 181

Lynne Marie Johnson and Ryan

RONALD GARFIELD JOHNSTON was born July 20, 1960, in Baltimore, MD. He is educated through 9th grade, followed by GED. He is a truck driver, and married Joyce Johnston on June 5, 1982. **His comments:** My source of inspiration is hardship, people, and hard times. Emotional thoughts that can only come from experience of life, through the mind of one striving to do what is right... 163

Ronald Garfield Johnston

AMY JONES was born Dec. 21, 1965, in Ottumwa, Iowa. She has a B.S. Pharmacy from University of Arizona and will receive a doctorate degree in pharmacy from University of Arizona, 1990. She married Gary Grizzle on May 20, 1989, and is a member of Community Theatre, several pharmacy/university organizations (academic/social). Her awards include Iowa Poetry Contest, 1984, and College Poetry Presentation, 1986. **Her comments:** My family (Gary, Mom, Dad, two sisters: Kelli and Whitney) provides inspiration and encouragement. Plan to continue writing—combine with a career in pharmacy.. 276

Amy Jones

DOROTHY JEAN (HAMMON) KIMBALL was born Dec. 10, 1926, in Versailles, IN. Her education includes: high school graduate, 1944; one semester aviation; three semesters car tune-up and overhauling. Her occupation is farming and housewife. She married Robert W. Kimball on Feb. 3, 1946, and is a member of Dabney Baptist Church, Riley Cheer Guilds, Pilots Association, Senior Citizens. Her poem was published in **American Poetry**, 1989. Her awards include first place, Street Kana, Womens Hot Rod Nationals, 1984. **Her comments:** This poem was inspired by the trouble we've had with I.R.S. since my husband retired in 1981 and we tried to start our two businesses...... 104

Dorothy Jean (Hammon) Kimball

DESTINY KINAL was born Sept. 9, 1943, in Buffalo, NY. She has a B.A. from Indiana University and is working on her Masters in International Development. She is a Marketing Consultant; President, DKMC (nine years), and married Barry Skeist, M.D., on Oct. 13, 1985. She is a member of American Marketing Association. She says she is a "late bloomer. Though I write, I have not submitted for publication (other than articles) poetry or prose." **Her comments:** I come from a line of women who are oral or written historians/poetesses, my mother Constance and daughters Gilian and Solange. I am dedicated to both personal and planetary transformation. I garden as an additional source of inspiration..................................... 6

Destiny Kinal

Wanda Kinzie

WANDA KINZIE was born July 15, 1954, in Camp Lejeune, NC. She has a Bachelor of Science in Elementary Education from Old Dominion University in Norfolk, VA, and is a Free-Lance Lettering Artist. She married Michael R. Kinzie on Feb. 19, 1977. Her memberships include: Calligraphers' Guild of the (Virginia) Peninsula, The Washington (D.C.) Calligraphers' Guild, The Greater Cincinnati (Ohio) Calligraphers' Guild, and The Guild of the Golden Quill (Dayton, Ohio). Her two calligraphy pieces, **Calligraphers Are** by Gunnlauger SE Brien and **Man's Mind** by Oliver Wendell Holmes, were published in "Letterforum's" Perpetual Calendar **Put It In Writing,** 1988. She received an award in the Juried "Letterforum" International Calligraphy Conference Exhibit, 1988. **Her comments:** My children, Nicholas and Daniel were an inspiration to me in writing **A Young Boy...** While rocking one of my sons during a restless night, the verse came together. Later I executed a combined watercolor and calligraphy piece of artwork using **A Young Boy...** that was exhibited in the joint Metropolitan Museum of Art (N.E.) and The Washington (D.C.) Calligraphers' Guild Exhibit. Today the work hangs in my son's room.. 36

Michael Kluznik

MICHAEL KLUZNIK was born March 9, 1946, in Cleveland, Ohio. His education includes B.A. & M.A., University of Minnesota; graduate work in education at E. Mich. U.; graduate work school psychology, U. of Wisc. He is a Learning Disabilities Specialist, and married his wife, Darlene, in 1973. He is a member of National Association of School Psychologists (NASP). His publications include: **Incident at Pickerel Lake** (short story) in **Voice** newspaper, 1988; **NASP Urged to Take Position on Gun Control** and **Action Needed: A Gun-Burning Amendment** in **Communiqué,** 1989; numerous columns and letters to the editor in **Voice** newspaper and others, 1978-1989. His awards include Patron of Youth (YMCA), 1989; Chapman Award—Oustanding Achievement, 1965, U. of Minn.; Boy Scout of the Year, 1958. **His comments:** I write a column for a community newspaper, the **Voice.** I am interested in current political events, history, events in the natural world, the American Indian (especially the Dakota nation), dreams, love and self-discovery. I guess that's a lot, and certainly enough to write about for a long time. **Communiqué** is the newsletter of the National Assoc. of School Psychologists. I am also a licensed school psychologist but do not work in that title................. 8

Bert Knowles

BERT KNOWLES was born in Orange, NJ, on Jan. 6, 1915 (age 74). He has a BA Degree from Rutgers University College, New Brunswick, NJ in Literature and History, and a Diploma, American Law and Procedure, LaSalle, Chicago, IL. He served in N.J. National Guard and U.S. Marine Corps Reserve and is a retired Major, U.S. Marine Corps Reserve; N.J. National Guard Federalized—WW II—Korean. **His comments:** I've been writing poetry, about 630 poems, for the past 25 years. Am working on two novels of historical myth, a series of children's poems, Sea Saga Series of poetry, picture story poems. I am permanently disabled and retired since 1975. I'm interested in collecting fine books in Literature, History, Art, Horticulture and Religion... 207

Step Lavern Boles, IV

LAVERNE is the pen name of **STEP LAVERN BOLES, IV,** who was born May 20, 1952, in Hampton, SC. He is a graduate of Wade Hampton High in Hampton, SC, now attending Technical College of the Low Country in Beauford, SC. He married Ivy Lee Boles on Nov. 11, 1972, and is a minister at Cainhoy Miracle Revival Ctr. Inc. and a saxophonist. **His comments:** A few of sources of inspiration are from mythological gardens, historical landmarks, walks alone in the wilderness, but most from just listening and thinking from any atmosphere. I usually search my inner feeling............................. 29

B. H. LEE was born Dec. 20, 1951, in Galena Park, TX. She has a B.A. and M.A. from Texas Southern University, Houston, TX (English major, History minor), She is a teacher, and married Roy E. Lee on March 18, 1982. **Her comments:** My source of inspiration was my Dad, Attorney Millard C. Heath Sr. Although he died on September 1, 1988, he still brings happiness, peace and joy to my heart today.. 216

B. H. Lee

DEBRA E. LEONARD was born in Wichita, Kansas. She has a B.S. in Elementary Education, and is a teacher. **Her comments:** This poem is capsular in the aspect of emotions and thoughts following a high school reunion.—A veritable wealth of inspiration.. 281

Debra E. Leonard

KATHERINE LOCKWOOD was born Nov. 19, 1956 in Chicago, IL; significant place: Beckley, W.Va. (where parents are buried). Her education includes BA, Lake Forest College, 1979; attended Mount Holyoke College, 1974-77, with graduate courses at Smith, and at Lake Forest, in Art and Education. She is a parent, competitive horsewoman, poet and artist, novelist, (ex-teacher). She married Brion Miller on Nov. 24, 1976. Her memberships include National Arts Society, American Horse Shows Association, New England Horsemens Council. Her poems have been published in several anthologies. **Edwin and Johanna**, her book

Katherine Lockwood

of poems, was published in January 1979 by Great Lakes Poetry Press, Harwood Heights, IL. She was a finalist, Thorn Tree Press Competition, 1987, for **Edwin and Johanna**; won second place, Great Lakes Poetry Press Holiday Contest, 1987; received a poetry award from Lake Forest Country Day School, 1968. **Her comments:** I'm obsessed with life, death, and the laws of nature. The daughter of a writer and of an engineer, who shared a bed with a book of Rilke (odd sport for an engineer), I'm tangled into the destinies of my parents, my planet, my children. It's as though I want to know the why behind the rose. . . Restless, restful, obsessed and pacific, I write because I must. It's a necessary culmination to the process of digestion................ 16

MARY FRANCIS LEAMON LONG was born April 21, 1923, in Glasgow, Barren County, KY. She has an eighth grade education, and is retired from Gerber Babywear as an examiner. She is a widow. Her late husband, Cecil D. Long, whom she married March 1, 1941, died 15 years ago. She is a member and Sunshine girl of Three Oaks Church of Christ and President of Ladies Aid, also sunshine girl. **Her comments:** I enjoy writing short poems and I get my inspiration from God and my heart.. 42

Mary Francis Leamon Long

HELEN LOUISE was born April 2, 1954, in Rockford, IL. She is a graduate of Auburn Sr. High School (Rockford), Practicing License Practical Nurse, working on Association Degree in Applied Science. She is employed as a nurse. **Her comments:** My poetry is inspired by the Holy Bible and the faith that I have in Jesus Christ. The themes are inspired by family, patients I care for in the hospital setting as well as Private Duty, experiences in my own personal life and world affairs.. 49

Helen Louise

CARL M. LOVE was born Nov. 29, 1950, in Baker County, GA. His education includes: A.A. Degree, Bainbridge Junior College; B.A., Albany State College (Albany, GA); Graduate Studies at Albany State College and Ga. Southwestern (Americus, GA). He is a High School Teacher (Social Studies) and Policeman for The City of Edison, GA. **His comments:** Poetry is the ultimate expressions of my innermost thoughts. I am inspired by "real life" situations and most of my friends. Most of my poems are about something that happened to a dear friend or to me. This entry was inspired by Bernard Buster, who is the best friend I've ever known.. 233

Carl M. Love

DELLA MAY MARSH is the pen name of MARTHA M. PERSON, who was born Mar. 22, 1900 in Hazel Dell, PA. Her education includes eighth grade in country schools, one year at night school at business college and music school. She is retired; former music teacher. She married Herman Person on Dec. 25, 1928. She has played the violin in various orchestras. Her publications include: **Sand Point Park** in a local newspaper, 1984; **Columbia the Gem of Space**, read over the radio, 1985; **Seasoned Seniors**, published by National Art Society, 1989. **Her comments:** I was born with red, curly hair on Mar. 22, 1900 in Hazel Dell, PA, into a family of six older brothers and sisters and one younger brother. I was moved to a farm and attended school in the country through the eighth grade. At sixteen I went to work in a greenhouse and later became a floral designer. I worked through the

Della May Marsh day and attended business college at night. I also studied violin at a music

school. In later years I taught violin and piano. I also did some orchestra work. I now have one daughter and one grandson. I live alone at the top of a highrise on the intercoastal waterway where I can look across at all the shuttle launches. I wrote my first poem at the first launch of the Columbia at age 81 years and wrote 1638 poems from '81 to '86. I am proud to have a poem published by the Sparrowgrass Poetry Forum.. 95

STEPHEN JOHN McCARTHY was born Dec. 27, 1953, in Bath Township, Green County, Ohio. He attended Baker High School, 200 Lincoln Dr., Fairborn, OH, and is a Janitor at Jack Huelsman Chevy Olds, 1001 N. Broad St., Fairborn.. 266

DIXIE MACK McDANIEL was born Oct. 24, 1957 in Cordova, SC. She graduated in 1974 from Edisto High School, Cordova, SC. She is a homemaker and mother of three boys. She married her husband, Walter, on Nov. 27, 1981. Her memberships include Bethel Fellowship Church Secretary; Orangeburg Citizens For Life. **Her comments:** My purpose in writing poetry is to express my deep love and gratitude to Jesus Christ who died and rose again so that I might live.. 207

Dixie Mack McDaniel

Robert R. McEllhiney

ROBERT R. McELLHINEY was born Sept. 22, 1927, in Princeton, IN. He has a B.S. from Purdue University, 1952, an M.B.A. from Indiana University, 1953, and is a Professor, Dept. of Grain Science and Industry, Kansas State University. He married Theresa Hessig on Feb. 23, 1952, and is a member of Masonic Lodge, Scottish Rite, Shrine, Beta Theta Pi, Alpha Zeta, Eastern Star, American Legion. His publications include poetry and essays: **Kansas, A View From the Flint Hills**, published in booklet form in Manhattan, Kansas, 1988; **The Lamp and Star**, published in booklet form in Manhattan, Kansas, 1986; and **Feed Manufacturing Technology III**, published in Arlington, VA, 1985; **Truck Management**, Arlington, VA, 1983. His awards include: Who's Who in the West, 1976, 1977; International Who's Who in Engineering, 1984; DeMolay Hon. Legion of Honor, 1975. **His comments:** I consider myself as a "situation" poet with my inspiration being a human or national event, occasion, or situation—joyful or tragic. My best efforts have involved weddings, anniversaries, retirement, death, various ceremonies such as for Masonically related bodies as well as observation of natural phenomena.................... 283

Mike McLaughlin

MIKE McLAUGHLIN was born Sept. 1, 1948, in Fort Meade, MD. He has a Masters Degree in Theology and Philosophy from Fuller Theological Seminary, and is a Program Manager, Electronics Engineering. He married his wife, Valerie Ann, on April 23, 1983. His memberships include World of Poetry, Sparrowgrass Poetry Forum. **From My Back Porch During A Brief Rain** was published in **World of Poetry Anthology**, 1989. His awards include: Golden Poet Award, 1989; Honorable Mention, Free Contest, 1988; Honorable Mention, Just For You Contest, 1987. **His comments:** I try to write for the common man. In that sense my poems are "Brown-bag" poems. My chief inspirations are love lost or yet unrealized, the magical-mystical side of nature, and those special experiences which make us children once again........... 14

Harry Lee McNeil

HARRY LEE McNEIL was born Dec. 17, 1954, in Dillon County, SC. He attended Lake View High School, Lake View, SC, and is a truck driver. He married his wife, Casandra, on Dec. 9, 1978. He is a Baptist, Trustee Board, Member—Little Mt. Zion Baptist Church, Lake View, SC, and a member of St. Mark Masonic Lodge #71, Lake View, SC. **His comments:** It comes strictly from thought and the way I see things. I sometimes see things and feel things that others don't. Then I put my thoughts in poetic form. I have a whole collection I want to put into my own book or make into songs for someone... 102

Christina Miller

CHRISTINA MILLER was born Dec. 31, 1944, in Steamboat Springs, CO. She is a Homemaker and Part-time Assistant Librarian. Her husband is Michael Miller. She is a four-year member of NOVA (National Organization of Victim Assistance), 11-year member of National Order of Does; current member Douglas County RVA (Rape Victim Associates); Tri-City Horseman Club. **Her comments:** I owe my inspiration to my Mother, God rest her soul, who wrote poetry and short stories. Always encouraging me to use my natural talents. Almost all of my themes come from true experiences within my family of seven children, as well as coming from a family with seven siblings. Growing up on a ranch in the Colorado Rockies serves as my background for many short stories, as well as poetry describing my love for the outdoors and "country life" I'm so familiar with........................... 185

Jean H. Mills

JEAN H. MILLS was born April 2, 1965, in New Orleans, LA. She attended Collierville Elementary and Middle Schools, Collierville, TN, and Lafayette High School, Oxford, MS. She is employed by A-1 Carpet Cleaning and Janitorial Services, and married her husband, Terry D., on Nov. 7, 1981. She is a member of Abbeville United Methodist Church and Charge Treasurer for Abbeville United Methodist Church and Mt. Zion Methodist Church in Oxford. **Her comments:** My inspiration for writing poetry comes from my feelings about God, my husband (Terry), my children (Tonya and Stephanie), my mom (Valerie), and the people and events in my life that evolve around me on a day-to-day basis... 148

KENNITH LAMOR MITCHELL was born Jan. 10, 1974, in Mound Bayou, MS. He is a ninth grade student at Greenville High School, and a 4-H Club member, Bell Grove M.B. Church member, and High School Choir member. **Can It Be Fair?** was published in Sistersville, WV, 1990. His awards include: Citizenship Award, 1988-89; Anti-Drug Poster Contest, Dec. 23, 1988. **His Comments:** The T.V. was on and a thought popped in my head. **Can It Be Fair** to the youth of today; that we have to pay for something, we didn't do? So, I thought, how can you find the answer if you don't know the problem.. 228

Kennith Lamor Mitchell

JUNE K. MONTGOMERY was born May 25, 1917, in Perth, Scotland. She is a Retired Business Manager, Public Water Supply, and a member of American Water Works Assoc. She married her husband, Robert W., on April 4, 1953. **Her comments:** I write poetry from sentiment or events that touch my life, always only from a spiritual point of view. I was widowed early in life with two little boys, remarried in 1953. God has blessed us abundantly as a family, we have four grandsons and one lovely granddaughter................ 98

June K. Montgomery

EVA TAYLOR MOODY was born March 8, 1928, in Greenville, SC. She is a high school graduate, with one year business school. She is owner and director of a child care center (12 years). Her husband Claude, whom she married April 30, 1950, died in 1973. **Her comments:** Loved poetry since age eight and nine—written many poems about many subjects; God and (family—friends—animals—loved ones—"situations," etc.) most are written from actual situations—but some as dreams—thoughts. I find poetry to be a great source of therapy "the kind that keeps me going forward"............................... 225

Eva Taylor Moody

AMANDA TERRY MOORE was born Nov. 23, 1975, in Jackson, MS. She is an eighth grader at St. Andrew's Episcopal School in Jackson, MS. Her awards include: 3rd place in St. Andrew's Literary Contest, 1988; 7th grade English, 1989. **Her comments:** All my poetry is inspired by someone. Almost all of it is sad. I can't help it; that's just the way my words come out best. But I love to write and all my family and friends and teachers encourage me.. 182

Amanda Terry Moore

MARY J. MOURA was born Feb. 9, 1953, in Mount Vernon, NY. She graduated from Mount Vernon High School in 1971, and is a full-time mother and homemaker. From 1971-1977 she was a Dental Assistant. She married Avelino Moura on July 18, 1973. She is Treasurer and Fundraising Chairperson of Westchester-Putnam Scout Council's Carmel Pack #1, a member of Carmel Fitness Club and an avid swimmer. **Her comments:** This poem was written as a message of encouragement for my two sons, Brian Jason (age 11) and Adam James (age 7½).. 171

Mary J. Moura

MARGARET (MONTGOMERY) MUIRHEAD was born Dec. 14, 1917, in Longmont, CO. Her education includes Business College, some Law School. She is a Homemaker, and married Harvey Muirhead on Dec. 16, 1945. **Her comments:** I write about the simple things in life. There is so much beauty in our every day surroundings, if a person will just stop and look... My eight children have inspired me to write poems and short stories about each one at different times in their lives... The sorrow and disappointments, as well as their happiness and joys... Forty years of my life was spent in the beautiful Colorado Rockies, which also spurred my writings and poetry.... 90

Margaret (Montgomery) Muirhead and Melissa

John Richard Murphy

JOHN RICHARD MURPHY was born May 22, 1967, in Beaumont, TX. He graduated from French High School, Beaumont, TX, 1986; attended and graduated with an A in General Education from Navarro Jr. College, Corsicana, TX. He is a full time student, starting his junior semester at Sam Houston State University, Huntsville, TX, Fall 1989. **His comments:** As a poet, my career as a writer has been brief. I began writing my sophomore year at Navarro Jr. College. The inspiration for my poems has come from God, the beauty that He has put on this earth, and inside of me. One of the main themes that I express in my poetry, and is most important in my life, is that of friendship. I have been greatly inspired by many of the friends whose love touched my life at Navarro. There is however, one person that stands high above all my many wonderful friends, and that is my best friend and roommate for two years at Navarro, Chris Henderson, a criminal justice major. He was always there to give me support when I was down, and to share in my triumphs as well. One other person who is a very special friend and inspiration, is my friend Sandra Kay Summerhill, a music major, and very accomplished artist in her field. If I could say one thing to her in thanks, it would be that meeting her was one of the best things that God ever allowed to happen to me. I would also like to wish her a very happy 20th birthday. Thank you Chris and Sandra for helping me to grow up just a little bit more. I love you both. As a poet I have been blessed with many different themes. These include faith, hope, love, despair, and pain. Poetry has been a great release for me, and it has helped me to grasp a part of me that I hadn't known before, and to me that is what poetry is really supposed to do.. 252

Charles James Myers

CHARLES JAMES MYERS was born Jan. 21, 1963, in Wayne, MI. He has an A.A. in Economics from Manatee Community College, Venice, FL, and is a student at University of South Florida, Ft. Myers, FL. He is a member of Florida Board of Realtors. **His comments:** I am inspired with all the things of nature, about mankind and brotherhood, and keeping our world a safe heritage for all.. 47

Lisa Faye Nelson

LISA FAYE NELSON was born Jan. 19, 1976, in Iowa City, IA. She is in eighth grade, hoping to go on to college at UCLA or Harvard. She plans to go into Journalism or Law. Her awards include Young Writers Conference, 1988, 1985, 1984. This is her first attempt at publication. **Her comments:** Obviously I am a very inexperienced writer. I write mostly when my mood changes (happy, sad, angry, etc.) I've always had a vivid imagination............... 277

Jan Neville

JAN NEVILLE was born Oct. 3, 1934, in Chicago, IL. Her education includes: B.A. (Theatre), University of Denver; M.A. (Librarianship), University of Denver; Ph.D. (Speech Communication), University of Denver. She is a Public School Librarian/Media Specialist, and married George Russell Neville (now deceased) on June 13, 1959. She is a member of League of Historic American Theatres, Speech Communication Association, and Toastmasters International. Her play, **Elizabeth Palmer Peabody**, was performed in 1975. **Power, Interpersonal Needs, and Communication Behavior** was her Doctoral Dissertation in 1989. Her awards include: nominated, Best Actress Fanny Award, 1974; winner, Elwood Murray Best Speaker Award, 1979; winner, Area Toastmasters Tall Tale Contest, 1988. **Her comments:** My inspiration comes from life around me which triggers in my memory quotes from playwrights, authors, poets, and song writers who become echoes in my writing. My mother, Margaret A. Chapman introduced me to the bluebird of happiness.... 94

Megan J. O'Connell

MEGAN J. O'CONNELL was born Oct. 25, 1970, in Cherry Point, NC. She completed Graham High School, trained at Lucas Travel School, will complete December '89 and anticipates employment as an Airline Reservationist. Her poem **Southern Summer Silence** was published in **Great Poems of the South**, 1989. Her awards include: Burlington Writers Club High School, for poetry, '86, '88, '89; Burlington Women's Jaycees Club, '89. **Her comments:** Now that my work has been published, I have the chance to explain my work. Water, as a subject is an excellent source of mystery for which I can relate to mankind. The source of my poetry is the testimony from a witness of love and my love for the land. Through more learning, my work will be more to share.................... 180

EVERETT ODOMS was born June 22, 1911, in Kearney, NE. He has a college degree, and is a retired school teacher. He married his wife, Edith, in 1937. His memberships include: N.E.A., state and local, Square Dancing. He received the Golden Poet Award (2) in 1988 and Award of Merit Certificate (2) in 1989. **His comments on his poetry:** Mostly mundane, simple, every-day happenings and topics. Some are non-sensical and even absurd but jolly and amusing. My themes are numerous—no one particular avenue of thought. My daughter, Mary Ann was, and is, a great inspirational source for my writing.. 43

Everett Odoms

KATHERINE ELIZABETH ORLOFF was born July 6, 1979, in Renton, WA. She is a student, currently attending Sutter Elementary in the fifth grade.. 94

Katherine Elizabeth Orloff

JOHN H. O'STEPHENSON was born Dec. 19, 1911 in South Fulton, TN. His education includes: Grammar School at St. Josephs, Cleveland, TN; three years at Eng. Res. and Dev. Lab., Fort Belvoir, VA. He is a Plant Breeder and Propigator, and married Bessie Shelton on Aug. 5, 1935. He is a member of Moose and Knights of Columbus. His publications include **Whiff's of Nostalgia**, published in August 1986. **His comments:** In high school, I read the works of Milton, Ben Johnson, Thomas Moore, Longfellow, and Burns... 224

John H. O'Stephenson

JAMIE OSTLAND was born Nov. 29, 1964, in Mt. Clemens, MI. He graduated from Oscoda High School, Oscoda, MI, and attended two years college at Alpena Community College for Business Management. He is an electrician and married his wife, Jeanine, on Nov. 12, 1988.................................... 69

Jamie Ostland

RENATA ANNA OSTROWICKI was born Jan. 8, 1977, in Jersey City, NJ. She is a seventh grade student at Taunton School, Howell, NJ, and a member of YMCA/Brick. **Her comments:** I think poems are a great way to express people's feelings and dreams in a creative way. I like to write poems, whether it's for my family and friends on special occasions, such as birthdays, holidays, etc.; or crazy poems like one I wrote called **Meatballs & Salami** or to express my feelings about the world called **The Dream.** Writing poems helps get my thoughts out in the open. When people read them, it makes me feel GREAT.................................... 61

Renata Anna Ostrowicki

MS. JESSIE COOPER OWENS was born Oct. 16, 1942, in Hayti, MO. Her education includes a high school diploma, some college credits, one year in Licensed Vocational Nursing School (L.V.N.). She is a Postal Worker; Distribution Window Clerk at Post Office. Her memberships are: Mt. Pleasant Art Society, Northeast Texas Writers Organization, Toastmaster of Longview, TX, Post Toastees of Longview. She won third place in the non-fiction category for her manuscript **I Had the Best of Two Centuries** in a contest held by the N.E.T.W.O. in 1989. **Her comments:** I have written poems and short stories all my life. I am now working on a novel. I hope someday to have a novel published

Ms. Jessie Cooper Owens

and/or a small book of poems by myself, published. My life, my family and children inspire me. I am single (divorced) at this time. I have two children and two grandchildren. I work at Mt. Pleasant Texas Post Office. I am also a nurse, L.V.N........................... 94

JASMIN PEÑA-McGILL was born June 6, 1954 in Corpus Christi, TX. She earned a Bachelor of Science, Liberal Studies, in 1986, and an Associate in Arts, Business Management, in 1982. She is a Computer Programmer Analyst/Contract Administrator. **Her comments:** My poetic writings began as of 1988. Special people or day-by-day events affecting me inwardly are my true sources of inspiration. Ideas, phrases and words begin to flow out abruptly mostly at night time during my quiet hours. Moving themes such as loneliness, past hurts and future hopes and dreams are the essential motivators to my writings.................................... 284

Jasmin Peña-McGill

JUAN JOSE PEREZ was born Aug. 8, 1970, in Brownfield, TX. He graduated from Medina Valley H.S., which is about 20 miles west of San Antonio. He is currently attending Texas A&I University as a full time student majoring in communications. **His comments:** My interest in literature started to grow when I took drama in high school. I have to give credit to my English professor Celeste P. Whiting, who helped expose what literature really meant to me.................................... 269

Juan Jose Perez

MARCIA NELSON PERONE was born March 23, 1955, in Marquette, MI. She married Neil Perone on April 23, 1989. Her publications include **Paradise** in **World Poetry Anthology,** 1987; **Country Shadows** in **Our Western World's Most Beautiful Poems,** 1985. She received the World of Poetry Golden Poet Award in 1985, 1986 and 1987. Poet awards are won and published under her other name, Marcia Nelson Greene. She has recently married and now writes under the name of Perone. **Her comments:** I like to observe life and to tell about my observations in the form of poetry. I would like to call myself a seeker of Truths. The short poem **Husband** is dedicated to my husband, Neil.. 279

Marcia Nelson Perone

DIANA PICK was born Nov. 1, 1960, in Batesville, AR. She has a G.E.D. and is a Licensed Vocational Nurse. She married Woodrow David Pick on April 22, 1988. Her awards include Florence Nightingale, 1981; Young Careerist, 1987. **Her comments:** I have to be inspired by someone or something that happens to be able to write poetry. I think what's neat about poetry is that I can write the way I really feel inside. I have always enjoyed reading poetry too... 211

Diana Pick

PIE is the pen name of **RACHYLL DEMPSEY** who was born July 23, 1974, in Manhasset, Long Island, NY. She is currently enrolled at Odem High School, Odem, Texas, Sophomore/10th grade, and a member of International Thespian Society, National Forensic League, Business Professionals of America and Teenage Library Association. **Her comments:** For some reason, I seem to be most inspired to write when I am depressed. The things that depress me the most are lies, hypocrisy, cruelty and hate. Fortunately, or maybe unfortunately, I am not depressed too often so I perform other artists' work more often than I write... 222

Rachyll Dempsey

JENNIFER A. POOLE was born June 20, 1977. She is a student at Daniels Middle School and a member of Raleigh School of Gymnastics. **Her comments about her themes and sources of inspiration:** Wildlife, Nature Places, People, Pets, etc.. 150

Jennifer A. Poole

PHADRA POWELL was born June 27, 1971, in Roanoke, VA. She just graduated from high school and plans to attend college sometime next year. **Her comments:** My source of inspiration is the things that are around me every day. Therefore, many of my poems are about nature or how I feel on the inside.. 84

Phadra Powell

SHARON KAY MAHER PRICE was born March 10, 1952, in Pekin, IL. Her education includes eight years Catholic grammar school, graduating 1966; four years public high school, graduating 1970 in Taylorville, IL; three years college in Springfield, IL, degree in Associate Arts 1973. She is a day care provider and general housewife. She married Michael Allan Price on Nov. 3, 1973. Her awards include Knights of Columbus Poetry Award (third place), 1963. **Her comments:** Inspired by: experiences throughout my life and places I have been, also my immediate family, especially my mother, Margie Campbell, and last but not least, a man whom I have yet to meet, Ron Perlman, but whose work truly touched me, and was perhaps the one who inspired me the most.. 83

Sharon Kay Maher Price

DONNA LYNN (GUIRE) REED was born Oct. 17, 1955, in Terre Haute, IN. She graduated from Staunton High School, Staunton, IN, and is a housewife. She married Gregory A. Reed on Nov. 8, 1988, and is a member of Evers Road Christian Church. **Her comments:** The source of my inspiration comes from Jesus Christ my Lord. It is He who dwells in me that inspires the feelings that come from my soul.. 191

Donna Lynn (Guire) Reed

ROBBIE is the pen name of ROBERTA J. JOHNSON, who was born Aug. 16, 1965, in Barnhart, MO. She is a 1983 graduate of Farmington High School and a 1985 graduate of Missouri Beauty Academy. She is employed as a Biltwell Factory Worker, buttonhole machine. She received an award in KTJJ Radio Fathers Day Contest, 1987. **Her comments: Camouflaged Competition** was inspired by my boyfriend, Dennis D. Gonz... 146

Roberta J. Johnson

YINKA SABREE was born July 13, 1951, in Victoria, VA. She is a Nurse's Aide. Her publications include articles and poem in **Muslim Journal**, 1989, and **Forward Times**, 1987; poem in **New Voices in America Poetry**, 1989, and a poem published in Whitter, Alaska, 1987. **Her comments:** I give praise to God for giving me the talent to read and write. I start reciting poetry first at home. My father used to sing and recite poetry at home. I have uncles and aunts, who love to read and write poetry. I used to recite poetry in church and school.. 191

Yinka Sabree

MARY ELIZABETH SANDERS was born March 28, 1920, in Ft. Madison, Iowa. She was educated at Central High School, Flint, MI, four years Writers Conference, Edison College, Ft. Myers, FL. She is a housewife, who married her husband, Robert B., on Nov. 4, 1989. She is a Docent, Art Gallery, Edison Community College. **Her comments:** I have been writing all my life for friends and family. Now it is a thrill to share with others. A fan of Georgia O'Keefe I have painted in Abiquiu, New Mexico, amid all the splendor at Ghost Ranch. Now the mountains of N.C. keep my brush and pen busy in the summer, with the Florida sunshine adding to my joy in the Winter.. 207

Mary Elizabeth Sanders

DAVID JOHN SCHNEIDER, JR., height 6'0", weight 190, was born Sept. 14, 1960, in Lindstrom, MN. He is a graduate of Chisago Lakes Senior High School and a Game Farm Manager. His memberships include NRA (National Rifle Association), Ducks Unlimited and Chisago Lakes Lutheran Church. **His comments:** I have been under the care of Nurses several times and I feel that they are truly dedicated for the work that they give, and I wanted to write a tribute to all of them!.. 225

David John Schneider, Jr.

LISA RENAE SCHWENK was born July 1, 1976, in Bloomington, IN. She is 13 and will be in the eighth grade this fall at Jasper Middle School. She is a member of National Wildlife Federation, World Wildlife Fund. Her awards include: First Place Academic Bowl in Poetry, in 1988 and 1989. **Her comments:** This poem was written so that the people who read it will understand my feelings and actually try to be nicer to animals.. 228

Lisa Renae Schwenk

STANLEY N. SEARLES, SR. was born Aug. 15, 1919, in Malden, MA. His education includes B.A. Program, New England Aeronautical Institute. He is retired, and a member of AF&AM and American Legion. He married his wife, Maria, on Dec. 27, 1947. His publications include: **The Price of Love** in **World of Poetry**, 1975; **Ignis Fathus, This is My Land** and **Zero in Tennis** in **Vol. II, Season of Somber,** 1976. He received the Silver Poet Award in 1986 and 1984, and the Golden Poet Award in 1985. **His comments:** My poetry is mostly of the Romantic and Emotional theme. I write best when completely alone whether working or reflecting. Poetry to me is a mirror reflecting the inner thoughts and the deepest emotions..................................... 190

Stanley N. Searles, Sr.

KATIE SHERRILL was born June 8, 1958 in Orange, TX. She has a BA from Texas A&M University, English/Technical Writing, 1981; and an MA to be awarded August 1990 from University of Texas at Dallas, Humanities. She is a Flight Attendant for Continental Airlines, and a member of Union of Flight Attendants, International Association of Business Communicators, National Association of Female Executives, Texas Abortion Rights Action League. Her husband is Jim Minor. **Her comments:** My travels and experiences as a flight attendant are my inspiration. Through my work and my writing, I'd like to share a little piece of the sky... 9

Katie Sherrill

PAUL SILVA is the pen name of PAUL FLORES, who was born April 2, 1970, in Corpus Christi, TX. He is a graduate of William Howard Taft High School, attended The University of Texas at San Antonio, further schooling provided by U.S. Navy. His occupation: United States Navy/Navy Hospital Corps and the United States Navy. His publications include: **The Red Man** in **Holmes Edition**, 1985; **The Wish for Innocence** in **Saacte Journal**, 1988; **Visions of Life** in **Writer's Block**, 1988; **The Unheard Cries** in **The Patriot**, 1988. **His comments:** The greatest source of inspiration for me, would have to be the victories that I have obtained over the struggles of life and the love I receive from my family... 238

Paul Flores

BOB SIMPSON is the pen name of ROBERT SIMPSON, who was born May 1, 1952, in Thornton, MS. His education includes: 1969—High School Diploma (Valedictorian), Durant, MS; 1972—B.A. in Sociology and Social Work—University of Miss. He is a Poet/Social Worker and a member of World of Poetry, 1988—. His publications include: **Dread Inferno**, published in Oxford, MS, 1977; **Motogusinele**, published in Chicago, IL, 1978; **Amazon Woman** in **World Treasury of Great Poems**, 1989; **!FREEDOM** in **Great Poems of the Western World**, 1989. He received the Golden Poet Award from the World of Poetry in 1988 and 1989, and Award of Merit from the World of Poetry, October 1988 and March 1989. **His comments:** My poetry is at the pulse beat of today's embryonic consciousness and is prepared to race with it through the "Cretinous recidivistic gauntlet" of fear and indecision to the freedom of "Awareness.".. 87

Robert Simpson

CAROLYN LORENE SMITH was born Feb. 2, 1943, in Tulare, CA. She graduated from Tulare Union High, 1961; College of the Sequoias, graduated with A.A. Secretarial, 1963; re-entered college, 1983; Major--Spanish, writing. She is a housewife and student, and married Davie Edward Smith on July 5, 1963. Her poem **Alone** is published in **Treasured Poems of America**, 1989. Her awards include Distinguished Poet Award, 1989. **Her comments:** The joy of living and loving, a roadside scene, a weathered face, clouds threatening the hills and light slicing through trees are a few of the things that stir a rumble of emotions within. I'm driven by a strong force to untangle, reweave, and preserve these emotions on paper. For me writing is a great joy!.. 22

Carolyn Lorene Smith

MARY SPINKS was born Jan. 29, 1950, in Fayette County. She has 13½ years of education, graduating from the 12th grade at W.P. Ware High School, Somerville, TN, in 1969, and attending 1½ years at Eastern Cuyahoga Community College, Warrensville, Ohio. She is licensed in Dental Assisting, graduating in 1971 from Bay City College, Eulid, Cleveand, Ohio. Her occupation is: professional writer, performance, dental assisting, assembly. She has two children, Charles Jr. and Charla O'Neal, and is divorced. **Her comments:** God's gifts He gave to us are so inspiring to us on earth. If we make one step He will make many more.............. 33

KENDRA KAY SPRINGER was born June 14, 1961, in Witchita Falls, TX. She has an Associate of Arts in English at Lin Benton Community College. She is a housewife, and married David M. Springer on July 2, 1983. She is a contributing poet to National Alliance for the Mentally Ill. Her poem **To Myself** is published in **Treasured Poems**, 1990. **Her comments:** It is my firm desire to express my great love for humanity and the mentally ill population in America through my rhyming verse... 63

Kendra Kay Springer

JEANNINE SPURLOCK was born Aug. 11, 1953, in Branson, MO. She is currently a senior at Drury College in Springfield, MO, and will earn a B.S. in English/Education in 1990. She is a Clerk and Substitute Teacher, and married her husband, Reginald, on Nov. 26, 1976. Her memberships are: National Council of Teachers of English, Douglas County Genealogical Society, Squires Volunteer Fire Dept. Auxiliary. Her publications include: **Meet Beth Highfill,** a feature profile in **Drury College Newsletter,** 1989; **To Emerson's Over-Soul** and **Presence** in **American Poetry Anthology,** 1990. She was selected for Who's Who Among American University and College Students, 1986-87, 1987-88, and received a Student Recognition Award in 1988

BARBARA ANN CSIK STADVEC was born April 28, 1952. Her education includes Elementary School—Holy Assumption; Florence High School, Florence Township, NJ. She is a cleaner for Holy Assumption School. Her publications include **Time** in **Great Poems of The Western World Vol. II,** 1989, and a children's story, **Johnny Flies To The Clouds,** in the process of being published in 1989. Her poem **Time** received the Golden Poet Award in 1989. **Her comments:** I love writing, about any subject. Writing is very important to me. My source of inspiration is children and watching people. I find a peace when I write. I am starting to write children stories. I will write on any theme or anything, anyplace. Children are important to me! I am in the starting process of publishing four children stories

Barbara Ann Csik Stadvec

PATRICIA ROBERTSON STEM was born Feb. 22, 1935, in Milton-Freewater, OR. She graduated from McLouglin Union High School, Milton-Freewater, OR, 1953, and attended 1½ years Secretarial Science, Westark Community College, Ft. Smith, AR. She is a homemaker, and married Roland Stem April 16, 1982. Her poem **Forevermore** is scheduled for publication in anthology **Great Poems of The Western World,** 1990, and received an Honorable Mention in 1989. She received the Golden Poet Award from World of Poetry Assoc. in 1989. **Her comments:** I write a variety of verse and style; inspired by seasons, holidays, people, and life in general. I began writing poetry in 1988 and entered my first and only poem, **Forevermore,** at that time (1989) in a poetry contest. I have since written close to a dozen or more poems—a few as tributes to friends and family

MICHELLE FRANCES STEVENS was born Sept. 29, 1957 in New York City. Her education includes: St. Clare's Academy High School, two years at Iona College, one year at Concordia College. She is Assistant Supervisor in a bank; a member of CCD Program and Sunday School teacher at Immaculate Conception Church. **Her comments:** This poem was inspired by a sightseeing cruise some years ago on "The Pioneer" in New York Harbor and when it was shown to the captain was put in the ship's log book for that day

Michelle Frances Stevens

JIM SWEET was born March 1, 1929, in Coulterville, IL. He graduated from Southern Illinois University, 1957, and has earned additional credit in 16 colleges and universities. He is a school teacher—crafts person, and married his wife, Audrey, on July 22, 1948. **His comments:** Life is good but life involves changes: It's wise to be aware of life's meaning and adapt joyously. "Why borrow tomorrow when I can own today."

Jim Sweet

LEE SHACKLEFORD TRIMBLE, JR. was born March 14, 1923, in Griffin, GA. His education includes: Lanier High School, Macon, GA (1936-41), University of Florida (1941-1943), Duke University (1943-44), University of Georgia (1946-48), Tulane University (1949), Emory University (1952-54), BAJ, BA, MA. He is a retired Library Director and a member of GLA, SCLA, Sigma Chi. He married Mary Cobb Trimble on Dec. 22, 1947. He served in U.S. Marine Corps, 1943-46. **His comments about his themes and sources of inspiration:** My family, friends, pets, social issues.. 44

Lee Shackleford Trimble, Jr.

MICHAEL S. VELKO was born April 6, 1949, in Akron, Ohio. He is a 1967 graduate of Savanna High School, Anaheim, CA, with continued coursework in Criminal Justice. He is a Police Officer, Tustin, CA (16 years in law enforcement), and a member of American Legion and California Peace Officer's Association. His publications include **The Fallen Shield** in **California Peace Officer Newsletter,** March '73, and **Once A Steelworker** in **Orange County Register,** June '89. He received the Golden Poet Award in '88 and the Silver Poet Award in '89. **His comments:** I began writing "free verse" out of high school as a means of expression in personal/family relationships. I would later draw inspiration from my experiences in Vietnam with the Navy and continue to write about the day to day activities of my position as a police officer for the past 16 years............... 267

Michael S. Velko

ANJALI VISWANATHAN was born April 9, 1974, in Rochester, NY. She is a Junior in high school—11th grade student in Mt. St. Mary's Academy, and a member of Forensics Club in Mt. St. Mary's Academy; Editorial Board of **Echoes,** school literary magazine. Her poem **Midsummer Dream** is accepted for publication in **Treasured Poems of America,** 1990. Her awards include: Johns Hopkins Scholarship for Academically Gifted and Talented Youth, 1985; First Prize in Forensics Competition in Kent Place School Summit NJ, 1986; "High Honors" Piano Teachers Association of America, 1985 to present. **Her comments:** I find poetry to be the most articulate means of expressing what I feel. Everyday occurrences can often acquire a new perspective and fresh outlook when looked at through the lens of poetry. I like the make-believe aspect of poetry. The inner life interests me generally. I am also deeply moved by themes such as the destruction of nature, and the environment. I am appalled by the toxic wastes that are destroying our planet. I wrote a poem entitled **Bhopal** on the tragedy brought about by Union Carbide at Bhopal... 234

Anjali Viswanathan

S. BRYEANS VON SCHMACHT was born Feb. 6, 1961, in Whittier, CA. She has a B.A. in English from California State University, Fullerton, and is a Writer and Mom. She married James A. von Schmacht on Jan. 5, 1985. Her publications include: **Broken Dreams** in **Punctuation,** 1984; **Habit** and **Lovers** in **American Poetry Anthology,** 1989. **Her comments:** I write because I must, to keep myself intact, to honor a never-ending request: "Tell me what you see."... 20

SARAH WEST was born March 2, 1958, in Warren Co, NC. She is a graduate of Vance-Granville Community College of Henderson, NC, and a graduate of Deliverance Bible College of Rocky Mt., NC. She is a school teacher. **Her comments:** I'm a vegetarian and I love writing poetry. It's a gift from God. I write poems for all occasions. Most of my poems are written from my life style. I'm also a pianist. Sometimes I recite some of my poems while playing the piano.. 265

Sarah West

CHARLES J. WHITE was born Feb. 2, 1925, in Pine Hill, NJ. He has an eighth grade education, and is an artist/poet. He married his wife, Evelyn, on July 10, 1970, and is a member of Submarine Veterans World War II. His publications include: **Original Poems by CJW**, published in Pennsylvania, 1985; **Cherry Blossoms**, a lithograph published in New York, 1985; **The Garden**, five-color print published in Pennsylvania, 1987; **The Stubborn Mare**, five-color print published in Pennsylvania, 1988, and many more prints. **His comments:** I write poem first then paint the painting it describes. My work is hanging in the Jacob Javitts Building, GSA Office New York and appears in Printworld Directory 3rd Edition. I am self taught after heart attack, 1979—was on Channel 6 TV in 1986—national... 48

Charles J. White

DOROTHY WIESLER was born July 19, 1927, in New York City. Her education includes high school and two years of college. She is a retired surgical technician, and married Rudolph Wiesler (now deceased) on Feb. 8, 1985. She is a member of American Legion Post 291, Newport Beach, CA. She received Honorable Mention in 1989 for her work, **Reality**, which was published in October 1989. **Her comments:** I have written lyrics for 15 years and was a member of BMI under the name Dorothy Gorman. I have, with a friend, Ernestine Goldman, a book of music, namely songs, ie: Country—Middle of the Road tunes. Also, was in Lehman Engles' Broadway-Musical-Theatre Class in the '70's. I plan, in the future, to put my poems in book form and publish.. 103

Dorothy Wiesler

SHIRLEY A. WINNER was born Oct. 15, 1937, in Kentucky. She has a high school education and is a housewife. She married her husband, Glenn, on Dec. 31, 1975. Her publications include: **Infinity** in **Windows on the World**, 1989; **Memories** published by Sparrowgrass, 1989; **My Plea** in **Lady of Lord's**, 1989. She won outstanding award for poem, **Miracle**, in April 1989. **Her comments:** My poetry is written in honor of my son Philip Lennie Miller, born July 4, 1962, died October 30, 1988.. 145

Shirley A. Winner

GILBERT MARCUS WOTEN "MARC" was born Jan. 14, 1953, in Lima, OH. He is a graduate of Lima Senior High School, attended Apollo Joint Vocational Center at Lima, and studied theology at Goshen College, IN. He is a free-lance artist and musician for schools and weddings. He married Germaine R. Spicer on Sept. 11. 1977, and is a member of the Ohio National Guard, The Musicians Union, and a Proud Sponsor of "Children International." His song, **Testimony**, was included in **Maple Grove Church Hymns**, 1974, Topeka, IN. **His comments:** My poetry is inspired by the strength we all show through life's trials and tribulations, and how I compare that strength with the efforts and love of children as they grow, and nature as it changes through the seasons... 213

Gilbert Marcus Woten "Marc"

MALA LUCRETIA WRIGHT was born May 19, 1970, in Trenton, NJ. She attended Villa Victoria Academy since kindergarten—graduated June 1988, currently attending Mercer County College. She is a student, part-time peer counselor and one-time actress. She is a 1988 member of LaDebu Debutantes' Society; Poet from Great Lakes Poetry Association, 1989. Her publications include: **My School Day Session** in **American Anthology of Contemporary Poetry**, 1989; **Deep Inside** in **American Anthology of Midwestern Poetry**, 1989. Her awards are: Father Godfrey Scholarship Award, 1984; "All-American Look" in Acting, 1984; PCD&D Achievement Award in Acting (second place), 1983. **Her comments:** I like to use my poetry as a means of communication and a way of expressing myself. Many of my poems are derived from songs

Mala Lucretia Wright

Continued on next page

I've written. I really don't have a source of inspiration, but, if I'm in a good mood, I can "knock off" a poem in about 15-20 mins. I love to read and to interpret works by Geoffrey Chaucer and William Shakespeare... 279

JEFFREY LAMAR YANCY was born November 26, 1969, in Mesquite, Texas. He is a Student of Life. **His comments:** Family, friends and society in general inspired this poem.. 187

Jeffrey Lamar Yancy

STEPHEN WEBB YATES was born March 27, 1966, in Pascagoula, MS. He is a 12-year student, Ocean Springs High; graduate of MGCJC; currently enrolled at Mississippi State University. **His comments:** I consider my writings to be very sensitive. Each time I begin to escape reality through my writings I revert back to nature and visualize a wonderland full of excitement. Henry David Thoreau—what an inspiration... 99

WESLEY YONTS was born March 2, 1921 on Millstone Creek, Letcher County, Kentucky. Both parents died before he was eight years old and he was raised by relatives in Pike and Knott Counties. He entered the Army in September, 1939, and served five years, eight months; 27 months overseas in England, North Africa, Sicily and Italy. He was honorably discharged in 1945. Shortly after this he met and married Maulta Sizemore of Hazard, Kentucky, on November 23, 1946, and raised two sons, Jerry and Charles. In 1947 he joined the Regular Baptist Church and in 1956 he was ordained to the Ministry. He is presently pastor of the Irvine Eversole Memorial Church, Bonnyman, Kentucky. He is a former Scout Master and Cub Master and was active in Little League Baseball. He was employed with Kentucky Power Company 36½ years and is presently retired. His publications include: **Life's Fleeting Moments,** published in Letcher Co., KY, 1976; **A Few More Glimpses** and **The Wheels of Time,** published in Perry Co., KY, 1980. **His comments:** My poetry, I believe, is a gift from God; to Him be the glory........ 156

Wesley Yonts

LISA ANN ZIMMERMAN was born Aug. 8, 1964, in Lewisburg, PA. She is a graduate of Mifflinburg High School, Mifflinburg, PA, and a Sewing Machine Operator. **Her comments:** I have always enjoyed writing. Poetry is just one outlet that I use as a means of expressing myself. I find it is easiest to write poetry when I am sad, or want to say something to someone in particular. My poems are about sorrow or romance.......................... 59

Lisa Ann Zimmerman

Index of Authors

Authors are indexed under the name or pen name that appears with their poem.